The Foundations of the New Institutional Economics

The International Library of the New Institutional Economics

Editor: Claude Ménard

> *Professor of Economics*
> *and Director of ATOM (Center for Analytical Theory of Organizations and Markets)*
> *University of Paris Panthéon-Sorbonne, France*

Wherever possible, the articles in these volumes have been reproduced as originally published using facsimile reproduction, inclusive of footnotes and pagination to facilitate ease of reference.

For a list of all Edward Elgar published titles visit our site on the World Wide Web at
www.e-elgar.com

The Foundations of the New Institutional Economics

Edited by

Claude Ménard

*Professor of Economics
and Director of ATOM (Center for Analytical Theory of Organizations and Markets)
University of Paris Panthéon-Sorbonne, France*

THE INTERNATIONAL LIBRARY OF THE NEW INSTITUTIONAL ECONOMICS

An Elgar Reference Collection
Cheltenham, UK • Northampton, MA, USA

Published by
Edward Elgar Publishing Limited
Glensanda House
Montpellier Parade
Cheltenham
Glos GL50 1UA
UK

Edward Elgar Publishing, Inc.
136 West Street
Suite 202
Northampton
Massachusetts 01060
USA

A catalogue record for this book is available from the British Library.

ISBN   1 84376 660 4
        1 84064 382 X (7 volume set)

Printed and bound in Great Britain by MPG Books Ltd, Bodmin, Cornwall.

Contents

Acknowledgements

The editor and publishers wish to thank the authors and the following publishers who have kindly given permission for the use of copyright material.

American Economic Association for articles: Armen A. Alchian and Harold Demsetz (1972), 'Production, Information Costs, and Economic Organization', *American Economic Review*, **62** (5), December, 777–95; James M. Buchanan (1975), 'A Contractarian Paradigm for Applying Economic Theory', *American Economic Review, Papers and Proceedings*, **65** (2), May, 225–30; Ronald Coase (1998), 'The New Institutional Economics', *American Economic Review, Papers and Proceedings*, **88** (2), May, 72–4.

American Philosophical Society for article: Herbert A. Simon (1962), 'The Architecture of Complexity', *Proceedings of the American Philosophical Society*, **106** (6), December, 467–82.

Masahiko Aoki for his own excerpt: (2000), 'Institutional Evolution as Punctuated Equilibria', in Claude Ménard (ed.), *Institutions, Contracts and Organizations: Perspectives from New Institutional Economics*, Chapter 3, 11–33.

Blackwell Publishing Ltd for articles: R.H. Coase (1937), 'The Nature of the Firm', *Economica*, **4** (16), New Series, November, 386–405; R.C.O. Matthews (1986), 'The Economics of Institutions and the Sources of Growth', *Economic Journal*, **96** (384), December, 903–18; Leonid Hurwicz (1987), 'Inventing New Institutions: The Design Perspective', *American Journal of Agricultural Economics*, **69** (2), May, 395–402; Masahiko Aoki (1996), 'Towards a Comparative Institutional Analysis: Motivations and Some Tentative Theorizing', *Japanese Economic Review*, **47** (1), March, 1–19; Leonid Hurwicz (1996), 'Institutions as Families of Game Forms', *Japanese Economic Review*, **47** (2), June, 113–32.

Cambridge University Press for excerpts: Lance E. Davis and Douglass C. North with the assistance of Calla Smorodin (1971), 'A Theory of Institutional Change: Concepts and Causes', in *Institutional Change and American Economic Growth*, Chapter 1, 3–25; Andrew Schotter (1981), 'The Nature and Function of Social Institutions', in *The Economic Theory of Social Institutions*, Chapter 1, 1–17, 165–6, references.

Elsevier for articles: Michael H. Riordan and Oliver E. Williamson (1985), 'Asset Specificity and Economic Organization', *International Journal of Industrial Organization*, **3** (4), 365–78; Claude Ménard (1995), 'Markets as Institutions versus Organizations as Markets? Disentangling Some Fundamental Concepts', *Journal of Economic Behavior and Organization*, **28** (3), 161–82.

Eirik G. Furubotn and Rudolf Richter for their own excerpt: (1997), 'Introductory Observations', in *Institutions and Economic Theory: The Contribution of the New Institutional Economics*, Chapter 1, 1–37, references.

Houghton Mifflin Company for excerpt: Kenneth J. Arrow (1970), 'The Organization of Economic Activity: Issues Pertinent to the Choice of Market versus Nonmarket Allocation', in Robert H. Haveman and Julius Margolis (eds), *Public Expenditures and Policy Analysis*, Chapter 2, 59–73.

Journal of Law and Economics and the University of Chicago Law School for articles: Steven N.S. Cheung (1973), 'The Fable of the Bees: An Economic Investigation', *Journal of Law and Economics*, **XVI** (1), April, 11–33; Oliver E. Williamson (1979), 'Transaction-Cost Economics: The Governance of Contractual Relations', *Journal of Law and Economics*, **XXII** (2), October, 233–61.

Kluwer Academic/Plenum Publishers for articles: Kenneth A. Shepsle and Barry R. Weingast (1981), 'Structure-Induced Equilibrium and Legislative Choice', *Public Choice*, **37**, 503–19; Elinor Ostrom (1986), 'An Agenda for the Study of Institutions', *Public Choice*, **48** (1), 3–25.

MIT Press Journals and the President and Fellows of Harvard College for article: H.B. Malmgren (1961), 'Information, Expectations and the Theory of the Firm', *Quarterly Journal of Economics*, **75** (3), August, 399–421.

Oxford University Press for excerpt and article: Adam Smith ([1776] 1976), 'Of the Division of Labour', 'Of the Principle Which Gives Occasion to the Division of Labour' and 'That the Division of Labour is Limited by the Extent of the Market', in R.H. Campbell, A.S. Skinner and W.B. Todd (eds), *An Inquiry into the Nature and Causes of the Wealth of Nations,* Glasgow Edition, Volume I, Book I, Chapters I, II and III, 13–24, 25–30, 31–6; David M. Kreps (1996), 'Markets and Hierarchies and (Mathematical) Economic Theory', *Industrial and Corporate Change*, **5** (2), 561–95.

RAND for article: Patrick Bajari and Steven Tadelis (2001), 'Incentives versus Transaction Costs: A Theory of Procurement Contracts', *RAND Journal of Economics*, **32** (3), Autumn, 387–407.

Sage Publications Ltd and the Scandinavian Sociological Association for article: Mark Granovetter (1992), 'Economic Institutions as Social Constructions: A Framework for Analysis', *Acta Sociologica*, **35** (1), 3–11.

Every effort has been made to trace all the copyright holders but if any have been inadvertently overlooked the publishers will be pleased to make the necessary arrangement at the first opportunity.

In addition the publishers wish to thank the Marshall Library of Economics, Cambridge University, the Library of the University of Warwick and the Library of Indiana University at Bloomington, USA for their assistance in obtaining these articles.

General Introduction

Claude Ménard

A Remarkable Development

From a historical standpoint, the New Institutional Economics (NIE) is a very young theory. With the exception of the now famous article from Ronald Coase, 'The Nature of the Firm' (1937), this new approach slowly took shape in the 1960s, but really took off in the 1970s, with major contributions from Alchian, Coase, Demsetz, North, Williamson, and many others. It was only in the 1980s and 1990s that it established itself as a fully developed and acknowledged research program.[1] Looking retrospectively at this short period of time, the accomplishments are quite remarkable. The contributions collected in these seven volumes illustrate the variety and richness of the analyses elaborated during that period. The difficulties in selecting the articles reprinted in the series provide an indication of the quality of these contributions.

The developments occurred mostly along two complementary and interdependent axes; one oriented towards the analysis of the modes of organization, while the other focused on the institutional environment in which these arrangements are embedded.

The transaction costs analysis of the tradeoff among modes of organization, the explanation provided to vertical integration, the centrality of contractual arrangements, and the insights on some fundamental characteristics of the different modes of organization have all become standard references in economics (and beyond), even among those who do not share the NIE interpretation. Similarly, the recognition of the central role played by the institutional environment in making possible the development of market economies, the importance of laws and political rules in order to have lower transaction costs and a larger volume of transactions, and the comparative analysis of the impact of different political regimes on development and growth, have now permeated all social sciences as well as mainstream economics. The present series is intended to show how NIE has contributed to these developments.

Main Axes of Analysis

In a recent synthesis reproduced in the last volume of this series,[2] Williamson proposed a distinction between four levels of analysis, corresponding to different time perspectives. Although the chronology suggested may be debatable, the general scheme provides a helpful framework for encapsulating the varied set of contributions that developed under the NIE umbrella.

In the *very long run*, spanning over centuries, customs, traditions, and beliefs tend to predominate. Although they change very slowly, they contribute to shaping the institutional environment, as illustrated in many articles of this series. Their importance comes from their role in defining rules and support in the organization of transactions and in contributing to the determination of the level of transaction costs, particularly in environments with no public enforcers or very weak ones. However, they can also create obstacles to the development of transactions, as with customs that isolate a social group from its environment. Douglass North has repeatedly brought attention to the importance of these factors for understanding the evolution of transactions over time and, ultimately, on development and growth. Several recent researches, particularly by historians and anthropologists, have substantiated this view and some of them are presented in the following volumes.

Over a more restricted time span, but still in a *long run* perspective, political and legal institutions define rules within which transactions can develop, thus creating possibilities or inhibitions for trading activities. Coase has opened the way here in showing the significance of laws and the legal regime in a world with positive transaction costs. Three aspects have particularly captured the attention of new institutionalists in that respect. First, a comparative approach to political systems, using transaction costs and contractual lenses, has allowed substantial progress in our understanding of how the polity interacts with the organization of exchanges. At the same time, Douglass North has also played an important role here, by showing the way political systems operate can be analysed as a 'market' of a specific type, on which political transactions occur that explain the adoption of certain forms and the reasons why some have been more successful than others in supporting development and growth. The many articles on federalism collected in this series illustrate this.

Second, parallel to and interacting with political institutions, the legal system also plays a major role in determining how transactions can be organized and at what costs. Legal issues have been part of the research program in NIE from very early on, particularly under the influence of Ronald Coase. One important lesson of these studies is that they tend to show that no legal system is superior to another one per se, contrary to what has been suggested by competing theories. What really matters is the fitness of a legal system, that is: (1) its adaptation to what we can call the institutional endowments of a society at some point in its history, particularly its endowments in public servants and personnel with legal competences; (2) its relevance to the nature of transactions at stake, since institutions adapted to some activities, for example the financial system, do no necessarily correspond to those needed for regulating other activities, for example markets for perishable goods; (3) its reliability in defining, implementing, and enforcing property rights.

Last, a flow of recent studies has substantiated this concern for the long-run impact of political and legal regimes through the analysis of the successes and failures of regulations, with a special attention to the reform of public utilities. All these faces of the durable influence of institutions on the way transactions are organized are represented in this series. They constitute the hard core of that part of the NIE research program that North and Davis have synthesized as the 'institutional environment'.

In the *medium* and short run, the analysis concentrates on the variety of modes of organization that shape an economy and that North and Davis encapsulated as 'institutional arrangements'. These arrangements are embedded in existing legal and political institutions as well as in ideologies and traditions that shape the behavior of transactors. However, their time horizon is shorter and they are more malleable, and more prone to voluntary changes. Coase opened the way to the analysis of these modes of organization that provide differentiated supports to transactions, and Williamson has become the leading figure here.

By using a transaction costs lens, this approach has exhibited the diversity of ways in which to organize trading activities in order to take advantage of specialization. The booming literature on modes of organization has switched us from a bipolar perspective, focusing on the tradeoff between markets and 'hierarchies' (or integrated organizations), to a multi-polar vision with the increasing acknowledgement of the importance of intermediate or 'hybrid' forms. However, and even more importantly, NIE has provided a theoretical framework that has become a point of reference for explaining the tradeoff among these modes of organization, that is, why one form is preferred to another one under the specific attributes that characterize a transaction. The initial attention went to the explanation of vertical integration, as an alternative to market solutions, and it is now widely acknowledged that this represented both an important theoretical breakthrough and an empirical 'success story'. More recently, the attention has turned to ways of organizing transactions that correspond neither to integration nor to the usual features characterizing market relations. The analysis of these non-standard contractual relationships has become an important component of the NIE research program.

Also related to a medium-run perspective, there is an increasing interest for identifying and examining the internal structures and characteristics of alternative modes of organizations. The idea here, reflected in many articles in this series, is that using the concepts developed in NIE could help to understand better why one mode fits better than another with the attributes of transactions at stake. One important issue concerns the theoretical status of these factors in the effort to explain the tradeoff among modes of organizations. Are these factors orthogonal to an explanation of the tradeoff, for example are costs of bureaucracy orthogonal to transaction costs? If they must be mobilized for substantiating the transaction costs explanation, how can we model them so as to avoid getting trapped into a tautology, that is, a mode of organization prevails because it has a superior mode of organization!

Lastly, *short run* elements and variations also influence the way transactions are organized, and the way relative costs are incurred. According to Williamson, and most new institutionalists would likely agree on this, the short-run perspective focuses on marginal adaptation, as in the price theory or with incentives issues, and it prevails in mainstream economics. NIE has surely contributed less to this aspect than other theories, for example agency theory. However, it has paid attention to the role of these variations in comparing modes of organization. It has also contributed to refocusing on the short perspective in pointing out the need to examine how these variables of adjustments are embedded in specific modes of organizations. One illustration, developed in this series, concerns the role of organizational motivations and values, beyond monetary incentives and their variations.

All these developments result in a complex and highly diversified research program, as illustrated by this series. At the same time it is a unified research program.

A Unifying Set of Concepts Paired to a Methodological Vision

Indeed, a striking aspect of the NIE research program is the presence under this diversity of object and levels of analysis of a coherent set of concepts that provides unity to the whole. Transaction costs, contracts, and property rights form the core of this analytical apparatus.

Within this triad, *transaction costs* occupy a very central position, for historical as well as theoretical reasons. The historical priority goes back to the pioneering role of Coase's article on 'The Nature of the Firm'. The theoretical centrality of the concept refers to more subtle reasons, as so many misinterpretations testify (for example the idea that transaction costs would at best neglect, at worst ignore production costs). Several chapters in this series explicitly point out why transaction costs matter so much in the NIE perspective. It all boils down to an argument rooted in Adam Smith: there is no possibility of taking advantage of the division of labor and of specialization without organizing transactions, and all arrangements that can be implemented for doing so have a cost. This approach gives its full sense to the definition of transaction costs as 'the cost of running the economic system' (Arrow, 1970).

How exactly to pin down these costs and how to approximate them is a more complex question, and is one that is discussed in several chapters of the series. At least two different views have developed. One considers that transaction costs make sense only for analysing market exchanges, thus transaction costs are what it costs to trade on markets. A more extensive definition considers transaction costs as the costs of transferring rights of usage, which makes the concept a relevant tool for analysing modes of organization alternative to markets as well. However, whether the restrictive or the wider interpretation prevails, the concept remains a powerful tool for examining micro arrangements as well as global institutions and for exploring the interaction between these levels. At the same time, the issue of measuring transaction costs remains an open one, that is, whether it is relevant or not to try measuring them remains debatable; and if it is relevant to measure them, then the question arises of how this can be done. Again, several chapters in the series discuss these issues.

Whatever are the answers to these important and difficult questions, there is a general agreement among new institutionalists that transaction costs particularly matter when in comes to the establishment and transfer of *property rights*. Identifying the different types of property rights and the consequences of their allocation has been on the agenda of NIE since very early in its development. Indeed, in a world of positive transaction costs, the distribution of rights and the devices for transferring them are of the utmost importance and have a significant impact on the performance of the alternative modes of organization as well as on growth. Therefore, the two concepts of transaction costs and of property rights have been linked from the very beginning of the research program, as is already visible in 'The Problem of Social Costs' (Coase, 1960). NIE has continuously contributed to a better understanding of the nature and role of property rights. It has also continuously emphasized the centrality of their enforcement, that is, the need for institutions to implement and secure property rights, thus reducing contractual hazards and risk of opportunism. In doing so it establishes a link with the microfoundations of transaction costs, as well illustrated with the credibility issue, discussed in several papers of this series.[3]

In a developed market economy, *contracts* represent one of the major supports for transferring property rights and, more generally, for organizing transactions. Coase had the intuition of the importance of contracts in his pioneering discussion (1937) of the integration issue and of what differentiates the allocation of resources and tasks in a firm by contrast with markets. However, Williamson deserves the main credit here because he has led the crowd in establishing the centrality of contracts for organizing and coordinating transactions. In an apparent paradox he has done so while exhibiting the incompleteness of contracts. In a world in which uncertainties combine with positive transaction costs, contracts remain inevitably incomplete, thus generating hazards that require safeguards. These safeguards may be entrenched in the contracts themselves; they may also rely on complementary governing devices or on external enforcers, among which courts and governments are major actors. An entire branch of NIE has developed this research program and is well represented in this series.

One element that contributes to explain the incompleteness of contracts, besides the importance of unanticipated events, may lie in the *behavior* of parties to contractual arrangements. NIE paid early attention to the strategizing behavior of agents and, more generally, to exploring a more complex representation of agents than the one dominating the standard approach in economics. References to bounded rationality and to opportunistic behavior may be considered as relatively primitive efforts in this direction. They have been seriously substantiated by more recent researches, mainly coming from two different perspectives: experimental economics on the one hand, and cognitive sciences on the other hand. Several chapters of the series illustrate this movement. Among others, Ostrom provides particularly important insights based on experiments and field studies; and North indicates how cognitive sciences may help in developing sound microfoundations to the analysis of organizations and institutions through the analytical explanation of how agents combine rational calculation and beliefs in their behavior and their choices.

Hence, the NIE research program reposes on a solid and dense web of concepts tightly interwoven. These fundamental concepts and assumptions, and their refinements developed in numerous chapters in the series, are complemented by a *methodological approach* quite universally shared among new institutionalists. Indeed, the NIE approach is deliberately and systematically comparative. Institutions and modes of organizations cannot be assessed in isolation; they can only be evaluated through comparison. New institutionalists go even further in considering that all institutions and all modes of organizations have their own flaws. This happens quite naturally from the concepts introduced above. As soon as the existence of positive transaction costs is acknowledged, and that the efficiency in the allocation and reallocation of rights depends on the characteristics of the devices required by these transfers, no one optimal solution that could serve as a benchmark exists. The only way to assess successes and failures, and to estimate costs and benefits, is through comparisons.

An Open Approach

In implementing this comparative approach on these kinds of issues, NIE has necessarily developed major intersections with other disciplines. Among the different and often competing paradigms that characterize modern economics, NIE figures as exceptionally interactive with legal scholars, social scientists, management scientists, and so on. Because NIE regards agents and organizations as socially embedded in institutions, the intersection with non-economic disciplines has become increasingly significant. Since it acknowledges the fact that agents are calculators and that costs matter in their choice, bridges have also remained open with mainstream economists. NIE is all but an isolated and closed paradigm.

Open to other disciplines as well as to other approaches in economics, new institutionalists naturally acknowledge weaknesses and problems in their paradigm. Numerous articles selected for this series identify problems and flaws; some even challenge corner stones of the edifice. This is precisely what in my view makes NIE a 'progressive' research program, that is, a research program turned in the direction of problems to be explored further and of domains to develop. Understanding institutional and organization changes, establishing more rigorously the channels through which modes of organization and institutions interact, and integrating the analysis of technology and technological dynamics are some of the challenges facing NIE. Several contributions show that these issues, and others, are high on the agenda of NIE researchers. If one main goal should be assigned to this series, it is to help the readers identify these terrains that are open to future research.

Organization of the Series: Some Caveats

The series is organized in seven books structured by themes so that each one forms an autonomous entity. Volume 1 collects articles that provided foundations to the field and opened the domain of NIE, and more recent articles that identify the major axes that have since developed and review some important issues, many of which remain under-explored. Volume 2 summarizes the behavioral assumptions that distinguish NIE from other approaches. Then, it proceeds to examine two building blocks of the theory: the nature and role of transaction costs, and the status of property rights. Volume 3 completes the golden triangle of NIE by thoroughly reviewing what contracts are, their characteristics, and how they are enforced. Volume 4 assembles articles on a leading theme in NIE, that is, the existence of alternative modes of organization and the tradeoff among them. The emblematic case of vertical integration definitively occupies a central place here. However, I have also included some exploratory articles on hybrid arrangements. Volume 5 develops the specific case of large modern corporations, since this case provides the support of most of what has been published in a NIE perspective on the internal characteristics of firms, an underdeveloped topic in NIE (and more generally in economic theory). Part of this volume also explores the impact of institutions on structural choices made within or among modes of organization. In Volume 6, I have assembled a set of articles focusing on the analysis of institutions, with a particular attention to what relates institutions to development and growth. Therefore, the emphasis here is less on the general impact of institutions at the organizational level, as in the previous volume, and more on the impact of political institutions and legal systems on the dynamics of transactions over time. Volume 7 concludes the series with articles examining critical issues in NIE and, for some of them, challenging the relevance of the approach. The confrontation of these different and often controversial perspectives should not only help to determine some of the main problems and flaws in NIE, but also identify where the action is or should be expected.

    Through all seven volumes, I have selected articles that emphasize the testability of the theory. Indeed, one major characteristic of NIE from the very beginning has been its reluctance towards 'blackboard economics' and its emphasis on the urgent need to build a theory that continually confronts facts and adjusts to observed realities.

    One last thing deserves clarification here. The introductions to the different volumes are intended to explain the logic underlying my choices. Ordering the chapters and suggesting specific links among them obviously involves interpretation. I have done my best to not distort or bias the main messages the authors wanted to get across. However, I have put the articles in a perspective that authors may not always share. Moreover, there is clearly a selection bias. Although the series is quite extensive, I was forced to discard some articles that would have deserved being here.

Acknowledgements

A project like this one develops over a long period of time. It requires support and encouragement. In preparing the series, I have benefited from a particularly generous environment.

First, I owe a lot to numerous friends and colleagues who made suggestions regarding the selection of articles for the series. I am particularly indebted to Ronald Coase, Philip Keefer, Gary Libecap, Douglass C. North, Emmanuel Raynaud, Stephane Saussier, Mary Shirley, and Oliver E. Williamson. Of course none of them is responsible for errors or omissions in the final selection. I have also received technical support from research assistants (Caroline Berteau, Stephanie Polin, and Anne Yvrande-Billon) and from the staff at Edward Elgar (particularly Nicola Mills and Ben Booth, whom I thank for their patience). Several institutions have supported and/or hosted me at different times in this project. The University of Paris (Panthéon-Sorbonne), the French Ministry of Education and Research, the Centre National de la Recherche Scientifique, the University of California at Berkeley, and the Massachusetts Institute of Technology have all provided facilities and support without which this project could not have been achieved.

However, my most significant debt is towards the contributors who all enthusiastically supported the project and helped to attain the copyrights. I want to express them my deepest gratitude.

Notes

1. The creation of the International Society for New Institutional Economics at a Conference held in St. Louis in 1997, with almost all major contributors to the field attending, can be considered as the institutional consolidation of the developments of the previous period.
2. Williamson (2000); Chapter 30, Volume 7.
3. All these aspects clearly distinguish NIE from the so-called 'new' property rights theory in which the existence and definition of these rights as well as the institutions required are assumed as given and costless.

References

Arrow, Kenneth (1970), 'The Organization of Economic Activity: Issues Pertinent to the Choice of Market versus Non-market Allocation', in Robert Haveman and Julius Margolis (eds), *Public Expenditures and Policy Analysis*. Chicago: Markham Pub. Co., pp. 39–73.
Coase, R.H. (1937), 'The Nature of the Firm', *Economica*, New Series, **4** (16), November, 386–405.
Coase, R.H. (1960), 'The Problem of Social Costs', *Journal of Law and Economics*, **3**, October, 1–44.
Williamson, O.E. (2000), 'The New Institutional Economics: Taking Stock, Looking Ahead', *Journal of Economic Literature*, **XXXVIII** (3), September, 596–613.

Introduction

Claude Ménard

New Institutional Economics (NIE) proposes a research program that developed essentially over the last 30 years. Although this is quite a short period of time for a theory to assess itself, the progress made is quite remarkable. It is rooted in a set of articles of exceptional quality, the bulk of which were published in the 1960s and early 1970s. Premonitory contributions can be identified, of course. The term 'institutions' existed long before the new approach emerged. However, what defines the specificity of New Institutional Economics is the elaboration of a set of concepts that provide powerful tools for analysing questions largely neglected, if not totally ignored before.

The readings collected in this volume combine some of the most influential articles that contributed to define the domain, as well as recent articles summarizing major axes of its development. They set the ground for the vast array of issues analysed in the series. They introduce the behavioral assumptions on which NIE is built, they present the basic concepts that are necessary for delineating what this approach is about, they provide attempts at modeling aspects of the theory, and they identify some of the major problems new institutional economics deals with.

The volume is organized in four parts. Part I fixes the background. Part II assembles the leading contributions that opened the new field and oriented its development. Part III reflects the efforts made at modeling some central concepts. Part IV identifies major issues that will be explored further in the next volumes.

Part I Background

This series is not intended to provide a historical overview of how NIE emerged or how it connects to past efforts. Only two historical references are reproduced, because they relate to two key issues in the development of NIE; one has to do with behavioral assumptions and the other with the importance and significance of putting transactions at the core of the analysis.

In Mandeville (Chapter 1), the point of entry is behavioral and developed through a fable. Mandeville intends 'to skew the Vileness of the ingredients that all together compose the wholesome mixture of a well order'd society' (Preface, p. 6). By rejecting an idealistic view of society and human beings, based on benevolence and altruism, he provocatively proposes to consider a society founded on passions and interests. In that context, institutions make sense: the central analytical problem becomes the explanation of how complex social mechanisms can be implemented, making possible the well-being of all to come out of dishonest, selfish, vicious individuals. What has been called the 'Mandevillian paradox' is the quest for institutions, or 'skillful management' in Mandeville terms, that can transform 'those very Vices of every Particular Persons' into the 'Grandeur and worldly Happiness of the whole' (p. 7).

Although later he comes back to behavioral assumptions, Smith begins his analysis of the sources of the *Wealth of Nations* with an organizational perspective, based on stylized facts (Chapter 2). Identifying the division of labor as the key to economic progress, he develops a more 'structural' approach to institutions that asks under what conditions could a 'well governed society' take advantage of specialization? His answer focuses on institutions that support the human propensity to exchange, of which the famous 'Invisible Hand' is only an example. The division of labor and the adequate organization of transactions go together, as later developed by Coase (Chapter 26).

Part II   Classic References

Part II collects articles that have deeply influenced the shaping of NIE. More could have been selected, of course, but I think the articles in this section cover the main contributions that gave its impulse to the new approach. Exceptionally, in order to give a flavor of the emergence of the field, the chapters are organized chronologically. They could be grouped under three headings that define significant aspects of the research program in NIE: the nature of the firm and the role of transaction costs in explaining it (Chapters 3, 4, and 8); the role of contracts as coordinating devices in a context of bounded rationality (Chapters 5, 9, and 10); and the nature of institutions in which transactions are embedded (Chapters 7 and 11).

Ronald Coase (Chapter 3) remains the fundamental reference in discussing the nature of the firm. The article is so often quoted that its basic argument has become common knowledge: firms exist because of the high costs of organizing some transactions through the price system. However, other aspects of the article have been neglected, or even ignored, which is unfortunate. Two of them deserve particular attention in my view. One relates to Coase's conception of society as an organization, requiring choices by agents among alternative arrangements, as opposed to the 'organic' perspective of a self-sufficient economy that is entirely ruled by prices. Another important point concerns the conception of the firm as 'a system of relationship', with the entrepreneur at the core, in charge of command and planning; however, this comes with limited capabilities, which explains the limits of the firm.

Malmgren (Chapter 4) develops the Coasian argument about the transaction cost origin of the firm. However, he challenges the idea of the division of labor and the resulting coordination problems as the explanation to these costs. In an economy that changes along predictable patterns, so that future events can accurately be foreseen, the Invisible Hand (or complete contracts in contemporary parlance) could do the job. The real source of transaction costs lies in uncertainty, which explains the role of entrepreneurs as well as the selection process of firms. Arrow (Chapter 6) totally concurs when he attributes transaction costs to market failures, part of which results from uncertainty, as when markets for risk bearing or for future transactions do not exist. Therefore, transaction costs represent 'the costs of running the economic system' in an imperfect world. Social institutions, such as vertically integrated firms, develop for overcoming these failures while taking advantage of collective actions. However, Malmgren's chapter goes a step further when it relates uncertainty to the types of information processed in a market economy, with the comparative advantage of some firms resulting from their capacity to produce adequate knowledge.

Information and knowledge provide the core of the controversial article by Alchian and Demsetz (Chapter 8), in which they challenge the transaction costs perspective. In their view, reducing transaction costs is a secondary determinant. What really characterizes a firm is its capacity to take advantage of specialization through the organization of collective action. A firm is therefore an institution that relies on the entrepreneur acting as the 'centralized contractual agent in a team production process'. His or her central role is not the exercise of authority, but the collection and interpretation of information, the coordination of the team, and the reduction of shirking, all of which he or she has an incentive to do efficiently because he or she is the residual claimant. Their controversial conclusion is that a firm is nothing but a nexus of contracts, 'a highly specialized surrogate market'. One remaining problem of this approach is of course the explanation of the modern corporation as multiple layers of hierarchically organized employees.

Notwithstanding the problems it raises, Alchian and Demsetz's article largely contributed in combination with an almost simultaneous article by Williamson (1971; Chapter 8, Volume 4), to attract the attention on the key role of contracts. Cheung soon illustrated this in a subtle empirical study of the relationship between beekeepers and farmers (Chapter 9). Following suggestions from Coase (1960; Chapter 15, Volume 2), Cheung intended to show that market failures and externalities might not have the importance suggested by Arrow and others. In many situations, relatively simple contractual agreements can be designed and implemented that allow transactors to take advantage of their mutual specialization. The article also exhibited the importance of norms and customs in the enforcement of these contracts.

The importance of social interaction was already suggested in Simon's article on 'The Architecture of Complexity' (Chapter 5). By adopting a decision-making approach, the article emphasizes the now well-known idea that agents have a very limited capacity to process information and to deal with complex situations. Therefore, they behave as adapters rather than maximizers, thus decomposing problems and finding rules of behavior. Some results show that new institutionalists capitalized later on. First, agents generate uncertainty in responding to external events that they analyse imperfectly. Second, their bounded rationality may provide them incentives to the 'team'.[1] Simon thus makes room for an interpretation of alternative modes of organization as ways to overcome bounded rationality.

Building on these premises, Williamson (Chapter 10) represents a major step in the development of transaction costs economics and more generally of NIE. The chapter integrates dispersed pieces into a coherent framework, thus providing a model that can generate testable predictions. Assuming that agents are boundedly rational and that they have an opportunistic propensity to take advantage of uncertainties and information 'impactedness', Williamson emphasizes the importance of contractual agreements for dealing with these situations. However, contracts are incomplete and contractual hazards can develop. The chapter then establishes a relationship between the sources of these hazards, rooted in the attributes of transactions, and their impact on the choice of contractual forms and their related modes of governance. He thus opens the door to a systematic analysis of alternative modes of governance, with contracts at the core.

Contractual hazards may also result from the institutional environment in which these arrangements are rooted. The distinction between institutional environment and institutional arrangements (or modes of governance) comes from Davis and North (Chapter 7). To this now classical distinction, corresponds the two major branches in NIE. The institutional environment defines the rules of the game in which economic units act. It encapsulates the political, social, and legal factors under which choices are made, contracts are implemented, and organizations evolved. Hurwicz (Chapter 11) provides a nice illustration of efforts at modeling the concept of institutions as rules of the game. Using a game theoretic framework, he identifies institutions as mechanisms designed for processing information. The approach is clearly distinct from the one that prevails in NIE, particularly because of the standard behavioral assumptions underlying it. However, it exhibits interesting properties and problems in a 'northian' perspective, particularly the possibility of multiple equilibria and the question of how a specific equilibrium is selected. Also, it illustrates the potential role of game theory in exploring properties of institutions and modeling them.

Part III   Modeling Institutions and Institutional Arrangements

Part III is about some major modeling efforts. One reiterated critique to NIE and more generally to the analysis of institutions, mostly by mainstream economists, points out an alleged inability to provide models encapsulating rigorously the proposed concepts. I would certainly not argue that the situation is satisfying in that respect. The rudimentary state in which we still are may not be that surprising: after all, NIE is essentially one generation old. However, the articles selected for this section show the serious steps made in modeling the theory, and very significantly the models developed have a close connection to applied models and to tests, a point the next volumes will substantiate.

The section is organized along the two major axes of investigation suggested by Davis and North. Chapters 12–14 formalize the concept of institution understood as institutional environment while Chapters 15–17 focus on microanalytical issues, particularly the tradeoff among institutional arrangements. Chapter 18 extends to political issues.

Notwithstanding its limitations in capturing the richness of the problems raised in NIE, a point nicely discussed by Kreps (Chapter 15) in his discussion of the relationship between transaction-costs and mathematical economics, game theoretical approaches have nevertheless provided substantial insights on the nature of institutions and how they change. Several articles illustrate this. Schotter's chapter (Chapter 12) introduces a pioneering study in the field. By adopting an evolutionary game perspective, he interprets institutions as conventions resulting from common knowledge that is developed through the interaction of individual strategies. This approach raises many questions, particularly with regard to the implementation and enforcement of these conventions, a point also noted by Hurwicz (Chapter 11), but it helps identify some major problems, that is the coordination function of institutions, the role of interacting strategies in the emergence of institutions, the nature of equilibria at stake, and so on. Schotter also openly discusses the relevance of using a game theoretic language for analysing institutions.

Years later, more recent articles by Hurwicz (Chapter 13) and Aoki (Chapter 14) illustrate the progress made and the difficulties encountered. This progress comes from a better specification of the attributes of institutions (for example, specification of the strategy domains and of the outcome functions, enforcement issues, the key role of the information system, and so on). However, the two chapters also identify severe difficulties, including oversimplified behavioral assumptions; underdeveloped analysis of the emergence and enforcement of institutions, with a risk of infinite regression emphasized by Hurwicz; heterogeneous concepts of equilibrium identified as institutions; and the question of what equilibrium is selected and how and when multiple equilibria are at stake.

Similar difficulties emerge with game theory when applied at the micro level of organizational issues. While discussing how to model the tradeoff between markets and hierarchies from a game strategic perspective, Kreps (Chapter 15) meets Schotter and Hurwicz in his emphasis on how game theory, in order to provide the adequate language, might have to learn as much from the frameworks it intends to encapsulate as NIE can gain in endorsing a game perspective.

Riordan and Williamson (Chapter 16) adopt a more 'pedestrian' approach. By using standard analytical tools, that is well-defined functions and a maximizing rule, they developed a model of the tradeoff between make or buy that provides a rigorous yet simple framework for analysing the alignment of governance structures with attributes of transactions, particularly the specificity of assets involved. In their discussion, they also exhibit the potential role of intermediate arrangements ('hybrids'), a point largely documented later in the literature (see Volume 4). The model also explicitly intended to establish bridges with mainstream economics. Bajari and Tadelis (Chapter 17) go a step further and provide a sophisticated version of the previous model. While the 1985 article used a reduced form model, their contribution proposes a structural version, with costs and benefits from different contractual forms endogenized. The model explains nicely why procurement problems in the private sector as well as the public are problems of ex-post adaptation rather than ex-ante screening.

Shepsle and Weingast (Chapter 18) close the section in extending transaction costs analysis to an important issue in political sciences, the nearly complete instability of Pure Majority Rule, a problem somewhat similar to the stability problem in a Pure Exchange Economy. They suggest that failures of solutions, based on legislative exchanges (for example, vote trading) or contingent contracts among legislators, are due to reasons similar to those explaining failures of pure exchange or complete contracts in establishing a stable economic equilibrium; political transaction costs are ignored. They also argue the solution to instability may well depend on the development of institutions restricting the domain of choices and the modes of functioning of a Pure Majority Rule. Hence, the idea of a structure-induced equilibrium they developed.

The models selected above do not cover all the complex problems developed in the next volumes but they do show some of the difficulties involved in a modeling strategy.

Part IV   Some Major Issues

The last part of this volume summarizes some major issues that will likely define the agenda of NIE for a significant period of time. The articles selected reveal some diverging views and show that notwithstanding the unifying role of the transaction costs concept, boundaries of the field remain blurred. For example, Furubotn and Richter (Chapter 19) adopt a broad and inclusive perspective, while Coase (Chapter 25) defends a more focused approach. The former motivate their broad view in identifying three building blocks in NIE: transaction costs, property rights, and (incomplete) contracts. Most new institutionalists likely agree with this conception but the progressive diffusion of these themes in economics and social sciences makes the delineation of NIE more difficult. For example, Richter and Furubotn include public choice and agency theory in the field of NIE, a relationship that some leading figures of these approaches may not feel comfortable with. Notwithstanding constant interactions among these paradigms, substantial differences remain, some of which should become more visible in the coming volumes.[2] The review provided here helped to fix the elements of the global picture.

Buchanan's article on 'A Contractarian Paradigm' comes next (Chapter 20). It is included here because of its representation of the economy as a 'social organization', in contrast to the standard view of economics as a science of choice. In the former perspective, interactions among agents become the core of the analysis requiring that economics be transformed into a science of contracts. A substantial number of new institutional economists share this view.

In establishing her agenda for the study of institutions, Ostrom (Chapter 21) goes in the same direction and extends it to the social sciences, particularly political sciences. As in Davis and North (Chapter 7), she emphasizes the importance of rules and norms in defining institutions. She interprets rules as social artifacts embedded in arrangements that give them a prescriptive force, thus shaping actions. Granovetter is not far from this view when he defines institutions as social constructions (Chapter 22). Although this author has often adopted a controversial approach to NIE, and particularly to Williamson that he accused of developing an 'undersocialized' approach similar to neoclassical economics (1985; see Chapter 27, Volume 7), his interpretation of institutions and organizations as embedded in social networks does not sound unfamiliar to neo-institutionalists (see for example Volume 6). The divergence may concern more the methodology than the content. The comparison with Ostrom is very useful in that respect, particularly with regard to the argument developed by Granovetter that neo-institutionalists would have an approach based exclusively on individual choices. Granovetter may not have fully registered progress made in NIE.

The last four chapters of this volume focus on aspects of the interactions among institutional components that deserve more research. Matthews (Chapter 23) is among the first macroeconomists to have explicitly acknowledged the importance of the emerging approach for understanding the factors that determine development and growth. His article can be read as a signal of changes that were beginning to penetrate standard models. He rightly pointed out the importance of interactions among different levels at which institutions operate and the resulting difficulties for developing empirical studies that are much needed.

Published exactly ten years later, the article by Aoki (Chapter 24) illustrates part of the progress made. In his analysis, Aoki re-emphasizes the role of institutions for understanding proper development and growth, and the difficult experiences of many developing countries as well as transition economies. The benign neglect of institutions has had major negative impact but Aoki argues that we have learned much in that process. A comparative analysis of different experiences shows not only the important role played by institutions, but also their interdependence. Economic systems should be better understood as 'a cluster of institutions'. The article also defends the idea that institutional diversity can represent the potential source of social gains, a view shared by many contributors to these volumes.

While the Aoki chapter is mainly about the impact of the institutional environment, the chapter by Ménard (Chapter 25) focuses on more conceptual issues, and mostly at the micro level. The emphasis is on what we have learned that can help better understand the diversity of institutional arrangements (or modes of governance) that characterize a market economy, and the properties that differentiate these arrangements. In trying to delineate the concepts better, the article exhibits how institutional arrangements are deeply embedded in their environment and suggest some mechanisms of interactions between these two levels.

Coase (Chapter 26) concludes the volume in restating the position of NIE as a way to think about how institutions and their interactions explain and determine the capacity to implement and take advantage of the division of labor, which determine the possibilities of growth and welfare. He thus reminds us of the fundamental reason why institutions matter so much in economics; agents could not benefit from the division of labor and its ensuing specialization without the complex set of devices required for organizing transactions. This establishes a neat link with Adam Smith (Chapter 2).

Notes

1. One of the very first attempts at modeling bounded rationality significantly came from a leading proponent of team theory (Radner, 1975).
2. Some fundamental divergences are discussed in Williamson (2002).

References

Coase, R. (1960), 'The Problem of Social Cost', *Journal of Law and Economics*, **III** (1), October, 1–44.
Granovetter, M. (1985), 'Economic Action and Social Structure: The Problem of Embeddedness', *American Journal of Sociology*, **91** (3), November, 481–510.
Radner, R. (1975), 'Satisficing', *Journal of Mathematical Economics*, **2** (2), 253–62.
Williamson, O.E. (1971), 'The Vertical Integration of Production: Market Failure Considerations', *American Economic Review, Papers and Proceedings*, **LXI** (2), May, 112–23.
Williamson, O.E. (2002), 'The Theory of the Firm as Governance Structure: From Choice to Contract', *Journal of Economic Perspective*, **16** (3), 171–94.

Part I
Background

THE   [1]

GRUMBLING HIVE:

OR,

KNAVES *turn'd Honest.*[a]

Spacious Hive well stockt with Bees,
That liv'd in Luxury and Ease ;
And yet as fam'd for Laws and
    Arms,
As yielding large and early Swarms;
Was counted the great Nursery
Of Sciences and Industry.
No Bees had better Government,
More Fickleness, or less Content :
They were not Slaves to Tyranny,
Nor rul'd by wild *Democracy* ;
But Kings, that could not wrong, because   [2]
Their Power was circumscrib'd by Laws.

   a: or, KNAVES *turn'd Honest*] *om. in heading, although present on title-page*, 05

18   *The Grumbling Hive : Or,*

THESE Insects liv'd like Men, and all
Our Actions they perform'd in small :
They did whatever's done in Town,
And what belongs to Sword or Gown :
Tho' th' Artful Works, by nimble Slight
Of minute Limbs, 'scap'd Human Sight ;
Yet we've no Engines, Labourers,
Ships, Castles, Arms, Artificers,
Craft, Science, Shop, or Instrument,
But they had an Equivalent :
Which, since their Language is unknown,
Must be call'd, as we do our own.
As grant, that among other Things,
They wanted Dice, yet they had Kings ;
And those had Guards ; from whence we may
Justly conclude, they had some Play ;
Unless a Regiment be shewn
Of Soldiers, that make use of none.

[3]   VAST Numbers throng'd the fruitful Hive ;
Yet those vast Numbers made 'em thrive ;
Millions endeavouring to supply
Each other's Lust and Vanity ;
While other Millions were employ'd,
To see their Handy-works destroy'd ;
They furnish'd half the Universe ;
Yet had more Work than Labourers.

Knaves turn'd Honest.   19

Some with vast Stocks, and little Pains,

Jump'd into Business of great Gains ;

And some were damn'd to Sythes and Spades,

And all those hard laborious Trades ;

Where willing Wretches daily sweat,

And wear out Strength and Limbs to eat :

(*A.*) [a] While others follow'd Mysteries,

To which few Folks bind 'Prentices ;

That want no Stock, but that of Brass,

And may set up without a Cross ; [1]

As Sharpers, Parasites, Pimps, Players,

Pick-pockets, Coiners, Quacks, South-sayers, [2]

And all those, that in Enmity,   [4]

With downright Working, cunningly

Convert to their own Use the Labour

Of their good-natur'd heedless Neighbour.

(*B.*) These were call'd Knaves, but bar the Name,

The grave Industrious were the same :

[a] (*A.*), (*B.*), *etc.*]   *No reference letters in* 05

[1] Without money. A cross was a small coin.

[2] Cf. Butler's posthumous *Upon the Weakness and Misery of Man*:
... bawds, whores, and usurers,
Pimps, scriv'ners, silenc'd ministers,
That get estates by being undone
For tender conscience, and have none,
Like those that with their credit drive
A trade, without a stock, and thrive . . . .
Had Mandeville perhaps seen a MS. of Butler's poem (published 1759)? The poem, incidentally, stated,
Our holiest actions have been Th' effects of wickedness and sin . . .

B 2

20   *The Grumbling Hive : Or,*

All Trades and Places knew some Cheat,
No Calling was without Deceit.

T H E Lawyers, of whose Art the Basis
Was raising Feuds and splitting Cases,
Oppos'd all Registers, that Cheats
Might make more Work with dipt Estates ; [1]
As wer't unlawful, that one's own,
Without a Law-Suit, should be known.
They kept off Hearings wilfully,
To finger the refreshing [a] Fee ;
And to defend a wicked Cause,
Examin'd and survey'd the Laws,
As Burglars Shops and Houses do,
To find out where they'd best break through.

[5]   P H Y S I C I A N S valu'd Fame and Wealth
Above the drooping Patient's Health,
Or their own Skill : The greatest Part
Study'd, instead of Rules of Art,
Grave pensive Looks and dull Behaviour,
To gain th' Apothecary's Favour ;
The Praise of Midwives, Priests, and all
That serv'd at Birth or Funeral.

[a] retaining *05*

[1] Mortgaged estates.

Knaves turn'd Honest. 21

To bear with th' ever-talking Tribe,
And hear my Lady's Aunt prescribe;
With formal Smile, and kind How d'ye,
To fawn on all the Family;
And, which of all the greatest Curse is,
T' endure th' Impertinence of Nurses.

A M O N G the many Priests of *Jove*,
Hir'd to draw Blessings from Above,
Some few were Learn'd and Eloquent,
But thousands Hot and Ignorant:
Yet all pass'd Muster that could hide
Their Sloth, Lust, Avarice and Pride;
For which they were as fam'd as Tailors   [6]
For Cabbage, or for Brandy Sailors: [a]
Some, meagre-look'd, and meanly clad,
Would mystically pray for Bread,
Meaning by that an ample Store,
Yet lit'rally received no more;
And, while these holy Drudges starv'd,
The [b] lazy Ones, for which they serv'd,
Indulg'd their Ease, with all the Graces
Of Health and Plenty in their Faces.

[a] Sailors :] Sailors, *32*   [b] Some *05–23*

22   *The Grumbling Hive : Or,*

(*C.*) T H E Soldiers, that were forc'd to fight,
If they surviv'd, got Honour by't ;
Tho' some, that shunn'd the bloody Fray,
Had Limbs shot off, that ran away :
Some valiant Gen'rals fought the Foe ;
Others took Bribes to let them go :
Some ventur'd always where 'twas warm,
Lost now a Leg, and then an Arm ;
Till quite disabled, and put by,
They liv'd on half their Salary ;
[7] While others never came in Play,
And staid at Home for double Pay.

T H E I R Kings were serv'd, but Knavishly,
Cheated by their own Ministry ;
Many, that for their Welfare slaved,
Robbing the very Crown they saved :
Pensions were small, and they liv'd high,
Yet boasted of their Honesty.
Calling, whene'er they strain'd their Right,
The slipp'ry Trick a Perquisite ;
And when Folks understood their Cant,
They chang'd that for Emolument ;
Unwilling to be short or plain,
In any thing concerning Gain ;
(*D.*) For there was not a Bee but would
Get more, I won't say, than he should ;

Knaves turn'd Honest.   23

But than he dar'd to let them know,
(*E.*) That pay'd for't ; as your Gamesters do,
That, tho' at fair Play, ne'er will own
Before the Losers what they've won.

    B U T who can all their Frauds repeat ?   [8]
The very Stuff, which in the Street
They sold for Dirt t'enrich the Ground,
Was often by the Buyers found
Sophisticated with a quarter
Of good-for-nothing Stones and Mortar ;
Tho' *Flail* had little Cause to mutter,
Who sold the other Salt for Butter.

    J U S T I C E her self, fam'd for fair Dealing,
By Blindness had not lost her Feeling ;
Her Left Hand, which the Scales should hold,
Had often dropt 'em, brib'd with Gold ;
And, tho' she seem'd Impartial,
Where Punishment was corporal,
Pretended to a reg'lar Course,
In Murther, and all Crimes of Force ;
Tho' some, first pillory'd for Cheating,
Were hang'd in Hemp of their own beating ;
Yet, it was thought, the Sword she bore
Check'd but the Desp'rate and the Poor ;

24   *The Grumbling Hive : Or,*

[9] That, urg'd by meer Necessity,
     Were ty'd up to the wretched Tree [1]
     For Crimes, which not deserv'd that Fate,
     But to secure the Rich and Great.

     T H U S every Part was full of Vice,
     Yet the whole Mass a Paradise ;
     Flatter'd in Peace, and fear'd in Wars,
     They were th' Esteem of Foreigners,
     And lavish of their Wealth and Lives,
     The Balance of all other Hives.
     Such were the Blessings of that State ;
     Their Crimes conspir'd to make them [a] Great :
     (*F.*) And Virtue, who from Politicks
     Had learn'd a Thousand Cunning Tricks,
     Was, by their happy Influence,
     Made Friends with Vice : And ever since,
     (*G.*) The worst of all the Multitude
     Did something for the Common Good.

[10]   T H I S was the State's Craft, that maintain'd
     The Whole of which each Part complain'd :
     This, as in Musick Harmony,[b]
     Made Jarrings in the main agree ; [c]

          [a] 'em *05*   [b] Harmony,] Harmony *25–32*
                    [c] agree ;] agree, *32*

     [1] Cf. Livy i. 26 : 'infelici arbori reste suspendito' ; also Cicero,
Pro C. Rabirio iv. 13.

Knaves turn'd Honest.   25

(*H.*) Parties directly opposite,
Assist each other ª, as 'twere for Spight;
And Temp'rance with Sobriety,
Serve Drunkenness and Gluttony.

(*I.*) T H E Root of Evil, Avarice,
That damn'd ill-natur'd baneful Vice,
Was Slave to Prodigality,
(*K.*) That noble Sin; (*L.*) whilst Luxury
Employ'd a Million of the Poor,
(*M.*) And odious Pride a Million more:
(*N.*) ᵇ Envy it self, and Vanity,
Were Ministers of Industry;
Their darling Folly, Fickleness,
In Diet, Furniture and Dress,
That strange ridic'lous Vice, was made
The very Wheel that turn'd the Trade.
Their Laws and Clothes were equally   [11]
Objects of Mutability;
For, what was well done for a time,
In half a Year became a Crime;
Yet while they alter'd thus their Laws,
Still finding and correcting Flaws,
They mended by Inconstancy
Faults, which no Prudence could foresee.

ª oth'r *05*   ᵇ (*N.*) *om. 14*

26   *The Grumbling Hive: Or,*

T H U S Vice nurs'd Ingenuity,

Which join'd with Time and Industry,

Had carry'd Life's Conveniencies [a],

(*O.*) [b] It's real Pleasures, Comforts, Ease,

(*P.*) [c] To such a Height, the very Poor

Liv'd better than the Rich before,[1]

And nothing could be added more.

H o w Vain is Mortal Happiness !

Had they but known the Bounds of Bliss ;

And that Perfection here below

Is more than Gods can well bestow ;

[12] The Grumbling Brutes had been content

With Ministers and Government.

But they, at every ill Success,

Like Creatures lost without Redress,

Curs'd Politicians, Armies, Fleets ;

While every one cry'd, *Damn the Cheats*,

And would, tho' conscious of his own,

In others barb'rously bear none.

---

[a] Conveniences *32*   [b] (*N.*) *14*   [c] (*O.*) *14*

[1] Of these lines and their elaboration in Remark P, I note two anticipations (not necessarily sources): '...a king of a large and fruitful territory there [America] feeds, lodges, and is clad worse than a day-labourer in England' (Locke, *Of Civil Government* II. v. 41); and '...a King of *India* is not so well lodg'd, and fed, and cloath'd, as a Day-labourer of *England*' (*Considerations on the East-India Trade*, in *Select Collection of Early English Tracts on Commerce*, ed. Political Economy Club, 1856, p. 594).

Knaves turn'd Honest. 27

O N E, that had got a Princely Store,
By cheating Master, King and Poor,
Dar'd cry aloud, *The Land must sink*
For all its Fraud ; And whom d'ye think
The Sermonizing Rascal chid?
A Glover that sold Lamb for Kid.

    The least thing was not done amiss,
Or cross'd the Publick Business ;
But all the Rogues cry'd brazenly,
Good Gods, Had we but Honesty !
Merc'ry smil'd at th' Impudence,   [13]
And others call'd it want of Sense,
Always to rail at what they lov'd :
But *Jove* with Indignation mov'd,
At last in Anger swore, *He'd rid*
The bawling Hive of Fraud ; and did.
The very Moment it departs,
And Honesty fills all their Hearts ;
There shews 'em, like th' Instructive Tree,
Those Crimes which they're asham'd to see ;
Which now in Silence they confess,
By blushing at their Ugliness :
Like Children, that would hide their Faults,
And by their Colour own their Thoughts :

28   *The Grumbling Hive : Or,*

Imag'ning, when they're look'd upon,
That others see what they have done.

    B u t, Oh ye Gods ! What Consternation,
How vast and sudden was th' Alteration !
In half an Hour, the Nation round,
Meat fell a Peny in the Pound.

[14] The Mask Hypocrisy's flung down,
From the great Statesman to the Clown :
And some in borrow'd Looks well known,
Appear'd like Strangers in their own.
The Bar was silent from that Day ;
For now the willing Debtors pay,
Ev'n what's by Creditors forgot ;
Who quitted them that had it not.
Those, that were in the Wrong, stood mute,
And dropt the patch'd vexatious Suit :
On which since nothing less ª can thrive,
Than Lawyers in an honest Hive,
All, except those that got enough,
With Inkhorns by their sides troop'd off.

    J u s t i c e hang'd some, set others free ;
And after Goal delivery,
Her Presence being ᵇ no more requir'd,
With all her Train and Pomp retir'd.

      ª else *32*   ᵇ be'ng *14-25*

Knaves turn'd Honest. 29

First march'd some Smiths with Locks and Grates,

Fetters, and Doors with Iron Plates :

Next Goalers, Turnkeys and Assistants :   [15]

Before the Goddess, at some distance,

Her chief and faithful Minister,

'Squire C A T C H,[1] the Law's great Finisher,

Bore not th' imaginary Sword,[2]

But his own Tools, an Ax and Cord :

Then on a Cloud the Hood-wink'd Fair,

J U S T I C E her self was push'd by Air :

About her Chariot, and behind,

Were Serjeants, Bums [3] of every kind,

Tip-staffs, and all those Officers,

That squeeze a Living out of Tears.

T H o' Physick liv'd, while Folks were ill,

None would prescribe, but Bees of skill,

Which through the Hive dispers'd so wide,

That none of them [a] had need to ride ;

Wav'd vain Disputes, and strove to free

The Patients of their Misery ;

[a] 'em *05*

[1] ' Jack Ketch ' had become a generic term for executioners.

[2] Probably the sword of justice, although a note in the French translation explains it differently (ed. 1750, i. 21) : 'On ne se sert dans les executions en *Angleterre* que de la hache pour trancher la tête, jamais de l'Epée. C'est pour cela qu'il donne le nom d'imaginaire à cette Epée qu'on attribue au Bourreau.'

[3] Bumbailiffs.

30   *The Grumbling Hive : Or,*

Left Drugs in cheating Countries grown,

And us'd the Product of their own ;

[16] Knowing the Gods sent no Disease

To Nations without Remedies.

T H E I R Clergy rous'd from Laziness,

Laid not their Charge on Journey-Bees ; [1]

But serv'd themselves, exempt from Vice,

The Gods with Pray'r and Sacrifice ;

All those, that were unfit, or knew

Their Service might be spar'd, withdrew :

Nor was there Business for so many,

(If th' Honest stand in need of any,)

Few only with the High-Priest staid,

To whom the rest Obedience paid :

Himself employ'd in Holy Cares,[a]

Resign'd to others State-Affairs.

He chas'd no Starv'ling from his Door,

Nor pinch'd the Wages of the Poor ;

But at his House the Hungry's fed,

The Hireling finds unmeasur'd Bread,

The needy Trav'ler Board and Bed.

[a] Cares,] Cares ; *24–32*

[1] ' Journeyman parson ' was a slang term for a curate.

Knaves turn'd Honest.   31

A M O N G the King's great Ministers,
And all th' inferior Officers
The Change was great ; (&.) ª for frugally
They now liv'd on their Salary :
That a poor Bee should ten times come
To ask his Due, a trifling Sum,
And by some well-hir'd Clerk be made
To give a Crown, or ne'er be paid,
Would now be call'd a downright Cheat,
Tho' formerly a Perquisite.
All Places manag'd first by Three,
Who watch'd each other's Knavery,
And often for a Fellow-feeling,
Promoted one another's stealing,
Are happily supply'd by One,
By which some thousands more are gone.

(*R*) ᵇ No Honour now could be content,
To live and owe for what was spent ;
Liv'ries in Brokers Shops are hung,
They part with Coaches for a Song ;
Sell stately Horses by whole Sets ;
And Country-Houses, to pay Debts.

ª (*P.*) *14*   ᵇ (*Q.*) *14*

32   *The Grumbling Hive : Or,*

VAIN Cost is shunn'd as much as Fraud ;
They have no Forces kept Abroad ;
Laugh at th' Esteem of Foreigners,
And empty Glory got by Wars ;
They fight, but for their Country's sake,
When Right or Liberty's at Stake.

Now mind the glorious Hive, and see
How Honesty and Trade agree.
The Shew is gone, it thins apace ;
And looks with quite another Face.
For 'twas not only that They went,
By whom vast Sums were Yearly spent ;
But Multitudes that liv'd on them,
Were daily forc'd to do the same.
In vain to other Trades they'd fly ;
All were o'er-stock'd accordingly.

[19]   THE Price of Land and Houses falls ;
Mirac'lous Palaces, whose Walls,
Like those of *Thebes*, were rais'd by Play,[1]
Are to be let ; while the once gay,

[1] A footnote in the French translation (ed. 1750, i. 27) says : ' L'Auteur veut parler des bâtimens élevés pour l'Opera & la Comédie. *Amphion*, après avoir chassé *Cadmus & sa Femme* du lieu de leur demeure, y bâtit la Ville de *Thèbes*, en y attirant les pierres avec ordre & mesure, par l'harmonie merveilleuse de son divin Luth.' It is possible, however, that Mandeville intended a pun on ' Play ' as meaning both music and gambling.

Knaves turn'd Honest. 33

Well-seated Houshold Gods would be
More pleas'd to expire [a] in Flames, than see
The mean Inscription on the Door
Smile at the lofty ones they bore.
The building Trade is quite destroy'd,
Artificers are not employ'd ;
(*S.*) [b] No Limner for his Art is fam'd,
Stone-cutters, Carvers are not nam'd.

T H O S E, that remain'd, grown temp'rate, strive,
Not how to spend, but how to live,
And, when they paid their Tavern Score,
Resolv'd to enter it no more :
No Vintner's Jilt in all the Hive
Could wear now Cloth of Gold, and thrive ;
Nor *Torcol* such vast Sums advance,
For *Burgundy* and *Ortelans* ;
The Courtier's gone, that with his Miss   [20]
Supp'd at his House on *Christmas* Peas ;
Spending as much in two Hours stay,
As keeps a Troop of Horse a Day.

T H E haughty *Chloe*, to live Great,
Had made her (*T.*) [c] Husband rob the State :

---

[a] to expire] t'expire *05–25*   [b] (*R.*) *14*
        [c] (*T.*) *om. 14*

C

34   *The Grumbling Hive : Or,*

But now she sells her Furniture,

Which th' *Indies* had been ransack'd for ;

Contracts th' expensive Bill of Fare,

And wears her strong Suit a whole Year :

The slight and fickle Age is past ;

And Clothes, as well as Fashions, last.

Weavers, that join'd rich Silk with Plate,

And all the Trades subordinate,

Are gone.   Still Peace and Plenty reign,

And every Thing is cheap, tho' plain :

Kind Nature, free from Gard'ners Force,

Allows all Fruits in her own Course ;

But Rarities cannot be had,

Where Pains to get them ᵃ are not paid.

[21]   A s Pride and Luxury decrease,

So by degrees they leave the Seas.

Not Merchants now, but ᵇ Companies

Remove whole Manufactories.

All Arts and Crafts neglected lie ;

(*V.*) ᶜ Content, the Bane of Industry,¹

ᵃ 'em *05–29*   ᵇ But *32*   ᶜ (*S.*) *14*

¹ Compare Locke's reflection : thus we see our all-wise Maker, ' When a man is perfectly content suitably to our constitution and with the state he is in—which is frame, and knowing what it is when he is perfectly without any that determines the will, has put uneasiness—what industry, what into man the uneasiness of hunger action, what will is there left, and thirst, and other natural de- but to continue in it ? . . . And sires, that return at their seasons,

Knaves turn'd Honest.　　35

Makes 'em admire their homely Store,
And neither seek nor covet more.

S o few in the vast Hive remain,
The hundredth Part they can't maintain
Against th' Insults of numerous Foes ;
Whom yet they valiantly oppose :
'Till some well-fenc'd Retreat is found,
And here they die or stand their Ground.
No Hireling in their Army's known ;
But bravely fighting for their own,
Their Courage and Integrity
At last were crown'd with Victory.
　　They triumph'd not without their Cost,
For many Thousand Bees were lost.
Hard'ned with Toils and Exercise,　　　　　　　[22]
They counted Ease it self a Vice ;
Which so improv'd their Temperance ;
That, to avoid Extravagance,
They flew into a hollow Tree,
Blest with Content and Honesty.

to move and determine their of their species ' (*Essay concerning*
wills, for the preservation of *Human Understanding,* ed. Fraser,
themselves, and the continuation 1894, II. xxi. 34).

[23]   T H E

M O R A L.

T HEN *leave Complaints : Fools only strive*
    (X.) [a] *To make a Great an Honest Hive*
(Y.) [b] *T' enjoy the World's Conveniencies,*[c]
Be fam'd in War, yet live in Ease,
Without great Vices, is a vain
EUTOPIA *seated in the Brain.*
Fraud, Luxury and Pride must live,
While we the Benefits receive :
Hunger's a dreadful Plague, no doubt,
Yet who digests or thrives without ?
Do we not owe the Growth of Wine
To the dry shabby crooked [d] *Vine ?*
Which, while its Shoots neglected stood,
Chok'd other Plants, and ran to Wood ;
But blest us with its noble Fruit,
As soon as it was ty'd and cut :

    [a] *(T.) 14*   [b] *(V.) 14*   [c] *Conveniences 32*
    [d] *shabby crooked] crooked, shabby 05*

The *MORAL*.   37

So Vice is beneficial found,   [24]

When it's by Justice lopt and bound ;

Nay, where the People would be great,

As necessary to the State,

As Hunger is to make 'em eat.

Bare Virtue can't make Nations live

In Splendor ; they, that would revive

A Golden Age, must be as free,

For Acorns, as for Honesty.[1]

[1] In its use of feminine endings the *Grumbling Hive* is less Hudibrastic than is Mandeville's other verse, containing only some seven per cent of these endings as against the twenty per cent of Mandeville's verse as a whole and the thirty-five per cent of his translations from Scarron in *Typhon* (1704) and *Wishes to a Godson* (1712). Perhaps Mandeville consciously imitated this feature of *Hudibras*, a poem which he twice quoted (*Treatise*, ed. 1711, p. 94, and *Origin of Honour*, p. 134) and whose author he called 'the incomparable Butler' (*Treatise*, p. 94).

F I N I S.

[2]

BOOK I

Of the Causes of Improvement in the productive Powers of Labour, and of the Order according to which its Produce is naturally distributed among the different Ranks of the People

CHAPTER I

Of the Division of Labour

1 THE greatest *a*improvement*a* in the productive powers of labour, and the greater part of the skill, dexterity, and judgment with which it is any where directed, or applied, seem to have been the effects of the division of labour.[1]

a-a improvements *1*

---

[1] The first considered exposition of the term division of labour by a modern writer was probably by Sir William Petty: 'Those who have the command of the Sea Trade, may Work at easier Freight with more profit, than others at greater: for as Cloth must be cheaper made, when one Cards, another Spins, another Weaves, another Draws, another Dresses, another Presses and Packs; than when all the Operations above-mentioned, were clumsily performed by the same hand; so those who command the Trade of Shipping, can build long slight Ships for carrying Masts, Fir-Timber, Boards, Balks, etc.' (*Political Arithmetick* (London, 1690), 19, in C. H. Hull, *The Economic Writings of Sir William Petty* (Cambridge, 1899), i. 260). 'For in so vast a City *Manufactures* will beget one another, and each *Manufacture* will be divided into as many parts as possible, whereby the work of each *Artisan* will be simple and easie: As for Example. In the making of a *Watch*, If one Man shall make the *Wheels*, another the *Spring*, another shall Engrave the *Dial-plate*, and another shall make the *Cases*, then the *Watch* will be better and cheaper, than if the whole Work be put upon any one Man.' (*Another Essay in Political Arithmetick, concerning the Growth of the City of London* (London, 1683), 36–7, in C. H. Hull, ii.473.)

Later use was by Mandeville and Harris: 'There are many Sets of Hands in the Nation, that, not wanting proper Materials, would be able in less than half a Year to produce, fit out, and navigate a First-Rate [Man of War]: yet it is certain, that this Task would be impracticable, if it was not divided and subdivided into a great Variety of different Labours; and it is as certain, that none of these Labours require any other, than working Men of ordinary Capacities.' (B. Mandeville, *The Fable of the Bees*, pt. ii.149, ed. F. B. Kaye (Oxford, 1924), ii.142.) 'No number of Men, when once they enjoy Quiet, and no Man needs to fear his Neighbour, will be long without learning to divide and subdivide their Labour.' (Ibid., pt. ii.335, ed. Kaye ii.284.) 'The advantages accruing to mankind from their betaking themselves severally to different occupations, are very great and

2   The effects of the division of labour, in the general business of society, will be more easily understood, by considering in what manner it operates in some particular manufactures. It is commonly supposed to be carried furthest in some very trifling ones; not perhaps that it really is carried further in them than in others of more importance: but in those trifling manufactures which are destined to supply the small wants of but a small number of people, the whole number of workmen must necessarily be small; and those employed in every different branch of the work can often be collected into the same [7] workhouse, and placed at once under the view of the spectator. In those great manufactures, on the contrary, which are destined to supply the great wants of the great body of the people, every different branch of the work employs so great a number of workmen, that it is impossible to collect them all into the same workhouse. We can seldom see more, at one time, than those employed in one single branch. Though *b*in such manufactures,*b* therefore, the work may really be divided into a much greater number of parts, than in those of a more trifling nature, the division is not near so obvious, and has accordingly been much less observed.

3   To take an example, therefore, from a very trifling manufacture; but one in which the division of labour has been very often taken notice of, the trade of the pin-maker; a workman not educated to this business (which the division of labour has rendered a distinct trade), nor acquainted with the use of the machinery employed in it (to the invention of which the same division of labour has probably given occasion), could scarce, perhaps, with his utmost industry, make one pin in a day, and certainly could not make twenty.[2] But in the way in which this business is now carried on, not only the whole work is a peculiar trade, but it is divided into a number of branches, of which the greater part are likewise peculiar

---

b-b in them *I*

obvious: For thereby, each becoming expert and skilful in his own particular art; they are enabled to furnish one another with the products of their respective labours, performed in a much better manner, and with much less toil, than any one of them could do of himself.' (J. Harris, *An Essay upon Money and Coins* (London, 1757), i. 16.)

The advantages of the division of labour are also emphasized by Turgot in sections III and IV of his *Reflections on the Formation and Distribution of Riches* (1766). The translation used is by R. L. Meek and included in his *Turgot on Progress, Sociology and Economics* (Cambridge, 1973).

[2] Cf. ED 2.4: 'to give a very frivolous instance, if all the parts of a pin were to be made by one man, if the same person was to dig the metall out of the mine, seperate it from the ore, forge it, split it into small rods, then spin these rods into wire, and last of all make that wire into pins, a man perhaps could with his utmost industry scarce make a pin in a year.' Smith added that even where the wire alone was furnished an unskilled man could probably make only about 20 pins a day. Similar examples occur in LJ (A) vi.29–30 and LJ (B) 213–14, ed. Cannan 163. It is remarked in LJ (A) vi.50 that the wire used in pin manufacture generally came from Sweden.

trades. One man draws out the wire, another straights it, a third cuts it, a fourth points it, a fifth grinds it at the top for receiving the head; to make the head requires [8] two or three distinct operations; to put it on, is a peculiar business, to whiten the pins is another; it is even a trade by itself to put them into the paper; and the important business of making a pin is, in this manner, divided into about eighteen distinct operations,[3] which, in some manufactories, are all performed by distinct hands, though in others the same man will sometimes perform two or three of them. I have seen a small manufactory of this kind where ten men only were employed, and where some of them consequently performed two or three distinct operations. But though they were very poor, and therefore but indifferently accommodated with the necessary machinery, they could, when they exerted themselves, make among them about twelve pounds of pins in a day.[4] There are in a pound upwards of four thousand pins of a middling size. Those ten persons, therefore, could make among them upwards of forty-eight thousand pins in a day. Each person, therefore, making a tenth part of forty-eight thousand pins, might be considered as making four thousand eight hundred pins in a day. But if they had all wrought separately and independently, and without any of them having been educated to this peculiar business, they certainly could not each of them have made twenty, perhaps not one pin in a day; that is, certainly, not the two hundred and fortieth, perhaps not the four thousand eight hundredth part of what they are at present capable of performing, in consequence of [9] a proper division and combination of their different operations.

4   In every other art and manufacture, the effects of the division of labour are similar to what they are in this very trifling one; though, in many of them, the labour can neither be so much subdivided, nor reduced to so great a simplicity of operation. The division of labour, however, so far as it can be introduced, occasions, in every art, a proportionable increase of the productive powers of labour. The separation of different trades and employments from one another, seems to have taken place, in consequence of this advantage. This separation too is generally carried furthest in those countries which enjoy the highest degree of industry and improvement; what is the work of one man, in a rude state of society, being generally that of several in an improved one. In every improved society, the

----

[3] Eighteen operations are described in the *Encyclopédie* (1755), v.804–7. See also *Chambers' Cyclopaedia* (4th ed. 1741), s.v. Pin.

[4] A very similar passage occurs in ED 2.4 which also concludes that where the processes of manufacture are divided among 18 persons, each should in effect be capable of producing 2,000 pins in a day. These figures are also cited in LJ (A) vi.30 and 51 and LJ (B) 214, ed. Cannan 163. In referring to the disadvantages of the division of labour in LJ (B) 329, ed. Cannan 255, the lecturer mentions the example of a person engaged on the 17th part of a pin or the 80th part of a button. See below, V.i.f.50.

farmer is generally nothing but a farmer; the manufacturer, nothing but a manufacturer.⁵ The labour too which is necessary to produce any one complete manufacture, is almost always divided among a great number of hands. How many different trades are employed in each branch of the linen and woollen manufactures, from the growers of the flax and the wool, to the bleachers and smoothers of the linen, or to the dyers and dressers of the cloth! The nature of agriculture, indeed, does not admit of so many subdivisions of labour, nor of so complete a separation of one business from another, as manufactures.⁶ It is impossible to separate so entirely, the business of [10] the grazier from that of the corn-farmer, as the trade of the carpenter is commonly separated from that of the smith. The spinner is almost always a distinct person from the weaver; but the ploughman, the harrower, the sower of the seed, and the reaper of the corn, are often the same.⁷ The occasions for those different sorts of labour returning with the different seasons of the year, it is impossible that one man should be constantly employed in any one of them. This impossibility of making so complete and entire a separation of all the different branches of labour employed in agriculture, is perhaps the reason why the improvement of the productive powers of labour in this art, does not always keep pace with their improvement in manufactures. The most opulent nations, indeed, generally excel all their neighbours in agriculture as well as in manufactures; but they are commonly more distinguished by their superiority in the latter than in the former.⁸ Their lands are in general better cultivated, and having more labour and expence bestowed upon them, produce more, in proportion to the extent and natural fertility of the ground. But ᶜthisᶜ superiority of produce is seldom much more than in proportion to the superiority of labour and expence. In agriculture, the labour of the rich country is not always much more productive than that of the poor; or, at least, it is never so much more productive, as it commonly is in manufactures. The corn of the rich country, therefore, will not always, in the same degree of goodness, come cheaper to [11] market than that of the poor. The corn of Poland, in the same degree of goodness, is as cheap as that of France, notwithstanding

ᶜ⁻ᶜ the *1*

---

⁵ See below, I.x.b.52.

⁶ The same point is made at IV.ix.35. The limitation imposed on the division of labour in agriculture is stated to require greater knowledge on the part of the workman at I.x.c.24. At the same time, agriculture was regarded by Smith as the most productive form of investment, II.v.12.

⁷ LJ (A) vi.30–1 comments that: 'Agriculture however does not admit of this separation of employment in the same degree as the manufactures of wool or lint or iron work. The same man must often be the plougher of the land, sower, harrower, reaper and thresher of the corn (tho' here there may be some distinctions.)' Similar points are made in LJ (B) 214, ed. Cannan 164.

⁸ The two preceding sentences follow the text of ED 2.5 very closely.

the superior opulence and improvement of the latter country. The corn of France is, in the corn provinces, fully as good, and in most years nearly about the same price with the corn of England, though, in opulence and improvement, France is perhaps inferior to England. The ᵈcorn-landsᵈ of England, however, are better cultivated than those of France, and the ᵉcorn-landsᵉ of France are said to be much better cultivated than those of Poland. But though the poor country, notwithstanding the inferiority of its cultivation, can, in some measure, rival the rich in the cheapness and goodness of its corn, it can pretend to no such competition in its manufactures; at least if those manufactures suit the soil, climate, and situation of the rich country. The silks of France are better and cheaper than those of England, because the silk manufacture, ᶠat least under the present high duties upon the importation of raw silk,ᶠ does not ᵍso wellᵍ suit the climate of England ʰas that of France.ʰ But the hard-ware and the coarse woollens of England are beyond all comparison superior to those of France, and much cheaper too in the same degree of goodness.⁹ In Poland there are said to be scarce any manufactures of any kind, a few of those coarser household manufactures excepted, without which no country can well subsist.

5   This great increase ⁱofⁱ the quantity of work, which, ʲin consequence of the division of labour,ʲ [12] the same number of people are capable of performing, ᵏ is owing to three different circumstances; first, to the increase of dexterity in every particular workman; secondly, to the saving of the time which is commonly lost in passing from one species of work to another; and lastly, to the invention of a great number of machines which facilitate and abridge labour, and enable one man to do the work of many.¹⁰

6   First, the improvement of the dexterity of the workman necessarily

---

ᵈ⁻ᵈ lands *1*   ᵉ⁻ᵉ lands *1*   ᶠ⁻ᶠ *2–6*   ᵍ⁻ᵍ *2–6*   ʰ⁻ʰ *2–6*   ⁱ⁻ⁱ in *6*
ʲ⁻ʲ *2–6*   ᵏ in consequence of the division of labour, *1*

---

⁹ ED 2.5 ends with the statement that: 'The corn of France is fully as good and in the provinces where it grows rather cheaper than that of England, at least during ordinary seasons. But the toys of England, their watches, their cutlery ware, their locks & hinges of doors, their buckles and buttons are in accuracy, solidity, and perfection of work out of all comparison superior to those of France, and cheaper too in the same degree of goodness.' A précis of this argument appears in LJ (A) vi.31–2, and LJ (B) 214, ed. Cannan 164; and see below, I.xi.o.4, where Smith states that manufactures which use the coarser metals have probably the greatest scope for the division of labour.

ED 2.6 and 7 are omitted from the WN. In these passages Smith elaborated on the advantages of the division of labour in pin making and added that these advantages were such as to suggest that any rich country which faced a loss of markets in international trade to a poor one 'must have been guilty of some great error in its police.' There is no corresponding passage in LJ (B), but a similar argument occurs in LJ (A) vi.34.

¹⁰ This paragraph is evidently based on ED 2.8. Similar points appear in LJ (A) vi.38; LJ (B) 215–16, ed. Cannan 166. The advantages are also cited in the *Encyclopédie* (1755), i.713–17.

increases the quantity of the work he can perform, and the division of labour, by reducing every man's business to some one simple operation, and by making this operation the sole employment of his life, necessarily increases very much the dexterity of the workman. A common smith, who, though accustomed to handle the hammer, has never been used to make nails, if upon some particular occasion he is obliged to attempt it, will scarce, I am assured, be able to make above two or three hundred nails in a day, and those too very bad ones. A smith who has been accustomed to make nails, but whose sole or principal business has not been that of a nailer, can seldom with his utmost diligence make more than eight hundred or a thousand nails in a day. I have seen several boys under twenty years of age who had never exercised any other trade but that of making nails, and who, when they exerted themselves, could make, each of them, upwards of two thousand three hundred nails in a day. The making of a nail, however, is by no means one [13] of the simplest operations. The same person blows the bellows, stirs or mends the fire as there is occasion, heats the iron, and forges every part of the nail: In forging the head too he is obliged to change his tools. The different operations into which the making of a pin, or of a metal button, is subdivided, are all of them much more simple, and the dexterity of the person, of whose life it has been the sole business to perform them, is usually much greater. The rapidity with which some of the operations of those manufactures are performed, exceeds what the human hand could, by those who had never seen them, be supposed capable of acquiring.[11]

7 Secondly, the advantage which is gained by saving the time commonly lost in passing from one sort of work to another, is much greater than we should at first view be apt to imagine it. It is impossible to pass very quickly from one kind of work to another, that is carried on in a different place, and with quite different tools. A country weaver, who cultivates a small farm, must lose a good deal of time in passing from his loom to the field, and from the field to his loom. When the two trades can

[11] This whole paragraph follows ED 2.9, save that the boy is there said to have been 19 years old. A similar argument occurs in LJ (A) vi.38, where a nailsmith of 15 is said to be capable of producing 3,000–4,000 nails in a day. See also LJ (B) 216, ed. Cannan 166:

A country smith not accustomed to make nails will work very hard for 3 or 400 a day, and these too very bad. But a boy used to it will easily make 2000 and these incomparably better; yet the improvement of dexterity in this very complex manufacture can never be equal to that in others. A nail-maker changes postures, blows the bellows, changes tools etca. and therefore the quantity produced cannot be so great as in manufactures of pins and buttons, where the work is reduced to simple operations.

(The manufacture of nails was common in central and east Scotland. In the village of Pathhead and Gallatown near Kirkcaldy a number of nailers worked domestically, using iron supplied by merchants from Dysart. The growth of the iron industry in central Scotland provided local supplies later.)

be carried on in the same workhouse, the loss of time is no doubt much less. It is even in this case, however, very considerable. A man commonly saunters a little in turning his hand from one sort of employment to another. When he first begins the new work he is seldom very keen and hearty; his mind, as they say, does not go to it, and for some time he rather trifles than applies to good purpose.[12] The [14] habit of sauntering and of indolent careless application, which is naturally, or rather necessarily[13] acquired by every country workman who is obliged to change his work and his tools every half hour, and to apply his hand in twenty different ways almost every day of his life; renders him almost always slothful and lazy, and incapable of any vigorous application even on the most pressing occasions. Independent, therefore, of his deficiency in point of dexterity, this cause alone must always reduce considerably the quantity of work which he is capable of performing.[14]

8   Thirdly, and lastly, every body must be sensible how much labour is facilitated and abridged by the application of proper machinery. It is unnecessary to give any example.[15] I shall *l* only observe, *ᵐtherefore,ᵐ*

---

l therefore, *1*   *m–m* 2–6

---

[12] Cf. ED 2.10: 'A man of great spirit and activity, when he is hard pushed upon some particular occasion, will pass with the greatest rapidity from one sort of work to another through a great variety of businesses. Even a man of spirit and activity, however, must be hard pushed before he can do this.'

[13] Smith often juxtaposes the terms 'naturally' and 'necessarily'. See, for example, I.viii.57, III.i.3, IV.i.30, IV.ii.4, 6, IV.vii.c.80, V.i.b.12, V.i.f.24, V.i.g.23.

[14] The preceding two sentences follow the concluding passages of ED 2.10 very closely. Similar arguments appear in LJ (A) vi.39–40 and LJ (B) 216–17, ed. Cannan 166–7.

[15] Smith cites three major improvements apart from the fire engines mentioned below, in I.xi.o.12, and see also II.ii.7. The 'condensing engine' and 'what is founded upon it, the wind gun' are cited as 'ingenious and expensive machines' in External Senses, 16. Cf. ED 2.11: 'By means of the *plough* two men, with the assistance of three horses, will cultivate more ground than twenty could do with the spade. A miller and his servant, with a wind *or* water mill, will at their ease, grind more corn than eight men could do, with the severest labour, by hand mills.' A similar example occurs in LJ (B) 217, ed. Cannan 167, save that it is said that the miller and his servant 'will do more with the water miln than a dozen men with the hand miln, tho' it too be a machine'. LJ (B) does not mention the windmill and it is also interesting to note that the example provided at LJ (A) vi.40 is exactly the same as that provided in ED. It is stated at I.xi.o.12 that neither wind nor water mills were known in England at the beginning of the sixteenth century.

Cf. Montesquieu, *Esprit des Lois*, trans. Thomas Nugent, ed. F. Neumann (New York, 1959), XXIII.xv.3, where it is stated that machines are not always useful, for example, in cases where their effect is to reduce employment. He added that 'if water-mills were not everywhere established, I should not have believed them so useful as is pretended'. In commenting on this remark Sir James Steuart confirmed that the advantages of using machines were 'so palpable that I need not insist upon them', especially in the current situation of Europe. He did, however, agree that the introduction of machines could cause problems of employment in the very short run, and that they might have adverse consequences in an economy incapable of further growth. See especially the *Principles of Political Oeconomy* (London, 1767), I.xix.

that the invention of all those machines by which labour is so much facilitated and abridged, seems to have been originally owing to the division
of labour. Men are much more likely to discover easier and readier methods
of attaining any object, when the whole attention of their minds is directed
towards that single object, than when it is dissipated among a great variety
of things. But in consequence of the division of labour, the whole of every
man's attention comes naturally to be directed towards some one very
simple object. It is naturally to be expected, therefore, that some one or
other of those who are employed in each particular branch of labour should
soon find out easier and readier methods of performing their own particular work, wherever the nature of it admits of such [15] improvement.[16]
A great part of the machines ⁿmade use ofⁿ in those manufactures in which
labour is most subdivided, were originally the inventions of common
workmen, who, being each of them employed in some very simple operation, naturally turned their thoughts towards finding out easier and
readier methods of performing it.[17] Whoever has been much accustomed
to visit such manufactures, must frequently have been shewn very pretty
machines, which were the inventions of ᵒsuchᵒ workmen, in order to
facilitate and quicken their own particular part of the work.[18] In the
first fire-engines,[19] a boy was constantly employed to open and shut
alternately the communication between the boiler and the cylinder,
according as the piston either ascended or descended. One of those boys,
who loved to play with his companions, observed that, by tying a string
from the handle of the valve, which opened this communication, to
another part of the machine, the valve would open and shut without his
assistance, and leave him at liberty to divert himself with his play-fellows.
One of the greatest improvements that has been made upon this machine,

ⁿ⁻ⁿ employed *1*   ᵒ⁻ᵒ common *1*

[16] Exactly these views are expressed in ED 2.11 and LJ (B) 217, ed. Cannan 167.
The brief statement in LJ (A) vi.41 reads that 'When one is employed constantly on one
thing his mind will naturally be employed in devising the most proper means of improv-
ing it.'

[17] It is stated at IV.ix.47 that invention of this kind is generally the work of freemen.
On the other hand Smith argues at V.i.f.50 that the mental faculties of the workers are
likely to be damaged by the division of labour, thus affecting the flow of invention from
this source.

[18] Cf. LJ (A) vi.54: 'if we go into the workhouse of any manufacturer in the new
works at Sheffield, Manchester, or Birmingham, or even some towns in Scotland, and
enquire concerning the machines, they will tell you that such or such an one was invented
by some common workman.' See also Astronomy, II.11: 'When we enter the work-houses
of the most common artizans; such as dyers, brewers, distillers; we observe a number
of appearances, which present themselves in an order that seems to us very strange and
wonderful.'

[19] In the Fourth Dialogue, Cleo refers to 'those Engines that raise Water by the Help
of Fire; the Steam you know, is that which forces it up.' Mandeville, *The Fable of the
Bees*, pt. ii.181–2, ed. Kaye ii.167. Fire engine was the name for the earliest steam
engines. The story that follows seems untrue. See T. K. Derry and T. I. Williams, *A
Short History of Technology* (Oxford, 1960), 316–19.

since it was first invented, was in this manner the discovery of a boy who wanted to save his own labour.[20]

9   All the improvements in machinery, however, have by no means been the inventions of those who had occasion to use the machines. Many improvements have been made by the ingenuity of the makers of the machines, when [16] to make them became the business of a peculiar trade;[21] and some by that of those who are called philosophers or men of speculation, whose trade it is, not to do any thing, but to observe every thing; and who, upon that account, are often capable of combining together the powers of the most distant and dissimilar objects.[22] In the progress of society, philosophy or speculation becomes, like every other employment, the principal or sole trade and occupation of a particular class of citizens. Like every other employment too, it is subdivided into a great number of different branches, each of which affords occupation

[20] In general, Smith concluded that machines would tend to become simpler as the result of improvement; a point made in Astronomy, IV.19 and First Formation of Languages, 41. He also commented in LRBL i.v.34, ed. Lothian 11, that 'machines are at first vastly complex but gradually the different parts are more connected and supplied by one another.' In ED 2.11 Smith ascribes the invention of the Drill Plow to the farmer while claiming that some 'miserable slave' probably produced the original hand-mill (cf. below, IV.ix.47). On the other hand, some improvements were ascribed to those who made the instruments involved, as distinct from using them, and to the 'successive discoveries of time and experience, and of the ingenuity of different artists'. This subject is briefly mentioned in LJ (B) 217–18, ed. Cannan 167. LJ (A) vi.42–3 provides a more elaborate illustration of the kind found in ED, while stating that the inventions of the mill and plough are so old that history gives no account of them (54).
[21] The 'fabrication of the instruments of trade' is described as a specialized function at IV.viii.1.
[22] Cf. ED. 2.11. Smith here suggests that it was probably a philosopher who first thought of harnessing both wind and water, especially the former, for the purposes of milling. Smith added that while the application of powers already known was not beyond the ability of the ingenious artist, innovation amounting to 'the application of new powers, which are altogether unknown' is the contribution of the philosopher (i.e. scientist):

> When an artist makes any such discovery he showes himself to be not a meer artist but a real philosopher, whatever may be his nominal profession. It was a real philosopher only who could invent the fire-engine, and first form the idea of producing so great an effect by a power in nature which had never before been thought of. Many inferior artists, employed in the fabric of this wonderful machine, may afterwards discover more happy methods of applying that power than those first made use of by its illustrious inventer.

In a note to the passage just cited W. R. Scott suggested that Smith was probably referring to James Watt. Similar points regarding the role of the philosopher are made in LJ (A) vi.42–3, and more briefly in LJ (B) 218, ed. Cannan 167–8.
Mandeville (*The Fable of the Bees*, pt. ii.152, ed. Kaye ii.144) was more sceptical with regard to the rôle of the philosopher: 'They are very seldom the same Sort of People, those that invent Arts, and Improvements in them, and those that enquire into the Reason of Things: this latter is most commonly practis'd by such, as are idle and indolent, that are fond of Retirement, hate Business, and take delight in Speculation: whereas none succeed oftener in the first, than active, stirring, and laborious Men, such as will put their Hand to the Plough, try Experiments, and give all their Attention to what they are about.'

to a peculiar tribe or class of philosophers; and this subdivision of employment in philosophy, as well as in every other business, improves dexterity,
and saves time. Each individual becomes more expert in his own peculiar
branch, more work is done upon the whole, and the quantity of science
is considerably increased by it.[23]

10   It is the great multiplication of the productions of all the different arts,
in consequence of the division of labour, which occasions, in a well-
governed society, that universal opulence which extends itself to the
lowest ranks of the people.[24] Every workman has a great quantity of his
own work to dispose of beyond what he himself has occasion for; and every
other workman being exactly in the same situation, he is enabled to exchange a great quantity of his own goods for a great quantity, or, what
comes to the same thing, for the price of a great quan-[17]tity of theirs.
He supplies them abundantly with what they have occasion for, and they
accommodate him as amply with what he has occasion for, and a general
plenty diffuses itself through all the different ranks of the society.

11   Observe the accommodation of the most common artificer or day-
labourer in a civilized and thriving country, and you will perceive that
the number of people of whose industry a part, though but a small part,
has been employed in procuring him this accommodation, exceeds all
computation. The woollen coat, for example, which covers the day-
labourer, as coarse and rough as it may appear, is the produce of the
joint labour of a great multitude of workmen.[25] The shepherd, the sorter
of the wool, the wool-comber or carder, the dyer, the scribbler, the
spinner, the weaver, the fuller, the dresser, with many others, must all
join their different arts in order to complete even this homely production.

[23] The last two paragraphs are considered in ED 2.11, but in a form which suggests
that this section of the WN was considerably redrafted, although the preceding three
sentences correspond very closely to the concluding sentences of ED 2.11. In the ED
Smith provides examples drawn from the separate trades of 'mechanical, chemical,
astronomical, physical, metaphysical, moral, political, commercial, and critical philosophers'. LJ (A) vi.43 includes a shorter list, but mentions 'ethical' and 'theological'
philosophers.

[24] This sentence corresponds to the opening sentence of ED 2.6 save that Smith there
refers to an 'immense multiplication' and 'all civilised societies'. He also alluded to 'the
great inequalities of property' in the modern state. See below, p. 24 n. 29.

[25] Related arguments occur in LJ (A) vi.16–17; LJ (B) 211–12, ed. Cannan 161–3.
The example of the 'coarse blue woolen coat' is cited in ED 2.1, LJ (A) vi.21 and LJ (B)
211, ed. Cannan 161. Cf. Mandeville (*The Fable of the Bees*, pt. i.182–3, ed. Kaye
i.169–70): 'A Man would be laugh'd at, that should discover Luxury in the plain Dress
of a poor Creature that walks along in a thick Parish Gown and a coarse Shirt underneath it; and yet what a number of People, how many different Trades, and what a variety
of Skill and Tools must be employed to have the most ordinary *Yorkshire* Cloth? What
depth of Thought and Ingenuity, what Toil and Labour, and what length of Time
must it have cost, before Man could learn from a Seed to raise and prepare so useful a
Product as Linen.' Cf. ibid., part i.411, ed. Kaye i.356: 'What a Bustle is there to be made
in several Parts of the World, before a fine Scarlet or crimson Cloth can be produced,
what Multiplicity of Trades and Artificers must be employ'd!'

How many merchants and carriers, besides, must have been employed in transporting the materials from some of those workmen to others who often live in a very distant part of the country! How much commerce and navigation in particular, how many ship-builders, sailors, sail-makers, rope-makers, must have been employed in order to bring together the different drugs made use of by the dyer, which often come from the remotest corners of the world! What a variety of labour too is necessary in order to produce the tools of the meanest of those workmen! To say nothing of such complicated ma-[18]chines as the ship of the sailor, the mill of the fuller, or even the loom of the weaver, let us consider only what a variety of labour is requisite in order to form that very simple machine, the shears with which the shepherd clips the wool.[26] The miner, the builder of the furnace for smelting the ore, the feller of the timber, the burner of the charcoal to be made use of in the smelting-house, the brick-maker, the brick-layer, the workmen who attend the furnace, the mill-wright, the forger, the smith, must all of them join their different arts in order to produce them. Were we to examine, in the same manner, all the different parts of his dress and household furniture, the coarse linen shirt which he wears next his skin, the shoes which cover his feet, the bed which he lies on, and all the different parts which compose it, the kitchen-grate at which he prepares his victuals, the coals which he makes use of for that purpose, dug from the bowels of the earth, and brought to him perhaps by a long sea and a long land carriage, all the other utensils of his kitchen, all the furniture of his table, the knives and forks, the earthen or pewter plates upon which he serves up and divides his victuals, the different hands employed in preparing his bread and his beer, the glass window which lets in the heat and the light, and keeps out the wind and the rain, with all the knowledge and art requisite for preparing that beautiful and happy invention, without which these northern parts of the world could scarce have afforded a very [19] comfortable habitation, together with the tools of all the different workmen employed in producing those different conveniencies; if we examine, I say, all these things, and consider what a variety of labour is employed about each of them, we shall be sensible that without the assistance and co-operation of many thousands, the very meanest person in a civilized country could not be provided, even according to, what we very falsely imagine, the easy and simple manner in which he is commonly accommodated.[27] Compared, indeed, with the more extravagant luxury of the

[26] ED 2.1 refers to the variety of labour needed to 'produce that very simple machine, the sheers of the clipper'.

[27] ''tis obvious that for the support of human life, to allay the painful cravings of the appetites, and to afford any of those agreeable external enjoyments which our nature is capable of, a great many external things are requisite; such as food, cloathing, habitations, many utensils, and various furniture, which cannot be obtained without a great

great, his accommodation must no doubt appear extremely simple and easy; and yet it may be true, perhaps, that the accommodation of an European prince does not always so much exceed that of an industrious and frugal peasant,[28] as the accommodation of the latter exceeds that of many an African king, the absolute master of the lives and liberties of ten thousand naked savages.[29]

deal of art and labour, and the friendly aids of our fellows.' (Francis Hutcheson, *A System of Moral Philosophy* (London, 1755), i.287). John Locke (*Essay on Civil Government* (3rd ed. 1698), *Works* (London, 1823), v.363) also noted that:

> 'Twoud be a strange catalogue of things, that industry provided and made use of, about every loaf of bread, before it came to our use, if we could trace them; iron, wood, leather, bark timber, stone, bricks, coals, lime, cloth, dyeing, drugs, pitch, tar, masts, ropes, and all the materials made use of in the ship, that brought any of the commodities used by any of the workmen, to any part of the work: all which it would be almost impossible, at least too long, to reckon up. See also Thomas Mun, *England's Treasure by Forraigne Trade* (London, 1664), iii.12.

[28] Cf. Mandeville (*The Fable of the Bees*, pt. i.181, ed. Kaye i.169): 'If we trace the most flourishing Nations in their Origin, we shall find that in the remote Beginnings of every Society, the richest and most considerable Men among them were a great while destitute of a great many Comforts of Life that are now enjoy'd by the meanest and most humble Wretches.'

[29] The phrase 'absolute master' occurs in ED 2.1 in contrasting the luxury of the common day-labourer in England with that of 'many an Indian prince, the absolute master of the lives and liberties of a thousand naked savages'. The same paragraph also contains a contrast with the 'chief of a savage nation in North America'. LJ (A) vi.21, 23 repeats the former example. Cf. LJ (B) 212, ed. Cannan 162. It is also remarked at 287, ed. Cannan 223, that one explanation of the contrast is to be found in the fact that 'An Indian has not so much as a pick-ax, a spade, nor a shovel, or any thing else but his own labour.'

There is a considerable difference in the order in which the argument of ED and this part of the WN develops. For example, ED opens chapter 2 with an analysis which is very similar to that set out in the last two paragraphs of this chapter. It is then argued that while it cannot be difficult to explain the contrast between the poor savage and the modern rich (i.e. by reference to the division of labour), yet 'how it comes about that the labourer and the peasant should likewise be better provided is not perhaps so easily understood'. Smith further illustrates the difficulty by reference to the 'oppressive inequality' of the modern state; a theme which is developed at considerable length (mainly in 2.2,3) before the paradox is resolved by reference to arguments similar to those developed in the first nine paragraphs of this chapter. In LJ (A) and (B) the argument follows a similar order to that found in ED, save that the discussion opens in each case with an account of the 'natural wants of mankind', introducing by this means the general point that even the simplest wants require a multitude of hands before they can be satisfied. The 'natural wants' thesis would, presumably, have figured in the (missing) first chapter of ED. See LJ (A) vi.8–18; LJ (B) 206–13, ed. Cannan 157–63. The link between the development of productive forces and the natural wants of man also features in Hume's essays 'Of Commerce' and 'Of Refinement in the Arts'.

CHAPTER II

Of the Principle which gives occasion to the Division of Labour

1 THIS division of labour, from which so many advantages are derived, is not originally the effect of any human wisdom, which foresees and intends that general opulence to [20] which it gives occasion.[1] It is the necessary, though very slow and gradual consequence of a certain propensity in human nature which has in view no such extensive utility; the propensity to truck, barter, and exchange one thing for another.[2]

2 　　Whether this propensity be one of those original principles in human nature, of which no further account can be given; or whether, as seems more probable, it be the necessary consequence of the faculties of reason and speech, it belongs not to our present subject to enquire.[3] It is common to all men, and to be found in no other race of animals, which seem to know neither this nor any other species of contracts. Two greyhounds, in running down the same hare, have sometimes the appearance of acting in some sort of concert. Each turns her towards his companion, or endeavours to intercept her when his companion turns her towards himself. This, however, is not the effect of any contract, but of the accidental

---

[1] LJ (B) 218–19, ed. Cannan 168 reads: 'We cannot imagine this to have been an effect of human prudence. It was indeed made a law by Sesostratis that every man should follow the employment of his father. But this is by no means suitable to the dispositions of human nature and can never long take place. Everyone is fond of being a gentleman, be his father what he would.' The law is also mentioned in LJ (A) vi.54. See below, I.vii.31 and IV.ix.43.

[2] This paragraph closely follows the first three sentences in ED 2.12. The propensity to truck and barter is also mentioned in LJ (A) vi.44, 48 and LJ (B) 219 ff., ed. Cannan 169. Cf. LJ (B) 300–1, ed. Cannan 232: 'that principle in the mind which prompts to truck, barter and exchange, tho' it is the great foundation of arts, commerce and the division of labour, yet it is not marked with any thing amiable. To perform any thing, or to give any thing without a reward is always generous and noble, but to barter one thing for another is mean.' In a *Letter from Governor Pownall to Adam Smith, being an Examination of Several Points of Doctrine laid down in his Inquiry, into the Nature and Causes of the Wealth of Nations* (London, 1776), the author objected that the analysis of this chapter stopped short in ascribing the division of *labour directly* to a propensity to barter (4–5). Pownall, a former Governor of Massachusetts, also criticized Smith's views on labour as a measure of value, paper money, the employments of capital, colonies, etc. Smith acknowledged Pownall's work in Letter 182 addressed to Pownall, dated 19 January 1777. In Letter 208 addressed to Andreas Holt, dated 26 October 1780 Smith remarked that: 'In the second edition I flattered myself that I had obviated all the objections of Governor Pownal. I find however, he is by no means satisfied, and as Authors are not much disposed to alter the opinions they have once published, I am not much surprized at it.' There is very little evidence to suggest that Smith materially altered his views in response to Pownall, but see below, p. 50, n. 15.

[3] In LJ (B) 221, ed. Cannan 171, Smith argued in referring to the division of labour that 'The real foundation of it is that principle to persuade which so much prevails in human nature.' The same point is made in LJ (A) vi.56.

concurrence of their passions in the same object at that particular time.[4] Nobody ever saw a dog make a fair and deliberate exchange of one bone for another with another dog. Nobody ever saw one animal by its gestures and natural cries signify to another, this is mine, that yours; I am willing to give this for that. When an animal wants to obtain something either of a man or of another animal, it has no other means of persuasion but to gain the favour of those whose service it requires. A puppy fawns upon its dam, and a spaniel endea-[21]vours by a thousand attractions to engage the attention of its master who is at dinner, when it wants to be fed by him. Man sometimes uses the same arts with his brethren, and when he has no other means of engaging them to act according to his inclinations, endeavours by every servile and fawning attention to obtain their good will. He has not time, however, to do this upon every occasion. In civilized society he stands at all times in need of the co-operation and assistance of great multitudes, while his whole life is scarce sufficient to gain the friendship of a few persons. In almost every other race of animals each individual, when it is grown up to maturity, is intirely independent, and in its natural state has occasion for the assistance of no other living creature.[5] But man has almost constant occasion for the help of his brethren, and it is in vain for him to expect it from their benevolence only.[6] He will be more likely to prevail if he can interest their self-love in his favour, and shew them that it is for their own advantage to do for him what he requires of them. Whoever offers to another a bargain of any kind, proposes to do this. Give me that which I want, and you shall have this which you want, is the meaning of every such offer; and it is in this manner that we obtain from one another the far greater part of those good offices which we stand in need of. It is not from

---

[4] The example of the greyhounds occurs in LJ (B) 219, ed. Cannan 169. LJ (A) vi.44 uses the example of 'hounds in a chace' and again at 57. Cf. LJ (B) 222, ed. Cannan 171: 'Sometimes, indeed, animals seem to act in concert, but there is never any thing like a bargain among them. Monkeys when they rob a garden throw the fruit from one to another till they deposit it in the hoard, but there is always a scramble about the division of the booty, and usually some of them are killed.' In LJ (A) vi.57 a similar example is based on the Cape of Good Hope.

[5] In ED 2.12 an additional sentence is added at this point: 'When any uncommon misfortune befals it, its piteous and doleful cries will sometimes engage its fellows, and sometimes prevail even upon man, to relieve it.' With this exception, and the first sentence of this paragraph, the whole of the preceding material follows ED 2.12 very closely and in places verbatim. The remainder of the paragraph follows ED 2.12 to its close.

[6] 'To expect, that others should serve us for nothing, is unreasonable; therefore all Commerce, that Men can have together, must be a continual bartering of one thing for another. The Seller, who transfers the Property of a Thing, has his own Interest as much at Heart as the Buyer, who purchases that Property; and, if you want or like a thing, the Owner of it, whatever Stock of Provision he may have of the same, or how greatly soever you may stand in need of it, will never part with it, but for a Consideration, which he likes better, than he does the thing you want.' (Mandeville, *The Fable of the Bees*, pt. ii. 421–2, ed. Kaye, ii.349.)

the benevolence of the butcher, the brewer, or the baker, that we expect our dinner, but from their [22] regard to their own interest. We address ourselves, not to their humanity but to their self-love, and never talk to them of our own necessities but of their advantages.[7] Nobody but a beggar chuses to depend chiefly upon the benevolence of his fellow-citizens. Even a beggar does not depend upon it entirely. The charity of well-disposed people, indeed, supplies him with the whole fund of his subsistence. But though this principle ultimately provides him with all the necessaries of life which he has occasion for, it neither does nor can provide him with them as he has occasion for them. The greater part of his occasional wants are supplied in the same manner as those of other people, by treaty, by barter, and by purchase. With the money which one man gives him he purchases food. The old cloaths which another bestows upon him he exchanges for other old cloaths which suit him better, or for lodging, or for food, or for money, with which he can buy either food, cloaths, or lodging, as he has occasion.

3   As it is by treaty, by barter, and by purchase, that we obtain from one another the greater part of those mutual good offices which we stand in need of, so it is this same trucking disposition which originally gives occasion to the division of labour. In a tribe of hunters or shepherds a particular person makes bows and arrows, for example, with more readiness and dexterity than any other. He frequently exchanges them for cattle or for venison with his companions; and [23] he finds at last that he can in this manner get more cattle and venison, than if he himself went to the field to catch them. From a regard to his own interest, therefore, the making of bows and arrows grows to be his chief business, and he becomes a sort of armourer.[8] Another excels in making the frames and covers of their

[7] Cf. LJ (B) 220, ed. Cannan 169: 'The brewer and the baker serve us not from benevolence but from selflove. No man but a beggar depends on benevolence, and even they would die in a week were their entire dependance upon it.' Also LJ (A) vi.46: 'You do not adress his [the brewer's and baker's] humanity but his self-love. Beggars are the only persons who depend on charity for their subsistence; neither do they do so alltogether. For what by their supplications they have got from one, they exchange for something else they more want. They give their old cloaths to a one for lodging, the mony they have got to another for bread, and thus even they make use of bargain and exchange.'

[8] Cf. LJ (A) vi.46: 'This bartering and trucking spirit is the cause of the separation of trades and the improvements in arts. A savage who supports himself by hunting, having made some more arrows than he had occasion for, gives them in a present to some of his companions, who in return give him some of the venison they have catched; and he at last finding that by making arrows and giving them to his neighbour, as he happens to make them better than ordinary, he can get more venison than by his own hunting, he lays it aside unless it be for his diversion, and becomes an arrow-maker.' Similar points are made in LJ (B) 220, ed. Cannan 169–70, and a similar passage occurs in ED 2.13. Mandeville (*The Fable of the Bees*, pt. ii. 335–6, ed. Kaye ii.284) also noted that: 'Man', as I have hinted before, naturally loves to imitate what he sees others do, which is the reason that savage People all do the same thing: This hinders them from meliorating their Condition, though they are always wishing for it: But if one will wholly apply himself to the making of Bows and Arrows, whilst another provides Food, a third builds

little huts or moveable houses. He is accustomed to be of use in this way to his neighbours, who reward him in the same manner with cattle and with venison, till at last he finds it his interest to dedicate himself entirely to this employment, and to become a sort of house-carpenter. In the same manner a third becomes a smith or a brazier, a fourth a tanner or dresser of hides or skins, the principal part of the clothing of savages.[9] And thus the certainty of being able to exchange all that surplus part of the produce of his own labour, which is over and above his own consumption, for such parts of the produce of other men's labour as he may have occasion for, encourages every man to apply himself to a particular occupation, and to cultivate and bring to perfection whatever talent or genius he may possess for that particular species of business.[10]

4   The difference of natural talents in different men is, in reality, much less than we are aware of; and the very different genius which appears to distinguish men of different professions, when grown up to maturity, is not upon many occasions so much the cause, as the effect of the division of labour.[11] The difference between the [24] most dissimilar characters, between a philosopher and a common street porter, for example,

Huts, a fourth makes Garments, and a fifth Utensils, they do not only become useful to one another, but the Callings and Employments themselves will in the same Number of Years receive much greater Improvements, than if all had been promiscously follow'd by every one of the Five.'

[9] Cf. Hutcheson (*System*, i.288–9): ' 'Nay 'tis well known that the produce of the labours of any given number, twenty, for instance, in providing the necessaries or conveniences of life, shall be much greater by assigning to one, a certain sort of work of one kind, in which he will soon acquire skill and dexterity, and to another assigning work of a different kind, than if each one of the twenty were obliged to employ himself, by turns, in all the different sorts of labour requisite for his subsistence, without sufficient dexterity in any. In the former method each procures a great quantity of goods of one kind, and can exchange a part of it for such goods obtained by the labours of others as he shall stand in need of. One grows expert in tillage, another in pasture and breeding cattle, a third in masonry, a fourth in the chace, a fifth in iron-works, a sixth in the arts of the loom, and so on throughout the rest. Thus all are supplied by means of barter with the work of complete artists. In the other method scarce any one could be dextrous and skilful in any one sort of labour.'

[10] This paragraph is based on ED 2.13, which it follows very closely.

[11] 'When we consider how nearly equal all men are in their bodily force, and even in their mental powers and faculties, till cultivated by education; we must necessarily allow, that nothing but their consent could, at first, associate them together, and subject them to any authority.' (D. Hume, 'Of the Original Contract', in *Political Discourses* (1752); *Essays Moral, Political and Literary*, ed. T. H. Green and T. H. Grose (London, 1882), i.444–5.) Cf. *Treatise of Human Nature*, III.i: 'The skin, pores, muscles, and nerves of a day-labourer, are different from those of a man of quality: so are his sentiments, actions, and manners. The different stations of life influence the whole fabric, external and internal; and these different stations arise necessarily, because uniformly, from the necessary and uniform principles of human nature.' On the other hand, Harris (*Essay*, i.15) believed that: 'Men are endued with various talents and propensities, which naturally dispose and fit them for different occupations; and are ... under a necessity of betaking themselves to particular arts and employments, from their inability of otherwise acquiring all the necessaries they want, with ease and comfort. This creates a dependance of one man upon another, and naturally unites men into societies.'

seems to arise not so much from nature, as from habit, custom, and education.[12] When they came into the world, and for the first six or eight years of their existence, they were*[a]*, perhaps,*[a]* very much alike, and neither their parents nor play-fellows could perceive any remarkable difference. About that age, or soon after, they come to be employed in very different occupations. The difference of talents comes then to be taken notice of, and widens by degrees, till at last the vanity of the philosopher is willing to acknowledge scarce any resemblance. But without the disposition to truck, barter, and exchange, every man must have procured to himself every necessary and conveniency of life which he wanted. All must have had the same duties to perform, and the same work to do, and there could have been no such difference of employment as could alone give occasion to any great difference of talents.[13]

5   As it is this disposition which forms that difference of talents, so remarkable among men of different professions, so it is this same disposition which renders that difference useful. Many tribes of animals acknowledged to be all of the same species, derive from nature a much more remarkable distinction of genius, than what, antecedent to custom and

a–a 1, *4e–6*

---

[12] Cf. V.i.f 51. LJ (A) vi.47–8 reads: 'No two persons can be more different in their genius as a philosopher and a porter, but there does not seem to have been any original difference betwixt them. For the five or six first years of their lives there was hardly any apparent difference: their companions looked upon them as persons of pretty much the same stamp. No wisdom and ingenuity appeared in the one superior to that of the other. From about that time a difference was thought to be perceived in them. Their manner of life began to affect them, and without doubt had it not been for this they would have continued the same.' Similar arguments appear in LJ (B) 220, ed. Cannan 170. There is an interesting variant on this point in LJ (B) 327, ed. Cannan 253, where Smith commented on the fact that 'probity and punctuality' generally accompany the introduction of commerce. He added that varying degrees of these qualities were 'not at all to be imputed to national character as some pretend. There is no natural reason why an Englishman or a Scotchman should not be as punctual in performing agreements as a Dutchman. It is far more reduceable to self interest, that general principle which regulates the actions of every man . . .'

[13] The whole of the preceding paragraph follows ED 2.14 to this point. In ED, however, the sentence ends with '. . . any great difference in character' and goes on: 'It is upon this account that a much greater uniformity of character is to be observed among savages than among civilized nations. Among the former there is scarce any division of labour and consequently no remarkable difference of employments; whereas among the latter there is an almost infinite variety of occupations, of which the respective duties bear scarce any resemblance to one another. What a perfect uniformity of character do we find in all the heroes described by Ossian? And what a variety of manners, on the contrary, in those who are celebrated by Homer? Ossian plainly describes the exploits of a nation of hunters, while Homer paints the actions of two nations, who, tho' far from being perfectly civilised, were yet much advanced beyond the age of shepherds, who cultivated lands, who built cities, and among whom he mentions many different trades and occupations, such as masons, carpenters, smiths, merchants, soothsayers, priests, physicians.' The texts then assume a similar form until the end of the following paragraph of the WN. The uniformity of character found among savages is also mentioned in LJ (A) vi.48, LJ (B) 221, ed. Cannan 170.

education, appears to take place among men. By nature a philosopher is not in genius and disposition half so different from a street porter, as a mastiff is from a greyhound, or a greyhound from a spaniel, or this [25] last from a shepherd's dog. Those different tribes of animals, however, though all of the same species, are of scarce any use to one another. The strength of the mastiff is not, in the least, supported either by the swiftness of the greyhound, or by the sagacity of the spaniel, or by the docility of the shepherd's dog. The effects of those different geniuses and talents, for want of the power or disposition to barter and exchange, cannot be brought into a common stock, and do not in the least contribute to the better accommodation and conveniency of the species. Each animal is still obliged to support and defend itself, separately and independently, and derives no sort of advantage from that variety of talents with which nature has distinguished its fellows. Among men, on the contrary, the most dissimilar geniuses are of use to one another; the different produces of their respective talents, by the general disposition to truck, barter, and exchange, being brought, as it were, into a common stock, where every man may purchase whatever part of the produce of other men's talents he has occasion for.[14]

[14] The text of ED continues beyond this point to include an additional folio (N8) which elaborates on the interdependence between the philosopher and the porter and the advantages to be gained from these separate trades. This passage opens with the statement that 'Every thing would be dearer if before it was exposed to sale it had been carried packt and unpackt by hands less able and less dexterous, who for an equal quantity of work, would have taken more time, and must consequently have required more wages, which must have been charged upon the goods.' It is interesting to note that FA begins with the words '. . . who for an equal quantity of work' and then continues in parallel with ED for some 25 lines. The fragment then proceeds to elaborate on the link between the division of labour and the extent of the market (a subject which is not mentioned in ED) whereas ED continues with the preceding theme. It is possible that the fragments represent an alternative, and a later, rewriting of this section of Smith's work. The interdependence of philosopher and porter is briefly mentioned in LJ (A) vi.49, LJ (B) 221, ed. Cannan 171.

CHAPTER III

[26] *That the Division of Labour is limited by the Extent of the Market*[1]

1   As it is the power of exchanging that gives occasion to the division of labour, so the extent of this division must always be limited by the extent of that power, or, in other words, by the extent of the market.[2] When the market is very small, no person can have any encouragement to dedicate himself entirely to one employment, for want of the power to exchange all that surplus part of the produce of his own labour, which is over and above his own consumption, for such parts of the produce of other men's labour as he has occasion for.

2   There are some sorts of industry, even of the lowest kind, which can be carried on no where but in a great town. A porter, for example, can find employment and subsistence in no other place. A village is by much too narrow a sphere for him; even an ordinary market town is scarce large enough to afford him constant occupation. In the lone houses and very small villages which are scattered about in so desert a country as the Highlands of Scotland, every farmer must be butcher, baker and brewer for his own family.[3] In such situations we can scarce expect to find even a smith, a carpenter, or a mason, within less than twenty miles of another of the same trade. The scattered families that [27] live at eight or ten miles distance from the nearest of them, must learn to perform themselves a great number of little pieces of work, for which, in more populous countries, they would call in the assistance of those workmen.[4] Country workmen

---

[1] The subjects of this chapter, as observed in the previous note, do not figure in ED. In LJ (A) vi Smith did develop the argument that the division of labour depends on the extent of the market, but did so in the course of offering a recapitulation of his treatment of price, i.e. outwith his main discussion of the division of labour. In LJ (B) the discussion of the extent of the market is brief, but integrated with the wider discussion of the division of labour. FA and FB thus provide the most elaborate examination of the subject; a fact which lends some support to the view that the fragments may have been written after ED. Paragraphs 1 and 2 of this chapter appear to be based on FA from the first complete paragraph of the latter 'As it is the power of exchanging . . .' while paragraphs 3–7 show the same close connection with the whole of FB.

[2] LJ (B) 222, ed. Cannan 172: 'From all that has been said we may observe that the division of labour must always be proportioned to the extent of commerce.' In LJ (A) vi.63 it is remarked that the division of labour 'is greater or less according to the market'.

[3] Cf. LJ (A) ii.40: 'It is found that society must be pretty far advanced before the different trades can all find subsistence: . . . And to this day in the remote and deserted parts of the country, a weaver or a smith, besides the exercise of his trade, cultivates a small farm, and in that manner exercises two trades; that of a farmer and that of a weaver.'

[4] The degree of correspondence between the preceding passages and FA ceases at this point and there is a long passage from the beginning of the following sentence, and ending 22 lines below ('a ship navigated by six') which has no counterpart in the fragment. This passage amounts to about three hundred words, which would make about one folio page in the hand of the amanuensis used. Smith may, therefore, have decided to omit the two final

are almost every where obliged to apply themselves to all the different branches of industry that have so much affinity to one another as to be employed about the same sort of materials.[5] A country carpenter deals in every sort of work that is made of wood: a country smith in every sort of work that is made of iron. The former is not only a carpenter, but a joiner, a cabinet-maker, and even a carver in wood, as well as a wheel-wright, a plough-wright, a cart and waggon maker. The employments of the latter are still more various.[6] It is impossible there should be such a trade as even that of a nailer in the remote and inland parts of the High-lands of Scotland. Such a workman at the rate of a thousand nails a day, and three hundred working days in the year, will make three hundred thousand nails in the year. But in such a situation it would be impossible to dispose of one thousand, that is, of one day's work in the year.[7]

3   As by means of water-carriage a more extensive market is opened to every sort of industry than what land-carriage alone can afford it, so it is upon the sea-coast, and along the banks of navigable rivers, that industry of every kind naturally begins to subdivide and improve itself, and it is frequently not till a long time after that [28] those improvements extend themselves to the inland parts of the country.[8] A broad-wheeled waggon, attended by two men, and drawn by eight horses, in about six weeks time carries and brings back between London and Edinburgh near four ton

pages of FA and introduce a new page which is now lost. The passage from FA which is omitted from the WN had gone on to illustrate the link between the division of labour and the extent of the market by reference to primitive communities such as the North American Indians and the Hottentots, Arabs, and Tartars. In speaking of the Hottentots he pointed out that there was some separation of employments such as the tailor, physician, and smith, but that the people involved were *principally*, but not *entirely* supported by them. It was in this connection that Smith made the interesting point that 'The compleat division of labour however, is posteriour to the invention even of agriculture.'

[5] See I.x.c.8 where it is stated that country labourers were excluded from the statute of apprenticeship by judicial interpretation, as a result of the nature of the employment.

[6] LJ (A) vi.64 notes that 'A wright in the country is a cart-wright, a house carpenter, a square wright or cabinet maker and a carver in wood; each of which in a town makes a separate business. A merchant in Glasgow or Aberdeen who deals in linnen will have in his ware-house, Irish, Scots and Hamburg linnens, but at London there are separate dealers in each of these.'

[7] Smith provides a further example, that of the shoemaker, at IV.ix.45.

[8] 'Great Cities are usually built on the seacoast or on the banks of large Rivers for the convenience of transport; because water-carriage of the produce and merchandise neces-sary for the subsistence and comfort of the inhabitants is much cheaper than Carriages and Land Transport.' (R. Cantillon, *Essai sur la Nature du Commerce* (1755), 22–3; edited and translated by Henry Higgs (London, 1931), 19.) See below, II.v.33 and III.iii.20. While Smith gives a prominent place to navigation in explaining the historical origins of cities and manufactures in III.iii, he did not neglect the importance of land carriage. It is pointed out in LJ (B) 223, ed. Cannan 172, that 'Since the mending of roads in England 40 or 50 years ago, its opulence has increased extremely.' In LJ (A) vi.65 he commented on the problem of bad roads and remarked that 'hence we see that the turnpikes of England have within these 30 or 40 years increased the opulence of the inland parts'. The advantages of good roads are also emphasized in I.xi.b.5 and V.i.d.17.

weight of goods. In about the same time a ship navigated by six or eight men, and sailing between the ports of London and Leith, frequently carries and brings back two hundred ton weight of goods. Six or eight men, therefore, by the help of water-carriage, can carry and bring back in the same time the same quantity of goods between London and Edinburgh, as fifty broad-wheeled waggons, attended by a hundred men, and drawn by four hundred horses.[9] Upon two hundred tons of goods, therefore, carried by the cheapest land-carriage from London to Edinburgh, there must be charged the maintenance of a hundred men for three weeks, and both the maintenance, and, what is nearly equal to the maintenance, the wear and tear of four hundred horses as well as of fifty great waggons. Whereas, upon the same quantity of goods carried by water, there is to be charged only the maintenance of six or eight men, and the wear and tear of a ship of two hundred tons burden, together with the value of the superior risk, or the difference of the insurance between land and water-carriage. Were there no other communication between those two places, therefore, but by land-carriage, as no goods could be transported from the one to the other, except such whose price was very consi-[29]derable in proportion to their weight, they could carry on but a small part of that commerce which *a* at present *b*subsists*b* between them, and consequently could give but a small part of that encouragement which they at present mutually afford to each other's industry.[10] There could be little or no commerce of any kind between the distant parts of the world. What goods could bear the expence of land-carriage between London and Calcutta? Or if there *c*were*c* any so precious as to be able to support this expence, with what

---

a is *I*   *b–b* carried on *I*   *c–c* was *I*

[9] The remainder of this paragraph finds a close parallel in the opening passages of FB, save that 8 or 10 men sailing from the port of Leith can transport 200 tons between Edinburgh and London more cheaply than 'Sixty six narrow wheeled wagons drawn by three hundred & ninety horses & attended by a hundred & thirty two men; or than forty broad wheeled wagons drawn by three hundred & twenty horses & attended by eighty men.' Cf. LJ (B) 223, ed. Cannan 172: 'Water carriage is another convenience as by it 300 ton can be conveyed at the expence of the tare and wear of the vessel, and the wages of 5 or 6 men, and that too in a shorter time than by a 100 waggons which will take 6 horses and a man each.' In LJ (A) vi.66 Smith compares the expense of a ship of 200 tons navigated by four or five men with that incurred in the use of wagons.

[10] Smith may exaggerate the relative advantage of water-carriage, particularly in his example of the costs of carriage between London and Edinburgh. Carriage by sea had its own dangers: natural hazards; pilfering; privateering in time of war. Fine woollen goods were often sent by land in spite of its other disadvantages (cf. IV.viii.21). Smith was writing at the end of the first major phase of passing turnpike acts, but before the improvements which followed were fully evident. Coaching times, a fairly reliable indicator of improvement, show the change. Edinburgh and London were about four days apart in the mid-eighteenth century; only 60 hours by 1786. Smith's concern over the contribution of navigable rivers is more to the point. He was writing at the end of an age when rivers played a more important part in the economic life of Britain than they had ever done before or since.

safety could they be transported through the territories of so many bar-barous nations? Those two cities, however, at present carry on ^{d} a very considerable commerce ^{e}with each other^e, and by mutually affording a market, give a good deal of encouragement to each other's industry.

4   Since such, therefore, are the advantages of water-carriage, it is natural that the first improvements of art and industry should be made where this conveniency opens the whole world for a market to the produce of every sort of labour, and that they should always be much later in extending them-selves into the inland parts of the country. The inland parts of the country can for a long time have no other market for the greater part of their goods, but the country which lies round about them, and separates them from the sea-coast, and the great navigable rivers. The extent of their market, therefore, must for a long time be in proportion to the riches and populous-ness of that country, and consequently their improvement must always be pos-[30]terior to the improvement of that country. In our North American colonies the plantations have constantly followed either the sea-coast or the banks of the navigable rivers, and have scarce any where extended them-selves to any considerable distance from both.[11]

5   The nations that, according to the best authenticated history, appear to have been first civilized, were those that dwelt round the coast of the Medi-terranean sea. That sea, by far the greatest inlet that is known in the world, having no tides, nor consequently any waves except such as are caused by the wind only, was, by the smoothness of its surface, as well as by the multitude of its islands, and the proximity of its neighbouring shores, extremely favourable to the infant navigation of the world; when, from their ignorance of the compass, men were afraid to quit the view of the coast, and from the imperfection of the art of ship-building, to abandon them-selves to the boisterous waves of the ocean.[12] To pass beyond the pillars of Hercules, that is, to sail out of the Streights of Gibralter, was, in the antient world, long considered as a most wonderful and dangerous ex-ploit of navigation. It was late before even the Phenicians and Carthagin-ians, the most skilful navigators and shipbuilders of those old times, at-tempted it, and they were for a long time the only nations that did attempt it.

6   Of all the countries on the coast of the Mediterranean sea, Egypt seems to have been the first in which either agriculture or manufactures were [31]

---

^{d} together 1 $^{e-e}$ $2-6$

---

[11] This sentence appears verbatim in FB, which adds: 'What James the sixth of Scotland said of the county of Fife, of which the inland parts were at that time very ill while the sea coast was extremely well cultivated, that it was like a coarse woollen coat edged with gold lace, might still be said of the greater part of our North American colonies.' See below, I.ix.11.

[12] The passage from the beginning of this paragraph follows FB very closely, and often verbatim, although there is nothing corresponding to the two following sentences.

cultivated and improved to any considerable degree.[13] Upper Egypt extends itself nowhere above a few miles from the Nile, and in Lower Egypt that great river breaks itself into many different canals, which, with the assistance of a little art, seem to have afforded a communication by water-carriage, not only between all the great towns, but between all the considerable villages, and even to many farm-houses in the country; nearly in the same manner as the Rhine and the Maese do in Holland at present. The extent and easiness of this inland navigation was probably one of the principal causes of the early improvement of Egypt.[14]

7   The improvements in agriculture and manufactures seem likewise to have been of very great antiquity in the provinces of Bengal in the East Indies, and in some of the eastern provinces of China; though the great extent of this antiquity is not authenticated by any histories of whose authority we, in this part of the world, are well assured. In Bengal the Ganges and several other great rivers *form a great number of navigable* canals in the same manner as the Nile does in Egypt. In the Eastern provinces of China too, several great rivers form, by their different branches, a multitude of canals, and by communicating with one another afford an inland navigation much more extensive than that either of the Nile or the Ganges, or perhaps than both of them put together.[15] It is remarkable that neither the antient Egyptians, nor the Indians, nor the Chinese, encouraged foreign commerce, but [32] seem all to have derived their great opulence from this inland navigation.

8   All the inland parts of Africa, and all that part of Asia which lies any

---

ˢ⁻ˢ break themselves into many *ɪ*

[13] In LJ (A) iv.60–2 and LJ (B) 31, ed. Cannan 22 the early economic development of Greece is attributed to its natural advantages including ease of communication. Smith added that 'Most of the European countries have most part of the same advantages. They are divided by rivers and branches of the sea, and are naturally fit for the cultivation of the soil and other arts.' The development of the arts and sciences in classical Greece was attributed to its early economic advance in LJ (A) iv.60, Astronomy, III.4 and, LRBL ii.117–9, ed. Lothian 132–3.

[14] This paragraph is evidently based on FB, which goes on, however, to conclude with the statement that 'Agriculture and manufactures too seem to have been of very great antiquity in some of the maritime provinces of China & in the province of Bengal in the East Indies. All these were countries very much of the same nature with Egypt, cut by innumerable canals which afford them an immense inland navigation.' LJ (A) iii.47 also remarks with regard to China, Egypt, and Bengal that 'These countries are all remarkably fruitful. The banks of the Nile and the Ganges are overflowed by . . . rivers and yield immense crops, 3 or 4 in a year. This as there must be plenty of food and subsistence for man must . . . promote population, as the number of men is proportion'd to the quantity of subsistence.'

[15] Smith comments on the inland navigation of China and Indostan at I.xi.g.28, and links the concern of these governments with canal and road improvement to their reliance on land-taxes at V.ii.d.5. He mentions that China was not eminent for foreign trade at II.v.22 and IV.iii.c.11, and comments on the limitations thereby imposed on her economic growth at I.ix.15, IV.ix.40,41. However, it is stated that at least some trade was carried on by foreigners at III.i.7 and IV.ix.45.

considerable way north of the Euxine and Caspian seas, the antient Scythia, the modern Tartary and Siberia, seem in all ages of the world to have been in the same barbarous and uncivilized state in which we find them at present.[16] The sea of Tartary is the frozen ocean which admits of no navigation, and though some of the greatest rivers in the world run through that country, they are at too great a distance from one another to carry commerce and communication through the greater part of it. There are in Africa none of those great inlets, such as the Baltic and Adriatic seas in Europe, the Mediterranean and Euxine seas in both Europe and Asia, and the gulphs of Arabia, Persia, India, Bengal, and Siam, in Asia, to carry maritime commerce into the interior parts of that great continent: and the great rivers of Africa are at too great a distance from one another to give occasion to any considerable inland navigation. The commerce besides which any nation can carry on by means of a river which does not break itself into any great number of branches or canals, and which runs into another territory before it reaches the sea, can never be very considerable; because it is always in the power of the nations who possess that other territory to obstruct the communication between the upper country and the sea. The navigation of the Danube is of very little use to the different [33] states of Bavaria, Austria and Hungary, in comparison of what it would be if any *ᵍ* of them possessed the whole of its course till it falls into the Black Sea.

ᵍ one *I*

---

[16] Smith comments on the limited improvement in Arabia due to the poorness of the soil and difficulties of transport and uses this point to explain why the Arabs had not advanced beyond the shepherd state in LJ (A) iv.36, 56–62; see also LJ (B) 303, ed. Cannan 234: 'in Asia and other eastern countries; all inland commerce is carried on by great caravans, consisting of several thousands, for mutual defence, with waggons etca.' The passages from LJ (A) iv above cited make it plain that the preconditions for economic development include fertility of the soil, ease of defence, and of communication where the latter provides an opportunity for the export of surpluses. In LJ (A) iv.53 Smith also comments that the Tartars 'have indeed some of the largest rivers in the world' while adding that they 'have always been a state of shepherds, which they will always be from the nature of their country, which is dry and raised above the sea, with few rivers, tho' some very large ones, and the weather and the air is too cold for the produce of any grain.' See also 62, and cf. LJ (B) 30–1, ed. Cannan 22.

Part II
Classic References

[3]

The Nature of the Firm

By R. H. Coase

ECONOMIC theory has suffered in the past from a failure
to state clearly its assumptions. Economists in building
up a theory have often omitted to examine the foundations
on which it was erected. This examination is, however,
essential not only to prevent the misunderstanding and
needless controversy which arise from a lack of knowledge
of the assumptions on which a theory is based, but also
because of the extreme importance for economics of good
judgment in choosing between rival sets of assumptions.
For instance, it is suggested that the use of the word " firm "
in economics may be different from the use of the term
by the " plain man."[1] Since there is apparently a trend
in economic theory towards starting analysis with the
individual firm and not with the industry,[2] it is all the
more necessary not only that a clear definition of the word
" firm " should be given but that its difference from a
firm in the " real world," if it exists, should be made clear.
Mrs. Robinson has said that " the two questions to be
asked of a set of assumptions in economics are : Are they
tractable ? and : Do they correspond with the real world ? "[3]
Though, as Mrs. Robinson points out, " more often one set
will be manageable and the other realistic," yet there may
well be branches of theory where assumptions may be
both manageable and realistic. It is hoped to show in
the following paper that a definition of a firm may be obtained
which is not only realistic in that it corresponds to what
is meant by a firm in the real world, but is tractable by
two of the most powerful instruments of economic analysis
developed by Marshall, the idea of the margin and that of
substitution, together giving the idea of substitution at

[1] Joan Robinson, *Economics is a Serious Subject*, p. 12.
[2] See N. Kaldor, " The Equilibrium of the Firm," *Economic Journal*, March, 1934.
[3] Op. cit., p. 6.

the margin.[1]   Our definition must, of course, " relate to formal relations which are capable of being *conceived* exactly."[2]

I

It is convenient if, in searching for a definition of a firm, we first consider the economic system as it is normally treated by the economist.   Let us consider the description of the economic system given by Sir Arthur Salter.[3]   " The normal economic system works itself.   For its current operation it is under no central control, it needs no central survey.   Over the whole range of human activity and human need, supply is adjusted to demand, and production to consumption, by a process that is automatic, elastic and responsive."   An economist thinks of the economic system as being co-ordinated by the price mechanism and society becomes not an organisation but an organism.[4]   The economic system " works itself."   This does not mean that there is no planning by individuals.   These exercise foresight and choose between alternatives.   This is necessarily so if there is to be order in the system.   But this theory assumes that the direction of resources is dependent directly on the price mechanism.   Indeed, it is often considered to be an objection to economic planning that it merely tries to do what is already done by the price mechanism.[5]   Sir Arthur Salter's description, however, gives a very incomplete picture of our economic system.   Within a firm, the description does not fit at all.   For instance, in economic theory we find that the allocation of factors of production between different uses is determined by the price mechanism.   The price of factor A becomes higher in X than in Y.   As a result, A moves from Y to X until the difference between the prices in X and Y, except in so far as it compensates for other differential advantages, disappears.   Yet in the real world, we find that there are many areas where this does not apply.   If a workman moves from department Y to department X, he does not go because of a change in relative prices, but because he is ordered to do so.   Those who

[1] J. M. Keynes, *Essays in Biography*, pp. 223-4.
[2] L. Robbins, *Nature and Significance of Economic Science*, p. 63.
[3] This description is quoted with approval by D. H. Robertson, *Control of Industry*, p. 85, and by Professor Arnold Plant, "Trends in Business Administration," ECONOMICA, February, 1932. It appears in *Allied Shipping Control*, pp. 16-17.
[4] See F. A. Hayek, "The Trend of Economic Thinking," ECONOMICA, May, 1933.
[5] See F. A. Hayek, op. cit.

object to economic planning on the grounds that the problem is solved by price movements can be answered by pointing out that there is planning within our economic system which is quite different from the individual planning mentioned above and which is akin to what is normally called economic planning. The example given above is typical of a large sphere in our modern economic system. Of course, this fact has not been ignored by economists. Marshall introduces organisation as a fourth factor of production; J. B. Clark gives the co-ordinating function to the entrepreneur; Professor Knight introduces managers who co-ordinate. As D. H. Robertson points out, we find "islands of conscious power in this ocean of unconscious co-operation like lumps of butter coagulating in a pail of buttermilk."[1] But in view of the fact that it is usually argued that co-ordination will be done by the price mechanism, why is such organisation necessary? Why are there these "islands of conscious power"? Outside the firm, price movements direct production, which is co-ordinated through a series of exchange transactions on the market. Within a firm, these market transactions are eliminated and in place of the complicated market structure with exchange transactions is substituted the entrepreneur-co-ordinator, who directs production.[2] It is clear that these are alternative methods of co-ordinating production. Yet, having regard to the fact that if production is regulated by price movements, production could be carried on without any organisation at all, well might we ask, why is there any organisation?

Of course, the degree to which the price mechanism is superseded varies greatly. In a department store, the allocation of the different sections to the various locations in the building may be done by the controlling authority or it may be the result of competitive price bidding for space. In the Lancashire cotton industry, a weaver can rent power and shop-room and can obtain looms and yarn on credit.[3] This co-ordination of the various factors of production is, however, normally carried out without the intervention of the price mechanism. As is evident, the amount of "vertical" integration, involving as it does

---

[1] Op. cit., p. 85.
[2] In the rest of this paper I shall use the term entrepreneur to refer to the person or persons who, in a competitive system, take the place of the price mechanism in the direction of resources.
[3] *Survey of Textile Industries*, p. 26.

the supersession of the price mechanism, varies greatly from industry to industry and from firm to firm.

It can, I think, be assumed that the distinguishing mark of the firm is the supersession of the price mechanism. It is, of course, as Professor Robbins points out, " related to an outside network of relative prices and costs,"[1] but it is important to discover the exact nature of this relationship. This distinction between the allocation of resources in a firm and the allocation in the economic system has been very vividly described by Mr. Maurice Dobb when discussing Adam Smith's conception of the capitalist : " It began to be seen that there was something more important than the relations inside each factory or unit captained by an undertaker ; there were the relations of the undertaker with the rest of the economic world outside his immediate sphere . . . . the undertaker busies himself with the division of labour inside each firm and he plans and organises consciously," but " he is related to the much larger economic specialisation, of which he himself is merely one specialised unit. Here, he plays his part as a single cell in a larger organism, mainly unconscious of the wider rôle he fills."[2]

In view of the fact that while economists treat the price mechanism as a co-ordinating instrument, they also admit the co-ordinating function of the " entrepreneur," it is surely important to enquire why co-ordination is the work of the price mechanism in one case and of the entrepreneur in another. The purpose of this paper is to bridge what appears to be a gap in economic theory between the assumption (made for some purposes) that resources are allocated by means of the price mechanism and the assumption (made for other purposes) that this allocation is dependent on the entrepreneur-co-ordinator. We have to explain the basis on which, in practice, this choice between alternatives is effected.[3]

---

[1] Op. cit., p. 71.

[2] *Capitalist Enterprise and Social Progress*, p. 20. Cf., also, Henderson, *Supply and Demand*, pp. 3–5.

[3] It is easy to see when the State takes over the direction of an industry that, in planning it, it is doing something which was previously done by the price mechanism. What is usually not realised is that any business man in organising the relations between his departments is also doing something which could be organised through the price mechanism. There is therefore point in Mr. Durbin's answer to those who emphasise the problems involved in economic planning that the same problems have to be solved by business men in the competitive system. (See " Economic Calculus in a Planned Economy," *Economic Journal*, December, 1936.) The important difference between these two cases is that economic planning is imposed on industry while firms arise voluntarily because they represent a more efficient method of organising production. In a competitive system, there is an " optimum " amount of planning !

II

Our task is to attempt to discover why a firm emerges at all in a specialised exchange economy. The price mechanism (considered purely from the side of the direction of resources) might be superseded if the relationship which replaced it was desired for its own sake. This would be the case, for example, if some people preferred to work under the direction of some other person. Such individuals would accept less in order to work under someone, and firms would arise naturally from this. But it would appear that this cannot be a very important reason, for it would rather seem that the opposite tendency is operating if one judges from the stress normally laid on the advantage of " being one's own master."[1] Of course, if the desire was not to be controlled but to control, to exercise power over others, then people might be willing to give up something in order to direct others ; that is, they would be willing to pay others more than they could get under the price mechanism in order to be able to direct them. But this implies that those who direct pay in order to be able to do this and are not paid to direct, which is clearly not true in the majority of cases.[2] Firms might also exist if purchasers preferred commodities which are produced by firms to those not so produced ; but even in spheres where one would expect such preferences (if they exist) to be of negligible importance, firms are to be found in the real world.[3] Therefore there must be other elements involved.

The main reason why it is profitable to establish a firm would seem to be that there is a cost of using the price mechanism. The most obvious cost of " organising " production through the price mechanism is that of discovering what the relevant prices are.[4] This cost may be reduced but it will not be eliminated by the emergence of specialists who will sell this information. The costs of negotiating and

[1] Cf. Harry Dawes, " Labour Mobility in the Steel Industry," *Economic Journal*, March, 1934, who instances " the trek to retail shopkeeping and insurance work by the better paid of skilled men due to the desire (often the main aim in life of a worker) to be independent " (p. 86).

[2] None the less, this is not altogether fanciful. Some small shopkeepers are said to earn less than their assistants.

[3] G. F. Shove, " The Imperfection of the Market : a Further Note," *Economic Journal*, March, 1933, p. 116, note 1, points out that such preferences may exist, although the example he gives is almost the reverse of the instance given in the text.

[4] According to N. Kaldor, " A Classificatory Note on the Determinateness of Equilibrium," *Review of Economic Studies*, February, 1934, it is one of the assumptions of static theory that " All the relevant prices are known to all individuals." But this is clearly not true of the real world.

concluding a separate contract for each exchange transaction which takes place on a market must also be taken into account.[1] Again, in certain markets, e.g., produce exchanges, a technique is devised for minimising these contract costs ; but they are not eliminated. It is true that contracts are not eliminated when there is a firm but they are greatly reduced. A factor of production (or the owner thereof) does not have to make a series of contracts with the factors with whom he is co-operating within the firm, as would be necessary, of course, if this co-operation were as a direct result of the working of the price mechanism. For this series of contracts is substituted one. At this stage, it is important to note the character of the contract into which a factor enters that is employed within a firm. The contract is one whereby the factor, for a certain remuneration (which may be fixed or fluctuating), agrees to obey the directions of an entrepreneur *within certain limits*.[2] The essence of the contract is that it should only state the limits to the powers of the entrepreneur. Within these limits, he can therefore direct the other factors of production.

There are, however, other disadvantages—or costs— of using the price mechanism. It may be desired to make a long-term contract for the supply of some article or service. This may be due to the fact that if one contract is made for a longer period, instead of several shorter ones, then certain costs of making each contract will be avoided. Or, owing to the risk attitude of the people concerned, they may prefer to make a long rather than a short-term contract. Now, owing to the difficulty of forecasting, the longer the period of the contract is for the supply of the commodity or service, the less possible, and indeed, the less desirable it is for the person purchasing to specify what the other contracting party is expected to do. It may well be a matter of indifference to the person supplying the service or commodity which of several courses of action is taken, but not to the purchaser of that service or commodity. But the purchaser will not know which of these several courses he will want the supplier to take. Therefore,

---

[1] This influence was noted by Professor Usher when discussing the development of capitalism. He says : " The successive buying and selling of partly finished products were sheer waste of energy." (*Introduction to the Industrial History of England*, p. 13). But he does not develop the idea nor consider why it is that buying and selling operations still exist.

[2] It would be possible for no limits to the powers of the entrepreneur to be fixed. This would be voluntary slavery. According to Professor Batt, *The Law of Master and Servant*, p. 18, such a contract would be void and unenforceable.

the service which is being provided is expressed in general terms, the exact details being left until a later date. All that is stated in the contract is the limits to what the persons supplying the commodity or service is expected to do. The details of what the supplier is expected to do is not stated in the contract but is decided later by the purchaser. When the direction of resources (within the limits of the contract) becomes dependent on the buyer in this way, that relationship which I term a " firm " may be obtained.[1] A firm is likely therefore to emerge in those cases where a very short term contract would be unsatisfactory. It is obviously of more importance in the case of services— labour—than it is in the case of the buying of commodities. In the case of commodities, the main items can be stated in advance and the details which will be decided later will be of minor significance.

We may sum up this section of the argument by saying that the operation of a market costs something and by forming an organisation and allowing some authority (an " entrepreneur ") to direct the resources, certain marketing costs are saved. The entrepreneur has to carry out his function at less cost, taking into account the fact that he may get factors of production at a lower price than the market transactions which he supersedes, because it is always possible to revert to the open market if he fails to do this.

The question of uncertainty is one which is often considered to be very relevant to the study of the equilibrium of the firm. It seems improbable that a firm would emerge without the existence of uncertainty. But those, for instance, Professor Knight, who make the *mode of payment* the distinguishing mark of the firm—fixed incomes being guaranteed to some of those engaged in production by a person who takes the residual, and fluctuating, income— would appear to be introducing a point which is irrelevant to the problem we are considering. One entrepreneur may sell his services to another for a certain sum of money, while the payment to his employees may be mainly or wholly a share in profits.[2] The significant question would

---

[1] Of course, it is not possible to draw a hard and fast line which determines whether there is a firm or not. There may be more or less direction. It is similar to the legal question of whether there is the relationship of master and servant or principal and agent. See the discussion of this problem below.

[2] The views of Professor Knight are examined below in more detail.

appear to be why the allocation of resources is not done directly by the price mechanism.

Another factor that should be noted is that exchange transactions on a market and the same transactions organised within a firm are often treated differently by Governments or other bodies with regulatory powers. If we consider the operation of a sales tax, it is clear that it is a tax on market transactions and not on the same transactions organised within the firm. Now since these are alternative methods of " organisation "—by the price mechanism or by the entrepreneur—such a regulation would bring into existence firms which otherwise would have no *raison d'être*. It would furnish a reason for the emergence of a firm in a specialised exchange economy. Of course, to the extent that firms already exist, such a measure as a sales tax would merely tend to make them larger than they would otherwise be. Similarly, quota schemes, and methods of price control which imply that there is rationing, and which do not apply to firms producing such products for themselves, by allowing advantages to those who organise within the firm and not through the market, necessarily encourage the growth of firms. But it is difficult to believe that it is measures such as have been mentioned in this paragraph which have brought firms into existence. Such measures would, however, tend to have this result if they did not exist for other reasons.

These, then, are the reasons why organisations such as firms exist in a specialised exchange economy in which it is generally assumed that the distribution of resources is " organised " by the price mechanism. A firm, therefore, consists of the system of relationships which comes into existence when the direction of resources is dependent on an entrepreneur.

The approach which has just been sketched would appear to offer an advantage in that it is possible to give a scientific meaning to what is meant by saying that a firm gets larger or smaller. A firm becomes larger as additional transactions (which could be exchange transactions co-ordinated through the price mechanism) are organised by the entrepreneur and becomes smaller as he abandons the organisation of such transactions. The question which arises is whether it is possible to study the forces which determine the size of the firm. Why does the entrepreneur not organise one less transaction or one more ?   It is interesting to note that Professor Knight considers that :

> "the relation between efficiency and size is one of the most serious problems of theory, being, in contrast with the relation for a plant, largely a matter of personality and historical accident rather than of intelligible general principles.   But the question is peculiarly vital because the possibility of monopoly gain offers a powerful incentive to *continuous and unlimited* expansion of the firm, which force must be offset by some equally powerful one making for decreased efficiency (in the production of money income) with growth in size, if even boundary competition is to exist."[1]

Professor Knight would appear to consider that it is impossible to treat scientifically the determinants of the size of the firm.   On the basis of the concept of the firm developed above, this task will now be attempted.

It was suggested that the introduction of the firm was due primarily to the existence of marketing costs.   A pertinent question to ask would appear to be (quite apart from the monopoly considerations raised by Professor Knight), why, if by organising one can eliminate certain costs and in fact reduce the cost of production, are there any market transactions at all ?[2]   Why is not all production carried on by one big firm ?   There would appear to be certain possible explanations.

First, as a firm gets larger, there may be decreasing returns to the entrepreneur function, that is, the costs of organising additional transactions within the firm may rise.[3]   Naturally, a point must be reached where the costs of organising an extra transaction within the firm are equal to the costs involved in carrying out the transaction in the open market, or, to the costs of organising by another entrepreneur.   Secondly, it may be that as the transactions which are organised increase, the entrepreneur fails to place the factors of production in the uses where their value

---

[1] *Risk, Uncertainty and Profit*, Preface to the Re-issue, London School of Economics Series of Reprints, No. 16, 1933.

[2] There are certain marketing costs which could only be eliminated by the abolition of "consumers' choice" and these are the costs of retailing. It is conceivable that these costs might be so high that people would be willing to accept rations because the extra product obtained was worth the loss of their choice.

[3] This argument assumes that exchange transactions on a market can be considered as homogeneous; which is clearly untrue in fact. This complication is taken into account below.

is greatest, that is, fails to make the best use of the factors of production. Again, a point must be reached where the loss through the waste of resources is equal to the marketing costs of the exchange transaction in the open market or to the loss if the transaction was organised by another entrepreneur. Finally, the supply price of one or more of the factors of production may rise, because the "other advantages" of a small firm are greater than those of a large firm.[1] Of course, the actual point where the expansion of the firm ceases might be determined by a combination of the factors mentioned above. The first two reasons given most probably correspond to the economists' phrase of "diminishing returns to management."[2]

The point has been made in the previous paragraph that a firm will tend to expand until the costs of organising an extra transaction within the firm become equal to the costs of carrying out the same transaction by means of an exchange on the open market or the costs of organising in another firm. But if the firm stops its expansion at a point below the costs of marketing in the open market and at a point equal to the costs of organising in another firm, in most cases (excluding the case of "combination"[3]), this will imply that there is a market transaction between these two producers, each of whom could organise it at less than the actual marketing costs. How is the paradox to be resolved ? If we consider an example the reason for this will become clear. Suppose *A* is buying a product from *B* and that both *A* and *B* could organise this marketing transaction at less than its present cost. *B*, we can assume, is not organising one process or stage of production, but several. If *A* therefore wishes to avoid a market transaction, he will have to take over all the processes of production controlled by *B*. Unless *A* takes over all the processes of

---

[1] For a discussion of the variation of the supply price of factors of production to firms of varying size, see E. A. G. Robinson, *The Structure of Competitive Industry.* It is sometimes said that the supply price of organising ability increases as the size of the firm increases because men prefer to be the heads of small independent businesses rather than the heads of departments in a large business. See Jones, *The Trust Problem,* p. 531, and Macgregor, *Industrial Combination,* p. 63. This is a common argument of those who advocate Rationalisation. It is said that larger units would be more efficient, but owing to the individualistic spirit of the smaller entrepreneurs, they prefer to remain independent, apparently in spite of the higher income which their increased efficiency under Rationalisation makes possible.

[2] This discussion is, of course, brief and incomplete. For a more thorough discussion of this particular problem, see N. Kaldor, "The Equilibrium of the Firm," *Economic Journal,* March, 1934, and E. A. G. Robinson, "The Problem of Management and the Size of the Firm," *Economic Journal,* June, 1934.

[3] A definition of this term is given below.

production, a market transaction will still remain, although it is a different product that is bought. But we have previously assumed that as each producer expands he becomes less efficient; the additional costs of organising extra transactions increase. It is probable that A's cost of organising the transactions previously organised by B will be greater than B's cost of doing the same thing. A therefore will take over the whole of B's organisation only if his cost of organising B's work is not greater than B's cost by an amount equal to the costs of carrying out an exchange transaction on the open market. But once it becomes economical to have a market transaction, it also pays to divide production in such a way that the cost of organising an extra transaction in each firm is the same.

Up to now it has been assumed that the exchange transactions which take place through the price mechanism are homogeneous. In fact, nothing could be more diverse than the actual transactions which take place in our modern world. This would seem to imply that the costs of carrying out exchange transactions through the price mechanism will vary considerably as will also the costs of organising these transactions within the firm. It seems therefore possible that quite apart from the question of diminishing returns the costs of organising certain transactions within the firm may be greater than the costs of carrying out the exchange transactions in the open market. This would necessarily imply that there were exchange transactions carried out through the price mechanism, but would it mean that there would have to be more than one firm ? Clearly not, for all those areas in the economic system where the direction of resources was not dependent directly on the price mechanism could be organised within one firm. The factors which were discussed earlier would seem to be the important ones, though it is difficult to say whether " diminishing returns to management " or the rising supply price of factors is likely to be the more important.

Other things being equal, therefore, a firm will tend to be larger :

(*a*) the less the costs of organising and the slower these costs rise with an increase in the transactions organised.

(*b*) the less likely the entrepreneur is to make mistakes and the smaller the increase in mistakes with an increase in the transactions organised.

(*c*) the greater the lowering (or the less the rise) in the supply price of factors of production to firms of larger size.

Apart from variations in the supply price of factors of production to firms of different sizes, it would appear that the costs of organising and the losses through mistakes will increase with an increase in the spatial distribution of the transactions organised, in the dissimilarity of the transactions, and in the probability of changes in the relevant prices.[1] As more transactions are organised by an entrepreneur, it would appear that the transactions would tend to be either different in kind or in different places. This furnishes an additional reason why efficiency will tend to decrease as the firm gets larger. Inventions which tend to bring factors of production nearer together, by lessening spatial distribution, tend to increase the size of the firm.[2] Changes like the telephone and the telegraph which tend to reduce the cost of organising spatially will tend to increase the size of the firm. All changes which improve managerial technique will tend to increase the size of the firm.[3-4]

It should be noted that the definition of a firm which was given above can be used to give more precise meanings to the terms "combination" and "integration."[5] There is a combination when transactions which were previously

---

[1] This aspect of the problem is emphasised by N. Kaldor, op. cit. Its importance in this connection had been previously noted by E. A. G. Robinson, *The Structure of Competitive Industry*, pp. 83–106. This assumes that an increase in the probability of price movements increases the costs of organising within a firm more than it increases the cost of carrying out an exchange transaction on the market—which is probable.

[2] This would appear to be the importance of the treatment of the technical unit by E. A. G. Robinson, op. cit., pp. 27–33. The larger the technical unit, the greater the concentration of factors and therefore the firm is likely to be larger.

[3] It should be noted that most inventions will change both the costs of organising and the costs of using the price mechanism. In such cases, whether the invention tends to make firms larger or smaller will depend on the relative effect on these two sets of costs. For instance, if the telephone reduces the costs of using the price mechanism more than it reduces the costs of organising, then it will have the effect of reducing the size of the firm.

[4] An illustration of these dynamic forces is furnished by Maurice Dobb, *Russian Economic Development*, p. 68. "With the passing of bonded labour the factory, as an establishment where work was organised under the whip of the overseer, lost its *raison d'être* until this was restored to it with the introduction of power machinery after 1846." It seems important to realise that the passage from the domestic system to the factory system is not a mere historical accident, but is conditioned by economic forces. This is shown by the fact that it is possible to move from the factory system to the domestic system, as in the Russian example, as well as *vice versa*. It is the essence of serfdom that the price mechanism is not allowed to operate. Therefore, there has to be direction from some organiser. When, however, serfdom passed, the price mechanism was allowed to operate. It was not until machinery drew workers into one locality that it paid to supersede the price mechanism and the firm again emerged.

[5] This is often called " vertical integration," combination being termed " lateral integration."

organised by two or more entrepreneurs become organised by one. This becomes integration when it involves the organisation of transactions which were previously carried out between the entrepreneurs on a market. A firm can expand in either or both of these two ways. The whole of the " structure of competitive industry " becomes tractable by the ordinary technique of economic analysis.

III

The problem which has been investigated in the previous section has not been entirely neglected by economists and it is now necessary to consider why the reasons given above for the emergence of a firm in a specialised exchange economy are to be preferred to the other explanations which have been offered.

It is sometimes said that the reason for the existence of a firm is to be found in the division of labour. This is the view of Professor Usher, a view which has been adopted and expanded by Mr. Maurice Dobb. The firm becomes " the result of an increasing complexity of the division of labour . . . . The growth of this economic differentiation creates the need for some integrating force without which differentiation would collapse into chaos ; and it is as the integrating force in a differentiated economy that industrial forms are chiefly significant."[1] The answer to this argument is an obvious one. The " integrating force in a differentiated economy " already exists in the form of the price mechanism. It is perhaps the main achievement of economic science that it has shown that there is no reason to suppose that specialisation must lead to chaos.[2] The reason given by Mr. Maurice Dobb is therefore inadmissible. What has to be explained is why one integrating force (the entrepreneur) should be substituted for another integrating force (the price mechanism).

The most interesting reasons (and probably the most widely accepted) which have been given to explain this fact are those to be found in Professor Knight's *Risk, Uncertainty and Profit*. His views will be examined in some detail.

---

[1] Op. cit., p. 10. Professor Usher's views are to be found in his *Introduction to the Industrial History of England*, pp. 1–18.

[2] Cf. J. B. Clark, *Distribution of Wealth*, p. 19, who speaks of the theory of exchange as being the " theory of the organisation of industrial society."

Professor Knight starts with a system in which there is no uncertainty :

"acting as individuals under absolute freedom but without collusion men are supposed to have organised economic life with the primary and secondary division of labour, the use of capital, etc., developed to the point familiar in present-day America. The principal fact which calls for the exercise of the imagination is the internal organisation of the productive groups or establish-ments. With uncertainty entirely absent, every individual being in possession of perfect knowledge of the situation, there would be no occasion for anything of the nature of responsible management or control of productive activity. Even marketing transactions in any realistic sense would not be found. The flow of raw materials and productive services to the consumer would be entirely automatic."[1]

Professor Knight says that we can imagine this adjustment as being " the result of a long process of experimentation worked out by trial-and-error methods alone," while it is not necessary " to imagine every worker doing exactly the right thing at the right time in a sort of ' pre-established harmony ' with the work of others. There might be managers, superintendents, etc., for the purpose of co-ordinating the activities of individuals," though these managers would be performing a purely routine function, " without responsi-bility of any sort."[2]

Professor Knight then continues :

"With the introduction of uncertainty—the fact of ignorance and the necessity of acting upon opinion rather than knowledge—into this Eden-like situation, its character is entirely changed . . . . With uncertainty present doing things, the actual execution of activity, becomes in a real sense a secondary part of life ; the primary problem or function is deciding what to do and how to do it."[3]

This fact of uncertainty brings about the two most important characteristics of social organisation.

" In the first place, goods are produced for a market, on the basis of entirely impersonal prediction of wants, not for the satisfaction of the wants of the producers themselves. The producer takes the responsibility of

---

[1] *Risk, Uncertainty and Profit*, p. 267.
[2] Op. cit., pp. 267-8.   [3] Op. cit., p. 268.

c

forecasting the consumers' wants. In the second place, the work of forecasting and at the same time a large part of the technological direction and control of production are still further concentrated upon a very narrow class of the producers, and we meet with a new economic functionary, the entrepreneur. . . . . When uncertainty is present and the task of deciding what to do and how to do it takes the ascendancy over that of execution the internal organisation of the productive groups is no longer a matter of indifference or a mechanical detail. Centralisation of this deciding and controlling function is imperative, a process of ' cephalisation ' is inevitable."[1] The most fundamental change is :

" the system under which the confident and venturesome assume the risk or insure the doubtful and timid by guaranteeing to the latter a specified income in return for an assignment of the actual results. . . . With human nature as we know it it would be impracticable or very unusual for one man to guarantee to another a definite result of the latter's actions without being given power to direct his work. And on the other hand the second party would not place himself under the direction of the first without such a guarantee. . . . The result of this manifold specialisation of function is the enterprise and wage system of industry. Its existence in the world is the direct result of the fact of uncertainty."[2]

These quotations give the essence of Professor Knight's theory. The fact of uncertainty means that people have to forecast future wants. Therefore, you get a special class springing up who direct the activities of others to whom they give guaranteed wages. It acts because good judgment is generally associated with confidence in one's judgment.[3]

Professor Knight would appear to leave himself open to criticism on several grounds. First of all, as he himself points out, the fact that certain people have better judgment or better knowledge does not mean that they can only get an income from it by themselves actively taking part in production. They can sell advice or knowledge. Every business buys the services of a host of advisers. We can imagine a system where all advice or knowledge was bought

---

[1] Op. cit., pp. 268–95.   [2] Op. cit., pp. 269–70.
[3] Op. cit., p. 270.

as required. Again, it is possible to get a reward from better knowledge or judgment not by actively taking part in production but by making contracts with people who are producing. A merchant buying for future delivery represents an example of this. But this merely illustrates the point that it is quite possible to give a guaranteed reward providing that certain acts are performed without directing the performance of those acts. Professor Knight says that " with human nature as we know it it would be impracticable or very unusual for one man to guarantee to another a definite result of the latter's actions without being given power to direct his work." This is surely incorrect. A large proportion of jobs are done to contract, that is, the contractor is guaranteed a certain sum providing he performs certain acts. But this does not involve any direction. It does mean, however, that the system of relative prices has been changed and that there will be a new arrangement of the factors of production.[1] The fact that Professor Knight mentions that the " second party would not place himself under the direction of the first without such a guarantee " is irrelevant to the problem we are considering. Finally, it seems important to notice that even in the case of an economic system where there is no uncertainty Professor Knight considers that there would be co-ordinators, though they would perform only a routine function. He immediately adds that they would be " without responsibility of any sort," which raises the question by whom are they paid and why ? It seems that nowhere does Professor Knight give a reason why the price mechanism should be superseded.

IV

It would seem important to examine one further point and that is to consider the relevance of this discussion to the general question of the " cost-curve of the firm."

It has sometimes been assumed that a firm is limited in size under perfect competition if its cost curve slopes upward,[2] while under imperfect competition, it is limited

---

[1] This shows that it is possible to have a private enterprise system without the existence of firms. Though, in practice, the two functions of enterprise, which actually influences the system of relative prices by forecasting wants and acting in accordance with such forecasts, and management, which accepts the system of relative prices as being given, are normally carried out by the same persons, yet it seems important to keep them separate in theory. This point is further discussed below.

[2] See Kaldor, op. cit., and Robinson, *The Problem of Management and the Size of the Firm.*

in size because it will not pay to produce more than the output at which marginal cost is equal to marginal revenue.[1] But it is clear that a firm may produce more than one product and, therefore, there appears to be no *prima facie* reason why this upward slope of the cost curve in the case of perfect competition or the fact that marginal cost will not always be below marginal revenue in the case of imperfect competition should limit the size of the firm.[2] Mrs. Robinson[3] makes the simplifying assumption that only one product is being produced. But it is clearly important to investigate how the number of products produced by a firm is determined, while no theory which assumes that only one product is in fact produced can have very great practical significance.

It might be replied that under perfect competition, since everything that is produced can be sold at the prevailing price, then there is no need for any other product to be produced. But this argument ignores the fact that there may be a point where it is less costly to organise the exchange transactions of a new product than to organise further exchange transactions of the old product. This point can be illustrated in the following way. Imagine, following von Thunen, that there is a town, the consuming centre, and that industries are located around this central point in rings. These conditions are illustrated in the following diagram in which *A*, *B* and *C* represent different industries.

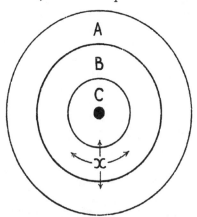

[1] Mr. Robinson calls this the Imperfect Competition solution for the survival of the small firm.
[2] Mr. Robinson's conclusion, op. cit., p. 249, note 1, would appear to be definitely wrong. He is followed by Horace J. White, Jr., " Monopolistic and Perfect Competition," *American Economic Review*, December, 1936, p. 645, note 27. Mr. White states " It is obvious that the size of the firm is limited in conditions of monopolistic competition."
[3] *Economics of Imperfect Competition.*

Imagine an entrepreneur who starts controlling exchange transactions from x. Now as he extends his activities in the same produce (B), the cost of organising increases until at some point it becomes equal to that of a dissimilar product which is nearer. As the firm expands, it will therefore from this point include more than one product (A and C). This treatment of the problem is obviously incomplete,[1] but it is necessary to show that merely proving that the cost curve turns upwards does not give a limitation to the size of the firm. So far we have only considered the case of perfect competition ; the case of imperfect competition would appear to be obvious.

To determine the size of the firm, we have to consider the marketing costs (that is, the costs of using the price mechanism), and the costs of organising of different entrepreneurs and then we can determine how many products will be produced by each firm and how much of each it will produce. It would, therefore, appear that Mr. Shove[2] in his article on " Imperfect Competition " was asking questions which Mrs. Robinson's cost curve apparatus cannot answer. The factors mentioned above would seem to be the relevant ones.

V

Only one task now remains ; and that is, to see whether the concept of a firm which has been developed fits in with that existing in the real world. We can best approach the question of what constitutes a firm in practice by considering the legal relationship normally called that of " master and servant " or " employer and employee."[3] The essentials of this relationship have been given as follows :

" (1) the servant must be under the duty of rendering personal services to the master or to others on behalf

---

[1] As has been shown above, location is only one of the factors influencing the cost of organising.

[2] G. F. Shove, " The Imperfection of the Market," *Economic Journal*, March, 1933, p. 115. In connection with an increase in demand in the suburbs and the effect on the price charged by suppliers, Mr. Shove asks " . . . . why do not the old firms open branches in the suburbs ? " If the argument in the text is correct, this is a question which Mrs. Robinson's apparatus cannot answer.

[3] The legal concept of " employer and employee " and the economic concept of a firm are not identical, in that the firm may imply control over another person's property as well as over their labour. But the identity of these two concepts is sufficiently close for an examination of the legal concept to be of value in appraising the worth of the economic concept.

of the master, otherwise the contract is a contract for sale of goods or the like.

(2) The master must have the right to control the servant's work, either personally or by another servant or agent. It is this right of control or interference, of being entitled to tell the servant when to work (within the hours of service) and when not to work, and what work to do and how to do it (within the terms of such service) which is the dominant characteristic in this relation and marks off the servant from an independent contractor, or from one employed merely to give to his employer the fruits of his labour. In the latter case, the contractor or performer is not under the employer's control in doing the work or effecting the service; he has to shape and manage his work so as to give the result he has contracted to effect."[1]

We thus see that it is the fact of direction which is the essence of the legal concept of " employer and employee," just as it was in the economic concept which was developed above. It is interesting to note that Professor Batt says further :

"That which distinguishes an agent from a servant is not the absence or presence of a fixed wage or the payment only of commission on business done, but rather the freedom with which an agent may carry out his employment."[2]

We can therefore conclude that the definition we have given is one which approximates closely to the firm as it is considered in the real world.

Our definition is, therefore, realistic. Is it manageable? This ought to be clear. When we are considering how large a firm will be the principle of marginalism works smoothly. The question always is, will it pay to bring an extra exchange transaction under the organising authority? At the margin, the costs of organising within the firm will be equal either to the costs of organising in another firm or to the costs involved in leaving the transaction to be " organised " by the price mechanism. Business men will be constantly experimenting, controlling more or less, and in this way, equilibrium will be maintained. This gives the position of equilibrium for static analysis. But

---

[1] Batt, *The Law of Master and Servant*, p. 6.
[2] Op. cit., p. 7.

it is clear that the dynamic factors are also of considerable importance, and an investigation of the effect changes have on the cost of organising within the firm and on marketing costs generally will enable one to explain why firms get larger and smaller. We thus have a theory of moving equilibrium. The above analysis would also appear to have clarified the relationship between initiative or enterprise and management. Initiative means forecasting and operates through the price mechanism by the making of new contracts. Management proper merely reacts to price changes, rearranging the factors of production under its control. That the business man normally combines both functions is an obvious result of the marketing costs which were discussed above. Finally, this analysis enables us to state more exactly what is meant by the " marginal product " of the entrepreneur. But an elaboration of this point would take us far from our comparatively simple task of definition and clarification.

[4]

INFORMATION, EXPECTATIONS AND THE THEORY OF THE FIRM*

By H. B. MALMGREN

This paper is concerned with the rationale of decentralized decision-making in a market economy. In particular it raises a somewhat unusual question: Why do multi-person, multi-process firms exist in a competitive economy? In the past, firms were generally taken for granted in working out theoretical problems[1] and the question was only rarely raised as to why firms should take over a number of conceivably independent activities and allocate resources among them. The firm is, after all, an allocating mechanism over the entire set of economic activities between the purchase of inputs and the sale of outputs. The market operates between firms, but the entrepreneur is the planning and co-ordinating agent within the bounds of any one firm. Why then do we find, as Sir Dennis Robertson so nicely put it, "islands of conscious power in this ocean of unconscious co-operation like lumps of butter coagulating in a pail of butter-milk?"[2]

I. THE PRICE SYSTEM AND THE FIRM

There must, of course, be firms in a market economy, for consumers alone could not establish, by their own decisions, the market prices. But the question is why firms should take on a specific size which entails more than one person and one process. Suppose, to begin with, that individuals came into a market, or clearing house,

* I am grateful in particular to Professor J. Marschak, C. L. Lloyd, and P. P. Streeten for detailed comments on an earlier version of this paper, and also to P. W. S. Andrews, M. H. Dobb, C. P. Kindleberger, I. M. D. Little, R. Lubitz, E. J. Nell, L. L. Pasinetti and E. T. Penrose for remarks. I am also grateful to the Social Science Research Council for a Research Training Fellowship which made this and related work possible.

1. Mrs. Robinson's definition of a firm, which served her very well, is a case in point: "a concern very similar to the firms of the real world." Joan Robinson, *The Economics of Imperfect Competition* (London: Macmillan, 1933).

2. D. H. Robertson, *The Control of Industry* (Rev. ed.; London: Nisbet, 1928), p. 85.

each day prepared to perform productive services at some price. Among these individuals would be specialists in specific functions and specialists in co-ordination. Is there any *economic* reason why each person could not then perform his service in return for a market-determined price without tying himself to other persons by long-term contracts? Certainly, one might say, for capital in the form of productive implements has to be provided in order that the workers can produce an "efficient" quantity of output. But suppose then that in this perfectly competitive market future events are fairly accurately foreseen. That is, suppose that the market is stationary, or changing over time in a perceptible pattern, so that prices for tomorrow and the next day and so on are determinate today. Then owners of capital goods could offer the services of such goods each day just like the specialist workers, and the market price mechanism would allocate resources and services to their most efficient uses. Each man could arrive at the right place at the right time each day to perform his task, to produce his product.

Coase proposed an explanation why firms should arise in such markets in a well-known article.[3] He suggested that the distinguishing characteristic of the firm is the supersession of the price mechanism. The most obvious reason for this is that there are *costs of using the price mechanism*. This does run counter to the traditional view that the major advantage of a competitively determined price system is that the signals of how much to produce, prices, were freely available and therefore the economies of information handling were secured free of charge.[4] Nonetheless I think we must face up to Coase's argument. He suggested that there were a number of costs of using the mechanism, among which were the cost of finding out what the relevant prices are and the cost of negotiating and concluding a contract. Thus in his view division of labor and specialization are not really valid explanations of multi-person firms if taken independently of the relative costs of organizing production by means of the market (that is, the costs of using a highly decentralized price mechanism) or the large firm. To say that firms exist because co-ordination of production is required is to miss the point entirely. What has to be explained is why firms, in the form of wilful entre-

3. R. H. Coase, "The Nature of the Firm," *Economica*, N.S., IV (1937), reprinted in *Readings in Price Theory*, American Economic Association (Chicago: Irwin, 1952).

4. Cf. T. C. Koopmans, *Three Essays on the State of Economic Science* (New York: McGraw-Hill, 1957), p. 23.

THEORY OF THE FIRM   401

preneurs, organize production in areas where the market could do so also.[5]

Coase's view depends upon uncertainty about the current and future states of events, since if events were predictable the price mechanism would render its signalling service at no cost. It is because of uncertainty that the competitive price mechanism in a market of individual producers and consumers breaks down. For at least some producers who came to the market each day there would only be a vague hope of finding buyers, for some of the producers would be specialists in uncommon tasks, and have to search laboriously for buyers of those special services. Knowing in advance where to look for a buyer or seller on any day of this week or next is necessary for the functioning of such a market. It is because of this lack of information on a range of events that firms are put together, where long-term contracts and regulated markets for clearly defined services can be developed. Taking this perspective we can say that there are definite transaction costs in using the price mechanism, costs of collecting information on relevant sets of events.

For purposes of theorizing about a perfectly competitive static economy we generally assume that all buyers and sellers know all the relevant prices in the system in order that equilibrium be attained.[6] There still remains the problem of the determination of the "correct" prices if the market is not initially at equilibrium. Both Walras and Edgeworth encountered this problem and decided that, in the absence of universal omniscience, buyers and sellers would have to be allowed to explore the market, by crying out prices without transacting or by making provisional contracts until a stable equilibrium was reached. Only then could transactions be made if the same price was to rule

5. In a letter to me Mr. Dobb questioned whether the *raison d'etre* of the firm could be confined to this argument, suggesting that each system of production has its own requirements as regards discipline, "and the firm as a managerial unit, exercising powers of control, coordination and coercion, embodies these requirements, and presumably exists by reason of them." Whereas I agree that this is fundamental, I think that what is involved from the *economic* point of view is the bringing about of a convergence of expectations about the time pattern of services to be supplied where an uncontracted, and therefore uncontrolled, pattern of services would be erratic over time because prices were insufficient indicators of future events. This argument is developed further in subsequent pages.

6. Cf. G. J. Stigler's excellent review of the literature, "Perfect Competition, Historically Contemplated," *Journal of Political Economy*, LXV (Feb. 1957). He suggests that all buyers and sellers need not be in communication with all other buyers and sellers (p. 12), but the less restrictive condition does not alter my argument.

for all. Such a solution is hardly acceptable, but if nothing better is offered we have to let a trial and error process run its course. But if equilibrium is gradually established the possibility of exploding cobwebs has to be eliminated from the picture somehow. Only experience can be allowed to influence the various buyers and sellers, and not physical carry-overs from previous periods, or changes in taste or the marginal utility of money, as Kaldor has shown.[7] But even then we must bear in mind that there are costs of finding out the best prices at any one moment and of making contracts, and, indeed, during a trial and error process the information costs may be very high because of the uncertainty about where everyone stands at any moment and where everyone is going. And in fact we have to assume that it is expected prices and quantities which are relevant, and not current data (except insofar as current data determine expectations).[8]

II. The Control of Information

If there are transaction costs, particularly in a free market where transactions are heterogeneous and the search for a buyer or seller may be lengthy, there may be an incentive to combine a number of events or activities into one bundle by arranging long-term contracts. As a result, events would be made to behave according to plan, in the sense that closely allied activities are isolated from the market and balanced one against another in a planned system.[9] A number of producers and purchasers become one market unit by integrating, and the firm which arises does not have to hunt for buyers and sellers in its internal transactions as a result. The currently relevant price changes are reduced in number by internal contracts. Activities which tended to fluctuate, causing fluctuations in prices and outputs in the market, could be integrated and balanced against one another

7. N. Kaldor, "The Determinateness of Equilibrium," *Review of Economic Studies*, I (Feb. 1934).

8. Even when all this is granted there still arise problems in the determination of equilibrium, as discussed, for example, in a recent paper by Arrow, "Toward a Theory of Price Adjustment" in *The Allocation of Economic Resources, Essays in Honor of Bernard Francis Haley* by Moses Abramovitz and others (Stanford University Press, 1959).

9. Both Cassel and Dobb suggested that control was substituted for "anarchy" in the combinations of which firms are comprised, but their arguments did not go far enough to make the necessary link between this idea and the very nature of the firm. G. Cassel, *The Theory of Social Economy* (London: T. F. Unwin, 1923), I, p. 120. M. H. Dobb, *Capitalist Enterprise and Social Progress* (London: Routledge, 1925), p. 387.

and thus reduce the fluctuations in required information. The entrepreneur resorts to the law of large numbers by producing for many consumers, each of whom may or may not know what he will want, and how much, and how strongly at some time in the future.[1] Where fluctuations in demand, or in the time required for supply, or both are important the firm can consolidate production and carry the necessary average level of idle capacity to achieve long-term stability in production and price.[2] Stability in turn reduces the cost of finding and making transactions.

If this is true we may now ask what kind of activities can be expected to be integrated, and, of course, the traditional view of technical interdependence and economies of scale comes immediately to mind. Certainly where services are closely related in their technical effect upon one another it would be important to be assured of the availability of such services when needed, at predictable prices. To dash off to the market place to locate a specific factor of production might prove a costly activity in itself. But what is a technically interdependent bundle of services? Is it the complete production function from purchase of inputs to sale of outputs, or is it some set of activities which taken together have no apparent physical effect on any other activities in the firm? Or is it a bundle of activities which is related to other such bundles only insofar as it uses a common, but limited resource, as in linear programming? In a factory where does one process end and another begin? What *is* a technically independent production function? I raise these questions in order to bring out the fact that in many cases it is not at all clear what group of interdependent activities constitute a single production function. Take, for example, Carlson's suggestion that the production function be thought of in relation to the "technical unit," "the unit for which the entrepreneur calculates the costs of production."[3] It would seem that this unit, and Carlson himself says this, is defined in terms of accounting convenience, that is, in terms of *informational advantage*, and is so defined in actual business practice. There remains a great deal to be said in economic theory about the nature or concept of an industrial process or production function, but a study of that

1. F. H. Knight, *Risk, Uncertainty and Profit* (Boston: Houghton Mifflin, 1921), p. 241.

2. Cf. A. B. Aráoz and H. B. Malmgren, "Congestion and Idle Capacity in an Economy," *Review of Economic Studies*, XXVIII (June, 1961).

3. S. Carlson, *A Study on the Pure Theory of Production* (New York: Kelley and Millman, 1956), p. 10.

kind must be put aside now, or left to others, in order to get on with the argument of this essay.   The essential point is that technical interdependence is not at all unambiguous when thought of in traditional terms.   In addition, when one does have a good notion of what a "technical unit" is in some particular situation, the question ought immediately to be put why such units are not linked by market relationships rather than executive directives.

I wish now to suggest that multi-person and multi-process firms arise in a market economy for a number of reasons which are corollary to the existence of transaction, or information, costs.   To begin with, they gain an advantage over the market in certain areas of production and sales by reducing or eliminating the costs of finding out relevant prices.   As a result a number of long-term contracts, which may well cost no more than each individual short-term contract which might instead be made, are arranged.   This in turn provides a large amount of *controlled information:* Not only are a number of events predictable over the duration of the entire production plan, but also less information is required to describe that set of events for control purposes. A number of events which must fall within a prescribed range can be identified by a single observation when it is known in advance that there is a necessary link between them (in this case as a result of contracting ahead for a series of related activities).[4]   The "principle of exceptions" and other operating rules of quite simple nature replace a more thorough analysis of every possible transaction which might arise in market-determined allocation of resources over the set of activities which make up the firm.   This stabilization of events extends into the market transactions which remain, for the firm reduces its customers costs of waiting or going without,[5] and thus its own costs (the costs of reclaiming buyers who go elsewhere) by acting as an integrated market, holding inventories and buying and selling in a way which tends to reduce fluctuations, and thus costs. (This function could, of course, be provided by an organized futures

4. To the information theorist, this is related to coding.   Marschak's concept of "optimal inexact information" is also somewhat similar. J. Marschak, "Towards an Economic Theory of Organization and Information," in *Decision Processes*, R. M. Thrall, C. H. Coombs, and R. L. Davis, eds. (New York: Wiley, 1954).   I am trying to work this notion out in a different study to which this article is in some ways introductory, and have therefore refrained from elaborating here.

5. I.e., they reduce the congestion, or "queueing," which occurs when arrivals of demand, or time required to service or supply goods, or both, fluctuate. For an elementary discussion of the congestion phenomenon, see Aráoz and Malmgren, *op. cit.*

market, but such markets can operate only under very special conditions.) Finally, the firm predicts the costs of production of its commodities better than the market could over its set of activities by eliminating the divergence of expectations which may arise when interdependent decisions are taken by independent decision-makers.

III. INFORMATION AND EXPECTATIONS

If we think of a production plan for the duration of activities up to the relevant profit horizon we must consider what equilibrium consists of. In relation to the difficulties about reaching equilibrium discussed earlier, we may prefer to consider equilibrium in terms of the individual firm's plan. Equilibrium for the individual firm exists only for actions which make up a consistent plan. We may call this kind of equilibrium *expectational equilibrium*. Any change in information would disrupt that equilibrium and create conditions for a new one. Therefore it can be said that equilibrium can exist only so long as the actions planned prove correct. If they prove incorrect, the change in planning data would require a rearrangement of the plan according to the new information if the plan were to be efficient.[6] Among many firms, a market equilibrium, as opposed to a personal equilibrium, would, of course, require more. Everyone would have to base his expectations on the same set of events as everyone else, and come to the same conclusions, or plans would have to be quite independent with respect to their consequences. It is the necessity for convergence of expectations when plans are not independent which is difficult to handle. The question I should now like to tackle is whether interdependence of decision sets is significant, and if so whether it makes a difference in the way we look at allocation decisions within and among firms.

If we suppose for the moment that a number of multi-person firms exist in a market economy, by virtue of historical accident or the argument in the previous section or whatever the reader wishes, what kinds of interdependence in decisions can we expect to find? The most obvious type of interdependence is that between buyer and seller, since the price and output set between them will depend on the offer, counter-offer bargaining of a market economy (the reader should keep in mind that I am considering a market where information is limited and the seeking out of a buyer or seller is a

6. This is Hayek's notion of how we should look at equilibrium given an uneven distribution of knowledge. F. A. von Hayek, "Economics and Knowledge," *Economica*, N.S., IV (1937), p. 36.

costly activity).[7] This kind of interdependence in expectations could also occur between a firm and a number of buyers and sellers, many of whom may not even be known in advance to the firm.[8] This kind of uncertainty extends through time and over a chain of purchases and sales, since most commitments undertaken in the producers' goods sector of the economy are undertaken on an expectation that further, and in general, later, investment for which the original equipment is needed will also take place.[9] I should like to call this general class of interdependence *multi-lateral exchange uncertainty*.

The second kind of interdependence which might be thought of is due to the effects which plans of other firms who are not direct (or indirect) buyers or sellers have on the outcome of one's own expectations. The simplest case of this is oligopolistic interdependence, in its most elementary form, where each person's outcomes depend upon what other people plan. It is well known that no satisfactory solution to the problem of how converging expectations can be brought about in such a situation has been offered, at least theoretically. But oligopolistic uncertainty of the simplest type is only a special case of a more general class of interdependence in which success is achieved by anticipating other people's expectations. At a fairly simple level this problem is described by Keynes's famous newspaper contest in which competitors were to pick the six faces which most other competitors would select as prettiest — a problem of "anticipating what average opinion expects the average opinion to be."[1] But as Keynes suggested, this is only the third degree or order of expectations (the first being a guess at the prettiest faces, and the second a guess at what other people will think to be the prettiest faces), and there are fourth, fifth and higher orders as well. In fact it is possible to think of a set of degrees of sophistication which extends indefinitely. If expectations proceed to the n'th degree, where n is very large, there is no reason to suppose that expectations must converge. They may or may not. It is difficult to draw a line

7. Svennilson suggested that variables under such conditions be called "bilaterally directed," as opposed to "unilaterally directed," variables as in internal planning of the firm. I. Svennilson, *Ekonomisk Planering* (Uppsala: Almquist and Wiksells, 1938), p. 27.

8. This was called "social uncertainty" by Houthakker in "The Scope and Limits of Futures Trading," in *The Allocation of Economic Resources, op. cit.*, p. 141.

9. Cf. F. A. von Hayek, "Investment that Raises the Demand for Capital," *Review of Economic Statistics*, XIX (Nov. 1937).

1. Keynes, *General Theory of Employment, Interest and Money*, p. 156.

somewhere between the third and n'th degrees and say this is where one will rest, for there is no reason to suppose that everyone will stop at the same degree of sophistication. The problem of converging expectations in the mixed-motive decision situations which are described as "non-zero-sum games" has been explored at length by Schelling, and the analogy between the problems he considers and what I have in mind here is so close that an extensive discussion is unnecessary.[2] It is sufficient for the purposes of this essay to indicate the nature of this type of interdependence and its influence on expectations. Clearly it leads to a great deal of uncertainty, unless expectations do converge. Schelling proposed that precedents, custom, and unique or asymmetrical qualities of a situation could bring about convergence, and we can certainly see such an influence at work in speculation within the "acceptable range of fluctuation,"[3] in the settling of falling or rising stock market prices at "resistance levels," in the practice of pricing in line with a "leader," in the maintenance of stability in an oligopolistic market where any change could lead to chaos, and in many other areas where lack of convergence is costly, if not disastrous.[4] Tentatively we might call this type of linkage between independently made decisions an *interdependent planning uncertainty* (keeping in mind that the effects of interdependence may be complementary or competitive or both).

Clearly these kinds of interdependence are important — all the more so when we consider production plans over a number of periods and the exchange and planning interdependence takes on a linked form over time in which the success of what one firm does depends upon decisions taken in other firms now and, in particular, in later periods when the product goes into its next use in the flow of production or when the gestation period of the decision is completed. Firms must plan in relation to the market if expectational equilibrium is

2. T. C. Schelling, *The Strategy of Conflict* (Harvard University Press, 1960).

3. Cf. L. M. Lachmann, *Capital and Its Structure* (London: London School of Economics and Political Science, 1956), pp. 30–34.

4. It should be noted that this kind of interdependence can be found sometimes in what might appear at first to be straightforward independent decision-making. For example, the location problem turns out to be indeterminate unless at least one site is predetermined independently. The price mechanism in its traditional form just breaks down when decisions on various sites are made independently of one another. Cf. T. C. Koopmans, *Three Essays on the State of Economic Science, op. cit.*, p. 154 and Koopmans and M. Beckmann, "Assignment Problems and the Location of Economic Activities," *Econometrica*, Vol. 27 (1957).

to be achieved and "windfalls"[5] are to be avoided. Its internal knowledge is definitive in forming its expectations only if the firm is in no way dependent upon expectations and plans elsewhere in the market. But if information about other firms' plans is limited, and if consumers' desires and expectations are only partly known, or guessed at, the firm's long-run success will depend upon its informational advantage over the market in its own area of production and upon its ability to achieve expectations which are consistent with other firms' expectations.

A distinction between the kinds of variables which the firm can control and those which are dependent on other firms' or consumers' plans is fairly often made in economic theory.[6] A recent, and for present purposes, rather fruitful distinction has been offered by G. B. Richardson.[7] He proposed that we distinguish information about variables which are independent of the type or structure of the market, as in the case of internal technical planning of the firm, and information which explicitly depends on the structure of the communication system of the market and on what related firms will do within that system. The first type he calls primary information and the second secondary information. The distinction will be adopted in this essay, except that I shall call primary information *controlled information*.[8]

If we consider the state of information in which a firm's decision is taken it is clear that the quality of that information is generally limited in one or more ways. Omniscience, or *perfect information*, is quite impossible, given the various kinds of interdependence and the difficulties in reaching equilibrium mentioned earlier, and given an environment which is not always predictable, to say the least. We

5. In Lindahl's sense, e.g., in "The Concept of Gains and Losses," *Festskrift til Frederik Zeuthen*, 1958.

6. The best known distinction is made according to whether a variable is set according to self-decision or whether other firms control its outcome, as in the case of Frisch's "parameters of action" and "conjectural variables." R. Frisch, "Monopole-Polypole-La notion de force dans l'economie, *"Nationaløkonomisk Tidsskrift*, Vol. 71 (1933). Sometimes the distinction is made between "particular" and "general" expectations, the latter being considered as expectations of variables generally held in common by the business community, as in Keirstead's work. B. S. Keirstead, *An Essay in the Theory of Profits and Income Distribution* (Oxford: Blackwell, 1953), pp. 21–24.

7. G. B. Richardson, "Equilibrium, Expectations, and Information," *Economic Journal*, LXIX (June 1959).

8. Richardson told me that he has adopted the name "technical information" in his forthcoming book, but considers my term better. G. B. Richardson, *Information and Investment*, to be published.

can still think of *complete information*, where everyone at least thinks he knows what everyone else knows, even though they may all turn out to be wrong in some degree when the various plans mature. *Incomplete information* is the usual state of affairs, when each firm decides on the basis of a limited amount of information relative to the total amount dispersed throughout the economy.[9] Since incomplete information is the general case in any realistic conception of the market economy it would be advisable to develop a theory of planning, at least from the firm's point of view, which takes uncertainty and the possibility of completely incorrect expectations for granted. People may make mistakes in forming their expectations, because they use too little of the information which is readily available to them, or because they use incorrect or conflicting information, or because random or unpredictable events occur which prove their expectations wrong. They must certainly simplify very complex situations in order to form any expectations at all, if there is any time limit on decisions. If events are changing over time as the economy, or sectors of it, adjust from one static state to another or along some growing or fluctuating path, there will be an incentive to collect information and decide before the information goes out of date. But the imposition of a time limit means that decisions will be based on a restricted quantity of information or the firm will have to employ more specialists in information collection (that is, more people with the requisite know-how). Information collection not only takes time, but is also costly.[1] In general, we may suppose that information cost can be reckoned in terms of the labor time consumed in collecting it. But even in a static state where time is not particularly important to decisions we must assume that information has a cost (even cost accountants who tell you where you are at cost something). In simplifying the environment in order not to waste time observing every possible event a set of rules will probably be established which will be partly informational (what one should consider and what disregard) and partly expectational (what one

9. So as not to mislead some readers I wish to add that the meanings of complete and incomplete information used here are different from those of Marschak in his recent work, especially in "Role of Liquidity under Complete and Incomplete Information," *American Economic Review*, XXXIX (May 1949).

1. Marschak has worked out a number of aspects of the cost and value of information in "Remarks on the Economics of Information," *Contributions to Scientific Research in Management* (Los Angeles: University of California, 1959), and also in "Towards an Economic Theory of Organization and Information," *op. cit.*

should do in relation to what he thinks others, both producers and consumers, will do). Precisely how expectations are formed and plans made need not detain us in this essay, so long as it is realized that some kind of consistent decision system has to be set up in firms which will bring about expectational equilibrium.

Richardson's distinction between primary, or *controlled* information, and secondary information is of considerable assistance in analyzing the communication problem and the interdependence of decisions in a market economy where incomplete information is the general case. If the economic system is constructed in such a way that people's expectations and plans are readily communicated to each other the difficulties in making plans are reduced. The less the communication, given an equal amount of interdependence and uncertainty due to unpredictable events, the greater the difficulty of planning. The secondary information which is relevant to a plan is a function of the communication system which operates. Richardson suggested that firms could improve communication or otherwise gain information in three ways: through explicit collusion, implicit collusion or through discovery of the restraints to which other firms are subjected. Explicit collusion needs little discussion, except to remark that a colluding partner has scope for manipulating his information to his advantage, as Schelling has shown.[2] Implicit collusion, Richardson thinks, is a mystery, but I think that the Schelling notion of visible convergence points mentioned already clears the air considerably. In addition to the use of mutually visible points of convergence, firms will have a strong incentive to behave in a stable and predictable manner so that each firm is able to plan on a basis consistent with other firms' plans. The last case, where firms try to find the "boundaries" of other firms' possible activities by finding out what limits are operative (such as shortage of reserves or inability to obtain necessary finance) or by estimating the "degree of attachment" of customers of competitors is perhaps not sufficiently explained by Richardson.[3] He suggested that in a perfectly competitive situation where many entrepreneurs simultaneously discovered a productive opportunity, no one entrepreneur would invest if all others could invest simultaneously. As a result, he was interested in explaining why one firm could take up the opportunity while others

2. *Op. cit.*
3. "Demand and Supply Reconsidered," *Oxford Economic Papers*, VIII (June 1956).

could not. The notion of "restraints" is useful, but it might be better to turn the argument around and say that one or more firms have a cost advantage over the others. This enables us to discuss the phenomenon in terms of conventional theory, rather than rely on physical restraints as an explanation. We could do this if we could discover how a firm can have a cost advantage over the market (that is, over the alternative means of allocating tasks through a market price system for the same set of activities) and over other firms in terms of its unique information, or perhaps its greater amount of information, and its superior ability to communicate some of that information to sources of finance.

IV. THE DIVISION OF KNOWLEDGE

This leads us into one of the more general problems about which this paper is concerned. Given a state of limited information in which that information is not equally distributed among all possible productive units, what can be said about the nature of the firm? Why a firm composed of a number of producers should arise in such an economic system was discussed in previous pages (but even if the reader wishes to retain a different view of the *raison d'etre* itself, it still remains true that the information and decision apparatus of the firm is a fundamental aspect of its structure). It will be worthwhile now to look into this informational aspect in order to see how the firm exploits its informational advantages in relation to the market. Like our old friend "the division of labor," this is clearly a problem of the division of knowledge in the market.

One of the most interesting types of interdependence between firms is the presence of external economies. External economies have always been a rather difficult problem. The Marshallian kind, where cost is a function of the firm's and the industry's level of output taken together, is really only one of a number of types. In fact it is probably more fruitful to think in terms of the more general notion of external economies which Rosenstein-Rodan and Scitovsky had in mind.[4] This notion is that an investment which two or more firms could undertake simultaneously may often be profitable for all, although no one firm could realize this profit acting independently, without the explicit assurance that the others would follow. If the

4. P. N. Rosenstein-Rodan, "Problems of Industrialization of Eastern and South-Eastern Europe," *Economic Journal*, LIII (June–Sept. 1943). T. Scitovsky, "Two Concepts of External Economies," *Journal of Political Economy*, LXII (April 1954).

firms in this interdependent group were integrated, the pecuniary external economies would become internal economies, with a resulting gain in profits to the investors of the integrated firm. This argument has been extended in dynamic terms with respect to leading sectors and "growth poles" where interdependence affects decisions not only in the static sense but also according to the sequence of investments undertaken.[5] All of the external effects are not due merely to complementary demand and the psychological attractions of "keeping up." Technical complementarity is probably a significant element, in which case an investment appears profitable only if certain other investments are undertaken simultaneously. In fact, market prices fail to recognize such kinds of interdependence when decisions are made by independent firms. Just as social overhead projects by governments require an estimate of the social product, including all the external effects, in order to assess the need for such projects, so in private economic decisions the external effects ought to be calculated insofar as interdependence is present. I wish to suggest, moreover, that where output and profitability of various production units are closely interdependent, the firm is formed to undertake decisions concerning all or some of the production units simultaneously, so as to maximize the joint profit and total output. What would have been "external economies" and therefore not registered in the price system become internalized. Surely the reason that we see so few instances in the real world of "technical external economies"[6] is that the most obvious of these have been perceived by businessmen who have *internalized* them.

The competitive producer in conventional theory has no way of knowing what a competitor's *future* output will be, even when this is determined already by present plans,[7] for he knows only the current price (even then only if he is lucky enough to be in a market with a long history which has had a chance to settle down at one price) which may be quite irrelevant, or unstable. But the firm with different, indeed, better information can use this "monopoly power" in reducing the number of variables of secondary information which will be relevant, judging that others will not perceive the same oppor-

5. Cf. A. O. Hirschman, *The Strategy of Economic Development* (Yale University Press, 1958), Chap. 6.

6. Cf. J. E. Meade, "External Economies and Diseconomies in a Competitive Situation," *Economic Journal*, LXII (Mar. 1952), and Scitovsky, "Two Concepts of External Economies," *op. cit.*

7. Cf. Scitovsky, *Welfare and Competition* (Chicago: Irwin, 1951), pp. 237 ff.

tunity in the same way, or if they do, that they will not be able to act as fast because of their need to acquire the necessary know-how. In this way we can explain Richardson's dilemma of many producers perceiving the same opportunity in a competitive market not being able to invest because if they all invested there would be general overproduction.[8] Any one firm with a particular combination of technical resources and know-how is in a favorable position, either to take the opportunity at all, or to take it sooner with less expenditure in gaining knowledge of markets and techniques. When new opportunities, or *market vacua* as Myrdal has called them,[9] appear the uneven distribution of initially required information and the faulty communication of the new information enable one or more firms to enter the vacua while others do not.

Since acquiring information takes time and is a costly activity[1] some firms will have a relative advantage in their knowledge of internal transactions or techniques of production, market requirements, or the types of administrative activity necessary to adapt to particular kinds of fluctuations or uncertainties in demand or supply. How often we hear a business man say that he would not invest in a certain opportunity because that is "not his line of business," while he would invest in another because he could use his special know-how. Firms frequently diversify, and more often than not they diversify according to their special knowledge of the new area. If the same techniques of production can be applied to a completely new product, say if both the old and new are assembled in similar ways, the firm can utilize its special knowledge of the costs involved, costs which are not reflected in market prices for other potential producers without that know-how. Engineering or scientific knowledge accumulates over time, and unlike other kinds of investment, knowledge can be consumed without using it up. Indeed, the cost of research could be treated as a joint cost over time, with the marginal cost of use of

8. A word of warning may be necessary here: if everyone perceiving the new opportunity started out with heavy prior commitments, it might be true that no one of them could move out to the optimum scale very fast, and they all might be able to achieve a satisfactory position, either in or not in the new area, by step by step adjustment. But if some of them start fresh these will be able to act simultaneously, and Richardson's dilemma remains.

9. Cf. F. Zeuthen, *Economic Theory and Method* (Harvard University Press, 1955), pp. 182–83.

1. It should be clear that there is a strategic problem regarding information since one can choose to have more information more quickly by hiring more market experts and research specialists, or less information much less rapidly, or more information less rapidly or less information more rapidly.

knowledge in many cases zero. In addition, the marginal cost of new information added to the old stock of knowledge is probably very much lower when the accumulated stock is large. A new idea takes a long time to develop, but when it crystallizes all sorts of applications and ramifications usually follow with a little additional effort. There is a fair amount of empirical evidence that for many manufacturing processes costs are a function not only of volume per unit of time but also of the cumulated number of units produced. It would appear that for many processes there is a definite, ascertainable mathematical function, often called the learning curve or the technical progress curve, relating unit cost (either average or marginal) to cumulated production.[2] Because of all this we may suppose that firms already in a related area are at a distinct advantage, both with respect to cost and time (for if entry were undertaken faster by someone with less know-how at the start the cost of entry would be proportionately greater).

Firms may also produce or finish a number of different products which go to the same market, particularly the final consumer market, because they are familiar with the number and types of customers and their particular requirements. They may have a number of customers attached to them through contract, or through good will Good will in these terms is a more tangible concept than in traditional analysis, since what it means is that buyers and sellers are familiar with each other, and need not hunt around to make a transaction They need take no risk, for they are familiar with what they buy Good will has, in other words, a rationale based on economic costs.

Relative advantage appears over time with respect to the administrative mechanism of the firm also. The more often a particular transaction is made the more information the firm may have about that transaction. Expectations based upon past experience become more and more conditioned by probabilities inferred from past data, and less and less by uncertain judgments based on instinct. A variety of transactions require a great deal of administrative time to interpret and decide on, but as these transactions are

2. A thorough study is found in H. Asher, "Cost-Quantity Relationships in the Airframe Industry," RAND Report R-291, 1956. Since this concept has no been integrated into economic theory, with one exception in an important articl by A. Alchian, "Costs and Outputs," in *The Allocation of Economic Resources op. cit.*, the reader is also referred to F. J. Andress, "The Learning Curve as a Production Tool," *Harvard Business Review*, Vol. 32 (Jan.–Feb. 1954) and W. Z. Hirsch, "Manufacturing Progress Functions," *Review of Economics and Statistics*, XXXIV (May 1952).

repeated a system of criteria, such as "policies," "standing orders," and statistical sampling rules, is evolved. Less information is necessary to describe the "controlled" variables with experience in the pattern of occurrence. Decision-makers are then released to perform new activities. The growing firm at the same time brings new people into the firm and trains them in the particular types of decisions with which the firm is concerned. Their value to the organization increases as they become more and more familiar with the communication system and the peculiarities of their own special tasks.[3]

It is in any firm's interest to keep secret any of the knowledge which is part of its relative advantage.[4] For even though one does not lose any knowledge by giving some of it to someone else, nonetheless the benefits of that knowledge can only be had if others do not have it. As long as a firm possesses special advantages, it can act as a monopolist. But as soon as it becomes worthwhile for other firms to gain the knowledge required to enter the same area, the firm will lose its advantage. Since continuity of production and sales is extremely important to the firm, because of the incentive to utilize fully the accumulated stock of knowledge and decision rules, the firm will probably not exercise the monopolistic advantage unless it judges that entry by others is more costly than the gain to be had by them, and such others who might enter know this. Moreover, other firms are always accumulating information and discovering new uses to which it can be put, some of which may obviate the first firm's transactions and hence its advantage.

Over time, even secondary information settles down enough to make plans on the basis of expectations, for the accumulation of experience will enable firms to make decisions which are correct more often in relation to uncontrolled variables. A *modus vivendi* becomes established among firms as responses become habituated. Change calls forth chaos, and so stability is sought after and actively pre-

3. This is, of course, Kaldor's argument in the extremely important article ("The Equilibrium of the Firm," *Economic Journal*, XLIV, Mar. 1934) concerning limits to the size of the firm. The dynamic aspect of his argument is often overlooked, though it is one of the most important insights into the theory of the growth of the firm ever made. Mrs. Penrose has built a book on this foundation which also puts forward many of the arguments about the advantages of specialized know-how which I have used here. E. T. Penrose, *The Theory of the Growth of the Firm* (New York: Wiley, 1959).

4. Unless there are complementary effects to be realized by informing other firms about certain techniques or goods, in which case certain advantages of co-ordinated decisions can be had without full merger between two or more firms.

served. The more stable the secondary information, the more time to devote energies to exploitation of controlled information, and the larger the firm can become, provided its efficiency in interpreting and deciding on expectations and in controlling its primary data does not fall, which will happen either if the firm grows too fast or if its personnel fall off in quality, as we shall see in a moment.

We are now in a position to explain profits, and variations in profit rates in various firms and industries. If not everyone in the market can take up a new opportunity because they do not perceive it, or perceiving it cannot profitably assimilate the transaction as fast, there exists a gain for those "in the know."[5] Some firms will see opportunities, but be unable to communicate their own information and expectations favorably to bankers, and thus be unable to acquire finance, or need to pay a higher charge for the capital borrowed. Bankers and investors of funds in turn will be attracted to those firms which have shown in the past an ability to perceive and exploit effectively new opportunities, as against new firms which can only give their word that what they think is good is in fact good.

If the firm is an innovator or imitator there will still remain a certain amount of indeterminacy in the production plan, regardless of how much else is done to regularize information collection and decisions. Whatever knowledge is to be had from one innovation may be useful for many other possible innovations, but the "external effects" (external to the specific project for which research was undertaken) cannot be exploited all at once. Some of this information is fully developed, and ready to be utilized in active transactions or internal activities, and much of it is partially developed, on the drawing boards, in the laboratories, and in the heads of the decision-makers. Among many possible alternatives, there will be an efficient strategy (or perhaps several) of introduction of new activities according to the amount of information available about the activities, the cost of assimilating new transactions at each of various rates of growth, and the likelihood of competitors gaining similar information and being able to use it more quickly. A choice will have to be made between a faster, but more costly introduction of new activities and a slower, less costly introduction which might enable competitors to take up the opportunity.[6]

5. Cf. P. P. Streeten, "The Theory of Profit," *Manchester School*, XVII (Sept. 1949), 283.
6. See my note on long-run cost curves, "How Long is the Long Run?" *Economic Journal*, LXX (June 1960).

It would seem, if the argument about the division of knowledge holds true, that costs will mean different things to different people. The firm will have its own judgment of costs in terms of alternative activities foregone. The market will value the planned activities of a firm differently if it is investing in a market vacuum, so that from the point of view of the market there is a different cost involved.[7] More informed people will have different levels of expected costs than less informed people. From the firm's point of view it is its own evaluation of opportunities which matters, but it must also persuade at least some others if it goes outside for finance.

V. The Firm's Decision Mechanism

It must now be asked why the firm stops growing. This is a thorny old problem about which there have been many suggestions, most of which are concerned about restraints to size at any one moment rather than with absolute size as such. The exception, of course, was the argument that "management" was the limiting agent, and since we have been concerned so much with the efficiency of the decision system in the firm it is necessary to face up to that argument now. If it were true that all decisions had to be made by one executive or board of executives at the top of the hierarchy of the firm, we could probably develop an argument for fairly small efficient size. But suppose that we look at the firm in the following way. Each person in the firm is a specialist in a small number of activities. The knowledge of each person is in some ways different from the knowledge of others. The executive at the top of the hierarchy does not know everything that each of the specialists knows. Indeed, just because the executive can neither be an expert in every activity nor know all the necessary information for all possible decisions simultaneously, he allocates many activities, including decisions, to specialists. The firm, in other words, does not abandon the principle of division of labor in information and decision activities any more than it does in other kinds of activities. But an allocation problem then appears because, as in the market, effective decisions depend on the communication system which transmits information from one person to another. Inside the firm we must suppose that interdependence between decision sets is rather significant. After all, the firm owes its existence to the consolidation of interdependent decision sets, and

7. Mr. Thirlby's recent discussion of the various views of costs which can be taken in certain situations is relevant here, "Economists' Cost Rules and Equilibrium Theory," *Economica*, N.S., XXVII (May 1960).

if it were to "suboptimize"[8] we might well ask why the subsets of tasks which were decided on independently were ever integrated into the firm. But if communication is necessary to ensure that decisions are consistent with one another, the question is how much communication? The costs of communicating information (including the costs of delay in a model dealing with time) have to be balanced against the value of decisions taken without full consultation with other decision-makers who might have relevant information.[9]

We may not expect, therefore, that division of labor in information and decision activities proceeds without any force working in the opposite direction. The various decisions must be consistent with one another so that the production plan of the firm may be in expectational equilibrium, and consistency requires communication. We might suppose that one possible decision network consisted of a number of observation centers each of which transmitted all its information to some central board which then sent out a series of directives, much like some socialists' view of the centrally planned economy. Since each observation center would have no way of knowing what might be relevant information to the central board it would have to send everything it was allowed to observe. The central board would then issue directives concerning every possible contingency (including machine breakdowns). We might then suppose that this kind of mechanism, admittedly an extreme, was very costly, either because it took a long time to assimilate everything in order to decide or because it employed an extremely large staff and expensive computers in order to make fast decisions. It might then be the case that if the central board were thrown out and the firm broken up into smaller units the cost of allocating activities among the smaller units by means of a market-determined price system would be less. At the other extreme, we might suppose complete decentralization, in which each person in the firm acted independently on independent information. As we have seen, this is unsatisfactory.

Suppose, then, that somewhere between the two extremes an optimum decision system can be found.[1] That system must in general satisfy a market test: If the market could arrange an allocation of all

8. Cf. "Economics and Operations Research: A Symposium," *Review of Economics and Statistics,* XL (Aug. 1958).

9. This is, of course, the heart of Marschak's theory of "teams." Cf. J. Marschak, "Elements for a Theory of Teams," *Management Science,* Vol. 1 (1955).

1. Besides Jacob Marschak's formulation, see Thomas Marschak's study of this problem, which brings up the difficulty of a cut-off time and its effect on

or some of these tasks with a net gain over the value of production when organized by the firm, then the "market" in the form of other, differently organized firms of different sizes will take over the activities. Market information is, as we have seen, inaccurate when interdependent activities are decentralized independently of one another. On the other hand, information which the firm uses will also not be wholly accurate. Some relationships are ignored in the communication and decision network. Some information is ignored because observations would be more costly than the net gain to be had from decisions based on the information.[2] When events are changing over time, decisions must be made before whatever information is used is out of date. Informational and expectational strategies of the kind mentioned earlier will then be introduced to help sort out the environment, but the information then employed is only of limited accuracy. The firm's efficiency in allocation decisions is not, therefore, absolute, but rather relative — relative to alternative internal and market information systems.

Over time as the firm grows there will be the dynamic restraint mentioned earlier that new activities take a disproportionately long time to evaluate and decide on, since there are no visible patterns of behavior or history to rely on, but as decisions become routinized new activities can be taken on. As Mrs. Penrose has pointed out,[3] new personnel can be assimilated only at a certain pace. This pace, I think, is determined relatively to the time strategies of the firm, since faster assimilation is possible at some cost, regardless of the rate when starting out. The higher cost of taking on transactions faster has to be balanced against the possible loss of opportunity, or reduction in its value, because of faster moves by competitors. The information strategies and decision rules adopted over time are partly dependent upon information in previous periods, and are conditioned by it, with the result that the rate of adjustment to new kinds of activities is dependent upon the universality, or lack of it, in the information structure of previous periods. Besides, the rate of accumulation of new information from research activities is limited

the decision system, "Centralization and Decentralization in Economic Organizations," *Econometrica*, Vol. 27 (July 1959).

2. This is not as simple as it seems at first, and I do not subscribe to the view that the only problem is to collect information up to the point at which marginal gain equals marginal cost. Information is not neatly ordered in advance according to increasing value. However, I hope to discuss at another time the actual working out of an information structure, and will not do so here.

3. *Op. cit.*

by the cost the firm is willing to incur and the time strategy adopted. More can be had faster, but more people have to be employed to work it out.

The more heterogeneous the transactions assimilated by the firm, the greater the cost. Although economic interdependence, direct or indirect, is universal, that interdependence varies in kind and degree throughout the system. Where the linkage between activities begins to thin out and transactions become more heterogeneous, the cost of assimilating such transactions begins at some point to exceed the gain to be had (the cost of organizing the same transactions elsewhere in the market falls below one's own costs). I have not tried to argue that the best of all possible worlds is that where all planning is centralized. On the contrary, there will be some degree of integration which will be most efficient for any bundle of interdependent activities, and this degree may vary as among "bundles." There comes a point at which the firm must rely on secondary information for its expectations about external transactions. Such information is *uncontrolled*, and the firm must develop a system of evaluating whatever information of this type filters through. Experience coupled with an ability to bring about consistency between one's own plans and those of others ensures expectational equilibrium.

VI. Conclusion

I have suggested in this paper a rationale for the efficiency of a market system containing many firms which are really small planning agencies in themselves. For at least the small area of economic production inside the firm, plans can be made which are based on consistent expectations. Various production units need no longer have convergent expectations to be in equilibrium, for the plan of which they are a part is itself an integrated, consistent plan based on *controlled information*.

If this argument holds true, we are able, for example, to explain some of the observations made by Erik Lundberg in his recent Marshall Lectures at Cambridge University.[4] For then variations in rates of return among firms and in internal rates of return within firms are a natural conclusion of the division of knowledge. We can also agree with Lundberg that investment in capital goods normally occurs in partial disequilibrium situations, or market vacua, and we can now also see the rationale of continuously evolving market vacua

4. "The Profitability of Investment," *Economic Journal*, LXIX (Dec. 1959).

THEORY OF THE FIRM   421

which are taken up by some firms, and not others. Does this mean that general equilibrium is not a useful concept? Recalling Hayek's definition of expectational equilibrium, I think we can consider general equilibrium in terms of the satisfaction of expectations. (This does not mean that firms will always be surprised by adversity, since the strategies adopted can guarantee success only on the average, in the long run.) Market vacua related to the firm's own activities will be its main concern, but it will act on the knowledge that pockets of disequilibrium situations throughout the economy are part of the natural progression of events, and that the hard core of stable development of the economy is sufficiently large to give reliability to general expectations. The entrepreneur can then be regarded, as Lundberg suggested, as an expert on the technical progress function of the firm, aware of particular paths of development and growth for which the firm has an advantage, and aware of the problems of strategy of planning in relation to expected developments.

Finally, I have tried to lay a foundation for generalizing the work of the many organization theorists in economic terms. One might, in pursuit of this kind of generality, reformulate my argument as follows:[5] In the theory of the perfect market each firm is associated with a particular set of production possibilities. The list of all sets, and therefore the *number of firms*, is given. My argument suggests that the number of firms is not given. Instead, the fundamental "givens" are data on the dispersion of information in the society and data on the cost of information. There are then two problems to be treated: (1) How is the number of firms determined? (2) What is the most efficient allocation of information-processing and decision-making functions among the various members of each firm?

NUFFIELD COLLEGE,
OXFORD

5. Prof. J. Marschak suggested this reformulation to me.

[5]

THE ARCHITECTURE OF COMPLEXITY

HERBERT A. SIMON*

Professor of Administration, Carnegie Institute of Technology

(*Read April 26, 1962*)

A NUMBER of proposals have been advanced in recent years for the development of "general systems theory" which, abstracting from properties peculiar to physical, biological, or social systems, would be applicable to all of them.[1] We might well feel that, while the goal is laudable, systems of such diverse kinds could hardly be expected to have any nontrivial properties in common. Metaphor and analogy can be helpful, or they can be misleading. All depends on whether the similarities the metaphor captures are significant or superficial.

It may not be entirely vain, however, to search for common properties among diverse kinds of complex systems. The ideas that go by the name of cybernetics constitute, if not a theory, at least a point of view that has been proving fruitful over a wide range of applications.[2] It has been useful to look at the behavior of adaptive systems in terms of the concepts of feedback and homeostasis,

and to analyze adaptiveness in terms of the theory of selective information.[3] The ideas of feedback and information provide a frame of reference for viewing a wide range of situations, just as do the ideas of evolution, of relativism, of axiomatic method, and of operationalism.

In this paper I should like to report on some things we have been learning about particular kinds of complex systems encountered in the behavioral sciences. The developments I shall discuss arose in the context of specific phenomena, but the theoretical formulations themselves make little reference to details of structure. Instead they refer primarily to the complexity of the systems under view without specifying the exact content of that complexity. Because of their abstractness, the theories may have relevance—application would be too strong a term—to other kinds of complex systems that are observed in the social, biological, and physical sciences.

In recounting these developments, I shall avoid technical detail, which can generally be found elsewhere. I shall describe each theory in the particular context in which it arose. Then, I shall cite some examples of complex systems, from areas of science other than the initial application, to which the theoretical framework appears relevant. In doing so, I shall make reference to areas of knowledge where I am not expert—perhaps not even literate. I feel quite comfortable in doing so before the members of this society, representing as it does the whole span of the scientific and scholarly endeavor. Collectively you will have little difficulty, I am sure, in distinguishing instances based on idle fancy or sheer ignorance from instances that cast some light on the ways in which complexity exhibits itself wherever it is found in nature. I shall leave to you the final judgment of relevance in your respective fields.

I shall not undertake a formal definition of

* The ideas in this paper have been the topic of many conversations with my colleague, Allen Newell. George W. Corner suggested important improvements in biological content as well as editorial form. I am also indebted, for valuable comments on the manuscript, to Richard H. Meier, John R. Platt, and Warren Weaver. Some of the conjectures about the nearly decomposable structure of the nucleus-atom-molecule hierarchy were checked against the available quantitative data by Andrew Schoene and William Wise. My work in this area has been supported by a Ford Foundation grant for research in organizations and a Carnegie Corporation grant for research on cognitive processes. To all of the above, my warm thanks, and the usual absolution.

[1] See especially the yearbooks of the Society for General Systems Research. Prominent among the exponents of general systems theory are L. von Bertalanffy, K. Boulding, R. W. Gerard, and J. G. Miller. For a more skeptical view—perhaps too skeptical in the light of the present discussion—see H. A. Simon and A. Newell, Models: their uses and limitations, *in* L. D. White, ed., *The state of the social sciences*, 66–83, Chicago, Univ. of Chicago Press, 1956.

[2] N. Wiener, *Cybernetics*, New York, John Wiley & Sons, 1948. For an imaginative forerunner, see A. J. Lotka, *Elements of mathematical biology*, New York, Dover Publications, 1951, first published in 1924 as *Elements of physical biology*.

[3] C. Shannon and W. Weaver, *The mathematical theory of communication*, Urbana, Univ. of Illinois Press, 1949; W. R. Ashby, *Design for a brain*, New York, John Wiley & Sons, 1952.

"complex systems."[4] Roughly, by a complex system I mean one made up of a large number of parts that interact in a nonsimple way. In such systems, the whole is more than the sum of the parts, not in an ultimate, metaphysical sense, but in the important pragmatic sense that, given the properties of the parts and the laws of their interaction, it is not a trivial matter to infer the properties of the whole. In the face of complexity, an in-principle reductionist may be at the same time a pragmatic holist.[5]

The four sections that follow discuss four aspects of complexity. The first offers some comments on the frequency with which complexity takes the form of hierarchy—the complex system being composed of subsystems that, in turn, have their own subsystems, and so on. The second section theorizes about the relation between the structure of a complex system and the time required for it to emerge through evolutionary processes: specifically, it argues that hierarchic systems will evolve far more quickly than non-hierarchic systems of comparable size. The third section explores the dynamic properties of hierarchically-organized systems, and shows how they can be decomposed into subsystems in order to analyze their behavior. The fourth section examines the relation between complex systems and their descriptions.

Thus, the central theme that runs through my remarks is that complexity frequently takes the form of hierarchy, and that hierarchic systems have some common properties that are independent of their specific content. Hierarchy, I shall argue, is one of the central structural schemes that the architect of complexity uses.

---

[4] W. Weaver, in: Science and complexity, *American Scientist* **36**: 536, 1948, has distinguished two kinds of complexity, disorganized and organized. We shall be primarily concerned with organized complexity.

[5] See also John R. Platt, Properties of large molecules that go beyond the properties of their chemical sub-groups, *Jour. Theoret. Biol.* **1**: 342–358, 1961. Since the reductionism-holism issue is a major *cause de guerre* between scientists and humanists, perhaps we might even hope that peace could be negotiated between the two cultures along the lines of the compromise just suggested. As I go along, I shall have a little to say about complexity in the arts as well as in the natural sciences. I must emphasize the pragmatism of my holism to distinguish it sharply from the position taken by W. M. Elsasser in *The physical foundation of biology*, New York, Pergamon Press, 1958.

HIERARCHIC SYSTEMS

By a *hierarchic system*, or hierarchy, I mean a system that is composed of interrelated subsystems, each of the latter being, in turn, hierarchic in structure until we reach some lowest level of elementary subsystem. In most systems in nature, it is somewhat arbitrary as to where we leave off the partitioning, and what subsystems we take as elementary. Physics makes much use of the concept of "elementary particle" although particles have a disconcerting tendency not to remain elementary very long. Only a couple of generations ago, the atoms themselves were elementary particles; today, to the nuclear physicist they are complex systems. For certain purposes of astronomy, whole stars, or even galaxies, can be regarded as elementary subsystems. In one kind of biological research, a cell may be treated as an elementary subsystem; in another, a protein molecule; in still another, an amino acid residue.

Just why a scientist has a right to treat as elementary a subsystem that is in fact exceedingly complex is one of the questions we shall take up. For the moment, we shall accept the fact that scientists do this all the time, and that if they are careful scientists they usually get away with it.

Etymologically, the word "hierarchy" has had a narrower meaning than I am giving it here. The term has generally been used to refer to a complex system in which each of the subsystems is subordinated by an authority relation to the system it belongs to. More exactly, in a hierarchic formal organization, each system consists of a "boss" and a set of subordinate subsystems. Each of the subsystems has a "boss" who is the immediate subordinate of the boss of the system. We shall want to consider systems in which the relations among subsystems are more complex than in the formal organizational hierarchy just described. We shall want to include systems in which there is no relation of subordination among subsystems. (In fact, even in human organizations, the formal hierarchy exists only on paper; the real flesh-and-blood organization has many inter-part relations other than the lines of formal authority.) For lack of a better term, I shall use hierarchy in the broader sense introduced in the previous paragraphs, to refer to all complex systems analyzable into successive sets of subsystems, and speak of "formal hierarchy" when I want to refer to the more specialized concept.[6]

---

[6] The mathematical term "partitioning" will not do for what I call here a hierarchy; for the set of subsystems,

SOCIAL SYSTEMS

I have already given an example of one kind of hierarchy that is frequently encountered in the social sciences: a formal organization. Business firms, governments, universities all have a clearly visible parts-within-parts structure. But formal organizations are not the only, or even the most common, kind of social hierarchy. Almost all societies have elementary units called families, which may be grouped into villages or tribes, and these into larger groupings, and so on. If we make a chart of social interactions, of who talks to whom, the clusters of dense interaction in the chart will identify a rather well-defined hierarchic structure. The groupings in this structure may be defined operationally by some measure of frequency of interaction in this sociometric matrix.

BIOLOGICAL AND PHYSICAL SYSTEMS

The hierarchical structure of biological systems is a familiar fact. Taking the cell as the building block, we find cells organized into tissues, tissues into organs, organs into systems. Moving downward from the cell, well-defined subsystems—for example, nucleus, cell membrane, microsomes, mitochondria, and so on—have been identified in animal cells.

The hierarchic structure of many physical systems is equally clear-cut. I have already mentioned the two main series. At the microscopic level we have elementary particles, atoms, molecules, macromolecules. At the macroscopic level we have satellite systems, planetary systems, galaxies. Matter is distributed throughout space in a strikingly non-uniform fashion. The most nearly random distributions we find, gases, are not random distributions of elementary particles but random distributions of complex systems, i.e. molecules.

A considerable range of structural types is subsumed under the term hierarchy as I have defined it. By this definition, a diamond is hierarchic, for it is a crystal structure of carbon atoms that can be further decomposed into protons, neutrons, and electrons. However, it is a very "flat" hierarchy, in which the number of first-order subsystems belonging to the crystal can be indefinitely large. A volume of molecular gas is a flat hierarchy in the same sense. In ordinary usage, we

and the successive subsets in each of these defines the partitioning, independently of any systems of relations among the subsets. By hierarchy I mean the partitioning in conjunction with the relations that hold among its parts.

tend to reserve the word hierarchy for a system that is divided into a *small or moderate number* of subsystems, each of which may be further subdivided. Hence, we do not ordinarily think of or refer to a diamond or a gas as a hierarchic structure. Similarly, a linear polymer is simply a chain, which may be very long, of identical subparts, the monomers. At the molecular level it is a very flat hierarchy.

In discussing formal organizations, the number of subordinates who report directly to a single boss is called his *span of control*. I will speak analogously of the *span* of a system, by which I shall mean the number of subsystems into which it is partitioned. Thus, a hierarchic system is flat at a given level if it has a wide span at that level. A diamond has a wide span at the crystal level, but not at the next level down, the molecular level.

In most of our theory construction in the following sections we shall focus our attention on hierarchies of moderate span, but from time to time I shall comment on the extent to which the theories might or might not be expected to apply to very flat hierarchies.

There is one important difference between the physical and biological hierarchies, on the one hand, and social hierarchies, on the other. Most physical and biological hierarchies are described in spatial terms. We detect the organelles in a cell in the way we detect the raisins in a cake—they are "visibly" differentiated substructures localized spatially in the larger structure. On the other hand, we propose to identify social hierarchies not by observing who lives close to whom but by observing who interacts with whom. These two points of view can be reconciled by defining hierarchy in terms of intensity of interaction, but observing that in most biological and physical systems relatively intense interaction implies relative spatial propinquity. One of the interesting characteristics of nerve cells and telephone wires is that they permit very specific strong interactions at great distances. To the extent that interactions are channeled through specialized communications and transportation systems, spatial propinquity becomes less determinative of structure.

SYMBOLIC SYSTEMS

One very important class of systems has been omitted from my examples thus far: systems of human symbolic production. A book is a hierarchy in the sense in which I am using that term. It is generally divided into chapters, the chapters into sections, the sections into paragraphs, the paragraphs into sentences, the sentences into clauses and phrases, the clauses and phrases into words. We may take the words as our elementary units, or further subdivide them, as the linguist often does, into smaller units. If the book is narrative in character, it may divide into "episodes" instead of sections, but divisions there will be.

The hierarchic structure of music, based on such units as movements, parts, themes, phrases, is well known. The hierarchic structure of products of the pictorial arts is more difficult to characterize, but I shall have something to say about it later.

THE EVOLUTION OF COMPLEX SYSTEMS

Let me introduce the topic of evolution with a parable. There once were two watchmakers, named Hora and Tempus, who manufactured very fine watches. Both of them were highly regarded, and the phones in their workshops rang frequently —new customers were constantly calling them. However, Hora prospered, while Tempus became poorer and poorer and finally lost his shop. What was the reason?

The watches the men made consisted of about 1,000 parts each. Tempus had so constructed his that if he had one partly assembled and had to put it down—to answer the phone say—it immediately fell to pieces and had to be reassembled from the elements. The better the customers liked his watches, the more they phoned him, the more difficult it became for him to find enough uninterrupted time to finish a watch.

The watches that Hora made were no less complex than those of Tempus. But he had designed them so that he could put together subassemblies of about ten elements each. Ten of these subassemblies, again, could be put together into a larger subassembly; and a system of ten of the latter subassemblies constituted the whole watch. Hence, when Hora had to put down a partly assembled watch in order to answer the phone, he lost only a small part of his work, and he assembled his watches in only a fraction of the man-hours it took Tempus.

It is rather easy to make a quantitative analysis of the relative difficulty of the tasks of Tempus and Hora: Suppose the probability that an interruption will occur while a part is being added to an incomplete assembly is p. Then the probability that Tempus can complete a watch he has started without interruption is $(1-p)^{1000}$—a very small number unless p is .001 or less. Each interruption will cost, on the average, the time to as-

semble $1/p$ parts (the expected number assembled before interruption). On the other hand, Hora has to complete one hundred eleven sub-assemblies of ten parts each. The probability that he will not be interrupted while completing any one of these is $(1-p)^{10}$, and each interruption will cost only about the time required to assemble five parts.[7]

Now if p is about .01—that is, there is one chance in a hundred that either watchmaker will be interrupted while adding any one part to an assembly—then a straightforward calculation shows that it will take Tempus, on the average, about four thousand times as long to assemble a watch as Hora.

We arrive at the estimate as follows:

1. Hora must make 111 times as many complete assemblies per watch as Tempus; but,

2. Tempus will lose on the average 20 times as much work for each interrupted assembly as Hora [100 parts, on the average, as against 5]; and,

3. Tempus will complete an assembly only 44 times per million attempts ($.99^{1000} = 44 \times 10^{-6}$), while Hora will complete nine out of ten ($.99^{10} = 9 \times 10^{-1}$). Hence Tempus will have to make 20,000 as many attempts per completed assembly as Hora. $(9 \times 10^{-1})/(44 \times 10^{-6}) = 2\times 10^4$. Multiplying these three ratios, we get:

$$1/111 \times 100/5 \times .99^{10}/.99^{1000}$$
$$= 1/111 \times 20 \times 20,000 \sim 4,000.$$

---

[7] The speculations on speed of evolution were first suggested by H. Jacobson's application of information theory to estimating the time required for biological evolution. See his paper, Information, reproduction, and the origin of life, in *American Scientist* **43**: 119–127, January, 1955. From thermodynamic considerations it is possible to estimate the amount of increase in entropy that occurs when a complex system decomposes into its elements. (See, for example, R. B. Setlow and E. C. Pollard, *Molecular biophysics*, 63–65, Reading, Mass., Addison-Wesley Publishing Co., 1962, and references cited there.) But entropy is the logarithm of a probability, hence information, the negative of entropy, can be interpreted as the logarithm of the reciprocal of the probability—the "improbability," so to speak. The essential idea in Jacobson's model is that the expected time required for the system to reach a particular state is inversely proportional to the probability of the state—hence increases exponentially with the amount of information (negentropy) of the state. Following this line of argument, but not introducing the notion of levels and stable subassemblies, Jacobson arrived at estimates of the time required for evolution so large as to make the event rather improbable. Our analysis, carried through in the same way, but with attention to the stable intermediate forms, produces very much smaller estimates.

VOL. 106, NO. 6, 1962]
THE ARCHITECTURE OF COMPLEXITY

BIOLOGICAL EVOLUTION

What lessons can we draw from our parable for biological evolution? Let us interpret a partially completed subassembly of k elementary parts as the coexistence of k parts in a small volume—ignoring their relative orientations. The model assumes that parts are entering the volume at a constant rate, but that there is a constant probability, p, that the part will be dispersed before another is added, unless the assembly reaches a stable state. These assumptions are not particularly realistic. They undoubtedly underestimate the decrease in probability of achieving the assembly with increase in the size of the assembly. Hence the assumptions understate—probably by a large factor—the relative advantage of a hierarchic structure.

Although we cannot, therefore, take the numerical estimate seriously the lesson for biological evolution is quite clear and direct. The time required for the evolution of a complex form from simple elements depends critically on the numbers and distribution of potential intermediate stable forms. In particular, if there exists a hierarchy of potential stable "subassemblies," with about the same span, s, at each level of the hierarchy, then the time required for a subassembly can be expected to be about the same at each level—that is proportional to $1/(1-p)^s$. The time required for the assembly of a system of n elements will be proportional to $\log_s n$, that is, to the number of levels in the system. One would say—with more illustrative than literal intent—that the time required for the evolution of multi-celled organisms from single-celled organisms might be of the same order of magnitude as the time required for the evolution of single-celled organisms from macromolecules. The same argument could be applied to the evolution of proteins from amino acids, of molecules from atoms, of atoms from elementary particles.

A whole host of objections to this oversimplified scheme will occur, I am sure, to every working biologist, chemist, and physicist. Before turning to matters I know more about, I shall mention three of these problems, leaving the rest to the attention of the specialists.

First, in spite of the overtones of the watchmaker parable, the theory assumes no teleological mechanism. The complex forms can arise from the simple ones by purely random processes. (I shall propose another model in a moment that shows this clearly.) Direction is provided to the scheme by the stability of the complex forms, once these come into existence. But this is nothing more than survival of the fittest—i.e., of the stable.

Second, not all large systems appear hierarchical. For example, most polymers—e.g., nylon—are simply linear chains of large numbers of identical components, the monomers. However, for present purposes we can simply regard such a structure as a hierarchy with a span of one—the limiting case. For a chain of any length represents a state of relative equilibrium.[8]

Third, the evolution of complex systems from simple elements implies nothing, one way or the other, about the change in entropy of the entire system. If the process absorbs free energy, the complex system will have a smaller entropy than the elements; if it releases free energy, the opposite will be true. The former alternative is the one that holds for most biological systems, and the net inflow of free energy has to be supplied from the sun or some other source if the second law of thermodynamics is not to be violated. For the evolutionary process we are describing, the equilibria of the intermediate states need have only local and not global stability, and they may be stable only in the steady state—that is, as long as there is an external source of free energy that may be drawn upon.[9]

Because organisms are not energetically closed systems, there is no way to deduce the direction, much less the rate, of evolution from classical thermodynamic considerations. All estimates indicate that the amount of entropy, measured in physical units, involved in the formation of a one-celled biological organism is trivially small—about -10^{-11} cal/degree.[10] The "improbability" of evolution has nothing to do with this quantity of entropy, which is produced by every bacterial cell every generation. The irrelevance of quantity of

---

[8] There is a well-developed theory of polymer size, based on models of random assembly. See for example P. J. Flory, *Principles of polymer chemistry*, ch. 8, Ithaca, Cornell Univ. Press, 1953. Since *all* subassemblies in the polymerization theory are stable, limitation of molecular growth depends on "poisoning" of terminal groups by impurities or formation of cycles rather than upon disruption of partially-formed chains.

[9] This point has been made many times before, but it cannot be emphasized too strongly. For further discussion, see Setlow and Pollard, *op. cit.*, 49–64; E. Schrodinger, *What is life?* Cambridge Univ. Press, 1945; and H. Linschitz, The information content of a bacterial cell, in H. Questler, ed., *Information theory in biology*, 251–262, Urbana, Univ. of Illinois Press, 1953.

[10] See Linschitz, *op. cit.* This quantity, 10^{-11} cal/degree, corresponds to about 10^{13} bits of information.

information, in this sense, to speed of evolution can also be seen from the fact that exactly as much information is required to "copy" a cell through the reproductive process as to produce the first cell through evolution.

The effect of the existence of stable intermediate forms exercises a powerful effect on the evolution of complex forms that may be likened to the dramatic effect of catalysts upon reaction rates and steady state distribution of reaction products in open systems.[11] In neither case does the entropy change provide us with a guide to system behavior.

PROBLEM SOLVING AS NATURAL SELECTION

Let us turn now to some phenomena that have no obvious connection with biological evolution: human problem-solving processes. Consider, for example, the task of discovering the proof for a difficult theorem. The process can be—and often has been—described as a search through a maze. Starting with the axioms and previously proved theorems, various transformations allowed by the rules of the mathematical systems are attempted, to obtain new expressions. These are modified in turn until, with persistence and good fortune, a sequence or path of transformations is discovered that leads to the goal.

The process usually involves a great deal of trial and error. Various paths are tried; some are abandoned, others are pushed further. Before a solution is found, a great many paths of the maze may be explored. The more difficult and novel the problem, the greater is likely to be the amount of trial and error required to find a solution. At the same time, the trial and error is not completely random or blind; it is, in fact, rather highly selective. The new expressions that are obtained by transforming given ones are examined to see whether they represent progress toward the goal. Indications of progress spur further search in the same direction; lack of progress signals the abandonment of a line of search. Problem solving requires *selective* trial and error.[12]

[11] See H. Kacser, Some physico-chemical aspects of biological organization, Appendix, pp. 191–249 in C. H. Waddington, *The strategy of the genes*, London, George Allen & Unwin, 1957.

[12] See A. Newell, J. C. Shaw, and H. A. Simon, Empirical explorations of the logic theory machine, *Proceedings of the 1957 Western Joint Computer Conference*, February, 1957, New York: Institute of Radio Engineers; Chess-playing programs and the problem of complexity, *IBM Journal of Research and Development* 2: 320–335, October, 1958; and for a similar view of problem solving, W. R. Ashby, Design for an intelligence

A little reflection reveals that cues signaling progress play the same role in the problem-solving process that stable intermediate forms play in the biological evolutionary process. In fact, we can take over the watchmaker parable and apply it also to problem solving. In problem solving, a partial result that represents recognizable progress toward the goal plays the role of a stable subassembly.

Suppose that the task is to open a safe whose lock has ten dials, each with one hundred possible settings, numbered from 0 to 99. How long will it take to open the safe by a blind trial-and-error search for the correct setting? Since there are 100^{10} possible settings, we may expect to examine about one-half of these, on the average, before finding the correct one—that is, fifty billion billion settings. Suppose, however, that the safe is defective, so that a click can be heard when any one dial is turned to the correct setting. Now each dial can be adjusted independently, and does not need to be touched again while the others are being set. The total number of settings that has to be tried is only 10×50, or five hundred. The task of opening the safe has been altered, by the cues the clicks provide, from a practically impossible one to a trivial one.[13]

A considerable amount has been learned in the past five years about the nature of the mazes that represent common human problem-solving tasks—proving theorems, solving puzzles, playing chess, making investments, balancing assembly lines, to mention a few. All that we have learned about these mazes points to the same conclusion: that human problem solving, from the most blundering to the most insightful, involves nothing more than varying mixtures of trial and error and selectivity. The selectivity derives from various rules of

amplifier, 215–233 in C. E. Shannon and J. McCarthy, *Automata studies*, Princeton, Princeton Univ. Press, 1956.

[13] The clicking safe example was supplied by D. P. Simon. Ashby, *op. cit.*, 230, has called the selectivity involved in situations of this kind "selection by components." The even greater reduction in time produced by hierarchization in the clicking safe example, as compared with the watchmaker's metaphor, is due to the fact that a random *search* for the correct combination is involved in the former case, while in the latter the parts come together in the right order. It is not clear which of these metaphors provides the better model for biological evolution, but we may be sure that the watchmaker's metaphor gives an exceedingly conservative estimate of the savings due to hierarchization. The safe may give an excessively high estimate because it assumes all possible arrangements of the elements to be equally probable.

The Foundations of the New Institutional Economics

THE ARCHITECTURE OF COMPLEXITY

thumb, or heuristics, that suggest which paths should be tried first and which leads are promising. We do not need to postulate processes more sophisticated than those involved in organic evolution to explain how enormous problem mazes are cut down to quite reasonable size.[14]

THE SOURCES OF SELECTIVITY

When we examine the sources from which the problem-solving system, or the evolving system, as the case may be, derives its selectivity, we discover that selectivity can always be equated with some kind of feedback of information from the environment.

Let us consider the case of problem solving first. There are two basic kinds of selectivity. One we have already noted: various paths are tried out, the consequences of following them are noted, and this information is used to guide further search. In the same way, in organic evolution, various complexes come into being, at least evanescently, and those that are stable provide new building blocks for further construction. It is this information about stable configurations, and not free energy or negentropy from the sun, that guides the process of evolution and provides the selectivity that is essential to account for its rapidity.

The second source of selectivity in problem solving is previous experience. We see this particularly clearly when the problem to be solved is similar to one that has been solved before. Then, by simply trying again the paths that led to the earlier solution, or their analogues, trial-and-error search is greatly reduced or altogether eliminated.

What corresponds to this latter kind of information in organic evolution? The closest analogue is reproduction. Once we reach the level of self-reproducing systems, a complex system, when it has once been achieved, can be multiplied indefinitely. Reproduction in fact allows the inheritance of acquired characteristics, but at the level of genetic material, of course; i.e., only characteristics acquired by the genes can be inherited. We shall return to the topic of reproduction in the final section of this paper.

ON EMPIRES AND EMPIRE-BUILDING

We have not exhausted the categories of complex systems to which the watchmaker argument can reasonably be applied. Philip assembled his

[14] A. Newell and H. A. Simon, Computer simulation of human thinking, *Science* 134: 2011–2017, December 22, 1961.

Macedonian empire and gave it to his son, to be later combined with the Persian subassembly and others into Alexander's greater system. On Alexander's death, his empire did not crumble to dust, but fragmented into some of the major subsystems that had composed it.

The watchmaker argument implies that if one would be Alexander, one should be born into a world where large stable political systems already exist. Where this condition was not fulfilled, as on the Scythian and Indian frontiers, Alexander found empire building a slippery business. So too, T. E. Lawrence's organizing of the Arabian revolt against the Turks was limited by the character of his largest stable building blocks, the separate, suspicious desert tribes.

The profession of history places a greater value upon the validated particular fact than upon tendentious generalization. I shall not elaborate upon my fancy, therefore, but will leave it to historians to decide whether anything can be learned for the interpretation of history from an abstract theory of hierarchic complex systems.

CONCLUSION: THE EVOLUTIONARY EXPLANATION OF HIERARCHY

We have shown thus far that complex systems will evolve from simple systems much more rapidly if there are stable intermediate forms than if there are not. The resulting complex forms in the former case will be hierarchic. We have only to turn the argument around to explain the observed predominance of hierarchies among the complex systems nature presents to us. Among possible complex forms, hierarchies are the ones that have the time to evolve. The hypothesis that complexity will be hierarchic makes no distinction among very flat hierarchies, like crystals, and tissues, and polymers, and the intermediate forms. Indeed, in the complex systems we encounter in nature, examples of both forms are prominent. A more complete theory than the one we have developed here would presumably have something to say about the determinants of width of span in these systems.

NEARLY DECOMPOSABLE SYSTEMS

In hierarchic systems, we can distinguish between the interactions *among* subsystems, on the one hand, and the interactions *within* subsystems —i.e., among the parts of those subsystems—on the other. The interactions at the different levels may be, and often will be, of different orders of

	A1	A2	A3	B1	B2	C1	C2	C3
A1	—	100	—	2	—	—	—	—
A2	100	—	100	1	1	—	—	—
A3	—	100	—	—	2	—	—	—
B1	2	1	—	—	100	2	1	—
B2	—	1	2	100	—	—	1	2
C1	—	—	—	2	—	—	100	—
C2	—	—	—	1	—	100	—	100
C3	—	—	—	—	2	—	100	—

FIG. 1. A hypothetical nearly-decomposable system. In terms of the heat-exchange example of the text, A1, A2, and A3 may be interpreted as cubicles in one room, B1 and B2 as cubicles in a second room, and C1, C2, and C3 as cubicles in a third. The matrix entries then are the heat diffusion coefficients between cubicles.

A1		C1
	B1	
A2		C2
	B2	
A3		C3

magnitude. In a formal organization there will generally be more interaction, on the average, between two employees who are members of the same department than between two employees from different departments. In organic substances, intermolecular forces will generally be weaker than molecular forces, and molecular forces than nuclear forces.

In a rare gas, the intermolecular forces will be negligible compared to those binding the molecules —we can treat the individual particles, for many purposes, as if they were independent of each other. We can describe such a system as *decomposable* into the subsystems comprised of the individual particles. As the gas becomes denser, molecular interactions become more significant. But over some range, we can treat the decomposable case as a limit, and as a first approximation. We can use a theory of perfect gases, for example, to describe approximately the behavior of actual gases if they are not too dense. As a second approximation, we may move to a theory of *nearly decomposable* systems, in which the interactions among the subsystems are weak, but not negligible.

At least some kinds of hierarchic systems can be approximated successfully as nearly decomposable systems. The main theoretical findings from the approach can be summed up in two propositions:

(*a*) in a nearly decomposable system, the short-run behavior of each of the component subsystems is approximately independent of the short-run behavior of the other components; (*b*) in the long run, the behavior of any one of the components depends in only an aggregate way on the behavior of the other components.

Let me provide a very concrete simple example of a nearly decomposable system.[15] Consider a building whose outside walls provide perfect thermal insulation from the environment. We shall take these walls as the boundary of our system. The building is divided into a large number of rooms, the walls between them being good, but not perfect, insulators. The walls between rooms are the boundaries of our major subsystems. Each room is divided by partitions into a number of cubicles, but the partitions are poor insulators. A thermometer hangs in each cubicle. Suppose that at the time of our first observation of the system there is a wide variation in temperature from cubicle to cubicle and from room to room—the various cubicles within the building are in a state of thermal disequilibrium. When we take new temperature readings several hours later, what shall we find? There will be very little variation in temperature among the cubicles within each single room, but there may still be large temperature variations *among* rooms. When we take readings again several days later, we find an almost uniform temperature throughout the building; the temperature differences among rooms have virtually disappeared.

We can describe the process of equilibration formally by setting up the usual equations of heat flow. The equations can be represented by the matrix of their coefficients, r_{ij}, where r_{ij} is the rate at which heat flows from the ith cubicle to the jth cubicle per degree difference in their temperatures. If cubicles i and j do not have a common wall, r_{ij} will be zero. If cubicles i and j have a common wall, and are in the same room, r_{ij} will be large. If cubicles i and j are separated by the wall of a

[15] This discussion of near-decomposability is based upon H. A. Simon and A. Ando, Aggregation of variables in dynamic systems, *Econometrica* 29: 111–138, April, 1961. The example is drawn from the same source, 117–118. The theory has been further developed and applied to a variety of economic and political phenomena by Ando and F. M. Fisher. See F. M. Fisher, On the cost of approximate specification in simultaneous equation estimation, *Econometrica* 29: 139–170, April, 1961, and F. M. Fisher and A. Ando, Two theorems on *Ceteris Paribus* in the analysis of dynamic systems, *American Political Science Review* 61: 103–113, March, 1962.

room, r_{ij} will be nonzero but small. Hence, by grouping all the cubicles together that are in the same room, we can arrange the matrix of coefficients so that all its large elements lie inside a string of square submatrices along the main diagonal. All the elements outside these diagonal squares will be either zero or small (see figure 1). We may take some small number, ϵ, as the upper bound of the extradiagonal elements. We shall call a matrix having these properties a *nearly decomposable matrix*.

Now it has been proved that a dynamic system that can be described by a nearly decomposable matrix has the properties, stated above, of a nearly decomposable system. In our simple example of heat flow this means that in the short run each room will reach an equilibrium temperature (an average of the initial temperatures of its offices) nearly independently of the others; and that each room will remain approximately in a state of equilibrium over the longer period during which an over-all temperature equilibrium is being established throughout the building. After the intra-room short-run equilibria have been reached, a single thermometer in each room will be adequate to describe the dynamic behavior of the entire system—separate thermometers in each cubicle will be superfluous.

NEAR DECOMPOSABILITY OF SOCIAL SYSTEMS

As a glance at figure 1 shows, near decomposability is a rather strong property for a matrix to possess, and the matrices that have this property will describe very special dynamic systems—vanishingly few systems out of all those that are thinkable. How few they will be depends, of course, on how good an approximation we insist upon. If we demand that epsilon be very small, correspondingly few dynamic systems will fit the definition. But we have already seen that in the natural world nearly decomposable systems are far from rare. On the contrary, systems in which each variable is linked with almost equal strength with almost all other parts of the system are far rarer and less typical.

In economic dynamics, the main variables are the prices and quantities of commodities. It is empirically true that the price of any given commodity and the rate at which it is exchanged depend to a significant extent only on the prices and quantities of a few other commodities, together with a few other aggregate magnitudes, like the average price level or some over-all measure of

economic activity. The large linkage coefficients are associated, in general, with the main flows of raw materials and semi-finished products within and between industries. An input-output matrix of the economy, giving the magnitudes of these flows, reveals the nearly decomposable structure of the system—with one qualification. There is a consumption subsystem of the economy that is linked strongly to variables in most of the other subsystems. Hence, we have to modify our notions of decomposability slightly to accommodate the special role of the consumption subsystem in our analysis of the dynamic behavior of the economy.

In the dynamics of social systems, where members of a system communicate with and influence other members, near decomposability is generally very prominent. This is most obvious in formal organizations, where the formal authority relation connects each member of the organization with one immediate superior and with a small number of subordinates. Of course many communications in organizations follow other channels than the lines of formal authority. But most of these channels lead from any particular individual to a very limited number of his superiors, subordinates, and associates. Hence, departmental boundaries play very much the same role as the walls in our heat example.

PHYSICO-CHEMICAL SYSTEMS

In the complex systems familiar in biological chemistry, a similar structure is clearly visible. Take the atomic nuclei in such a system as the elementary parts of the system, and construct a matrix of bond strengths between elements. There will be matrix elements of quite different orders of magnitude. The largest will generally correspond to the covalent bonds, the next to the ionic bonds, the third group to hydrogen bonds, still smaller linkages to van der Waals forces.[16] If we select an epsilon just a little smaller than the magnitude of a covalent bond, the system will decompose into subsystems—the constituent molecules. The smaller linkages will correspond to the intermolecular bonds.

It is well known that high-energy, high-fre-

---

[16] For a survey of the several classes of molecular and inter-molecular forces, and their dissociation energies see Setlow and Pollard, *op. cit.*, chapter 6. The energies of typical covalent bonds are of the order of 80–100 k cal/mole, of the hydrogen bonds, 10 k cal/mole. Ionic bonds generally lie between these two levels, the bonds due to van der Waals forces are lower in energy.

quency vibrations are associated with the smaller physical subsystems, low-frequency vibrations with the larger systems into which the subsystems are assembled. For example, the radiation frequencies associated with molecular vibrations are much lower than those associated with the vibrations of the planetary electrons of the atoms; the latter, in turn, are lower than those associated with nuclear processes.[17] Molecular systems are nearly decomposable systems, the short-run dynamics relating to the internal structures of the subsystems; the long-run dynamics to the interactions of these subsystems.

A number of the important approximations employed in physics depend for their validity on the near-decomposability of the systems studied. The theory of the thermodynamics of irreversible processes, for example, requires the assumption of macroscopic disequilibrium but microscopic equilibrium,[18] exactly the situation described in our heat-exchange example. Similarly computations in quantum mechanics are often handled by treating weak interactions as producing perturbations on a system of strong interactions.

SOME OBSERVATIONS ON HIERARCHIC SPAN

To understand why the span of hierarchies is sometimes very broad—as in crystals—sometimes narrow, we need to examine more detail of the interactions. In general, the critical consideration is the extent to which interaction between two (or a few) subsystems excludes interaction of these subsystems with the others. Let us examine first some physical examples.

Consider a gas of identical molecules, each of which can form covalent bonds, in certain ways, with others. Let us suppose that we can associate with each atom a specific number of bonds that it is capable of maintaining simultaneously. (This number is obviously related to the number we usually call its valence.) Now suppose that two atoms join, and that we can also associate with the combination a specific number of external bonds it is capable of maintaining. If this number is the same

[17] Typical wave numbers for vibrations associated with various systems (the wave number is the reciprocal of wave length hence proportional to frequency):
  steel wire under tension—10^{-10} to 10^{-9} cm^{-1}
  molecular rotations—10^{0} to 10^{2} cm^{-1}
  molecular vibrations—10^{2} to 10^{3} cm^{-1}
  planetary electrons—10^{4} to 10^{5} cm^{-1}
  nuclear rotations—10^{8} to 10^{10} cm^{-1}
  nuclear surface vibrations—10^{11} to 10^{12} cm^{-1}.

[18] S. R. de Groot, *Thermodynamics of irreversible processes*, 11–12, New York, Interscience Publishers, 1951.

as the number associated with the individual atoms, the bonding process can go on indefinitely—the atoms can form crystals or polymers of indefinite extent. If the number of bonds of which the composite is capable is less than the number associated with each of the parts, then the process of agglomeration must come to a halt.

We need only mention some elementary examples. Ordinary gases show no tendency to agglomerate because the multiple bonding of atoms "uses up" their capacity to interact. While each oxygen atom has a valence of two, the O_2 molecules have a zero valence. Contrariwise, indefinite chains of single-bonded carbon atoms can be built up because a chain of any number of such atoms, each with two side groups, has a valence of exactly two.

Now what happens if we have a system of elements that possess both strong and weak interaction capacities, and whose strong bonds are exhaustible through combination? Subsystems will form, until all the capacity for strong interaction is utilized in their construction. Then these subsystems will be linked by the weaker second-order bonds into larger systems. For example, a water molecule has essentially a valence of zero—all the potential covalent bonds are fully occupied by the interaction of hydrogen and oxygen molecules. But the geometry of the molecule creates an electric dipole that permits weak interaction between the water and salts dissolved in it—whence such phenomena as its electrolytic conductivity.[19]

Similarly, it has been observed that, although electrical forces are much stronger than gravitational forces, the latter are far more important than the former for systems on an astronomical scale. The explanation, of course, is that the electrical forces, being bipolar, are all "used up" in the linkages of the smaller subsystems, and that significant net balances of positive or negative charges are not generally found in regions of macroscopic size.

In social as in physical systems there are generally limits on the simultaneous interaction of large numbers of subsystems. In the social case, these limits are related to the fact that a human being is more nearly a serial than a parallel information-processing system. He can carry on only one conversation at a time, and although this does not limit the size of the audience to which a mass communication can be addressed, it does

[19] See, for example, L. Pauling, *General chemistry*, ch. 15.

limit the number of people simultaneously involved in most other forms of social interaction. Apart from requirements of direct interaction, most roles impose tasks and responsibilities that are time consuming. One cannot, for example, enact the role of "friend" with large numbers of other people.

It is probably true that in social as in physical systems, the higher frequency dynamics are associated with the subsystems, the lower frequency dynamics with the larger systems. It is generally believed, for example, that the relevant planning horizon of executives is longer the higher their location in the organizational hierarchy. It is probably also true that both the average duration of an interaction between executives and the average interval between interactions is greater at higher than at lower levels.

SUMMARY: NEAR DECOMPOSABILITY

We have seen that hierarchies have the property of near-decomposability. Intra-component linkages are generally stronger than intercomponent linkages. This fact has the effect of separating the high-frequency dynamics of a hierarchy—involving the internal structure of the components—from the low frequency dynamics—involving interaction among components. We shall turn next to some important consequences of this separation for the description and comprehension of complex systems.

THE DESCRIPTION OF COMPLEXITY

If you ask a person to draw a complex object—e.g., a human face—he will almost always proceed in a hierarchic fashion.[20] First he will outline the face. Then he will add or insert features: eyes, nose, mouth, ears, hair. If asked to elaborate, he will begin to develop details for each of the features—pupils, eyelids, lashes for the eyes, and so on—until he reaches the limits of his anatomical knowledge. His information about the object is arranged hierarchicly in memory, like a topical outline.

When information is put in outline form, it is easy to include information about the relations among the major parts and information about the internal relations of parts in each of the suboutlines. Detailed information about the relations of subparts belonging to different parts has no place

[20] George A. Miller has collected protocols from subjects who were given the task of drawing faces, and finds that they behave in the manner described here (private communication). See also E. H. Gombrich, *Art and illusion*, 291–296, New York, Pantheon Books, 1960.

in the outline and is likely to be lost. The loss of such information and the preservation mainly of information about hierarchic order is a salient characteristic that distinguishes the drawings of a child or someone untrained in representation from the drawing of a trained artist. (I am speaking of an artist who is striving for representation.)

NEAR DECOMPOSABILITY AND COMPREHENSIBILITY

From our discussion of the dynamic properties of nearly decomposable systems, we have seen that comparatively little information is lost by representing them as hierarchies. Subparts belonging to different parts only interact in an aggregative fashion—the detail of their interaction can be ignored. In studying the interaction of two large molecules, generally we do not need to consider in detail the interactions of nuclei of the atoms belonging to the one molecule with the nuclei of the atoms belonging to the other. In studying the interaction of two nations, we do not need to study in detail the interactions of each citizen of the first with each citizen of the second.

The fact, then, that many complex systems have a nearly decomposable, hierarchic structure is a major facilitating factor enabling us to understand, to describe, and even to "see" such systems and their parts. Or perhaps the proposition should be put the other way round. If there are important systems in the world that are complex without being hierarchic, they may to a considerable extent escape our observation and our understanding. Analysis of their behavior would involve such detailed knowledge and calculation of the interactions of their elementary parts that it would be beyond our capacities of memory or computation.[21]

[21] I believe the fallacy in the central thesis of W. M. Elsasser's *The physical foundation of biology*, mentioned earlier, lies in his ignoring the simplification in description of complex systems that derives from their hierarchic structure. Thus (p. 155): "If we now apply similar arguments to the coupling of enzymatic reactions with the substratum of protein molecules, we see that over a sufficient period of time, the information corresponding to the structural details of these molecules will be communicated to the dynamics of the cell, to higher levels of organization as it were, and may influence such dynamics. While this reasoning is only qualitative, it lends credence to the assumption that in the living organism, unlike the inorganic crystal, the effects of microscopic structure cannot be simply averaged out; as time goes on this influence will pervade the behavior of the cell 'at all levels.'"

But from our discussion of near-decomposability it would appear that those aspects of microstructure that control the slow developmental aspects of organismic

I shall not try to settle which is chicken and which is egg: whether we are able to understand the world because it is hierarchic, or whether it appears hierarchic because those aspects of it which are not elude our understanding and observation. I have already given some reasons for supposing that the former is at least half the truth—that evolving complexity would tend to be hierarchic—but it may not be the whole truth.

SIMPLE DESCRIPTIONS OF COMPLEX SYSTEMS

One might suppose that the description of a complex system would itself be a complex structure of symbols—and indeed, it may be just that. But there is no conservation law that requires that the description be as cumbersome as the object described. A trivial example will show how a system can be described economically. Suppose the system is a two-dimensional array like this:

$$
\begin{array}{llllllll}
A & B & M & N & R & S & H & I \\
C & D & O & P & T & U & J & K \\
M & N & A & B & H & I & R & S \\
O & P & C & D & J & K & T & U \\
R & S & H & I & A & B & M & N \\
T & U & J & K & C & D & O & P \\
H & I & R & S & M & N & A & B \\
J & K & T & U & O & P & C & D
\end{array}
$$

Let us call the array $\begin{vmatrix} AB \\ CD \end{vmatrix}$ a, the array $\begin{vmatrix} MN \\ OP \end{vmatrix}$ m, the array $\begin{vmatrix} RS \\ TU \end{vmatrix}$ r, and the array $\begin{vmatrix} HI \\ JK \end{vmatrix}$ h. Let us call the array $\begin{vmatrix} am \\ ma \end{vmatrix}$ w, and the array $\begin{vmatrix} rh \\ hr \end{vmatrix}$ x. Then the entire array is simply $\begin{vmatrix} wx \\ xw \end{vmatrix}$. While the original structure consisted of 64 symbols, it requires only 35 to write down its description:

$$
S = \frac{wx}{xw}
$$

$$
w = \frac{am}{ma} \qquad x = \frac{rh}{hr}
$$

$$
a = \frac{AB}{CD} \qquad m = \frac{MN}{OP} \qquad r = \frac{RS}{TU} \qquad h = \frac{HI}{JK}
$$

We achieve the abbreviation by making use of the redundancy in the original structure. Since

---

dynamics can be separated out from the aspects that control the more rapid cellular metabolic processes. For this reason we should not despair of unravelling the web of causes. See also J. R. Platt's review of Elsasser's book in *Perspectives in biology and medicine* 2: 243-245, 1959.

the pattern $\frac{AB}{CD}$, for example, occurs four times in the total pattern, it is economical to represent it by the single symbol, a.

If a complex structure is completely unredundant—if no aspect of its structure can be inferred from any other—then it is its own simplest description. We can exhibit it, but we cannot describe it by a simpler structure. The hierarchic structures we have been discussing have a high degree of redundancy, hence can often be described in economical terms. The redundancy takes a number of forms, of which I shall mention three:

1. Hierarchic systems are usually composed of only a few different kinds of subsystems, in various combinations and arrangements. A familiar example is the proteins, their multitudinous variety arising from arrangements of only twenty different amino acids. Similarly, the ninety-odd elements provide all the kinds of building blocks needed for an infinite variety of molecules. Hence, we can construct our description from a restricted alphabet of elementary terms corresponding to the basic set of elementary subsystems from which the complex system is generated.

2. Hierarchic systems are, as we have seen, often nearly decomposable. Hence only aggregative properties of their parts enter into the description of the interactions of those parts. A generalization of the notion of near-decomposability might be called the "empty world hypothesis" —most things are only weakly connected with most other things; for a tolerable description of reality only a tiny fraction of all possible interactions needs to be taken into account. By adopting a descriptive language that allows the absence of something to go unmentioned, a nearly empty world can be described quite concisely. Mother Hubbard did not have to check off the list of possible contents to say that her cupboard was bare.

3. By appropriate "recoding," the redundancy that is present but unobvious in the structure of a complex system can often be made patent. The most common recoding of descriptions of dynamic systems consists in replacing a description of the time path with a description of a differential law that generates that path. The simplicity, that is, resides in a constant relation between the state of the system at any given time and the state of the system a short time later. Thus, the structure of the sequence, 1 3 5 7 9 11 . . ., is most simply expressed by observing that each member is obtained by adding 2 to the previous one. But

VOL. 106, NO. 6, 1962]   THE ARCHITECTURE OF COMPLEXITY   479

this is the sequence that Galileo found to describe the velocity at the end of successive time intervals of a ball rolling down an inclined plane.

It is a familiar proposition that the task of science is to make use of the world's redundancy to describe that world simply. I shall not pursue the general methodological point here, but shall instead take a closer look at two main types of description that seem to be available to us in seeking an understanding of complex systems. I shall call these *state description* and *process description*, respectively.

STATE DESCRIPTIONS AND PROCESS DESCRIPTIONS

"A circle is the locus of all points equidistant from a given point." "To construct a circle, rotate a compass with one arm fixed until the other arm has returned to its starting point." It is implicit in Euclid that if you carry out the process specified in the second sentence, you will produce an object that satisfies the definition of the first. The first sentence is a state description of a circle, the second a process description.

These two modes of apprehending structure are the warp and weft of our experience. Pictures, blueprints, most diagrams, chemical structural formulae are state descriptions. Recipes, differential equations, equations for chemical reactions are process descriptions. The former characterize the world as sensed; they provide the criteria for identifying objects, often by modeling the objects themselves. The latter characterize the world as acted upon; they provide the means for producing or generating objects having the desired characteristics.

The distinction between the world as sensed and the world as acted upon defines the basic condition for the survival of adaptive organisms. The organism must develop correlations between goals in the sensed world and actions in the world of process. When they are made conscious and verbalized, these correlations correspond to what we usually call means-end analysis. Given a desired state of affairs and an existing state of affairs, the task of an adaptive organism is to find the difference between these two states, and then to find the correlating process that will erase the difference.[22]

Thus, problem solving requires continual trans-

lation between the state and process descriptions of the same complex reality. Plato, in the *Meno*, argued that all learning is remembering. He could not otherwise explain how we can discover or recognize the answer to a problem unless we already know the answer.[23] Our dual relation to the world is the source and solution of the paradox. We pose a problem by giving the state description of the solution. The task is to discover a sequence of processes that will produce the goal state from an initial state. Translation from the process description to the state description enables us to recognize when we have succeeded. The solution is genuinely new to us—and we do not need Plato's theory of remembering to explain how we recognize it.

There is now a growing body of evidence that the activity called human problem solving is basically a form of means-end analysis that aims at discovering a process description of the path that leads to a desired goal. The general paradigm is: given a blueprint, to find the corresponding recipe. Much of the activity of science is an application of that paradigm: given the description of some natural phenomena, to find the differential equations for processes that will produce the phenomena.

THE DESCRIPTION OF COMPLEXITY IN SELF-REPRODUCING SYSTEMS

The problem of finding relatively simple descriptions for complex systems is of interest not only for an understanding of human knowledge of the world but also for an explanation of how a complex system can reproduce itself. In my discussion of the evolution of complex systems, I touched only briefly on the role of self-reproduction.

Atoms of high atomic weight and complex inorganic molecules are witnesses to the fact that the evolution of complexity does not imply self-reproduction. If evolution of complexity from simplicity is sufficiently probable, it will occur repeatedly; the statistical equilibrium of the system will find a large fraction of the elementary particles participating in complex systems.

If, however, the existence of a particular complex form increased the probability of the creation of another form just like it, the equilibrium between complexes and components could be greatly altered in favor of the former. If we have a description of an object that is sufficiently clear and

---

[22] See H. A. Simon and A. Newell, Simulation of human thinking, *in* M. Greenberger (ed.), *Management and the computer of the future*, 95–114, esp. pp 110 ff., New York, Wiley, 1962.

[23] *The works of Plato*, B. Jowett, trans., 3: 26–35, New York, Dial Press.

complete, we can reproduce the object from the description. Whatever the exact mechanism of reproduction, the description provides us with the necessary information.

Now we have seen that the descriptions of complex systems can take many forms. In particular, we can have state descriptions or we can have process descriptions; blueprints or recipes. Reproductive processes could be built around either of these sources of information. Perhaps the simplest possibility is for the complex system to serve as a description of itself—a template on which a copy can be formed. One of the most plausible current theories, for example, of the reproduction of deoxyribonucleic acid (DNA) proposes that a DNA molecule, in the form of a double helix of matching parts (each essentially a "negative" of the other), unwinds to allow each half of the helix to serve as a template on which a new matching half can form.

On the other hand, our current knowledge of how DNA controls the metabolism of the organism suggests that reproduction by template is only one of the processes involved. According to the prevailing theory, DNA serves as a template both for itself and for the related substance ribonucleic acid (RNA). RNA, in turn, serves as a template for protein. But proteins—according to current knowledge—guide the organism's metabolism not by the template method but by serving as catalysts to govern reaction rates in the cell. While RNA is a blueprint for protein, protein is a recipe for metabolism.[24]

ONTOGENY RECAPITULATES PHYLOGENY

The DNA in the chromosomes of an organism contains some, and perhaps most, of the information that is needed to determine its development and activity. We have seen that, if current theories are even approximately correct, the information is recorded not as a state description of the organism but as a series of "instructions" for the construction and maintenance of the organism from nutrient materials. I have already used the metaphor of a recipe; I could equally well compare it with a computer program, which is also a sequence of instructions, governing the construction

[24] C. B. Anfinsen, *The molecular basis of evolution*, chs. 3 and 10, New York, Wiley, 1959, will qualify this sketchy, oversimplified account. For an imaginative discussion of some mechanisms of process description that could govern molecular structure, see H. H. Pattee, On the origin of macromolecular sequences, *Biophysical Journal* 1: 683–710, 1961.

of symbolic structures. Let me spin out some of the consequences of the latter comparison.

If genetic material is a program—viewed in its relation to the organism—it is a program with special and peculiar properties. First, it is a self-reproducing program; we have already considered its possible copying mechanism. Second, it is a program that has developed by Darwinian evolution. On the basis of our watchmaker's argument, we may assert that many of its ancestors were also viable programs—programs for the subassemblies.

Are there any other conjectures we can make about the structure of this program? There is a well-known generalization in biology that is verbally so neat that we would be reluctant to give it up even if the facts did not support it: ontogeny recapitulates phylogeny. The individual organism, in its development, goes through stages that resemble some of its ancestral forms. The fact that the human embryo develops gill bars and then modifies them for other purposes is a familiar particular belonging to the generalization. Biologists today like to emphasize the qualifications of the principle—that ontogeny recapitulates only the grossest aspects of phylogeny, and these only crudely. These qualifications should not make us lose sight of the fact that the generalization does hold in rough approximation—it does summarize a very significant set of facts about the organism's development. How can we interpret these facts?

One way to solve a complex problem is to reduce it to a problem previously solved—to show what steps lead from the earlier solution to a solution of the new problem. If, around the turn of the century, we wanted to instruct a workman to make an automobile, perhaps the simplest way would have been to tell him how to modify a wagon by removing the singletree and adding a motor and transmission. Similarly, a genetic program could be altered in the course of evolution by adding new processes that would modify a simpler form into a more complex one—to construct a gastrula, take a blastula and alter it!

The genetic description of a single cell may, therefore, take a quite different form from the genetic description that assembles cells into a multi-celled organism. Multiplication by cell division would require, as a minimum, a state description (the DNA, say), and a simple "interpretive process"—to use the term from computer language —that copies this description as a part of the larger copying process of cell division. But such a mechanism clearly would not suffice for the differentiation of cells in development. It appears more natural to conceptualize that mechanism as based on a process description, and a somewhat more complex interpretive process that produces the adult organism in a sequence of stages, each new stage in development representing the effect of an operator upon the previous one.

It is harder to conceptualize the interrelation of these two descriptions. Interrelated they must be, for enough has been learned of gene-enzyme mechanisms to show that these play a major role in development as in cell metabolism. The single clue we obtain from our earlier discussion is that the description may itself be hierarchical, or nearly decomposable, in structure, the lower levels governing the fast, "high-frequency" dynamics of the individual cell, the higher level interactions governing the slow, "low-frequency" dynamics of the developing multi-cellular organism.

There are only bits of evidence, apart from the facts of recapitulation, that the genetic program is organized in this way, but such evidence as exists is compatible with this notion.[25] To the extent that we can differentiate the genetic information that governs cell metabolism from the genetic information that governs the development of differentiated cells in the multi-cellular organization, we simplify enormously—as we have already seen —our task of theoretical description. But I have perhaps pressed this speculation far enough.

The generalization that in evolving systems whose descriptions are stored in a process language, we might expect ontogeny partially to recapitulate phylogeny has applications outside the

---

[25] There is considerable evidence that successive genes along a chromosome often determine enzymes controlling successive stages of protein syntheses. For a review of some of this evidence, see P. E. Hartman, Transduction: a comparative review, *in* W. D. McElroy and B. Glass (eds.), *The chemical basis of heredity*, Baltimore, Johns Hopkins Press, 1957, at pp. 442–454. Evidence for differential activity of genes in different tissues and at different stages of development is discussed by J. G. Gall, Chromosomal Differentiation, *in* W. D. McElroy and B. Glass (eds.), *The chemical basis of development*, Baltimore, Johns Hopkins Press, 1958, at pp. 103–135. Finally, a model very like that proposed here has been independently, and far more fully, outlined by J. R. Platt, A 'book model' of genetic information transfer in cells and tissues, *in* Kasha and Pullman (eds.), *Horizons in biochemistry*, New York, Academic Press, forthcoming. Of course, this kind of mechanism is not the only one in which development could be controlled by a process description. Induction, in the form envisaged in Spemann's organizer theory, is based on process description, in which metabolites in already formed tissue control the next stages of development.

realm of biology. It can be applied as readily, for example, to the transmission of knowledge in the educational process. In most subjects, particularly in the rapidly advancing sciences, the progress from elementary to advanced courses is to a considerable extent a progress through the conceptual history of the science itself. Fortunately, the recapitulation is seldom literal—any more than it is in the biological case. We do not teach the phlogiston theory in chemistry in order later to correct it. (I am not sure I could not cite examples in other subjects where we do exactly that.) But curriculum revisions that rid us of the accumulations of the past are infrequent and painful. Nor are they always desirable—partial recapitulation may, in many instances, provide the most expeditious route to advanced knowledge.

SUMMARY: THE DESCRIPTION OF COMPLEXITY

How complex or simple a structure is depends critically upon the way in which we describe it. Most of the complex structures found in the world are enormously redundant, and we can use this redundancy to simplify their description. But to use it, to achieve the simplification, we must find the right representation.

The notion of substituting a process description for a state description of nature has played a central role in the development of modern science. Dynamic laws, expressed in the form of systems of differential or difference equations, have in a large number of cases provided the clue for the simple description of the complex. In the preceding paragraphs I have tried to show that this characteristic of scientific inquiry is not accidental or superficial. The correlation between state description and process description is basic to the functioning of any adaptive organism, to its capacity for acting purposefully upon its environment. Our present-day understanding of genetic mechanisms suggests that even in describing itself the multi-cellular organism finds a process description—a genetically encoded program—to be the parsimonious and useful representation.

CONCLUSION

Our speculations have carried us over a rather alarming array of topics, but that is the price we must pay if we wish to seek properties common to many sorts of complex systems. My thesis has been that one path to the construction of a nontrivial theory of complex systems is by way of a theory of hierarchy. Empirically, a large proportion of the complex systems we observe in nature exhibit hierarchic structure. On theoretical grounds we could expect complex systems to be hierarchies in a world in which complexity had to evolve from simplicity. In their dynamics, hierarchies have a property, near-decomposability, that greatly simplifies their behavior. Near-decomposability also simplifies the description of a complex system, and makes it easier to understand how the information needed for the development or reproduction of the system can be stored in reasonable compass.

In both science and engineering, the study of "systems" is an increasingly popular activity. Its popularity is more a response to a pressing need for synthesizing and analyzing complexity than it is to any large development of a body of knowledge and technique for dealing with complexity. If this popularity is to be more than a fad, necessity will have to mother invention and provide substance to go with the name. The explorations reviewed here represent one particular direction of search for such substance.

[6]

THE ORGANIZATION OF ECONOMIC ACTIVITY: ISSUES PERTINENT TO THE CHOICE OF MARKET VERSUS NONMARKET ALLOCATION

Kenneth J. Arrow

INTRODUCTION

The concept of public goods has been developed through a process of successive refinement over a long period of time. Yet surprisingly enough there does not seem to exist anywhere in the literature a clear general definition of this concept or the more general one of "externality." The accounts given are usually either very general and discursive, difficult of interpretation in specific contexts, or else they are rigorous accounts of very special situations. What exactly is the relation between externalities and such concepts as "appropriability" or "exclusion"?

Also, there is considerable ambiguity in the purpose of the analysis of externalities. The best developed part of the theory relates to only a single question: the statement of a set of conditions, as weak as possible, which insure that a competitive equilibrium exists and is Pareto efficient.[1] Then the denial of any of these hypotheses is presumably a sufficient condition for considering resort to non-market channels of resource allocation—usually thought of as government expenditures, taxes, and subsidies.

At a second level the analysis of externalities should lead to criteria for nonmarket allocation. We are tempted to set forth these criteria in terms analogous to the profit-and-loss statements of private business; in this form, we are led to benefit-cost analysis. There are, moreover, two possible aims for benefit-cost analysis; one, more ambitious but theoretically simpler, is specification of the nonmarket actions which will restore Pareto efficiency; the second involves the recognition that the instruments available to the government or other nonmarket forces are scarce resources for one reason or another, so that all that can be achieved is a "second-best."

Other concepts that seem to cluster closely to the concept of public

Kenneth J. Arrow is Professor of Economics at Harvard University and is associated with the Project on Efficiency of Decisionmaking in Economic Systems at that institution.

goods are those of "increasing returns" and "market failure." These are related to Pareto inefficiency on the one hand and to the existence and optimality of competitive equilibrium on the other; sometimes the discussions in the literature do not adequately distinguish these two aspects. I contend that market failure is a more general category than externality; and both differ from increasing returns in a basic sense, since market failures in general and externalities in particular are relative to the mode of economic organization, while increasing returns are essentially a technological phenomenon.

Current writing has helped bring out the point that market failure is not absolute; it is better to consider a broader category, that of transaction costs, which in general impede and in particular cases completely block the formation of markets. It is usually though not always emphasized that transaction costs are costs of running the economic system. An incentive for vertical integration is replacement of the costs of buying and selling on the market by the costs of intrafirm transfers; the existence of vertical integration may suggest that the costs of operating competitive markets are not zero, as is usually assumed in our theoretical analysis.

Monetary theory, unlike value theory, is heavily dependent on the assumption of positive transaction costs; the recurrent complaint about the difficulty of integrating these two branches of theory is certainly governed by the contradictory assumptions made about transaction costs. The creation of money is in many respects an example of a public good.

The identification of transaction costs in different contexts and under different systems of resource allocation should be a major item on the research agenda of the theory of public goods and indeed of the theory of resource allocation in general. Only the most rudimentary suggestions are made here. The "exclusion principle" is a limiting case of one kind of transaction cost, but another type, the costliness of the information needed to enter and participate in any market, has been little remarked. Information is closely related on the one hand to communication and on the other to uncertainty.

Given the existence of Pareto inefficiency in a free market equilibrium, there is a pressure in the market to overcome it by some sort of departure from the free market; i.e., some form of collective action. This need not be undertaken by the government. I suggest that in fact there is a wide variety of social institutions, in particular generally accepted social norms of behavior, which serve in some means as compensation for failure or limitation of the market, though each in turn involves transaction costs of its own. The question also arises how the behavior of individual economic agents in a social institution (especially in voting) is related to their behavior on the market. A good deal of theoretical literature has arisen in recent years which seeks to describe political behavior as analogous to economic, and we may hope for a general theory of socioeconomic equilibrium. But it must always be kept in mind that the contexts of choice are radically different, particularly when the hypotheses of perfectly costless action and information are relaxed. It is not accidental that economic analysis has been successful only in certain limited areas.

COMPETITIVE EQUILIBRIUM AND PARETO EFFICIENCY

A quick review of the familiar theorems on the role of perfectly competitive equilibrium in the efficient allocation of resources will be useful. Perfectly competitive equilbrium has its usual meaning: households, possessed of initial resources, including possibly claims to the profits of firms, choose consumption bundles to maximize utility at a given set of prices; firms choose production bundles so as to maximize profits at the same set of prices; the chosen production and consumption bundles must be consistent with each other in the sense that aggregate production plus initial resources must equal aggregate consumption. The key points in the definition are the parametric role[2] of the prices for each individual and the identity of prices for all individuals. Implicit are the assumptions that all prices can be known by all individuals and that the act of charging prices is not itself a consumer of resources.

A number of additional assumptions are made at different points in the theory of equilibrium, but most are clearly factually valid in the usual contexts and need not be mentioned. The two hypotheses frequently not valid are (C), the convexity of household indifference maps and firm production possibility sets,[3] and (M), the universality of markets. While the exact meaning of the last assumption will be explored later at some length, for the present purposes we mean that the consumption bundle which determines the utility of an individual is the same as that which he purchases at given prices subject to his budget constraint, and that the set of production bundles among which a firm chooses is a given range independent of decisions made by other agents in the economy.

The relations between Pareto efficiency and competitive equilibrium are set forth in the following two theorems:

1. *If (M) holds, a competitive equilibrium is Pareto-efficient.* This theorem is true even if (C) does not hold.

2. *If (C) and (M) hold, then any Pareto-efficient allocation can be achieved as a competitive equilibrium by a suitable reallocation of initial resources.*

When the assumptions of proposition 2 are valid, then the case for the competitive price system is strongest. Any complaints about its operation can be reduced to complaints about the distribution of income, which should then be rectified by lump-sum transfers. Of course, as Pareto already emphasized, the proposition provides no basis for accepting the results of the market in the absence of accepted levels of income equality.

The central role of competitive equilibrium both as a normative guide and as at least partially descriptive of the real world raises an analytically difficult question: does a competitive equilibrium necessarily exist?

3. *If* (C) *holds, then there exists a competitive equilibrium.* This theorem is true even if (M) does not hold.

If both (C) and (M) hold, we have a fairly complete and simple picture of the achievement of desirable goals, subject always to the major qualification of the achievement of a desirable income distribution. The price system itself determines the income distribution only in the sense of preserving the status quo. Even if costless lump-sum transfers are possible, there is needed a collective mechanism reallocating income if the status quo is not regarded as satisfactory.

Of course (C) is not a necessary condition for the existence of a competitive equilibrium, only a sufficient one. From proposition 1, it is possible to have an equilibrium and therefore efficient allocation without convexity (when (M) holds). However, in view of the central role of (C) in these theorems, the implications in relaxing this hypothesis have been examined intensively in recent years by Farrell (1959), Rothenberg (1960), Aumann (1966), and Starr (1969). Their conclusions may be summarized as follows: Let (C') be the weakened convexity assumption that there are no indivisibilities large relative to the economy.

4. *Propositions 2 and 3 remain approximately true if* (C) *is replaced by* (C').

Thus, the only nonconvexities that are important for the present purposes are increasing returns over a range large relative to the economy. In those circumstances, a competitive equilibrium cannot exist.

The price system, for all its virtues, is only one conceivable form of arranging trade, even in a system of private property. Bargaining can assume extremely general forms. Under the assumptions (C') and (M), we are assured that not everyone can be made better off by a bargain not derived from the price system; but the question arises whether some members of the economy will not find it in their interest and within their power to depart from the perfectly competitive price system. For example, both Knight (1921, pp. 190–194) and Samuelson (1967, p. 120) have noted that it would pay all the firms in a given industry to form a monopoly. But in fact it can be argued that unrestricted bargaining can only settle down to a resource allocation which could also be achieved as a perfectly competitive equilibrium, at least if the bargaining itself is costless and each agent is small compared to the entire economy. This line of argument originated with Edgeworth (1881, pp. 20–43) and has been developed recently by Shubik (1959), Debreu and Scarf (1963), and Aumann (1964).

More precisely, it is easy to show:

5. *If (M) holds and a competitive equilibrium prevails, then no set of economic agents will find any resource allocation which they can accomplish by themselves (without trade with the other agents) which they will all prefer to that prevailing under the equilibrium.*

Proposition 5 holds for any number of agents. A deeper proposition is the following converse:

6. *If (C′) and (M) hold, and if the resources of any economic agent are small compared with the total of the economy, then, given any allocation not approximately achievable as a competitive equilibrium, there will be some set of agents and some resource allocation they can achieve without any trade with others which each one will prefer to the given allocation.*

These two propositions, taken together, strongly suggest that when all the relevant hypotheses hold, (*a*) a competitive equilibrium, if achieved, will not be upset by bargaining even if permitted, and (*b*) for any bargain not achievable by a competitive equilibrium there is a set of agents who would benefit by change to another bargain which they have the full power to enforce.

The argument that a set of firms can form a monopoly overlooks the possibility that the consumers can also form a coalition, threaten not to buy, and seek mutually advantageous deals with a subset of the firms; such deals are possible since the monopoly allocation violates some marginal equivalences.

In real life, monopolizing cartels are possible for a reason not so far introduced into the analysis: bargaining costs between producers and consumers are high, those among producers low—a point made most emphatically by Adam Smith (1937, p. 128); "People of the same trade seldom meet together, even for merriment or diversion, but the conversation ends in a conspiracy against the public, or in some contrivance to raise prices." *It is not the presence of bargaining costs per se but their bias that is relevant.* If all bargaining costs are high, but competitive pricing and the markets are cheap, then we expect the perfectly competitive equilibrium to obtain, yielding an allocation identical with that under costless bargaining. But if bargaining costs are biased, then some bargains other than the competitive equilibrium can be arrived at which will not be upset by still other bargains if the latter but not the former are costly.

Finally, in this review of the elements of competitive equilibrium theory, let me repeat the obvious and well-known fact that in a world where time is relevant, the commodities which enter into the equilibrium system include those with future dates. In fact, the bulk of meaningful future transactions cannot be carried out on any existing present market, so that assumption (M), the universality of markets, is not valid.

EXTERNALITIES ILLUSTRATED

After this long[4] excursus into the present state of the theory of equilibrium and optimality, it is time to discuss some of the standard concepts of externality, market failure, and public goods generally. The clarification of these concepts is a long historical process, not yet concluded, in which the classic contributions of Knight (1924), Young (1913, pp. 676–684), and Robertson (1924) have in more recent times been enriched by those of Meade (1952), Scitovsky (1954), Coase (1960), Buchanan and Stubblebine (1962), and Demsetz (1966). The concept of externality and the extent to which it causes nonoptimal market behavior will be discussed here in terms of a simple model.

Consider a pure exchange economy. Let x_{ik} be the amount of the kth commodity consumed by the ith individual ($i = 1, \ldots, n; \ k = 1, \ldots, m$) and $\bar{x}_k$ be the amount of the kth commodity available. Suppose in general that the utility of the ith individual is a function of the consumption of all individuals (not all types of consumption for all individuals need actually enter into any given individual's utility function); the utility of the ith individual is $U_i(x_{11}, \ldots, x_{mn})$. We have the obvious constraints:

$$(1) \qquad \sum_i x_{ik} \leqq \bar{x}_k$$

Introduce the following definitions:

$$(2) \qquad x_{jik} = x_{ik}.$$

With this notation a Pareto-efficient allocation is a vector maximum of the utility functions $U_j(x_{j11}, \ldots, x_{jmn})$, subject to the constraints (1) and (2). Because of the notation used, the variables appearing in the utility function relating to the jth individual are proper to him alone and appear in no one else's utility function. If we understand now that there are n^2m commodities, indexed by the triple subscript jik, then the Pareto-efficiency problem has a thoroughly classical form. There are n^2m prices, p_{jik}, attached to the constraints (2), plus m prices, q_k, corresponding to constraints (1). Following the maximization procedure formally, we see, much as in Samuelson (1954), that Pareto efficiency is characterized by the conditions:

(3) $$\lambda_j(\partial U_j / \partial x_{ik}) = p_{jik},$$

and

(4) $$\sum_j p_{jik} = q_k,$$

where λ_j is the reciprocal of the marginal utility of income for individual j. (These statements ignore corner conditions, which can easily be supplied.)

Condition (4) can be given the following economic interpretation: Imagine each individual i to be a producer with m production processes, indexed by the pair (i,k). Process (i,k). has one input, namely commodity k, and n outputs, indexed by the triple (j,i,k). In other words, what we ordinarily call individual i's consumption is regarded as the production of joint outputs, one for each individual whose utility is affected by individual i's consumption.

The point of this exercise is to show that by suitable and indeed not unnatural reinterpretation of the commodity space, externalities can be regarded as ordinary commodities, and all the formal theory of competitive equilibrium is valid, including its optimality.

It is not the mere fact that one man's consumption enters into another man's utility that causes the failure of the market to achieve efficiency. There are two relevant factors which cannot be discovered by inspection of the utility structures of the individual. One, much explored in the literature, is the appropriability of the commodities which represent the external repercussions; the other, less stressed, is the fact that markets for externalities usually involve small numbers of buyers and sellers.

The first point, Musgrave's "exclusion principle," (1959, p. 86) is so well known as to need little elaboration. Pricing demands the possibility of excluding nonbuyers from the use of the product, and this exclusion may be technically impossible or may require the use of considerable resources. Pollution is the key example; the supply of clean air or water to each individual would have to be treated as a separate commodity, and it would have to be possible in principle to supply to one and not the other (though the final equilibrium would involve equal supply to all). But this is technically impossible.

The second point comes out clearly in our case. Each commodity (j,i,k) has precisely one buyer and one seller. Even if a competitive equilibrium could be defined, there would be no force driving the system to it; we are in the realm of imperfectly competitive equilibrium.

In my view, the standard lighthouse example is best analyzed as a problem of small numbers rather than of the difficulty of exclusion, though both elements are present. To simplify matters, I will abstract from uncertainty so that the lighthouse keeper knows exactly when each ship will need its services, and also abstract from indivisibility (since the light is either on or off). Assume further that only one ship will be within range of the lighthouse at any moment. Then exclusion is perfectly possible; the lighthouse need only shut off its light when a nonpaying ship is coming into range. But there would be only one buyer and one seller and no competitive forces to drive the two into a competitive equilibrium. If in addition the costs of bargaining are high, then it may be most efficient to offer the service free.

If, as is typical, markets for the externalities do not exist, then the allocation from the point of view of the "buyer" is determined by a rationing process. We can determine a shadow price for the buyer; this will differ from the price, zero, received by the seller. Hence, formally, the failure of markets for externalities to exist can also be described as a difference of prices between buyer and seller.

In the example analyzed, the externalities related to particular named individuals; individual i's utility function depended on what a particular individual, j, possessed. The case where it is only the total amount of some commodity (e.g., handsome houses) in other people's hands that matters is a special case, which yields rather simpler results. In this case, $\partial U_j / \partial x_{ik}$ is independent of i for $i \neq j$, and hence, by (3), p_{jik} is independent of i for $i \neq j$. Let,

$$p_{iik} = p_{ik}, p_{jik} = \bar{p}_{jk} \text{ for } i \neq j.$$

Then (4) becomes,

$$p_{ik} + \sum_{j \neq i} \bar{p}_{jk} = q_k,$$

or,

$$(p_{ik} - \bar{p}_{ik}) + \sum_{j} \bar{p}_{jk} = q_k,$$

from which it follows that the difference, $p_{ik} - \bar{p}_{ik}$, is independent of i. There are two kinds of shadow prices, a price $\bar{p}_{ik}$, the price that individual i is willing to pay for an increase in the stock of commodity k in any other individual's hands, and the premium, $p_{ik} - \bar{p}_{ik}$, he is willing to pay to have the commodity in his possession rather than someone else's. At the optimum, this premium for private possession must be the same for all individuals.

Other types of externalities are associated with several commodities simultaneously and do not involve named individuals, as in the case of neighborhood effects, where an individual's utility depends both on others' behavior (e.g., esthetic, criminal) and on their location.

There is one deep problem in the intepretation of externalities which can only be signaled here. What aspects of others' behavior to we consider as affecting a utility function? If we take a hard-boiled revealed preference attitude, then if an individual expends resources in supporting legislation regulating another's behavior, it must be assumed that that behavior affects his utility. Yet in the cases that students of criminal law call "crimes without victims," such as homosexuality or drug-taking, there is no direct relation between the parties. Do we have to extend the concept of externality to all matters that an individual cares about? Or, in the spirit of John Stuart Mill, is there a second-order value judgment which excludes some of these preferences from the formation of social policy as being illegitimate infringements of individual freedom?

MARKET FAILURE

The problem of externalities is thus a special case of a more general phenomenon, the failure of markets to exist. Not all examples of market failure can fruitfully be described as externalities. Two very important examples have already been alluded to; markets for many forms of risk-bearing and for most future transactions do not exist and their absence is surely suggestive of inefficiency.

Previous discussion has suggested two possible causes for market failures: (1) inability to exclude; (2) lack of necessary information to permit market transactions to be concluded.

The failure of futures markets cannot be directly explained in these terms. Exclusion is no more a problem in the future than in the present. Any contract to be executed in the future is necessarily contingent on some events (for example, that the two agents are still both in business), but there must be many cases where no informational difficulty is presented. The absence of futures markets may be ascribed to a third possibility: (3) supply and demand are equated at zero; the highest price at which anyone would buy is below the lowest price at which anyone would sell.

This third case of market failure, unlike the first two, is by itself in no way presumptive of inefficiency. However, it may usually be assumed that its occurrence is the result of failures of the first two types on complementary markets. Specifically, the demand for future steel may be low because of uncertainties of all types; sales and technological uncertainty for the buyer's firm, prices and existence of competing goods, and the quality specification of the steel. If, however, adequate markets for risk-bearing existed, the uncertainties could be removed, and the demand for future steel would rise.

TRANSACTION COSTS

Market failure has been presented as absolute, but in fact the situation is more complex than this. A more general formulation is that of transaction costs, which are attached to any market and indeed to any mode of resource allocation. Market failure is the particular case where transaction costs are so high that the existence of the market is no longer worthwhile. The distinction between transaction costs and production costs is that the former can be varied by a chance in the mode of resource allocation, while the latter depend only on the technology and tastes, and would be the same in all economic systems.

The discussions in the preceding sections suggest two sources of transaction costs. (1) exclusion costs; (2) costs of communication and information, including both the supplying and the learning of the terms on which transactions can be carried out. An additional source is (3) the costs of disequlibrium; in any complex system, the market or authoritative allocation, even under perfect information, it takes time to compute the optimal allocation, and either transactions take place which are inconsistent with the final equilibrium or they are delayed until the computation are completed (see T. Marschak, 1959).

These costs vary from system to system; thus, one of the advantages of a price system over either bargaining or some form of authoritative allocation is usually stated to be the economy in costs of information and communication. But the costs of transmitting and especially of receiving a large number of price signals may be high; thus, there is a tendency not to differentiate prices as much as would be desirable from the efficiency viewpoint; for example, the same price is charged for peak and offpeak usage of transportation or electricity.

In a price system, transaction costs drive a wedge between buyer's and seller's prices and thereby give rise to welfare losses as in the usual analysis. Removal of these welfare losses by changing to another system (for example, governmental allocation on benefit-cost critera) must be weighed against any possible increase in transaction costs (for example, the need for elaborate and perhaps impossible studies to determine demand functions without the benefit of observing a market).

The welfare implications of transaction costs would exist even if they were proportional to the size of the transaction, but in fact they typically exhibit increasing returns. The cost of acquiring a piece of information, for example, a price, is independent of the scale of use to which it will be put.

COLLECTIVE ACTION: THE POLITICAL PROCESS

The state may frequently have a special role to play in resource allocation because, by its nature, it has a monopoly of coercive power, and coercive power can be used to economize on transaction costs. The most important use of coercion in the economic context is the collection of taxes; others are regulatory legislation and eminent domain proceedings.

The state is not an entity but rather a system of individual agents, a widely extensive system in the case of a democracy. It is appealing and fruitful to analyze its behavior in resource allocation in a manner analogous to that of the price system. Since the same agents appear in the two systems, it becomes equally natural to assume they have the same motives. Hotelling (1929, pp. 54–55) and Schumpeter (1942, ch. XXII) had sketched such politicoeconomic models, and von Neumann and Morgenstern's monumental work is certainly based on the idea that all social phenomena are governed by essentially the same motives as economics. The elaboration of more or less complete models of the political process along the lines of economic theory is more recent, the most prominent contributors being Black (1958), Downs (1957), Buchanan and Tullock (1962), and Rothenberg (1965).

I confine myself here to a few critical remarks on the possibilities of such theories. These are not intended to be negative but to suggest problems that have to be faced and are raised by some points in the preceding discussion.

1. If we take the allocative process to be governed by majority voting, then, as we well know, there are considerable possibilities of paradox. The possible intransitivity of majority voting was already pointed out by Condorcet (1785). If, instead of assuming that each individual votes according to his preferences it is assumed that they bargain freely before voting (vote-selling), the paradox appears in another form, a variant of the bargaining problems already noted in section 2. If a majority could do what it wanted, then it would be optimal to win with a bare majority and take everything; but any such bargain can always be broken up by another proposed majority.

Tullock (1967) has recently argued convincingly that if the distribution of opinions on social issues is fairly uniform and if the dimensionality of the space of social issues is much less than the number of individuals, then majority voting on a sincere basis will be transitive. The argument is not, however applicable to income distribution, for such a policy has as many dimensions as there are individuals, so that the dimensionality of the issue space is equal to the number of individuals.

This last observation raises an interesting question. Why, in fact, in democratic systems has there been so little demand for income redistribution? The current discussion of a negative income tax is the first serious attempt at a purely redistributive policy. Hagström (1938) presented a mathematical model predicting on the basis of a self-interest model for voters that democracy would inevitably lead to radical egalitarianism.

2. Political policy is not made by voters, not even in the sense that they choose the vector of political actions which best suits them. It is in fact made by representatives in one form or another. Political representation is an outstanding example of the principal-agent relation. This means that the link between individual utility functions and social action is tenuous, though by no means completely absent. Representatives are no more a random sample of their constituents than physicians are of their patients.

Indeed, the question can be raised: to what extent is the voter, when acting in that capacity, a principal or an agent? To some extent, certainly, the voter is cast in a role in which he feels some obligation to consider the social good, not just his own. It is in fact somewhat hard to explain otherwise why an individual votes at all in a large election, since the probability that his vote will be decisive is so negligible.

COLLECTIVE ACTION: SOCIAL NORMS

It is a mistake to limit collective action to State action; many other departures from the anonymous atomism of the price system are observed regularly. Indeed, firms of any complexity are illustrations of collective action, the internal allocation of their resources being directed by authoritative and hierarchical controls.

I want, however, to conclude by calling attention to a less visible form of social action: norms of social behavior, including ethical and moral codes. I suggest as one possible interpretation that they are reactions of society to compensate for market failures. It is useful for individuals to have some trust in each other's word. In the absence of trust, it would become very costly to arrange for alternative sanctions and guarantees, and many opportunities for mutually beneficial cooperation would have to be foregone. Banfield (1958) has argued that lack of trust is indeed one of the causes of economic underdevelopment.

It is difficult to conceive of buying trust in any direct way (though it can happen indirectly, for example, a trusted employee will be paid more as being more valuable); indeed, there seems to be some inconsistency in the very concept. Nonmarket action might take the form of a mutual agreement. But the arrangement of these agreements and especially their continued extension to new individuals entering the social fabric can be costly. As an alternative, society may proceed by internalization of these norms to the achievement of the desired agreement on an unconscious level.

There is a whole set of customs and norms which might be similarly interpreted as agreements to improve the efficiency of the economic system (in the broad sense of satisfaction of individual values) by providing commodities to which the price system is inapplicable.

These social conventions may be adaptive in their origins, but they can become retrogressive. An agreement is costly to reach and therefore costly to modify; and the costs of modification may be especially large for unconscious agreements. Thus, codes of professional ethics, which arise out of the principal-agent relation and afford protection to the principals, can serve also as a cloak for monopoly by the agents.

NOTES

[1] A competitive equilibrium is defined below. An allocation of resources through the workings of the economic system is said to be Pareto efficient if there is no other allocation which would make every individual in the economy better off.

[2] By "parametric role" is meant that each household and firm takes the market prices as given, not alterable by its consumption or production decisions.

[3] For households, "convexity" means that if we consider two different bundles of consumption, a third bundle defined by averaging the first two commodity by commodity is not inferior in the household's preferences to both of the first two. For a firm, "convexity" means that if we consider two different specifications of inputs and outputs, either of which is possible to the firm (in that the inputs suffice to produce the outputs), then a third specification defined by averaging the inputs and outputs of the first two is also possible for the firm to carry out.

[4] The extended version of this paper which appeared in the Compendium of the Joint Economic Committee contained sections on Imperfectly Competitive Equilibrium and Risk and Information.

72   *The Economic Basis of Public Expenditures*

REFERENCES

Aumann, R. J. 1964. Markets with a continuum of traders. *Econometrica* 32:39–50.

Aumann, R. J. 1966. The existence of competitive equilibria in markets with a continuum of traders. *Econometrica* 34:1–17.

Banfield, E. C. 1958. *The Moral Basis of a Backward Society.* The Free Press.

Black, D. 1958. *The Theory of Committees and Elections.* Cambridge, U.K.: Cambridge University Press.

Buchanan, J. and W. C. Stubblebine. 1962. Externality. *Economica* 29:371–384.

Buchanan, J. and G. Tullock. 1962. *The Calculus of Consent.* Ann Arbor, Michigan: University of Michigan Press.

Coase, R. H. 1960. The problem of social cost. *Journal of Law and Economics* 3:1–44.

Condorcet, Marquis de. 1785. *Essai sur l'application de l'analyse à la probabilitié des décisions rendues à la pluralité des voix.* Paris.

Demsetz, H. 1966. Some aspects of property rights. *Journal of Law Economics* 9:61–70.

Downs, A. 1957. *An Economic Theory of Democracy.* New York: Harper.

Hagström, K. G. 1938. A mathematical note on democracy. *Econometrica* 6:381–383.

Hotelling, H. 1929. Stability in competition. *Economic Journal* 39:41–57.

Knight, F. H. 1921. *Risk, Uncertainty, and Profit.* Boston and New York: Houghton-Mifflin. Reprinted by London School of Economics and Political Science, 1948.

Knight, F. H. 1924. Some fallacies in the interpretation of social cost. *Quarterly Journal of Economics* 38:582–606.

Marschak, T. 1959. Centralization and decentralization in economic organizations. *Econometrica* 27:399–430.

Meade, J. E. 1952. External economies and diseconomies in a competitive situation. *Economic Journal* 62:54–67.

Musgrave, R. A. 1959. *The Theory of Public Finance: A Study in Public Economy.* New York: McGraw-Hill Book Company.

von Neumann, J., and O. Morgenstern. 1944. *Theory of Games and Economic Behavior.* Princeton, N.J.: Princeton University Press. Second edition, 1947.

Robertson, D. H. 1924. Those empty boxes. *Economic Journal* 34:16–30.

Rothenberg, J. 1960. Non-convexity, aggregation, and Pareto optimality. *Journal of Political Economy* 68:435–468.

Rothenberg, J. 1965. A model of economic and political decision-making. In J. Margolis (ed.) *The Public Economy of Urban Communities.* Washington, D.C.: Resources for the Future.

Samuelson, P. A. 1954. The pure theory of public expenditures, *Review of Economic Statistics* 36:387–389.

Samuelson, P. A. 1967. The monopolistic competition revolution. In R. E. Kuenne (ed.) *Monopolistic Competition Theory: Studies in Impact.* New York, London, and Sydney: Wiley, pp. 105–138.

Schumpeter, J. 1942. *Capitalism, Socialism, and Democracy.* New York: Harper. Third Edition, 1950.

Scitovsky, T. 1954. Two concepts of external economies. *Journal of Political Economy* 62:143–151

Shapley, L. S., and M. Shubik. 1967. Ownership and the production function. *Quarterly Journal of Economics* 81:88–111.

Shubik, M. 1959. Edgeworth market games. In A. W. Tucker and R. D. Luce (eds.) *Contributions to the Theory of Games IV. Annals of Mathematics Study.* Princeton, New Jersey: Princeton University Press, 40:267–278.

Smith, A. 1937. *An Enquiry Concerning the Causes of the Wealth of Nations.* New York: Modern Library.

Starr, R. 1969. Quasi-equilibria in markets with nonconvex preferences. *Econometrica* 37:25–38.

Tullock, G. 1967. *Toward a Mathematics of Politics.* Ann Arbor, Michigan: University of Michigan Press.

Young, A. A. 1913. Pigou's Wealth and Welfare. *Quarterly Journal of Economics* 27:672–686.

[7]

A THEORY OF INSTITUTIONAL CHANGE: CONCEPTS AND CAUSES[1]

(I) Introduction

Historians have traditionally displayed an interest in the institutions within which human action occurs, and much of their work has involved an examination of the interaction between people and these institutions. Economic historians, especially the 'new' group, have, on the other hand, focused their efforts on economically rational behavior as an explanation of past events; institutions have been taken as given, and the 'antiquarian' interests of the more traditional historians have sometimes been scorned.[2] Perhaps because of their concern with long-run change, traditional historians have recognized that institutions do have something to do with the speed and pattern of economic growth (a relationship that was obvious to them but one that economists have only gradually perceived). Much of written history is devoted to the study of the evolution and development of political, military, and social institutions; and just as these sophisticated institutions have evolved through history, so have complex economic institutions emerged to provide a part of the framework within which a highly technical society can survive and flourish. While there are few pieces of history that do not lean heavily upon some form of theory, unfortunately, there has been little theory to help understand the phenomena of institutional change. In the absence of such theory, history is limited to narration, classification, and description. There are relatively few historians who would willingly accept such a limitation.

[1] This chapter draws heavily on the work of J. Buchanan and G. Tullock, *The Calculus of Consent* (Ann Arbor, Mich., 1962); K. Arrow, 'Political and Economic Evaluations of Social Effect and Externalities', paper given at the NBER Conference on the Economics of Public Output, April 1968; and A. Downs, *An Economic Theory of Democracy* (New York, 1957).

[2] For a discussion of the 'new' economic history, its method, proponents, and critics, see either L. Davis, 'And It Will Never Be Literature', *Explorations in Economic History*, 2nd ser., vol. 6, Fall 1968, or R. Fogel, 'The New Economic History: Its Findings and Methods', *Economic History Review*, December 1968.

The theory developed

If the historian's explanation of the process of economic development has been less insightful than one might wish, a substantial part of the blame must rest on the set of blueprints of the causal structure that the economists have provided. The best of the historian's work has all too often been rooted not in sound logical deductions from explicit premises but in brilliant historical intuition. This triumph of intuition over mathematics rests not on the blind refusal of the historian to kneel at the altar of science, but on the fact that the theories that he might have used have been poorly specified, totally irrelevant, and, at times, marked by errors in logic. Until 'better' theories are created, no one can blame him for depending on the intuition that has served him so well in the past.

It is unlikely, however, that these theories will spring full-grown from the forehead of some ivory-towered theorist. It is more probable that theories capable of predicting the future and explaining the past will emerge in bits and pieces from some interaction between the theorist who worries about logic and the historian concerned with explaining the past. In his search for a theory that explains the process of economic evolution, the scholar must continually move from theory to fact and back again to theory.

This book is a 'day-by-day' account of an intellectual journey through American economic history. The journey was planned to provide a description of the processes that have produced the present structure of economic institutions. That description, in turn, is the basis for a first (and very primitive) attempt at the formulation of a specified, relevant, and logical theory of the birth, growth, mutation, and, perhaps, death of these institutions. The book is a study of the sources of institutional change in American history. It is specifically concerned with the relationship between economic organization and economic growth, but it is no more than a preliminary study. The theory is at some points woefully weak and the explanations at times incredibly simplistic. The book does, however, represent a first step towards a useful theory of economic growth, and it does provide some new interpretations of the American economic experience.

Since the book is written for historians (as well as economists), it may be well to digress briefly on the role of models and theories in the writing of history. Although it is technically inaccurate to do so, for simplicity's sake we will use the words 'model' and 'theory' interchangeably. They will both refer to a logical structure that relates a set of assumptions to a certain set of conclusions. In economics, it is initially assumed that a firm attempts to maximize its profits and that it is constrained in its production possibilities by a combination of its technological capabilities and existing resources, and in its sales opportunities by certain market conditions. From these assumptions it follows that if it pays a firm to produce at all, it will choose to

4

A theory of institutional change

operate at a level that will return the greatest possible profit – i.e. where the difference between total revenue and total cost is the greatest. This assertion is only a logical deduction, and like any such conclusion it has predictive or explanatory power in the real world only if, in addition to being logically valid, its initial conditions are met. It is under these circumstances that the theory is said to be 'operational'. If, for example, we were attempting to explain the production decision of a Soviet firm whose goals were the maximization of output, rather than profit, the theory would not be very useful.

Even if the theory is conjoined with a relevant set of initial conditions and is in principle operational, the historian must realize that the 'laws' (i.e. predictive or explanatory statements) that can be derived from the theory are probabilistic, not mechanical. In the same way that a physicist cannot predict the behavior of an individual sub-atomic particle but is quite able to predict the average behavior of large groups of such particles, the economic theorist can predict the behavior of typical firms and consumers but cannot make meaningful predictions about the behavior of single decision-making units.

If the model is to be completely useful, ideally it ought to be able to predict two kinds of things:

(1) Given any established set of institutions and some disequilibrating force, the model ought to predict whether the newly emerging institutions will be purely individual (i.e. involve only a single decision maker), depend upon some form of voluntary cooperation, or rely on the coercive power of government.

(2) It should provide some estimate of the period of time that is likely to elapse between the initiating disequilibrium and the establishment of the new (or mutated) institutions.

In the remainder of Part One (Chapters 1–4), we attempt to spell out the model and the initial condition in their simplest form. In Part Two (Chapters 5–10), the model is applied to a number of facets of the American economy, and its ability to explain institutional developments in those sectors is evaluated. In the final part (Chapters 11–12), we summarize the impact that institutional innovation has had on the public–private mix and attempt to reformulate the model along the lines suggested by the experience of Part Two. This particular form of exposition was chosen to make it easier for the reader to follow the argument, as well as to show him why the modifications were important.

This book, then, attempts to specify a theory of institutional change and to apply that theory to certain facets of American development. It is hoped that the theory will contribute to our understanding of that process and that

5

The theory developed

such an experiment might make it possible to modify the model so that in the future it can be used to explain change in certain non-economic institutions and in certain non-American environments. The model has been formulated in a manner that makes it in principle operational, although, like many models in the social sciences, it predicts much less than we would like. As our narrative unfolds it will become increasingly clear that the model yields particularly poor results: when the potential gains and losses are large and relatively equal, but received and/or incurred by different groups; when the predictions involve a mixed result – an institution that is not purely public or purely private; when the fundamental legal and social rules that govern economic and political behavior are altered by the 'predicted' changes in the institutional structure. Despite these qualifications and limitations, we argue that the exercise is worthwhile. It focuses attention on the need for some theory of institutional change if we are ever to have a useful theory of economic growth; and, even in its present crude form, the model has, we feel, allowed us to take a new and productive look at certain aspects of the American historical experience.

(II) Some definitions

While Humpty Dumpty was obviously correct when he said, 'When I use a word it means just what I choose it to mean', Alice also had a point when she complained that words should not mean so many different things. In deference to Alice, it seems appropriate to define some terms as we intend to use them in the remainder of this study and to draw some distinctions between concepts that are sometimes lumped together.

(1) The *institutional environment* is the set of fundamental political, social, and legal ground rules that establishes the basis for production, exchange, and distribution. Rules governing elections, property rights, and the right of contract are examples of the type of ground rules that make up the economic environment. In the American economy, the environment is established by: a written document, the Constitution, and the interpretations that the judiciary have placed on it in decisions dating back to the earliest years of the Republic; and the views of the nation's citizens about the type of institutions that they prefer.[1]

The environment can, of course, be altered. In the context of the American

---

[1] In other countries the environment is set in other ways and different rules for amendment apply. In the United Kingdom, for example, there is no written constitution, and court decisions alone establish the rules of the game. In a totalitarian country, the rules are established by political fiat and altered by decree. We distinguish between fundamental legal ground rules and other types of legislation. The former we treat as exogenous; the latter as endogenous. However, we admit that the line between the two is not always clear cut, and to that extent the analysis contains an element of ambiguity.

A theory of institutional change

legal structure such changes can come from an amendment to the Constitution either by political action or a change in judicial interpretation, or from a shift in citizens' preferences. Thus, for example, property rights were fundamentally altered both by the Thirteenth Amendment and by the court decision in the case of *Ogden* v. *Saunders*. Similarly, election rules have been changed both by constitutional amendment (the Fifteenth, for example) and by judicial reinterpretation. (The twin decisions in *Baker* v. *Carr* and *Reynolds* v. *Sims* are cases in point.) In this study we make no attempt to explain changes in the economic environment. Such changes have certainly occurred and any study of their causes would be interesting. They are, however, exogenous to this model of institutional innovation.[1]

(2) An *institutional arrangement* is an arrangement between economic units that govern the ways in which these units can cooperate and/or compete. The institutional arrangement is probably the closest counterpart of the most popular use of the term 'institution'. The arrangement may be either a formal or an informal one, and it may be temporary or long-lived. It must, however, be designed to accomplish *at least one* of the following goals: to provide a structure within which its members can cooperate to obtain some added income that is not available outside that structure; or to provide a mechanism that can effect a change in laws or property rights designed to alter the permissible ways that individuals (or groups) can legally compete.

The laws legalizing the corporation provide an example of an institutional arrangement that is designed to accomplish both of these ends. The corporate form provides an organizational structure that makes it possible for management to control a much larger and more diverse set of economic activities than could be effectively directed within a more primitive organizational form; and it gives the organization itself legal life. A business so constituted can, therefore, compete in areas that are closed to other types of organizations.

The arrangement may involve a single individual, a group of individuals voluntarily cooperating together, or the government (alone or in cooperation with one or more individuals). The last mentioned innovation frequently implies some legal change, but the first two, while resting on the legal structure that constitutes the environment, involve only the private sector directly; and it is possible that innovation could occur without a change in the law.[2] It is the process of innovation of these institutional arrangements

---

[1] A survey of changes in the environment is presented in Chapter 4.

[2] The government can act, for example, through executive fiat (as the President did in ordering black employment in the defense industries) and in these cases one might say no legal change has occurred.

7

The theory developed

that the model of 'institutional change' is designed to predict – specifically it is designed to predict their level (individual, voluntary cooperative, or governmental) and the timing of their emergence.

(3) A *primary action group* is a decision-making unit whose decisions govern the process of arrangemental innovation. The unit may be a single individual or a group of individuals, but it is the action group that recognizes there exists some income – income that their members are not presently receiving – that *they* could accrue, if only they could alter the arrangemental structure. At least one member of any primary action group is an innovating entrepreneur in the Schumpeterian sense, and within the context of this model the group initiates the process of arrangemental innovation. The action group always increases its income if its innovation survives the test of competition. The group pays a portion of the innovation costs, but it may or may not have to bear all or part of the operating costs of the new arrangement (if, in fact, there are operating costs).

The New York manufacturers who informally banded together in 1811 to lobby for the passage of a general incorporation law provide an example of a successful primary action group. They saw that income could be earned if easy incorporation were possible, they paid the costs involved in pushing the revised law through the legislature, and they reaped the profits from their innovation.[1]

(4) A *secondary action group* is a decision-making unit that has been established by some change in the institutional arrangement to help effect the capture of income for the primary action group. The secondary action group makes some of the tactical decisions that bring about the capture, but it does not accrue all of the additional income (it may, in fact, quite likely accrue none).

If the New York law had established the office of Commissioner of Corporations charged with the task of receiving, reviewing, and approving applications for corporate charters, the commissioner (together with his staff) would have constituted a secondary action group. In the normal course of events the secondary action group might accrue none of the income arising from the innovation, but if the law granted them some discretionary powers, they might be able to effect a transfer of a portion of that extra income from the primary action group to themselves. If one wishes, it is possible to view the American tradition of bribing public officials as an arrangement

---

[1] Although the history is not clear, it is possible that the lobbyists might have effected an even more profitable innovation had they been able to convince the legislature to pass a *temporary* general incorporation law. However, the costs of such an arrangement may have been prohibitive either because of the legislative response or because of the rules laid out in the institutional environment.

8

A theory of institutional change

designed to redistribute income between primary and secondary action groups.

(5) *Institutional instruments* are documents or devices employed by action groups to effect the capture of income external to the existing arrangemental structures when those instruments are applied within the new arrangemental structure. The corporate charter granted to a manufacturing company under the New York general incorporation act is an example of an institutional instrument.

The arrangement, if it is a governmental one, will directly involve the coercive power of government; if it is a voluntary one, it may have underlying it the coercive power of an existing structure of property rights. The effectiveness of the instruments may depend on some fundamental legal concept that is part of the economic environment. An officer of a corporation may sign a contract and in so doing effect a decision to buy a machine. While the contract once signed can be enforced in the courts, the enforcement power does not rest with the institutional arrangement, but depends upon some fundamental constitutional rule.

In an attempt to make the reader more familiar with these definitions, consider for a moment the case of a factory that produces smog as well as products. The smoke is part of the production process; it would be costly to eradicate it, but the people living near the factory find it very disagreeable. Assume that the real cost to them of the smoke (as measured by the amount they would be willing to pay to eliminate it) is greater than the cost the factory owner would have to incur if he were to install a smog control device. Clearly total income could be increased if the smog were eliminated; however, it may well be that there is no way the bargain can be effected within the existing institutional arrangement (where the costs of the smoke accrue to one group, the costs of elimination to another). This problem is typical of those faced by residents of most every city in the United States, and often it appears that some type of government institution should be innovated to effect the smoke abatement.[1] At least two alternatives are open to those who seek the additional income. They could band together to form a political coalition (a *primary action group*), and, if successful at the polls, they (or their representatives) could enact a law (an *institutional arrangement*) that prohibited the factory from emitting smoke. Alternatively the successful political coalition could underwrite legislation establishing a zoning board (a *secondary action group*), and that board could, in turn, issue a cease and

---

[1] The explanation for the choice of government as opposed to some other form of institution is the thrust of the argument in the next three chapters. Here for simplicity we merely assume that that choice is 'best' in some sense.

9

The theory developed

desist order against excessive air pollution.[1] The cease and desist order is an *institutional instrument* backed by the coercive power of the government. Either plan, however, depends on an *economic environment* within which it is possible by political action to abrogate certain of the 'rights of private property'. If the fundamental rules of society prohibited such interference (as in fact they did in the United States until the late nineteenth century), either arrangement (and its complement of instruments and secondary action groups) would be ruled out unless (or until) the rules were changed.

(III) A theory of institutional innovation: a first approximation

Economic institutions and property rights are assigned distinct and constant values in most economic models, but in the study of long-term economic growth, these values are always subject to fundamental change. We postulate that economic institutions are innovated or property rights are revised because it appears desirable for individuals or groups to undertake the costs of such changes; they hope to capture some profit which is unattainable under the old arrangement.

An institutional arrangement will be innovated if the expected net gains exceed the expected costs.[2] Only when this condition is met would we expect to find attempts being made to alter the existing structure of institutions and property rights within a society. For example, if production can be carried on more cheaply by large firms than small, it may be cheaper for a corporation to operate than for a sole proprietorship; if prices differ widely between two markets, it may be profitable to organize a third market to move goods from the low-priced to the high-priced market; if theft and brigandage are widespread, the creation of an efficient police force will raise the value of private property. If an entrepreneur contemplates the construction of a dam designed to produce hydroelectric power that also reduces flood damage downstream, the builder might appropriate a share of these benefits by the prior purchase of some of the downstream property. On the other hand, he might appeal to government to impose a tax on the downstream beneficiaries to help subsidize his construction costs.

As to form, arrangements can range from purely voluntary to totally government controlled and operated. Between these extremes exists a wide

---

[1] Alternatively they could band together to pay off the factory owner. As we shall see, the alternative of choice depends, like the choice between government and private arrangement, on the costs incurred and the revenues accruing to each.

[2] To avoid confusion we will use the term 'innovation' to refer to any change in the institutional technology embodied in an institutional arrangement and the term '*new innovation*' to the first such application.

A theory of institutional change

variety of semi-voluntary, semi-government structures. Voluntary arrangements are simply cooperative arrangements between consenting individuals, and any individual can legally withdraw.[1] This ability implies, of course, that decisions must be unanimous, as the costs of acceding to the decisions are less than those incurred by withdrawal. Government arrangements, on the other hand, do not provide the withdrawal option. Action, therefore, does not require unanimous consent but only conformity with some decision rule.[2] In a democracy, for example, a simple majority frequently determines the course of action.

Both voluntary and government arrangements have been innovated to realize economies of scale, gains from transaction costs, internalization of externalities, the reduction of risk, and the redistribution of income.[3] For example, the corporation has aided the realization of the benefits of the economies of scale sometimes inherent in large-scale operations, and the TVA has yielded similar benefits from power generation and distribution. The stock exchange is an example of a voluntary arrangement whose innovation has reduced transaction costs, and an insurance company is an example of a voluntary arrangement designed to reduce risk. At the same time government employment exchanges and the Federal Deposit Insurance Corporation are examples of parallel government innovations. The Union Pacific's development of Sun Valley, Idaho – a development that turned a primitive area into a major resort – is an example of a voluntary cooperative group effectively capturing the externalities associated with the development of a complex of diverse economic activities. The enactment of a zoning ordinance, a government solution, might be aimed at the same goals in an already established community.[4] Trade unions and the American Medical

[1] We recognize that the costs of withdrawal from both voluntary and government arrangements can vary from zero to infinity (i.e. death of the withdrawing individual). Typically, however, the costs of withdrawal from voluntary organizations have been substantially lower than from government ones. Therefore, for purposes of simplicity in exposition, we have followed Buchanan and Tullock in assuming that voluntary organizations abide by unanimity rule and the cost of withdrawal is zero, whereas government arrangements abide by some political decision rule and do not permit withdrawal.

[2] In line with the argument in footnote 1 above, since emigration is always an alternative, withdrawal from governmental decisions are possible, but the larger is the area of sovereignty, the higher are the costs.

[3] These sources of reorganizational profits are spelled out in detail in Section IV of this chapter.

[4] In William Baumol's *Welfare Economics and the Theory of the State*, 2nd ed. (Cambridge Mass., 1968), he explores the rise of government as the method by which externalities may be internalized in a society. But in his second edition he acknowledges the point developed by Buchanan and Tullock in *Calculus of Consent*; it may be equally possible to internalize externalities, in many cases, through the use of voluntary organization as well as via government.

The theory developed

Association are examples of voluntary arrangements designed to redistribute income. Tariff laws and the progressive income tax are governmental illustrations. What factors underlie the choice between individual, voluntary cooperative, and government arrangements?

The choice rests upon the benefits and costs of each, and on the relative market and non-market power of the affected groups. There are neither organization nor coercive costs associated with individual arrangements, but the revenues are limited to only those that can accrue to an individual. There are organizational costs in the innovation of both the other types of arrangement. In voluntary and in democratic governmental arrangements, the total costs of organization tend to rise with the number of participants.[1] However, in the former case, the need for unanimity may further increase the organizational costs. Given the same number of participants, the organizational costs may be lower for government arrangements than for voluntary arrangements; however, there is an additional element of cost inherent in government arrangements. Each participant is subject to the coercive power of government, and no matter how much he may dislike the government-imposed solution, he may not withdraw.[2] It is possible, however, that a government-imposed solution may yield higher revenues, as a government can utilize its coercive power and impose a solution that might not be achieved by any voluntary bargain.

(IV) The sources of external gains

Let us now be more specific about the sources of gains which could induce people to strive toward changes in their institutional arrangements. In theory there are many outside events that can lead to the generation of profits which, given the existing state of economic arrangements, remain unharvested. We refer to such gains as 'external profits'. In this book we shall limit our analysis to only four: (A) economies of scale, (B) externalities, (C) risk, and (D) transaction costs, since they appear to have played the most important role in American development. If an arrangemental innovation can successfully internalize these profits, then total income is increased, and it is possible that the innovator can gain without anyone having lost.

(A) *Economies of scale*

Economies of scale in production are a technological phenomenon and reflect the fact that the most efficient (lowest cost per unit) output may entail a size

---

[1] In the case of totalitarian institutions, the organization's costs may not rise proportionately, but political and policing costs may be quite high.
[2] The costs and benefits of voluntary organization versus the use of government are discussed in detail in Buchanan and Tullock, *Calculus of Consent*, Chapter 6.

A theory of institutional change

of firm so large that it requires more complex organization than the single proprietor or partnership type of firm can underwrite.

In the jargon of the economist, a firm is faced at any moment in time by a technological constraint. To the layman, this statement need mean no more than given any state of the arts, limits are set by the existing technology on the ways inputs can be combined to form output. The economist's short-hand for the technical relationship between physical inputs and outputs is the term 'production function', an expression often written:

$$O = P(L, K, T)$$

where O refers to output and L, K and T to Labor, Capital and Land. P refers to the technical function that governs the transformation of those inputs into output. There are no *a priori* constraints on the form of this relation; thus it is possible that a doubling of all inputs might lead to less than a doubling of output, exactly a doubling of output, or more than a doubling of output. If the former holds, the production function is said to be subject to *decreasing returns* to scale (it takes more and more inputs to produce equal changes in output); if the second condition holds, it is said to be subject to *constant returns* to scale; and in the last condition, to *increasing returns* to scale (you need fewer inputs to produce an extra unit of output at high levels of production than at low levels). Moreover, since the relationship is unconstrained, it may be subject to increasing returns with regard to some part or range of the output, constant returns over another, and decreasing returns over yet a third. In particular, if the process requires investment in a large and complex plant that must be erected on an all or nothing basis, one might expect increasing returns until the capacity of that plant is reached, at which time decreasing returns set in.

For example, the petroleum refining industry in the 1850s was character-ized by something close to constant returns to scale. All that was required to operate was a still (basically a copper boiler and several hundred feet of tubing). Small firms had one still and larger firms more than one, but costs per unit of output were not a function of the size of the operation. Over the next two decades, however, a new technology was innovated, and this technology was subject to increasing returns over a wide range of outputs. The new techniques required very heavy investment in a sophisticated refining plant. That plant, in turn, could produce a large volume of refined petroleum much more cheaply than under the old technology, but the entire plant was needed (i.e. it was 'indivisible') even if the output were very small. As a result, large firms could produce much more cheaply than small, and there was great pressure for small firms to adopt the new technology, increase their size, and capture the profits inherent in the lower costs of

13

The theory developed

production. Most efficient firm size and the number of firms in the industry were, of course, a function of the technology and the relevant market size.

If all firms had equal access to capital and knowledge, there would be no way of predicting which firms would grow and which would die. In the real world, however, capital is not equally available to all firms. The firm's own organizational form may well be the determining factor in the supply of capital available to it. Since both sole proprietorships and partnerships are characterized by limited life and unlimited liability, the supply of long-term external finance available to such firms is frequently quite restricted. Equity finance tends to be scarce because of the unlimited liability attached to such investments; and debt finance, because the enterprise may die (with its owner) while the capital still has a portion of its life remaining. The latter constraint becomes more binding the more specific is the capital[1]. The innovation of the corporation with its unlimited life and limited liability lifts the restrictions on obtaining capital and therefore allows its innovators to reap the profits inherent in the economies of scale.

In terms of the American experience, the last third of the nineteenth century was marked by the development of a number of manufacturing technologies which required large-scale production in order to obtain the lowest per unit cost. At the same time, the limited supply of capital available to the traditional single owner or partnership firm prevented the expansion of these types of organizations into the large-scale firm which was a prerequisite to the utilization of the new technologies. Thus technology made it more economical to produce on a very large scale, but the unavailability of capital to enterprises organized in traditional fashion prevented them from attaining those 'efficient' levels of production. The corporation had access to capital and was able to take full advantage of scale economies; its innovation permitted the capture of the external profits existing in the new technology.

(B) *Externalities – changes in external costs and revenues*[2]

Traditional micro economic theory can be used to explore the relationship between some exogenous event (i.e. an event external to the theory), the reaction to some manifestation of that event by a decision-making unit, and

---

[1] If the finance is invested in capital for which there is a ready market, the problems exist but their effect is minimized. If, however, the capital has no market, the demise of the owner may signal the default of the loan.

[2] In a recent article that appeared after most of this manuscript had been completed, Stephen Cheung suggests that there be substituted for the term externalities, the degree to which a contract is inclusive of all potential gains and costs to the transacting parties.

14

A theory of institutional change

the ultimate reestablishment of an equilibrium position as the system adjusts to the new decision. Within the structure of a free enterprise system, for example, a change in consumer tastes (an exogenous change) may result in an increase in demand for some commodity. A businessman (a decision-making unit) notes the higher prices that result and in an attempt to increase his profits responds by increasing his output. The result of the rise in demand, therefore, has been an increase in the quantity of the commodity supplied – that increase followed from the recognition by the businessman that the increase in demand gave him a chance to make more profits if he responded in the correct manner. The search for profits, then, provides the drive that pushes the economy towards a new equilibrium.

The system works less well if the potential profits (or the costs of the expansion in output) are not received (or borne) by the unit that makes the output decision. The term 'externality' refers to the fact that some costs or revenues are external to the decision-making unit. Whenever these external costs and revenues exist it is possible that unaided the market may not yield the most·efficient result. If such is the case, some new institutional arrangement that does permit a counting of all costs and revenues (both private and external; i.e. social) would increase the total net revenue accruing to society.

Every homeowner realizes that the value of his property reflects not only his own building, upkeep, and improvement decisions, but those of his neighbors as well. In fact, these 'neighborhood' effects are the basis for community improvement drives, for anti-litter laws, and for the profit potential in 'block busting' in areas undergoing racial integration. What every homeowner may not realize is that these neighborhood effects are only one example of a large class of 'externalities' and that institutional reorganization can increase total income when other types of externalities are present in the same way that a community improvement drive (an institutional innovation) can increase the value of everyone's home.

Leaving economics for a moment, consider the following situation: A college professor finds that his research output is closely linked with his ability to interact with his secretary. Although she is hired only to type manuscripts, it becomes clear that her contribution is far in excess of the number of pages pushed through the typewriter. In this case, since a part of the research process lies outside of the control of the decision maker, an externality exists. Since the secretary bears no additional costs because of

---

This may be a useful alternative, but it appeared too late to permit us to change our terminology. Moreover, our terminology is in line with the economists' traditional vocabulary. See Stephen Cheung, 'The Structure of a Contract and the Theory of a Non-Exclusive Resource', *The Journal of Law and Economics*, 13, no. 1, 49–70.

The theory developed

her extra contribution (her costs may be negative if she views interacting as more fun than typing), no problems are raised and the system operates as it should.[1] A problem does arise if the secretary's husband becomes jealous and tells her to quit her job. The costs (a jealous husband to face each evening) are borne by the secretary while the revenues (fame in the profession, promotion, and salary increases) accrue to the professor. Faced by her dis-equilibrating resignation, the proper response should be an offer of an in-creased salary (a bribe), and if she accepts, the external costs have been internalized (i.e. assumed by the decision-making unit), and production – albeit higher cost production – continues. The new equilibrium is Pareto efficient. If the highest bribe that the professor can afford is less than the costs she incurs by remaining on the job, the production will cease, but the result will still be Pareto efficient. If, however, something in the existing institutional arrangement makes it impossible to pay the bribe – a bribe that the professor can afford and that if paid would be sufficient to keep her on the job – then the result will not be efficient. Such a situation might occur if, for example, university regulations forbad personal payments between employees or if the scandal engendered by such side payments would cause the professor to lose his job. In these circumstances some institutional arrangement would be necessary if the external profits are again to be realized, and it is the analysis of the processes through which these rearrange-ments are invented and innovated that constitute an important part of the subject matter of this book.[2]

Externalities in production exist whenever the firm making the production decision does not bear all the costs inherent in the decision or whenever it is unable to accrue all the revenues from selling the output that results from that decision. Similarly, consumption externalities exist whenever the utility of the consuming unit depends not only on that unit's consumption but on the consumption of some other unit as well.[3] In each case the pro-duction or consumption decision will have been made without a full assess-ment of the relevant costs and revenues. As a result the decision may not be Pareto efficient (that is, it might be possible to make a different decision that would make at least one person better off without making anyone worse off). To better describe the potential source of profits from reorganization, let us examine a few examples of externalities.

[1] An economist would call it Pareto efficient, which is nothing but a fancy word for a situation that cannot be altered to make someone better off without making anyone worse off.

[2] The rearrangement could take the form of out-of-office interacting or, perhaps, a suitable bribe might make the husband 'less jealous'.

[3] Utility is a word that economists use to refer to a measure of consumer satisfaction or well being. The greater the utility derived from any commodity the greater the satisfaction.

A theory of institutional change

Returning to the manufacturing plant that produced not only its saleable output, but a large volume of black noxious smoke as well, assume that the volume of the smoke increases as output rises. Moreover, assume that while the smoke is not poisonous, people would prefer to breathe clean rather than polluted air.[1] Since, by assumption, the utility of everyone who breathes the smoke is adversely affected, this reduction in utility is certainly a part of the *total* cost of the firm's production. In addition, since people prefer less smoke to more smoke, that element of cost rises as the firm's output increases. The utility reduction, however, is a cost item that, while real, is not borne by the firm, and it is, therefore, not included in the calculations undertaken to determine the firm's most profitable level of output. Since the firm will choose an output level that maximizes its profits, the failure to include a cost item that increases as output rises will cause the firm to choose an output level greater than the one they would have selected had they been forced to consider all costs. Some reorganization that would induce the firm to include all relevant costs in its calculations would increase total revenues accruing to all of society (although it might reduce those accruing to the firm), and it would pay those who now bear the cost of the smoke to innovate some new institution that would induce the manufacturing plant to include all cost items in its profit calculations.

Although it is always possible that a private side market will develop which will make it possible for some group to capture the potential external profit (i.e. to 'internalize' the profit), at times the costs of such private innovations are prohibitive. In this case, the reorganization is likely to occur outside the market – through the interposition of government. When the institutional rearrangement involves some political action, there are no longer any guarantees that the new arrangement is superior to the old. It may just be different.

In the case of the factory, if the plant had not already been built, it would be possible for the owners to buy all of the surrounding land and sell it at costs low enough to compensate for the loss of utility. The firm, by absorbing the differential in land prices, is forced to bear the cost of its smoke-generating activities. If, however, property rights are already vested, the solution becomes more complicated. On the one hand, the company might attempt to bribe the landowners to put up with the smoke. If production is dependent upon agreement, though, each property holder has a potential veto, and is therefore in a position to demand all the increase in income. Since *every* landowner has this potential veto, any time there is more than

[1] This preference is, of course, only an assumption. If people are indifferent, there is no difference, and if they prefer smoke to clean air, they will be better off and we are back to our 'interacting is more fun than typing' example.

17

The theory developed

one affected property holder the sum of the demands for possible profit exceeds the total profits available for distribution. Under these conditions, it is unlikely that any agreement could be reached – at least not without a long delay. On the other hand, if the law permits a firm to pollute the air, the property owners might join together to bribe the firm to desist or reduce its pollution. Since, however, it is impossible for the plant to reduce the pollution over some pieces of property but not over all, it would pay each potential member of the coalition to stay outside and get a 'free ride' from the payments of the others. Once again, it is likely that agreement would be impossible or at least long delayed.

When exclusion is difficult or when any potential member of a coalition has a potential monopoly veto, it is costly to organize the private side markets needed to effectively internalize the externalities. If these conditions do not exist, however, private reorganization is possible. In the case of employee training, it might be possible for the firm to tie training to some contractual obligation, but this solution is not without cost and may not be very effective. The reader should not forget that reorganization, although potentially profitable, must also be viewed as a resource-using activity. In this case, for example, contracts must be written and then they must be enforced.

Such costs often make private reorganization uneconomic. In these cases, it is common to turn to the government's coercive powers to effect an institutional rearrangement. In the case of the factory, strict zoning laws prohibiting pollution may be passed. In the case of labor training, the educational system may be socialized or an appeal may be made to courts to enjoin employees from taking their skills to competitive firms. Finally, in the case of the army and fire protection, the functions tend to be socialized and their costs spread throughout the body politic.

Nowhere, however, in these government solutions is there any guarantee that the resulting reorganization, although certainly profitable from someone's point of view, will be Pareto superior to the old.[1] Instead, they may make someone better off only by making someone else worse off. The zoning board's decision to prohibit smoke may be as far, if not farther, from an optimal solution as was the firm's original decision; the existence of a socialized educational system does not necessarily lead towards an optimal output of that product.[2]

Institutional reorganization aimed at internalizing externalities can,

---

[1] An economist would say that *A* is Pareto superior to *B* if a move from *B* to *A* would make someone better off and no one worse off.

[2] Certainly not all voluntary cooperative solutions lead to Pareto superior results either – in fact, in the redistributive case we will find many examples of arrangemental innovation that make someone better off only at the cost of making someone worse off.

18

A theory of institutional change

therefore, increase total revenues to society, but it can also reduce them. This fact should be kept in mind throughout this entire analysis.

(C) *Overcoming risk aversion*

The prevalence of risk – the inability to be certain of terms on which future transactions can be made – is yet another factor that curtails economic activity.

We may assert that most persons are risk averters. In the absence of risk aversion, an individual would be as willing to risk a dollar for a possible return of a million if the odds were a million to one as he would to risk a dollar for a potential profit of a dollar when the outcome is certain. In fact, with the exception of the very poor, most people appear to prefer the certain to the uncertain outcome for large gambles. If, as appears likely, risk aversion becomes stronger as the odds increase, its presence tends further to bias activities toward those with more certain outcomes and away from those marked by a high variance of returns. Clearly, since the expected value of the profits is higher in the high variance activities that are not being undertaken than in the low variance activities that are, total profits could be increased if some mechanism could overcome the tendency towards risk aversion (i.e. by concentrating the risk among those who are not averters), or make risky outcomes appear more certain in regards to the income to be obtained. The former types of solutions are usually achieved through the development of some speculative side market (and are considered in this section under 'Market Failures'), but the latter can often be achieved through insurance.

Not all risks are insurable, but when they are, institutional reorganization aimed at innovating insurance schemes can frequently permit an increase in total profits. For insurance to be successful, however, there must be some basis on which to assess the risks accurately, and the insurance base must be broad enough to permit that the risks be spread. Moreover, the insurance cannot be so complete that all management risks are removed since such insurance would, by dulling management decisions, undercut the very basis on which the insurance was written. After all, if the only cost of a poor management decision is that profits are collected from the insurance company rather than from the customer, there is little incentive to make good decisions.

Insurance schemes can be intra-firm, but more often innovation produces firms specialized in supplying the requisite insurance. To be effective, however, someone must first be able to assess the risks. Thus, while the idea of life insurance dates back into the seventeenth century, it was almost the middle of the nineteenth before it was successfully innovated in the United

The theory developed

States. Innovation, in this case, awaited the construction of an adequate mortality table – the basis for risk assessment. Even then, however, firms refused to sell insurance in the South because for that subset of the population they did not have an adequate basis for rate making. Second, the insurance base must be large enough to adequately spread the risk. In the late nineteenth and early twentieth centuries, for example, a number of states passed bank insurance laws designed to protect depositors from bank failure.[1] Unfortunately, the plans were innovated in farm states where the primary cause of bank failure was bad weather. Since the weather tended to be region-wide, the state unit was insufficiently broad to provide the necessary insurance base (all banks tended to get into trouble at the same time), and the schemes were universal failures. Thirty years later, the innovation of a similar scheme with a nation-wide base (the Federal Deposit Insurance Corporation) made the insurance plan viable.

Insurance from the effects of fluctuations in the price of a single security is the characteristic of the services offered potential investors by a wide range of financial institutions. The goal of 'diversification' so revered in investment textbooks is nothing but a technical term for insurance. A diversified portfolio implies that an institution has invested in a wide range of activities and while not insured against general business failure (as the experience of the 1930s proved), is protected against individual (or even industry-wide) failure.

American development has been marked by the growth of a large number of firms specializing in some phase of insurance, and almost certainly these innovations have increased total revenues. They have not, however, been cost-free. There are organizational costs, there are costs in assessing risk, and there are costs in effecting the insurance contract. Despite these costs, innovation was still profitable.

(D) *Market failures and improvements in imperfect markets*

The implications of positive transaction costs have only recently been extensively explored by economists. The organization and improvement of the flow of relevant economic information (one of many types of transaction costs) has probably been the major area of arrangemental innovation. If

[1] Although the schemes were partly politically motivated, there was an economic rationale as well. It was hoped that by increasing the certainty of the returns from bank deposits it would be possible to increase the total volume of savings. While insurance would reduce the expected value of the return (the schemes were not cost-free) they would also reduce the variance. Insofar as the depositors were both risk averters and willing to save more at higher rates of interest, the reduction in variance could have increased the volume of deposits.

20

A theory of institutional change

there were no costs to acquiring information, then prices in all markets would differ only by transport costs. In fact, information is costly and the widespread existence of purely local markets reflects in good part simply a lack of information about profitable trading opportunities in more distant areas. As information about prices in distant regions becomes available, merchants will send their products to markets where net price differentials (i.e. adjusted for transport costs) are highest.

Economists are wont to assume that all markets are perfect, and this assumption, by definition, rules out any possible potential profits arising from the failure of markets to operate. In the real world, however, information is not cost-free, and therefore, perfect markets (whose existence depends on perfect knowledge) do not exist. The lower the cost of information, of course, the better markets will operate. Even in developed countries they are far from perfect, and in an underdeveloped country the costs of information may be so high that the markets do not operate at all.

In general, not only is information costly, but it is subject to increasing returns. That is, one must frequently pay for information, but the cost does not change much whether that information is used to effect one, one hundred, or one thousand transactions. If information costs are substantial and if they are subject to decreasing costs, it is likely that substantial profits are to be earned from increasing information flows that reduce uncertainty. The arrangemental innovation that is most economical will likely be a specialized firm capable not only of supplying the information but also of achieving the potential economies of scale.

While there is no logical reason to assume that the high cost of information might not lead to market failure even if the market deals only with a single location and a single time period, the fact is that market failure most often occurs when the markets must reach across spatial or temporal barriers. In the absence of an adequate information network (and other things being equal) the discounts that entrepreneurs put on potential income because of the uncertainty tend to be higher the farther the potential buyer is (either in time or space) from the location of the transaction. In fact, these uncertainty discounts may be so high that the discounted equilibrium price may be below zero and the markets not operate at all.

Spatial or industrial relocation of economic activity involves the establishment of new markets for inputs and outputs. Most economic literature on foreign trade (where it has long been recognized that the world is characterized by more than one market for each commodity) tends to assume that only transport costs prevent complete intermarket arbitrage.[1] Thus, it is

---

[1] Arbitrage is another piece of economist's shorthand. To the uninitiated let it be said that it merely refers to the purchase of goods in a market with lower prices and their resale

The theory developed

frequently argued that price differences between two markets for the same commodity can never exceed the cost of transporting that commodity from the lower to the higher priced market.

Such a formulation, since it implicitly assumes that potential arbitragers exist and that they know with certainty the prices prevailing in each market and the potential transport routes between the markets, is largely irrelevant to a discussion of the process of economic growth. Historical experience suggests that the lower the level of economic development in any country and the newer the relevant markets, the less are such assumptions justified and the greater are the uncertainty discounts the potential arbitrager will make. Moreover, since different individuals stand in different relation to the markets, one would not expect that the same uncertainty discounts would be applied by all. Thus, it might be possible that discounts are so high no arbitrage takes place (the case of market failure); or, if an individual arbitrager's resources are limited, partial arbitrage may reduce the intermarket price differentials, but these differentials may still exceed transportation costs.

Given the fact that there are certain indivisibilities in search costs, that markets lack complete information flows, and that different people are differently situated in relation to those markets, one would expect the level of uncertainty to differ markedly between individuals. Thus one might expect a person located closer either spatially or geographically to the new markets to be more willing to engage in some arbitrage relation. Such was clearly the case in United States development. In the case of capital, for example, persons with specific knowledge of the West frequently were willing to lend in that area when others were not; similarly, men connected with the iron industry were more ready to lend to the incipient steel industry than were the bankers and the other more 'traditional' sources of loan finance. Thus it is possible that for some persons the uncertainty discounts are low enough that they recognize the potential benefits from arbitrage, although they themselves cannot move enough goods or factors to completely arbitrage the markets.

If such imperfect markets exist, it is possible that some institutional

---

in a market with higher prices. The result is to assure that the price of the same commodity in two different markets will never differ by more than the cost of transport between them. At the same time it is also possible to conduct arbitrage transactions between two markets that are temporally separated. In this case arbitrage will prevent prices from differing by more than interest and storage costs. If the prices should diverge by more than that amount (and if transaction costs are zero) then it will pay someone to engage in arbitrage. Needless to say, any legal barrier that prohibits (or interferes with) the arbitrage transactions can lead to 'overly large' intermarket price differentials. Here, however, we are considering the effect of certain transaction costs (e.g. uncertainty discounts) that have traditionally been ignored.

A theory of institutional change

rearrangement can set them to operating more easily, and such an innovation can increase total income by permitting the movement of inputs and commodities to the market in which they receive the highest return. For example, while it pays no individual to accumulate up-to-date information on investment opportunities in some far distant place if he only wishes to invest a small amount, it does pay a brokerage house to make that expenditure since the costs can be spread over a large number of transactions. Again, a market service can provide price information from many markets to a large number of customers at very low cost, but any attempt by an individual shipper to get that information for himself would probably be prohibitively expensive.

Although the empirical problems are probably less and the implications for economic development fewer, many of the same problems that arose in the process of arbitrage between markets that are spatially removed appear also in contracts that have a time dimension. Just as prices in a market a distance away tend to be heavily discounted in the absence of information, so are similar uncertainty discounts applied to prices of future transactions. Moreover, as institutional changes can reduce the effective spatial distance between buyers and sellers, so a different set of institutions can reduce the temporal distance.

Total income can be increased by moving goods spatially to the activities of greatest return; similarly, resources can be redistributed through time to increase the stream of output or satisfaction. In the latter case, however, goods are not moved physically, but are redistributed between competitive activities today to achieve the alteration in the flow of output through time. For example, assume a businessman has the option of investing in a steel mill or of consuming some stock of resources. The investment is a long-term one, and he will compare the present value of that investment with the satisfaction he can achieve through present consumption. The present value of the mill, however, depends in part on his expectations about the prices he will receive in the future for his steel. Since the future is uncertain, he will tend to discount his price expectations, and, if the degree of uncertainty is high, the discounts, too, will be large. As a result, he may choose not to invest even though the 'expected value' of his price expectations might suggest that the investment was a profitable one (once again we find an example of the bias introduced by risk aversion). In theory, however, the innovation of a side market (in this case a market for future steel) could reduce his uncertainty (at least that relating to future steel prices) and he might find the investment a viable one. For such a market to develop, however, it is necessary that someone (a nonrisk averter) be willing to assume the uncertainty and that the uncertainty itself can be assessed with some

23

The theory developed

reliability.[1] That such a market has not grown up suggests that it is un-profitable to innovate a side market; but the question of why it is unprof-itable remains an interesting one.[2]

While future markets for steel have not developed, such markets do appear in other intertemporal transactions. In both the securities and the agri-cultural commodities markets, side markets have evolved to overcome some of the problems of intertemporal market failure. In both cases the markets are essentially short term (and in this way they avoid the classic uncertainty of long-term transactions) and in both cases they depend on the existence of a class of speculators willing to take the uncertain side in the intertemporal transaction. The speculators are persons whose aversion to risk is less than the average and/or who specialize in speculative transactions and are able, therefore, to effect these intermarket exchanges at lower costs than the farmers or stock holders, just as a miller who specializes in flour milling can grind wheat more cheaply than the farmer who grows the grain. In the case of wheat futures, for example, a mill may want to function solely as production and sales units and to insulate its profits from the vagaries of the future price of wheat. Thus, its management will buy wheat for delivery in the future at the present price of future wheat. The 'speculator', on the other hand, will gamble that future wheat prices will be below the present quotation, and that the deliveries he contracts to make can be purchased at this lower price. The market, then, merely concentrates the risk in the hands of those who are willing to assume it, and those that are not, pay some 'certain' charge for the service.

The fact that markets have not developed in other areas suggests that the uncertainties in these transactions are subject to such large discounts that no one is willing to offer the risk-bearing service at a price the risk averters are willing to pay. Temporal uncertainties, like spatial uncertainty discounts, however, are partly a function of information costs. One may, therefore, expect that cheaper information would reduce uncertainty and permit a side market to develop. Unless there is considerable improvement in crystal balls, however, it appears unlikely that improvements in intertemporal mar-kets will be as substantial as they have been in the spatial dimension. Still, the existence of futures markets in commodities and securities suggests that

---

[1] Alternatively, large inventories could be held to provide intertemporal price insurance; however, these stocks are costly.

[2] The steel example is drawn from Arrow, 'Political and Economic Evaluations'. It has been suggested that the example is not a good one, since the absence of a future market for steel may flow from the high degree of certainty about future prices that follows from the structure of the industry. This criticism may or may not be relevant but in general the Arrow point is a very good and important one.

A theory of institutional change

it is possible to improve the temporal distribution of economic activity by improvements in these side markets.

(V) Conclusion

We have seen that the innovation of a new institution can permit the capture of potential increases in income arising from externalities, economies of scale, risk and transaction costs when this income cannot be internalized within the existing institutional structure. Moreover, we have argued that the choice between levels of institutions (individual, voluntary cooperative, or governmental) is dictated by the costs and revenues associated with each alternative.

Given these potential profits, it paid someone or some group to innovate a new arrangement to capture them. In each of these cases, successful innovation caused total income to grow and in principle made it possible for no one to lose in the process.

The model that we have outlined, when more precisely specified and when conjoined with a set of initial conditions relating to the economic environment, can be used to 'explain' this process of arrangemental innovation as it occurred in the American past.

[8]

Production, Information Costs, and Economic Organization

By Armen A. Alchian and Harold Demsetz*

The mark of a capitalistic society is that resources are owned and allocated by such nongovernmental organizations as firms, households, and markets. Resource owners increase productivity through cooperative specialization and this leads to the demand for economic organizations which facilitate cooperation. When a lumber mill employs a cabinetmaker, cooperation between specialists is achieved within a firm, and when a cabinetmaker purchases wood from a lumberman, the cooperation takes place across markets (or between firms). Two important problems face a theory of economic organization—to explain the conditions that determine whether the gains from specialization and cooperative production can better be obtained within an organization like the firm, or across markets, and to explain the structure of the organization.

It is common to see the firm characterized by the power to settle issues by fiat, by authority, or by disciplinary action superior to that available in the conventional market. This is delusion. The firm does not own all its inputs. It has no power of fiat, no authority, no disciplinary action any different in the slightest degree from ordinary market contracting between any two people. I can "punish" you only by withholding future business or by seeking redress in the courts for any failure to honor our exchange agreement. That is exactly all that any employer can do. He

can fire or sue, just as I can fire my grocer by stopping purchases from him or sue him for delivering faulty products. What then is the content of the presumed power to manage and assign workers to various tasks? Exactly the same as one little consumer's power to manage and assign his grocer to various tasks. The single consumer can assign his grocer to the task of obtaining whatever the customer can induce the grocer to provide at a price acceptable to both parties. That is precisely all that an employer can do to an employee. To speak of managing, directing, or assigning workers to various tasks is a deceptive way of noting that the employer continually is involved in renegotiation of contracts on terms that must be acceptable to both parties. Telling an employee to type this letter rather than to file that document is like my telling a grocer to sell me this brand of tuna rather than that brand of bread. I have no contract to continue to purchase from the grocer and neither the employer nor the employee is bound by any contractual obligations to continue their relationship. Long-term contracts between employer and employee are not the essence of the organization we call a firm. My grocer can count on my returning day after day and purchasing his services and goods even with the prices not always marked on the goods —because I know what they are—and he adapts his activity to conform to my directions to him as to what I want each day . . . he is not my employee.

Wherein then is the relationship between a grocer and his employee different from that between a grocer and his cus-

* Professors of economics at the University of California, Los Angeles. Acknowledgment is made for financial aid from the E. Lilly Endowment, Inc. grant to UCLA for research in the behavioral effects of property rights.

tomers? It is in a *team* use of inputs and a centralized position of some party in the contractual arrangements of *all* other inputs. It is the *centralized contractual agent in a team productive process*—not some superior authoritarian directive or disciplinary power. Exactly what is a team process and why does it induce the contractual form, called the firm? These problems motivate the inquiry of this paper.

I. The Metering Problem

The economic organization through which input owners cooperate will make better use of their comparative advantages to the extent that it facilitates the payment of rewards in accord with productivity. If rewards were random, and without regard to productive effort, no incentive to productive effort would be provided by the organization; and if rewards were negatively correlated with productivity the organization would be subject to sabotage. Two key demands are placed on an economic organization—metering input productivity and metering rewards.[1]

Metering problems sometimes can be resolved well through the exchange of products across competitive markets, because in many situations markets yield a high correlation between rewards and productivity. If a farmer increases his output of wheat by 10 percent at the prevailing market price, his receipts also increase by 10 percent. This method of organizing economic activity meters the *output directly*, reveals the marginal product and apportions the *rewards* to resource owners in accord with that direct measurement of their outputs. The success of this decentralized, market exchange in promoting productive specialization requires that changes in market rewards fall

on those responsible for changes in *output*.[2]

The classic relationship in economics that runs from marginal productivity to the distribution of income implicitly *assumes* the existence of an organization, be it the market or the firm, that allocates rewards to resources in accord with their productivity. The problem of economic organization, the economical means of metering productivity and rewards, is not confronted directly in the classical analysis of production and distribution. Instead, that analysis tends to assume sufficiently economic—or zero cost—means, as if productivity automatically created its reward. We conjecture the direction of causation is the reverse—the specific sys-

---

[1] Meter means to measure and also to apportion. One can meter (measure) output and one can also meter (control) the output. We use the word to denote both; the context should indicate which.

[2] A producer's wealth would be reduced by the present capitalized value of the future income lost by loss of reputation. Reputation, i.e., credibility, is an asset, which is another way of saying that reliable information about expected performance is both a costly and a valuable good. For acts of God that interfere with contract performance, both parties have incentives to reach a settlement akin to that which would have been reached if such events had been covered by specific contingency clauses. The reason, again, is that a reputation for "honest" dealings—i.e., for actions similar to those that would probably have been reached had the contract provided this contingency—is wealth.

Almost every contract is open-ended in that many contingencies are uncovered. For example, if a fire delays production of a promised product by A to B, and if B contends that A has not fulfilled the contract, how is the dispute settled and what recompense, if any, does A grant to B? A person uninitiated in such questions may be surprised by the extent to which contracts permit either party to escape performance or to nullify the contract. In fact, it is hard to imagine any contract, which, when taken solely in terms of its stipulations, could not be evaded by one of the parties. Yet that is the ruling, viable type of contract. Why? Undoubtedly the best discussion that we have seen on this question is by Stewart Macaulay.

There are means not only of detecting or preventing cheating, but also for deciding how to allocate the losses or gains of unpredictable events or quality of items exchanged. Sales contracts contain warranties, guarantees, collateral, return privileges and penalty clauses for specific nonperformance. These are means of assignment of *risks* of losses of cheating. A lower price without warranty—an "as is" purchase—places more of the risk on the buyer while the seller buys insurance against losses of his "cheating." On the other hand, a warranty or return privilege or service contract places more risk on the seller with insurance being bought by the buyer.

tem of rewarding which is relied upon stimulates a particular productivity response. If the economic organization meters poorly, with rewards and productivity only loosely correlated, then productivity will be smaller; but if the economic organization meters well productivity will be greater. What makes metering difficult and hence induces means of economizing on metering costs?

II. Team Production

Two men jointly lift heavy cargo into trucks. Solely by observing the total weight loaded per day, it is impossible to determine each person's marginal productivity. With team production it is difficult, solely by observing total output, to either define or determine *each* individual's contribution to this output of the cooperating inputs. The output is yielded by a team, by definition, and it is not a *sum* of separable outputs of each of its members. Team production of Z involves at least two inputs, X_i and X_j, with $\partial^2 Z/\partial X_i \partial X_j \neq 0$.[3] The production function is *not* separable into two functions each involving only inputs X_i or only inputs X_j. Consequently there is no *sum* of Z of two separable functions to treat as the Z of the team production function. (An example of a *separable* case is $Z = aX_i^2 + bX_j^2$ which is separable into $Z_i = aX_i^2$ and $Z_j = bX_j^2$, and $Z = Z_i + Z_j$. This is not team production.) There exist production techniques in which the Z obtained is greater than if X_i and X_j had produced separable Z. Team production will be used if it yields an output enough larger than the sum of separable production of Z to cover the costs of organizing and disciplining team members—the topics of this paper.[4]

[3] The function is separable into additive functions if the cross partial derivative is zero, i.e., if $\partial^2 Z/\partial X_i \partial X_j = 0$.

[4] With sufficient generality of notation and conception this team production function could be formulated as a case of the generalized production function interpretation given by our colleague, E. A. Thompson.

Usual explanations of the gains from cooperative behavior rely on exchange and production in accord with the comparative advantage specialization principle with separable additive production. However, as suggested above there is a source of gain from cooperative activity involving working as a *team*, wherein individual cooperating inputs do not yield identifiable, separate products which can be *summed* to measure the total output. For this cooperative productive activity, here called "team" production, measuring *marginal* productivity and making payments in accord therewith is more expensive by an order of magnitude than for separable production functions.

Team production, to repeat, is production in which 1) several types of resources are used and 2) the product is not a sum of separable outputs of each cooperating resource. An additional factor creates a team organization problem—3) not all resources used in team production belong to one person.

We do not inquire into why all the jointly used resources are not owned by one person, but instead into the types of organization, contracts, and informational and payment procedures used among owners of teamed inputs. With respect to the one-owner case, perhaps it is sufficient merely to note that (a) slavery is prohibited, (b) one might assume risk aversion as a reason for one person's not borrowing enough to purchase all the assets or sources of services rather than renting them, and (c) the purchase-resale spread may be so large that costs of short-term ownership exceed rental costs. Our problem is viewed basically as one of organization among different people, not of the physical goods or services, however much there must be selection and choice of combination of the latter.

How can the members of a team be rewarded and induced to work efficiently?

In team production, marginal products of cooperative team members are not so directly and separably (i.e., cheaply) observable. What a team offers to the market can be taken as the marginal product of the team but not of the team members. The costs of metering or ascertaining the marginal products of the team's members is what calls forth new organizations and procedures. Clues to each input's productivity can be secured by observing *behavior* of individual inputs. When lifting cargo into the truck, how rapidly does a man move to the next piece to be loaded, how many cigarette breaks does he take, does the item being lifted tilt downward toward his side?

If detecting such behavior were costless, neither party would have an incentive to shirk, because neither could impose the cost of his shirking on the other (if their cooperation was agreed to voluntarily). But since costs must be incurred to monitor each other, each input owner will have more incentive to shirk when he works as part of a team, than if his performance could be monitored easily or if he did not work as a team. If there is a net increase in productivity available by team production, net of the metering cost associated with disciplining the team, then team production will be relied upon rather than a multitude of bilateral exchange of separable individual outputs.

Both leisure and higher income enter a person's utility function.[5] Hence, each person should adjust his work and realized reward so as to equate the marginal rate of substitution between leisure and production of real output to his marginal rate of substitution in consumption. That is, he would adjust his rate of work to bring his demand prices of leisure and output to equality with their true costs. However,

[5] More precisely: "if anything other than pecuniary income enters his utility function." Leisure stands for all nonpecuniary income for simplicity of exposition.

with detection, policing, monitoring, measuring or metering costs, each person will be induced to take more leisure, because the effect of relaxing on *his realized* (reward) rate of substitution between output and leisure will be less than the effect on the *true* rate of substitution. His realized cost of leisure will fall more than the true cost of leisure, so he "buys" more leisure (i.e., more nonpecuniary reward).

If his relaxation cannot be detected perfectly at zero cost, part of its effects will be borne by others in the team, thus making *his* realized cost of relaxation less than the true total cost to the team. The difficulty of detecting such actions permits the private costs of his actions to be less than their full costs. Since each person responds to his private realizable rate of substitution (in production) rather than the true total (i.e., social) rate, and so long as there are costs for other people to detect his shift toward relaxation, it will not pay (them) to force him to readjust completely by making him realize the true cost. Only enough efforts will be made to equate the marginal gains of detection activity with the marginal costs of detection; and that implies a lower rate of productive effort and more shirking than in a costless monitoring, or measuring, world.

In a university, the faculty use office telephones, paper, and mail for personal uses beyond strict university productivity. The university administrators could stop such practices by identifying *the* responsible person in each case, but they can do so only at higher costs than administrators are willing to incur. The extra costs of identifying each party (rather than merely identifying the presence of such activity) would exceed the savings from diminished faculty "turpitudinal peccadilloes." So the faculty is allowed some degree of "privileges, perquisites, or fringe benefits." And the total of the pecuniary wages paid is lower because of this irreducible (at acceptable costs) degree of amenity-seizing activity. Pay is lower in pecuniary terms and higher in leisure, conveniences, and ease of work. But still every person would prefer to see detection made more effective (if it were somehow possible to monitor costlessly) so that he, as part of the now more effectively producing team, could thereby realize a higher pecuniary pay and less leisure. If everyone could, at zero cost, have his reward-realized rate brought to the true production possibility real rate, all could achieve a more preferred position. But detection of the responsible parties is costly; that cost acts like a tax on work rewards.[6] Viable shirking is the result.

What forms of organizing team production will lower the cost of detecting "performance" (i.e., marginal productivity) and bring personally realized rates of substitution closer to true rates of substitution? Market competition, in principle, could monitor some team production. (It already *organizes* teams.) Input owners who are not team members can offer, in return for a smaller share of the team's rewards, to replace excessively (i.e., overpaid) shirking members. Market competition among potential team members would determine team membership and individual rewards. There would be no team leader, manager, organizer, owner, or employer. For such decentralized organizational control to work, outsiders, possibly after observing each team's total output, can speculate about their capabilities as team members and, by a market competitive process, revised teams with greater productive ability will be formed and sustained. Incumbent members will be constrained by threats of replacement by outsiders offering services for lower reward shares or offering greater rewards to the other members of the team. Any team member who shirked in the expectation that the reduced output effect would not be attributed to him will be displaced if his activity is detected. Teams of productive inputs, like business units, would evolve in apparent spontaneity in the market—without any central organizing agent, team manager, or boss.

But completely effective control cannot be expected from individualized market competition for two reasons. First, for this competition to be completely effective, new challengers for team membership must know where, and to what extent, shirking is a serious problem, i.e., know they can increase net output as compared with the inputs they replace. To the extent that this is true it is probably possible for existing fellow team members to recognize the shirking. But, by definition, the detection of shirking by observing team output is costly for team production. Secondly, assume the presence of detection costs, and assume that in order to secure a place on the team a new input owner must accept a smaller share of rewards (or a promise to produce more). Then his incentive to shirk would still be at least as great as the incentives of the inputs replaced, because he still bears less than the entire reduction in team output for which he is responsible.

III. The Classical Firm

One method of reducing shirking is for someone to specialize as a monitor to check the input performance of team members.[7]

---

[6] Do not assume that the sole result of the cost of detecting shirking is one form of payment (more leisure and less take home money). With several members of the team, each has an incentive to cheat against each other by engaging in more than the average amount of such leisure if the employer can not tell at zero cost which employee is taking more than average. As a result the total productivity of the team is lowered. Shirking detection costs thus change the form of payment and also result in lower total rewards. Because the cross partial derivatives are positive, shirking reduces other people's marginal products.

[7] What is meant by performance? Input energy, initiative, work attitude, perspiration, rate of exhaustion?

(*Continued*)

But who will monitor the monitor? One constraint on the monitor is the aforesaid market competition offered by other monitors, but for reasons already given, that is not perfectly effective. Another constraint can be imposed on the monitor: give him title to the net earnings of the team, net of payments to other inputs. If owners of cooperating inputs agree with the monitor that he is to receive any residual product above prescribed amounts (hopefully, the marginal value products of the other inputs), the monitor will have an added incentive not to shirk as a monitor. Specialization in monitoring plus reliance on a residual claimant status will reduce shirking; but additional links are needed to forge the firm of classical economic theory. How will the residual claimant monitor the other inputs?

We use the term monitor to connote several activities in addition to its disciplinary connotation. It connotes measuring output performance, apportioning rewards, observing the input behavior of inputs as means of detecting or estimating their marginal productivity and giving assignments or instructions in what to do and how to do it. (It also includes, as we shall show later, authority to terminate or revise contracts.) Perhaps the contrast between a football coach and team captain is helpful. The coach selects strategies and tactics and sends in instructions about what plays to utilize. The captain is essentially an observer and reporter of

Or output? It is the latter that is sought—the *effect* or output. But performance is nicely ambiguous because it suggests both input and output. It is *nicely* ambiguous because as we shall see, sometimes by inspecting a team member's input activity we can better judge his output effect, perhaps not with complete accuracy but better than by watching the output of the *team*. It is not always the case that watching input activity is the only or best means of detecting, measuring or monitoring output effects of each team member, but in some cases it is a useful way. For the moment the word performance glosses over these aspects and facilitates concentration on other issues.

the performance at close hand of the members. The latter is an inspector-steward and the former a supervisor manager. For the present all these activities are included in the rubric "monitoring." All these tasks are, in principle, negotiable across markets, but we are presuming that such market measurement of marginal productivities and job reassignments are not so cheaply performed for team production. And in particular our analysis suggests that it is not so much the costs of spontaneously negotiating contracts in the markets among groups for team production as it is the detection of the performance of individual members of the team that calls for the organization noted here.

The specialist *who receives the residual rewards* will be the monitor of the members of the team (i.e., will manage the use of cooperative inputs). The monitor earns his residual through the reduction in shirking that he brings about, not only by the prices that he agrees to pay the owners of the inputs, but also by observing and directing the actions or uses of these inputs. *Managing or examining the ways to which inputs are used in team production is a method of metering the marginal productivity of individual inputs to the team's output.*

To discipline team members and reduce shirking, the residual claimant must have power to revise the contract terms and incentives of *individual* members without having to terminate or alter every other input's contract. Hence, team members who seek to increase their productivity will assign to the monitor not only the residual claimant right but also the right to alter individual membership and performance on the team. Each team member, of course, can terminate his own membership (i.e., quit the team), but only the monitor may unilaterally terminate the membership of any of the

other members without necessarily ter-
minating the team itself or his association
with the team; and he alone can expand or
reduce membership, alter the mix of
membership, or sell the right to be the
residual claimant-monitor of the team. It
is this entire bundle of rights: 1) to be a
residual claimant; 2) to observe input
behavior; 3) to be the central party common to all contracts with inputs; 4) to
alter the membership of the team; and
5) to sell these rights, that defines the
ownership (or the employer) of the *classical*
(capitalist, free-enterprise) firm. The
coalescing of these rights has arisen, our
analysis asserts, because it resolves the
shirking-information problem of team
production better than does the noncen-
tralized contractual arrangement.

The relationship of each team member
to the *owner* of the firm (i.e., the party
common to all input contracts *and* the
residual claimant) is simply a "quid pro
quo" contract. Each makes a purchase
and sale. The employee "orders" the owner
of the team to pay him money in the same
sense that the employer directs the team
member to perform certain acts. The
employee can terminate the contract as
readily as can the employer, and long-
term contracts, therefore, are not an essential attribute of the firm. Nor are
"authoritarian," "dictational," or "fiat"
attributes relevant to the conception of the
firm or its efficiency.

In summary, two necessary conditions
exist for the emergence of the firm on the
prior assumption that more than pecuniary
wealth enter utility functions: 1) It is
possible to increase productivity through
team-oriented production, a production
technique for which it is costly to directly
measure the marginal outputs of the cooperating inputs. This makes it more
difficult to restrict shirking through simple
market exchange between cooperating inputs. 2) It is economical to estimate mar-

ginal productivity by observing or specifying input behavior. The simultaneous occurrence of both these preconditions leads
to the contractual organization of inputs,
known as the *classical capitalist firms* with
(a) joint input production, (b) several input owners, (c) one party who is common
to all the contracts of the joint inputs, (d)
who has rights to renegotiate any input's
contract independently of contracts with
other input owners, (e) who holds the
residual claim, and (f) who has the right
to sell his central contractual residual
status.[8]

Other Theories of the Firm

At this juncture, as an aside, we briefly
place this theory of the firm in the contexts
of those offered by Ronald Coase and
Frank Knight.[9] Our view of the firm is not
necessarily inconsistent with Coase's; we
attempt to go further and identify refut-
able implications. Coase's penetrating insight is to make more of the fact that
markets do not operate costlessly, and he
relies on the cost of using markets to *form*
contracts as his basic explanation for the
existence of firms. We do not disagree with
the proposition that, *ceteris paribus*, the
higher is the cost of transacting across
markets the greater will be the comparative advantage of organizing resources
within the firm; it is a difficult proposition
to disagree with or to refute. We could
with equal ease subscribe to a theory of
the firm based on the cost of managing,
for surely it is true that, *ceteris paribus*,
the lower is the cost of managing the
greater will be the comparative advantage
of organizing resources within the firm. To
move the theory forward, it is necessary
to know what is meant by a firm and to

[8] Removal of (b) converts a capitalist proprietary firm
to a socialist firm.

[9] Recognition must also be made to the seminal in-
quiries by Morris Silver and Richard Auster, and by
H. B. Malmgren.

explain the circumstances under which the cost of "managing" resources is low relative to the cost of allocating resources through market transaction. The conception of and rationale for the classical firm that we propose takes a step down the path pointed out by Coase toward that goal. Consideration of team production, team organization, difficulty in metering outputs, and the problem of shirking are important to our explanation but, so far as we can ascertain, not in Coase's. Coase's analysis insofar as it had heretofore been developed would suggest open-ended contracts but does not appear to imply anything more—neither the residual claimant status nor the distinction between employee and subcontractor status (nor any of the implications indicated below). And it is not true that employees are generally employed on the basis of long-term contractual arrangements any more than on a series of short-term or indefinite length contracts.

The importance of our proposed additional elements is revealed, for example, by the explanation of why the person to whom the control monitor is responsible receives the residual, and also by our later discussion of the implications about the corporation, partnerships, and profit sharing. These alternative forms for organization of the firm are difficult to resolve on the basis of market transaction costs only. Our exposition also suggests a definition of the classical firm—something crucial that was heretofore absent.

In addition, sometimes a technological development will lower the cost of market transactions while, at the same time, it expands the role of the firm. When the "putting out" system was used for weaving, inputs were organized largely through market negotiations. With the development of efficient central sources of power, it became economical to perform weaving in proximity to the power source and to engage in team production. The bringing in of weavers surely must have resulted in a reduction in the cost of negotiating (forming) contracts. Yet, what we observe is the beginning of the factory system in which inputs are organized within a firm. Why? The weavers did not simply move to a common source of power that they could tap like an electric line, purchasing power while they used their own equipment. Now team production in the joint use of equipment became more important. The measurement of marginal productivity, which now involved interactions between workers, especially through their joint use of machines, became more difficult though contract negotiating cost was reduced, while managing the *behavior* of inputs became easier because of the increased centralization of activity. The firm as an organization expanded even though the cost of transactions was reduced by the advent of centralized power. The same could be said for modern assembly lines. Hence the emergence of central power sources expanded the scope of productive activity in which the firm enjoyed a comparative advantage as an organizational form.

Some economists, following Knight, have identified the bearing of risks of wealth changes with the director or central employer without explaining why that is a viable arrangement. Presumably, the more risk-averse inputs become employees rather than owners of the classical firm. Risk averseness and uncertainty *with regard to the firm's fortunes* have little, if anything, to do with our explanation although it helps to explain why all resources in a team are not owned by one person. That is, the role of risk taken in the sense of absorbing the windfalls that buffet the firm because of unforeseen competition, technological change, or fluctuations in demand are not central to our theory, although it is true that imperfect knowledge and, therefore, risk, in *this* sense of risk, underlie the problem of monitoring team behavior. We deduce the system of paying the manager with a residual claim (the equity) from the desire to have efficient means to reduce shirking so as to make team production economical and not from the smaller aversion to the risks of enterprise in a dynamic economy. We conjecture that "distribution-of-risk" is not a valid rationale for the *existence* and organization of the *classical* firm.

Although we have emphasized team production as creating a costly metering task and have treated team production as an essential (necessary?) condition for the firm, would not other obstacles to cheap metering also call forth the same kind of contractual arrangement here denoted as a firm? For example, suppose a farmer produces wheat in an easily ascertained quantity but with subtle and difficult to detect quality variations determined by how the farmer grew the wheat. A vertical integration could allow a purchaser to control the farmer's behavior in order to more economically estimate productivity. But this is not a case of joint or team production, unless "information" can be considered part of the product. (While a good case could be made for that broader conception of production, we shall ignore it here.) Instead of forming a firm, a buyer can contract to have his inspector on the site of production, just as home builders contract with architects to supervise building contracts; that arrangement is not a firm. Still, a firm might be organized in the production of many products wherein no team production or jointness of use of separately owned resources is involved.

This possibility rather clearly indicates a broader, or complementary, approach to that which we have chosen. 1) As we do in this paper, it can be argued that the firm is the particular policing device utilized when joint team production is present. If other sources of high policing costs arise, as in the wheat case just indicated, some other form of contractual ar-

rangement will be used. Thus to each source of informational cost there may be a different type of policing and contractual arrangement. 2) On the other hand, one can say that where policing is difficult across markets, various forms of contractual arrangements are devised, but there is no reason for that known as the firm to be uniquely related or even highly correlated with team production, as defined here. It might be used equally probably and viably for other sources of high policing cost. We have not intensively analyzed other sources, and we can only note that our current and readily revisable conjecture is that 1) is valid, and has motivated us in our current endeavor. In any event, the test of the theory advanced here is to see whether the conditions we have identified are necessary for firms to have long-run viability rather than merely births with high infant mortality. Conglomerate firms or collections of separate production agencies into one owning organization can be interpreted as an investment trust or investment diversification device—probably along the lines that motivated Knight's interpretation. A holding company can be called a firm, because of the common association of the word firm with any ownership unit that owns income sources. The term firm as commonly used is so turgid of meaning that we can not hope to explain every entity to which the name is attached in common or even technical literature. Instead, we seek to identify and explain a particular contractual arrangement induced by the cost of information factors analyzed in this paper.

IV. Types of Firms

A. Profit-Sharing Firms

Explicit in our explanation of the capitalist firm is the assumption that the cost of *managing* the team's inputs by a central monitor, who disciplines himself because he is a residual claimant, is low relative to the cost of metering the marginal outputs of team members.

If we look within a firm to see who monitors—hires, fires, changes, promotes, and renegotiates—we should find him being a residual claimant or, at least, one whose pay or reward is more than any others correlated with fluctuations in the residual value of the firm. They more likely will have options or rights or bonuses than will inputs with other tasks.

An implicit "auxiliary" assumption of our explanation of the firm is that the cost of team production is increased if the residual claim is not held entirely by the central monitor. That is, we assume that if profit sharing had to be relied upon for *all* team members, losses from the resulting increase in central monitor shirking would exceed the output gains from the increased incentives of other team members not to shirk. If the optimal team size is only two owners of inputs, then an equal division of profits and losses between them will leave each with stronger incentives to reduce shirking than if the optimal team size is large, for in the latter case only a smaller percentage of the losses occasioned by the shirker will be borne by him. Incentives to shirk are positively related to the optimal size of the team under an equal profit-sharing scheme.[10]

The preceding does not imply that profit sharing is never viable. Profit sharing to encourage self-policing is more appropriate for small teams. And, indeed, where input owners are free to make whatever contractual arrangements suit them, as generally is true in capitalist economies, profit sharing seems largely limited to partnerships with a relatively small number of *active*[11] partners. Another advantage of such arrangements for smaller teams is that it permits more effective reciprocal monitoring among inputs. Monitoring need not be entirely specialized.

Profit sharing is more viable if small team size is associated with situations where the cost of specialized management of inputs is large relative to the increased productivity potential in team effort. We conjecture that the cost of managing team inputs increases if the productivity of a team member is difficult to correlate with his behavior. In "artistic" or "professional" work, watching a man's activities is not a good clue to what he is actually thinking or doing with his mind. While it is relatively easy to manage or direct the loading of trucks by a team of dock workers where input activity is so highly related in an obvious way to output, it is more difficult to manage and direct a lawyer in the preparation and presentation of a case. Dock workers can be directed in detail without the monitor himself loading the truck, and assembly line workers can be monitored by varying the speed of the assembly line, but detailed direction in the preparation of a law case would require in much greater degree that the monitor prepare the case himself. As a result, artistic or professional inputs, such as lawyers, advertising specialists, and doctors, will be given relatively freer reign with regard to individual behavior. If the management of inputs is relatively costly, or ineffective, as it would seem to be in these cases, but, nonetheless if team effort is more productive than separable production with exchange across markets, then there will develop a tendency to use profit-sharing schemes to provide incentives to avoid shirking.[12]

[10] While the degree to which residual claims are centralized will affect the size of the team, this will be only one of many factors that determine team size, so as an approximation, we can treat team size as exogenously determined. Under certain assumptions about the shape of the "typical" utility function, the incentive to avoid shirking with unequal profit-sharing can be measured by the Herfindahl index.

[11] The use of the word active will be clarified in our discussion of the corporation, which follows below.

[12] Some sharing contracts, like crop sharing, or rental

B. Socialist Firms

We have analyzed the classical proprietorship and the profit-sharing firms in the context of free association and choice of economic organization. Such organizations need not be the most viable when political constraints limit the forms of organization that can be chosen. It is one thing to have profit sharing when professional or artistic talents are used by small teams. But if political or tax or subsidy considerations induce profit-sharing techniques when these are not otherwise economically justified, then additional management techniques will be developed to help reduce the degree of shirking.

For example, most, if not all, firms in Jugoslavia are owned by the employees in the restricted sense that all share in the residual. This is true for large firms and for firms which employ nonartistic, or nonprofessional, workers as well. With a decay of political constraints, most of these firms could be expected to rely on paid wages rather than shares in the residual. This rests on our auxiliary assumption that general sharing in the residual results in losses from enhanced shirking by the monitor that exceed the gains from reduced shirking by residual-sharing employees. If this were not so, profit sharing with employees should have occurred more frequently in Western societies where such organizations are neither banned nor preferred politically. Where residual sharing by employees is politically imposed, as in Jugoslavia, we are led to expect that some management technique will arise to reduce the shirking by the central monitor, a technique that will not be found frequently in Western societies since the monitor retains all (or much) of the re-

payments based on gross sales in retail stores, come close to profit sharing. However, it is gross output sharing rather than profit sharing. We are unable to specify the implications of the difference. We refer the reader to S. N. Cheung.

sidual in the West and profit sharing is largely confined to small, professional-artistic team production situations. We do find in the larger scale residual-sharing firms in Jugoslavia that there are employee committees that can recommend (to the state) the termination of a manager's contract (veto his continuance) with the enterprise. We conjecture that the workers' committee is given the right to recommend the termination of the manager's contract precisely because the general sharing of the residual increases "excessively" the manager's incentive to shirk.[13]

C. The Corporation

All firms must initially acquire command over some resources. The corporation does so primarily by selling promises of future returns to those who (as creditors or owners) provide financial capital. In some situations resources can be acquired in advance from consumers by promises of future delivery (for example, advance sale of a proposed book). Or where the firm is a few artistic or professional persons, each can "chip in" with time and talent until the sale of services brings in revenues. For the most part, capital can be acquired more cheaply if many (risk-averse) investors contribute small portions to a large investment. The economies of raising large sums of equity capital in this way suggest that modifications in the relationship among corporate inputs are required to cope with the shirking problem

[13] Incidentally, investment activity will be changed. The inability to capitalize the investment value as "take-home" proviate property *wealth* of the members of the firm means that the benefits of the investment must be taken as annual income by those who are employed at the time of the income. Investment will be confined more to those with shorter life and with higher rates or pay-offs if the alternative of investing is paying out the firm's income to its employees to take home and use as private property. For a development of this proposition, see the papers by Eirik Furobotn and Svetozar Pejovich, and by Pejovich.

that arises with profit sharing among large numbers of corporate stockholders. One modification is limited liability, especially for firms that are large relative to a stockholder's wealth. It serves to protect stockholders from large losses no matter how they are caused.

If every stock owner participated in each decision in a corporation, not only would large bureaucratic costs be incurred, but many would shirk the task of becoming well informed on the issue to be decided, since the losses associated with unexpectedly bad decisions will be borne in large part by the many other corporate shareholders. More effective control of corporate activity is achieved for most purposes by transferring decision authority to a smaller group, whose main function is to negotiate with and manage (renegotiate with) the other inputs of the team. The corporate stockholders retain the authority to revise the membership of the management group and over major decisions that affect the structure of the corporation or its dissolution.

As a result a new modification of partnerships is induced—the right to sale of corporate shares without approval of any other stockholders. Any shareholder can remove his wealth from control by those with whom he has differences of opinion. Rather than try to control the decisions of the management, which is harder to do with many stockholders than with only a few, unrestricted salability provides a more acceptable escape to each stockholder from continued policies with which he disagrees.

Indeed, the policing of managerial shirking relies on across-market competition from new groups of would-be managers as well as competition from members within the firm who seek to displace existing management. In addition to competition from outside and inside managers, control is facilitated by the temporary

congealing of share votes into voting blocs owned by one or a few contenders. Proxy battles or stock-purchases concentrate the votes required to displace the existing management or modify managerial policies. But it is more than a change in policy that is sought by the newly formed financial interests, whether of new stockholders or not. It is the capitalization of expected future benefits into stock prices that concentrates on the innovators the wealth gains of their actions if they own large numbers of shares. Without capitalization of future benefits, there would be less incentive to incur the costs required to exert informed decisive influence on the corporation's policies and managing personnel. Temporarily, the structure of ownership is reformed, moving away from diffused ownership into decisive power blocs, and this is a transient resurgence of the classical firm with power again concentrated in those who have title to the residual.

In assessing the significance of stockholders' power it is not the usual diffusion of voting power that is significant but instead the frequency with which voting congeals into decisive changes. Even a one-man owned company may have a long term with just one manager—continuously being approved by the owner. Similarly a dispersed voting power corporation may be also characterized by a long-lived management. The question is the probability of replacement of the management if it behaves in ways not acceptable to a majority of the stockholders. The unrestricted salability of stock and the transfer of proxies enhances the probability of decisive action in the event current stockholders or any outsider believes that management is not doing a good job with the corporation. We are not comparing the corporate responsiveness to that of a single proprietorship; instead, we are indicating features of the corporate structure that are induced by the problem of

delegated authority to manager-moni-
tors.[14]

D. Mutual and Nonprofit Firms

The benefits obtained by the new management are greater if the stock can be purchased and sold, because this enables *capitalization* of anticipated future im-

provements into present *wealth* of new managers who bought stock and created a larger capital by their management changes. But in nonprofit corporations, colleges, churches, country clubs, mutual savings banks, mutual insurance companies, and "coops," the future consequences of improved management are not

---

[14] Instead of thinking of shareholders as joint *owners*, we can think of them as investors, like bondholders, except that the stockholders are more optimistic than bondholders about the enterprise prospects. Instead of buying bonds in the corporation, thus enjoying smaller risks, shareholders prefer to invest funds with a greater realizable return if the firm prospers as expected, but with smaller (possibly negative) returns if the firm performs in a manner closer to that expected by the more pessimistic investors. The pessimistic investors, in turn, regard only the bonds as likely to pay off.

If the entrepreneur-organizer is to raise capital on the best terms to him, it is to his advantage, as well as that of prospective investors, to recognize these differences in expectations. The residual claim on earnings enjoyed by shareholders does not serve the function of enhancing their efficiency as monitors in the general situation. The stockholders are "merely" the less risk-averse or the more optimistic member of the group that finances the firm. Being more optimistic than the average and seeing a higher mean value future return, they are willing to pay more for a certificate that allows them to realize gain on their expectations. One method of doing so is to buy claims to the distribution of returns that "they see" while bondholders, who are more pessimistic, purchase a claim to the distribution that they see as more likely to emerge. Stockholders are then comparable to warrant holders. They care not about the voting rights (usually not attached to warrants); they are in the same position in so far as voting rights are concerned as are bondholders. The only difference is in the probability distribution of rewards and the terms on which they can place their bets.

If we treat bondholders, preferred and convertible preferred stockholders, and common stockholders and warrant holders as simply different classes of investors—differing not only in their risk averseness but in their beliefs about the probability distribution of the firm's future earnings, why should stockholders be regarded as "owners" in any sense distinct from the other financial investors? The entrepreneur-organizer, who let us assume is the chief operating officer and sole repository of control of the corporation, does not find his authority residing in common stockholders (except in the case of a take over). Does this type of control make any difference in the way the firm is conducted? Would it make any difference in the kinds of behavior that would be tolerated by competing managers and investors (and we here deliberately refrain from thinking of them as owner-stockholders in the traditional sense)?

Investment old timers recall a significant incidence of nonvoting common stock, now prohibited in corporations whose stock is traded on listed exchanges. (Why prohibited?) The entrepreneur in those days could hold voting shares while investors held nonvoting shares, which in every other respect were identical. Nonvoting share holders were simply investors devoid of ownership connotations. The control and behavior of inside owners in such corporations has never, so far as we have ascertained, been carefully studied. For example, at the simplest level of interest, does the evidence indicate that nonvoting shareholders fared any worse because of not having voting rights? Did owners permit the nonvoting holders the normal return available to voting shareholders? Though evidence is prohibitively expensive to obtain, it is remarkable that voting and nonvoting shares sold for essentially identical prices, even during some proxy battles. However, our casual evidence deserves no more than interest-initiating weight.

One more point. The facade is deceptive. Instead of nonvoting shares, today we have warrants, convertible preferred stocks all of which are solely or partly "equity" claims without voting rights, though they could be converted into voting shares.

In sum, is it the case that the stockholder-investor relationship is one emanating from the *division* of *ownership* among several people, or is it that the collection of investment funds from people of varying anticipations is the underlying factor? If the latter, why should any of them be thought of as the owners in whom voting rights, whatever they may signify or however exercisable, should reside in order to enhance efficiency? Why voting rights in any of the outside, participating investors?

Our initial perception of this possibly significant difference in interpretation was precipitated by Henry Manne. A reading of his paper makes it clear that it is hard to understand why an investor who wishes to back and "share" in the consequences of some new business should necessarily have to acquire voting power (i.e., power to change the manager-operator) in order to invest in the venture. In fact, we invest in some ventures in the hope that no other stockholders will be so "foolish" as to try to toss out the incumbent management. We want him to have the power to stay in office, and for the prospect of sharing in his fortunes we buy nonvoting common stock. Our willingness to invest is enhanced by the knowledge that we can act legally via fraud, embezzlement and other laws to help assure that we outside investors will not be "milked" beyond our initial discounted anticipations.

capitalized into present wealth of stock-holders. (As if to make more difficult that competition by new would-be monitors, mutiple shares of ownership in those enterprises cannot be bought by one person.) One should, therefore, find greater shirking in nonprofit, mutually owned enterprises. (This suggests that nonprofit enterprises are especially appropriate in realms of endeavor where more shirking is desired and where redirected uses of the enterprise in response to market-revealed values is less desired.)

E. Partnerships

Team production in artistic or professional intellectual skills will more likely be by partnerships than other types of team production. This amounts to market-organized team activity and to a non-employer status. Self-monitoring partnerships, therefore, will be used rather than employer-employee contracts, and these organizations will be small to prevent an excessive dilution of efforts through shirking. Also, partnerships are more likely to occur among relatives or long-standing acquaintances, not necessarily because they share a common utility function, but also because each knows better the other's work characteristics and tendencies to shirk.

F. Employee Unions

Employee unions, whatever else they do, perform as monitors for employees. Employers monitor employees and similarly employees monitor an employer's performance. Are correct wages paid on time and in good currency? Usually, this is extremely easy to check. But some forms of employer performance are less easy to meter and are more subject to employer shirking. Fringe benefits often are in non-pecuniary, contingent form; medical, hospital, and accident insurance, and retirement pensions are contingent payments

or performances partly in *kind* by employers to employees. Each employee cannot judge the character of such payments as easily as money wages. Insurance is a contingent payment—what the employee will get upon the contingent event may come as a disappointment. If he could easily determine what other employees had gotten upon such contingent events he could judge more accurately the performance by the employer. He could "trust" the employer not to shirk in such fringe contingent payments, but he would prefer an effective and economic monitor of those payments. We see a specialist monitor—the union employees' agent—hired by them and monitoring those aspects of employer payment most difficult for the employees to monitor. Employees should be willing to employ a specialist monitor to administer such hard-to-detect employer performance, even though their monitor has incentives to use pension and retirement funds not entirely for the benefit of employees.

V. Team Spirit and Loyalty

Every team member would prefer a team in which no one, not even himself, shirked. Then the true marginal costs and values could be equated to achieve more preferred positions. If one could enhance a common interest in nonshirking in the guise of a team loyalty or team spirit, the team would be more efficient. In those sports where team activity is most clearly exemplified, the sense of loyalty and team spirit is most strongly urged. Obviously the team is better, with team spirit and loyalty, because of the reduced shirking—not because of some other feature inherent in loyalty or spirit as such.[15]

[15] *Sports Leagues:* Professional sports contests among teams is typically conducted by a *league* of teams. We assume that sports consumers are interested not only in absolute sporting skill but also in skills *relative* to other teams. Being slightly better than opposing teams enables one to claim a major portion of the receipts; the

Corporations and business firms try to instill a spirit of loyalty. This should not be viewed simply as a device to increase profits by *over*-working or misleading the employees, nor as an adolescent urge for belonging. It promotes a closer approximation to the employees' potentially available true rates of substitution between production and leisure and enables each team member to achieve a more preferred

inferior team does not release resources and reduce costs, since they were expected in the play of contest. Hence, absolute skill is developed beyond the equality of marginal investment in sporting skill with its true social marginal value product. It follows there will be a tendency to overinvest in training athletes and developing teams. "Reverse shirking" arises, as budding players are induced to overpractice hyperactively relative to the social marginal value of their enhanced skills. To prevent overinvestment, the teams seek an agreement with each other to restrict practice, size of teams, and even pay of the team members (which reduces incentives of young people to overinvest in developing skills). Ideally, if all the contestant teams were owned by one owner, overinvestment in sports would be avoided, much as ownership of common fisheries or underground oil or water reserve would prevent overinvestment. This hyperactivity (to suggest the opposite of shirking) is controlled by the league of teams, wherein the league adopts a common set of constraints on each team's behavior. In effect, the teams are no longer really owned by the team owners but are supervised by them, much as the franchisers of some product. They are not full-fledged owners of their business, including the brand name, and can not "do what they wish" as franchises. Comparable to the franchiser, is the league commissioner or conference president, who seeks to restrain hyperactivity, as individual team supervisors compete with each other and cause external diseconomies. Such restraints are usually regarded as anticompetitive, antisocial, collusive-cartel devices to restrain free open competition, and reduce players' salaries. However, the interpretation presented here is premised on an attempt to avoid hyperinvestment in team sports production. Of course, the team operators have an incentive, once the league is formed and restraints are placed on hyperinvestment activity, to go further and obtain the private benefits of monopoly restriction. To what extent overinvestment is replaced by monopoly restriction is not yet determinable; nor have we seen an empirical test of these two competing, but mutually consistent interpretations. (This interpretation of league-sports activity was proposed by Earl Thompson and formulated by Michael Canes.) Again, athletic teams clearly exemplify the specialization of monitoring with captains and coaches; a captain detects shirkers while the coach trains and selects strategies and tactics. Both functions may be centralized in one person.

situation. The difficulty, of course, is to create economically that team spirit and loyalty. It can be preached with an aura of moral code of conduct—a morality with literally the same basis as the ten commandments—to restrict our conduct toward what we would choose if we bore our full costs.

VI. Kinds of Inputs Owned by the Firm

To this point the discussion has examined why firms, as we have defined them, exist? That is, why is there an owner-employer who is the common party to contracts with other owners of inputs in team activity? The answer to that question should also indicate the kind of the jointly used resources likely to be owned by the central-owner-monitor and the kind likely to be hired from people who are not team-owners. Can we identify characteristics or features of various inputs that lead to their being hired or to their being owned by the firm?

How can residual-claimant, central-employer-owner demonstrate ability to pay the other hired inputs the promised amount in the event of a loss? He can pay in advance or he can commit wealth sufficient to cover negative residuals. The latter will take the form of machines, land, buildings, or raw materials committed to the firm. Commitments of labor-wealth (i.e., human wealth) given the property rights in people, is less feasible. These considerations suggest that · residual claimants—owners of the firm—will be investors of resalable capital equipment in the firm. The goods or inputs more likely to be invested, than rented, by the owners of the enterprise, will have higher resale values relative to the initial cost and will have longer expected use in a firm relative to the economic life of the good.

But beyond these factors are those developed above to explain the existence of the institution known as the firm—the costs of detecting output performance. When a durable resource is used it will have a marginal product and a depreciation. Its use requires payment to cover at least use-induced depreciation; unless that user cost is specifically detectable, payment for it will be demanded in accord with *expected* depreciation. And we can ascertain circumstances for each. An indestructible hammer with a readily detectable marginal product has zero user cost. But suppose the hammer were destructible and that careless (which is easier than careful) use is more abusive and causes greater depreciation of the hammer. Suppose in addition the abuse is easier to detect by observing the way it is used than by observing only the hammer after its use, or by measuring the output scored from a hammer by a laborer. If the hammer were rented and used in the absence of the owner, the depreciation would be greater than if the use were observed by the owner and the user charged in accord with the imposed depreciation. (Careless use is more likely than careful use—if one does not pay for the greater depreciation.) An absentee owner would therefore ask for a higher rental price because of the higher *expected* user cost than if the item were used by the owner. The expectation is higher because of the greater difficulty of observing specific user cost, by inspection of the hammer after use. Renting is therefore in this case more costly than owner use. This is the valid content of the misleading expressions about ownership being more economical than renting—ignoring all other factors that may work in the opposite direction, like tax provision, short-term occupancy and capital risk avoidance.

Better examples are tools of the trade. Watch repairers, engineers, and carpenters tend to own their own tools especially if

they are portable. Trucks are more likely to be employee owned rather than other equally expensive team inputs because it is relatively cheap for the driver to police the care taken in using a truck. Policing the use of trucks by a nondriver owner is more likely to occur for trucks that are not specialized to one driver, like public transit busses.

The factor with which we are concerned here is one related to the costs of monitoring not only the gross product performance of an input but also the abuse or depreciation inflicted on the input in the course of its use. If depreciation or user cost is more cheaply detected when the owner can see its use than by only seeing the input before and after, there is a force toward owner use rather than renting. Resources whose user cost is harder to detect when used by someone else, tend on this count to be owner-used. Absentee ownership, in the lay language, will be less likely. Assume momentarily that labor service cannot be performed in the absence of its owner. The labor owner can more cheaply monitor any abuse of himself than if somehow labor-services could be provided without the labor owner observing its mode of use or knowing what was happening. Also his incentive to abuse himself is increased if he does not own himself.[16]

[16] Professional athletes in baseball, football, and basketball, where athletes having sold their source of service to the team owners upon entering into sports activity, are owned by team owners. Here the team owners must monitor the athletes' physical condition and behavior to protect the team owners' wealth. The athlete has *less* (not, *no*) incentive to protect or enhance his athletic prowess since capital value changes have less impact on his own wealth and more on the team owners. Thus, some athletes sign up for big initial bonuses (representing present capital value of future services). Future salaries are lower by the annuity value of the prepaid "bonus" and hence the athlete has *less* to lose by subsequent abuse of his athletic prowess. Any decline in his subsequent service value would in part be borne by the team owner who owns the players' future service. This does not say these losses of future salaries have no effect on preservation of athletic talent (we are not making a "sunk cost" error). Instead, we assert that the

The similarity between the preceding analysis and the question of absentee landlordism and of sharecropping arrangements is no accident. The same factors which explain the contractual arrangements known as a firm help to explain the incidence of tenancy, labor hiring or sharecropping.[17]

VII. Firms as a Specialized Market Institution for Collecting, Collating, and Selling Input Information

The firm serves as a highly specialized surrogate market. Any person contemplating a joint-input activity must search and detect the qualities of available joint inputs. He could contact an employment agency, but that agency in a small town would have little advantage over a large firm with many inputs. The employer, by virtue of monitoring many inputs, acquires special superior information about their productive talents. This aids his *directive* (i.e., market hiring) efficiency. He "sells" his information to employee-inputs as he aids them in ascertaining good input combinations for team activity. Those who work as employees or who rent services to him are using him to discern superior combinations of inputs. Not only

does the director-employer "decide" what each input will produce, he also estimates which heterogeneous inputs will work together jointly more efficiently, and he does this in the context of a privately owned market for forming teams. The department store is a firm and is a superior private market. People who shop and work in one town can as well shop and work in a privately owned firm.

This marketing function is obscured in the theoretical literature by the assumption of homogeneous factors. Or it is tacitly left for individuals to do themselves via personal market search, much as if a person had to search without benefit of specialist retailers. Whether or not the firm arose because of this efficient information service, it gives the director-employer more knowledge about the productive talents of the team's inputs, and a basis for superior decisions about efficient or profitable combinations of those heterogeneous resources.

In other words, opportunities for profitable team production by inputs already within the firm may be ascertained more economically and accurately than for resources outside the firm. Superior combinations of inputs can be more economically identified and formed from resources already used in the organization than by obtaining new resources (and knowledge of them) from the outside. Promotion and revision of employee assignments (contracts) will be preferred by a firm to the hiring of new inputs. To the extent that this occurs there is reason to expect the firm to be able to operate as a conglomerate rather than persist in producing a single product. Efficient production with heterogeneous resources is a result not of having *better* resources but in *knowing more accurately* the relative productive performances of those resources. Poorer resources can be paid less in accord with their inferiority; greater accuracy of

---

preservation is reduced, not eliminated, because the amount of loss of wealth suffered is smaller. The athlete will spend less to maintain or enhance his prowess thereafter. The effect of this revised incentive system is evidenced in comparisons of the kinds of attention and care imposed on the athletes at the "expense of the team owner" in the case where atheletes' future servies are owned by the team owner with that where future labor service values are owned by the athlete himself. Why athletes' future athletic services are owned by the team owners rather than being hired is a question we should be able to answer. One presumption is cartelization and monopsony gains to team owners. Another is exactly the theory being expounded in this paper—costs of monitoring production of athletes; we know not on which to rely.

[17] The analysis used by Cheung in explaining the prevalence of sharecropping and land tenancy arrangements is built squarely on the same factors—the costs of detecting output performance of jointly used inputs in team production and the costs of detecting user costs imposed on the various inputs if owner used or if rented.

knowledge of the potential and actual productive actions of inputs rather than having high productivity resources makes a firm (or an assignment of inputs) profitable.[18]

VIII. Summary

While ordinary contracts facilitate efficient specialization according to comparative advantage, a special class of contracts among a group of joint inputs to a team production process is commonly used for team production. Instead of multilateral contracts among all the joint inputs' owners, a central common party to a set of bilateral contracts facilitates efficient organization of the joint inguts in team production. The terms of the contracts form the basis of the entity called the firm—especially appropriate for organizing team production processes.

Team productive activity is that in which a union, or joint use, of inputs yields a larger output than the sum of the products of the separately used inputs. This

[18] According to our interpretation, the firm is a specialized surrogate for a market for team use of inputs; it provides superior (i.e., cheaper) collection and collation of knowledge about heterogeneous resources. The greater the set of inputs about which knowledge of performance is being collated within a firm the greater are the present costs of the collation activity. Then, the larger the firm (market) the greater the attenuation of monitor control. To counter this force, the firm will be divisionalized in ways that economize on those costs— just as will the market be specialized. So far as we can ascertain, other theories of the reasons for firms have no such implications.

In Japan, employees by custom work nearly their entire lives with one firm, and the firm agrees to that expectation. Firms will tend to be large and conglomerate to enable a broader scope of input revision. Each firm is, in effect, a small economy engaging in "intranational and international" trade. Analogously, Americans expect to spend their whole lives in the United States, and the bigger the country, in terms of variety of resources, the easier it is to adjust to changing tastes and circumstances. Japan, with its lifetime employees, should be characterized more by large, conglomerate firms. Presumably, at some size of the firm, specialized knowledge about inputs becomes as expensive to transmit across divisions of the firms as it does across markets to other firms.

team production requires—like all other production processes—an assessment of marginal productivities if efficient production is to be achieved. Nonseparability of the products of several differently owned joint inputs raises the cost of assessing the marginal productivities of those resources or services of each input owner. Monitoring or metering the productivities to match marginal productivities to costs of inputs and thereby to reduce shirking can be achieved more economically (than by across market bilateral negotiations among inputs) in a firm.

The essence of the classical firm is identified here as a contractual structure with: 1) joint input production; 2) several input owners; 3) one party who is common to all the contracts of the joint inputs; 4) who has rights to renegotiate any input's contract independently of contracts with other input owners; 5) who holds the residual claim; and 6) who has the right to sell his central contractual residual status. The central agent is called the firm's owner and the employer. No authoritarian control is involved; the arrangement is simply a contractual structure subject to continuous renegotiation with the central agent. The contractual structure arises as a means of enhancing efficient organization of team production. In particular, the ability to detect shirking among owners of jointly used inputs in team production is enhanced (detection costs are reduced) by this arrangement and the discipline (by revision of contracts) of input owners is made more economic.

Testable implications are suggested by the analysis of different types of organizations—nonprofit, proprietary for profit, unions, cooperatives, partnerships, and by the kinds of inputs that tend to be owned by the firm in contrast to those employed by the firm.

We conclude with a highly conjectural

but possibly significant interpretation. As a consequence of the flow of information to the central party (employer), the firm takes on the characteristic of an efficient market in that information about the productive characteristics of a large set of specific inputs is now more cheaply available. Better recombinations or new uses of resources can be more efficiently ascertained than by the conventional search through the general market. In this sense inputs compete with each other within and via a firm rather than solely across markets as conventionally conceived. Emphasis on interfirm competition obscures intrafirm competition among inputs. Conceiving competition as the *revelation and exchange* of knowledge or information about qualities, potential uses of different inputs in different potential applications indicates that the firm is a device for enchancing competition among sets of input resources as well as a device for more efficiently rewarding the inputs. In contrast to markets and cities which can be viewed as publicly or nonowned market places, the firm can be considered a privately owned market; if so, we could consider the firm and the ordinary market as competing types of markets, competition between private proprietary markets and public or communal markets. Could it be that the market suffers from the defects of communal property rights in organizing and influencing uses of valuable resources?

REFERENCES

M. Canes, "A Model of a Sports League," unpublished doctoral dissertation, UCLA 1970.

S. N. Cheung, *The Theory of Share Tenancy*, Chicago 1969.

R. H. Coase, "The Nature of the Firm," *Economica*, Nov. 1937, *4*, 386–405; reprinted in G. J. Stigler and K. Boulding, eds., *Readings in Price Theory*, Homewood 1952, 331–51.

E. Furobotn and S. Pejovich, "Property Rights and the Behavior of the Firm in a Socialist State," *Zeitschrift für Nationalökonomie*, 1970, *30*, 431–454.

F. H. Knight, *Risk, Uncertainty and Profit*, New York 1965.

S. Macaulay, "Non-Contractual Relations in Business: A Preliminary Study," *Amer. Sociological Rev.*, 1968, *28*, 55–69.

H. B. Malmgren, "Information, Expectations and the Theory of the Firm," *Quart J. Econ.*, Aug. 1961, *75*, 399–421.

H. Manne, "Our Two Corporation Systems: Law and Economics," *Virginia Law Rev.*, Mar. 1967, *53*, No. 2, 259–84.

S. Pejovich, "The Firm, Monetary Policy and Property Rights in a Planned Economy," *Western Econ. J.*, Sept. 1969, *7*, 193–200.

M. Silver and R. Auster, "Entrepreneurship, Profit, and the Limits on Firm Size," *J. Bus. Univ. Chicago*, Apr. 1969, *42*, 277–81.

E. A. Thompson, "Nonpecuniary Rewards and the Aggregate Production Function," *Rev. Econ. Statist.*, Nov. 1970, *52*, 395–404.

[9]

THE FABLE OF THE BEES: AN ECONOMIC INVESTIGATION*

STEVEN N. S. CHEUNG
University of Washington

> Economists possess their full share of the common ability to invent and commit errors. . . . Perhaps their most common error is to believe other economists.
>
> GEORGE J. STIGLER

EVER since A. C. Pigou wrote his books on "welfare,"[1] a divergence between private and social costs has provided the main argument for instituting government action to correct allegedly inefficient market activities. The analysis in such cases has been designed less to aid our understanding of how the economic system operates than to find flaws in it to justify policy recommendations. Both to illustrate the argument and to demonstrate the nature of the actual situation, the quest has been for real-world examples of such defects.

Surprisingly enough, aside from Pigou's polluting factory and Sidgwick's lighthouse, convincing examples were hard to come by.[2] It was not until 1952, more than thirty years after Pigou's initial analysis, that J. E. Meade proposed further examples and revitalized the argument for corrective govern-

* Facts, like jade, are not only costly to obtain but also difficult to authenticate. I am therefore most grateful to the following beekeepers and farmers: Leonard Almquist, Nat Giacomini, Ancel Goolsbey, L. W. Groves, Rex Haueter, Harold Lange, Lavar Peterson, Elwood Sires, Clarence Smith, Ken Smith, John Steg, P. F. Thurber, and Mrs. Gerald Weddle. All of them provided me with valuable information; some of them made available to me their accounting records and contracts. R. H. Coase inspired the investigation, Yoram Barzel saw that it was conducted thoroughly, and Mrs. Lina Tong rendered her assistance. The investigation is part of a proposed research in the general area of contracts, financially supported by the National Science Foundation.

[1] A. C. Pigou, Wealth and Welfare (1912); and The Economics of Welfare (1920).

[2] Pigou had offered other examples. The example of two roads was deleted from later editions of The Economics of Welfare, presumably in an attempt to avoid the criticism by F. H. Knight in Some Fallacies in the Interpretation of Social Cost, 38 Q. J. Econ. 582 (1924). The railroad example has not enjoyed popularity. Most of Pigou's examples, however, were drawn from land tenure arrangements in agriculture, but an exhaustive check of his source references has revealed no hard evidence at all to support his claim of inefficient tenure arrangements.

ment actions.[3] Meade's prime example, which soon became classic, concerned the case of the apple farmer and the beekeeper. In his own words:

> Suppose that in a given region there is a certain amount of apple-growing and a certain amount of bee-keeping and that the bees feed on the apple blossom. If the apple-farmers apply 10% more labour, land and capital to apple-farming they will increase the output of apples by 10%; but they will also provide more food for the bees. On the other hand, the bee-keepers will not increase the output of honey by 10% by increasing the amount of land, labour and capital to bee-keeping by 10% unless at the same time the apple-farmers also increase their output and so the food of the bees by 10%. . . . We call this a case of an unpaid factor, because the situation is due simply and solely to the fact that the apple-farmer cannot charge the beekeeper for the bees' food. . . .[4]

And Meade applied a similar argument to a reciprocal situation:

> While the apples may provide the food of the bees, the bees may fertilize the apples. . . . By a process similar to that adopted in the previous case we can obtain formulae to show what subsidies and taxes must be imposed. . . .[5]

In another well-known work, Francis M. Bator used Meade's example to infer "market failure":

> It is easy to show that if apple blossoms have a positive effect on honey production . . . any Pareto-efficient solution . . . will associate with apple blossoms a positive Lagrangean shadow-price. If, then, apple producers are unable to protect their equity in apple-nectar and markets do not impute to apple blossoms their correct shadow value, profit-maximizing decisions will fail correctly to allocate resources . . . at the margin. There will be failure "by enforcement." This is what I would call an *ownership* externality.[6]

It is easy to understand why the "apples and bees" example has enjoyed widespread popularity. It has freshness and charm: the pastoral scene, with its elfin image of bees collecting nectar from apple blossoms, has captured the imagination of economists and students alike. However, the universal credence given to the lighthearted fable is surprising; for in the United States, at least, contractual arrangements between farmers and beekeepers have long been routine. This paper investigates the pricing and contractual arrangements of the beekeeping industry in the state of Washington, the location having been

---

[3] See J. E. Meade, External Economies and Diseconomies in a Competitive Situation, 52 Econ. J. 54 (1952).

[4] *Id.* at 56-57.

[5] *Id.* at 58.

[6] Francis M. Bator, The Anatomy of Market Failure, 72 Q. J. Econ. 351, 364 (1958).

selected because the Pacific Northwest is one of the largest apple-growing areas in the world.

Contrary to what most of us have thought, apple blossoms yield little or no honey.[7] But it is true that bees provide valuable pollination services for apples and other plants, and that many other plants do yield lucrative honey crops. In any event, it will be shown that the observed pricing and contractual arrangements governing nectar and pollination services are consistent with efficient allocation of resources.

I. SOME RELEVANT FACTS OF BEEKEEPING

Although various types of bees pollinate plants, beekeeping is confined almost exclusively to honeybees.[8] The hive used by beekeepers in the state of Washington is of the Langstroth design which consists of one or two brood chambers, a queen excluder, and from zero to six supers. A brood chamber is a wooden box large enough to contain eight or ten movable frames, each measuring 9-⅛ by 17-⅝ by 1-⅜ inches. Within each frame is a wax honeycomb built by the bees. In the hexagonal cells of this comb the queen lays her eggs and the young bees, or "brood," are raised. It is here also that the bees store the nectar and pollen which they use for food. Honey is not usually extracted from this chamber but from the frames of a shallower box, called a super, placed above the brood chamber. The queen excluder, placed between the super and the brood chamber, prevents the laying of eggs in the upper section.[9]

The bees, and consequently the beekeepers, work according to a yearly cycle. Around the beginning of March, a Washington beekeeper will decide whether he wants to prepare for the pollination season by ordering booster packages of bees from California to strengthen his colonies, depleted and

---

[7] The presence of apple honey in the market is therefore somewhat mysterious. While occasionally apple orchards in the Northwest do yield negligible amounts of nectar, beekeepers are frank to point out that the dandelion and other wild plants in the orchard are often the sources of "apple" honey, so called. Elsewhere, as in New York, it was reported that apple orchards yielded slightly more nectar. See, for example, A. I. & E. R. Root, The ABC and XYZ of Bee Culture 386 (1923). The explanation for this divergence of facts, to my mind, lies in the different lengths of time in which the hives are placed in the apple orchards: in Root's day the hives were probably left in the orchards for longer periods than today.

[8] See George E. Bohart, Management of Wild Bees, in U. S. Dep't of Agriculture, Beekeeping in the United States 109 (Ag. Handbook No. 335, 1971). [Hereinafter cited as Beekeeping. . .]. Leafcutters, for example, have recently been introduced for the pollination of alfalfa and clover seeds. But these bees yield no honey crop and are seldom kept.

[9] For further details see Spencer M. Riedel, Jr., Development of American Beehive, in Beekeeping. . . 8-9; A. I. & E. R. Root, *supra* note 7, at 440-58; Carl Johansen, Beekeeping (PNW Bulletin No. 79, rev. ed. March 1970).

weakened during the winter and early spring. Alternatively, he may decide to build up the colony by transporting the hives to farms or pastures in warmer areas, such as Oregon and California. The colony hatches continuously from spring to fall, and the growth rate is rapid. Reared on pollen, the infant bees remain in the brood stage for about three weeks before entering the productive life of the colony for five or six weeks. Active workers spend three weeks cleaning and repairing the brood cells and nursing the young, then live out the remainder of their short lives foraging for pollen and nectar.[10]

Because of the bees' quick growth, the working "strength" of a colony includes both brood and workers, and increases from about five frames in early spring to about twelve by late summer. Spring is the primary season for fruit pollination, and beekeepers usually market a standard colony strength of roughly four frames of bees and two to three frames of brood for pollination services. But since empty frames are needed to accommodate the expanding colony, two-story hives, with 16 or 20 frames, are used. The swarming period, beginning in mid-summer and lasting until early fall, is the peak honey season, and the yield per hive will vary positively with the colony strength. Because the maximization of honey yield requires that the colonies be of equal strength, they are usually reassorted in preparation for the major honey season, so that the number of colonies at the "peak" is generally larger than the number in spring.[11]

When pollen fails in late fall, the hives become broodless and the bee population begins to decline. During the idle winter months adult bees live considerably longer than in the active season, and they can survive the winter if about 60 pounds of nectar are left in the hive. But in the northern part of the state and in Canada, where cold weather makes the overwintering of bees more costly, the common practice is to eliminate the bees and extract the remaining honey. It should be noted here that bees can be captured, and that they can be easily eliminated by any of a large number of pesticide sprays.[12] The cost of enforcing property rights in nectar is therefore much lower than economists have been led to believe.

[10] For further details see Carl Johansen, *supra* note 9; F. E. Moeller, Managing Colonies for High Honey Yields, in Beekeeping. . . 23; E. Oertel, Nectar and Pollen Plants, in Beekeeping. . . 10.

[11] According to a survey conducted by Robert K. Lesser in 1968, based on a sample of 30 out of 60 commercial beekeepers in the state of Washington, the total number of peak colonies is 14.6% higher than that of spring colonies. See Robert K. Lesser, An Investigation of the Elements of Income from Beekeeping in the State of Washington 74 (unpublished thesis, Sch. of Bus. Admin., Gonzaga Univ., 1969).

[12] See, for example, A. I. & E. R. Root, *supra* note 9, at 97-103; Eugene Keyarts, Bee Hunting, Gleanings in Bee Culture 329-33 (June 1960); U.S. Dep't of Agriculture, Protecting Honey Bees from Pesticides (Leaflet 544, 1972); Carl A. Johansen, How to Reduce Poisoning of Bees from Pesticides (Pamphlet EM 3473, Wash. St. Univ., College of Ag., May 1971); Philip F. Torchio, Pesticides, in Beekeeping. . . 97.

Few agricultural crops, to my knowledge, exhibit a higher year-to-year variance of yield than does the honey crop. Several natural factors contribute. Cold weather and rain discourage the bees from working, and winds alter their direction of flight. Also, the nectar flows of plants are susceptible to shocks of heat and cold.[13] The plants yielding most honey are mint, fireweed, and the legumes, such as alfalfa and the clovers. Fruit trees usually have low nectar flows, although orange blossoms (in California) are excellent. Indeed, the pollination of fruits, especially the cherry in early spring, may actually detract from the yield of honey: less honey may be in the hive after pollination than was there initially, owing to the bees' own consumption. Another reason for the low honey yield from fruit trees is the relatively short time that the hives are left in the orchards.

Cross-pollination is accidentally effected as the bees forage for nectar and pollen. Pollination services were not marketed before World War I, primarily because small farms had enough flowering plants and trees to attract wild insects. It was not until 1910 and the advent of modern orcharding, with its large acreage and orderly planting, that markets for pollination services began to grow rapidly.[14] Today, the services are demanded not only for production of fruits but also for the setting (fertilizing) of seeds for legumes and vegetables. Evidence is incontrovertible that the setting of fruits and seeds increases with the number of hives per acre, that the pollination productivity of bees is subject to diminishing returns, and, despite some beekeepers' claims to the contrary, beyond some point the marginal productivity may even be negative.[15] There is also strong evidence that pollination yield will improve if the hives are placed strategically throughout the farm rather

---

[13] See E. Oertel, *supra* note 10; C. R. Ribbands, The Behaviour and Social Life of Honeybees 69-75 (1953); Roger A. Morse, Placing Bees in Apple Orchards, Gleanings in Bee Culture 230-33 (April 1960). Owing to its weather, Washington is not one of the better honey yielding states in the Union. Data made available to me by the U. S. Dep't of Agriculture indicates that over the years (1955-1971) Washington ranks 24th among 48 states in yield per colony and 20th in the total number of colonies. The U.S. Dep't of Agriculture data, like those obtained by Lesser, provide no information on the different honey yields and pollination requirements of various plants and are therefore of little use for our present purpose. It should be noted that the U.S. Dep't of Agriculture overall yield data are significantly lower than those obtained by Lesser and by me. See Robert K. Lesser, *supra* note 11.

[14] See M. D. Levin, Pollination, in Beekeeping. . . 77.

[15] *Id.*; 9th Pollination Conference, Report, The Indispensable Pollinators (Ag. Extension Serv., Hot Springs, Ark., October 12-15, 1970); G. E. Bohart, Insect Pollination of Forage Legumes, 41 Bee World 57-64, 85-97 (1960); J. B. Free, Pollination of Fruit Trees, 41 Bee World 141-51, 169-86 (1960); U.S. Dep't of Agriculture, Using Honey Bees to Pollinate Crops (Leaflet 549, 1968); Get More Fruit with Honey Bee Pollinators (Pamphlet EM 2922, Wash. St. Univ., March 1968); Protect Berry Pollinating Bees (Pamphlet EM 3341, Wash. St. Univ., February 1970); Increase Clover Seed Yields with Adequate Pollination (Pamphlet EM 3444, Wash. St. Univ., April 1971); Honey Bees Increase Cranberry Production (Pamphlet EM 3468, Wash. St. Univ., April 1971).

than set in one spot.[16] The closer a particular area is to a hive, the more effective will be the pollination within that area. Although each individual bee will forage only a few square yards, the bees from one hive will collectively pollinate a large circular area,[17] and this gives rise to a problem: given a high cost to control fully the foraging behavior of bees, if similar orchards are located close to one another, one who hires bees to pollinate his own orchard will in some degree benefit his neighbors. This complication will be further discussed in the next section.

In the state of Washington, about 60 beekeepers each own 100 colonies or more; at the peak season the state's grand total of colonies is about 90,000. My investigation, conducted in the spring of 1972, covered a sample of nine beekeepers and a total of approximately 10,000 spring colonies. (One of these beekeepers specialized in cut-comb honey and he will be treated separately in a footnote.) Table 1 lists the bee-related plants covered by my investigation. As seen from Columns (3) and (4), some plants (such as cherry trees) require pollination services for fruit setting but yield no honey; some (such as mint) yield honey while requiring no pollination service; and some (such as alfalfa) are of a reciprocal nature. Note that when alfalfa and the clovers are grown only for hay, pollination services are not required, although these plants yield honey.

The practice of relocating hives from farm to farm, by truck, enables the beekeeper to obtain multiple crops a year, either in rendering pollination service or in extracting honey. However, while the maximum observed number of crops per hive per year is four and the minimum is two, my estimate is that a hive averages only 2.2 crops a year. More frequent rotation not only involves greater costs of moving and of standardizing hives, but abbreviates the honey yield per crop. In the southern part of the state, where the relatively warm climate permits an early working season, beekeepers usually begin by pollinating either cherry or almond (in California) in early spring. The hives may or may not then be moved northward in late spring, when apple and soft fruits (and some late cherry) begin to bloom.[18]

The lease period for effective pollination during spring bloom is no more than a week. But then, for a month or two between the end of fruit pollina-

[16] See, for example, Douglas Oldershaw, The Pollination of High Bush Blueberries, in The Indispensable Pollinators, *supra* note 15, at 171-76; Roger A. Morse, *supra* note 13.

[17] There is, however, little agreement as to how far a bee could fly: estimated range is from one to three miles. For general foraging behavior, see M. D. Levin, *supra* note 14, at 79; O. W. Park, Activities of Honeybees, in The Hive and the Honeybee 125, 149-206 (Roy A. Grout ed., 1946); C. R. Ribbands, *supra* note 13.

[18] Following the practice of local beekeepers, we use the term "soft fruit" to refer to peaches, pears, and apricots, generally grown in the same area, and often in the same orchard, as apples. (By standard usage, the term refers only to the various berry plants.)

TABLE 1
BEE-RELATED PLANTS INVESTIGATED
(State of Washington, 1971)

(1) Plants	(2) Number of Beekeepers	(3) Pollination Services Rendered	(4) Surplus Honey Expected	(5) Approximate Season	(6) Number of Hives Per Acre (range)
Fruits & Nuts					
Apple & Soft Fruits[a]	7	Yes	No	Mid-April—Mid-May	0.4 to 2
Blueberry (with maple)	1	Yes	Yes	May	2
Cherry (early)	1	Yes	No	March—Early April	0.5 to 2
Cherry	2	Yes	No	April	0.5 to 2
Cranberry	2	Yes	Negligible	June	1.5
Almond (Calif.)	2	Yes	No	February—March	2
Legumes					
Alfalfa	5	Yes and No[c]	Yes	June—September	0.3 to 3
Red Clover	4	Yes and No	Yes	June—September	0.5 to 5
Sweet Clover	1	No[d]	Yes	June—September	0.5 to 1
Pasture[b]	4	No	Yes	Late May—September	0.3 to 1
Other Plants					
Cabbage	1	Yes	Yes	Early April—May	1
Fireweed	2	No	Yes	July—September	n.a.
Mint	3	No	Yes	July—September	0.4 to 1

[a] Soft fruits include pears, apricots, and peaches.
[b] Pasture includes a mixture of plants, notably the legumes and other wild flowers such as dandelions.
[c] Pollination services are rendered for alfalfa and the clovers if their seeds are intended to be harvested; when they are grown only for hay, hives will still be employed for nectar extraction.
[d] Sweet clover may also require pollination service, but such a case is not covered by this investigation.

tion and the beginning of summer nectar flow, the hives have little alternative usage. Since this period is substantially longer than the time needed for the beekeeper to check and standardize his hives for the honey crops, he will generally be in no hurry to move them and will prefer to leave them in the orchards with no extra charge, unless the farmer is planning to spray with insecticide. The appropriate seasons for the various plants listed in Column (5) of Table 1, may not, therefore, match the lengths of hive leases. Lease periods are generally longer for honey crops, for the collection of nectar takes more time.

The sixth column in Table 1 indicates the various hive-densities employed. The number of hives per acre depends upon the size of the area to be serviced, the density of planting, and, in the case of fruit pollination, the age of the orchards. For the pollination of fruits, the hives are scattered throughout the farm, usually with higher densities employed in older orchards because the trees are not strategically placed to facilitate the crossing of pollen. The most popular choices are one hive per acre and one hive per two acres. It is interesting, and easily understood, that farmers demand significantly fewer hives for pollination than the number recommended by entomologists:[19] both are interested in the maximization of yield, but for the farmer such maximization is subject to the constraint of hive rentals. When bees are employed to produce honey only, the hives are placed together in one location, called an apiary, for greater ease of handling.[20] The relatively large variation in hive densities required if legumes are, or are not, to be pollinated is discussed in the next section.

Before we turn to an analysis of the pricing and contractual behavior of beekeepers and farmers, I must point out that the two government programs which support the beekeeping industry did not constitute relevant constraints for the period under investigation. The honey price-support program, initiated in 1949, involves purchase of honey at supported prices by the Commodity Credit Corporation.[21] For the period under investigation, however, the supported price was about 20 per cent lower than the market price.[22] Section 804 of the Agricultural Act of 1970, effectuated in 1971 and designed to reimburse beekeepers for any loss due to pesticide sprays, has been largely ignored by

[19] See note 15 *supra*.

[20] See, for example, W. P. Nye, Beekeeping Regions in the United States, in Beekeeping . . . 17.

[21] See Harry A. Sullivan, Honey Price Support Program, in Beekeeping . . . 136.

[22] From 1970 to 1972 the supported prices were near 11.5 cents per pound, whereas the market wholesale price was above 14 cents per pound. Between 1950 and 1965 were seven years in which the CCC purchased no honey, and two years of negligible amounts. See Harry A. Sullivan, *supra* note 21, at 137.

beekeepers because of the difficulty of filing effective claims with the federal government.[23]

II. The Observed Pricing and Contractual Behavior

It is easy to find conclusive evidence showing that both nectar and pollination services are transacted in the marketplace: in some cities one need look no further than the yellow pages of the Telephone Directory. But the existence of prices does not in itself imply an efficient allocation of resources. It is, therefore, necessary to demonstrate the effectiveness of the market in dictating the use even of those resources—bees, nectar, and pollen—which, admittedly, are elusive in character and relatively insignificant in value. In doing so, I shall not attempt to estimate the standard sets of marginal values which an efficient market is said to equate: the burden of such a task must rest upon those who believe the government can costlessly and accurately make these estimates for the imposition of the "ideal" tax-subsidy schemes. Rather, I offer below an analysis based on the equimarginal principle. To the extent that the observed pricing and contractual behavior fails to falsify the implications derived from this analysis we conclude that (1) the observed behavior is explained, and (2) the observations are consistent with efficient allocation of resources.

A. *The Analysis*

The reciprocal situation in which a beekeeper is able to extract honey from the same farm to which he renders pollination services poses an interesting theoretic riddle. The traditional analysis of such a condition relies on some interdependent production functions, and is, I think, unnecessarily complex.[24] The method employed here simply treats pollination services and honey yield as components of a joint product generated by the hive. That is, the rental price per hive received by a beekeeper for placing his hives on a farm may be paid in terms of honey, of a money fee, or of a combination of both. The money fee or the honey yield may be either positive or negative, but their total measures the rental value of the hive.

[23] See 7 U.S.C. § 135 b, note (1970); Pub. L. No. 91-524 § 804. My judgment is based both on the behavior of beekeepers (see next section) after the initiation of the Act and on the complexity of relevant claim forms which I have at hand. In April 1972 beekeepers associations were still lobbying for easier claiming conditions.

[24] In J. E. Meade, *supra* note 3, at 58, this problem is set up in terms of the interdependent functions $x_1 = H_1 (l_1, c_1, x_2)$ and $x_2 = H_2 (l_2, c_2, x_1)$. I find Meade's analysis difficult to follow. Elsewhere, Otto A. Davis and Andrew Whinston employ the functions $C_1 = C_1 (q_1, q_2)$ and $C_2 = C_2 (q_1, q_2)$ in their treatment of certain "externalities." It is not clear, however, that the authors had the bee example in mind. See Otto A. Davis & Andrew Whinston, Externalities, Welfare, and the Theory of Games, 70 J. Pol. Econ. 241 (1962).

20   THE JOURNAL OF LAW AND ECONOMICS

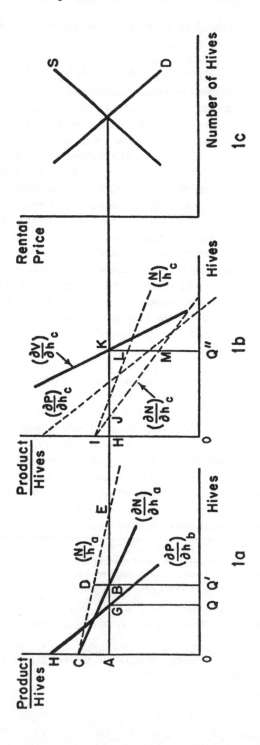

Figure I

The solution is illustrated in Figure I. We assume that the hives are always strategically placed. In Figure Ia the curve $(\partial N/\partial h)_a$ depicts the value of the marginal nectar product of a farm in which beehives are used *only* for the extraction of nectar (as with fireweed, mint, or alfalfa grown only for hay), with the farming assets held constant. Given the market-determined rental price of OA per hive, constrained wealth maximization implies that OQ′ of hives will be employed. In this case, the beekeeper will be remunerated only in honey, and will pay an *apiary rent* equal to area ABC (or DB per hive) to the farmer. The curve $(\partial P/\partial h)_b$, on the other hand, depicts the value of the marginal pollination product for a farm which employs hives for pollination *only* (as with cherry or apple orchards). Here the number of hives employed will be OQ, which again is the result of wealth maximization. With zero honey yield, the money pollination fee per hive is again OA, and the *orchard rent* is represented by the area AGH.

We now turn to the joint product case in Figure Ib, where hives are used both for pollination and for the extraction of nectar (as in the setting of alfalfa and clover seeds). The curves $(\partial P/\partial h)_c$ and $(\partial N/\partial h)_c$ respectively are the values of marginal pollination and of marginal nectar products. Their *vertical* summation, the solid line $(\partial V/\partial h)_c$, is the total marginal value. Wealth maximization implies the employment of OQ″ of hives, the point where the rental price per hive equals the aggregate marginal value. As drawn, area HIJ is smaller than area JKM. This implies that the value of the *average* nectar product, $(N/h)_c$, must pass below point K, as it does here at L. In this case the rental price per hive, KQ″, will consist of LQ″ in honey yield and KL in pollination fee. For this joint product situation, of course, it is possible to construct a case in which $(N/h)_c$ passes above point K, thus yielding an apiary rent. It is also possible to construct cases where the number of hives employed yields zero or negative marginal productivity, in either nectar or pollination. In other words, *zero or negative marginal productivity in one component of the joint product is consistent with efficient allocation of resources*.

Under open competition, there are large numbers of potential participants in each of the cases above. The aggregate total marginal value curve for the market, or the market demand for hives, is therefore the horizontal summation of a large number of the *solid* curves in Figures Ia and Ib. Similarly, the market supply of hives is the horizontal summation of the marginal costs of producing and keeping hives of all actual and potential beekeepers. Both market curves are shown in Figure Ic.[25] Assuming no costs for collating bids

[25] More variables are usually used in the derivation of these curves, but for our present purpose little is gained by incorporating them.

and asks or for forming rental contracts among all actual and potential participants, the price per hive, OA, is determined in the market. The Pareto condition is satisfied: the value of the marginal product of a hive is the same
on every farm, and in turn equals the rental price and the marginal opportunity cost of producing the hive.

B. Tests of Implications

Before we derive and test some implications of the above analysis, it is
necessary to point out the limitations of the information at hand. Since no
attempt is made to estimate the marginal values or the elasticities of the
marginal products, we will seek to confirm the marginal equalities with some
observed average values. These include apiary rent, pollination fees, honey
yields per hive, and the wholesale price of honey. We also have information
on the number of hives employed on different farms, and some other numerical data. My choice of data for the honey yield per hive, however, must be
qualified. The large fluctuations in yield from year to year and even from
farm to farm caused by uncontrollable natural phenomena makes the use
of the actual observed yields of a particular year, or even of a few years,
irrelevant for our purposes. Take, for example, the exceptionally poor
year of 1971 when, in many cases, the yield per hive was just one-third of
that in a normal year. This windfall loss is irrelevant for decision-making
(although the expected variance is relevant), and it cannot be attributed to
market "failure." Lacking sufficient data to compute the honey yield per
hive extracted from various plants over time, I resort to the expected
yields as reported by beekeepers. Fortunately, their estimates for yields under comparable conditions exhibit remarkable consistency.

An overall view of the pricing structure is shown in Table 2. Since a hive
has different rental values for different seasons, we divide the time period into
three productive seasons: early spring, late spring, and the honey season
(summer to fall). Surplus honey is not expected in the early spring season,
although nectar may accumulate in the brood chamber and there may be a
gain in brood strength. Most beekeepers in the state are idle during this
season, and pollination is confined to almond in California or cherry in the
southern part of Washington. The rental value of hives is the highest in
the major pollination season of late spring (April to June), second highest
in the major honey season, and lowest in the early spring (March).

The pollination fees listed in Table 2 are based on 1971 data, but they
have remained roughly constant from 1970 to 1972. The wholesale honey
prices, however, are based on 1970 and early 1971 data, as the unexpectedly
low honey yield throughout the country in 1971 generated a a sharp rise in
prices (from 14 cents a pound in April 1971 to 32 cents a pound in March

TABLE 2

PRICING SCHEMES AND EXPECTED HONEY YIELDS OF BEE-RELATED PLANTS

(State of Washington, 1970–1971)

Seasons	Plants	Surplus Honey Expected (pounds per hive)	Honey Prices Per Pound (whole-sale, 1970)	Pollination Fees (range, 1971)	Approximate Apiary Rent Per Hive (range, 1970-1)
Early Spring	Almond (Calif.)	0	—	$5–$8	0
	Cherry	0	—	$6–$8	0
Late Spring (major pollination season)	Apple & Soft Fruits	0	—	$9–10	0
	Blueberry (with maple)	40	14¢	$5	0
	Cabbage	15	13¢	$8	0
	Cherry	0	—	$9–$10	0
	Cranberry	5	13¢	$9	0
Summer and Early Fall (major honey season)	Alfalfa	60	14.5¢	0	13¢–60¢
	Alfalfa (with pollination)	25–35	14.5¢	$3–$5	0
	Fireweed	60	14.5¢	0	25¢–63¢
	Mint	70–75	11¢	0	15¢–65¢
	Pasture	60	14¢	0	15¢–65¢
	Red Clover	60	14¢	0	65¢
	Red Clover (with pollination)	0–35	14¢	$3–$6	0
	Sweet Clover	60	14¢	0	20¢–25¢

1972). The apiary rents are paid mostly in refined and bottled honey, and are therefore converted into money values according to 1970 retail honey prices. To maintain consistency with pollination fees, the apiary rents are computed per hive, although in the latter contracts the number of hives is not stipulated.

The following test implications are derived from our analysis:

(1) Our first implication is that, at the same season and with colonies of the same strength, the rental price per hive obtained from different farms or by different beekeepers will be roughly the same whether the hive is employed for pollination, for honey production, or for a combination of both. By "roughly the same" I do not mean that hive rentals are invariable among different beekeepers. Rather, I mean that (a) any differences which do occur are statistically no more significant than those for most other commodities in the market, and that (b) there is a strong *negative* correlation between the pollination fee (hive rental in money) and the expected honey yield (hive rental in kind).

Data from the early spring season are not suitable to test this implication because during this period there are great variations in colony strength, in the gains in brood and unextracted nectar, and in distances travelled by bee-keepers to deliver the hives.[26] Lacking sufficient information to make appropriate adjustments for these variations in calculating the rental price per hive, we concentrate on data from the late spring and summer seasons.

In contracting for pollination services, beekeepers offer discounts for larger numbers of hives and for less elaborate hive dispersals. Of the four beekeepers from whom detailed records are available, for example, each served from 10 to 14 farms of apples and soft fruits; their mean hive rentals in the major pollination season ranged from $9.20 to $9.68 and their coefficients of variation from 0.025 to 0.053.[27] To reduce the effects on price generated by discounts, we use the mean rentals for the above four beekeepers and the reported means from beekeepers who did not maintain records. Our data thus comprise separate observations of the mean hive rental of each bee-keeper, of each different plant, and (for the summer season) of each different

---

[26] In the pollination of almond, for example, $5.00 is charged for a one-story hive and $6.00 to $8.00 for a two-story hive. On the one hand, Washington beekeepers have to travel to California to obtain this amount when they could have earned the same fee locally in the pollination of early cherry. On the other hand, however, the brood gain is greater with almond than with cherry; also, unextracted nectar in the brood chamber gains significantly in the case of almond but is likely to suffer a net loss with early cherry.

[27] An analysis of variance performed for these four beekeepers shows no significant difference in their mean rentals in the pollination of apple and soft fruits. However, the coefficient of variation of their means, 0.018, is lower than those computed from a larger body of data. This simply indicates a very low variation among the four who provided detailed records.

expected honey yield for the same plant. The latter separation is requisite because the expectation of honey yield varies greatly depending on whether pollination is, or is not, required in the case of such plants as alfalfa.

The coefficient of variation of the mean hive rentals among beekeepers who engaged in the pollination of apples (including soft fruits) and cherries (9 observations in total) is 0.035. The expected honey yield for these observations is zero. When we extend the computation to include cranberry, blueberry and cabbage pollination (13 observations in total), with expected honey yields converted into monetary terms and added to the pollination fees, the coefficient of variation is 0.042. We may meaningfully compare our coefficients of variations with those cited by George Stigler:[28] automobile prices (0.017) and anthracite coal prices (0.068).

Another, and more illuminating, way of testing our implication is through the relationship

$$x_0 = x_1 + x_2, \qquad (1)$$

where x_0 is the total rent per hive, x_1 is the rent paid in money, and x_2 is the expected rent paid in nectar. During the major pollination season, x_1 is positive for all our observations, but during the summer honey season negative values for x_1 (that is, payments in apiary rents) are common. As noted earlier, x_2 may also be positive or negative, but it is generally either zero or positive for the late spring and summer seasons. In the major pollination season, the mean values of equation (1) are $9.65 = $9.02 + $0.64.

The variance of x_0 can be broken down to

$$\sigma^2_{x_0} = \sigma^2_{x_1} + \sigma^2_{x_2} + 2 \text{ Cov } (x_1, x_2). \qquad (2)$$

With a total of 13 observations in late spring, the corresponding values are

$$0.166 = 1.620 + 2.317 - 3.771.$$

The variability in x_1 is almost entirely accounted for by the variability in x_2, as reflected by the large negative covariance term. The coefficient of correlation between x_1 and x_2 is −0.973.

Turning to the summer honey season, we have a total of 23 observations, covering mint (3), fireweed (2), pasture (4), sweet clover (1), red clover (6), and alfalfa (7). The mean values of equation (1) are $8.07 = $1.30 + $6.77. The values corresponding to equation (2) are

$$0.806 = 5.414 + 6.182 - 10.791.$$

Again, most of the variability in x_1 is strongly and negatively correlated with that of x_2. The remaining variance for x_0 (with a coefficient of variation of

[28] George J. Stigler, The Economics of Information, 69 J. Pol. Econ. 213 (1961).

0.111) is larger here than in the major pollination season. This can be explained as follows. First, high risks are associated with the expected honey yields, and beekeepers seem willing to settle for lower, but more certain, incomes. Since x_1 is more certain than x_2, beekeepers seem willing to accept a lower x_0 with a higher ratio of x_1 to x_2,[29] and the variability in this ratio is larger in summer than in spring. Similarly, they will accept a lower expected mean of x_2 for mint than for other honey crops, since mint is generally known to have the smallest variance in expected honey yield of any crop in the state.[30] A second, and more important, factor contributing to the larger variance of x_0 is the premium paid to beekeepers to assume the risk of pollinating crops (notably red clover) where the use of pesticide sprays on neighboring farms poses the danger of loss of bees. Since our information is inadequate to support adjustments for these factors, the resultant distortions must remain. Even so, the coefficient of correlation between x_1 and x_2 computed from the data is -0.933.

(2) The preceding evidence confirms that the rental prices of hives employed in different uses by different beekeepers lie on a roughly horizontal line. However, it does not confirm that these prices are equated to the marginal productivities. Refer to Figure I, for example: the employment of hives might be at a point such as E rather than at G, B, or K. We now turn to some testable implications regarding the tendency toward the equalization of price and marginal productivity.

One obvious implication is that, if the employment of hives renders no valuable pollination services, then an apiary rent will always be observed. In the entire body of evidence available to me, there is not a single observation to the contrary,[31] and this means, referring to Figure Ia, that the employment

[29] This statement is drawn only from casual conversations with beekeepers; no attempt was made to seek refuting evidence.

[30] Inconclusive evidence indicates that hive rentals (paid in honey) obtained from mint is about 40 cents less than those obtained from other honey-yielding plants. Although available information is insufficient for us to compute the year-to-year variances of the honey yields of different plants, ranges of yields as recalled by beekeepers are larger than most agricultural crops.

Because honey from mint has an undesirably strong flavor that excludes it from the retail market, it is either sold to bakeries or used to feed bees during the winter. Quite understandably, onion honey shares the distinction of being much cheaper than any other. Generally rated as the best is orange honey, which commands a wholesale premium of about 1 to 2 cents a pound. Between the extremes, different varieties of honey have roughly the same value and are graded more by clarity than by taste.

[31] One beekeeper specializing in cut-comb honey reported that he pays apiary rents even though no surplus honey is expected, provided that gains in brood strength and in unextracted nectar are expected to be substantial, as when the hives are placed in a farm with maples. This beekeeper is excluded from our first test of implication because he did not engage in pollination and his colonies were of greater strengths.

THE FABLE OF THE BEES   27

of hives is to the left of point E. It should be noted here that even in the absence of demand for pollination some is effected when bees forage for nectar from alfalfa and the clovers, but this is not to be treated as a service unless the seeds are harvested.

Less obvious implications can be obtained from the case of a farm where hives may be employed for nectar extraction only *or* jointly with pollination services. When we discussed the reciprocal case, as depicted in Figure Ib, it was noted that either an apiary rent or a pollination fee may be paid. With simple manipulation, the following implications are evident:

(a) If an apiary rent is paid in the case of a joint product, and if the marginal pollination product is positive, the number of hives employed per acre is necessarily greater than where bees are used only for nectar extraction on the same or a similar farm.

(b) If a pollination fee is paid in the case of a joint product, the number of hives employed per acre is necessarily greater than where bees are used only for nectar extraction on the same or a similar farm.

While both implications indicate a tendency toward point K (in Figure Ib), we lack sufficient information regarding the marginal pollination product to test (a) above. But since in every available observation involving pollination and nectar extraction a pollination fee is paid, only implication (b) is relevant for our purposes.

The evidence, obtained from red clover and alfalfa farms, strongly confirms the implication. The density of hives employed is at least twice as great when the bees are used for both pollination service and nectar extraction as when used for nectar extraction only. As a rule, this increase in hive density leads to a sharp decrease in the expected honey yield per hive. In the typical case, the density of hives in alfalfa and clover farms for pollination services is about 2.5 times what would be employed for nectar extraction only, and the expected honey yield per hive is reduced by 50 per cent. This indicates the marginal nectar product of a hive is close to zero and possibly negative. In

Cut-comb honey is more expensive than ordinary honey because the comb wax, which goes with the honey, is about three times the price of honey per pound. Only honey of top grades (very clear) will be extracted. This observation is implied by the law of demand, since with the comb top-grade honey becomes relatively cheap. Implied by the same law also is that this beekeeper chooses to forgo pollination contracts so that a higher honey yield can be obtained (see evidence in implication test 2). Even during the major pollination season, when little honey can be expected, he prefers to place his hives in farms where the colonies will gain greater strength than would occur if they were used for pollination. For a related discussion on similar implications of the law of demand, see Armen A. Alchian & William R. Allen, Exchange and Production: Theory in Use 78–79 (1969). These implications are accepted here in spite of the criticisms in John P. Gould & Joel Segall, The Substitution Effects of Transportation Costs, 77 J. Pol. Econ. 130 (1969).

one extreme case, in a red clover farm the hive density with pollination services is reported at about seven or eight times that for nectar extraction only; since the expected honey yield is then reduced to zero, the marginal nectar product of the hive is clearly negative! But, as noted earlier, zero or negative marginal product in one component of a joint product is consistent with efficient allocation of resources.

(3) It remains for us to show that the rental price of a hive is roughly equal to the marginal cost of keeping it. Lacking data on marginal cost, we will show that the price approximates the average cost, as implied by competition. We will make the comparison in terms of some general considerations. The expected annual income of a spring colony under a normal rate of utilization, as of 1970-1971, is about $19.00. This includes rentals from a pollination crop, a honey crop, an occasional extra crop (for some hives), and a small amount from the sale of beeswax.[32] The costs of delivering or moving a hive and of finding and contracting the farmers for its use are estimated to total about $9.00 per year.[33] This figure is obtained as follows. Some beekeepers lease some of their hives to other beekeepers on a share contract basis; the lessor receives 50 to 55 per cent of whatever income in money and in kind the lessee obtains from the farmers. Since the lessor could have contracted to serve the farmers himself and obtained the entire income of the $19.00, the fact that he has chosen to take 45 to 50 per cent less indicates that $9.00 must approximate such costs. The interest forgone in keeping a hive is about $3.00 per year.[34] The cost of renewing the colony strength in early spring is about $4.50, the price of a standard booster package of bees.[35] This leaves about $2.50 to cover the costs of depreciation of the hive value, the labor involved in checking and standardizing hives, space for keeping hives in the winter, and the equipment used for honey extraction.

[32] In Lesser's investigation (*supra* note 11) the actual mean annual income of a spring colony for the year 1967 was estimated to be $14.71, and the actual honey yields of that year were slightly larger than our expected honey yields. But in 1967 the price of honey was about 16% lower than that in 1970; and Lesser's estimate of pollination income per hive is about 37% lower than mine, owing both to a rise in pollination fees in recent years and to different samplings of beekeepers. According to Lesser's estimate, beeswax constitutes 4.4% of the beekeeper's total income.

[33] The moving costs cover labor, truck, and other hive-handling equipment. Depending on the time of the year, a complete hive (with supers) weighs somewhere between 80 and 250 pounds.

[34] A complete hive, used but in good condition, sells for about $35.00. The borrowing rate of interest for the beekeepers is around 8%.

[35] The nectar left unextracted in the brood chamber, which constitutes the major cost of overwintering, is not counted as part of income and therefore is not counted as part of the cost.

C. *Characteristics of the Contractual Arrangements*

Contracts between beekeepers and farmers may be oral or written. I have at hand two types of written contracts. One is formally printed by an association of beekeepers; another is designed for specific beekeepers, with a few printed headings and space for stipulations to be filled in by hand.[36] Aside from situations where a third party demands documented proof of the contract (as when a beekeeper seeks a business loan), written contracts are used primarily for the initial arrangement between parties; otherwise oral agreements are made. Although a written contract is more easily enforceable in a court of law, extra-legal constraints are present: information travels quickly through the closely knit society of beekeepers and farmers,[37] and the market will penalize any party who does not honor his contracts. Oral contracts are rarely broken.

Pollination contracts usually include stipulations regarding the number and strength of the colonies, the rental fee per hive, the time of delivery and removal of hives, the protection of bees from pesticide sprays, and the strategic placing of hives. Apiary lease contracts differ from pollination contracts in two essential aspects. One is, predictably, that the amount of apiary rent seldom depends on the number of colonies, since the farmer is interested only in obtaining the rent per apiary offered by the highest bidder. Second, the amount of apiary rent is not necessarily fixed. Paid mostly in honey, it may vary according to either the current honey yield or the honey yield of the preceding year.[38]

In general, contractual arrangements between beekeepers and farmers do not materially differ from other lease contracts. However, some peculiar arrangements resulting from certain complications are worth noting. First, because of the foraging behavior of the bees a farmer who hires bees may benefit his neighbors. Second, the use of pesticide sprays by one farmer may cause

[36] Some beekeepers use just postal cards. The general contractual details reported below are similar to those briefly mentioned in Grant D. Morse, How About Pollination, Gleanings in Bee Culture 73–78 (February 1970).

[37] During my conversations with beekeepers, I was impressed by their personal knowledge of one another, including details such as the number of hives owned, the kinds of farms served, and the rents received.

[38] While we may attribute this behavior to the aversion of risks, the apiary contracts are not the same as share contracts. Rather, they resemble fixed-rent contracts with what I have called "escape clauses." For discussion of the "escape clause" and the stipulations of the share contract, see Steven N. S. Cheung, The Theory of Share Tenancy, ch. 2 & 4 (1969). One impression I obtain is that apiary rents generally involve such low values in Washington that elaborate formations and enforcements of apiary contracts are not worthwhile. In further investigations of these contracts, states with higher honey yields are recommended.

damage to the bees on an adjacent farm. And third, fireweed, which yields good honey, grows wild in forests. Let us discuss each in turn.

The Custom of the Orchards. As noted earlier, if a number of similar orchards are located close to one another, one who hires bees to pollinate his own orchard will in some degree benefit his neighbors. Of course, the strategic placing of the hives will reduce the spillover of bees. But in the absence of any social constraint on behavior, each farmer will tend to take advantage of what spillover does occur and to employ fewer hives himself. Of course, contractual arrangements could be made among all farmers in an area to determine collectively the number of hives to be employed by each, but no such effort is observed.

Acknowledging the complication, beekeepers and farmers are quick to point out that a social rule, or custom of the orchards, takes the place of explicit contracting: during the pollination period the owner of an orchard either keeps bees himself or hires as many hives per area as are employed in neighboring orchards of the same type. One failing to comply would be rated as a "bad neighbor," it is said, and could expect a number of inconveniences imposed on him by other orchard owners.[39] This customary matching of hive densities involves the exchange of gifts of the same kind, which apparently entails lower transaction costs than would be incurred under explicit contracting, where farmers would have to negotiate and make money payments to one another for the bee spillover.[40]

The Case of Pesticide Sprays. At the outset, we must remember that to minimize the loss of bees from insecticide usage is not necessarily consistent with efficient allocation of resources. The relevant consideration is whether the gain from using the pesticide is greater than the associated loss of bees, in total and at the margin. Provided that the costs of forming con-

---

[39] The distinction between an oral or an implicit contract and a custom is not always clear. A common practice in some areas is that each farmer lets his neighbors know how many hives he employs. Perhaps the absence of a court of law to enforce what could in fact be a highly informal agreement is the reason why farmers deny the existence of any contract among them governing the employment of hives.

[40] Since with a sufficiently high reward the notoriety of being a "bad neighbor" will be tolerated, the likelihood of explicit contracting rises with increasing rental values of hives. Alternatively and concurrently, with a high enough rental price of hives the average size of orchards may increase through outright purchases, or the shapes of the orchards may be so tailored as to match the foraging behavior of the bees. By definition, given the gains the least costly arrangement will be chosen.

Some beekeepers reported that there are peculiar situations where the foraging behavior of the bees forces a one-way gift, but these situations are not covered by the present investigation. Even under these rare situations, the absence of both contractual and customary restraints may not result in a different allocation of resources. See Steven N. S. Cheung, The Theory of Inter-individual Effects and The Demand for Contracts (Univ. of Washington, Inst. of Econ. Res.).

tracts permits, beekeepers and farmers will seek cooperative arrangements such that the expected marginal gain from using the pesticide is equal to the value of the expected marginal bee loss. In the absence of the arrangements, however, the total gain from using the pesticide may still be greater than the associated loss; the greater the expected damage done to bees, the greater will be the gain from the cooperative arrangements.[41]

When a pollination contract is formed, the farmer usually agrees to inform the beekeeper before spraying his crop, but this assurance will not protect the bees from pesticide used on neighboring farms. In areas dominated by orchards which require pollination at roughly the same time, such as the apple-growing districts, this agreement will suffice, for no farmer will apply the spray during the pollination period. But in regions where adjacent farms require bee pollination at different times, or do not require it at all, a farmer with no present obligation to any beekeeper may spray his fields and inflict damages to the bees rented by other farms. In this situation, only cooperation over a large geographic area can avoid bee loss, and we find just such arrangements in the pollination of cranberries but not of red clover.

Cranberry farms near Seattle are usually found in clusters, and spraying is conducted shortly after the bloom, which may vary by as much as a week or two among neighboring farms. Although each cranberry grower agrees not to spray until the contracted beekeeper removes the bees from his farm, this does not protect bees which may still remain on adjacent farms. Therefore the beekeepers make a further arrangement among themselves to remove all hives on the same date, thus insuring that all the bees are protected.

Red clover presents a different situation. Since the plant is often grown in areas where neighboring farms require no bee pollination, the pesticide danger is reportedly high and beekeepers demand an additional $1.00 to $2.00 per hive to assume the risk. But just as the beekeepers cooperate with one another during cranberry pollination, a clover farmer could make arrangements with his neighbors. Given that neighboring farmers have the legal right to use pesticide, the clover farmer would be willing to pay them an amount not exceeding the beekeeper's risk premium if they would refrain from spraying during the pollination period. Although no such arrangements are observed, it would seem that the costs of reaching an agreement would be no higher than those encountered in the case of the cranberries, and we must infer, pending empirical confirmation, that the gain from using the sprays is greater than the associated loss. This would particularly apply when a single farm requiring pollination is located amidst a large number of farms which require spraying during that same period.

[41] For a fuller discussion, see Steven N. S. Cheung, *supra* note 40.

The Case of Fireweed. I have at hand two types of apiary contract pertaining to fireweed, a honey plant which grows wild in the forest. The first is between a beekeeper and the Weyerhaeuser Company, owner of private timber land; the second is between a beekeeper and the Water Department of the City of Seattle. Two distinctions between them are worth noting. First, while both contracts stipulate 25 cents per hive, Weyerhaeuser asks a minimum charge of $100, and the Water Department a minimum of $25. In the apiary for fireweed honey, the number of hives used by a beekeeper is more than 100 but less than 400. Thus it happens that in the case of Weyerhauser, the apiary rent is independent of the number of hives, whereas with the Water Department it is dependent. The "underpriced" rent levied by the Water Department would have implied some sort of queuing except that a second unique feature is incorporated in its apiary contracts: no beekeeper is granted the exclusive right to the fireweed nectar in a particular area. The implication is that competition among beekeepers will reduce the honey yield per hive until its apiary rent is no more than 25 cents; while no beekeeper attempts to exclude entrants, the parties do seek a mutual division of the total area to avoid chaotic hive placement. Finally, fireweed also grows wild in the national forests and for this case I have no contract at hand. My information is that apiary rent is measured by the hive, is subject to competitive bidding among beekeepers, and has a reported range of 25 to 63 cents with the winner being granted exclusive right to a particular area.

III. CONCLUSIONS

Whether or not Keynes was correct in his claim that policy makers are "distilling their frenzy" from economists, it appears evident that some economists have been distilling their policy implications from fables. In a desire to promote government intervention, they have been prone to advance, without the support of careful investigation, the notion of "market failure." Some have dismissed in cavalier fashion the possibility of market operations in matters of environmental degradation, as witnesses the assertion of E. J. Mishan:

With respect to bodies of land and water, extension of property rights may effectively internalize what would otherwise remain externalities. But the possibilities of protecting the citizen against such common environmental blights as filth, fume, stench, noise, visual distractions, etc. by a market in property rights are too remote to be taken seriously.[42]

[42] E. J. Mishan: A Reply to Professor Worcester, 10 J. Econ. Lit. 59, 62 (1972). As immediate refutation of Professor Mishan's claim, I refer the reader to a factual example: Professor John McGee has just purchased a house, separated from that of

THE FABLE OF THE BEES   33

Similarly, it has been assumed that private property rights cannot be enforced in the case of fisheries, wildlife, and whatever other resources
economists have chosen to call "natural." Land tenure contracts are routinely
taken as inefficient, and to some the market will fail in the areas of education, medical care, and the like.

Then, of course, there is the fable of the bees.

In each case, it is true that costs involved in enforcement of property
rights and in the formation of contracts will cause the market to function
differently than it would without such costs. And few will deny that government does afford economic advantages. But it is equally true that any government action can be justified on efficiency grounds by the simple expedient
of hypothesizing high enough transaction costs in the marketplace and low
enough costs for government control. Thus to assume the state of the world
to be as one sees fit is not even to compare the ideal with the actual but,
rather, to compare the ideal with a fable.

I have no grounds for criticizing Meade and other economists who follow
the Pigovian tradition for their use of the bee example to illustrate a theoretical point: certainly, resource allocation would in general differ from what
is observed if the factors were "unpaid." My main criticism, rather, concerns
their approach to economic inquiry in failing to investigate the real-world
situation and in arriving at policy implications out of sheer imagination.
As a result, their work contributes little to our understanding of the actual
economic system.

---

his neighbor by a vacant lot. That the space would remain vacant had been assured
by the previous owner who (upon learning that a third party was planning to buy
the lot and construct a house there) had negotiated with the neighbor to make a joint
purchase of the ground, thus protecting their two households from the "filth, fumes,
stench, noise, visual distractions, etc." which would be generated by a new neighbor.

[10]

TRANSACTION-COST ECONOMICS: THE GOVERNANCE OF CONTRACTUAL RELATIONS*

OLIVER E. WILLIAMSON
University of Pennsylvania

T HE new institutional economics is preoccupied with the origins, incidence, and ramifications of transaction costs. Indeed, if transaction costs are negligible, the organization of economic activity is irrelevant, since any advantages one mode of organization appears to hold over another will simply be eliminated by costless contracting. But despite the growing realization that transaction costs are central to the study of economics,[1] skeptics remain. Stanley Fischer's complaint is typical: "Transaction costs have a well-deserved bad name as a theoretical device . . . [partly] because there is a suspicion that almost anything can be rationalized by invoking suitably specified transaction costs."[2] Put differently, there are too many degrees of freedom; the concept wants for definition.

* This paper has benefited from support from the Center for Advanced Study in the Behavioral Sciences, the Guggenheim Foundation, and the National Science Foundation. Helpful comments by Yoram Ben-Porath, Richard Nelson, Douglass North, Thomas Palay, Joseph Sax, David Teece, and Peter Temin and from the participants at seminars at the Yale Law School and the Institute for Advanced Study at Princeton are gratefully acknowledged. The paper was rewritten to advantage after reading Ben-Porath's discussion paper, the F-Connection: Family, Friends, and Firms and the Organization of Exchange, and Temin's discussion paper, Modes of Economic Behavior: Variations on Themes of J. R. Hicks and Herbert Simon.

[1] Ronald Coase has forcefully argued the importance of transaction costs at twenty-year intervals. See R. H. Coase, The Nature of the Firm, 4 Economica 386 (n.s. 1937), reprinted in Readings in Price Theory 331 (George J. Stigler & Kenneth E. Boulding eds. 1952) and R. H. Coase, The Problem of Social Cost, 3 J. Law & Econ. 1 (1960). Much of my own work has been "preoccupied" with transaction costs during the past decade. See especially Oliver E. Williamson, Markets and Hierarchies: Analysis and Antitrust Implications (1975). Other works in which transaction costs are featured include: Guido Calabresi, Transaction Costs, Resource Allocation, and Liability Rules: A Comment, 11 J. Law & Econ. 67 (1968); Victor P. Goldberg, Regulation and Administered Contracts, 7 Bell J. Econ. 426 (1976); Benjamin Klein, Robert G. Crawford, and Armen A. Alchian, Vertical Integration, Appropriable Rents, and the Competitive Contracting Process, 21 J. Law & Econ. 297 (1978); and Carl J. Dahlman, The Problem of Externality, 22 J. Law & Econ. 141 (1979). For an examination of Pigou in which transaction costs are featured, see Victor P. Goldberg, Pigou on Complex Contracts and Welfare Economics (1979) (unpublished manuscript).

[2] S. Fischer, Long-Term Contracting, Sticky Prices, and Monetary Policy: Comment, 3 J. Monetary Econ. 317, 322 n. 5 (1977).

Among the factors on which there appears to be developing a general consensus are: (1) opportunism is a central concept in the study of transaction costs;[3] (2) opportunism is especially important for economic activity that involves transaction-specific investments in human and physical capital;[4] (3) the efficient processing of information is an important and related concept;[5] and (4) the assessment of transaction costs is a comparative institutional undertaking.[6] Beyond these general propositions, a consensus on transaction costs is lacking.

Further progress in the study of transaction costs awaits the identification of the critical dimensions with respect to which transaction costs differ and an examination of the economizing properties of alternative institutional modes for organizing transactions. Only then can the matching of transactions with modes be accomplished with confidence. This paper affirms the proposition that transaction costs are central to the study of economics, identifies the critical dimensions for characterizing transactions, describes the main governance structures of transactions, and indicates how and why transactions can be matched with institutions in a discriminating way.

I am mainly concerned with intermediate-product market transactions. Whereas previously I have emphasized the incentives to remove transactions from the market and organize them internally (vertical integration),[7] the analysis here is symmetrical and deals with market, hierarchical, and intermediate modes of organization alike. The question of why there is so much vertical integration remains interesting, but no more so than the question of why there are so many market- (and quasi-market) mediated transactions. A discriminating analysis will explain which transactions are located where and give the reasons why. The overall object of the exercise essentially comes down to this: for each abstract description of a transaction, identify

---

[3] Opportunism is a variety of self-interest seeking but extends simple self-interest seeking to include self-interest seeking with guile. It is not necessary that all agents be regarded as opportunistic in identical degree. It suffices that those who are less opportunistic than others are difficult to ascertain ex ante and that, even among the less opportunistic, most have their price. For a more complete discussion of opportunism, see Oliver E. Williamson, *supra* note 1, at 7-10, 26-30. For a recent application see Benjamin Klein, Robert G. Crawford, & Armen A. Alchian, *supra* note 1.

[4] The joining of opportunism with transaction-specific investments (or what Klein, Crawford, and Alchian refer to as "appropriable quasi rents") is a leading factor in explaining decisions to vertically integrate. See Oliver E. Williamson, The Vertical Integration of Production: Market Failure Considerations, 61 Am. Econ. Rev. 112 (Papers & Proceedings, May 1971); Oliver E. Williamson, *supra* note 1, at 16-19, 91-101; and Benjamin Klein, Robert G. Crawford, & Armen A. Alchian, *supra* note 1.

[5] But for the limited ability of human agents to receive, store, retrieve, and process data, interesting economic problems vanish.

[6] See Carl J. Dahlman, *supra* note 1.

[7] See note 4 *supra*.

the most economical governance structure—where by governance structure I refer to the institutional framework within which the integrity of a transaction is decided. Markets and hierarchies are two of the main alternatives.

Some legal background to the study of transactions is briefly reviewed in Section I. Of the three dimensions for describing transactions that I propose, investment attributes are the least well understood and probably the most important. The special relevance of investments is developed in the context of the economics of idiosyncrasy in Section II. A general contracting schema is developed and applied to commercial contracting in Section III. Applications to labor, regulation, family transactions, and capital markets are sketched in Section IV. Major implications are summarized in Section V. Concluding remarks follow.

I. Some Contracting Background

Although there is widespread agreement that the discrete-transaction paradigm—"sharp in by clear agreement; sharp out by clear performance"[8]—has served both law and economics well, there is increasing awareness that many contractual relations are not of this well-defined kind.[9] A deeper understanding of the nature of contract has emerged as the legal-rule emphasis associated with the study of discrete contracting has given way to a more general concern with the contractual purposes to be served.[10]

---

[8] I. R. Macneil, The Many Futures of Contract, 47 S. Cal. L. Rev. 691, 738 (1974) [hereinafter cited without cross-reference as Macneil, Many Futures of Contract].

[9] With respect to commercial contracts, see Karl N. Llewellyn, What Price Contract?—An Essay in Perspective, 40 Yale L. J. 704 (1931); Harold C. Havighurst, The Nature of Private Contract (1961); Lon L. Fuller, Collective Bargaining and the Arbitrator, 1963 Wis. L. Rev. 3; *id.*, The Morality of Law (1964); Stewart Macaulay, Non-Contractual Relations in Business, 28 Am. Soc. Rev. 55 (1963); Lawrence M. Friedman, Contract Law in America (1965); Arthur Allen Leff, Contract as a Thing, 19 Am. U. L. Rev. 131 (1970); I. R. Macneil, Many Futures of Contracts; *id.*, Contracts: Adjustment of Long-Term Economic Relations under Classical, Neoclassical, and Relational Contract Law, 72 Nw. U. L. Rev. 854 (1978) [hereinafter cited without cross-reference as Macneil, Contracts]; and Victor P. Goldberg, Toward an Expanded Economic Theory of Contract, 10 J. Econ. Issues 45 (1976). Labor lawyers have made similar observations regarding contracts governing the employment relationship. See Archibald Cox, The Legal Nature of Collective Bargaining Agreements, 57 Mich. L. Rev. 1 (1958); Clyde W. Summers, Collective Agreements and the Law of Contracts, 78 Yale L. J. 525 (1969); and David E. Feller, A General Theory of the Collective Bargaining Agreement, 61 Cal. L. Rev. 663 (1973).

[10] The technical versus purposive distinction is made by Clyde Summers, *supra* note 9. He distinguishes between "black letter law," on the one hand (539, 543, 548, 566) and a more circumstantial approach to law, on the other (549-51, 561, 566). "The epitome of abstraction is the *Restatement,* which illustrates its black letter rules by transactions suspended in mid-air, creating the illusion that contract rules can be stated without reference to surrounding circumstances and are therefore generally applicable to all contractual transactions" (566). He observes that such a conception does not and cannot provide a "framework for integrating rules and principles applicable to all contractual transactions" (566) but that this must be sought in a more

Ian Macneil, in a series of thoughtful and wide-ranging essays on contract, usefully distinguishes between discrete and relational transactions.[11] He further supplies twelve different "concepts" with respect to which these differ.[12] Serious problems of recognition and application are posed by such a rich classificatory apparatus. More useful for my purposes is the three-way classification of contracts that Macneil offers in his most recent article, where classical, neoclassical, and relational categories of contract law are recognized.

A. *Classical Contract Law*

As Macneil observes, any system of contract law has the purpose of facilitating exchange. What is distinctive about classical contract law is that it attempts to do this by enhancing discreteness and intensifying "presentiation,"[13] where presentiation has reference to efforts to "make or render present in place or time; to cause to be perceived or realized at present."[14] The economic counterpart to complete presentiation is contingent-claims contracting—which entails comprehensive contracting whereby all relevant future contingencies pertaining to the supply of a good or service are described and discounted with respect to both likelihood and futurity.[15]

Classical contract law endeavors to implement discreteness and presentiation in several ways. For one thing, the identity of the parties to a transaction is treated as irrelevant. In this respect it corresponds exactly with the "ideal" market transaction in economics.[16] Second, the nature of the agreement is carefully delimited, and the more formal features govern when formal (for example, written) and informal (for example, oral) terms are contested. Third, remedies are narrowly prescribed such that, "should the initial presentiation fail to materialize because of nonperformance, the consequences are relatively predictable from the beginning and are not open-

---

affirmative view of the law in which effective governance relations are emphasized. Contract interpretation and completing contracts are among these affirmative functions.

[11] See especially Macneil, Many Futures of Contract; Macneil, Contracts; and references to related work of his cited therein.

[12] Macneil, Many Futures of Contracts 738-40; Macneil, Contracts 902-05.

[13] Macneil, Contracts 862.

[14] *Id.* at 863 n. 25.

[15] For a discussion of complex contingent-claims contracting and its mechanics, see Kenneth J. Arrow, Essays in the Theory of Risk Bearing 121-34 (1971); J. E. Meade, The Controlled Economy 147-88 (1971); and Oliver E. Williamson, *supra* note 1, at 20-40.

[16] As Lester G. Telser & Harlow N. Higinbotham put it: "In an organized market the participants trade a standardized contract such that each unit of the contract is a perfect substitute for any other unit. The identities of the parties in any mutually agreeable transaction do not affect the terms of exchange. The organized market itself or some other institution deliberately creates a homogeneous good that can be traded anonymously by the participants or their agents." Organized Futures Markets: Costs and Benefits 85 J. Pol. Econ. 969, 997 (1977).

ended."[17] Additionally, third-party participation is discouraged.[18] The emphasis, thus, is on legal rules, formal documents, and self-liquidating transactions.

B. *Neoclassical Contract Law*

Not every transaction fits comfortably into the classical-contracting scheme. In particular, long-term contracts executed under conditions of uncertainty are ones for which complete presentation is apt to be prohibitively costly if not impossible. Problems of several kinds arise. First, not all future contingencies for which adaptations are required can be anticipated at the outset. Second, the appropriate adaptations will not be evident for many contingencies until the circumstances materialize. Third, except as changes in states of the world are unambiguous, hard contracting between autonomous parties may well give rise to veridical disputes when state-contingent claims are made. In a world where (at least some) parties are inclined to be opportunistic, whose representations are to be believed?

Faced with the prospective breakdown of classical contracting in these circumstances, three alternatives are available. One would be to forgo such transactions altogether. A second would be to remove these transactions from the market and organize them internally instead. Adaptive, sequential decision making would then be implemented under common ownership and with the assistance of hierarchical incentive and control systems. Third, a different contracting relation which preserves trading but provides for additional governance structure might be devised. This last brings us to what Macneil refers to as neoclassical contracting.

As Macneil observes, "Two common characteristics of long-term contracts are the existence of gaps in their planning and the presence of a range of processes and techniques used by contract planners to create flexibility in lieu of either leaving gaps or trying to plan rigidly."[19] Third-party assistance in resolving disputes and evaluating performance often has advantages over litigation in serving these functions of flexibility and gap filling. Lon Fuller's remarks on procedural differences between arbitration and litigation are instructive:

> . . . there are open to the arbitrator . . . quick methods of education not open to the courts. An arbitrator will frequently interrupt the examination of witnesses with a request that the parties educate him to the point where he can understand the testimony being received. This education can proceed informally, with frequent interruptions by the arbitrator, and by informed persons on either side, when a point

[17] Macneil, Contracts 864.
[18] *Id.*
[19] *Id.* at 865.

238   THE JOURNAL OF LAW AND ECONOMICS

needs clarification. Sometimes there will be arguments across the table, occasionally even within each of the separate camps. The end result will usually be a clarification that will enable everyone to proceed more intelligently with the case. There is in this informal procedure no infringement whatever of arbitrational due process.[20]

A recognition that the world is complex, that agreements are incomplete, and that some contracts will never be reached unless both parties have confidence in the settlement machinery thus characterizes neoclassical contract law. One important purposive difference in arbitration and litigation that contributes to the procedural differences described by Fuller is that, whereas continuity (at least completion of the contract) is presumed under the arbitration machinery, this presumption is much weaker when litigation is employed.[21]

C. *Relational Contracting*

The pressures to sustain ongoing relations "have led to the spin-off of many subject areas from the classical, and later the neoclassical, contract law system, e.g., much of corporate law and collective bargaining."[22] Thus, progressively increasing the "duration and complexity" of contract has resulted in the displacement of even neoclassical adjustment processes by adjustment processes of a more thoroughly transaction-specific, ongoing-administrative kind.[23] The fiction of discreteness is fully displaced as the relation takes on the properties of "a minisociety with a vast array of norms beyond those centered on the exchange and its immediate processes."[24] By contrast with the neoclassical system, where the reference point for effecting adaptations remains the original agreement, the reference point under a truly relational approach is the "entire relation as it has developed . . . [through] time. This may or may not include an 'original agreement'; and if it does, may or may not result in great deference being given it."[25]

II. THE ECONOMICS OF IDIOSYNCRASY

Macneil's three-way discussion of contracts discloses that contracts are a good deal more varied and complex than is commonly realized.[26] It further-

[20] Lon L. Fuller, *supra* note 9, at 11-12.

[21] As Lawrence Friedman observes, relationships are effectively fractured if a dispute reaches litigation. *Supra* note 9, at 205.

[22] Macneil, Contracts 885.

[23] *Id.* at 901.

[24] *Id.*

[25] *Id.* at 890.

[26] To be sure, some legal specialists insist that all of this was known all along. There is a difference, however, between awareness of a condition and an understanding. Macneil's treatment heightens awareness and deepens the understanding.

more suggests that governance structures—the institutional matrix within which transactions are negotiated and executed—vary with the nature of the transaction. But the critical dimensions of contract are not expressly identified, and the purposes of governance are not stated. Harmonizing interests that would otherwise give way to antagonistic subgoal pursuits appears to be an important governance function, but this is not explicit in his discussion.

That simple governance structures should be used in conjunction with simple contractual relations and complex governance structures reserved for complex relations seems generally sensible. Use of a complex structure to govern a simple relation is apt to incur unneeded costs, and use of a simple structure for a complex transaction invites strain. But what is simple and complex in contractual respects? Specific attention to the defining attributes of transactions is evidently needed.

As developed in Section III, the three critical dimensions for characterizing transactions are (1) uncertainty, (2) the frequency with which transactions recur, and (3) the degree to which durable transaction-specific investments are incurred. Of these three, uncertainty is widely conceded to be a critical attribute;[27] and that frequency matters is at least plausible.[28] The governance ramifications of neither, however, have been fully developed—nor can they be until joined with the third critical dimension: transaction-specific investments. Inasmuch as a considerable amount of the "action" in the study of governance is attributable to investment differences, some explication is needed.

A. *General*

The crucial investment distinction is this: to what degree are transaction-specific (nonmarketable) expenses incurred. Items that are unspecialized among users pose few hazards, since buyers in these circumstances can easily turn to alternative sources, and suppliers can sell output intended for one order to other buyers without difficulty.[29] Nonmarketability problems arise

---

[27] For a recent study of contractual relations in which uncertainty is featured, see Peter Temin, Modes of Economic Behavior: Variations on Themes of J. R. Hicks and Herbert Simon (March 1979) (Working Paper No. 235, MIT Dep't of Econ.).

[28] Gordon Whinston emphasizes frequency in his "A Note on Perspective Time: Goldberg's Relational Exchange, Repetitiveness, and Free Riders in Time and Space" (October 1978) (unpublished paper).

[29] See Lester A. Telser & Harold N. Higinbotham, *supra* note 16; also Yoram Ben-Porath, The F-Connection: Families, Friends, and Firms and the Organization of Exchange (December 1978) (Report No. 29/78, The Hebrew University of Jerusalem) and Yoram Barzel, Measurement Cost and the Organization of Markets (April 1979) (unpublished paper). Note that Barzel's concern with standardization is mainly in connection with final-product markets, whereas I am more interested in nonstandard investments. The two are not unrelated, but identical quality can often be realized with a variety of inputs. I am concerned with specialized (transaction-specific) inputs.

when the *specific identity* of the parties has important cost-bearing consequences. Transactions of this kind will be referred to as idiosyncratic.

Occasionally the identity of the parties is important from the outset, as when a buyer induces a supplier to invest in specialized physical capital of a transaction-specific kind. Inasmuch as the value of this capital in other uses is, by definition, much smaller than the specialized use for which it has been intended, the supplier is effectively "locked into" the transaction to a significant degree. This is symmetrical, moreover, in that the buyer cannot turn to alternative sources of supply and obtain the item on favorable terms, since the cost of supply from unspecialized capital is presumably great.[30] The buyer is thus committed to the transaction as well.

Ordinarily, however, there is more to idiosyncratic exchange than specialized physical capital. Human-capital investments that are transaction-specific commonly occur as well. Specialized training and learning-by-doing economies in production operations are illustrations. Except when these investments are transferable to alternative suppliers at low cost, which is rare, the benefits of the set-up costs can be realized only so long as the relationship between the buyer and seller of the intermediate product is maintained.

Additional transaction-specific savings can accrue at the interface between supplier and buyer as contracts are successively adapted to unfolding events, and as periodic contract-renewal agreements are reached. Familiarity here permits communication economies to be realized: specialized language develops as experience accumulates and nuances are signaled and received in a sensitive way. Both institutional and personal trust relations evolve. Thus the individuals who are responsible for adapting the interfaces have a personal as well as an organizational stake in what transpires. Where personal integrity is believed to be operative, individuals located at the interfaces may refuse to be a part of opportunistic efforts to take advantage of (rely on) the letter of the contract when the spirit of the exchange is emasculated. Such refusals can serve as a check upon organizational proclivities to behave opportunistically.[31] Other things being equal, idiosyncratic exchange rela-

---

[30] This assumes that it is costly for the incumbent supplier to transfer specialized physical assets to new suppliers. On this, see Oliver E. Williamson, Franchise Bidding for Natural Monopolies—in General and with Respect to CATV, 7 Bell J. Econ. 73 (1976). Klein, Crawford, & Alchian use the term "appropriable quasi rent" to refer to this condition. Use versus user distinctions are relevant in this connection: "The quasi-rent value of the asset is the excess of its value over its salvage value, that is, its value in its next best *use* to another renter. The potentially appropriable specialized portion of the quasi rent is the portion, if any, in excess of its value to the second highest-valuing *user*." Benjamin Klein, Robert G. Crawford, & Armen A. Alchian, *supra* note 1, at 298.

[31] Thorstein Veblen's remarks on the distant relation of the head of a large enterprise to transactions are apposite. He observes that under these impersonal circumstances "The mitigating effect which personal conduct may have in dealings between man and man is . . . in great

tions which feature personal trust will survive greater stress and display greater adaptability.

Idiosyncratic goods and services are thus ones where investments of transaction-specific human and physical capital are made and, contingent upon successful execution, benefits are realized. Such investments can and do occur in conjunction with occasional trades where delivery for a specialized design is stretched out over a long period (for example, certain construction contracts). The transactions that I wish to emphasize here, however, are exchanges of the recurring kind. Although large-numbers competition is frequently feasible at the initial award stage for recurring contracts of all kinds, idiosyncratic transactions are ones for which the relationship between buyer and supplier is quickly thereafter *transformed* into one of bilateral monopoly—on account of the transaction-specific costs referred to above. This transformation has profound contracting consequences.

Thus, whereas recurrent spot contracting is feasible for standardized transactions (because large-numbers competition is continuously self-policing in these circumstances), such contracting has seriously defective investment incentives where idiosyncratic activities are involved. By assumption, cost economies in production will be realized for idiosyncratic activities only if the supplier invests in a special-purpose plant and equipment or if his labor force develops transaction-specific skills in the course of contract execution (or both). The assurance of a continuing relation is needed to encourage investments of both kinds. Although the requisite incentives might be provided if long-term contracts were negotiated, such contracts are necessarily incomplete (by reason of bounded rationality). Appropriate state-contingent adaptations thus go unspecified. Intertemporal efficiency nevertheless requires that adaptations to changing market circumstances be made.

How to effect these adaptations poses a serious contracting dilemma, though it bears repeating that, absent the hazards of opportunism, the difficulties would vanish—since then the gaps in long-term, incomplete contracts could be faultlessly filled in an adaptive, sequential way. A general clause, to which both parties would agree, to the effect that "I will behave responsibly rather than seek individual advantage when an occasion to adapt arises," would, in the absence of opportunism, suffice. Given, however, the unenforceability of general clauses and the proclivity of human agents to make false and misleading (self-disbelieved) statements, the follow-

---

measured eliminated. . . . Business management [then] has a chance to proceed . . . untroubled by sentimental considerations of human kindness or irritation or of honesty." The Theory of Business Enterprise 53 (1927). Veblen evidently assigns slight weight to the possibility that those to whom negotiating responsibilities are assigned will themselves invest the transactions with integrity.

ing hazard must be confronted: joined as they are in an idiosyncratic condition of bilateral monopoly, both buyer and seller are strategically situated to bargain over the disposition of any incremental gain whenever a proposal to adapt is made by the other party. Although both have a long-term interest in effecting adaptations of a joint profit-maximizing kind, each also has an interest in appropriating as much of the gain as he can on each occasion to adapt. Efficient adaptations which would otherwise be made thus result in costly haggling or even go unmentioned, lest the gains be dissipated by costly subgoal pursuit. Governance structures which attenuate opportunism and otherwise infuse confidence are evidently needed.

B. *Examples*

Some illustrations may help to motivate what is involved in idiosyncratic transactions. Specialized physical capital is relatively straightforward. Examples are (1) the purchase of a specialized component from an outside supplier or (2) the location of a specialized plant in a unique, proximate relation to a downstream processing stage to which it supplies vital input.

Thus assume (*a*) that special-purpose equipment is needed to produce the component in question (which is to say that the value of the equipment in its next-best alternative use is much lower), (*b*) that scale economies require that a significant, discrete investment be made, and (*c*) that alternative buyers for such components are few (possibly because of the organization of the industry, possibly because of special-design features). The interests of buyer and seller in a continuing exchange relation are plainly strong under these circumstances.

Plant-proximity benefits are attributable to transportation and related flow-process (inventory, thermal economy, and so on) economies. A specialized plant need not be implied, but long life and a unique location are. Once made, the investment preempts the unique location and is not thereafter moveable (except at prohibitive cost). Buyer and supplier again need to satisfy themselves that they have a workable, adaptable exchange agreement.[32]

Idiosyncratic investments in human capital are in many ways more interesting and less obvious than are those in physical capital. Polanyi's discussion of "personal knowledge" is illuminating:

The attempt to analyze scientifically the established industrial arts has everywhere led to similar results. Indeed even in the modern industries the indefinable knowledge is still an essential part of technology. I have myself watched in Hungary a new, imported machine for blowing electric lamp bulbs, the exact counterpart of which

---

[32] The *Great Lakes Carbon* case is an example of the latter, 1970-1973 Trade Reg. Rep. Transfer Binder ¶ 19,848 (FTC Dkt No. 8805).

was operating successfully in Germany, failing for a whole year to produce a single flawless bulb.[33]

And he goes on to observe with respect to craftsmanship that:

. . . an art which has fallen into disuse for the period of a generation is altogether lost. . . . It is pathetic to watch the endless efforts—equipped with microscopy and chemistry, with mathematics and electronics—to reproduce a single violin of the kind the half-literate Stradivarius turned out as a matter of routine more than 200 years ago.[34]

Polanyi's discussion of language also has a bearing on the argument advanced above that specialized code words or expressions can and do arise in the context of recurring transactions and that these yield economies. As he puts it, "Different vocabularies for the interpretation of things divide men into groups which cannot understand each other's way of seeing things and acting upon them."[35] And subsequently he remarks that:

To know a language is an art, carried on by tacit judgments and the practice of unspecifiable skills. . . . Spoken communication is the successful application by two persons of the linguistic knowledge and skill acquired by such apprenticeship, one person wishing to transmit, the other to receive, information. Relying on what each has learnt, the speaker confidently utters words and the listener confidently interprets them, while they mutually rely on each other's correct use and understanding of these words. A true communication will take place if, and only if, these combined assumptions of authority and trust are in fact justified.[36]

Babbage reports a remarkable example of transaction-specific value in exchange that occurred in the early 1800s. Although he attributes the continuing exchange in the face of adversity to values of "established character" (trust), I believe there were other specialized human and physical investments involved as well. In any event, the circumstance which he describes is the following:

The influence of established character in producing confidence operated in a very remarkable manner at the time of the exclusion of British manufactures from the Continent during the last war. One of our largest establishments had been in the habit of doing extensive business with a house in the centre of Germany; but, on the closing of the continental ports against our manufacturers, heavy penalties were inflicted on all those who contravened the Berlin and Milan decrees. The English manufacturer continued, nevertheless, to receive orders, with directions how to con-

[33] Michael Polanyi, *Personal Knowledge: Towards a Post-Critical Philosophy* 52 (2d ed. 1962).
[34] *Id.* at 53.
[35] *Id.* at 112.
[36] *Id.* at 206.

sign them, and appointments for the time and mode of payment, in letters, the handwriting of which was known to him, but which were never signed, except by the Christian name of one of the firm, and even in some instances they were without any signature at all. These orders were executed; and in no instance was there the least irregularity in the payments.[37]

While most of these illustrations refer to technical and commercial transactions, other types of transactions also have an idiosyncratic quality. Justice Rhenquist refers to some of these when speaking of the general class of cases where "the litigation of an individual's claim of deprivation of a right would bring parties *who must remain in a continuing relationship* into the adversarial atmosphere of a courtroom"[38]—which atmosphere he plainly regards as detrimental to the quality of the relationship. Examples that he offers include reluctance to have the courts mediate collective bargaining disputes[39] and to allow children to bring suit against parents.[40]

But surely we must ask what is distinctive about these transactions. I submit that transaction-specific human capital is central to each. Why else would it take the Hungarians so long to operate the German light-bulb machine? And what else explains the loss of Stradivarius's craftsmanship? Likewise the understanding and trust which evolve between Babbage's transmitter and receiver are valued human assets which, once developed, will be sacrificed with reluctance. And the disruption of continuing relationships to which Justice Rhenquist refers occasions concern precisely because there are no adequate substitutes for these idiosyncratic relations.[41]

The general argument of this paper is that special governance structures supplant standard market-cum-classical contract exchange when transac-

[37] Charles Babbage, On the Economy of Machinery and Manufacturers 220-21 (1832). More recent examples of contracts wherein private parties can and evidently do "ignore" the law, even at some peril, when the law and the interests of the parties are at variance are offered by Stewart Macaulay, The Use and Nonuse of Contracts in the Manufacturing Industry, 9 Practical Lawyer 13, 16 (1963): "Requirements contracts probably are not legally enforceable in Wisconsin and a few other States. Yet, chemicals, containers, and a number of other things are still bought and sold there on the basis of requirements contracts.

"Decisions of the United States Court of Appeals for the Seventh Circuit indicate that a clause calling for a 'seller's price in effect at time and place of delivery' makes a contract unenforceable. The Wisconsin cases are not clear. Yet steel and steel products usually are sold in this way."

[38] Remarks of Mr. Justice Rhenquist, The Adversary Society, Baron di Hirsch Meyer Lecture, University of Miami School of Law, February 2, 1978, at 19 (emphasis added).

[39] *Id.* at 11-13.

[40] *Id.* at 16-19.

[41] As Ben-Porath puts it, "The most important characteristic of the family contract is that it is embedded in the identity of the partners without which it loses its meaning. It is thus specific and non-negotiable or nontransferable." Yoram Ben-Porath, *supra* note 29, at 6.

tion-specific values are great. Idiosyncratic commercial, labor, and family relationships are specific examples.

III. COMMERCIAL CONTRACTING

The discussion of commercial contracting begins with a brief statement on economizing. The proposed schema for characterizing transactions and their governance is then developed, including the relation of the schema with Macneil's three-way classification of contract.

A. *Economizing*

The criterion for organizing commercial transactions is assumed to be the strictly instrumental one of cost economizing. Essentially this takes two parts: economizing on production expense and economizing on transaction costs.[42] To the degree that transaction costs are negligible, buying rather than making will normally be the most cost-effective means of procurement.[43] Not only can static scale economies be more fully exhausted by buying rather than making, but the supplier who aggregates uncorrelated demands can realize collective pooling benefits as well. Since external procurement avoids many of the bureaucratic hazards of internal procurement (which hazards, however, are themselves of a transaction-cost kind),[44] external procurement is evidently warranted.[45]

As indicated, however, the object is to economize on the *sum* of production and transaction costs. To the degree production-cost economies of external procurement are small and/or the transaction costs associated with external procurement are great, alternative supply arrangements deserve serious consideration. Economizing on transaction costs essentially reduces

---

[42] More generally, the economizing problem includes choice between a special-purpose and a general-purpose good or service. A general-purpose item affords all of the advantages of market procurement, but possibly at the sacrifice of valued design or performance characteristics. A special-purpose item has the opposite features: valued differences are realized but market procurement here may pose hazards. For the purposes of this paper, intermediate-product characteristics are mainly taken as given and I focus principally on production and transaction-cost economies. A more general formulation would include product characteristics in the optimization.

[43] This ignores transient conditions, such as temporary excess˙ capacity. (In a zero-transaction-cost world, such excesses vanish as assets can be deployed as effectively by others as they can by the owner.)

[44] On these hazards and their transaction-cost origins, see Oliver E. Williamson, *supra* note 1, at 117-31.

[45] Dennis Carlton shows that economies of "vertical integration" can frequently be realized in a market where, absent integration, buyers and suppliers are randomly paired. As he defines vertical integration, however, this can be accomplished as effectively by long-term contract as it can by in-house production. Dennis W. Carlton, Vertical Integration in Competitive Markets under Uncertainty, 27 J. Indus. Econ. 189 (1979).

to economizing on bounded rationality while simultaneously safeguarding the transactions in question against the hazards of opportunism. Holding the governance structure constant, these two objectives are in tension, since a reduction in one commonly results in an increase in the other.[46]

Governance structures, however, are properly regarded as part of the optimization problem. For some transactions, a shift from one structure to another may permit a simultaneous reduction in both the expense of writing a complex contract (which economizes on bounded rationality) and the expense of executing it effectively in an adaptive, sequential way (by attenuating opportunism). Indeed, this is precisely the attraction of internal procurement for transactions of a recurrent, idiosyncratic kind. Not only are market-aggregation economies negligible for such transactions—since the requisite investments are transaction-specific—but market trading in these circumstances is shot through with appropriable quasi-rent hazards. The issues here have been developed elsewhere.[47] The object of this paper is to integrate them into a larger contractual framework.

Note in this connection that the prospect of recovering the set-up costs associated with specialized governance structures varies with the frequency with which transactions recur. Specialized governance structures are much easier to justify for recurrent transactions than for identical transactions that occur only occasionally.

B. *Characterizing Transactions*

I asserted earlier that the critical dimensions for describing contractual relations are uncertainty, the frequency with which transactions recur, and the degree to which investments are idiosyncratic. To simplify the exposition, I will assume uncertainty exists in some intermediate degree and focus initially on frequency and the degree to which the expenses incurred are transaction-specific. The separate importance of uncertainty will then be developed in Section III.D. Three frequency and three investment categories will be recognized. Frequency can be characterized as one-time, occasional, and recurrent; and investments are classed as nonspecific, mixed, and idiosyncratic. To further simplify the argument, the following assumptions are made: (1) Suppliers intend to be in business on a continuing basis; thus the special hazards posed by fly-by-night firms can be disregarded. (2) Potential suppliers for any given requirement are numerous—which is to say that *ex ante* monopoly in ownership of specialized resources is assumed away. (3)

---

[46] Thus a reduction in monitoring commonly gives rise to an increase in opportunism. Monitoring the employment relation, however, needs to be done with special care. Progressively increasing the intensity of surveillance can elicit resentment and have counterproductive (for example, work-to-rule) results. Such perversities are less likely for interfirm trading.

[47] See note 30 *supra*.

The frequency dimension refers strictly to buyer activity in the market.[48] (4) The investment dimension refers to the characteristics of investments made by suppliers.[49]

Although discrete transactions are intriguing—for example, purchasing local spirits from a shopkeeper in a remote area of a foreign country to which one never again expects to visit nor to refer his friends—few transactions have this totally isolated character. For those that do not, the difference between one-time and occasional transactions is not apparent. Accordingly, only occasional and recurrent frequency distinctions will be maintained. The two-by-three matrix shown in Figure I thus describes the six types of transactions to which governance structures need to be matched. Illustrative transactions appear in the cells.

		Investment Characteristics		
		Nonspecific	Mixed	Idiosyncratic
Frequency	Occasional	Purchasing Standard Equipment	Purchasing Customized Equipment	Constructing a Plant
	Recurrent	Purohasing Standard Material	Purchasing Customized Material	Site-Speoifio Transfer of Intermediate Product Across Successive Stages

FIGURE I
ILLUSTRATIVE COMMERCIAL TRANSACTIONS

C. *Governance Structures*

Three broad types of governance structures will be considered: non-transaction-specific, semi-specific, and highly specific. The market is the classic nonspecific governance structure within which "faceless buyers and sellers . . . meet . . . for an instant to exchange standardized goods at

---

[48] This seems reasonable for most intermediate-product market transactions.

[49] Production aspects are thus emphasized. Investments in governance structure are treated separately.

equilibrium prices."[50] By contrast, highly specific structures are tailored to the special needs of the transaction. Identity here clearly matters. Semi-specific structures, naturally, fall in between. Several propositions are suggested immediately. (1) Highly standardized transactions are not apt to require specialized governance structure. (2) Only recurrent transactions will support a highly specialized governance structure.[51] (3) Although occasional transactions of a nonstandardized kind will not support a transaction-specific governance structure, they require special attention nonetheless. In terms of Macneil's three-way classification of contract, classical contracting presumably applies to all standardized transactions (whatever the frequency), relational contracting develops for transactions of a recurring and nonstandardized kind, and neoclassical contracting is needed for occasional, nonstandardized transactions.

1. *Market Governance: Classical Contracting.* Market governance is the main governance structure for nonspecific transactions of both occasional and recurrent contracting. Markets are especially efficacious when recurrent transactions are contemplated, since both parties need only consult their own experience in deciding to continue a trading relationship or, at little transitional expense, turn elsewhere. Being standardized, alternative purchase and supply arrangements are presumably easy to work out.

Nonspecific but occasional transactions are ones for which buyers (and sellers) are less able to rely on direct experience to safeguard transactions against opportunism. Often, however, rating services or the experience of other buyers of the same good can be consulted. Given that the good or service is of a standardized kind, such experience rating, by formal and informal means, will provide incentives for parties to behave responsibly.

To be sure, such transactions take place within and benefit from a legal framework. But such dependence is not great. As S. Todd Lowry puts it, "the traditional economic analysis of exchange in a market setting properly corresponds to the legal concept of *sale* (rather than contract), since sale presumes arrangements in a market context and requires legal support primarily in enforcing transfers of title."[52] He would thus reserve the concept of contract for exchanges where, in the absence of standardized market

---

[50] Yoram Ben-Porath, *supra* note 29, at 7.

[51] Defense contracting may appear to be a counterexample, since an elaborate governance structure is devised for many of these. This reflects in part, however, the special disabilities of the government as a production instrument. But for this, many of these contracts would be organized in-house. Also, contracts that are very large and of long duration, as many defense contracts are, do have a recurring character.

[52] S. Todd Lowry, Bargain and Contract Theory in Law and Economics, 10 J. Econ. Issues 1, 12 (1976).

alternatives, the parties have designed "patterns of future relations on which they could rely."[53]

The assumptions of the discrete-contracting paradigm are rather well satisfied for transactions where markets serve as a main governance mode. Thus the specific identity of the parties is of negligible importance; substantive content is determined by reference to formal terms of the contract; and legal rules apply. Market alternatives are mainly what protect each party against opportunism by his opposite.[54] Litigation is strictly for settling claims; concentrated efforts to sustain the relation are not made because the relation is not independently valued.[55]

2. Trilateral Governance: Neoclassical Contracting. The two types of transactions for which trilateral governance is needed are occasional transactions of the mixed and highly idiosyncratic kinds. Once the principals to such transactions have entered into a contract, there are strong incentives to see the contract through to completion. Not only have specialized investments been put in place, the opportunity cost of which is much lower in alternative uses, but the transfer of these assets to a successor supplier would pose inordinate difficulties in asset valuation.[56] The interests of the principals in sustaining the relation are especially great for highly idiosyncratic transactions.

Market relief is thus unsatisfactory. Often the setup costs of a transaction-specific governance structure cannot be recovered for occasional transactions. Given the limits of classical contract law for sustaining these transactions, on the one hand, and the prohibitive cost of transaction-specific (bilateral) governance, on the other, an intermediate institutional form is evidently needed.

Neoclassical contract law has many of the sought-after qualities. Thus rather than resorting immediately to strict reliance on litigation—with its

---

[53] *Id.* at 13.

[54] Although recurrent, standard transactions are ones for which an active spot market commonly exists, term contracting may also be employed—especially as planning economies are thereby realized by the parties. See Dennis W. Carlton, Price Rigidity, Forward Contracts, and Market Equilibrium, J. Pol. Econ. (forthcoming). The duration of these contracts will not be long, however, since the assets in question can be employed in other uses and/or in the service of other customers. The result is that changing market circumstances will be reflected relatively quickly in both price and quantity and relatively stringent contracting attitudes may be said to prevail.

[55] "Generally speaking, a serious conflict, even quite a minor one such as an objection to a harmlessly late tender of the delivery of goods, terminates the discrete contract as a live one and leaves nothing but a conflict over money damages to be settled by a lawsuit. Such a result fits neatly the norms of enhancing discreteness and intensifying . . . presentation." Macneil, Contracts 877.

[56] See the articles cited in note 30 *supra*.

transaction-rupturing features—*third-party assistance* (arbitration) in resolving disputes and evaluating peformance is employed instead. (The use of the architect as a relatively independent expert to determine the content of form construction contracts is an example.)[57] Also, the expansion of the specific-performance remedy in past decades is consistent with continuity purposes—though Macneil declines to characterize specific performance as the "primary neoclassical contract remedy."[58] The section of the Uniform Commercial Code which permits the "seller aggrieved by a buyer's breach . . . unilaterally to maintain the relation"[59] is yet another example.

3. *Transaction-specific Governance: Relational Contracting.* The two types of transactions for which specialized governance structures are commonly devised are recurring transactions of the mixed and highly idiosyncratic kinds. The nonstandardized nature of these transactions makes primary reliance on market governance hazardous, while their recurrent nature permits the cost of the specialized governance structure to be recovered.

Two types of transaction-specific governance structures for intermediate-production market transactions can be distinguished: bilateral structures, where the autonomy of the parties is maintained, and unified structures, where the transaction is removed from the market and organized within the firm subject to an authority relation (vertical integration). Bilateral structures have only recently received the attention they deserve and their operation is least well understood.

(a) *Bilateral Governance: Obligational Contracting.* Highly idiosyncratic transactions are ones where the human and physical assets required for production are extensively specialized, so there are no obvious scale economies to be realized through interfirm trading that the buyer (or seller) is unable to realize himself (through vertical integration). In the case, however, of mixed transactions, the degree of asset specialization is less complete. Accordingly, outside procurement for these components may be favored by scale-economy considerations.

As compared with vertical integration, outside procurement also is good in eliciting cost control for steady-state supply. Problems, however, arise when adaptability and contractual expense are considered. Whereas internal adaptations can be effected by fiat, outside procurement involves effecting adaptations across a market interface. Unless the need for adaptations has been contemplated from the outset and expressly provided for by the contract,

---

[57] Macneil, Contracts 866.

[58] *Id.* at 879.

[59] *Id.* at 880. The rationale for this section of the Code is that "identification of the goods to the contract will, within limits, permit the seller to recover the price of the goods rather than merely damages for the breach. . . , ([where the] latter may be far less in amount and more difficult to prove)." *Id.*

which often is impossible or prohibitively expensive, adaptations across a market interface can be accomplished only by mutual, follow-on agreements. Inasmuch as the interests of the parties will commonly be at variance when adaptation proposals (originated by either party) are made, a dilemma is evidently posed.

On the one hand, both parties have an incentive to sustain the relationship rather than to permit it to unravel, the object being to avoid the sacrifice of valued transaction-specific economies. On the other hand, each party appropriates a separate profit stream and cannot be expected to accede readily to any proposal to adapt the contract. What is needed, evidently, is some way for declaring admissible dimensions for adjustment such that flexibility is provided under terms in which both parties have confidence. This can be accomplished partly by (1) recognizing that the hazards of opportunism vary with the type of adaptation proposed and (2) restricting adjustments to those where the hazards are least. But the spirit within which adaptations are effected is equally important.[60]

Quantity adjustments have much better incentive-compatibility properties than do price adjustments. For one thing, price adjustments have an unfortunate zero-sum quality, whereas proposals to increase, decrease, or delay delivery do not. Also, except as discussed below, price-adjustment proposals involve the risk that one's opposite is contriving to alter the terms within the bilateral monopoly trading gap to his advantage. By contrast, a presumption that exogenous events, rather than strategic purposes, are responsible for quantity adjustments is ordinarily warranted. Given the mixed nature of the exchange, a seller (or buyer) simply has little reason to doubt the representations of his opposite when a quantity change is proposed.

Thus buyers will neither seek supply from other sources nor divert products obtained (at favorable prices) to other uses (or users)—because other sources will incur high setup costs and an idiosyncratic product is nonfungible across uses and users. Likewise, sellers will not withhold supply because better opportunities have arisen, since the assets in question have a specialized character. The result is that quantity representations for idiosyncratic products can ordinarily be taken at face value. Since inability to adapt both quantity and price would render most idiosyncratic exchanges nonviable, quantity adjustments occur routinely.

---

[60] As Stewart Macaulay observes, "Disputes are frequently settled without reference to the contract or to potential or actual legal sanctions. There is a hesitancy to speak of legal right or to threaten to sue in . . . negotiations" where continuing business is valued. Stewart Macaulay, *supra* note 9, at 61.

The material which follows in this subsection was originally developed in connection with the study of inflation. See Michael L. Wachter & Oliver E. Williamson, Obligational Markets and the Mechanics of Inflation, 9 Bell J. Econ. 549 (1978).

Of course, not all price adjustments pose the same degree of hazard. Those which pose few hazards will predictably be implemented. Crude escalator clauses which reflect changes in general economic conditions are one possibility. But since such escalators are not transaction-specific, imperfect adjustments often result when these escalators are applied to local conditions. We should therefore consider whether price adjustments that are more closely related to local circumstances are feasible. The issue here is whether interim price adjustments can be devised for some subset of conditions such that the strategic hazards described above do not arise. What are the preconditions?

Crises facing either of the parties to an idiosyncratic exchange constitute one class of exceptions. Faced with a viability crisis which jeopardizes the relationship, ad hoc price relief may be permitted. More relevant and interesting, however, is whether there are circumstances whereby interim price adjustments are made routinely. The preconditions here are two: first, proposals to adjust prices must relate to exogenous, germane, and easily verifiable events; and second, quantifiable cost consequences must be confidently related thereto. An example may help to illustrate. Consider a component for which a significant share of the cost is accounted for by a basic material (copper, steel). Assume, moreover, that the fractional cost of the component in terms of this basic material is well specified. An exogenous change in prices of materials would under these circumstances pose few hazards if partial but interim price relief were permitted by allowing pass-through according to formula. A more refined adjustment than aggregate escalators would afford thereby obtains.

It bears emphasis, however, that not all costs so qualify. Changes in overhead or other expenses for which validation is difficult and which, even if verified, bear an uncertain relation to the cost of the component will not be passed through in a similar way. Recognizing the hazards, the parties will simply forgo relief of this kind.

(b) *Unified Governance: Internal Organization.* Incentives for trading weaken as transactions become progressively more idiosyncratic. The reason is that, as the specialized human and physical assets become more specialized to a single use, and hence less transferable to other uses, economies of scale can be as fully realized by the buyer as by an outside supplier.[61] The choice of organizing mode then turns on which mode has superior adaptive

---

[61] This assumes that factor prices paid by buyer and outside supplier are identical. Where this is not true, as in some unionized firms, buyers may choose to procure outside because of a differential wage rate. This is a common problem in the automobile industry, which has a very flat and relatively high wage scale.

properties. As discussed elsewhere, vertical integration will invariably appear in these circumstances.[62]

The advantage of vertical integration is that adaptations can be made in a sequential way without the need to consult, complete, or revise interfirm agreements. Where a single ownership entity spans both sides of the transactions, a presumption of joint profit maximization is warranted. Thus price adjustments in vertically integrated enterprises will be more complete than in interfirm trading. And quantity adjustments, of course, will be implemented at whatever frequency serves to maximize the joint gain to the transaction.

Unchanging identity at the interface coupled with extensive adaptability in both price and quantity is thus characteristic of highly idiosyncratic transactions which are vertically integrated. Obligational contracting is supplanted by the more comprehensive adaptive capability afforded by administration.

The match of governance structures with transactions that results from these economizing efforts is shown in Figure II.

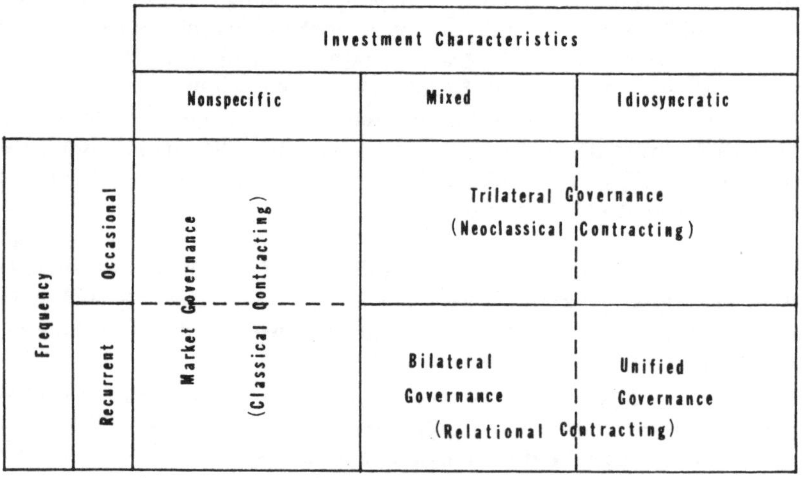

		Investment Characteristics		
		Nonspecific	Mixed	Idiosyncratic
Frequency	Occasional	Market Governance (Classical Contracting)	Trilateral Governance (Neoclassical Contracting)	
	Recurrent		Bilateral Governance (Relational Contracting)	Unified Governance

FIGURE II

MATCHING GOVERNANCE STRUCTURES WITH COMMERCIAL TRANSACTIONS

D. *Uncertainty*

Transactions conducted under certainty are relatively uninteresting. Except as they differ in the time required to reach an equilibrium-exchange

[62] See the references cited in note 4 *supra*.

configuration, any governance structure will do. More relevant are transactions where uncertainty is present to an intermediate or high degree. The foregoing has dealt with the first of these. The question here is how the governance of transactions is affected by increasing the degree of uncertainty.

Recall that nonspecific transactions are ones for which continuity has little value, since new trading relations are easily arranged. Increasing the degree of uncertainty does not alter this. Accordingly, market exchange continues and the discrete-contracting paradigm (classical contract law) holds across standardized transactions of all kinds, whatever the degree of uncertainty.

Matters are different with transaction-specific investments. Whenever investments are idiosyncratic in nontrivial degree, increasing the degree of uncertainty makes it more imperative that the parties devise a machinery to "work things out"—since contractual gaps will be larger and the occasions for sequential adaptations will increase in number and importance as the degree of uncertainty increases. This has special relevance for the organization of transactions with mixed investment attributes. Two possibilities exist. One would be to sacrifice valued design features in favor of a more standardized good or service. Market governance would then apply. The second would be to preserve the design but surround the transaction with an elaborated governance apparatus, thereby facilitating more effective adaptive, sequential decision making. Specifically, a more elaborate arbitration apparatus is apt to be devised for occasional, nonstandard transactions. And bilateral governance structures will often give way to unified ones as uncertainty is increased for recurrent transactions.

Reductions in uncertainty, of course, warrant shifting transactions in the opposite direction. To the extent that uncertainty decreases as an industry matures, which is the usual case, the benefits that accrue to integration presumably decline. Accordingly, greater reliance on obligational market contracting is commonly feasible for transactions of recurrent trading in mature industries.

IV. OTHER APPLICATIONS

The three dimensions for describing transactions—frequency, investment idiosyncrasy, and uncertainty—apply to transactions of all kinds. The same general considerations that apply to governance structures for commercial transactions carry over as well. The specific governance structures for organizing commercial transactions do not, however, apply without modification to the governance of other types of transactions. Applications of the framework to the study of labor markets, regulation, family law, and capital markets are briefly sketched here.

A. *Labor*

Occasional labor-market transactions typically take the form of repair or replacement services—the plumber, electrician, and so forth. Especially in older homes or structures, these transactions can take on an idiosyncratic quality. Although such transactions can be interesting, the transactions on which I want to focus are recurrent labor-market transactions of the nonspecific, mixed, and idiosyncratic kinds.

Clyde Summers's examination of collective agreements in relation to the law of contracts disclosed that, while the collective bargain differed greatly from the ordinary bargain of commerce, collective agreements are nonetheless a part of the "mainstream of contract."[63] He suggested that the study of contract proceed on two levels: the search for an underlying framework and, within that framework, an examination of the distinctive institutional attributes that distinguish each type of transaction. With respect to the first of these he conjectured that "the principles common to the whole range of contractual transactions are relatively few and of such generality and competing character that they should not be stated as legal rules at all."[64]

I am persuaded that Summers's two-part strategy for studying contract leads to a deeper understanding of the issues. And I believe that the framework set out in the preceding sections of this paper provides much of the underlying unity called for by Summers. What differs as one moves across various contracting activities is the institutional infrastructure.

(1) *Nonspecific Transactions.* Nonspecific labor-market transactions are ones where employer and employee are largely indifferent to the identity of each. Migrant farm labor is an example. Although an unchanging employment association between firm and worker may be observed to continue over long intervals for some of these employees, each party is essentially meeting bids in the spot market. A valuable ongoing relationship, in which specific training and on-the-job learning yield idiosyncratic benefits, is thus not implied. Both wages and employment are variable and market governance applies to transactions of this kind. Consider, therefore, mixed and idiosyncratic labor-market transactions.

(2) *Mixed Transactions.* Probably the most interesting labor-market transactions are those where large numbers of workers acquire an intermediate degree of firm-specific skill. Note that, inasmuch as the degree of idiosyncrasy is a design variable, firms would presumably redesign jobs to favor more standardized operations if it were impossible to devise governance structures which prevented antagonistic bargaining relations from developing between firms and idiosyncratically skilled employees. Although

[63] Clyde W. Summers, *supra* note 9, at 527.
[64] *Id.* at 568.

least-cost production technologies would be sacrificed in the process, net gains might nevertheless be realized since incumbent workers would realize little strategic advantage over otherwise qualified but inexperienced outsiders.

Justice Rhenquist has observed that "Adjudicatory review of the decisions of certain institutions, while perhaps insuring a 'better' decision in some objective sense, can only disrupt on-going relationships within the institution and thereby hamper the institution's ability to serve its designated societal function."[65] Examples of adjudicatory review with respect to which he counsels caution include collective bargaining agreements.

The reasons for this are that adjudicatory review is not easily apprised of the special needs of the transaction and the prospect of such review impairs the incentive of the parties to devise bilateral governance structure. The *Vaca v. Stipes* holding, which Justice Rhenquist cites, is fully consistent with this interpretation. There the Court held that an individual could not compel his union to take his grievance to arbitration, since if the law were otherwise "the settlement machinery provided by the contract would be substantially undermined, thus . . . [introducing] the vagaries of independent and unsystematic negotiations."[66] Archibald Cox elaborates as follows:[67]

. . . giving the union control over all claims arising under the collective agreement comports so much better with the functional nature of a collective bargaining agreement. . . . Allowing an individual to carry a claim to arbitration whenever he is dissatisfied with the adjustment worked out by the company and the union . . . discourages the kind of day-to-day cooperation between company and union which is normally the mark of sound industrial relations—a relationship in which grievances are treated as problems to be solved and contracts are only guideposts in a dynamic human relationship. When . . . the individual's claim endangers group interests, the union's function is to resolve the competition by reaching an accommodation or striking a balance.

The practice described by Cox of giving the union control over arbitration claims plainly permits group interests—whence the concern for system viability—to supersede individual interests, thereby curbing small-numbers opportunism.

General escalator or predetermined wage adjustments aside, wages are unchanging under collective bargaining agreements.[68] Interim adaptations are nonetheless essential. These take three forms: (1) quantity adjustments,

---

[65] Remarks of Mr. Justice Rhenquist, *supra* note 38, at 4.

[66] 386 U.S. 171, 191 (1967).

[67] Archibald Cox, *supra* note 9, at 24.

[68] The reason, of course, is that it is very costly and apt to be unproductive to reopen wage bargaining during the period covered by a contract. Since to reopen negotiations for one type of job is to invite it for all, and as objective differences among jobs may be difficult to demonstrate, wage bargaining is foreclosed except at contract-renewal intervals.

(2) assignment changes, and (3) refinement of working rules as a result of grievances.

Quantity adjustments are made in response to changing market opportunities. Either the level or the mix of employment is adjusted as economic events unfold. Given that valuable firm-specific training and learning reside in the workers, layoffs with a presumption of reemployment when conditions improve are common. Conformably, the degree to which the machinery governing access to jobs is elaborated ought to vary directly with the degree to which jobs in a firm are idiosyncratic. Thus promotion ladders in firms where a succession of interdependent jobs are highly idiosyncratic should be long and thin, with access mainly restricted to the bottom, whereas promotion ladders in nonidiosyncratic activities should be broadly structured.[69] Likewise, promotion on merit ought to be favored over promotion strictly by seniority in firms where jobs are more idiosyncratic.[70]

(3) *Highly Idiosyncratic Transactions.* Recall that idiosyncratic transactions involve not merely uniqueness but uniqueness of a transaction-specific kind. Also recall that our concern in this section is with recurring transactions. Thus, although there are many uniquely skilled individuals (artists, athletes, researchers, administrators), unique skills are rarely of a transaction-specific kind. On the contrary, most of these individuals could move to another organization without significant productivity losses.

The exceptions are those where the benefits which accrue to experience (inside knowledge) and/or team interaction effects are great. Whereas commercial transactions of a highly idiosyncratic nature are unified under a common ownership, limits on indenture foreclose this option for labor-market transactions. Instead of "merger," complex contracts designed to tie the interests of the individual to the organization on a long-term basis are negotiated. Severe penalties are provided should either party seek unilateral termination. Nonvested, long-term, contingent reward schemes are devised. More generally, transaction-specific infrastructure will be highly individuated for such transactions.

B. *Regulation of Natural Monopoly*

Again the argument is that specialized governance structure is needed to the degree efficient supply necessarily joins buyers and sellers in a bilateral

---

[69] Michael L. Wachter & Oliver E. Williamson, *supra* note 60, at 567.

[70] Thus although both nonidiosyncratic and idiosyncratic jobs may be organized collectively, the way in which the internal labor markets associated with each are organized should reflect objective differences between them. Additionally, the incentive to provide an orderly governance structure varies directly with the degree to which efficiencies are attributable thereto. *Ceteris paribus*, nonidiosyncratic jobs ought to be organized later and the governance structure less fully elaborated than for idiosyncratic jobs. Both propositions are borne out by the evidence.

trading relation of a continuing nature. And again, the object of governance is to (1) protect the interests of the respective parties and (2) adapt the relationship to changing circumstances.

Although differing in details, both Victor Goldberg[71] and I[72] have argued that specialized governance structure is needed for services for which natural monopoly features are great. Such structure presumably has the purpose of providing sellers (investors) and buyers with security of expectations, which is a protective function, while at the same time facilitating adaptive, sequential decision making. Rate-of-return regulation with periodic review has these features. To the extent, however, that such regulation is observed in conjunction with activities where transaction-specific investments are insubstantial (as, for example, in the trucking industry), the case for regulation is not at all apparent—or, if it is to be made, must appeal to arguments very different from those set out here.

C. Family Law

The issue here is whether the role of adjudication should be *expanded* to help govern family relationships. Granting that adjudication as ultimate relief can and often does serve a useful role for sustaining family relations, such relations are plainly idiosyncratic to an unusual degree and a specialized governance structure is surely the main mode of governance. As the role of adjudication is expanded, reliance upon internal structure is apt to be reduced. Therefore, except when individual rights are seriously threatened, withholding access to adjudication may be indicated.

Justice Rhenquist's remarks concerning the corrosive effects of adversary hearings on the family are apposite: "Any sort of adversary hearing which pits parent against child is bound to be disruptive, placing stresses and tensions on the intra-familial relationships which in turn weaken the family as an institution."[73] Whether, as this suggests, parent-child family relations are optimized where adjudication is zero or negligible is beyond the scope of this paper. It suffices for my purposes merely to note that valued family relations are recurrent and idiosyncratic and that a specialized, transaction-specific governance structure must be encouraged lest the parties withhold investing heavily in the institution.[74]

---

[71] Victor P. Goldberg, *supra* note 1.

[72] Oliver E. Williamson, *supra* note 30.

[73] Remarks of Mr. Justice Rhenquist, *supra* note 38, at 19.

[74] For a more extensive discussion of family transactions, see Yoram Ben-Porath, *supra* note 29, at 4-7.

D. *Capital Market Transactions*

The ease of verification is critical to the operation of capital markets.[75] Where verification is easy, markets work well and additional governance is unnecessary. Where verification is difficult or very difficult, however, additional governance may be indicated. Occasional transactions are apt to benefit from third-party assistance, while recurring transactions are ones for which bilateral or unified governance will presumably be observed. Assessing capital-market transactions within the proposed framework is thus accomplished by substituting "ease of verification" for "degree of transaction-specific investment." Once this is done, the governance structures appropriate to capital markets are broadly similar to those within which commercial transactions are organized.

V. IMPLICATIONS

Dimensionalizing transactions and examining the costs of executing different transactions in different ways generate a large number of institutional implications. Some of these are summarized here.

A. *General*

1. Nonspecific transactions, either occasional or recurrent, are efficiently organized by markets.

2. Occasional transactions that are nonstandardized stand most to benefit from adjudication.

3. A transaction-specific governance structure is more fully developed where transactions are (1) recurrent, (2) entail idiosyncratic investment, and (3) are executed under greater uncertainty.

B. *Commercial Transactions*

1. Optimization of commercial transactions requires simultaneous attention to (1) production economies, (2) transaction-cost economies, and (3) component design.

2. The reason why Macaulay observes so few litigated cases in business[76] is because markets work well for nonspecific transactions, while recurrent, nonstandard transactions are governed by bilateral or unified structures.

3. As uncertainty increases, the obligational market-contracting mode will not be used for recurrent transactions with mixed investment features. Such transactions will either be standardized, and shifted to the market, or organized internally.

[75] This feature was called to my attention by Sanford Grossman.
[76] Stewart Macaulay, *supra* note 9.

4. As generic demand grows and the number of supply sources increases, exchange that was once transaction-specific loses this characteristic and greater reliance on market-mediated governance is feasible. Thus vertical integration may give way to obligational market contracting, which in turn may give way to markets.

5. Where inventory and related flow-process economies are great, site-specific supply and transaction-specific governance (commonly vertical integration) will be observed. Generic demand here has little bearing.

6. The organization of the interface between manufacturing and distribution reflects similar investment considerations: goods and services that can be sold without incurring transaction-specific investment will be distributed through conventional marketing channels while those where such investments are great will be supported by specialized—mainly bilateral (for example, franchising) or unified (forward integration)—governance structures.

7. The governance of technical change poses special difficulties. The frequently noted limits of markets[77] often give way to more complex governance relations, again for the same general reasons and along the same general lines as are set out here.[78]

C. *Other Transactions*

1. The efficiency benefits of collective organization are negligible for nonspecific labor. Accordingly, such labor will be organized late, often only with the assistance of the political process.

2. Internal labor markets become more highly individuated as jobs become more varied and idiosyncratic.

3. Regulation can be interpreted in part as a response to the transactional dilemma posed by natural monopoly.

4. A transaction-cost justification for regulating activities for which transaction-specific investments are lacking (for example, trucking) is not apparent. The possibility that politics is the driving consideration in such industries warrants consideration.

5. Adjudication should proceed with caution in the area of family law lest valued transaction-specific investments be discouraged.

6. Ease of verification is the capital-market counterpart of transaction-specific investments. Upon making this substitution, the organization of capital markets and intermediate-product markets is broadly similar.

---

[77] Kenneth J. Arrow, Economic Welfare and the Allocation of Resources for Invention, in The Rate and Direction of Economic Activity 609 (1962).

[78] Aspects are discussed in Oliver E. Williamson, *supra* note 1, at 203-05.

VI. CONCLUDING REMARKS

Transaction-cost economics is an interdisciplinary undertaking that joins economics with aspects of organization theory and overlaps extensively with contract law. It is the modern counterpart of institutional economics and relies heavily on comparative analysis.[79] Frictionless ideals are useful mainly for reference purposes.

Although mathematical economics captures only a fraction of the transaction-cost phenomena of interest,[80] this has not been the only obstacle. Headway with the study of transaction-cost issues has been impeded by lack of verbal definitions. Identifying the critical dimensions with respect to which transactions differ has been a significant omission.

This paper attempts to rectify this deficiency and identifies uncertainty, frequency of exchange, and the degree to which investments are transaction-specific as the principal dimensions for describing transactions. The efficient organization of economic activity entails matching governance structures with these transactional attributes in a discriminating way.

Although the main applications in this paper are to commercial contracting, the proposed approach generalizes easily to the study of labor contracts. It also has ramifications for understanding both public utility regulation and family relations. A unified approach to contract thus emerges.

The fact that the broad features of so many varied transactions fit within the framework is encouraging. The importance of transaction costs to the organization of economic activity is thus confirmed. But the world of contract is enormously complex,[81] and the simple economizing framework proposed here cannot be expected to capture more than main features. Elaborating the framework to deal with microanalytic phenomena, however, should be feasible. And extending it to include additional or substitute dimensions (of which the ease of verification, in the case of capital-market transactions, is an example) may sometimes be necessary.

[79] Reliance on comparative analysis has been repeatedly emphasized by R. H. Coase, *supra* note 1.

[80] See Carl J. Dahlman, *supra* note 1, at 144-47.

[81] Benjamin Klein, Robert C. Crawford, & Armen A. Alchian, *supra* note 1, at 325.

[11]

Proceedings

Institutional Design and Innovation
(Vernon W. Ruttan, University of Minnesota, presiding)

Inventing New Institutions: The Design Perspective

Leonid Hurwicz

We live in an era of significant changes in the prevailing economic institutions, to a considerable extent in the direction of decentralization. In the West (U.S., U.K., France) steps have been taken toward deregulation as well as privatization or denationalization of public enterprises. In the People's Republic of China, in Hungary, and most recently in the Soviet Union, reforms have been carried out or proposed to move from command to market guidance of economic processes (see, for instance, Kornai). Earlier periods witnessed trends of the opposite type: establishment of regulatory agencies, nationalization of privately owned enterprises, and the substitution of decisions made by central organs of the state for market processes. Hence, although the early development of the design theory owes a great deal to the famous exchanges between Hayek, Lange, Lerner, and Mises, recent events alone justify interest in problems of design.

But design problems are not limited to those involving the grand systems for national economies. Indeed, some of the most valuable insights derive from an analysis of the internal problems of managing firms, issues raised by vertical or lateral integration of previously independent units, as well as the comparison of performance characteristics of price versus quantity guidance of production in integrated firms or other economic organizations.

Some institutional changes may be viewed

as purely evolutionary phenomena, induced (as analyzed by Ruttan) by changes in external factors (technological, political, or other). But often these changes contain an important element of conscious design and produce an institutional framework different from anything that existed before. It may not be incorrect to view the new institutions as "invented."

Although an invention involves a creative act, the science of economics should provide an analytical framework to aid in the design of new institutions or systems. Traditional economics does not do this. But two recent streams of thought, especially if integrated, can be useful for this purpose. The two are general theories (primarily normative in spirit) of resource allocation mechanisms and more specialized theories (mostly intended to explain observed phenomena) of the organizational structures of economic institutions, especially firms, markets, and hierarchies. Our purpose here is to indicate how these two approaches can be synthesized in order to strengthen each other.

To accomplish this we consider, against the background of the general theory of mechanisms, some of the problems raised by the specialized models.

Before discussing mechanism design, it may be helpful to look at a special but highly instructive case, that of a class of agricultural systems considered by Stiglitz. Stiglitz's model, unlike those considered below, fixes the formula according to which workers are rewarded. The formula is a simple linear one. With trivial notational changes it can be written as

$$y = aq + b,$$

where y is the worker's reward and q is his/her individual output, while a and b are parame-

The papers in the "Proceedings" section were presented at the AAEA sessions held at the annual meeting of the Allied Social Science Associations, New Orleans, Louisiana, 28–30 December 1986.

Leonid Hurwicz is a regents' professor of economics at the University of Minnesota.

Aid from National Science Foundation grants SES-8509547 and IST-8510042 is gratefully acknowledged by the author.

396 *May 1987*   *Amer. J. Agr. Econ.*

ters with *a* restricted to values between 0 and 1. Assigning specific values to the parameters yields certain familiar institutions. Thus *b* = 0, with *a* greater than 0 but less than one, yields the pure sharecropping system. With *a* = 0 and *b* positive, the worker is a wage earner. If *a* = 1 and *b* < 0, the worker is renting the land for the fixed fee of −*b*.

As Stiglitz points out, other cases are plausible. If the model itself is realistic, one could expect to observe various other combinations of parameter values. But from a normative point of view, one could imagine formulating an optimization problem with the formula fixed but the parameter values as the unknowns. In this example, the class of a priori admissible mechanisms is identified with a two-dimensional parameter space (*a*, *b*), and the simple design problem requires finding an optimizing pair of numbers (*a*, *b*). In a more general theory the formulas themselves are typically among the unknowns. Mathematically, design problems involve unknown functional relations: i.e., one is operating in a function space. Moreover, even the nature of the variables controlling the system, e.g., whether numerical or of some other type, must be included among the unknowns of a general design problem.

There are two main types of models of general resource allocation mechanisms: we shall call them message exchange models (also called adjustment processes) and (noncooperative, normal form) game-theoretic models. The former have primarily been used to study the informational aspects of economic mechanisms, the latter to explore the incentive aspects.

Message Exchange Models

A convenient form of such models may be described as a system of difference equations with individual messages as variables and the agents' characteristics as parameters. Actions to be taken are specified by the so-called outcome functions. To determine the outcome it is assumed either that the system is at rest (in equilibrium in the sense of stationarity) or if the process is subject to a time limit, that the time limit has been reached. The outcome function makes the action to be taken depend on the final or equilibrium messages. Since no actions are taken until the time limit or an equilibrium has been reached, the model is of the tâtonnement type.

Although there has been some work on the so-called non-tâtonnement models, most of the research follows the classical Walrasian tradition as formalized by Samuelson and uses tâtonnement models. But that is inadequate to account for phenomena described in specialized models where decisions concerning quantities, prices, or investments must be taken before equilibrium has been attained or a limit reached. Hence, to account for such phenomena, it is necessary to introduce actions as elements of the process: that is, to have a mixture of tâtonnement and non-tâtonnement. (Such a mixed model was constructed by Marschak in an unpublished paper presented at a decentralization conference held at Northwestern University in the early 1970s.)

Another frequent feature of message exchange models turns out to be too restrictive. Typically, one assumes the dynamics of the message exchange process to be temporally homogenous. This means that the relation of messages emitted at a given time to messages from previous time points remains the same at all times. But in applications, a particular time structure of information, communication, decisions, and actions is usually postulated. For instance, in a price-managed economy (such as considered in Weitzman 1974), the center specifies prices in the initial phase, while the level of output is decided by production managers in a later phase. Similarly, in the Grossman and Hart 1986 model, investment decisions are made at an early stage, while contracts and their implementation come later. Clearly, such processes are not temporally homogenous. Furthermore, while time runs ad infinitum in the usual models, the applied models are often characterized by a fixed time span, frequently just two or three periods. So, our model must also be enriched by permitting (although not requiring) temporal inhomogeneity.

The sacrifice of temporal homogeneity creates a problem. We may seem to lose the possibility of defining equilibrium in the sense of a stationary or rest value in a dynamic process. In a temporally homogenous process, its variables have stationary or rest values if those values remain unchanged once attained for a suitable number of periods. Without homogeneity this concept likely becomes vacuous.

But the notion of equilibrium, and in a sense even homogeneity, can be rescued by a formulation similar to that of a week in Hicks's *Value and Capital*. The different phases of decision making, bargaining, taking actions, and communicating may be thought of as occurring, say, on consecutive days of a single week. (In models with production, a year might be more appropriate.) However, there is a sequence of weeks. The agents' behavior in a given week is again a function of the events of one or more specified (finite) number of preceding weeks, and this functional relation does not change from week to week.

Hence, with a week as a point in time, and the events of a week as the new variable, the process is temporally homogenous, and it makes sense to speak of an equilibrium week. This would mean a pattern of events which, if prevailing for a specified (finite) number of weeks, would continue to prevail in subsequent weeks. This formulation would even permit speaking of equilibrium hierarchical structures, equilibrium degrees of vertical integration, and so forth. (The term "equilibrium," as used in the preceding paragraphs, meaning a stationary or rest position or value in a dynamic process, is distinct from—although not unrelated to—its usage in "competitive equilibrium" in much of the microeconomics literature, as well as from the notion of noncooperative game equilibrium, e.g., Nash equilibrium).

Message exchange models are useful in portraying phenomena where, for one reason or another, the patterns of the agents' responses under specified circumstances can be considered given. This applies, for instance, to the traditional descriptions of perfectly competitive (Walrasian) economies. Here prices and proposed quantities (supply or demand) are the messages; the traders' quantity responses are specified by the assumed maximization of utility or profit, with prices treated parametrically, while the auctioneer adjusts prices according to specified functions of excess demand. Again, message exchange models are applicable when agents operate according to specified rules (e.g., marginal cost pricing) and obey these rules. Indeed, it has been useful to study economic mechanisms viewed as message exchange systems in order to determine the feasibility of informational decentralization and minimal informational requirements to achieve efficient resource allocation.

But the message exchange models, with their a priori postulated response functions, may be inconsistent with natural motivations of the participating agents. To account for these motivations, we use models from game theory, especially from the theory of noncooperative games.

Noncooperative Games Models

A game, say chess, typically involves many moves. A player may be making decisions before every move. But, following the formulation due to von Neumann and Morgenstern, it is usually found convenient to think of each player as selecting a strategy, i.e., a rule prescribing behavior at every move given the information available to the player at the time the move is made. Hence, the choices of strategies by all players determine the physical outcome of the game. (To simplify exposition we ignore the possible randomization of moves or strategies.) Now the rules of the game determine the possible moves, hence the possible strategies, and—indirectly—the physical outcomes associated with any given choice of strategies by the players. The functional relation specifying the outcomes associated with strategy choices is called a game form or a (game) outcome function. In chess, the outcome specifies whether there is a draw or who wins. In economic models, the outcome may be the resulting resource allocation. It is important to distinguish the (physical) outcome from the players' utilities produced by that outcome. A game's payoff function (a composite of utility and outcome functions) specifies the players' utilities of the outcomes as functions of the chosen strategies. The formulation in terms of available strategies, outcome functions, and payoff functions is known as the normal form of a game—as distinct from the extensive form in which the detailed structure of information and decisions to be made at each move is explicitly brought out.

In the setting of noncooperative game models, the designer's role is to find game rules that would give an equilibrium outcome satisfying specified social goals or desiderata. By game rules we mean a specification of permissible moves (hence strategies) and of an outcome function. But the notion of social goals requires clarification. Simplistically, one

398   *May 1987*   *Amer. J. Agr. Econ.*

might think of such goals in terms of certain physical outcomes or ranges of outcomes, as with minimum standards of food, housing, or medical care. However, even these standards are subject to feasibility which, in turn, depends on the endowments and technologies of the participants. Furthermore, in general, outcomes are deemed desirable or not depending not only on their feasibility but also on the participants' preferences. Therefore, social goals constitute a relationship between the totality of individual characteristics on the one hand and (feasible) outcomes on the other. By a participant's characteristic we mean his/her endowment, preferences, and technology when the participant is a producer. The totality of such characteristics is usually called the (economic) environment or, more simply (but subject to misinterpretation), the economy.

Thus, social goals are formalized as a relation between the environment and outcomes. This relation is also called a social choice correspondence. It specifies a set of feasible outcomes considered desirable for a given economic environment, i.e., for a given totality (n-tuple when there are n participants) of individual characteristics. The most familiar social choice correspondence is that associating with each environment the set of all resource allocations that are Pareto-optimal in that environment.

We say that a set of game rules or mechanism (as specified by the strategy domains and the outcome function) implements a social choice correspondence over a given class of environments if the following two conditions are satisfied: (*a*) for any environment within the class there is an equilibrium outcome, and (*b*) the equilibrium outcomes for a given environment fall within the sets specified by that choice correspondence for that environment. (To distinguish it from other concepts, this definition is sometimes referred to as implementation in a weak sense.) By equilibrium we mean a solution of the noncooperative game defined by the specified strategies, outcome functions, and preferences. Different solution concepts are used either on normative or empirical grounds—Nash equilibria, dominance equilibria, minimax equilibria, and others. We shall primarily refer to Nash equilibria. (Strategies chosen by players constitute a Nash equilibrium if no unilateral change of strategy would result in an outcome preferable for the player making the unilateral change. A Nash equilibrium outcome is an outcome produced by an equilibrium set of strategies.) Our interpretation is that this is an assumption concerning the strategic behavior of participants, but the reader should be warned that this view is subject to considerable controversy.

The designer's role as just described reflects, of course, a normative point of view, since it takes the goals as given and seeks the means of implementing them. A difference between the normative theory of design and the more familiar branch of normative economic theory known as welfare economics is that in the design approach the unknown of the problem is the mechanism, while in welfare economics the unknown is typically the resource allocation. An approach that is a reverse of the design point of view is to take the mechanism as given and to explore the outcomes it generates. This is the case with those chapters of microeconomics textbooks that take the mechanism (perfect competition) as given and examine the Pareto-optimality properties of its equilibrium outcomes.

Among important contributions of design theory are the results concerning the implementability (in the sense of the above definition) of various social choice correspondences. It is not surprising that not every arbitrarily formulated set of social goals should be implementable. But it may have surprised some of us how narrow the boundaries of implementability turn out to be in some cases. Thus, dominance (truth-telling) equilibria, except in rare cases, violate the balance equalities and hence generate outcomes that are not, in general, Pareto-optimal. But even with the less stringent requirements of Nash equilibria, implementability is quite limited. In particular, if individual rationality as well as Pareto-optimality is among the goals, all competitive (Walrasian) outcomes must be among the equilibrium outcomes. (Individual rationality requires that nobody's final utility level should be lower than the initial level.) Hence a social choice correspondence viewing the competitive outcomes as undesirable, while insisting on Pareto-optimality and individual rationality, is not implementable. Again, the reader is warned that results of this type are sensitive to assumptions concerning strategic behavior and information available to the participants. Implementability under Bayesian postulates differs from those under pure Nash assumptions.

Even where implementability has been

shown to exist, serious difficulties may remain. (Thus the term is something of a misnomer.) Usually, implementability is demonstrated by constructing strategy domains and an outcome function generating desirable outcomes. In some cases, however, the strategies used in the proofs become so complex as to exceed any plausible bounds of human capacity to handle information. If one thinks of a strategy domain as a language (i.e., individual message space), the totality of the words it contains is greater than a finite-dimensional space. In some cases one might hope to find another mechanism implementing the same social goals but using a simpler strategy (message) space. But results obtained in the theory of message exchange mechanisms exhibit important economic classes of environments in which this hope is unjustified. In particular, this is the case in economies with increasing returns and those with infinite time horizons. In such economies efficiency (and hence Pareto-optimality) cannot be attained through any informationally decentralized message exchange mechanism, in particular not in a noncooperative game.

The excessive size of required strategy domains is only one example of issues of informational infeasibility (or, more generally, resource cost) of mechanisms. Another example arises in situations where the Arrow-Debreu model would call for a multitude of contingent commodities and a specification of quantities to be traded depending on which contingency (state of nature) occurs. Even if the numbers of contingencies and of commodities are finite, the solutions to the optimization problems may be very complex and may exceed the available information processing or computing capacity. These and similar limitations qualify under bounded rationality and have been used in explanatory (nonnormative) theory of the firm and of other organizations. They also have played a central role in the theory of message exchange processes, specifically in the concepts of informational decentralization, message space size, and process complexity. But there has been little integration between the study of the game model and the message exchange model. An important exception is the recent investigation by Reichelstein and Reiter of the minimal message space size requirements for the Nash implementation of certain social choice correspondences. It has shown that taking incentives into account through the postulate of Nash im-

plementability sometimes (but not in all cases) raises the message space size requirements, as compared with those called for by an informationally decentralized message exchange mechanism whose response functions yield the desired outcomes when the process is at rest but do not necessarily satisfy the Nash equilibrium conditions.

Message space requirements and complexity of required information processing procedures (including data acquisitions and mathematical calculations) are not the only information problems. A frequent assumption in organization theory work is an agent's limit on the number of others he/she is able to communicate with within a specified period of time. (When the agent is an executive, the limit on the number of subordinates he/she can communicate with is known as the span of control. See Williamson 1967.) Besides feasibility there are resource costs in information processing, the time required to carry out the procedures, and various errors that affect the solution. (For a consideration of the errors, see Hurwicz 1971, Sah and Stiglitz 1984, 1985.) Differences in the abilities to process information that distinguish some agents from others can also be considered (Geanakoplos and Milgrom).

An advantageous feature of certain mechanisms is that some of the functions are simply sums (or averages) of variables each of which refers to one individual, e.g., functions of aggregate demand or of averages of prices or quantities. The aggregation of quantities occurs in the usual models of perfect competition (both static and dynamic) and was used in Hurwicz 1960 under the label of aggregativeness as part of the definition of informational decentralization of concrete processes. (Aggregativeness is a special case of the symmetry property.) The fact that averages are sufficient in certain price-managed mechanisms, but not in quantity managed ones, was used by Milgrom and Weber to refute Weitzman's 1974 claim as to the symmetry of informational requirement of the two types of mechanisms. It appears that these symmetry and aggregation properties can be subsumed under the rubric of complexity, in the sense that, *ceteris paribus*, the computation of symmetric, and especially aggregative, functions is less complex for any plausible definition of complexity (see Mount and Reiter 1983, 1985). Similarly, the notion of informational efficiency, based on the fineness of

400 *May 1987*   *Amer. J. Agr. Econ.*

partitions induced by the response functions seems to represent a special case of a lower level of complexity, again subject to a *ceteris paribus* qualification.

The preceding discussion shows that while a number of informational or cognitive considerations encountered in the application-oriented literature may be contained implicitly in certain aspects of the existing message exchange models, others can only be accounted for by various enrichments of the structure of those models. The fact that these considerations have arisen in models of explanatory nature makes them no less valuable for normative or design purpose. Moreover, most of these considerations are sufficiently general to be as relevant for socialist as for capitalist systems of economic organization.

Their informational aspects are not the only features of mechanism structure in need of enrichment. Both the game theory model and the message exchange model take for granted that the physical consequences of the strategic decisions will be those prescribed by the outcome function, which is not subject to any restrictions other than perhaps those of mathematical regularity. But for those physical consequences to occur, an organizational structure must exist guaranteeing the implementation, essentially an enforcement system. This is particularly obvious for mechanisms that are not individually rational, say where the outcome function implies a loss of utility, perhaps through giving up some goods without obtaining anything in return. The enforcement aspect also becomes crucial in models where parties enter into contracts. Some agreements may be self-enforcing (that is how Nash equilibria are sometimes interpreted) but not all. Mechanisms relying on information flow but without enforcement, such as indicative planning, have a serious weakness (see Hurwicz 1977).

At one extreme, one could imagine societies (one would hesitate to call them organizations!) with no enforcement of contracts. At the other extreme, one could postulate automatic and unfailing enforcement of all agreements. In either case, no modeling problem arises. But reality is somewhere in between, and important theoretical insight is based on the distinction between those commitments that are enforceable and those that are not. Sometimes enforcement may be prohibited by law as, for instance, contracts involving involuntary servitude. In other cases the diffi-

culty or cost of proving relevant facts may render enforcement infeasible. But whatever the reasons, mechanism models must at least be able to reflect the possibility or impossibility of enforcement.

The enforcement aspects can be built into a model in two ways. One way, in principle the only correct one, is to enlarge the model by introducing as players agents constituting the enforcement system: judges, policemen, members of the executive and regulatory agencies, and by specifying their incentive structures, formally those parts of outcome functions applying to them. In turn one would look for equilibrium solutions to the expanded game. But this is a difficult task. A less ambitious approach is simply to specify in the model which agreements are enforceable and which are not. Similarly, on the informational side one can cope with the difficulty of anticipating and analyzing all conceivable contingencies in an analogous manner by grouping contingencies into ex ante indistinguishable classes. These two devices are implicit in, if not equivalent to, the notion of noncontractibility in Grossman and Hart. (The importance of and reasons for the incompleteness of contracts were previously stressed in Williamson 1975, 1985.) In a model that is not temporally homogenous, an action can be noncontractible at one stage (ex ante) but contractible at a later one.

To the extent that relationships between units are not explicitly regulated by enforceable contracts, there is a sphere where the range of possible actions is subject to other limitations—physical, legal, or those of social acceptability. In particular, these factors may endow certain decision makers with discretion (or rights, power, authority, control) in areas not limited by contractual or other obligations. As emphasized by Grossman and Hart, the ownership may confer such residual rights; but other sources of residual discretion may sometimes be more important, especially in bureaucratic and other noncapitalist organizational structures.

We can only provide here the briefest sketch of certain aspects of the formalization.

Each (Hicksian) week is modeled as an extensive form game, with a finite number of moves over time points $0, \ldots, T$, with T a nonnegative integer. Stationarity over a (potentially) infinite sequence of weeks may correspond to (say) a memory of the preceding week combined with a myopic lack of thought concerning future weeks. (Hence we do not have a supergame.) A week is a period during which commitments (contracts) are made and carried out. (There are no commitments for actions in future weeks.) A move, defined by its timing and the group undertaking it, is the behavior $b(S, t)$ of group S at time t. (S is a nonempty subset of the set $\{1, \ldots, n\} = N$ of participants.) The behavior $b(S, t)$ has two components: the message $m(S, t)$ and the action $a(S, t)$. The corresponding resource allocation is $z(S, t)$.

For each t there are defined sets of mutually compatible actions of which $A(S, t)$ is the S component, and the set $L(S, t)$ of actions enforceable on S at t. Let $C(t)$ be the set of all contingencies that could be envisaged at t. To express the notion of complexity we introduce a partitioning $\Gamma(t)$ of $C(t)$. Two contingencies belonging to the same set of $\Gamma(t)$ are considered indistinguishable. Similarly, there is a partitioning $\Sigma(S, t)$ of $A(S, t)$. If two actions belong to the same set of $\Sigma(S, t)$, they are considered indistinguishable for enforcement purposes, whether for observability, proof, or other reasons.

A commitment (or contract) is all or a part of a message consisting of a flag (signaling formal commitment) and a functional relation whose argument is a contingency and whose value is a set of presumably feasible actions. A commitment entered into by S at time t is contained in the message $m(S, t)$. For a commitment to be "valid," the following conditions must be satisfied. First, the above functional relation must be constant on every set of the partition $\Gamma(t')$ for every time t' for which actions are promised. This makes it contingency-verifiable. (See Postlewaite and Schmeidler for the definition of common knowledge.) Now let the commitment promise actions for time t' based on contingencies at that same time, and let $D(S, t')$ be the set of promised actions for the contingency k, i.e., $D(S, t') = \phi(k; t; t')$. (Here t indicates the time commitment was entered into, while t' is the time promised fulfillment; ϕ is the functional relation representing the commitment.) This means that S has promised, in case k (or an equivalent contingency) occurs, to carry out one of the actions in $D(S, t')$ at time t' and to refrain from action outside of this set. For the commitment to be enforceable $D(S, t')$ must be the intersection of the enforceable set $L(S, t')$ with some set of the partition $\Sigma(S, t')$. For the commitment to be "valid," it must be contin-

gency-verifiable and enforceable. An outcome function h specifies the resource allocation $z(S, \tau)$ for every time τ between 0 and T inclusive and for every subset S of N, based on behaviors up to and including time τ. How closely these notions correspond to the concept of contractibility remains to be examined in detail.

A possible formulation of the designer's problem might then be the following: given a social choice correspondence expressing the societal goals or desiderata, find game rules [i.e., an outcome function and a specification of permissible moves (behaviors—messages and actions)] implementing (in a noncooperative game equilibrium sense) that correspondence, subject to the "validity" of commitments, as well as to restrictions on message space size and on the complexity of computations to be performed by the participants. It is, of course, quite likely that only an approximate implementation is possible.

References

Geanakoplos, John, and Paul Milgrom. *A Theory of Hierarchies Based on Limited Managerial Attention.* Cowles Foundation Disc. Pap. No. 775, Yale University, 1985.

Grossman, Sanford J., and Oliver D. Hart. "The Costs and Benefits of Ownership: A Theory of Vertical and Lateral Integration." *J. Polit. Econ.* 94(1986):691–719.

Hart, Oliver, and Bengt Holmstrom. "The Theory of Contracts." *Advances in Economic Theory, 1985,* ed. T. Beweley. Cambridge: Cambridge University Press, forthcoming (July 1987).

Hicks, John R. *Value and Capital.* Oxford: Clarendon Press, 1939.

Hurwicz, Leonid. "Centralization and Decentralization in Economic Processes." *Comparison of Economic Systems, Theoretical and Methodological Approaches,* ed. A. Eckstein, pp. 79–102. Berkeley: University of California Press, 1971.

———. "Optimality and Informational Efficiency in Resource Allocation Processes." *Mathematical Methods in the Social Sciences,* ed. K. J. Arrow, S. Karlin, and P. Suppes, pp. 27–46. Stanford CA: Stanford University Press, 1959.

———. "Perspectives on Economics." *Perspectives on Economic Education,* ed. D. R. Wentworth, W. L. Hansen, and S. H. Hawke, pp. 21–40. Washington DC: Joint Council on Economic Education, 1977.

Kornai, János. "The Hungarian Reform Process: Visions, Hopes, and Reality." *J. Econ. Lit.* 24(1986):1687–1737.

Marschak, Thomas, and Stefan Reichelstein. "Informa-

402   *May 1987*   *Amer. J. Agr. Econ.*

tionally Efficient Hierarchies." Mimeographed. Berkeley: University of California, May 1986.

Milgrom, Paul, and Robert J. Weber. *Organizing Production in a Large Economy with Costly Communication.* Cowles Foundation Disc. Pap. No. 672, Yale University, 1983.

Mount, Kenneth, and Stanley Reiter. "Approximation in a Continuous Model of Computing." *J. Complexity* 1(1985):158–68.

———. "Computational Complexity of Resource Allocation Mechanisms." Mimeographed. Evanston IL: Northwestern University, 1983.

Postlewaite, Andrew, and David Schmeidler. "Implementation in Differential Information Economies." *J. Econ. Theory* 39(1986):14–33.

Reichelstein, Stefan, and Stanley Reiter. *Game Forms with Minimal Strategy Spaces.* Ctr. for Math. Stud. in Econ. and Manage. Sci. Disc. Pap. No. 525, Northwestern University, 1985.

Ruttan, Vernon W. "Induced Institutional Change." *Induced Innovation,* ed. H. P. Binswanger and V. W. Ruttan. Baltimore MD: Johns Hopkins University Press, 1978.

Sah, Raaj Kumar, and Joseph E. Stiglitz. "Human Fallibility and Economic Organization." *Amer. Econ. Rev.* 75(1985):292–97.

Stiglitz, Joseph E. "Incentives and Risk Sharing in Sharecropping." *Rev. Econ. Stud.* 41(1974):219–56.

———. *The Architecture of Economic Systems: Hierarchies and Polyarchies.* Cambridge MA: National Bureau of Economic Research Work. Pap. No. 1334, 1984.

Weitzman, Martin L. "Prices vs. Quantities." *Rev. Econ. Stud.* 41(1974):477–91.

Williamson, Oliver E. "Hierarchical Control and Optimum Firm Size." *J. Polit. Econ.* 75(1967):123–38.

———. *Markets and Hierarchies.* New York: Free Press, 1975.

———. *The Economic Institutions of Capitalism.* New York: Free Press, 1985.

Part III
Modeling Institutions and Institutional Arrangements

[12]

The nature and function of social institutions

This book considers the nature, function, and evolution of economic and social institutions. Most simply, it is a first step in an attempt to liberate economics from its fixation on competitive markets as an all-encompassing institutional framework. It views economic problems as evolutionary ones in which economic agents have finite lives and pass on to their successors a wide variety of social rules of thumb, institutions, norms, and conventions that facilitate the coordination of economic and social activities. In time, the institutional structure of the economy becomes more and more complex as more and more social and economic institutions are created and passed on from generation to generation. In some instances these institutions supplement competitive markets, and in some instances they totally replace them. Some of the institutions are explicitly agreed to and codified into law; others are only tacitly agreed to and evolve spontaneously from the attempts of the individual agents to maximize their own utility. Some lead to optimal social states; others are dysfunctional. In any case, each arises for a specific reason. It is the purpose of this book to investigate these reasons and analyze the types of institutions that evolve.

But what are social institutions, and what functions do they serve? These questions can be answered only by viewing economic problems in an evolutionary light. Doing this, as Veblen (1898) points out, takes the emphasis away from equilibrium analysis and places it on the disequilibrium aspects of the economic process.[1] The proper analogy to make is between the evolution of an economy and the evolution of a species. Biologists know that a particular animal reveals a variety of features that it has developed to solve specific evolutionary problems. If these problems cease to exist, the animal is left with vestigial features whose function is a mystery to us. But if the problems remain, the function of the feature may be obvious for all to see. The problem for the scientist is one of inferring from observed appearances the evolutionary problem that must have existed to produce what we observe today.

In the social world the problem is similar. Economic and social systems evolve the way species do. To ensure their survival and growth, they must solve

1

2   Economic theory of social institutions

a whole set of problems that arise as the system evolves. Each problem creates the need for some adaptive feature, that is, a social institution. Analogously, then, the problem facing social scientists is to infer the evolutionary problem that must have existed for the institution as we see it to have developed. Every evolutionary economic problem requires a social institution to solve it. For instance, the problem of multilateral exchange in neoclassical economies (economies satisfying all of the "proper" neoclassical assumptions) is solved by the creation of competitive markets, and the evolutionary source of this institutional feature is evident today. However, this is just one of many institutions that "successful" economies must develop. Those societies that create the proper set of social institutions survive and flourish; those that do not, falter and die. The distressing fact is that what is functional to meet today's problem may be totally inadequate in meeting the tests our society faces tomorrow. Social institutions are our adaptive tools; we cannot survive without them.

This point was made by Alfred Marshall in his *Principles of Economics*. Greatly influenced by the emerging biological sciences,[2] he perceived that those aspects of economic institutions that are most prominent today are those most likely to have developed recently and consequently will give no hint of the original purpose of the institution. He writes:

> In this matter economists have much to learn from the recent experiences of biology: and Darwin's profound discussion of the question throws a strong light on the difficulties before us. He points out that those parts of the structure which determine the habits of life and the general place of each being in the economy of nature, are as a rule not those which throw most light on its origin, but those that throw least.
>
> The qualities which a breeder or a gardener notices as eminently adapted to enable an animal or a plant to thrive in its environment, are for that very reason likely to have been developed in comparatively recent times. And in like manner, those properties of an economic institution which play the most important part in fitting it for the work which it has to do now, are for that very reason likely to be in a great measure of recent growth. [Marshall 1920, p. 50]

More recently, James Buchanan (1975) contends, in a book that is heavily institutional and evolutionary in its approach, that if one is to study institutions, one must study them in a historical–evolutionary context: "Once it is recognized that observed institutions of legal-political order exist in a historical setting, the attraction of trying to analyze conceptual origins independently of historical process is severely weakened" (Buchanan 1975, p. 53).

The following example should be illuminating. Consider the existence of a commodity money in an exchange economy. Clearly, the social convention that specifies a certain commodity as a means of exchange did not always exist. Furthermore, the particular commodity chosen is arbitrary except that we would expect it to be light in weight, durable, and relatively abundant. Consequently, if the proverbial creatures from outer space were to arrive and

Nature and function of social institutions   3

observe this phenomenon, they would have to explain why all trade is mone-
tized, and why, in addition, this one commodity out of the whole set of possible
commodities was the one chosen. The answer to the first part of the question
is simple. Money evolves because at some point in the history of an economy
the problem of efficient multilateral trade arises. Its solution requires a method
of exchange that uses as few social resources as possible to achieve a Pareto-
optimal set of trades. The obvious evolutionary solution, in addition to markets,
was to monetize trade by using one good as a means of exchange. Thus money
was a social convention that satisfied the important economic need for an efficient exchange of goods and services. Once this problem was solved, its solution
was passed on from generation to generation: money was institutionalized. This
explanation would, of course, not be obvious to our visiting creatures. They
would have no clue to the evolutionary problem for which money was the
solution. It is, therefore, the object of science to provide one for them.

If we attempted to answer the question of why one particular commodity
was chosen as money, we would find greater difficulties. Although, as we said,
the commodity must be durable, lightweight, and abundant, many commodities
have these qualities. Consequently, our explanation would have to involve a
certain amount of indeterminacy. This is not grounds for despair, however.
The nature of the analysis in this book is such that we can never expect to
isolate a unique institutional form as stable; rather, we must content ourselves
with a set of forms that, when taken together, are stable. This is all we can, or
should, expect from a theory.

1.1 Toward a new view of economics

The approach to economics outlined so far has dramatic consequences for the
way in which we look at the scope and method of economics. Before we discuss
this in detail, however, let us briefly look at some previous attempts at integrating institutions into economics.

There have been, historically, two distinct interpretations of the rise of social
institutions in economics. One explanation, put forth in John Commons's
Institutional Economics, may be called the "collectivist" explanation. The other
explanation, given in Karl Menger's *Untersuchungen über die Methode der
Sozialwissenschaften und der politischen Ökonomie insbesondere* (1883; translated by Francis J. Nock in 1963 as *Problems in Economics and Sociology*),
may be called the "organic" theory.

The difference between these two approaches is simple. Commons saw social
institutions as the expression of the conscious collective action of rational economic agents. For him, economics was to be freed from the "psychological" or
individualistic economics of Adam Smith and the neoclassical economists and

4   Economic theory of social institutions

put on a new foundation in which collective action and a "negotiational psychology" were to replace atomistic maximization. As Commons puts it:

> Collective action, as well as individual action, has always been there, but from Smith to the Twentieth Century it has been excluded or ignored, except as attacks on trade unions or postscripts on ethics or public policy. The problem now is not to create a different kind of economics-"institutional economics"-divorced from preceding schools, but how to give collective action, in all its varieties, its due place throughout economic theory. [Commons 1934, p. 5]

For Commons, then, the universal principle behind institutional behavior is the collective and purposeful action enforcing it: "If we endeavor to find a universal principle, common to all behavior known as institutional, we may define an institution as Collective Action in control of Individual Action" (Commons 1934, p. 69).

Menger's explanation of the rise of institutions is quite different. He saw them as arising out of the selfish interaction of a myriad of individual economic agents, each pursuing his own self-interest. They evolve "organically," not by collective design or will. Therefore, Menger believed that what Commons called "psychological economics" need not be thrown away in order to construct a theory of social institutions. Rather, this forms its theoretical superstructure. Just as Adam Smith's invisible hand can, in a decentralized fashion, lead economic agents to reach a Pareto-optimal competitive equilibrium, it can also lead them to create social institutions that will facilitate their interaction when competitive outcomes are not optimal.[3] Another way to phrase the same problem is to say that "competitive" economics deals with only one institution-the market-which arises organically out of the maximizing behavior of individual agents. However, a host of other institutions, norms, and rules are also created that help to allocate resources in an optimal fashion. It is the organic development of these other institutions with which Menger was concerned. He considered the "most noteworthy problem of the social sciences" to be the question of "how ... institutions which serve the common welfare and are extremely significant for its development came into being without a *common will* directed toward establishing them" (Menger 1883, p. 147). Menger went on to say: "The solution of the most important problems of the theoretical social sciences in general and of theoretical economics in particular is thus closely connected with the question of theoretically understanding the origin and change of 'organically' created social institutions" (Menger 1883, p. 147).

Interestingly, both Menger [in his *Principles of Economics* (1950) and in *Untersuchungen*] and Commons study the rise of the institutions of money and law as examples for their arguments. More recently, Robert Nozick (1975) has given an explanation of the rise of the state as a social institution in *Anarchy, State, and Utopia,* which is very close to Menger's conception of social insti-

Nature and function of social institutions   5

tutions arising organically.[4] James Buchanan (1975) has explained the rise of property and societal law in an analogous manner in *The Limits of Liberty*.

Our conception of the role of economics in social science is very close to Menger's, and it is on this conception that we will base our definition of *economics* as *the study of how individual economic agents pursuing their own selfish ends evolve institutions as a means to satisfy them*. This definition is quite distinct from the one offered by Lord Robbins in 1935, which is still the standard one in textbooks:

> The economist studies the disposal of scarce means. He is interested in the way different degrees of scarcity of different goods give rise to different ratios of valuation between them, and he is interested in the way in which changes in ends or changes in means–from the demand side or the supply side–affect these ratios. *Economics* is the science which studies human behavior as a relationship between ends and scarce means which have alternative uses. [Robbins 1935, p. 16]

Robbins's definition differs from ours in two distinct ways. First, it concentrates totally on the individual, whereas ours sees the individual as a selfish, maximizing agent who is capable of coordinated social action (i.e., institution building). Second, Robbins's definition, in his reference to the forces of supply and demand, clearly implies that he sees only one social mechanism through which human economic behavior can manifest itself–that of competitive markets; ours explicitly recognizes a variety of mechanisms or institutions. As a result, our definition is broader than his and our analysis sees competitive economics as an extreme case.

Using our definition of positive economics, welfare economics can be defined as the study of the welfare aspects of comparative social institutions. This definition then simply says that if our positive economic theory is going to study the effect of social institutions on resource allocation, the associated prescriptive theory should study comparative social institutions. This, however, includes within it neoclassical welfare economics, because if neoclassical theory deals only with perfectly competitive economies, the only institutions they deal with are markets, and welfare economics becomes the study of comparative market organizations.

1.2 Welfare economics and comparative social institutions: the optimal rules of the game

If, for a second, we let ourselves be all-powerful social planners who have the power to create any society or economic structure we want, what will that society or economy look like? In trying to answer this question, we would probably lay out some general rules or principles for the members of that society to follow. These rules could be codified into law and would prescribe the type of

6   Economic theory of social institutions

behavior that is acceptable in specific situations. In economics, such rules would include antitrust laws, safety requirements, and minimum-wage legislation.

John Rawls, in *A Theory of Justice* (1971), attacks just this problem. He seeks a set of rules to be the basis of a contract among selfish, maximizing social agents, which they would agree to under a "veil of ignorance." His view of social justice concentrates not so much on the comparison of social states as on the comparison of social systems and institutions. He states:

For us the primary subject of justice is the basic structure of society or more exactly, the way in which the major social institutions distribute fundamental rights and duties and determine the division of advantages from social cooperation. By major institutions I understand the political constitution and the principal economic and social arrangements. Thus the legal protection of freedom of thought and liberty, competitive markets, private property and the means of production, and the monogamous family are examples of major social institutions. Taken together as one scheme, the major institutions define men's rights and duties and influence their life prospects, what they can expect to be and how well they can hope to do. [Rawls 1971, p. 7]

When discussing institutions and formal justice, Rawls permits himself to be a social planner and shows that social planning involves not allocation by fiat but the development and administration of rules, laws, and institutions that lead to socially optimal states:

In designing and reforming social arrangements one must, of course, examine the schemes and tactics it allows and the forms of behavior which it tends to encourage. Ideally, the rules should be set up so that men are led by their predominant interests to act in ways which further socially desirable ends. The conduct of individuals guided by their rational plans should be coordinated as far as possible to achieve results which although not intended or perhaps even foreseen by them are nevertheless the best ones from the standpoint of social justice. [Rawls 1971, p. 57]

Our view of the role of theoretical welfare economics has much in common with Rawls's view of the study of justice. (Notice how close Rawls is here to Menger.) We view welfare economics not as a study that ranks social states or prescribes optimal resource allocations, but as one that ranks the system of rules which dictate social behavior. We view government in competitive and mixed economies as an agent whose role it is to prescribe a set of taxes, laws, and rules of behavior that limit the strategy sets of social agents in an optimal way. In essence, *welfare economics is the study of the optimal rules of the game for economic and social situations.* Its purpose is, like Rawls's rules and institutions, to structure competitive social and economic situations that further societal welfare while preserving individual sovereignty.[5]

The main point made here, then, is that welfare economics must study the comparative optimality of rules, laws, and institutions that form the rules of the game of social conduct, together with the outcomes that these rules help determine. The philosophical justification for such a view can be found in quite

Nature and function of social institutions 7

disparate works. John Rawls (1971) views justice through a "contractarian" point of view. He sees a just society as one whose rules, laws, and institutions are exactly those that would be chosen by its agents if they were placed under a "veil of ignorance" as to who they would be in that society. These rules are the rules that would form a contract by which the members of the society would agree to conduct themselves.

From the other side of the political spectrum comes additional support for our view. Robert Nozick (1975), in discussing fair income distributions, states that one cannot rank two income distributions–social states–by themselves in terms of social desirability, for the process by which the income distributions were achieved–the rules of the game determining them–is equally important. He argues that an extremely skewed income distribution can be fair as long as it is arrived at in a fair way and without coercion. In addition, a totally egalitarian income distribution could be undesirable if it were arrived at by immoral acts such as murder: "The entitlement theory of justice in distribution is historical; whether a distribution is just depends upon how it came about. In contrast, *current-time-slice* principles of justice hold that the justice of a distribution is determined by how things are distributed (who has what) as judged by some structural principle(s) of just distribution" (Nozick 1975, p. 153).

Still another philosophical view, "rule utilitarianism" (in contrast to the more typical "act utilitarianism" used widely by economists), can be called upon to support our institutional emphasis. This view ranks social actions not on the basis of the social states they alone determine, but on the basis of the eventual social state that would result if those types of actions became rules of conduct or conventions of behavior for the agents in the society. The rule-utilitarian view is, then, a type of Kantian approach, which views all human conduct in terms of the payoffs that would result if that conduct became a convention of behavior for all agents in society.[6]

Thus we have seen that welfare economics must be the study of the comparative "rules of the game" of social and economic behavior. Its role is not only to rank social states and prescribe which is best, but also to compare the rules of conduct by which those outcomes are determined.

1.3 Who should study social institutions?

Why should an economist be interested in social institutions? Why not leave the problem to the anthropologists and sociologists? The reason, as we will see more clearly in Chapter 2, is that economics as it exists today is hampered by an institutional short-sightedness that greatly inhibits its analysis of social problems. The short-sightedness results from our fixation on market institutions and our failure to introduce a more varied set of institutions into our

8   Economic theory of social institutions

analysis. This short-sightedness may lead to the advocacy of market solutions where other institutional arrangements might be more efficient.

To be a little more precise, economics focuses on the price relationships of commodities conditional on one particular institutional structure–competitive markets. When the phenomena in question fit appropriately into this frame-work–when there are no externalities or nonconvexities–its limited institutional assumptions are no hindrance. However, many institutions are created that allocate goods and services when competitive markets are not a realistic assumption to make, and a truly comprehensive theory must explain their creation together with the resulting value relationships, which may no longer be equivalent to equilibrium price ratios. As an illustration, consider the following rather fanciful game.

Game 1.1: The traffic game

Two cars, C and D, are driving toward each other on a street and are approaching an intersection, A. They are driving at the same speed and will approach the intersection at the same time. Both drivers are in a hurry and want to get to their destinations, which are marked g and f, respectively, in Figure 1.1. Therefore, C wants to make a left-hand turn and D wants to go straight ahead. The game that is determined by this scenario is a variant of the "battle of the sexes" game, pictured in Matrix 1.1. Clearly, the Pareto-optimal

Driver C

		Wait	Go ahead
Driver D	Wait	−3, −3	−2, 7
	Go ahead	5, 0	−4, −4

Matrix 1.1

states occur on the off-diagonal elements of the matrix, and some mechanism is needed for the agents in the economy to coordinate their activities. What mechanism should society use? To a theoretical economist, the obvious answer would be that a market should be set up that would sell the right to use the intersection. This right should be sold at auction. The argument here would be that the only reason a problem exists in the first place is because of a market failure in the right of way. Consequently, we may picture an auctioneer, who stands in the middle of the intersection and instantaneously accepts bids from both drivers, selling the right to use the intersection first to the higher bidder.

Nature and function of social institutions　　　　　　9

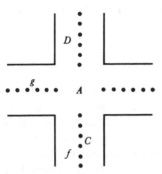

Figure 1.1. The traffic game.

Clearly, the price would be set between 5 and 7 and the car turning left would get the right to use the intersection first. This is, of course, a highly unlikely mechanism. However, even if it were feasible and the auctioning process were extremely efficient, this scheme would be cumbersome and costly.

Another scheme, however, would be to initiate traffic rules and force each person to learn them before he is allowed to drive on the streets. If this scheme were utilized, a rule of thumb would be established in which drivers wishing to make turns at intersections must wait for oncoming cars before proceeding. The person making the turn would wait, and the decisions would be costlessly coordinated.

The point of this example is that price mechanisms, except for the textbook variety, are not costless and are in many circumstances rather clumsy systems to run. Therefore, we might find situations in which decentralized informational schemes, such as rules and norms, are more efficient allocating mechanisms. However, if economic analysis is so fixated on the market that it ignores other institutional arrangements, it is destined to be analytically myopic.

1.4 Institutions defined

It is not an easy task to define social institutions, because they are amorphous and require a definition general enough to encompass all of them without being meaningless. Consequently, I have chosen a definition that is similar to David Lewis's definition of social conventions (1969): regularities in behavior which are agreed to by all members of a society and which specify behavior in specific recurrent situations. However, social institutions are different from social conventions in terms of the mechanisms necessary to enforce them. Social conventions, such as language, table manners, driving on the right side of the street, and allowing only one person to speak at a time in a conversation, are fundamentally self-policing. According to Lewis, they evolve as the noncooperative

10   Economic theory of social institutions

solution to social coordination games. For instance, consider the telephone game described by Lewis (1969, p. 42).

Game 1.2: The telephone game

In Oberlin, Ohio, the phone company used to cut all phone conversations off at the end of 3 minutes. Consequently, if party 1 called party 2 and was cut off, he faced the following problem: If I call him back, and he tries to call me, we will get a busy signal and will not be able to speak. If I do not call him back and he does not call me, we cannot speak either. We can speak only if I call him back and he does not call me, or if I do not call him back and he does call me. Party 2 has the same problem. Assuming that all calls are free, what will happen?

According to Lewis, the game can be represented as a coordination problem[7] (Matrix 1.2). The game, although simple, is by no means trivial. It can be

Callee

	Call back	Do not call back
Call back	0, 0	8, 8
Do not call back	8, 8	0, 0

Caller

Matrix 1.2

solved only if both parties can find a way to coordinate their activities. This coordination can be achieved by establishing a social convention or regularity in behavior to govern these situations, which specifies whether the caller or the person called is to call back. Which specific convention will evolve is indeterminate, yet both are in equilibrium, because not only does neither party have an incentive to deviate from the convention, both desire that the other not deviate either. The convention determines equilibrium behavior. More formally, Lewis defines a social convention as follows.

Definition 1.1: A social convention. A regularity R in the behavior of members of a population P when they are agents in a recurrent situation S is a *convention* if and only if it is true that and is common knowledge in P that (1) everyone conforms to R; (2) everyone expects everyone else to conform to R; and (3) everyone prefers to conform to R on the condition that the others do, since S is a coordination problem and uniform conformity to R is a coordination equilibrium in S (Lewis 1969, p. 58).

Nature and function of social institutions   11

Although social institutions are predominantly concerned with solving social coordination problems, they are not necessarily self-policing and may require some external authority, such as the state, to enforce them. For instance, a system of property rights is a social institution in which the behavior of individual agents is circumscribed to conform. It defines a regularity in behavior that is socially agreed to. Yet this institution is not in equilibrium because each person has an incentive to steal from others. As a result, some external authority must be instituted to enforce these rights–the state.[8] Consequently, we will have to modify Lewis's definition to read as follows: *A social institution is a regularity in social behavior that is agreed to by all members of society, specifies behavior in specific recurrent situations, and is either self-policed or policed by some external authority.* In these situations, the regularity may be the use of a particular commodity, such as money, in the exchange of goods and services or the regularity in prices charged by public utilities that specifies the behavior of regulated firms. In other situations, it might be a code that exists which dictates the contribution individuals make in paying for public or club goods, or it may be the percentage gratuity left as a tip for waiters in restaurants. Whatever it is, once it is incorporated in the study of economics, the institutional framework of our science is immediately expanded and we can proceed to rigorously analyze a great many problems in a fresh way without forcing the analysis into one particular institutional framework: competitive markets.

A social institution can then be more formally defined as follows.

Definition 1.2: A social institution. A regularity R in the behavior of members of a population P when they are agents in a recurrent situation Γ is an *institution* if and only if it is true that and is common knowledge in P that (1) everyone conforms to R; (2) everyone expects everyone else to conform to R; and (3) either everyone prefers to conform to R on the condition that the others do, if Γ is a coordination problem, in which case uniform conformity to R is a coordination equilibrium; or (4) if anyone ever deviates from R it is known that some or all of the others will also deviate and the payoffs associated with the recurrent play of Γ using these deviating strategies are worse for all agents than the payoff associated with R.[9]

Clearly, the class of social institutions is broader than the class of social conventions. For instance, it is common knowledge that the famous prisoners' dilemma game can be solved through the use of a binding contract that is enforceable by an external authority. Consequently, in an oligopolistic industry a particular pricing behavior may be instituted that specifies behavior for the firms in their recurrent play of prisoners' dilemma. This regularity, if violated, would be punished by some jointly randomized strategy on the part of the dou-

12   Economic theory of social institutions

ble-crossed firms. Consequently, although this pricing institution is not a convention in Lewis's sense because it is not self-policing, it is an institution under our definition.

1.5 Methodology

The chapters that follow present an approach to economic issues that is not typical. Although it is fundamentally game-theoretical, it differs from classical game-theoretical formulations in being evolutionary rather than static or dynamic. In classical game theory, players are treated as abstract entities totally described by their information and the strategy sets and by their preferences. They act strategically, given total information about the extensive form of a static or dynamic game. Consequently, in choosing strategies, the only information they are allowed to use is that which is formally contained in the description of the game before it is played.

We, however, start with the hypothesis that the most interesting games are not one-shot games or games that are played once and only once between a fixed set of players, but are, rather, recurrent supergames or games that are iterated over and over. In addition, the players in these recurrent situations are constantly changing as the agents who fill certain abstract roles in the game leave. Consequently, games, or the social situations they describe, are not viewed as static phenomena but as evolutionary situations with constantly changing players. The result of this approach is that, as the games we analyze are repeatedly played, the players develop certain societally agreed to rules of thumb, norms, conventions, and institutions which are passed on to succeeding generations of players. Consequently, our players have more information than classic players of n-person games, because they know not only the game in its extensive form but also a whole set of institutions that classic game theory ignores as being extra-game-theoretical. The rigorous inclusion of this information into a game-theoretical analysis is one of the contributions of this book.

In our analysis, players are real, not abstract beings. They are capable of developing trust, creating rules of thumb and social institutions, and following their dictates. In Chapter 3 we see the full impact of this approach.

1.6 Institutions and indeterminacy

As we saw earlier regarding the evolution of money, a theory of institutions may not yield unique results. In other words, although it can be expected to delimit a stable set of institutions that may evolve in an economy, there is no reason to expect the institutions that could theoretically evolve to be unique. Such determinacy should not be expected of any theory in the social sciences. This indeterminacy is not a weakness of the theory, however. As von Neumann

Nature and function of social institutions   13

and Morgenstern (1947) have said, the role of social science is not to find a solution to a problem but rather to define the set of all solutions. They state:

> Since solutions do not seem to be necessarily unique, the complete answer to any specific problem consists not in finding a solution, but in determining the set of all solutions. Thus the entity for which we look in any particular problem is really a set of imputations. This may seem to be unnaturally complicated in itself. . . . Concerning these doubts it suffices to say: First, the mathematical structure of the theory of games of strategy provides a formal justification of our procedure. Second, the previously discussed connections with "standards of behavior" (corresponding to sets of imputations) and the multiplicity of "standards of behavior" on the same physical background . . . makes just this amount of complicatedness desirable. [von Neumann and Morgenstern 1947, p. 44]

In this book we investigate the evolution of stable social institutions. Consequently, we will see that although there might be great indeterminacy in the predicted value of price relationships in some of our models, the range of institutional indeterminacy will be rather small. As an example, consider the following three-person constant-sum game.

Game 1.3: Buddies

Three players exist, eeny, meeny, and miny, and one external millionaire, moe. Moe offers the three players the following deal. If any two of them can agree on how they will split it, moe will give them $1 million. Or if they can all agree on how to split the million dollars, he will give it to all three of them.

The game can be depicted by the following characteristic function, which describes the payoff that any coalition, if it forms, can guarantee itself:

$$V(\text{eeny}) = V(\text{meeny}) = V(\text{miny}) = 0$$
$$V(\text{eeny, meeny}) = V(\text{eeny, miny}) = V(\text{meeny, miny}) = \$1,000,000$$
$$V(\text{eeny, meeny, miny}) = \$1,000,000$$

What should be the solution to this game or social situation? The answer can be found in the first chapter of von Neumann and Morgenstern's *The Theory of Games and Economic Behavior* (1947). It should consist of a set of payoffs–possibly infinite–together with a set of social institutions (called "standards of behavior" by von Neumann and Morgenstern) which are stable in the sense that no payoff/institution pair in the set dominates the other, and any payoff/institution pair not in the set is dominated by at least one pair in the set.

To be more precise, in our example there are two obvious institutional arrangements that might evolve. First, two players might join and split the reward in half, excluding the third player. The set of symmetric payoffs associated with this institutional arrangement is

14   Economic theory of social institutions

$$
V = \begin{cases}
\begin{array}{ccc}
\text{eeny} & \text{meeny} & \text{miny} \\
\overline{500{,}000} & \overline{500{,}000} & 0 \\
500{,}000 & 0 & 500{,}000 \\
0 & 500{,}000 & 500{,}000
\end{array}
\end{cases}
$$

In addition, we might envision a discriminatory institutional arrangement in which all three players join together; one is offered a fixed payment, possibly zero, and the other two split the remainder equally. This institution has the following set of symmetric payoffs associated with it:

$$
V' = \begin{cases}
\alpha_1 = \alpha_2 \; 0 < \alpha_3 < \$500{,}000 \\
\alpha_1 + \alpha_2 + \alpha_3 = \$1{,}000{,}000
\end{cases}
$$

where α_1, α_2, and α_3 are the payoffs to any of the players eeny, meeny, miny, respectively.

The result of the analysis is then indeterminate. However, although the set of imputations may be infinite, the analysis has greatly delimited the range of possible institutional arrangements. In fact, only two stable institutional arrangements exist.

The point that von Neumann and Morgenstern (1947) were making is that many distinct standards of behavior or institutions may evolve from the same physical background (i.e., from the same social situation or game as described by its rules) and that social science should be responsible for predicting that set of institutions that is in some sense stable.

Let us now assume that, as all mortals, eeny, meeny, and miny must some-day die, but that moe is immortal. Assume that when they do, their offspring will take their place in the game "Buddies," which is run by moe, and another division game will be played. If they are allowed to transfer the knowledge they have accumulated to their children, they will inform them of the particular payoff/institution pair chosen in their generation and it is likely, although not certain, that this will affect the solution to the next period's game. In other words, particular, arbitrary institutional arrangements may become fossilized in the economy, and these arrangements become parameters or permanent features of the society as it continues to evolve. Consequently, many generations later, a payoff/institution pair may exist that governs this game or situation, without it being obvious why that particular pair is chosen.

In oligopolistic markets, firms establish working relationships or industry ethics as they repeat the play of the same price, quality, or quantity game. Their working relationships are then institutionalized and passed on to their successors. Observing these industries, it is often hard to explain the origin of these institutions. Institutions are often bastard children whose true parents are hard to trace.

Nature and function of social institutions 15

1.7 Some game-theoretical terminology

Before describing how we will proceed with our analysis of social institutions in succeeding chapters, I think it appropriate to define some simple game-theoretical terms that will be used throughout. This is done because I hope the book will be accessible to all modern social scientists, not merely to the technically trained high theorist. Those who are already familiar with basic game-theoretical terms are urged to go directly to Section 1.8. I hope also that the game-theoretical purist will forgive my lack of rigor in this section.

To begin, a *game* is defined as a set of rules for a particular situation that delimits the actions available to the *players* (the agents engaged in the situation) and awards payoffs to them on the basis of the actions chosen. Each player has a set of actions or *strategies* from which to choose, which we will call his *strategy set*. The payoff he receives is determined not only by the strategy he chooses, but also by the strategies the other players have chosen. If the payoff to each player were independent of the actions or strategies of all the other players, the situation being investigated would not be called a game but, rather, would consist of a set of independent maximization problems–a situation of considerably less interest.

Now the rules of the game typically specify whether the players are allowed to communicate with each other and whether they are allowed to arrange binding contracts that will allow them to jointly correlate their strategies. If both communication and binding contracts are possible, the game is called a *cooperative game;* if no communication is possible, the game is called *noncooperative*. Cooperative and noncooperative games differ from each other not because the players in one cooperate whereas in the other they do not, but because the communication and contracting possibilities within them are different.

Consider the set of strategies available to player i. Call it S_i, player i's strategy set. If there are n players in the game and if we choose one strategy from each S_i, the resulting n choices will be called a *strategy n-tuple* and be denoted $s = (s_1, s_2, \ldots, s_n)$, $s_i \in S_i$, $i = 1, 2, \ldots, n$. The set of all such n-tuples is called the *strategy space* for the game.

To finish our description of a game we must define the payoffs that result when any given n-tuple is chosen. To do this we merely specify a *payoff function,* which is a function that assigns each player a payoff based on the strategy n-tuple chosen by the players. Hence a payoff function assigns a payoff vector $(\Pi_1(s), \ldots, \Pi_n(s))$ to each n-tuple $s = (s_1, \ldots, s_i, \ldots, s_n)$, where $\Pi_i(s)$ represents the payoff to player i resulting when the n-tuple s is chosen by the players.

With this background we can depict an abstract game by the triple (N; S; Π), where N is the set of players in the game, S the strategy space, and Π the

16   Economic theory of social institutions

payoff function. Describing the game in this way is called describing its *normal form*. In Chapters 2 and 3 we will be concerned almost exclusively with games in normal form. In Chapter 4 we turn our attention to games in what is called *extensive form,* and discuss them in detail.

From our discussion of the telephone game and our definitions of a social convention and a social institution, it should be clear that we will be engaged with problems or games that are recurrent or are played repeatedly by a fixed set of players. Consequently, we will be forced to analyze games that are created by the infinite iteration of static games described in normal form. The game that is defined by this infinite iteration is called a *supergame* and will be the focus of our attention in Chapter 3.

To finish our discussion of games in normal form, we must discuss two common equilibrium concepts–because games are usually studied for the specific purpose of discovering their equilibria. Let $\Pi_i(s_1, \ldots, s_i, \ldots, s_n)$ be the payoff function for player i. If this player has a strategy that yields a higher payoff than any other strategy, no matter what the other $n - 1$ players in the game do, this strategy is called a *dominant strategy* for player i. If in a game $(N; S; \Pi)$ all players have dominant strategies, a *dominant strategy equilibrium* exists. Typically, however, games do not have dominant strategy equilibria. For those situations in which dominant strategy equilibria do not exist, we are forced to fall back on a more general equilibrium notion called the *noncooperative, or Nash equilibrium*. This concept is quite easy to understand. We say that a game is in noncooperative or Nash equilibrium if, given the strategy n-tuple chosen by the players, no player has any incentive to deviate and choose another strategy. In other words, a strategy n-tuple $s^* = (s_1^*, \ldots, s_n^*)$ is in noncooperative or Nash equilibrium if no player, given the strategy choice of the other $n - 1$, could increase his payoff by changing his own strategy choice. As we will see, Nash equilibrium can be defined for games that are played once and only once as well as for iterated or supergames.

To complete this quick game-theoretical review, it is necessary to describe the notion of a cooperative game in *characteristic function form* and one solution concept for such a game, *the core*. In doing this, remember that in cooperative games the players are able to communicate with each other and make binding contracts. Let us assume that there is a set of N players in the cooperative game we are investigating and that a subset of them, $S \subseteq N$, decides to form a *coalition* and coordinate their strategy choices. If we denote $V(S)$ as the most this coalition can guarantee its members no matter what the other players in the game do against them, $V(S)$ is called the *value of the characteristic function for coalition S*. The *characteristic function* is a set-valued function that describes the best that any coalition $S \subseteq N$ can do for itself if it were to form. If there exists some good in the world for which all players have linear utilities, transferring this good becomes equivalent to transferring utility and

Nature and function of social institutions   17

the game is said to have *transferable utilities*. Let $x = (x_1, \ldots, x_n)$ be a payoff distribution awarding a payoff to each player in the game. If $\Sigma_i \, x_i = V(N)$ and $x_i \geq V(i)$, where $V(i)$ is the value of the characteristic function for player i, then $x = (x_1, \ldots, x_n)$ is called an *imputation*. The analysis of n-person cooperative games is nothing more than the search for imputations that are stable in some sense.

Suppose that we found an imputation $x = (x_1, \ldots, x_n)$ and that this imputation were proposed to the players with a request that they accept it. Clearly, if any coalition of players, S, could get together and do better for themselves [by distributing $V(S)$] than by accepting $x = (x_1, \ldots, x_n)$, they would *block* this imputation proposal. If an imputation exists that cannot be blocked by any coalition, that imputation is in the core of the game. The core can be defined as the set of imputations that cannot be blocked by any coalition.

With these concepts behind us, we can now discuss how we will proceed in succeeding chapters.

Notes

Chapter 1. The nature and function of social institutions

1. This emphasis on disequilibrium analysis is seen in the works of the neo-Austrian economists, best represented by Kirzner (1973). Shubik (1973) also places emphasis on what he calls a "process"-oriented approach as opposed to an equilibrium approach.

2. See Marshall (1920, app. B, pp. 764–5).

3. In the eighteenth century, David Hume (1888) presented a description of the way a system of legal justice evolved in a society that was strikingly similar to Menger's "organic" view.

4. Nozick's entire analysis in the first part of his book can be reformulated game-theoretically, and the state's evolution can easily be seen to be the core solution to a game that is convex (i.e., Nozick's protective associations contain increasing returns to scale).

5. Duncan Foley (1975), writing on institutions from a radical perspective, rejects this view entirely. He argues that institutions cannot be explained from a functionalist point of view as socially efficient mechanisms that are capable of fine tuning and change, but rather emerge historically from a class struggle. Consequently, they serve no particular purpose and cannot be altered in the way we envision in order to increase social welfare. Foley (1975, p. 235), writes: "The organization of society is not a technical question because institutions are not designed to perform certain functions; they are rather molded historically out of a process of struggle and compromise, so there is simply no place for a technician to intervene from outside to adjust and improve them."

6. Rule utilitarianism is discussed probably for the first time as such by an economist in R. F. Harrod's "Utilitarianism Revisited," *Mind,* vol. 45, 1936, pp. 137–56. Others, such as David Lyons in *The Forms and Limits of Utilitarianism* (New York: Oxford University Press, 1965), argue that rule utilitarianism collapses into act utilitarianism. The argument is simple. Say that there is a rule R that specifies behavior and a circumstance under which any individual should break this rule. Then a new rule, saying conform to R except in this situation, results. But the new rule is such that it results whenever the old rule should be violated, so that any time an act utilitarian would break a rule R, a rule utilitarian would change the rule. Hence the two are the same. See also *Utilitarianism For and Against* (New York: Cambridge University Press, 1973), Essay I, "An Outline of a System of Utilitarian Ethics," by J. J. C. Smart and Bernard Williams. This issue is still open, however.

7. For a further discussion of coordination problems, see Schelling (1960).

8. Of course, if the situation were modeled as a supergame, it could be shown, using certain discount rates, that property rights are a noncooperative equilibrium institution in the supergame and need no external enforcement. This basic point is made in a different manner by Buchanan (1975).

9. This definition is consistent with the following definition offered by Blaine Roberts and Bob Holdren (1972, p. 110):

An institution will be defined as a system of rules applicable to established practices (or situations) and generally accepted by the members of a social system. These guidelines of interaction may be either explicitly delineated by laws, charters, constitutions and so forth or they may be implicit to a particular culture, such as customs, mores, generally accepted ethics, and so forth. The essential point is that an institution specifies consequences of individual or group action which can be expected. Given an existing institution, an individual or group knows to some extent the reaction its activities will evoke.

References

Buchanan, James. *The Limits of Liberty: Between Anarchy and Leviathan.* Chicago: University of Chicago Press, 1975.

Commons, John. *Institutional Economics.* Madison, Wis.: University of Wisconsin Press, 1961 (first published in 1934).

Foley, Duncan, "Problems versus Conflicts: Economic Theory and Ideology," *American Economic Association Papers and Proceedings,* vol. 65, May 1975, pp. 231–7.

Hume, David. *Treatise on Human Nature.* New York: 1911 (first published in 1888).

Kirzner, Israel M. *Competition and Entrepreneurship.* Chicago: University of Chicago Press, 1973.

Lewis, D. *Convention: A Philosophical Study.* Cambridge, Mass.: Harvard University Press, 1969.

Marshall, Alfred. *Principles of Economics.* 8th ed. London: Macmillan, 1920.

Menger, Karl. *Untersuchungen über die Methode der Sozialwissenschaften und der politischen Ökonomie insbesondere* (1883). Translated by Francis J. Nock as *Problems in Economics and Sociology.* Urbana, Ill.: University of Illinois Press, 1963.

Principles of Economics. (J. Dingwall and B. F. Hoselitz, trans.). Glencoe, Ill.: Free Press, 1950 (first published 1923).

Nozick, Robert. *Anarchy, State and Utopia.* New York: Basic Books, 1975.

Rawls, John. *A Theory of Justice.* Cambridge, Mass.: Harvard University Press (Belknap), 1971.

Robbins, Lionel. *On the Nature and Significance of Economic Science.* London: Macmillan, 1935.

Roberts, Blaine, and Bob Holdren. *Theory of Social Process.* Ames, Iowa: University of Iowa Press, 1972.

Schelling, Thomas C. *The Strategy of Conflict.* New York: Oxford University Press, 1960.

Shubik, Martin. "The General Equilibrium Model Is the Wrong Model and a Noncooperative Strategic Process Model Is a Satisfactory Model for the Reconciliation of Micro and Macroeconomic Theory," *Cowles Foundation Discussion Paper 365,* November 1973.

Veblen, Thorstein. "Why Is Economics Not an Evolutionary Science?" *Quarterly Journal of Economics,* vol. 12, 1898.

von Neumann, J., and O. Morgenstern. *The Theory of Games and Economic Behavior,* 2nd ed. Princeton, N.J.: Princeton University Press, 1947.

[13]

The Japanese Economic Review
Vol. 47, No. 2, June 1996

INSTITUTIONS AS FAMILIES OF GAME FORMS*

By LEONID HURWICZ

University of Minnesota

1. Introduction

Recent decades have witnessed a revival of interest in the role of institutions in economic processes. The importance attached to the work of Coase, North, Williamson and others attests to this. The works of these authors contain illustrative examples of institutions: property rights (common or private property), the state as guarantor of rights, law, markets (competitive, oligopolistic, monopolistic), money (commodity or fiat money), liability for damage by smoke, state regulation of economic activities (e.g., price controls, anti-trust laws), various forms of land tenure (sharecropping, renting, utilization of wage-labour), various forms of business organization (corporations, partnerships, non-profits), company towns, franchise systems, and many others – including even the week, viewed as an institution.

Specific institutions have been studied with the help of familiar analytical tools: demand and cost functions, principal-agent, and game-theoretical models. The comparison of sharecropping (métayage or on "shares") system with renting (the "English" system) is already found in Marshall's 1890 edition of his *Principles of Economics* (Book VII, Ch. XI, §§ 4, 5, 6, pp. 682–689). But serious analytic study of institutions as a general phenomenon calls for a rigorous definition of the concept of an institution within the framework of a formal model. Ideally, the definition should fit most if not all of the examples such as those above.

Not all those stressing the importance of institutions have attempted to provide such a definition. Those who did, as pointed out by Ostrom (1986), had to face the multiplicity of meanings of the term and to make choices among them.

2. Institutions and game forms

2.1 Meanings A and B of the term 'institution'

For North (1990, pp. 3, 4), who views institutions as rules of the game in a society, a basic dichotomy is between the meaning of institutions as such rules and the players whom he calls "organizations". But these players are often also called institutions. They are entities or bodies, usually mission oriented and treated as juridical persons. Examples abound: a university, a church, a country's legislative body. Although most "player"-institutions involve many (physical) persons and can be classified as organizations, there are also one-person "player"-institutions, as for instance a

---

* The present paper is an expanded version of my comments at the First Decentralization Conference in Japan, held at Keio University in November 1994. Due to its expository nature, it overlaps parts of some of my earlier papers cited in the References. Thanks are due to Professors Tatsuyoshi Saijo and Takehiko Yamato for numerous helpful suggestions. Responsibility, as always, remains the author's.

country's presidency or an agency's ombudsman.[1] We shall refer to "player"-institutions as the *A-institutions*.

The other meaning of 'institution', to be referred as the B meaning, and often called an *institutional arrangement*, is a matter of some controversy. As noted above, for North and many others[2] it consists of rules (in the language of game theory, *game forms*). For others, in particular Schotter (1981, p. 155), social[3] institutions are regularities or standards of behaviour.[4] In the language of the game theory, they are for him the *solutions* rather than rules of the game.[5]

In what follows I shall be dealing primarily with the B meaning of the term "institution", i.e., with institutional arrangements. Hence in what follows "institution" is to be interpreted as synonymous with institutional arrangement (a *B-institution*), unless the contrary is specified.

As for a formal definition of a B-institution, mine will be close to the "rules (game forms)" interpretation, but when an institution's genesis is taken into account it will incorporate some of the regularities approach as well. To make this clear, some formal apparatus is needed.

2.2 Notation for games in normal form

In order to be clear about the formalization of the notion of rules of the game, we must be careful about distinguishing between a *game* and a *game-form*.[6] Games, as is well known, have different forms of representation, in particular the so-called *extensive form* specifying the individual moves and their consequences, and the *normal form* formulated in terms of admissible *strategies* and the outcomes they produce.

We shall mostly be dealing with the normal form, assuming a finite number n of players. The term "game" in its technical sense is applied to the ordered pair consisting of two n-tuples: that of *individual admissible strategy domains*, $S^1, \ldots, S^n$, and that of (real-valued) payoff functions, $\pi^1, \ldots, \pi^n$. Denote by $S = S^1 \times \ldots \times S^n$, the *(joint) strategy space*, i.e, the Cartesian product of the individual domains, and by $N = \{1, \ldots, n\}$ the set of players. For all i in N, the i-th payoff function has the (joint) strategy space S as its domain and takes its values in the reals. Let $s = (s^1, \ldots, s^n)$, s in S, s^i in S^i for all i in N, be the n-tuple of strategies adopted by the players. The result is that the i-th player obtains the payoff $\pi^i(s)$, usually interpreted as the utility derived by the i-th player when s prevails. It is its payoff that each player is trying to maximize.

---

1) In one-person player-institutions one must distinguish between the player-institution and its incumbent.

2) In particular Riker (1982, p. 4) and Ostrom (1986). For an approach synthesizing the different concepts see Crawford and Ostrom (1994)

3) Although North, unlike Schotter, does not use the term 'social', he speaks of the rules of the game *in society*, so the intent seems the same.

4) It is interesting to note that von Neumann and Morgenstern (1944, pp. 41, 512) use the term "standards of behavior" as representing the solution of a game. On the other hand, when using the term 'institutions' (as on p. 225, footnote 3), identified with forms of social organization (the example being *laissez-faire*), they seem to be referring to rules of the game rather than to solutions.

5) In (1989, pp. 50–1), Schotter speaks of institutions of type I (rules) and of type II (regularities of behaviour).

6) Although this is not customary, we sometimes hyphenate the term "game-form" in order to avoid misunderstandings that might arise, e.g., when we speak of game-forms in extensive form.

L. Hurwicz: Institutions as Families of Game Forms

Formally, a game Γ then is defined as the double n-tuple, $\Gamma = (S^1, \ldots, S^n; \pi^1, \ldots, \pi^n)$ where, for each i in N, $\pi^i: S \to \mathbb{R}$. (Here $\mathbb{R}$ represents the reals).

2.3 Game forms vs. games

Since the payoff values represent the players' utilities, they depend both on rules of the game and on the players' preferences. To represent this situation, we first introduce the notion of an *outcome space*, denoted by Z, whose elements are the (physical) outcomes of the strategic decisions. In economic environments, the generic element of Z might be a resource allocation; for example, in a pure-exchange economy with m goods, a point z of the outcome space is a vector with $m \cdot n$ real components z^i_j, where z^i_j is the total amount of good j held after trading by trader i, so that Z is a vector space of dimension $m \cdot n$. In a voting model, the outcome space might consist of the set of candidates. In a social game, Z might be the set of prizes that might be given to players. Just who gets which prize depends, of course, on the strategies chosen by the players. The relationship between the strategies chosen and the resulting outcomes is defined by the outcome function, denoted by h.

The *game form*[7] G is formally defined as $G = (S^1, \ldots, S^n, h)$, or more briefly as (S, h) where S is the Cartesian product of the S^i's and $h: S \to Z$.

To express the relationship between game forms and games, we introduce utility functions to represent preferences.[8] The i-th player's *utility function* ϕ^i associates a real number, say u^i, with the outcome (e.g., resource allocation[9] or candidate elected) resulting from the strategies s chosen by the players. I.e., $u^i = \phi^i(z)$ where $z = h(s)$ and so $u^i = \phi^i(h(s))$. Hence the real number u^i represents the i-th player's utility resulting when the strategy n-tuple s prevails, so that u^i is the value of the i-th payoff function associated with s. It follows that the payoff function is the composite of the utility function and the outcome function. This can be written as

$$\pi^i(s) = \phi^i(h(s)) \qquad \text{for all } i \text{ in } N \text{ and all } s \text{ in } S,$$

or, more compactly, as $\pi^i = \phi^i \circ h$.

2.4 "Rules of the game" are represented by game forms, not by games

We have been somewhat pedantic in formalizing the concepts of a game and of a game form, because the distinction between the two is crucial for understanding the meaning of the "rules of the game". Since the players' preferences are not part of the rules, it is the game form, rather than the game, that corresponds to the intuitive notion of the "rules of the game".[10] Hence "game form" is the important concept in defining institutions in terms of rules.[11]

---

7) In the economic literature often called the *mechanism*.

8) At the cost of complicating exposition it is possible to avoid the assumption (implicitly made here) that the preferences can be represented by utility functions.

9) This formulation allows for the possibility of non-selfish preferences. When preferences are selfish, the i-th player's utility in fact depends only on the subvector or "bundle" $z^i = (z^i_1, \ldots, z^i_m)$ of the resource allocation z.

10) On the other hand, since institutions will be defined as the results of human activities, not all aspects of the game-form are to be viewed as institutional.

11) I.e., corresponding to Schotter's "type"!

The Japanese Economic Review

In the literature, the models under consideration frequently involve numerical outcomes – e.g., monetary payments to individual consumers. Thus an element of the outcome space is $z = (z^1, \ldots, z^n)$ where z^i is the payment to person i (a real number). Further, suppose that every individual is selfish, so that i's utility depends only on the i-th component of z, say $u^i = \phi i(z) = \psi^i(z^i)$ where ψ^i is a strictly increasing function. Finally, suppose that every one is "risk-neutral", i.e., that the ψ^i is a linear (or affine) function of the payment z^i. Then, without loss of generality, one may take the function ψ^i to be identity, so that $u^i = \phi i(z) = \psi i(z^i = z^i$ for each person i. Let h denote the outcome function, so that $h(s) = (z^1, \ldots, z^n)$, and define $h^i(s) = z^i$. Then the payoff function in this model is given by $\pi^i(s) = z^i = h^i(s)$, and the n-tuple $\pi(s) = (\pi^1, \ldots, \pi^n)$ is identical with the outcome function $h(s) = (h^1(s), \ldots, h^n(s))$. It is easy to see that in this case the distinction between the outcome function (the n-tuple of the h^i's) and the i-th payoff function (identical with the i-th-component of the outcome function) does not seem very important. But, of course, this is a very special case.

2.5 Representation of institutions by game forms involves more than restrictions on strategy domains

When an institution is defined by restrictions on the individual strategy domains (the sets S^i) imposed by an authority, it is natural to call such an institution a *regulation*.[12] North's (1990, p. 3) initial definition of institutions appears to include little[13] beyond regulations so defined: "Institutions are the rules of the game in a society or, more formally, are the humanly devised constraints that shape human interaction."

But the notion of (B-) institutions as constraints is, in my view, too narrow – for two reasons. First, of the two components of a game form (S, h) they only deal with the first (the strategy domains) and, even among the properties of strategy domains, they seem to cover only restrictions of the individual strategy domains while ignoring the possibility of expansions[14] of these domains by institutional arrangements. Second, it is difficult to see how certain important institutions (e.g., markets, social insurance) could be described just in terms of strategy domains but without reference to the outcome functions. It is natural to represent arrangements such as taxes, penalties, or subsidies as properties of outcome functions.[15]

---

12) The concept of a regulated economy in Reiter and Hughes (1981) is broader: it includes not only "direct constraints on behaviour" (corresponding to our concept of regulation) but also parameters θ^{ij} determining the agents' incentives (e.g., taxes or subsidies).

13) It is somewhat broader because it refers to constraints that are "humanly devised" – but not necessarily by an authority. This might, for instance, cover commodity money regarded as a (spontaneously developed) institution but not qualifying as regulation.

14) Crawford and Ostrom (1994, p. 3), by contrast, do refer to opportunities as well as to constraints.
15) Admittedly, some of the arrangements mentioned above—such as taxes (or subsidies)—can alternatively be viewed as restrictions on (or expansions of) strategy domains, although this representation might make analysis more complicated. But in many cases, including these examples, there is additional machinery involved, needed for the processing and transmission of information as well as for enforcement. Representation through outcome functions (as well as addition of artificial players such as, e.g., the Internal Revenue Service agency, an A-institution) seems the appropriate way to represent such institutional arrangements.

L. Hurwicz: Institutions as Families of Game Forms

2.6   An institution is a class of game forms, not just a single game form

An examination of examples of any phenomenon typically called an institution (in the sense of rules) shows, however, that it would not be natural to identify it with a particular game form. For instance, the institution of sharecropping specifies that the crops will be divided so that the landlord gets a fraction, say k (with $0 < k < 1$) and the labourer $1 - k$.[16] Now when sharecropping is formulated as a game form, the value of the share parameter k (entering the outcome function) must be specified, say $k = 1/2$. But to qualify as the institution of sharecropping any fractional value of k is acceptable. Hence the institution of sharecropping corresponds not to a particular game-form, say $G_{1/2}$ (with k specified to equal $1/2$) but to a class of game forms, say $\mathbb{G} = \{G_k: 0 < k < 1\}$.[17]

Another illustration of the same point is provided by price controls, more specifically price ceilings. In game form representation, these define the seller's strategy (price) domain as having a finite upper bound, say p^{i*}, determined by the price control agency, say $S^i = \{p^i: p^i \leq p^{i*}\}$, where the seller is the i-th agent and p^i his/her strategy variable. To specify a game form requires a particular numerical value of p^{i*}. Denote such a game form by $G_{p^{i*}}$, characterized by a specific value of p^{i*} in the above formula for S^i. One would naturally say that price controls as an institution prevail regardless of the numerical value of the ceiling p^{i*}. Hence, again, the institution of (ceiling) price controls corresponds to a *class of game forms*, say $\mathbb{G} = \{G_{p^{i*}}: p^{i*} \text{ ranging over (finite!)} \text{ real numbers}\}$.[18]

Membership in a class of objects may be considered as equivalent to having a certain attribute (or collection of attributes) distinguishing members from non-members. Hence defining an institution as a class of game forms may be viewed as equivalent with defining a institution as an attribute (or collection of attributes) of game forms.

We may refer to the game forms belonging to the class representing the same institution (i.e., sharing certain attributes) as "institutionally equivalent". Typically, this equivalence is based on similarity of the incentive structure it engenders for the participants, but there is a great deal of arbitrariness, sometimes depending on the issues under consideration. As an illustration, much of the analysis of incentive

---

16) The 1969 *Nouveau Petit Larousse en couleurs* specifies (under *métayage*) that k should not exceed a third. Actually, the term *métayer* comes from a Latin word meaning 'a half'. Thus there might have been a time when $k = 1/2$ was the only permissible value under *métayage*. But in the present context, all values strictly between zero and one qualify as 'sharecropping'. (See Hurwicz (1979a, pp. 123–147, and esp. pp. 140–144, the section entitled 'Incentive structures for unilateral maximization', for a simple model in which one-half turns out to be the best value of k from the landlord's point of view when the labourer's effort cannot be measured or observed.)

17) Following Stiglitz (1974), let the labourer's reward, a component of the outcome function, be written as $r = ky + b$ where y is the size of the crop (regarded here as the worker's strategy variable) and k and b are real-valued parameters. Different forms of land tenure are defined by different regions in the (k, b)-parameter space. Thus (pure) sharecropping is defined by the conditions $b = 0$ and $0 < k < 1$; renting by $k = 1$, $b < 0$; wage-labour by $k = 0$, $b > 0$. Thus, under renting, $-b$ is the rental fee, while under wage-labour b is the wage.

18) Although the frameworks are different (dealing with imputations or strategy spaces), it is of interest to note the multiplicity of imputations in a single von Neumann-Morgenstern solution and the multiplicity of Nash solutions (e.g., in a coordination game) corresponding to the same institution in Schotter's treatment.

structures of the alternative land tenure form reaches conclusions that are valid for all pure sharecropping game forms, regardless of the value of the share parameter k (or a), provided it is strictly between 0 and 1; similarly for all rental arrangements, regardless of the value of the parameter $b < 0$, and all wage-labour arrangements regardless of the value of $b > 0$. (See footnote 17 for notation.) Hence we speak of all pure sharecropping game forms, regardless of the value of k as institutionally equivalent, etc.

2.7 Conditional game forms ("humanly devised" aspects of game forms)

2.7.1 Institutions as correspondences from environment's to game forms

Quite often a game form has two aspects: (1) those that are behavioural in nature and are (potentially at least) subject to alternative design and embody the essence of the institutional arrangements, and (2) those that are considered as given, either because they are determined by the laws of physics or, more generally, by what we call the (economic) environment (in particular by the existing resource endowments, and the current state of technology). In such cases it would be incorrect to identify the institutional arrangements with all of the game form (S, h), and therefore a more refined definition of an institution must be formulated.

One example of such a game form is seen in a mechanism proposed in Hurwicz, Maskin and Postlewaite (1995) for situations in which no player knows the other players' endowments. The rules of the game call for each player to announce his/her own endowment (as well as estimates of the other players' endowments). This announcement is permitted to be an understatement but not an overstatement. The prohibition against overstatement is enforced by the requirement that the player "put on the table" the resources claimed in the endowment. Assuming that borrowing is somehow ruled out, it is then physically impossible to exaggerate. But this means that a given player's strategy domain depends on his/her true endowment. (In the usual economic models the endowments, preferences, and technologies determine the environment.) Thus the i-th strategy domain S^i is a function of the true value, denoted by ω^{io}, of the i-th agent's endowment. Therefore, the i-th strategy domain is denoted more accurately by $S^i(\omega^{io})$. Since ω^{io} is a component of the i-th characteristic e^i, and, in turn, e^i is a component of the environment $e = (e^1, \ldots, e^n)$, we see that the rules of the game specify the i-th strategy domain by a functional relation from the space E of environments into the space of strategy domains, hence into the space of game forms. The institutional aspect, here the result of design ("humanly devised"), is this functional relation, rather than the strategy domain itself.

An instance where the outcome function of a mechanism depends on the existing technology, hence on the environment e, is given below in Section 6. Here the rules of the game specify (via the "reward functions") how players are rewarded given the output. With y denoting output, consider (as in footnote 17 – the Stiglitz model) the class of (the worker's) linear reward functions written $r^i = ky + b$. (However, unlike in footnote 17 and in Section 6, effort – not output – is considered the worker's strategy variable). As in footnote 17, special cases of the reward functions (i.e., of the parameters k and b) produce alternative institutional arrangements (e.g., sharecropping, wage labour, renting) and are "humanly devised". The player's strategy may be his/her intensity of effort; this will determine the output via the production function. The outcome function, relating reward (outcome) to effort (strategy), has a "humanly devised" aspect (the reward functions) and an aspect determined by the environment (the production function). Thus the institutional aspect is in this example represented by a functional relation from the space E of environments to the space of outcome functions, rather than the outcome function itself.

The preceding two examples illustrate the fact that institutional phenomena should, in general, be represented not as game forms but as relationships between game forms and the economic environment. But since we think of institutions as associated with *classes* of mechanisms, this relationship must be viewed as a correspondence rather than a function. Thus in the preceding example the institution of sharecropping involves the worker's reward function ("humanly devised") of the form $r^i = ky$ where y is the output and k a number between zero and one. But suppose the strategy variable s^i is the worker's effort x^i, so that $s^i = x^i$, and the output is determined by the production function $y = cx^i$, where c is the technologically determined productivity of effort parameter, considered as part of the environment and not institutional in nature. Then the worker's outcome function is $h^i(s) = dx^i = kcx^i$, involving both the institutional aspect (k) and the environment aspect (c). Thus it is not the outcome function h^i that represents the institution of sharecropping, but rather the correspondence that associates with each environment (productivity parameter c) is an outcome function $h^i(\cdot)$, where $h^i(s) = dx^i$ where d/c is a number between zero and one.

In formal notation we have the following situation. Let G denote the class of conceivable game forms. We may then consider an institution to be a correspondence, say Λ from the space of environments E into G, i.e., $\Lambda: E \to G$. Given an environment e, the resulting class of game forms, $G = \Lambda(e)$, embodies not only institutions but also the characteristics of the environment; it is the correspondence Λ itself that represents the purely institutional aspect of the game forms. (See footnote 41 in Section 6 for an example of such a correspondence).

We may note that a constant correspondence Λ may be identified with a class of game forms.

In fact, throughout the present paper, when we speak of institutions as represented by classes G of game forms, they should be interpreted as correspondences Λ. (Alternatively, one can interpret such references as dealing with the special case of constant Λ.)

For the sake of brevity we sometimes refer to *conditional game forms* or *classes* G when the institutional aspects are represented by functions or correspondences such as Λ above. (The case of constant Λ may then be termed an *unconditional* game form.)

2.7.2   *An alternative formalization of dependence on the environment*

As an alternative way of looking at the problem, consider again the class G of conceivable game forms. Further, let $G(e)$, a subset of G, be the class of game forms consistent with the laws of physics and other restrictions that cannot be modified by human action under the prevailing environment e. Thus human action can only result in choice among the game forms in $G(e)$. Thus an institution, say T, is represented by a subset, say G_T, of $G(e)$.

In our interpretation of institutions as classes of game forms, the set-theoretic difference $G(e) \backslash G_T$ represents the game forms that have been eliminated by human action. Full information about the effect of human action in this case is represented by the ordered pair $\langle G(e), G_T \rangle$, showing both the field of choice and the choice made through human action.

Now the set $G(e)$ is determined by the environment e. If the correspondence $G(\cdot)$ is regarded as known, we are back to the ordered pairs (e, G) representing institutions, i.e., to conditional game forms.

3. The defining attributes of institutions

Not all classes of game forms qualify as institutions. In this section we shall be considering some of the attributes of game forms that, by almost unanimous consensus, characterize institutions. These are:

a) The genesis of institutions: human actions (behaviour)
b) Ensuring the effectiveness of institutions.
c) The domain of applicability of institutional rules ("categoricity").

3.1 The genesis of institutions: human actions (behaviour)

Clearly, the constraints (or outcomes) due to laws of physics would not be considered institutions. In one fashion or another, this is recognized by all writers and incorporated into the definition of institutions. Thus, as seen from the above quotation, North defines institutions as *humanly devised* constraints.

Ostrom (1986, pp. 5–6) says: "Rules, as I wish to use the term, are distinct from physical and behavioral laws ... That rules can be changed by humans is one of their key characteristics."

Schotter's definition (1981, p. 11) reads as follows:

A social institution is a regularity in social behavior that is agreed to by all members of society, specifies behavior in specific recurrent situations, and is either self-policed or policed by some external authority.

Clearly, it is the human behaviour or actions that generate the institutions. In Section 3.1.2 we consider a formalization (the concept of conditional game forms) designed to separate the "human design" from the "environmental" aspects of game forms.

The Reiter-Hughes (1981) model contains a sequence of two games, the first of which generates the (institutional) rules for the second. Again, human choices are involved. This formalization will be elaborated in Section 4 below.

3.1.1 Conscious design vs. 'organic' (endogenous) origin

It is to be noted that human actions are not synonymous with conscious design. While North speaks of "humanly devised" constraints, Schotter (1981, p. 21) stresses the absence of conscious design (the "organic" or 'behavioural' view, with roots in Carl Menger's (1883) discussion almost a century earlier):

... the institutional form will be an endogenous variable in the model. It emerges without any agent or group of agents consciously designing it – through human action but not human design.

In this context Schotter cites Hayek's (1955, p. 39) statement in a similar spirit:

The problems which they [the social sciences] try to answer arise only in so far as regularities are observed which are not the result of anybody's design.

The point that not all institutions emerge without conscious design is made in Schotter, although he gives reasons (1981, pp. 28–9) (some quoted from Hayek (1955)) why he will not (subsequently) be discussing consciously created institutions. He says:

> ... many social institutions are created in one stroke by a social planner or by the agents of society meeting in a face-to-face manner and bargaining about the type of institution they would like to see created. Here the exact form of the institution that emerges is the result of explicit human design (in the case of a planner) or multilateral bargaining (in the case of a legislature).[19]

The "constitution creation game" is mentioned as an example of institutional rules created by such a process.

In his 1986 paper (pp. 117–118), Schotter correlates what he calls the "rules view" ("type I" in his 1989 terminology) of institutions with the notion of *consciously designed* game forms or mechanisms:

> The focus of attention here is on the possibility of designing sets of rules or game forms (to use Gibbard's terminology) that when imposed on a set of social agents, lead to prespecified equilibrium outcomes. ... Throughout this literature, social institutions are planned and designed mechanisms given exogenously to or imposed upon a society of agents. Institutional change is a process of social engineering that takes place through the manipulation of rules.

But there is no logical basis for identifying the "rules view" of institutions with the assumption of conscious design as genesis of the rules. Many questions studied in what is often called "mechanism design" or "implementation"[20] literature deal with the *logical* compatibility of various attributes of game forms or rules. The answers are as relevant to rules arrived at by consensus or majority vote of a group to whom the rules are to apply (and who respect the majority decision) as they are to rules "given exogenously or imposed upon a society of agents".

This is, in particular, true of the informational (im)possibility theorems, such as the theorem stating that Pareto optimality cannot be guaranteed by any informationally decentralized mechanism with a message space of dimension substantially lower than that needed to verify that perfectly competitive equilibrium prevails (see Mount and Reiter (1974), Hurwicz (1977) and Osana (1978)). It is also true of the theorem stating that the set of Nash equilibrium allocations of any mechanism guaranteeing Pareto optimality in an economy where participants are not forced to trade must include the perfectly competitive allocations.[21]

I see no reason why a set of rules under which a society or economy operates cannot

---

19) In fact, the first of two games in the Reiter-Hughes model, the (cooperative) political game Π [whose outcome (p. 1399) is the framework for the second game (played by firms and regulators)], is envisioned as a bargaining game involving coalition formation.

20) I probably am to blame for having popularized the "design" term, while "implementation" is probably due to Eric Maskin.

21) Subject to a condition of continuity and a sufficiently broad class of economies for which the guarantee is to hold. See Hurwicz (1979b).

The Japanese Economic Review

be the outcome of some "organic" process, free of conscious design. In fact, I believe that Schotter's (1981) supergame Nash equilibria may be viewed as an illustration of this possibility, showing that a rigorous game-theoretic formulation can constitute a model of "organic" or endogenous formation of rules governing behaviour. It is for this reason that I see no conflict between the rules interpretation of institutional arrangements and the possibility of "organic" genesis of such institutions.

However, the distinction between imposed and non-imposed rules does suggest a related and important dichotomy of institutions: (1. "external") those, like rules contained in laws, that are binding on persons other than their creators (e.g., legislators), and (2. "internal") those, like rules contained in contracts, that only bind those that participate in their creation (including heirs, assigns, etc.).[22] My intent is to formulate the concept of institution so that it covers both categories. Moreover, if I think of the process of creating an institution as a game (à la Reiter-Hughes, and perhaps even Schotter), this is not meant to exclude the possibility of less formalized genesis such as custom formation.

3.2 Ensuring the effectiveness of institutions

Although Schotter's concept of an institution differs from that proposed in the present paper[23], it is valuable because of its explicit reference (1981, p. 11) to behaviour being "either self-policed or policed by some external authority". North's definition does not mention enforcement but its importance is clear from subsequent discussion (e.g., 1990, pp. 28–33). Crawford and Ostrom (1994, p. 6) distinguish rules from norms by the role of sanctions for not following rules (their "or else" element).

Schotter's notion of "self-policed" may cover two phenomena: (1) behaviour being policed by members of the group rather than an external authority[24], and (2) internalization of appropriate behaviour, so that each person is, in effect, policing

---

22) It is interesting to note the part of Schotter's definition of a social institution as "... a regularity of social behavior that is agreed to by all members of society ..." Taken literally, this would imply that all social institutions belong to class (2) above. The models of institution generation constructed by Schotter, including property rights, do satisfy this requirement. But one might not want to say that the institution of property rights does not exist if some members of the society are opposed to it.

23) Schotter (1981, p. 11) defines an institution as regularity of behaviour and calls it in Schotter (1989, pp. 50–51) an institution of type II, while labelling institutions defined in terms of rules as institutions of type I. Both type I and II are institutions in the B sense. (The terminology used in Crawford and Ostrom (1994) is "institutions-as-equilibria" and "institutions-as-rules" corresponding, at least roughly, to Schotter's type II and type I respectively.)

In the terminology of game theory, an institution of type II is an equilibrium strategy (e.g., a Nash equilibrium) of a game, hence an element of the space S, while an institution of type I is formulated in terms of the game-form which, together with the players' utility functions, defines a game.

As will be seen below, we take into account the equilibrium aspect of institutional phenomena by following Reiter and Hughes (1981) using a model consisting of a sequence of two games where the rules governing the second game are obtained as the equilibrium outcome of the first game. Thus an institutional arrangement is both a class of game-forms (of the second game) and an equilibrium outcome (of the first game). Note, however, that—except in special cases—the equilibrium outcome of the first game need not be an element of its strategy space.

24) A situation studied by Elinor Ostrom and co-authors in a number of papers.

© Japan Association of Economics and Econometrics 1996.

himself/herself. In a variety of situations, any of these modes of enforcement (or their combinations) may be present. But it seems to me that enforcement is too narrow a category of phenomena serving to ensure the effectiveness of an institution (viewed as a class of game forms).[25]

Enforcement is aimed at making sure that the strategy domains prescribed by the game forms are being abided by. But to make a game form (mechanism) effective, the results specified by the outcome functions must also be "delivered". Mechanisms such as markets or social insurance, illustrate the need for special machinery required to carry out, in addition to enforcement, the informational functions (in particular, communication) as well as the physical flow of goods and financial instruments. The totality of these required activities corresponds, I believe, fairly closely to everyday usage of the term "implementation". But since in recent literature this term has been given a different meaning[26], I sometimes qualify it by an adjective and speak of "*genuine implementation*", with the intention of covering the complex of all activities designed to make the outcome function effective, thus including much in addition to enforcement.[27]

3.3 The domain of applicability of institutional rules ("categoricity")

Here again, Schotter's definition has the merit of explicitly referring to social institutions being concerned with "behaviour in specific recurrent situations". To put it in a somewhat more general form, a (B-) institution deals with a *category* of situations (whether recurrent or contemporaneous) and typically applies to a class (*category*) of actors rather than to specifically named persons.[28] Thus there are rules for buyers or sellers, for parents and children, for legislators, bureaucrats, etc. This is the property referred to as "*categoricity*".

To determine that an institution applies in a given case, it must be verified that the situation and the actors belong to appropriate categories.

---

25) One occasionally hears the opinion that a Nash equilibrium is self-enforcing. But that is only true (presumably, by definition) if one assumes that players abide by the rules of the game. To make sure that they do, enforcement machinery may be necessary.

  Another view exists, to the effect that enforcement is impossible because of the possibility of corruption on the part of those in charge of enforcement, as well as their superiors. ("Who will guard the guardians?") An infinite regress seems to be a possibility. A framework for avoiding this paradox, involving the notion of the "natural game form" is discussed in Hurwicz (1993a).

26) Following Eric Maskin, current literature uses the expression "to implement a social choice rule" in the sense of finding a game form which, within a specified class of players' preferences, would produce equilibrium outcomes consonant with the desiderata embodied in the social choice rule. (The use of the term "rule" in "social choice rule" to represent the desiderata, although widespread, is somewhat confusing in the present context; hence we sometimes use "goal correspondence" instead.)

27) One frequent aspect of genuine implementation is the creation of an agency (e.g., the Social Security Administration, an A-institution) whose function is precisely to make the outcome function operational, and in some cases also to enforce the constraints on the strategy domains.

28) As indicated above, some institutions (called above "internal") govern only their creators; others ("external") are binding on others as well.

4. A game sequence model

4.1 Three-game sequence model

To avoid ambiguity, we shall formalize some of the ideas discussed above. The formalization admittedly is narrower than the general situations discussed above; in particular, it may not cover the "organically" generated institutions that constitute Schotter's primary interest. Specifically, we follow to a considerable extent the schema used by Reiter and Hughes, although we shall use a sequence of three games where Reiter and Hughes use two. It is the first of these three games, Γ_1, called *preliminary*, that results in creating the institution, i.e., a class of game forms (denoted by $G_{23} = G_2 \times G_3$) intended to govern the subsequent games.[29)30)] The second game, Γ_2, called *administrative* (although it may be involve judicial as well as administrative bodies as players), formulates detailed regulations and so narrows down the *class* G_3 to a *single* game form G_3, required to be an element of G_3. This game form G_3 will then govern the third game, Γ_3, called *substantive*.

For example, the preliminary game Γ_1 may be the legislative process resulting in the prohibition of cartels, the institution being created; this legislation would define a class of game forms $G_{23} = G_2 \times G_3$, assuming a law abiding society, one can expect that the natural game forms of the two subsequent games change appropriately, thus assuring compliance. Based on this legislation, in the course of the administrative game Γ_2, the administrative (and/or judicial) bodies then formulate detailed regulations, e.g., defining the term "cartel" and specifying implementation and enforcement procedures consistent with the enabling legislation, thus producing a game form G_3 (an element of the class G_3). Again, we shall assume a law abiding society, so that game form G_3 will in fact be effective in governing the substantive game Γ_3. This game consists of interactions between the regulators and the firms being regulated, as well as among the firms themselves. (If compliance with law could not be taken for granted, additional actions would have to be taken in the course of the first two games to assure the effectiveness of the prohibition of cartels.) Thus, whatever the details, for the (desired) game form $G_3 = (S_3, h_3)$, the strategy domain S_3 excludes any 'legal' strategies that would result in the formation of a cartel among the participating firms, and h_3 imposes penalties for violations.

The question may be raised why a sequence of three separate games, is considered preferable to a single game with three stages. One reason is that the preliminary, administrative, and substantive phases are very likely to involve different sets of players. On the other hand for "internal" institutions a single multi-stage game model may be more appropriate.[31)] Much of our formulation could be adapted to such a model.

---

29) Unlike Reiter and Hughes, however, we do not require at this stage that the preliminary game be a cooperative game.

30) Here G_2 is assumed to be a one-element class (a singleton, its element denoted by G_2) representing the rules governing the administrative game Γ_2. (Otherwise, a longer cascade might be needed.) On the other hand, G_3 will in general have many elements, thus creating the need for the administrative stage, whose function is to narrow down the class G_3 to a single element G_3 of this class that will govern the substantive game Γ_3.

31) But even for "internal" institutions the sets of players in different phases may vary, as when, e.g., heirs of the contracting parties are involved.

L. Hurwicz: Institutions as Families of Game Forms

The fact that we restrict ourselves to a sequence of just three-game models is mainly an expository simplification. In general, we might consider a 'cascade' of T games, Γ_1, ..., Γ_T, $T \geqq 2$, where each predecessor restricts the game forms governing its successors, and it is only the last game, Γ_T, is substantive. As an illustration, the sequence could consist of the country's constitution, statutes of successively greater specificity, judicial interpretations of the law, as well as regulatory actions of administrative bodies.

Let us return to the three-game $(T = 3)$ sequence model. For $t = 1, 2, 3$, let the set of players of Γ_t be $N_t = \{(t, 1), ..., (t, n_t)\}$, the (joint) strategy space S_t, the outcome space Z_t, and the game-form $G_t = (S_t, h_t)$. (The symbol (t, i) denotes the i-th player in game Γ_t.) In game Γ_t, let the payoff function of player (t, i) be denoted by π_t^i. (It is obtained as the composition $\pi_t^i = \phi_t^i \circ h_t$, where ϕ_t^i is the utility function of player (t, i) and h_t the outcome function of Γ_t.) Then we may write $\Gamma_t = \langle N_t, S_t, (\pi_t^1, ..., \pi_t^n) \rangle$, or, for short, $\Gamma_t = \langle N_t, S_t, \pi_t \rangle$ where π_t is the n_t-tuple of payoff functions of the game Γ_t.

The generic element z_1 of Z_1 (the outcome space of the preliminary game) is assumed to consist of two elements, say $z_1 = (\mathbb{G}_{23}, b_{23})$, $\mathbb{G}_{23} = \mathbb{G}_2 \times \mathbb{G}_3$, with $\mathbb{G}_2$ consisting of the one element G_2. Here $\mathbb{G}_3$ is a class of "*desired game forms*" for the substantive game Γ_3. A rough interpretation of this concept is that players of the preliminary game want the substantive game Γ_3 to be governed by one of the game-forms in $\mathbb{G}_3$.[32] The b_{23} component of z_1 represents actions or behaviour of preliminary game players intended to have this effect on the environment prevailing during the subsequent games and hence the 'natural' game-forms $G^\wedge_2$ and $G^\wedge_3$[33] of the administrative and substantive games as to make some game-form from $\mathbb{G}_2$ effective for

---

32) More precisely, it is the result of strategy choices (bargaining, etc.) by members of N_1 each of whom is 'pushing' toward his/her favourite game-form for Γ_2. Of course the equilibrium outcome $\mathbb{G}_2$ need not be to every one's liking.

33) Write the 'natural' game-form as $G^\wedge = (S_\wedge, h^\wedge)$. The ("natural") strategy domain $S^\wedge$ of $G^\wedge$ contains not only the strategies permitted by a desired game-form, but also all others that are physically and psychologically feasible. If we think of the desired strategies as the legal ones, $S^\wedge$ contains not only the legal strategies but also all feasible illegal strategies. By definition, the ("natural") outcome function $h^\wedge$ of $G^\wedge$ represents those strategy choices from $S^\wedge$ that are in fact likely to occur. In general, even when desired strategies are used, the natural outcomes may differ from those desired. (See Hurwicz (1993a) for a fuller discussion of these concepts.)
Consider games with two players and finite strategy spaces, so that the outcome functions are represented by matrices. We may want to suppose that the desired outcome matrix is a submatrix of the natural outcome matrix, i.e., that at least the legal strategies have the desired outcomes. However, this need not always be so. It may easily happen that the desired outcome function is not effective, so that the actual (natural) outcome associated with a "legal" joint strategy s is different from the prescribed outcome; i.e., in symbols, for some $s \in S$, $h_\wedge(s) \neq h(s)$ where $h^\wedge$ denotes the natural outcome matrix and h the desired outcome matrix; thus in this case the desired outcome matrix h is not a submatrix of $h^\wedge$.
A desired game-form $G^* = (S^*, h^*)$ is said to be *effective* with respect to the natural game-form $G^\wedge$ over a class Φ of n-tuples of utility functions for players in N if, for every n-tuple of utility functions ϕ in Φ, the sets of equilibrium outcomes of the two games $\Gamma^\wedge$ and G^* are the same. (Here $\Gamma^\wedge$ is the composition of ϕ with the outcome function $h^\wedge$, while Γ^* is the composition of the same ϕ with the outcome function h^*; the set of players is N in both cases.)
The intent of this definition of the team "effective" is to formalize the idea that even though the actual game being played is always the natural game, the outcomes will be the same as those that would have resulted from the desired game. In particular, even though participants could have used illegal strategies, they will not do so at an equilibrium. Thus enforcement works and we have "genuine implementation".

The Japanese Economic Review

Γ_2 and some game form from G_3 effective for Γ_3. The introduction of the element b_{23} is motivated by the idea that the desired game-forms in G_2 might remain "on paper" and not become effective unless the natural game form of the substantive game was suitably changed by some action or behaviour. Examples of b_{23} components are: physical barriers (preventing or deterring the use of "illegal" strategies), education and propaganda, and, of course, the existence or creation of reliable and effective implementation (in particular, enforcement) organs.[34] These activities would involve diversion of resources (a component of transaction costs). A more sophisticated (probabilistic) model would explicitly take into account the fact that enforcement typically is less than 100% successful. It is interesting to note that in experimental settings great effort is made to make the rules of the game completely effective (there is genuine implementation), often by the nature of physical arrangements.

The outcome z_2 of G_2 is of the form (G^*_3, b_3), where G^*_3 is the game form (no longer a class!) designed to govern the substantive game Γ_3 and b^*_3 is again an action aimed at modifying the environment E_3 and hence the natural game form $G^\wedge_3$ prevailing during the substantive game so as to assure effectiveness.

In certain situations or societies, the mere fact that the preliminary game had produced the class G_{23} might have sufficient authority to make one of its constituent game-forms effective. (We speak of law-abiding societies and say that the rule of law prevails.) In such cases, b_{23} might be interpreted simply as the announcement of the class G_{23} as the equilibrium outcome of the preliminary game. (Formally, in this case, $z_1 = (G_{23}, b_{23})$, with $b_{23} =$ the announcement of G_{23}, and similarly $b^*_3 =$ the announcement of G^*_3.)

There is an important relationship between preferences of the players, N_1 and N_3, respectively in the preliminary and substantive games of the sequence. Typically, a player of the preliminary game is interested in the expected or likely outcome z_3 of the substantive game, perhaps because he/she identifies with the interests and/or preferences of some players of the substantive game. Hence while the utility function ϕ_1^i has Z_1 as its domain, the value of $\phi_1^i(z_1)$ depends on the expected outcome z_3 generated (indirectly) by z_1.

4.2 Main features of the model

To summarize, among the important features of the preceding model are these: (a) the sequential structure of the process; (b) the preliminary game, if effective (i.e., genuinely implemented), determines a class of game forms, here interpreted as the institutional arrangements, that will ultimately govern the "proper" phase of the substantive game; (c) in order to achieve genuine implementation, it is, in general, necessary for the preliminary game to produce actions or behaviour that will so modify the natural game form of the substantive game as to make the rules produced by the preliminary game effective.[35]

It should perhaps be emphasized that the model is intended for a broad class of institutions, even though in many cases it would not be natural to represent the

---

34) See Hurwicz (1993a) on the role of "intervenors", and "closed circles".

35) A formalization of "effective" is given above in footnote 33.

formative phase by game formalism. However, other aspects of the model might still be appropriate. Thus, for instance, the common features of the institution of marriage, with its many forms in many societies and historical periods, may be represented by a class G_3 of game forms, while the formative phase would be represented by an "organic" evolutionary process. However, the specific game form G^*_3 prevailing in a country or state during a particular period (e.g., the prohibition of polygamy) often is the product of legislative, administrative, or judicial actions.

As for the internal structure of the substantive game, whether or not it includes the administrative phase, it may be most natural to represent it in extensive form. One reason is that in practice, rules are usually[36] formulated in terms of moves rather than strategies. Moreover, extensive form would make it simpler to accommodate an important aspect of New Institutional Economics, viz. transaction costs. Therefore, for purposes of institutional analysis, it would be desirable to introduce the notion of *game-form in extensive form*. This could be represented by the usual tree diagram, but with outcomes (elements of the outcome space Z) instead of numerical (utility) payoffs. Furthermore, it would also seem desirable to depart from the usual procedure of associating the outcomes with terminal nodes only. In addition to the usual terminal outcomes, one could introduce *interim outcomes*, associated with progression from any node to the next. The various transaction costs would be among the components of such interim outcomes. An example might be the requirement of up-front payments for the filing of a law-suit.[37]

4.3 Definition of an institution

We have so far discussed different characteristics and models of (B-)institutions, but no formal definition of an institution has been given. A highly simplified definition might be that implied by the title of this paper: an institution is a class of game forms. In the preceding example of the institution prohibiting cartels, it would be a class G_3 of various game forms all of which exclude strategy domains involving cartel formation and, perhaps, some limits on penalties for violations. But such a definition fails to embody the various attributes that qualify a game-form class as an institution. To begin with, in line with our discussion in Section 2.7 above, in order to make sure that we are excluding the effects of the laws of physics, etc., we must use conditional game forms (in effect, specifying classes of game forms permitted by human actions given the prevailing environment). Second, there must be explicit reference to human actions creating the institution, the multi-stage or sequential aspect of the process. Third, since effectiveness (or genuine implementation) is considered to be essential, the element making for effectiveness must also be explicit in the formalization. Finally, there must be a formal expression of the categoricity aspect.

Clearly, this makes for a complex concept. In the interest of minimizing this complexity, we shall confine ourselves to the sequential structure described in Section

---

36) But not always: for instance, rules dealing with predatory competition concern strategies rather than separate moves.

37) Introducing interim outcomes is not a complete innovation. In games with infinite time horizon there are, of course, no terminal nodes; the so-called felicities are interim utilities associated with interim outcomes such as consumption in a given time period.

The Japanese Economic Review

4.1. Formally then, a (B-)institution is defined as the following ordered sequence of elements:

$$\langle E_1, \Gamma_1, z_1; E_2, \Gamma_2, z_2; E_3 \rangle,$$

with

$$z_1 = (\mathbb{G}_{23}, b_{23}), \ \mathbb{G}_{12} = \mathbb{G}_2 \times \mathbb{G}_3, \ z_2 = (\mathbb{G}_3^*, b_3^*),$$

$$E_2 = \eta_2(E_1, b_{23}); \ E_3 = \eta_3(E_2; b_{23}, b_3^*)$$

all game forms being "conditional" (in the sense of Section 2.7)[38] and "categorical" (in the sense of Section 3.3, i.e., applicable to categories of actors and situations rather than named individuals and situations), the unique element G_2 of $\mathbb{G}_2$ being effective in Γ_2, and the game form G_3^* being effective for the class $\mathbb{G}_3$ over E_3.[39]

The components b_{23} and b_3^* represent actions or behaviours so modifying the environment as to assure effectiveness in subsequent games. E_t represents the environment prevailing during game Γ_t and hence determines the natural game form $G_{\wedge t}$ prevailing during Γ_t. The symbols η^2 and η^3 denote functional relations representing the effects of the respective actions b_{23} and b_3^* on subsequent environments.

As it stands, the preceding formulation does not accommodate institutions whose "organic" genesis does not lend itself to game-theoretic representation of the preliminary phase ($t = 1$). To model this type of genesis, the preliminary game Γ_1 would have to be replaced by some non-game type of process. However, other elements of the above formal definition might still retain their relevance.

On the other hand there is a relationship, albeit imperfect, between Schotter's supergame model of institutions and our above framework, with the supergame corresponding to our preliminary game Γ_1, and the solution of the supergame corresponding to our game form G_3^*.

5. Contents of institutions

So far we have been discussing the more formal aspects of modelling institutions. But what of their substance? In particular, in economic settings, what aspects of the economic process do the rules deal with? The answer, of course, is: a tremendous diversity. Without attempting a complete treatment, it seems worthwhile to indicate two types of phenomena frequently treated in institutional literature: endowments and residuals.

---

38) Hence, strictly speaking, we should be using the symbols Λ representing correspondences from the respective environment spaces into the space of conceivable game forms rather than the symbols G representing classes of game forms. However, as indicated in Section 2.7, we have opted for the somewhat ambiguous notation because the G symbols seem more suggestive, and, of course, correct in the case when the Λ's are constant.

39) It may be noted that the class of environments, E_3 over which the institution represented by G_3 is effective may be different from what had been aimed at by players in the preliminary game.

5.1 Institutions assigning initial endowments

A broad class of institutions dealt with by economists can be formalized in terms of the assignment of initial *endowments*, especially endowments of rights (see Eggertsson (1990), especially ch. 4). Among many examples are the following.

The alternative liability rules for damage caused by pollution can be represented by alternative assignments of initial endowments of the right to pollute or the right to enjoy clean air and water (see Hurwicz (1993c)).

The distinction between common and (individual) private property (central to the "tragedy of the commons" problem) can be represented by distinguishing between endowments associated with a group of agents as against endowments obtained by individual agents. A property right may be viewed as a ternary relation involving a person, natural or artificial, the specific object owned, and a particular right, e.g., that of use, or alienation. Specifically, consider a particular aspect of property rights, the right of use, say the right of fishing in a commonly owned body of water. In general, more than one person may have the right of fishing there. But under exclusive individual property rights, only one person has such right. Denote by (i, x) the right of agent i to use the object x. In game-form formulation this means that (i, x) is an element of i's strategy domain S^i. The absence of common ownership means that, for any $j \neq i$, the element (j, x) does not belong to S^j. So absence of common ownership is a relationship between the different players' strategic domains, hence an attribute of the (joint) strategy space S, and therefore of the game form (S, h).

Primogeniture, considered by many an important institutional factor in England's economic history, is naturally represented as a rule concerning the endowment of heirs with the parents' estate. (Note that the rule is of "categorical" nature: it applies to the actor defined as the oldest son, not to a specific person.) In some cases the rights endowments are of procedural nature (e.g., the burden of proof in torts[40]), materially affecting transaction costs.

5.2 Institutions assigning certain residuals

Another class of institutional phenomena deals with certain *residuals*. Thus Grossman and Hart (1986) explain the effects of vertical or lateral integration of firms by the residual rights of ownership with respect to vague residuals due to the incompleteness of contracts caused by unavoidable complexity of contingencies. The different incentive effects of the various land tenure forms are due, at least in part, to the location of residual risks or opportunities. Similar considerations apply to alternative institutional structures of firms, both with respect to rewards (profits, etc.) and liabilities. The location of these residuals is often determined by the assignment of endowments, including those of liabilities. Hence there is a relationship between the two aspects of institutional phenomena, and much of the principal-agent literature deals with them. Very tentative and incomplete ideas for certain aspects of these phenomena are discussed in the next section.

---

40) In the Napoleonic code, as well as in ancient Roman Law, when damage was due to actions of children, cattle, or was "caused" by buildings, the burden of proof was on parent or owner, as an exception to the general rule. In French civil law before World War II this reversal also applied to most cases of damage caused by automobile accidents.

The Japanese Economic Review

5.3 Institutions governing particular aspects of behaviour

Institutions are not only due to human actions, they also deal with human actions, whether through the description of the strategy domains S^i or through the specified outcome functions h. One problem of formalization we have not yet faced is the fact that what is usually called an institution deals only with particular aspects of human activities, e.g., commerce, family status, punishment for crimes, etc., rather than with the totality of human behaviour. To formalize this, consider again an institution T (say, rules governing commerce) represented by the class G_T of game forms. Let the outcome space Z be the common range of all outcome functions in G_T, and let us think (in the present context only) of Z as a subset of a vector space, with sets of components of its elements corresponding to different aspects of human behaviour. For such an element z, write $z = (z_T, z_{T'})$, an element of the Cartesian product $Z = Z_T \times Z_{T'}$. Here z_T represents the components dealing with behaviour in commerce, while $z_{T'}$ represents all other aspects of behaviour. If $(S\#, h\#)$ is an element of G_T, and if, for some s in $S\#$, $h\#(s) = (a^*, b^*)$ in $Z_T \times Z_{T'}$, then G_T must also contain all game forms $(S\#, h)$ where $h(s) = (a^*, b)$ and b ranges over all of $Z_{T'}$.

Similar factoring of the elements s of the strategy domains S is also to be carried out. Thus if s is in S, write $s = (s_T, s_{T'})$, an element of the Cartesian product $S = S_T \times S_{T'}$. Then if $(S\#, h\#)$ is an element of G_T, and $s^* = (c^*, d^*)$ is in $S\#$, the G_T must also contain all game forms $(S, h\#)$ where S contains all elements of the form $s = (c^*, d)$, with d ranging over all of $S_{T'}$.

Let the different aspects of behaviour be indexed by the set Θ, and let the family G_θ of game forms represent the institution dealing with aspect θ of behaviour. Then, clearly, the aggregate impact of the totality of institutions G_θ, with θ ranging over Θ, is represented by their intersection $\bigcap_{\theta \,\mathrm{in}\, \Theta} G_\theta$. If the requirements of the various institutions are not mutually inconsistent, the intersection is non-empty.

6. The characteristic function, the support set, and the support function

As an illustration of some of the preceding concepts consider the following situation, closely related to the principal-agent model, with the Stiglitz land tenure example of Section 2.6 and footnote 17 as an illustration.

There are two persons 1, 2, with strategy domains S^1 and S^2. The set S^0 is the strategy domain of the exogenous factors (e.g., weather). S^i includes effort expended by person i, $i = 1, 2$. The joint strategy space is $S = S^1 \times S^2 \times S^0$.

Write $s = (s^1, s^2, s^0)$ for the generic element of S.

The generic outcome is written

$$z = (y, r^1, r^2),$$

where y is the output (or, e.g., value added) and r^i the reward (wealth increment) for person i.

The production function is

$$y = \eta(s);$$

in particular, the function η represents the extent to which the output depends on the level of effort of the two persons and on the exogenous factors. (The symbol η used here is not related to the same symbol used in Section 4.]

– 130 –

L. Hurwicz: Institutions as Families of Game Forms

The reward functions f^i (defined by the prevailing institutions) are given by

$$r^i = f^i(y; s), \qquad i = 1, 2.$$

(When the strategy, e.g., the level of effort, of person i is not observable to the other, it may be impractical to make the reward function f^i directly dependent on i's effort or, more generally, on s^i. A similar limitation applies to direct dependence of reward functions on exogenous factors, i.e., on s^0.)

Hence the outcome function $h(\cdot)$ can be written as

$$h(s) = \langle \eta(s), (f^i(\eta(s); s))_{i=1, 2} \rangle.^{41)} \qquad (*)$$

The utility functions are $u^i(r^i, s)$, $i = 1, 2$. It is natural to assume that u^i rises with r^i. The dependence of u^i on s represents phenomena such as the disutility of effort, the discomforts of bad weather, etc.

The production function η tells us who and to what extent strategies, in particular effort, can affect the output. On the other hand, the reward function f^i tells us to what extent i's reward is affected by variations in output, as well as directly by s. The relationship between the reward functions and the production function is a major factor in determining whether the given institutional setup does or does not promote "efficiency" (as measured by output).

The situation can be analysed with the help of certain concepts that seem of potential value in arriving at general propositions about the incentive structures engendered by alternative institutional arrangements.

The first of these is what we call the *characteristic function of an institution*, denoted by F. For instance, consider the Stiglitz land tenure example of Section 2.6 and footnote 17. Let the three forms of land tenure be abbreviated as $a = $ wages, $b = $ renting, $c = $ sharecropping, and let the two persons be the landlord ($i = 1$) and the worker ($i = 2$). Then we define $F(x/i) = 1$ (or -1, or 0) if i's reward depends positively (or negatively, or does not depend) on i's s^i (e.g., effort) via the production function.

Thus, assuming that the worker's effort can increase output, $F(2/a) = 0$ while $F(2/b) = 1$. On the other hand, if the landlord's actions can increase the worker's productivity, one might expect that $F(1/a) = 1$ while $F(1/b) = 0$. Finally, if both sharecroppers can raise output by their effort, $F(1/c) = F(2/c) = 1$.

The *support set of an institution* x is defined as the set of agents i, denoted by $\psi(x)$, such that $F(i/x) \neq 0$. The *support function for a class* X of institutions (with the same set of agents N) is the set-valued function $\psi(\cdot)$ where $\psi(x)$ is the support set of x, and the argument of $\psi(\cdot)$ ranges over the class X. I.e., $\psi: X \to N$, where for a given institution x in X, $\psi(x) = \{N'$ a subset of $N: F(i/x) \neq 0$ for i in $N'\}$.

Final version accepted November 24, 1995

---

41) Our interpretation here is that only the reward functions represent the institutional aspect of the model while the production function is an aspect of the environment. Consider, for example the class L of reward functions affine in y, i.e., $f = (f^1, f^2)$, $f^2(y, s) = ky + b$, $f^1(y, s) = y - f^2(y, s)$ where the landlord is agent 1, and let the subset L^* of L be the class of reward functions corresponding to sharecropping, i.e., where $f^2(y, s)) = ky$, with k ranging over the open interval $(0, 1)$.) Then the institution of sharecropping is formally represented by the correspondence $\Lambda: E \to G$ where an element e of the space E of environments can be identified with a particular production functions η and G is a class of game forms, and $\Lambda(e) = \Lambda(\eta) = h(s)$ where h is given by the formula $(*)$ in the text. (See Section 2.7 for a discussion of conditional game forms.)

The Japanese Economic Review

REFERENCES

Coase, R. (1960) "The Problem of Social Cost," *Journal of Law and Economics*, Vol. 3. pp. 1–44.

Crawford, S. and E. Ostrom (1994) "A Grammar of Institutions," 1994 [marked 7/8/94 and W93-1], Workshop in Political Theory and Policy Analysis, Indiana Univ., Bloomington, Indiana.

Eggertsson, T. (1990) *Economic Behavior and Institutions*, Cambridge: Cambridge University Press.

Gardner, R. and E. Ostrom (1991) "Rules and Games," *Public Choice*, Vol. 70, pp. 121–149.

Grossman, S. J. and O. D. Hart (1986) "The Costs and Benefits of Ownership: A Theory of Vertical and Lateral Integration," *Journal of Political Economy*, Vol. 94, pp. 691–719.

Hayek, F. A. (1955) *The Counterrevolution of Science*, New York: New York Free Press.

Hurwicz, Leonid (1972) "On Informationally Decentralized Systems," in McGuire, C. B. and R. Radner, eds., *Decision and Organization*, Amsterdam: North Holland, ch. 14.

— (1977) "On the Dimensional Requirements for Non-wasteful Resource Allocation Systems," in Arrow, K. J. and L. Hurwicz, eds., *Studies in Resource Allocation Processes*, Cambridge, Cambridge University Press.

— (1979a) "On the Interaction between Information and Incentives in Organizations," in Krippendorff, K., ed., *Communication and Control in Society*, New York: Gordon and Breach Science Publishers.

— (1979b) "On Allocations Attainable through Nash Equilibria," *Journal of Economic Theory*, Vol. 21, pp. 140–165.

— (1993a) "Implementation and Enforcement in Institutional Modelling," in Barnett, W. A., M. J. Hinich and N. J. Schofield, eds., *Political Economy: Institutions, Competition and Representation*, New York: Cambridge University Press, ch. 2.

— (1993b) "Toward a Framework for Analyzing Institutions and Institutional Change," in Bowles, S., H. Gintis and B. Gustafsson, eds., *Markets and Democracy: Participation, Accountability and Efficiency*, Cambridge: Cambridge University Press.

— (1993c) "What is the Coase Theorem?" presented at the Seventh Annual Japan-U.S. Technical Symposium, *The Coase Theorem: Competition and Bargaining*, held on March 5, 1993, at New York University; published in *Japan and the World Economy*. Vol. 7, (1995), pp. 49–74.

— (1994) "Institutional Change and the Theory of Mechanism Design," *Academia Economic Papers*, Vol. 22, No. 2. (September, 1994), Taipei, Taiwan: Institute of Economics, Academia Sinica.

—, E. Maskin and A. Postlewaite (1995) "Feasible Nash Implementation of Social Choice Rules when the Designer does not Know Endowments or Production Sets," in Ledyard, J. ed., *The Economics of International Decentralization: Complexity, Efficiency and Stability. Essays in Honor of Stanley Reiter*, Boston: Kluwer Academic Publishers.

Marshall, A. (1890) *Principles of Economics*, Vol. 1, London: Macmillan.

Menger, C. (1883) *Untersuchungen ueber die Methode der Sozialwissenschaften und der politischen Oekonomie insbesondere* (Investigation of the Methods of the Social Sciences especially Political Economy), Leipzig: Duncker and Humblot (reprinted by the London School of Economics, 1933).

Mount, K. and S. Reiter (1974) "The Informational Size of Message Spaces," *Journal of Economic Theory*, Vol. 8, pp. 161–192.

North, D. C. (1990) *Institutions, Institutional Change and Economic Performance*, Cambridge: Cambridge University Press.

— (1992) *Transaction Costs, Institutions, and Economic Performance*, San Francisco, CA: International Center for Economic Growth, ICS Press.

Osana, H. (1978) "On the Informational Size of Message Spaces for Resource Allocation Processes," *Journal of Economic Theory*, Vol. 17, pp. 66–78.

Ostrom, E. (1986) "An Agenda for the Study of Institutions," *Public Choice*, Vol. 48, pp. 3–25.

—, J. Walker, and R. Gardner (1992) "Covenants with and without a Sword: Self-governance is Possible," *American Political Science Review*, Vol. 86, No. 2, pp. 404–417.

Reiter, S. and J. Hughes (1981) "A Preface on Modeling the Regulated U.S. Economy," *Hofstra Law Review*, Vol. 9, No. 5, pp. 1381–1421.

Riker, W. H. (1982) "Implications from the Disequilibrium of Majority Rule for the Study of Institutions," in Ordeshook, P. C. and K. A. Shepsie, eds., *Political Equilibrium*, Boston: Kluwer-Nijhoff, pp. 3–24. Originally in *American Political Science Review*, 1980, pp. 432–447.

Schotter, A. (1981) *The Economic Theory of Social Institutions*, Cambridge: Cambridge University Press.

— (1986) "The Evolution of Rules," in Langlois, R. N., ed., *Economics as a Process*, Cambridge: Cambridge University Press. ch. 5.

— (1989) "Comment" (on "Market and Institutions" by Siro Lombardini), in Shiraishi, T. and S. Tsuru, eds., *Economic Institutions in Dynamic Society*, London: Macmillan and International Economic Association.

Stiglitz, J. (1974) "Incentives and Risk Sharing in Sharecropping," *Review of Economic Studies*, Vol. 41, pp. 219–256.

von Neumann, J. and O. Morgenstern (1944) *Theory of Games and Economic Behavior*, Princeton: Princeton University Press.

[14]

Institutional evolution as punctuated equilibria

Masahiko Aoki*

ECONOMISTS' VIEWS OF INSTITUTIONS

Where do institutions come from? What role do they play? How do they interrelate with one other within each economy and across economies? Can they be designed to change? Needless to say, these questions are impossible to answer without making explicit what is meant by institutions. However, leaving aside the old school of institutional economics, economists were largely content to leave the definition of institutions more or less vague. It is only recently that a few of them have taken up the task of conceptualizing institutions. Durkheim, a pioneer of modern sociology, once defined the discipline of sociology as the 'science of institutions' (1901) in contrast to that of economics as the 'science of markets'. Mainstream economists might have thought likewise that such a task was outside the realm of economics. However, economists can make unique contributions to understanding the nature, origin, roles and consequences of institutions, but we must first make clear what we are talking about. There are at least three different (although interrelated) meanings that economists attach to the word 'institution'. What we should be concerned with is obviously not a semantic clarification of the word as such, but a conceptualization that may be conducive to a better understanding of the workings of diverse economic systems by facilitating analytical insight.

In order to clarify the differences among the three meanings, or concept-ualizations, of institutions that economists use, an analogy of the economic process with a game is apt. The game theoretic apparatuses useful for institutional analysis, particularly those borrowed from the theory of evolutionary and repeated games, are of relatively recent vintage. However, the analogy of the economic process with a game can be dated back as far as Adam Smith, who stated: 'In the great chessboard of human society, every single piece has a principle of motion of its own, altogether different from that which the legislature might choose to impress upon them' (1775, Part 6, ch. 2).

11

12   *Foundations*

In the analogy of the economic process with a game, economists have regarded an institution as comparable to a player of the game, the rules of the game, or an outcome (equilibrium) of the game. When people casually talk about institutions in daily conversation, they normally mean (prominent) organizational establishments, such as the government, universities, corporations, foundations, religious organizations and so on. Some economists follow this convention, effectively identifying an institution with a specific player of the game. However, North (1990) argues for a second view: that institutions should be identified with the rules of the game as distinct from players of the game.[1] There are formal and informal rules of the game. By definition, the formal rules of the economic game cannot be constructed (changed) by the players of the game while they are playing, but need to have been determined prior to the playing of the game. As we are concerned with the origin of institutions, a question then immediately arises: who determines the economic rules? It is here that North draws a sharp distinction between the rules of the game and the players of the game (organizations and their political entrepreneurs) who can act as agents of institutional change, that is, as rule makers. According to North, the existing rules of the game shape the incentives of the players (organizations) as to how to transact and what to innovate, ultimately generating effective demands for new rules in response to changing relative prices. The new rules will then be negotiated and determined in the 'political market' that is structured according to political rules. North claims '[i]t is the polity that defines and enforces the economic rules of the game' (1995, p. 23) Informal norms of behavior come from socially transmitted information and thus constitute a part of the cultural heritage. Therefore the process of their formation and erosion must be slow and complex. The tension between politically determined formal rules and persistent informal constraints then may have important implications for the way economies change.

An equilibrium-theoretic approach to institutions was pioneered by Schotter (1981) and recently has been developed by Greif (1994, 1999), Milgrom et al. (1990), Greif et al. (1994), Weingast (1997) and Young (1998) among others, who rely on sophisticated concepts of equilibrium in repeated prisoner's dilemma games (such as subgame perfect equilibrium and a variant of sequential equilibrium) or long-run stochastically stable evolutionary equilibrium.

Basically, I subscribe to the equilibrium-of-the-game view of institutions. Depending on contexts, we may employ either evolutionary or repeated game approaches, and use correspondingly different equilibrium notions (some kinds of evolutionary equilibrium versus perfect equilibrium). Both approaches adopt rather extreme assumptions, in fact two polar opposite ones, regarding individual agents' rationality in analysing their motivations and choices. This may be interpreted as reflecting the present state of game theory, which has not yet succeeded in producing satisfactory models of the bounded rationality of individuals, that is, the trait of economic actors who are '*intendedly* rational, but only *limitedly* so' (Simon). Thus we may regard these two approaches as being not fundamentally opposed to each other, but complementary.[2] Regardless of which equilibrium notion we choose, the ones we employ are all Nash equilibria. That is, an institution is a socially constructed state from which agents are not motivated to depart as long as others do not do so.

Regarding the origin of an institution, we have seen that the rule-of-the-game theorists tend to subscribe to the design view; namely rule making is susceptible to conscious design, whether by legislators, political entrepreneurs, mechanism design economists and so on. Among the equilibrium-of-the-game theorists, in the beginning it appears that there was no clear consensus on this issue. Those who adopt the evolutionary game approach clearly subscribe to the view of an institution as a 'spontaneous order' (Hayek, 1973) or a characteristic of the self-organizing system. In contrast, the concept of subgame perfect equilibrium presumes that individual players are perfectly capable of deductive reasoning regarding a feedback mechanism between their own and others' choices. How can individuals jointly select strategies that are mutually consistent and lead to the construction of an institution, especially when there are multiple equilibria? There is nothing that the notion of subgame perfect equilibrium can reveal about why a certain institution evolves in one place and another evolves elsewhere. It seems natural then to consider that even those who adopt the super-rationality notions of equilibrium (such as subgame perfection) are doing so merely to show that a certain profile of strategies (actual plays and expectations) can become self-enforcing and sustainable, *once established*. Game theory provides a useful tool for understanding the self-enforcing nature of institutions. However, it is unlikely to provide a complete closed theory of institutions. To understand why one equilibrium is chosen but not others, we are required to make use of comparative and historical information and engage in inductive reasoning as well.

INSTITUTIONS AS THE ENDOGENOUS RULES OF THE GAME

I shall try to develop a game-theoretic approach to institutions that will synthesize the two views described above: rules and an equilibrium of the game as an institution. Since it is difficult to provide a succinct phrase for describing this approach, let me tentatively refer to it as the 'endogenous-rules-of-the-game' view. In this view, institutions are roughly identified with substantive characteristics of self-enforcing rules for action choices by agents that are universally believed to be relevant in a repeated game situation and thus able to govern agents' ongoing interactions. However, I do not regard these rules as exogenously given or conditioned by the polity or by culture, as the rules-of-the-game theorists do. I regard them as endogenously created through the interactions of agents in a relevant domain and thus self-enforcing, as the equilibrium-of-the-game theorists do. Although this view can be given a precise, analytical formalization,[3] I shall present here only a basic underlying idea.

In analysing institutions, I take a domain of transactions participated in by a set of agents as the unit of analysis and analyse their interactions as a game. The domain is defined by a set of the agents and the set of technologically feasible actions for each of them. Suppose that time consists of a sequence of (indefinite) periods and in each period every agent chooses an action. The combination of selected actions by all the agents – which I refer to as an action profile – in one period makes the internal state of the domain existing at the beginning of the period move to the new state by its end. The state refers to all the consequences of the action profile that are (observable and) welfare relevant to agents in the domain, say, the profile of the agents' actions themselves, the final distribution of their outputs, the level of common goods and so on, depending on context. Each agent wants to maximize his/her payoff, that is, to realize the best state for him/her (or more rationally the best sequence of future states). However, future states cannot be solely determined by his/her action. The best action choice of each agent ought to be contingent on others' action choices and the current state, but how can agents infer others' action choices in a given state?

Suppose for a moment that games are played repeatedly, out of which a stable state evolves and each agent has come to have a reasonably good idea, based on his/her experience, about how other agent(s) make action choices. Namely, agents may not be able to infer, or may not even need to infer, every detailed characteristic of the others' actual choices, but come to perceive some substantive characteristics of rules that the other relevant agents are believed to use in making their action choices. Relying on stabilized inferences, each agent may also develop his/her own rules for making an action choice in response to the state of the domain. However, it is intuitive that a complex feedback mechanism is operating here. All the agents form their own action-choice rules (as their strategies), while inferring others' action choice rules even though only in an incomplete and summary form. Only when their inferences about others' action-choice rules are stabilized and reproduced in response to an evolving state of the domain, can their own action-choice rules also become stabilized and serve as useful guides for playing the game, and vice versa. I capture such properties of consistency and stability evolving with respect to agents' inferences and strategic formation of action-choice rules as they are in equilibrium. Institutions are substantive characteristics of equilibrium action-choice rules that are universally recognized by agents in the domain and relevant to their own action choices. As equilibrium phenomena, they are endogenous constructs of repeated games and at the same time govern the strategic interactions of the agents in the domain. It is not beneficial for an agent to ignore or deviate from them. Although they are equilibrium phenomena, they should not be regarded as either a result of perfect deduction in a one-shot game, or of complete stasis to which any intended reasoning by agents is not applied. They represent a stable state of a process of strategic interactions among the agents who actually play the game repeatedly over time. Thus an institution is 'the product of long term experiences of a society of boundedly rational and retrospective individuals' (Kreps 1990, p. 183).

A couple of caveats are due regarding the above conceptualization of institutions. First, although my conceptualization is related to an equilibrium, obviously it is not appropriate to refer to every detail of a particular equilibrium action profile arising in response to a particular internal state and external environment of the domain as an institution. Rather, an institution ought to refer only to a substantive characteristic of equilibria that is robust to the mildly changing environments of the domain and universally relevant to all the agents in it. Thus I refer to equilibrium 'rules' for action choices, rather than an equilibrium choice of action in a particular state or a stationary action choice over periods, in my definition. Rules may prescribe different actions depending on the prevailing state of the domain. Furthermore, the agents cannot, and need not, form inferences about all the rules used by all other individual agents in the domain. However, they need to, and can, infer a substantive aspect of the relevant rules in a compressed form when making their own action choices. I provide a precise conceptualization of this notion of summary representation in my forthcoming book (Aoki, 2000).

Second, the (inferred) action-choice rules normally take the form of 'if the internal state of the domain is such and such, then agents in general, or a particular agent, would choose such and such action'.[4] An example is: 'If the ruler cheats merchants, then the merchants in the guild will boycott his castle town next year'. This appears to prescribe an action rule for the merchants to follow in the event of a ruler's cheating. However, as Greif et al. (1994) argued in their seminal paper on the guild, such an event may not actually happen, because a ruler's inferences about the merchant's action-choice rule prevents him from taking that action. Therefore, the rule above actually represents a belief of the ruler. It is often such beliefs that guide agents' actual action choices and constitute an institution.

A conceptualization of institutions is of course a matter of the theorist's taste and not a matter of right or wrong. However, in my view there are at least six reasons why the equilibrium-oriented, endogenous-rules-of-the-game conception of institutions is useful for comparative institutional analysis.

First, the equilibrium approach can deal with the issues of enforcement and the origins of institutions endogenously by making the dual nature of institutions clear: existing as an ongoing product of the strategic interactions of agents, but having a stable existence independent of individual agent's choice. If one subscribes to the traditional exogenous-rules-of-the-game view, then one must immediately face the issues of where and how the rules originated, as well as how they are enforced. Institutional origin may need to be found outside the domain of the economy in which the rules are applied: for example, in the polity outside the economic domain or, theoretically, in a meta game in which rational agents collectively choose a set of rules from many such possible sets.[5] But how, then, are the rules of the polity game set? How are all the possible rules known to the players of the meta game and how do they play it? Where are the rules of the meta game determined? Thus, a problem of infinite regression seems bound to arise. Perhaps the right way to resolve this problem is to regard an institution as originating as a stable endogenous product of the game, in the economic, social or political transaction domains, while leaving the rules of the game unspecified as much as possible at the outset. Even if legal rules are provided for a game, a stable pattern of choices by the agents may not be consistent with them. Then they can hardly be regarded as an institution. For example, even if the government prohibits the importation of some goods by law, and if it becomes a widespread practice to bribe customs officers to circumvent this regulation, then it seems appropriate to regard the bribery as an institution rather than the ineffectual law.

A similar problem of infinite regression can arise with respect to enforcement in the exogenous-rules-of-the-game approach. If the rules of the game are to be enforced by an augmented player (enforcer), the question of the enforcer's motivation needs to be addressed. Who enforces the enforcer? Do we need still another enforcer to enforce the rules of action prescribed for the original enforcer? A solution to this problem is again to analyse a game including the enforcer, if any, as a player, and see if the prescribed rules of action for the enforcer can become his/her equilibrium strategic choice, given an equilibrium constellation of strategic choices by other agents and vice versa. In other words, the equilibrium approach regards an institution as a substantive aspect of an equilibrium set of action-choice rules. Although institutions are constructed socially and are thus internal to the domain, once established, they nonetheless become objectified and 'taken for granted' by the agents and govern their action choices. Although endogenously created, they become rules of the game. We can understand this dual nature of institutions by relying on equilibrium analysis.

Second, by showing the possibility of multiple equilibria in specific models, the endogenous-rules-of-the-game approach is able to shed light on the 'humanly devised' (North 1990) nature of institutions rather than its ecologically, technologically or culturally driven aspects. If there is only one equilibrium corresponding to the technological specification of the structure of the game, then that equilibrium is little more than a disguised technological condition, and not an institution. For example, often the evolution of community norms in East Asia is attributed to the climatic and ecological conditions there, which presumably make peasant family farming and collective use of the irrigation system more productive. However, Korea and Japan, which are characterized by similar ecological conditions, had subtly divergent institutional evolutionary paths in terms of village social structures and social norms, which may have had profound and long-lasting impacts on the subsequent institutional trajectories of both economies.[6] Usually, a multiplicity of equilibria is regarded as troublesome by game theorists, and they have spent much research effort, without decisive success, in the so-called 'refinement' of the equilibrium concept to enable them to identify only one equilibrium out of the many possible Nash equilibria. However, I consider that the multiplicity of equilibria of games should not be regarded as a problem in comparative institutional analysis for the reason described above. We only need to carefully utilize empirical, comparative and historical information to identify the important historical, political and social factors that selected one equilibrium over the others in particular economies.

Third, the endogenous-rules-of-the-game approach to institutions provides an appropriate framework for analysing the interdependencies of institutions operating within the economy. When businesspeople design an organizational form with the purpose of emulating better practices abroad, or when the government drafts a statutory law for the purpose of introducing a so-far non-existent 'institution', their implementation in particular economic, political and social contexts can often have unintended consequences. For example, even if a government in a transition economy drafts a privatization law aimed at emulating markets for corporate control in the advanced economies, an outcome may be the widespread capture of corporate control by insiders, such as ex-party bureaucrats, directors of ex-state-owned enterprises and so on. This is analogous to a situation in which a medicine which has been tested in a laboratory may have unpredicted side-effects when it is administered to a human being because of the complexity of the living organic system. A major reason for such unintended outcomes is the absence of 'fits' between the designed plans and the existing institutional environments which reflect a unique historical trajectory of institutional development. This suggests the possibility that only institutional arrangements that are mutually consistent and/or reinforcing may be viable in an economy. We can conceptualize such ideas as institutionalized linkage and institutional complementarities. These intuitively appealing notions can become amenable to rigorous analysis when the endogenous-rules-of-the-game notion of institutions is applied. Specifically, we can consider games in different domains of the economy, such as organizational coordination, commodity trade, transactions of human asset services and financial asset services, political transactions, social exchange and so on, and can analyse how an equilibrium constellation of strategic choices of agents in one domain can become strategically complementary to, or conditional on, the equilibrium choices of the same or different agents in another domain.[7] In this way, we can understand the conditional robustness of an overall institutional arrangement of the economy as well as the multiplicity of such arrangements. In this way, we can understand why Pareto-inferior overall institutional arrangements can persist in spite of reform efforts in some domains in isolation.

Fourth, the endogenous-rules-of-the-game approach to institutions may also clarify the multifaceted roles of institutions. An institution is often conceptualized as constraints on the action choices of the agents. But in a world of incomplete and asymmetric information, an institution may also 'enable' the bounded-rational agents to economize on the information processing needed for decision making. Here, an analogy with the price mechanism familiar to economists may be useful. In the market mechanism, individuals do not need to know every detail of the economic environments in which they make their choices, but only the relative prices (Hayek 1945). Leaving aside the problem of the enforcement of contracts and property rights, if there are a complete set of markets, relative prices could be regarded as 'sufficient statistics' summarizing the data needed for society to achieve the social optimum in the most efficient way. The dimensionality of relative prices does not exceed the number of goods (Koopmans 1957; Hurwicz 1977). Needless to say, however, in actuality a complete set of markets does not exist. Individual agents therefore need alternative means to gain the useful information for making their choices. Various institutions other than markets then evolve in response to the failure of complete markets to exist. Thus Arrow maintains:

> [T]he absent contingent markets may be replaced by long-term relations. ... [T]he actual futures and contingent price will be replaced by expectations of future prices and quantities. Expectation *per se* can be thought of as an element of individual psychology, but in practice social institutions play a major role in guiding and forming expectations. There are ... understandings that others will not exploit every possible short-term profit opportunity, and elaborate financial services networks to provide forecasts and to smooth out temporary difficulties. (Arrow 1997, p. 6)

In short, individual agents are not only constrained but also informed by institutions. Just as markets transmit information regarding the economic environment (technologies, tastes and resource endowments) in the summary form of equilibrium relative prices, so do other institutions in alternative summary forms.[8] There are other, though related, aspects of the role of institutions. By providing common information in compressed forms that enable/constrain agents' choices, they serve in effect as a mechanism for coordinating the choices of individual agents in the domain *vis-à-vis* their environment, whether technological, natural or institutional (in surrounding domains). Also, the endogenous-rules-of-the-game view implies that an institution and the imputation of payoffs to the agents in the domain are co-determined. Thus an institution serves as an incentive mechanism for the agents to exercise effort and develop their individual capacities in a certain direction. The long-run implications of these two impacts lead us to the following point.

Fifth, the endogenous-rules-of-the-game approach to institutions may suggest a new perspective for analysing the mechanism of institutional change. Just as there can exist only an incomplete set of markets, the ability of any institution to transmit information regarding the changing environment and strategies of agents in a summary form is also incomplete. But for individual agents who are bounded in their ability to process information and compute their optimal choices, such incomplete information may be adequate for making reasonably satisfactory strategic choices in a relatively stable environment. However, this adequacy may become subjectively problematic when there is a drastic environmental, technological or demographic change, or when a path of continual change in the outcomes of games played by the agents endogenously creates an internal crisis. Individual agents may then perceive that the 'taken-for-grantedness' of institutional arrangements may not be tenable and begin to search for a new set of rules for action choices based on the collection of information, learning, experimentation and so on. As an aggregate outcome of such individual searching, agents' inferences and their perceptual representations of the internal and external states of the economy (or its subdomains) may gradually converge and a new institution may thus evolve. I shall explore this idea more later.

Finally but not least important, the difference in whether the rules of the game constituting institutions are viewed as exogenous or endogenous to the relevant domain may have significant implications for the role of public policy. If one subscribes to the view that institutions comprise polity-determined rules, leaving aside informal rules, yet institutions matter to the performance of an economy, then the implications could be that a badly performing economy might, and should, reform itself by designing and implementing better rules, possibly emulating best practices elsewhere. If this is not realized, blame could then be placed on politicians. For example, the standard reform prescription for an ex-socialist economy at the time of the demise of the USSR was to proceed as fast as possible on macroeconomic stabilization, the immediate and thorough liberalization of domestic trade and prices, and privatization of state-owned enterprises, while creating the legal framework for a market economy. However, the transformation of economic systems carried out along such policy recommendations has not been completely successful, particularly in the former USSR economies. Should only politicians be blamed, whether or not they are incompetent or ill-natured?

Meanwhile, the Chinese transition has been preceding in an institutional environment without a well-organized rule of law to constrain the ability of the state to prey on private property rights or massive one-time privatization of state-owned enterprises according to set rules. Yet China's per capita GDP has more than quadrupled in the last two decades, while the share of state-owned enterprises in industrial output has declined to about 30 percent, concentrated only in mining and metal industries. This contrast is a pointed challenge to the conventional advice for transplanting the rules of the game prevailing in advanced market economies as fast as possible to reform non-market or developing economies. It calls for a careful and systematic study of how the initial institutional conditions, such as the legacies of old institutions and the prevailing informal rules, affect policy impacts on subsequent institutional change, how rule setting in the polity interacts with the endogenous evolution of the rules of the games in other domains and so on.[9]

In summary, the equilibrium-oriented, endogenous-rules-of-the-game perspective may provide a promising approach to institutions because of (i) the endogenous treatment of institutions; (ii) the admission of their multiple existence; (iii) the provision of tools for analysing their interdependencies; (iv) insight into their multifaceted roles; and (v) the nature of their evolutionary change; as well as (vi) caution against the possibly harmful impacts of policy recommendations not consistent with the path of institutional evolution.

SUBJECTIVE-GAME MODELS AND PUNCTUATED EQUILIBRIA

Having submitted that institutions ought to be understood as an equilibrium phenomena – somewhat more precisely, as summary representations of an equilibrium profile of strategies of agents that are commonly recognized by, and relevant to, repeatedly interacting agents – the question naturally arises as to how we can understand the mechanism of institutional change from this perspective. Orthodox game theory, classical and evolutionary, defines its analytical framework in such a way as to regard the sets of actions by the agents fixed a priori. For both approaches, there can be multiple equilibria.

Then, an institution, viewed as an equilibrium, can be seen to change as a shift from one equilibrium to another. How can such a change occur? Although in Nash equilibrium no rational agent will find it beneficial to change his/her strategy individually, if agents' sets of all possible actions are objectively known and fixed, some rational agents may perceive the possibility of a 'better equilibrium', either through deductive reasoning or by learning from best practices elsewhere, and be engaged in an activity to make its choice a focal point. Often such a rational role is expected from the government. However, the government itself is an agent, with own incentives and limits in reasoning and persuasion. It is not clear at all that the government is able, or even willing, to lead the coordination necessary for a move from one equilibrium to another.[10] The government itself is a strategic player of the game in the polity domain.[11] Further the mechanism of institutional change seems often to involve a novelty or change in the agents' set of possible actions from which their strategy can be constructed.

Now I shall develop a conceptual framework, without completely abandoning the equilibrium approach, for understanding the mechanisms in which the agents try to discover a new way of doing things, and through their interactions new institutions become self-organized. Thus, I depart from the usual game-theoretic presumption that agents have complete (or incomplete) knowledge of the objective structure of game. Rather, they have subjective views of the structure of the game they play in the form of what I call the subjective game models.[12] In particular, individual agents subjectively activate only small subsets of possible actions and/or their combinations as menus of choice at any one time. Then we shall see how agents are induced to reassess and substantially revise 'subjective' sets of actions and rules for choices therefrom in a coordinated manner, consciously or unconsciously, thus eventually leading to a new profile of (moving) equilibria and their compressed subjective representations – new institutions.

Let me start by introducing a simple expository tool, called the COSE box, to describe the objective structure of the game and then discuss how it can be modified from the perspective of individual agents. As stated, we regard a *domain* of the economy as a unit of analysis. The domain consists of the set of a finite number of agents (players) – individuals or organizations, and the technologically feasible set of strategies (rules for action choices) for each agent.[13] The combination of strategy choices by all the agents is called a strategy profile. The data given to the domain are the technologically feasible sets of outcomes of strategic profiles relevant to agents' welfare, the environment that is not under the control of the agents, but affects the physical outcomes of their strategic choices parametrically, and a technological relationship that, given a state of the environment, assigns an outcome for each strategy profile. The set of agents, the sets of technologically feasible strategies for each agent, and the outcome function are the *exogenous rules* of the game. It is important to note that the strategy sets of agents include all technologically feasible strategies and do not exclude any strategies that may be constrained by human devices. The value of the outcome function depends implicitly on a set of parameters representing the state of the environment surrounding the domain. They may specify the state of technology, and the initial endowments of resources, as well as the states of other domains of the economy (institutional environments) than the one under consideration. However, I reserve an explicit reference to the institutional environment until the end. Thus, for the moment, we may proceed as if the exogenous rules of the game are completely technologically determined.

The objective structure of the game relevant to any individual agent in the domain may then be represented by a 2×2 tableau form, which we shall refer to as the COSE box (Table 3.1). The left column represents the data to an agent, while the right represents his/her variables. The first row refers to the dimension internal to the agent, and the second to that external to him/her. Each entry is self-explanatory. It is assumed that, given an expectation regarding others' strategies, each agent is assumed to choose a strategy that maximizes his/her own payoff. When there is consistency between agents' expectations about others' strategic choices and their actual choices, then we say the domain is in Nash equilibrium. The endogenous-rules-of-the-game approach regards institutions as social constructs that represent substantive characteristics of equilibrium strategic profiles of agents, and thus provides agents with stable expectations of others' strategic choices while constraining their own strategic choices. Schematically, they become entries in the E-cell of the COSE box, providing *endogenous rules of the game*.

However, if institutions are associated with equilibrium phenomena, what could be the mechanism for change? As already indicated, according to the

Table 3.1 *The COSE box representation of the objective structure of the game*

	Parametric data (exogenous rules of the game)	Endogenous variables
Internal to choice subject	(C) set of choices	(S) strategic choice
External constraints	(O) outcome function	(E) expectation of others' strategic choices; (institutions)

endogenous-rules-of-the game view of institutions, institutional change can be identified with a shift from one equilibrium (sequence) to another equilibrium (sequence) associated with a systematic, qualitative change in the strategies (in the choice of action-choice rules) of agents as well as in their common perceptual representations (beliefs) about them. At first, it may appear that there are two ways of realizing such a change of equilibrium. First, it may be thought of as occurring as a spontaneous ordering out of the *decentralized experiments* of agents trying new strategies from the given sets of choices. Alternatively, equilibrium change may be thought of as being introduced by the *collective design* of a law and/or that of a new type of agent – organizations – equipped with a fundamentally different set of action choices from the ones possessed by incumbent agents. This is related to the issue we have already touched on – that of spontaneity versus design as the origin of institutions.

However, from our perspective the introduction of a law *per se* and an associated new regulatory agency is nothing more than a change in the data – exogenous rules of the game – of the game form that the agents perceive. Such a change in a law or a policy may affect the process of institutional change by providing a focal point for agents in switching strategies or actually impacting the outcome of their (experimental) choices. Thus, a designed change in the game form can *induce* an institutional change. However, in understanding the role of a change in game form, we need to trace the process backwards as well as forwards. On the one hand, how does a law come to be changed? How do agents come to (collectively) recognize the need for a new (regulatory) organization? On the other hand, how does a new law and organization affect the expectations of agents, and accordingly their strategic choices, by changing the game form? Do they generate intended outcomes? If we pursue these questions, then we realize that, notwithstanding an apparent difference between spontaneous and induced institutional change, there is a common condition involved in bringing about a change by either route: a critical mass of the agents in the original or polity game need to begin to modify their representational perceptions about the internal structure of the domain, as well as its external environment, and conjointly adopt new strategies in a decentralized or coordinated manner to generate a new equilibrium (sequence). If we think in this way, the distinction made above between the two mechanisms of institutional change may become blurred. Even if there is a deliberate, collective choice of a new law and the introduction of a new agent (for example, a regulatory agency) to enforce it, the accumulation of decentralized private experiments or substantial agreement in thought experiments across agents in the polity domain needs to precede this, while a change in the game form needs to actually induce a new equilibrium, intended or unintended, to generate a new institution through the strategic interactions of all the agents in a relevant domain.

But how do agents perceive a new opportunity for a change in strategic choice? Does it merely occur as a chance event (mutation)? If so, how can one expect that such chance events will occur in a critical mass all at once? Alternatively, should the adoption of new strategies by individual agents be regarded as a rational response to environmental change from the known sets of actions? If so, is institutional change uniquely and steadfastly conditioned by the course of environmental change? As a conceptual frame for dealing with institutional change, let me now assume that individual agents cannot have full knowledge of the technologically determined rules of the game, nor can they make perfect inferences about other agents' strategic choices or environmental states. Instead we assume that each agent's perception of the structure of the game is represented by his/her 'subjective' game model.

- (C) The objective set of 'technologically feasible' strategic choices of an agent may be represented in a space of infinite dimension, but only a finite-dimensional subset is activated for possible choice at any moment in time. A subset may be chosen and sustained for a certain duration of period T in a manner specified below. We call this subset the *activated set* of actions (technically it is a hyperplane of the entire set of technologically feasible strategic choices).
- (E) The agents' common perceptual representation of the strategic profile believed to be prevailing in the domain over period T is given by the phenomenon of an institution.
- (O) Each agent has the subjective outcome function of the form over period T and, given the phenomena of institutions, infers the outcome of each strategic choice. The functional form of the subjective outcome function may be referred to as the agent's environmental *inference rule*, since it is considered to represent rules the agent is using for making inference about the environment of the domain.
- (S) The agent chooses a strategy from his/her activated set of strategies that, given a particular phenomenon of the institution and his/her inference of the environment, is predicted to maximize his/her utility (payoffs). Let us call this operation the *best-response choice rule*.

Then we have the COSE box representation of the subjective game model of an individual agent (Table 3.2).

When the agent repeatedly uses the same rules for environmental inference, payoff prediction, and (action) choice, under the same institutions (although their phenomena may be continually changing for continually changing environments), we say that his/her subjective game is reproduced (or in equilibrium). More generally and realistically, it may be that over periods the agent possesses multiple rules of inference and prediction, which are mutu-

Table 3.2   The COSE box representation of the subjective game model of an individual agent

	Parametric data (exogenous rules of the game)		Endogenous variables	
Internal to choice subject	(C)	activated subset of choices	(S)	best-response choice rule
External constraints	(O)	incomplete inference rule	(E)	phenomena of institutions

ally competitive in some respects, but complementary in others. Then, in response to the continually changing phenomena of institutions, the agent may experiment with each of them and choose the one that he/she considers appropriate under a given circumstance. He/she will develop a sort of meta rule as to which rule is to be triggered under which type of circumstance. However, when a fixed set of multiple rules are kept stored as a useful tool by the agent, we may still say that his/her subjective game model is reproduced. Note that the subjective game model in this sense roughly corresponds to the notion of 'mental models' in the induction theory of Holland et al. (1989). They conceive of the mental models as 'models of the problem space' that cognitive systems construct, and then 'mentally "run" or manipulate to produce expectations about the environment' (ibid., p. 12). But our conceptual framework emphasizes the interactions of such models with those of other agents who perceive and act in similar ways.[14]

Previously, an institution was regarded as being generated and self-enforced as a joint product of the strategic choices of agents who play an objective game. We now extend this notion to the present case where the agents each play their respective subjective games simultaneously. When all agents perceive the phenomenon of the institution generated by an equilibrium as a relevant constraint and act accordingly, then the equilibrium is sustained and thus the institution as its representation is reconfirmed and reproduced. The reproducibility of the institution may not necessarily require the rigid reproduction of the subjective games played by the agents. The agents might marginally change their sets of rules for personal perception, payoff prediction and (action) choice, or randomly experiment, but it is possible that the above 'general equilibrium' condition could still hold for a given institution.

When his/her existing set of rules does not produce satisfactory results relative to an agent's aspirations, however, the agent may start revising/

refining the existing set of rules more substantially, in particular, generating new strategic choice (rules) involving the expansion of the activated set of strategies. But when is such a gap between aspiration and prediction, that is, a subjective disequilibrium, likely to occur, especially in critical mass? One answer could be that this may happen in the case of a drastic environmental change, combined with cumulative impacts of internal equilibrium outcomes on the objective structure of the game. As environmental triggering conditions, we may think of the following events:

- new technological innovation occurs so that new actions become feasible (hitherto inactivated dimensions of the strategy sets can be invoked);
- external shocks, such as war, perceived productivity and innovation gaps with foreign competitors, or prolonged depression, compel agents to perceive a need for improvement in productivity or other performance characteristics;
- a large-scale institutional change occurs in a neighboring domain with which strong institutional complementarity exists;
- a big change in policy parameters of the outcome function occurs.

As internal cumulative impacts, we may think of the following states:

- experiments with new choice rules that do not follow customs, conventions, norms, institutional constraints, have occurred in a cluster;
- cumulative outcomes of repeated games have generated the disparity in the distribution of assets, power and social roles, that are conceived of as 'unjust' and 'unfair' by a critical mass of agents in the domain; and/or
- repeated play of games according to certain external and endogenous rules of the game has induced the accumulation of competence and the capacities of agents that cannot effectively be employed any more in the framework of those rules.

External shocks alone may not be enough to trigger the process of institutional change. Without the endogenous accumulation of seeds for change as listed above, the agents in the relevant domain may be able to adapt their choices only marginally in response to external shocks without changing the substantive characteristics of choice rules. On the other hand, when the performance characteristics of the domain are satisfactory and no significant gap between aspiration and achievement is perceived by the agents, the impacts of entrepreneurial mutation may be limited.[15] It is likely to be a general perception of large disequilibria in their respective subjective game models, generated by the combined effects of endogenous and external factors as described above, which initiates a synchronized search for the redefinition of subjective game models among agents. Some mutant choices that were not profitable under the stable external environment and internal state may become viable and yield higher payoffs. Other agents also may start to re-examine the effectiveness of their own activated choice sets and 'discover' new choice possibilities in the form of either new actions or new bundling of actions in the extant sets of actions, enlarging effectively the activated set of strategies. If proven successful, mutant choices, as well as new choices, may be emulated by other agents. This search and emulation are all directed by problem-solving incentives and their outcomes have feedback impacts on the process of search and emulation. The type of triggering conditions and feedback mechanisms obviates random searching. Instead, the agents direct their search and emulation according to an emergent problem situation, generating choices that are likely to be profitable for the emergent condition and hence possibly profitable in the future as well. Thus, search activity and selection becomes highly context specific.

Once simultaneous revision (innovation) by many agents of their activated choice sets and the systemic implementation of new choices therefrom starts, the hitherto existing institution will also cease to provide a useful guide/constraint for individual choices, because it is no longer an effective summary representation of newly emergent choice profiles that can reduce uncertainty in agents' expectations. The 'taken for granted' premises implied by the institution become questionable. Agents now need to process a larger amount of information regarding the internal state of the domain than they did under the rules of the old institution. In particular, they have to process information and form expectations regarding emergent patterns of choices by others that may be relevant to their payoffs. In association, agents also need to revise their rules for inference, prediction and action choice. In sum, the agents need to reconstruct their respective subjective game models. However, as synchronized search/emulation activities are induced by a common triggering condition, their directions are not randomly distributed, but may be highly correlated. Another factor that may play a significant role in the process of model revision could be that agents draw analogies from perceived existing models in other domains (including those in foreign economies) and from their (shared) history. Also, new experimental choices may prove to be more effective if there are some kind of fits (complementarities) with extant institutions or with emergent new experiments in other domains. For these and possibly other reasons, at most a few major competing types of subjective game models are likely to evolve in response to triggering conditions. Competition among them, within as well as across agents, characterizes the transitional process.

A new model of subjective game agent will be equilibrated for each agent, when (i) an application of new inference rules does not yield a big surprise;

and (ii) choices from a new activated choice set are perceived to be generating a satisfactory outcome as predicted. The transition process will come to a stop when the continually revised subjective game models of agents become consistent with one another, in the sense that they are simultaneously equilibrated. Then there will evolve a new institutional way of summarizing the substantive characteristics of new equilibrium strategic profiles – which may move continually and marginally in response to mildly changing environments – for succeeding periods. The transitional juncture of the institutional evolution process will come to an end and another spell of relative stability over periods will be initiated.

Figure 3.1 summarizes the mechanism of institutional evolution in terms of the COSE box. From the left it deals with the choice of endogenous variables in the 'old' subjective game model, its feedback to the data and redefinition of the old subjective game model, and finally the emergence of the 'new' institution.

Sustenance of the old institution		Feedback to, and redefinition of, the subjective game		Evolution of 'new' institution
(S) choice constrained by the existing activated set of choice	→	(A) gap between aspiration and achievement → context-specific search for a new subjective game model → redefinition of a new activated subset of choices	→	(S) novel strategic choice
⇓⇑		⇑		⇓⇑
(E) old institutions		(C) environmental change (technological change, external shocks, change in complementary institutions in neighboring domains)		(E) new institutions

Figure 3.1   The mechanism of institutional evolution

The actual process of institutional evolution may thus be seen analogous to the biological evolutionary process that biologists Stephen Jay Gould and Niles Eldredge (1977) conceptualized as *punctuated equilibria* rather than by a steady, gradual, Darwinian selection process.[16] An evolutionary process characterized by punctuated equilibria is one in which long periods of stasis are broken by short, in geologic time, episodes of rapid speciation. Although biological metaphors and analogies cannot be perfect, nonetheless these concepts are highly relevant and appropriate. Once a particular system (institutional or biological) is established, it tends to sustain itself. Change in the system may more likely be initiated by a large external shock that triggers the activation of internal change, cumulative or new, rather than something continual and gradual. The substantive characteristics of choice rules selected at the time of critical juncture are likely to impose constraints on future possibilities (path dependence). On the other hand, however, it is not certain whether the transition to the emergent institution was the only possible trajectory from the initial state of disequilibrium. Far from equilibria, branching out along multiple paths may be possible.[17] Thus institutional evolution may be characterized by both path dependence and novelty.

CONCLUDING REMARKS

In the previous section, I discussed the mechanism of institutional evolution from the angle of agents' subjective views of the rules of the game and their interactions. However, there is of course an objective aspect to the mechanism of institutional evolution. I suggested that during a period of institutional change (at the time of 'punctuation'), various experiments in agents' choices (in response to external shocks) take place and compete for selection as viable alternatives to well-worn strategies. We can identify three diachronic mechanisms which play an important role in realizing or selecting a strategic innovation and determining the nature of its consequences, or alternatively in deterring an institutional change, resulting in a system crisis or stagnation. I would like to suggest three possible mechanisms of diachronic linkage of institutions that may have impacts on institutional evolution.[18]

The first mechanism is what one may refer to as the mechanism of 'overlapping linkages' of domains. We can conceptualize the linkage of domains as the case in which agents can coordinate their strategies in two or more domains and thus a set of strategies not possible in each domain in isolation can become feasible and thus institutionalized. For example, honest trading may not be possible when the exchange game is played in isolation. However, if the exchange domain is linked with another social-exchange domain in which the reciprocal exchange of tacit social goods can take place, or if it is embedded in the political domain in which the government enforces private property rights, then it may become feasible. The spirit of contributions by sociologists such as Granovetter (1985) may be interpreted in that way in terms of a game-theoretic frame. Data characteristics of constituent domains (represented by the left-side column of the COSE box), such as policy and legal parameters, accumulated levels of institution-specific competence and assets, can change over time. However, the speed of change may differ significantly, depending on the types of domains. Characteristics of the so-cial-exchange domain may change more slowly, while new private transaction domains may emerge more frequently with new types of organizational agents and technology. Thus, the pattern of possible linkages of domains may vary over time, with some domains persisting longer and impacting on new do-mains while the latter exercise feedback repercussion on the former. This intergenerational overlapping of domains and possible linkages among them may suggest that institutional evolution has a highly path-dependent nature. Hence a satisfactory analysis of the mechanism of institutional change can be made only in a specific historical context.

The second mechanism, related to the first but possibly evolving more autonomously, is what may be referred to as the 'pattern reconfiguration of institutionalized linkage'. That is, an institutional innovation may emerge as a new type of linkage of domains, new and old, possibly entailing the dis-bundling of older institutionalized linkages. Conversely, institutional stagnation may occur as a result of the persistence of a worn-out linkage deterring the emergence of a new linkage. Indeed, according to Joseph Schumpeter (1934, 1947), an economic definition of innovation is a new combination of eco-nomic factors formed on the basis of creative destruction of older combinations and the entrepreneur is conceptualized as the agents who carry out this creative destruction. For example, we may understand the innovative nature of the Silicon Valley phenomena as a new type of linkage of R&D organiza-tions (entrepreneurial startup firms) mediated by the venture capitalists from this perspective.[19]

Third, there is an important mechanism of 'diachronic institutional complementarity'. A newly activated choice, or a mutant choice, may not be viable as a stand-alone choice, but if a complementary institution exists, or a change in that direction occurs in another domain, mutual reinforcement between the two may create momentum for new institutional building. Through this mechanism, exogenous changes in parameters of game forms, say sys-temic policy reforms, can propagate and amplify their impacts, sometimes leading to the emergence of a new overall institutional arrangement. How-ever, in order not to be trapped in a policy-deterministic view of institutions, this possibility needs to be subjected to analysis.

Combined together, these mechanisms may give the properties of path dependence to institutional evolution, as well as novelty and bifurcation at the time of disjuncture. However, in order to understand these mechanisms better, it seems that we need a theoretical and conceptual innovation that will go beyond the frame of traditional game theory, to say nothing of the impor-tance of careful accumulation and interpretations of comparative and historical information.

NOTES

*   This chapter is a slightly revised version of the closing lecture delivered at the Second Annual Conference of the International Society for New Institutional Economics, Paris, 17–19 September 1998. I am sincerely grateful to Professor Douglass North, the President of the Society, for giving me that opportunity. The lecture is based on materials more fully expounded upon in my forthcoming book, *Towards a Comparative Institutional Analysis* (to be published by MIT Press). I benefited greatly from competent research assistance by Christopher Kingston. However, the usual caveat applies.

1.   A technical formulation of the 'rules-of-the-game' view has been presented by Hurwicz (1993, 1996).
2.   I elaborate on this more in Aoki (2000, ch. 6.1).
3.   See ibid. (ch. 6.2).
4.   This relates to the notion of subgame perfect equilibrium.
5.   For the latter approach, see Reiter and Hugh (1981) and Hurwicz (1996). Also Young (1996) adopts this approach from the evolutionary game perspective.
6.   See Aoki (2000, ch. 2).
7.   I developed this idea in ibid. (ch. 7).
8.   We can formalize this idea based on the notion of 'summary representations' of moving equilibria as somewhat similar to that of 'sufficient statistics' in statistical inference theory (ibid., ch. 6.2).
9.   These issues are systematically analysed by Qian and his associates in a Chinese context from the comparative institutional analytic perspective. See Qian (1999) for a summary.
10. See Matsuyama (1997) for a thorough critique of such a view of the government.
11. From this perspective, I distinguish the government as a player of the game and 'states' as equilibria of the game. There can be many equilibria corresponding to various forms of the state (Aoki 2000, ch. 5). See also Weingast (1997).
12. See Kaneko and Matsui (1999) for a somewhat similar approach.
13. Acute readers may note that I am dealing here with sets of strategies rather than sets of actions as in the first section. Actually strategies can be built as rules of action choices possibly contingent on an internal state of the domain.
14. See also Denzau and North (1994).
15. Aoki (1998, proposition 6).
16. As noted in Aoki (2000), chapter 4, Denzau and North also refer to this analogy (1994). As far as I know, one of the first social scientific references to this analogy is by Krasner (1988). Also see Mokyr (1990) and Hodgson (1991).
17. See Aoki (1998, proposition 7).
18. I discuss these mechanisms more fully in Aoki (2000, ch. 8.2) with illustrative examples.
19. See ibid. (ch. 10).

REFERENCES

Aoki, M. (1998), 'Organizational conventions and the gains from diversity: an evolutionary game approach', *Corporate and Industrial Change*, **7**, 399–432.

Aoki, M. (2000), 'Toward a comparative institutional analysis', book manuscript, Stanford University.

Arrow, K.J. (1997), 'The place of institutions in the economy: a theoretical perspective', in Y. Hayami and M. Aoki (eds), *The Institutional Foundations of East Asian Economic Development*, London: Macmillan, pp. 39–48.

Denzau, A.T. and D. North (1994), 'Shared mental models: ideologies and institutions', *Kyklos*, vol 47, 3–31.

32   *Foundations*

Durkheim, E. (1901), *The Rules of Sociological Method*, New York: Free Press.

Gould, S.J. and N. Eldredge (1977), 'Punctuated equilibria: the tempo and mode of evolution reconsidered', *Paleobiology*, **3**, 115–51.

Granovetter, M. (1985), 'Economic action and social structure: the problem of embeddedness', *American Journal of Sociology*, **91**, 480–510.

Greif, A. (1994), 'Cultural beliefs and the organization of society: a historical and theoretical reflection on collectivist and individualist societies', *Journal of Political Economy*, **102**, 912–50.

Greif, A. (1999), *Genoa and the Maghribi Traders: Historical and Comparative Institutional Analysis*, Cambridge: Cambridge University Press, forthcoming.

Greif, A., P. Milgrom and B. Weingast (1994), 'Coordination, commitment, and enforcement: the case of the Merchant Guild', *Journal of Political Economy*, **102**, 745–76.

Hayek, F. (1945), 'The use of knowledge in society', *American Economic Review*, **35**, 519–30.

Hayek, F. (1973), *Law, Legislation and Liberty: Rules and Order*, vol 1., Chicago: University of Chicago Press.

Hodgson, G.M. (1991), 'Socio-political disruption and economic development', in G.M. Hodgson and E. Screpanti (eds), *Rethinking Economics: Markets, Technology and Economic Evolution*, Aldershot: Edward Elgar, pp. 153–71.

Holland, J.H., K.J. Holyoak, R.E. Nisbett and P.R. Thagard (eds) (1989), *Induction: Processes of Inference, Learning, and Discovery*, Cambridge, MA: MIT Press.

Hurwicz, L. (1977), 'On the dimensional requirements for non-wasteful resource allocation systems', in K.J. Arrow and L. Hurwicz (eds), *Studies in Resource Allocation Processes*, Cambridge: Cambridge University Press, pp. 413–24.

Hurwicz, L. (1993), 'Toward a framework for analysing institutions and institutional change', in S. Bowles, H. Gintis and B. Gustafsson (eds), *Markets and Democracy: Participation, Accountability, and Efficiency*, Cambridge: Cambridge University Press, pp. 51–67.

Hurwicz, L. (1996), 'Institutions as families of game forms', *Japanese Economic Review*, **47**, 113–32.

Kaneko, M. and A. Matsui (1999), 'Inductive game theory: discrimination and prejudices', *Journal of Public Economic Theory*, **1**, 1–37.

Koopmans, T. ([1957] 1990), *Three Essays on the State of Economic Sciences*, Reprints of Economic Classics, New York: Augustus Kelley.

Krasner, S. (1988), 'Sovereignty', *Comparative Political Studies*, **21**, 64–94.

Kreps, D. (1990), *Game Theory and Economic Modelling*, Oxford: Oxford University Press.

Matsuyama, K. (1997), 'Economic development as coordination problems', in M. Aoki, H. Kim and M. Okuno-Fujiwara (eds), *The Role of Government in East Asian Economic Development*, Oxford: Oxford University Press, pp. 134–60.

Milgrom, P., D. North and B. Weingast (1990), 'The role of institutions in the revival of trade: the law merchant, private judges, and the champagne fairs', *Economics and Politics*, **2**, 1–23.

Mokyr, J. (1990), 'Punctuated equilibria and technological progress', *American Economic Review (Papers and Proceedings)*, **80**(2), 350–54.

North, D. (1990), *Institutions, Institutional Change and Economic Performance*, Cambridge: Cambridge University Press.

North, D. (1995), 'Five propositions about institutional change', in J. Knight and I.

Sened (eds), *Explaining Social Institutions*, Ann Arbor, MI: University of Michigan Press, pp. 15–26.

Qian, Y. (1999), 'The institutional foundations of China's market transition', presented at the Annual Bank Conference on Development Economics, World Bank, April.

Reiter, S. and J. Hugh (1981), 'A preface on modelling the regulated United States economy', *Hofstra Law Review*, vol 9, 1381–421.

Schotter, A. (1981), *The Economic Theory of Social Institutions*, Cambridge: Cambridge University Press.

Schumpeter, J. (1934), *The Theory of Economic Development*, Cambridge, MA: Harvard University Press.

Schumpeter, J. (1947), 'The creative response in economic history', *Journal of Economic History*, **7**, 149–59.

Simon, H. (1961), *Administrative Behaviour*, second edition, New York: Macmillan.

Smith, A. ([1775] 1984), *The Theory of Moral Sentiments*, London: Liberty Fund, Inc.

Weingast, B. (1997), 'The political foundations of democracy and the rule of law', *American Political Science Review*, **91**, 245–63.

Young, H.P. (1996), 'Social coordination and social change', University of Maryland, mimeo.

Young, H.P. (1998), *Individual Strategy and Social Structure: An Evolutionary Theory of Institutions*, Princeton, NJ: Princeton University Press.

[15]

Markets and Hierarchies and (Mathematical) Economic Theory

DAVID M. KREPS

(Graduate School of Business, Stanford University, Stanford, CA 94305, USA)

Over the past decade transaction-cost economics has been partially translated in the more mathematical language of game theory, and understanding of the costs of trans- actions has been deepened, refined and extended. But the translation is incomplete: a great deal of human behaviour is missed, and doing game theory with more life-like models of individuals will bring theory closer to phenomena. Transaction-cost economics, particulary the economics of relational contracts, provides a major arena for these developments, since the important issues of bounded rationality and individual behavior are central to the topic.

1. Introduction

Consider the following bit of recent history of economic thought: When it appeared in 1975, Oliver Williamson's *Markets and Hierarchies* stood some- what outside the flow of mainstream economic theory. Initial developments in information economics were around five years old, the revelation principle was nearly contemporaneous, and the widespread embrace of the language of game theory for dealing with dynamics, small numbers, and incomplete information was about five years in the future. Without these tools to work with, it was perhaps inevitable that Williamson's theory would be rendered without the mathematical apparatus of mainstream theory. But as those tools worked their way into the mainstream, it was equally inevitable that the ideas set forth in *Markets and Hierarchies* would be reworked and further developed in symbols. And this has taken place; nowadays courses in contract theory are a mainstay of graduate microeconomics, and eminent symbol manipulators such as Oliver Hart and Jean Tirole choose this subject for their public lectures (Hart, The Clarendon Lectures; Tirole, the Walras- Bowley Lecture). As for the book itself, *Markets and Hierarchies* was a step along the way to a proper (mathematical) theory of contracts and trans-

Industrial and Corporate Change   Volume 5   Number 2   1996

——————— *Markets and Hierarchies and (Mathematical) Economic Theory* ———————

actions costs, but its place is now in the history of thought; it has been superceded by more precise and nuanced mathematical theories of these things. Notwithstanding the protests of Williamson (1993a), Richard Posner (1993) opines that Williamson's version of transaction-cost economics nowadays adds little more than neologisms to mainstream mathematical theory.[1] Since these neologisms can only serve to confuse students, it is time to consign *Markets and Hierarchies* to a relatively inaccessible shelf.

It is certainly true that important ideas in *Markets and Hierarchies* have been translated into the more mathematical language of non-cooperative game theory. Some of this is recalled below, although I will not give anything like a complete survey; for this, see Hart (1995) and Tirole (1995). But notwithstanding this work, the history given above is inaccurate. If *Markets and Hierarchies* has been translated into game theory using notions from information economics, it is a very poor translation. If some of the central and critical ideas in transaction-cost economics as formulated by Williamson have been captured, others, equally important, have been missed. In particular, mathematics-based theory still lacks the language needed to capture essential ideas of bounded rationality, which are central to Williamson's concepts of transaction costs and contractual form.[2] Anyone who relies on the translations alone misses large and valuable chunks of the original.

The missing pieces of theory are nearly within the grasp of mainstream theorists. To incorporate the missing pieces will take a bit of courage; further compromises with the high paradigm world of general equilibrium will be necessary. But it can be done, and to do it, we must continue to have *Markets and Hierarchies* on our desks; speaking as a tool-fashioner interested in developing tools that better deal with the world-as-it-is, I believe game theory (the tool) has more to learn from transaction-cost economics than it will have to give, at least initially.

But it will give something back. Specifically, regarding the principle of economizing—transactions *tend* to be arranged to maximize their benefits net of transaction costs—we may get a better sense of what bears on the strength of the economizing force; i.e. on how strong (relatively) is the tendency to move from inefficient transactional forms to those more efficient.

These ideas are developed in this paper. Because the hard work of theory development still remains to be done, I cannot claim to have a completely

---

[1] Posner's critique would be unfair even if now correct, since *Markets and Hierarchies* predated and in many ways provided the impetus for subsequent developments by Grossman, Hart, Holmstrom, etc.
[2] Posner (1993) goes on to say that bounded rationality is well handled within mainstream theory by incorporating the cost of information acquisition and processing; I will comment at the end.

──────── *Markets and Hierarchies and (Mathematical) Economic Theory* ────────

convincing story, but I believe that these ideas are worth pursuing and, at least, that the bit of history of thought in the first paragraph is wrong.

Why is this of interest? To tool developers like myself, the interest is clear; *Markets and Hierarchies* provides unreconciled puzzles which help us to produce more robust tools. But what of the much greater number of readers who are interested in the substance of transaction-cost economics? It is incontestable that mathematics-based theory has become the common language of economics (see Debreu, 1990 or Kreps, 1996). Most economists, and especially and most critically, new recruits in the form of graduate students, learn transaction-cost economics as translated and renamed (incomplete) contract theory. I hope it is not taken amiss if I claim that (for the prototypical graduate student) it is harder to read *Markets and Hierarchies* or *The Economic Institutions of Capitalism* than the classics-illustrated versions, written in the comfortable language of middle-brow theory. If the classics-illustrated versions miss subtleties connected with, say, bounded rationality and truly unforeseen contingencies, or they do not give any indication of how social embeddedness or internal consistency/simplicity affects a relational contract, then the consumer of the classics-illustrated editions has missed important pieces of the message. We should be clear on how (in)complete the translations are, to fight misguided tendencies to put *Markets and Hierarchies* away on that semi-accessible shelf.

2. *Game-theoretic versions of Markets and Hierarchies*

Game-theoretic renditions of the transaction-cost economics of *Markets and Hierarchies* have focused on contract incompleteness and *ex post* governance. Starting with the seminal paper Grossman and Hart (1986), in much of the literature the transaction is modeled as stretching over relatively few dates. Parties to a transaction face some well-understood uncertainty, typically bearing on the costs and benefits of the transaction if consummated. The parties to the transaction will make private investment decisions that (eventually) affect the costs and benefits of the transaction. Contracts between them may be written prior to the investment decisions, but it is assumed by fiat (with rationales usually given informally—see below) that contracts explicitly and fully contingent on the uncertain contingencies are impossible. Instead, *ex post* decision rights determine (implicitly) how the contract will be completed, with the *ex post* decision rights determined by aspects of the contract (most prevalently, the residual rights of control conferred by ownership).

For example, in the seminal paper by Grossman and Hart, two parties (A and B) must make four decisions, labelled a_x and q_x for $X = A, B$. Decisions

——————— *Markets and Hierarchies and (Mathematical) Economic Theory* ———————

a_x are *ex ante* investment/maintenance decisions; decision a_x must be taken by party X. Decisions q_x are *ex post* 'implementation' decisions. The right to take decision q_x, while initially belonging to party X, can be assigned to the other party contractually. (Think of q_x as the decision how to employ physical capital; *ex post* ownership of the capital confers the residual decision rights.) The gross outcome for party X is given by a benefit function $B_x(a_x, \phi_x(q_A, q_B))$, where ϕ_x is real-valued and B_x is strictly increasing in ϕ_x; in addition, utility is freely transferable between the parties. Negotiations over decision rights (or ownership) take place, then the private investment decisions a_x are taken, and then the q_x are chosen. Binding *ex ante* contracts involving the levels of the a_x or the gross benefit levels or the levels of the ϕ_x are not feasible. Final implementation decisions (q_A, q_B) are assumed to be chosen efficiently (to maximize the sum of the gross benefits, given the levels of a_A and a_B already chosen), with the benefits above the non-cooperative-equilibrium threat point divided 50-50 through an unmodeled negotiation process.

The question analyzed is, which pattern of ownership (assignment of implementation rights) leads to the most efficient outcome? Suppose that high levels of a_B are most effective given high levels of $\phi_B(q_A, q_B)$, and ϕ_B is very positively responsive to q_B and negatively responsive to q_A. If A is given decision rights to q_B, then A implicitly threatens a relatively low choice of q_B (insofar as ϕ_A depends on q_A and q_B in symmetric fashion). Since the choices of q_A and q_B are assumed to be *ex post* efficient, this threat is not carried out. But the threat determines the division of surplus from moving to efficient (q_A, q_B). Thus B will not fully internalize the benefit from his own investment in a_B (assuming this ownership structure); lack of *ex post* control and the particular negotiation process leads him to underinvest.

The model captures beautifully the idea that ownership-driven *ex post* decision rights can affect *ex ante* private investments decisions, hence the pattern of ownership can affect overall efficiency. Note that this is not driven by any supposed *ex post* inefficiency in residual decisions, but instead through a feedback into *ex ante* investments.

However, some important aspects of the original theory in *Markets in Hierarchies* are missing. Most importantly (for purposes of this paper), the notion of bounded rationality enters in a very peculiar way. Grossman and Hart assume by fiat within their model that binding contracts contingent on the investment levels and the levels of the ϕ_x and B_x are not possible; their verbal explanation for this is that the required contracts would be too complex to write. But within their model, the parties anticipate *ex ante* what decisions will be taken (contingent on observables).

In a subsequent paper, Hart and Moore (1990) write '. . . there is no inconsistency in assuming, on the one hand, that date 0 contingent *statements*

———— *Markets and Hierarchies and (Mathematical) Economic Theory* ————

are infeasible and, on the other hand, that agents have perfect foresight about the consequences of this lack of feasibility . . .' (emphasis added). Hart (1990), arguing that bounded rationality in the sense of Simon is unnecessary for contract theory, suggests that parties may suffer not from bounded rationality—he points out that per his analysis they must be quite rational and computationally able—but instead from 'bounded *writing* or *communication* skills' (emphasis in the original).

Maskin and Tirole (1995) extend this argument, showing that (even) truly unforeseen contingencies need not compromise the logic of economic (or Nash) equilibrium, if parties can anticipate the payoffs they will subsequently receive as a function of current decisions. To caricature their argument slightly, consider the pair of assertions: you and I correctly anticipate what is the distribution of utility that we will get next year from some joint venture we may enter into; but neither of us have any idea where that utility will come from and what we will be doing (specifically) in a year. As Maskin and Tirole observe, these two assertions are not logically inconsistent. But not everything that is logically consistent is credulous.[3]

Other authors have performed similar analyses, using somewhat different rationales for assumptions that contracts may not involve certain variables. In some instances the rationale is that the uncontractible variables are unobservable.[4] In others, they may be observable but unverifiable in a legal sense, hence not usable in implementable formal contracts. (Hart (1990) argues that unverifiability may stem from an initial inability to write out clearly the relevant clauses.)

Unobservability and unverifiability leads to a vast class of mainstream-theory models; viz., agency theory models, in which contracts are written in terms of signals that are (only) noisy indications of variables that would be used in a first-best (efficient) contract. That is, instead of an outright prohibition against including a variable in a contract, the parties to the transaction are able to contract on 'noisy' indicators of the variable and/or to rely on self-selection (subject, of course, to self-selection constraints). Of course, these analysis are almost always equilibrium analyses in the game-theoretic sense (I would say always, but there may be a part of this vast literature that I have missed).

My point is that although these models capture important aspects of con-

---

[3] I am somewhat wary of this caricature, because it implies that Maskin and Tirole are spouting nonsense. A written version of their paper does not exist yet, but based on comments in Tirole (1994), it is quite likely that they take the position that this result, while formally correct, indicates a modeling weakness of this general approach.

[4] When, say, private investment decisions are unobservable by the other party, some care in the equilibrium conditions is required. But a strength of game theoretic techniques is that it is clear on what care is required for this sort of thing.

──────── *Markets and Hierarchies and (Mathematical) Economic Theory* ────────

tract incompleteness, the sense in which the contracts are incomplete must be borne in mind. The contracts are incomplete in the Arrow-Debreuvian sense that there are contingencies on which *ex ante* efficient contracts would turn that do not turn up in the *ex ante* contract. In the Grossman-Hart model (and others), *ex post* decisions are taken based on ownership rights; these decisions are not contractually specified *ex ante*. Indeed, in Grossman-Hart, and in some pieces of the agency literature, such as Fudenberg and Tirole (1990), *ex post* renegotiation takes place based on 'threat points' determined *ex ante*; *ex ante* contracts certainly fail to reflect the outcomes of the renegotiations. But the analysis entails an equilibrium in anticipations and actions. Specifically, all participants are assumed able to say, *ex ante*, what will be the eventual 'terms of trade' based on the resolution of any physical uncertainty. (This is not true for Maskin and Tirole (1995), but then the argument that the participants anticipate perfectly the distribution of utility outcomes is particularly incredible.) As Hart (1990) observes, these models miss aspects of bounded rationality that are part of the original story. Are the missing parts important? This question will be discussed later.

Reputation, Reciprocity and Relational Contracts

A second type of model for translating ideas from transaction-cost economics into game-theoretic models concerns relational contracts modeled using (infinitely) repeated games and the Folk Theorem. This part of the theory will be recounted at substantial length, because (I believe) it is less well known than the short-horizon models and it is more important to the ideas I wish to develop.[5]

The seminal reference in this case predates both *Markets and Hierarchies* and most of the developments of the relevant pieces of game theory. Simon's 'A Formal Theory of the Employment Relationship' (1951) lacks some modern terminology and some of the formal polish that the subsequent 40-plus years have given to the topic, but the basic ideas are there.

Simon's model concerns an employment transaction between employer and employee. The employer offers a wage for the labor services of the employee, in return for which the employee agrees to accept the directions of the employer. The employee may retain the right to terminate the relationship whenever he chooses to; in simple language, the employee can always quit.[6] Except for that (in Simon's model), the employer makes all the

─────────────────────

[5] I am also convinced that long-horizon relational contracts are of underestimated importance in exchange generally, because they form the basis for most of the most important form of incomplete-contract exchange; viz., employment.

[6] But see the footnote following.

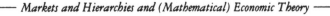

——— *Markets and Hierarchies and (Mathematical) Economic Theory* ———

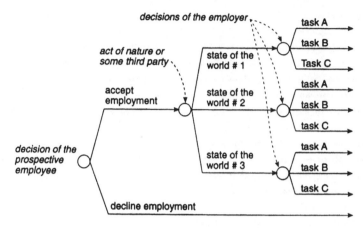

FIGURE 1. Simon's simple model of employment.

subsequent decisions about the nature of the relationship. The relationship is hierarchical, with the employer as the hierarchical superior and the employee as the hierarchical subordinate.

Figure 1 gives a simple example of Simon's model. The employment transaction is a three-stage affair. First, the employee must decide whether to accept employment. Then nature intervenes; uncertainty resolves, which determines the costs and benefits of the various tasks that might be done. Finally, the employer stipulates which task the employee will undertake. We have depicted a choice of three tasks, but in general there will be many more.[7]

Note that the contract is incomplete in that the employer and employee are presumed unable to write an enforceable contingent contract specifying what the employee will do as a function of the state of the world. Governance enters in the presumption that the employer will determine, *ex post*, what task the employee will undertake. The employee faces a simple 'accept employment/reject' decision, where accepting employment obligates the employee to accept the decision of the employer concerning what task must be done. Both presumptions need rationalization, to which we will return after exploring the model as formulated.

Why would the employee accept under these conditions? Simon tells two stories. The first is that the employee may anticipate that the assigned tasks

---

[7] To keep the analysis simple, we have not given the worker an option to quit after learning what the employer wants. If this option is included, the payoff to the worker of quitting after accepting employment should be less than the payoff if the worker declines employment at the outset; the employee must have something at risk if he accepts employment. The difference between pre- and post-acceptance payoffs could reflect, for example, costs of relocation, or simply the opportunity cost of lost time. On this general point, also see the next footnote.

——— *Markets and Hierarchies and (Mathematical) Economic Theory* ———

will not be so onerous on average as to make rejection of employment better than acceptance.

Assume that employer and employee evaluate options using expected payoffs. We have normalized payoffs so that no employment gives each party a payoff of zero. In Simon's first story, the employee reasons that the employer will demand whatever task makes her (the employer) as well off as possible, given the state of nature. In Figure 2, this means task A in state 1, task B in state 2, and task C in state 3. Although the employee finds task C quite onerous (he would not accept employment if he thought he would be given task C all or even most of the time), if the probability of state 3 is less than 1/11, getting tasks A and B in two states of the world and task C only in the third gives the employee a strictly positive expected payoff, which is better than he gets if he declines employment.

This story comes to grief if either it is in the interest of the employer to demand onerous actions with high probability or if the onerous tasks are exceedingly onerous; in either case the employee's average payoff may make employment worse than unemployment. Consider, for example, changing the example in Figure 2 so that the three states are equally likely. Task C is so onerous that a one-third chance of getting this assignment means a negative expected payoff for employment to the employee; in the unique Nash equilibrium outcome of this game, the employee declines employment.

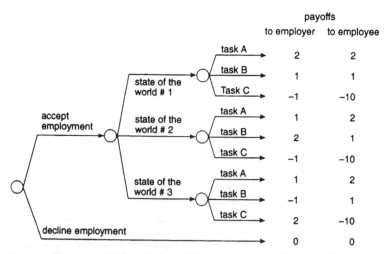

FIGURE 2. Simon's second story. If the employer asks for whichever task is best for her in each contingency, the employee may decline employment, depending on the probability of the three states. But if the employer will never ask for task C, in order to protect her reputation, then the employee will accept employment.

——————— *Markets and Hierarchies and (Mathematical) Economic Theory* ———————

Here Simon's second story comes into play. Imagine the situation is as in Figure 2 with equally likely probabilities for the three states, and also that the employer is engaged in this transaction (or others like it) repeatedly, either with this employee or with other employees.[8] If the situation is repeated indefinitely, and if the employer does not discount payoffs from future situations too severely, then we can construct reputational equilibria in which the employee will accept employment. In one such equilibrium, the employer does not ask for task C; she asks for task A in state 1 and task B in states 2 and 3. (Note that this makes her expected payoff 2/3.) She does not ask for task C in state 3 because asking any employee for task C would brand her as an exploitative employer; this would become generally known among (future) potential employees; and no one would ever work for her again. When and if state 3 arises, the employer must weigh the immediate payoff of 2 that she can get by wrecking her reputation followed by payoffs of zero forever after against absorbing the payoff of −1 this period, preserving her reputation, and an expected payoff of 2/3 in each subsequent period. If the future is not too heavily discounted, preservation of her reputation is more important, and she will refrain from asking for task C. For the employee, then, accepting employment is safe; task C will not be requested because the employer wishes to protect her reputation, and (with the numbers in Figure 2) accepting employment is better than declining no matter what is the state of the world. Simon concludes that workers can accept hierarchical subordination in some instances because they are protected by the employer's desire to safeguard her reputation.

It is fairly obvious (to anyone trained in game theory) where game theory enters into Simon's story.[9] Figures 1 and 2 describe an extensive form game, and Simon's two stories why the employee might trust the employer are no more or less than typical examples of Nash equilibrium analysis of the corresponding games and infinitely repeated versions of these games. Game

---

[8] The payoffs in Figure 2 work for the specification where the employer deals with a sequence of employees. Most of the remarks to follow work equally for the formulation of a long-term relationship with a single employee, but then to be closer to reality the model should be changed as follows: the employee makes an initial decision whether to accept employment and then has a quit option each period, either before or after that period's task assignment by the employer. After the initial decision to accept employment is taken, the utility of quitting is less than the zero-base level of never accepting employment at all, reflecting relocation costs, etc. Indeed, it might be sensible to assume that the costs of relocation (quitting) rise as the relationship matures, reflecting psychic costs of lost friendships, raised costs of moving a family, decreasingly attractive prospects back on the job market, and so on. We could also assume that the value to the employer of the employee rises as the relationship matures and the employee learns more about the employer's specific technology, builds a network within the employer's establishment, and so on. Such considerations add depth to the story that is missing in this very simple first-cut analysis.

[9] Simon wrote at a time where the formal language of game theory was, for his purposes, undeveloped. But anyone trained in game theory will find it hard to read his paper without considering it a piece of applied game theory.

——————— *Markets and Hierarchies and (Mathematical) Economic Theory* ———————

theory adds little or nothing to Simon's first story, but our understanding of the second story, which concerns a reputation construction in a repeated game setting, is enhanced by recalling some more-general analysis of these sorts of games:

(i) **Multiplicity of equilibria.** In a repeated game setting when reputational equilibria are feasible, there are usually many of them. For the payoffs of Figure 2, our description of the behaviour of the employer—ask for task A in state 1; ask for B in states 2 and 3—and the employee(s)—accept employment as long as the employer has never asked you or any other previous employee to undertake task C—describes a Nash equilibrium of the game when payoffs are discounted from one period to the next, the horizon is infinite, and the discount factor is close enough to one.[10] But in another equilibrium, the employer asks for task A in all contingencies and each employee declines employment if ever the employer asks (previously) for any task except A. Note that this raises the payoff to the employee and lowers the payoff to the employer, but (for discount factors close enough to one) the employer is better off always requesting A than asking for (and getting) B or C once and thereafter having all offers of employment declined; i.e. this is another Nash equilibrium.

This is just the tip of the iceberg. There are equilibria in which the employer asks for task B in every contingency, or where she asks for task A in states 1 and 2 and for B in state 3, and so on. There are equilibria in which the request in period t depends on the state in that period and the value of the tth digit in a decimal expansion of π. In another equilibrium, the employees decline employment at all dates (because the employer would request task C in state 3).

Is there any basis on which to choose among these equilibria? A theory that produces a continuum of possible answers gives weak testable propositions at best and so is not very useful. There are at least two things which can be said in this instance:

● Suppose the employer is simultaneously engaged in this sort of relationship with a large number of employees, each of whom deals with only the single employer but who observe how the employer treats other employees. Or suppose the employer deals sequentially with many employees,

---

[10] I will not be precise about the game theory used in this paper on grounds that for those who know the relevant theory, it is easy to provide the needed precision; while for those who do not, it is fruitless to begin to go into details. But while aficionados will know that I am being sloppy, novices might not, so let me add here that I have not described full strategies for the employer and employee. Enough is described to verify that however we fill out the strategies, we have a Nash equilibrium, but we would need more details to know that the strategy fragments described are pieces of a (subgame) perfect equilibrium.

—————— *Markets and Hierarchies and (Mathematical) Economic Theory* ——————

each of whom deals with the single employer only and each of whom sees how the employer has dealt in the past with earlier employees. Then it can be argued (in a somewhat more complex model) that the employer should have the power of a 'Stackelberg leader' in choosing among the equilibria; i.e. she can choose whichever equilibrium is best for her, subject to a participation constraint by the workers.[11]

- *Ex post* observability can be crucial. Suppose, for example, that the payoff to the employee of task B was -2 and the employer prefers B to A in state 3. Then in the simple model of Figure 3, a reputational equilibrium can be constructed (for high enough discount factors) in which the employer will select task A in states 1 and 2 and task B in state 3. But the enforcement of this equilibrium requires that the employee is able to observe the state of the world. If the employer (only) observes the state of the world, or if the employee observes the state of the world only imperfectly, then the employer might be tempted in state 2 to claim that the state is 3, so that task B is 'appropriate'. If the employee accepts this, and if, in consequence, the employer begins to ask for task B in states 2 and 3 both, the employee will find himself inadequately compensated on average for entering into employment. When employees can observe the state of the world only imperfectly (as best), equilibrium in which task B is sometimes requested can be constructed, but these equilibria are complex.

(ii) **Efficient governance forms.** General game-theoretic considerations also give us some leverage for choosing among different forms of governance in long-run relational contracts. Simon's model describes a hierarchical relationship, so called because the employer enjoys the preponderance of authority in determining how contingencies will be met as time passes. The employee retains the right to sunder the relationship—to quit—but (in this classic and extreme form of the employment relationship) that is the only decision left to the employee.

Contrast this with, say, the relationship between a physician and patient. The physician is in a very real sense the employee of the patient, but the distribution of *ex post* decision rights, including the right to specify the level of

---

[11] In the simultaneous-play formulation, we assume the employer is making continuous (or, at least, many) assignment decisions for each employee, who can quit as each decision is rendered. Thus taken separately, the employee and employer are 'symmetric' as regards threats, and we would normally be unable to discriminate among all the Folk-Theorem equilibria. But if the employer's reputation turns on incomplete information as to type, she has this sort of relationship with many employees simultaneously, and there is perfect (or strong) correlation in her 'type' from one relationship to the next, she is strengthened to the position of Stackelberg leader by the spillover effects each has on the others. See Fudenberg and Kreps (1987) for details. The analysis for the sequential-interaction variation is simpler (and stronger) and can be found in Fudenberg and Levine (1989). These two papers give Nash equilibrium analyses. Watson (1993) shows how somewhat weaker non-equilibrium analysis can be used to obtain the same conclusions.

————— *Markets and Hierarchies and (Mathematical) Economic Theory* —————

payment (wages), is much more heavily skewed towards the physician/ employee. Patients retain the right to get a second opinion or to decline recommended treatment; hence the physician is not a pure hierarchical superior in this transaction. But the physician is a lot closer to hierarchical superior than is his 'employer', the patient, in any practical sense. Why? From a game theoretic sense, the answer is clear. Insofar as party A is given decision-making authority in a relationship, authority that puts party B in danger of being exploited, party A must (i) have the information needed to take (relatively) efficient decisions[12] and (ii) be trustworthy; party B must believe that party A will not abuse her decision-making rights. In standard employment relationships, it is patent that the employer, who coordinates the efforts of many employees, enjoys the informational advantage. In the physician-patient relationship, it is equally clear that physician has the expertise/information requires. As for being trustworthy, for party A's reputation to constrain her effectively, she must have an ongoing interest in maintaining her reputation (she at least must repeat this or a similar transaction in the relatively near future), her efforts must be general observable to subsequent potential trading partners, and the stakes for her in any single transaction must not vary so much that she is enticed into exploitation in a single instance, if it means forfeiture of her reputation. Employers tend to be more permanent in location than employees, their behavior tends to be more observable by potential employees (than is the actions of a given employee by prospective employers), and their stakes with single employees tend to be relatively small (while a single employee can sometimes have enormous incentives to defraud and flee). These factors all reverse in the physician-patient relationship. Hence, the theory suggests the observed change in governance form.

In many employment relationships (beyond professional services), the employer does not have a monopoly on information; efficient transactions require that employees act with discretion. In such cases, we find governance that is more nearly balanced bilateral, where to support the incentives for the employee to behave in the transaction, employers will take steps to lengthen the duration of the employment relationship (e.g. as in Lazear, 1979), and/or to provide employees with increased costs of sundering the specific relationship.[13]

---

[12] On this point in particular, see Aghion and Tirole (1994).

[13] Note the standard efficiency-or-market-power dilemma: an employer puts a greenfield plant in a location where it will exercise a great deal of control over employees; e.g. Honda builds an assembly plant in Marysville, Ohio, instead of in Cleveland. Is this a case of (i) the employer attempting to exploit workers by increasing its (labor) market power, or (ii) an employer who aims to invest heavily in training and to give workers significant discretion, to make for more efficient labor exchange, but who therefore wishes to lengthen average employment tenures and to increase the cost to workers of voluntary turnover?

─────── *Markets and Hierarchies and (Mathematical) Economic Theory* ───────

In some cases the employer is insufficiently constrained by its reputation with workers as a class. Worker B101 may not be inclined to withdraw his labor services if worker B2 is mistreated by the employer, especially if the facts of mistreatment are in dispute. Insofar as it is costly to monitor the actions of the firm in its dealings with others, individual workers have little private incentive to expend the necessary resources. But if workers do not act collectively, either because they lack private incentives to act or to monitor, and if the firm's reputation is putatively based on the threat of collective action, the reputation equilibrium falls. A role is established in theory for trilateral governance, in which the workers bind themselves to act collectively, following the directions of a third-party monitor. That is, the theory suggests a role for a shop steward. (Compare with empirical studies of the union productivity effect and voice-based theories of unions. And note that, owing to the multiplicity of reputational equilibria, we have no problem rationalizing non-uniform effects of unionization.)

Trilateral governance is also suggested in cases where 'appropriate actions' are unclear, because of observability problems. Especially where these instances arise infrequently in a specific ongoing relationship, a role arises for an external trilateral authority (that can be trusted because it deals with this sort of issue in many relationships, hence relatively frequently, and derives rents from its reputation as a fair adjudicator in such circumstances). The equilibrium can be, when there is noise in the observables, the dispute is referred externally, and the decision of the external authority is accepted. It is not necessary in this construction that the external authority can penetrate the fog of noise better than either party, but only that by issuing a decision, it provides the two parties with a non-noisy signal of how to adapt. What is necessary is that the external authority is trusted by both sides to be 'fair', given the information it has, and its trustworthiness can arise at least in part by its independence from consequences of the specific decision it offers. (Consider, for example, the role of external auditors.)

In some settings, the momentary incentives for the employer to abuse its workers may on occasion outweigh the costs of lost reputation with those employees. An example of such an instance is a decision to move an entire manufacturing operation offshore. Reputation constructions alone will leave workers unprotected against such actions, and other forms of governance for this class of actions may be necessary, e.g. balanced-bilateral governance with a unanimity rule as in the Works Councils of Germany, or trilateral governance, either contractually provided or with the state as the trilateral authority.

The game theory that lies behind reputation-and reciprocity-based equilibria tells us that the bases of trust in such equilibria are enduring interest

——— *Markets and Hierarchies and (Mathematical) Economic Theory* ———

in the relationship, *ex post* observability, and single decisions that loom small relative to the overall value of the relationship (which speaks both to frequency and to variability in the immediate stakes). These bases in turn are quite informative about the different forms of governance found in specific relational contracts, when combined with considerations of who holds what information. Of course, this is nothing more than common sense, the theory is not telling us anything profound. Indeed, it cannot be profound, because a reputational equilibrium must, by its very nature, depend on the participants understanding how it works. But it allows us to organize our thinking about relational contracts and forms of governance.

A First-level Critique

Recall the earlier critique of the short-horizon models: contract incompleteness is rationalized by bounded rationality/communication (too hard to specify all the contingencies and the adaptation thereto), but the parties involved are sufficiently rational to anticipate accurately what will transpire in every possible contingency which includes, knowing every possible contingency. As per Maskin and Tirole, less than this is actually needed; parties need only have correct assessments concerning the flow of utility they will derive as a function of decisions taken today. But this is still rather a lot to swallow.

In the long-horizon, reputation/reciprocity models, this problem is if anything worse. Why is it impossible for employer and employee to specify a full contingent contract *ex ante*? The obvious and quite convincing story is that employment relationships can stretch over decades. No one seriously believes the parties involved can anticipate all the possibly relevant contingencies and draft a contract that covers them all. But then how can we convincingly use equilibrium analysis to study these relationships, where we assume that the parties involved understand at the outset what will happen over the course of the relationship as a function of all the contingencies that arise?

Multiplicity of equilibria in these settings compounds the problem. Consider the unrealistic situation in which the two parties literally play the game in Figure 2 repeatedly. Now an explicit contingent contract can be written. Indeed, some contracts are simple to write, such as: Task A in states #1 and #3 (period by period), task B in state #2.[14] Such an explicit contract,

---

[14] To be more exact, I have in mind a situation where the employee always retains the right to quit, although the employer cannot discharge the worker except for cause. Then this 'contract' specifies the path of equilibrium play, with the somewhat more implicit provision that the worker will depart if the firm does not follow the contractually-specified path of play. Of course, with the possibility of relatively cheap court enforcement, especially if sufficient punitive damage awards are possible, such contracts can go beyond the limitations of self-enforcing repeated-game equilibrium paths.

———— *Markets and Hierarchies and (Mathematical) Economic Theory* ————

assuming it is self-enforcing, has the advantage of spelling out what the equilibrium is going to be. In this unrealistic setting, if the parties are not explicit *ex ante*, can they implicitly agree on what the arrangement will be? Since repeated games have a continua of equilibria, it is hard to see how they might do so (unless for the reasons given earlier one party has the power of Stackelberg leader or noise-avoidance considerations points toward a particular equilibrium).

Returning to the real world where future contingencies are vague at best, we are unable to specify explicitly what will be the path of play. Hence, we are in a world where the parties must anticipate not only what will happen over time, as (unforeseeable!) contingencies arise, but they must do this foreseeing in a situation where a continua of specifications can give an equilibrium arrangement. Equilibrium analysis presumes, rather incredibly, that (i) they all do this foreseeing and (ii) their prediction coincide and turn out to be factually correct.

The problem of multiplicity arises in many of the short-horizon models as well; at least, in those that conclude the *ex post* renegotiation as, for example, in Grossman and Hart (1986). Grossman and Hart assume that the gains from renegotiation are split equally, where gains are measured relative to the threat point of a non-cooperative (subgame) equilibrium. (In subsequent work to accommodate more than two parties, Hart and Moore have used the Shapley Value.) The threat point is unique, but where does the 50-50 split come from? Many explicit bargaining models suffer from a multiplicity of equilibria. Some others, e.g. the Rubinstein (1982) alternating-offer bargaining model, have a unique subgame-perfect equilibrium. But uniqueness turns on the very delicate application of subgame perfection, and incomplete information as to the bargaining aspirations of the parties can muddy the pristine waters of a unique perfect equilibrium. Economics textbooks have, for quite a while, asserted that the outcome in a situation of bilateral monopoly is unclear—even taking the Panglossian view that efficiency will be attained—and my reading of recent work in bargaining theory is that Rubinstein notwithstanding, that intuition is theoretically supported.[15] Since expectations about the division of rents in the renegotiation stage drives almost completely the initial investment levels, the multiple-equilibria problem arises in the short-horizon models just as soon as we get serious (i.e. do something other than assume the result) about *ex post* renegotiation.

[15] I will also add that the lack of theoretical support for a specific bargaining outcome does not mean that, in controlled bargaining situations, we cannot predict what the outcome will be. We know from experimental work that by manipulating the expectations of subjects and by framing, we can influence the outcome of bargaining situations rather substantially, and somewhat in contradiction to what simple-minded application of game-theoretic ideas would predict for some protocols.

———— *Markets and Hierarchies and (Mathematical) Economic Theory* ————

Milton Friedman for the Defense

We can agree, I hope, that traditional game-theoretic models, with their assumptions of perfect (accurate) contingent foresight, do not do justice to boundedly rational behavior. Insofar as contract incompleteness is rationalized primarily by bounded rationality, important pieces are missing from our model.

There are those who will argue with the conclusion of the previous paragraph. Let me propose three lines of argument:

(i)   In a formal sense, it is not necessary (to invoke the predictions of Nash equilibrium) that players have perfect contingent foresight for all contingencies that arise, but only for those that are *relevant* in the technical sense that they can be reached by one deviation from the equilibrium by any one player (Fudenberg and Kreps, 1994, Proposition 4.1). Indeed, for two-player games, perfect contingent foresight is needed only along the path of play (Fudenberg and Kreps, 1995, Proposition 6.1). *Rejoinder*: These technical emendations do not really affect the argument above, insofar as it is hard to imagine that players have a good idea of what contingencies they will meet even assuming they stick to 'the agreement'. The path of play (all events that will be reached with positive probability if there are no deviations) itself is uncharted territory in a world of boundedly rational individuals.

(ii)   Following Maskin and Tirole (1995), in short-horizon situations, the parties do not need to describe accurately (in their mind's eye) what contingencies will arise and what actions will be taken given those contingencies. It is enough that they have an accurate feel for the distribution of 'utility' ramifications of the action-contingency pairs. For long-horizon models, we will need more than this; it must be feasible for them to assess *ex post* that their trading partners lived up to the implicit agreement. Justice Stewart's '[Although difficult if not impossible to define *ex ante*], I know [pornography] when I see it' is apposite. To extend the Maskin and Tirole argument to longer horizon models, this becomes: The participants cannot say *ex ante* precisely what is expected of each other in this agreement, but they recognize what it is as contingencies arise, and after the fact each is able to say whether the other fulfilled her obligations. *Rejoinder*: This simply compounds the original Maskin and Tirole assumptions. If they were not credulous before, they are surely less so compounded in this fashion.

(iii) It is not important that our models capture all aspects of the situation, as long as they give us testable predictions about the world that are not rejected by the data. That is, we have Milton Friedman's defense of positive economic theory.

3. Institutional Inertia

My rejoinder to argument (iii) is to list real-world phenomena that, I contend, are important and suggestive of boundedly rational behavior. To address these phenomena adequately, we should go beyond standard game theory. In this section and the next, I deal at some length with the first of these phenomena, institutional inertia. Section 5 presents further phenomena of this type.

It is widely held that organizations exhibit substantial inertia in what they do and how they do it (Hannan and Freeman, 1984). In the face of changing external circumstances, organizations adapt poorly or not at all; the economy and/or market evolves as much or more through changes in the population of live organizations than through changes in the organizations that are alive. Moreover, adaptations resemble a piecewise constant function; one sees little or no change and then a sudden discontinuous shift, which (often) involves many practices of the organization.[16] Organizational policies/procedures tend to be derived from the early history of the organization (Stinchcombe, 1965; Hannan and Freeman, 1977) and to be derived (or at least crystallized out of) specific noteworthy events in the early history of the organization (Schein, 1983).

Standard-theory Rationales

Granting its existence, can the phenomenon of institutional inertia be rationalized using standard economic/game theory? To answer, we first must be clear on how inertia connects to the models of Section 2.

Inertia is manifestly a phenomenon of long-enduring organizations and relationships. Thus, the short-horizon models of Section 2 are ill-suited to speak directly to inertia. The long-horizon models, on the other hand, seem very well suited to the task. (We could consider stacking together a sequence of short-horizon models, i.e. we imagine the two parties A and B engaged in a sequence of investment/employment interactions, but this would move us into the realm of repeated games and the Folk Theorem, in any case.)

---

[16] See, for example, Hannan and Freeman (1984) or Amburgey, Kelly, and Barnett (1993). At the level of the industry ecology, see Stinchcombe (1965). Small continuous changes do take place, and especially after a major jump in practices, there is a period during which new practices can adjust, seeking a new equilibrium. Hence, I use the formulation, adaptations *resemble* a piecewise constant function.

———— *Markets and Hierarchies and (Mathematical) Economic Theory* ————

Beginning with the long-horizon model of relational contracting, inertia might be viewed as simple equilibrium selection, which is orthogonal to standard game theory. That is, in the Simon model (specified as a repeated game version of Figure 2), there is a reputational equilibrium in which the employer calls for task A in each period, a second in which she asks for task A in state 1 and task B in states 2 and 3 in each period, and (for example) a third in which her request in period t depends on the period t state and, say, the tth element in a binary expansion of the number π. The first equilibrium certainly seems to be 'inertial', the second probably does, and the third almost certainly does not. But all are equilibria, and standard theory is mute on a selection among them.

The problem here is that inertia refers to the organization's adaptation to a changing environment; in the simple long-horizon model of Section 2, the environment is entirely time homogeneous. So to discuss how standard theory deals (or does not) with inertia, we must elaborate on the simple long-horizon model. The easiest way to do this is to imagine that the payoffs in period t depend on the actions taken by the actors on that date *and* on some random environmental parameter θ_t. We can imagine that the stochastic process $\{\theta_t\}$ is very slow moving (i.e. with high probability, the payoffs at date t as a function of the actions are nearly the same as the payoffs at date $t-1$) or that it jumps around somewhat. But however we think of this process, inertia then becomes: the employer and employee maintain the 'form' of their relationship for a long time—the employee expects, say, that the employer will ask for task A regardless of the state of nature—despite changes in the environment (in θ_t) that render this relationship fairly inefficient.

Recall from transaction-cost economics the fundamental precept that transactions tend to take the form that maximizes the net benefits of the transaction, net of the costs of the transaction. As a selection device for the game of Figure 2, this would seem to push for the reputational equilibrium in which the employer asks for that action in a given state that maximizes the sum of the payoffs (if utility is transferable), or at least does not ask for an action that is Pareto dominated by some other. As θ_t changes, this would argue for contingent-action requests that shift through time, and inertia would be observed if the actual requests shift markedly less quickly than this.

Can we generate inertia using standard-theory arguments? There are at least three ways to do so:

(i) Suppose first that θ_t is not observable by the employee(s), or is observable only with noise. Insofar as the employer's private interests diverge from the socially efficient choice of contingent action (even if the date-to-date state is fully observable), employee(s) will worry that the employer's modification of the state-contingent action rule is directed not at efficiency-enhancement but at maximizing her own welfare. Thus, fewer changes than are called for by full-observation efficiency would lead to greater efficiency under the informational constraints.

(ii) Suppose (in a more elaborate model) that employees seek employment with employers whose assignments/work conditions match well the tastes of the employee. Some employees seek employers who ask for many hours of work away from home (for premium pay), because these employees are relatively willing to take on such assignments; others seek employers who rigidly adhere to the rule no-more-than-one-day-away-a-month, because of the high personal value they put on being with their families. A particular employer, facing a particular environment, might find that she can live with the second, rigid rule, and still be fairly efficient. Thus, she puts that rule in place and attracts the corresponding work-force. Then her environment shifts, so that it would be more efficient to send employees out on the road much more (and more variably). If she changes her practices for extant employees, she must either compensate those employees, who will otherwise suffer (on average) from the increasing (average) mismatch, or suffer from high levels of turnover, with concomittent recruitment and training costs. Inertia in HR practices would seem to result. But why then should she not adopt better fitting practices for new hires? A complementary story concerning the need for homogeneity among employees will work: suppose (i) a significant portion of an employee's compensation is the psychic benefits of comradeship with other employees and (ii) one gets greater comradeship benefits from people who have similar tastes.

(iii) In Section 2 we relied on the models of reputation construction that depend on infinite horizon arguments. But there is another way to construct reputation equilibria (even with finite horizon models)— models based on incomplete information about the employer's 'type'— and these constructions can give a third standard theory argument for inertia.

In short, incomplete-information-about-type formulations assume that, at the outset, there is some chance that parties will behave in a way to conform to some behavioral type (with small probability, summing over the types) or they will behave in standard, utility-maximizing fashion (with large probability *ex ante*). Each participant knows his/her own type, but this is private information. Then with repeated play for stakes that are low relative to the overall stakes in the game, even a small chance that a participant

——————— *Markets and Hierarchies and (Mathematical) Economic Theory* ———————

behaves rigidly in a particular manner can affect equilibria dramatically. If (in equilibrium) the standard utility maximizer is to take some action that distinguishes herself from the pure type, then by mimicking the pure type instead she will be mistaken for the pure type and treated accordingly. (If no one but a paranoid person would hold a handgrenade on a bus, then anyone holding a handgrenade will be perceived as being paranoid and subsequently treated as such.) Hence, the standard utility maximizer must do (nearly) as well in expected payoff as she would do if mistaken for any type—either her behavior distinguishes herself from the pure type, in which case the mimicking argument works, or it does not, in which case she is treated exactly as one treats the pure type.[17]

The connection to inertia is: to be an attractive type to mimic, the type behavior must be predictable by the other side.[18] One can imagine, in theory, a predictable type whose behavior at date t depends on the tth digit of the binary expansion of π, but more plausible predictable types are those that are fairly steady in behavior. Having cultivated a reputation for such behavior, an employer (say) who suddenly 'shifts' loses her reputational asset; and a positive case for equilibrium inertia is made.

Note in passing that in this form of reputation construction, a lot of information about the reputation bearer's type is passed in the first few actions she takes. Hence we have a rationale for the observation that the early actions of the organization can be very influential concerning how it acts later.

4. Bounded Rationality and Organizational Inertia

The three standard-theory rationales of organizational inertia just advanced all work, in the sense that they hold together as theoretical constructs. There is probably some truth to them (or, at least, to the first and the second—I find the third rather far fetched). But, at the same time, alternative rationalizations/explanations of inertia can be advanced, using the (so-far) unmodeled concept of bounded rationality. Broadly, the connection between bounded rationality and inertia is something of a variation on the first rationale offered previously. The idea is that employees (in the Simon game)

---

[17] The formal argument first appears in Kreps and Wilson (1982) and Milgrom and Roberts (1982) and has been refined subsequently. For current purposes, good references are Fudenberg and Kreps (1987), Fudenberg and Levine (1989), and Watson (1993).

[18] In a confrontational setting, this certainly is not true. Someone who is perceived to act irrationally may get very gentle treatment in an otherwise harsh environment. But we are thinking here of contexts in which parties must cooperate to their mutual benefit; i.e. we are applying these ideas to beneficial exchange.

─────── *Markets and Hierarchies and (Mathematical) Economic Theory* ───────

must understand and anticipate what the employer is doing (in the Simon game, to monitor the employer's compliance with the implicit contract they have with her). Thus in the first rationale above, the employer cannot be shifting her demands at will, based on information that the employees lack. But even if the employees had access to this information, their ability to do the requisite equilibrium calculations are probably more limited than standard theory assumes. They forecast the employer's future actions (and check her compliance with the implicit contract) based more on her adherence to a pattern of behavior. If they learn adaptively in this sense, it is in her interests to confirm their adaptively-learned expectations; i.e. to adhere to her pattern or previous behavior even if that pattern is no longer an efficient response to the changing environment.

The first key to building a (mathematical) model of this is to construct the model of individual boundedly rational behavior. There are many alternative models that can be employed here, and it is beyond my abilities to survey them all or even a wide subset. Instead, one class of models of behavior that has been studied extensively, adaptive (co-)learning, will be described followed by a discussion of how this model of individual behavior might connect to inertia.

Adaptive Co-learning in Repeated Games

Imagine that individuals play a game at dates $t = 1, 2, \ldots$ At each date t, each player has an assessment concerning the play of her rivals, and she chooses her own action according to some criterion evaluated relative to those assessments. Some of the literature assumes that the choice criterion is precise and myopic; players form assessments of how their rivals will act in the current version of the game, and they then choose actions to maximize their (subjective) immediate payoffs.[19] In other analyses, myopia is assumed but a level of suboptimality is permitted; players can use any (mixed) strategy giving an immediate payoff that is suboptimal (in terms of immediate payoffs) by no more than an exogenously specified amount, an amount that vanishes as the player gains more experience. Other versions assume greater foresight; at the extreme, each player uses a fully specified assessment of how

---

[19] Myopia is sometimes justified by assuming that interactions come from random matches in a population so large that the rivals of Player X at date $t + k$ are very unlikely to have had any contact, direct or indirect, with rivals of Player X at dates t through $t + k - 1$, for k large enough so that α^k is very close to zero where α is the player's per period discount factor. Note that if each individual interaction involves M players and the total population size is N, the chances that a player will meet someone indirectly connected to one of her rivals from dates t to $t + k - 1$ at date t is bounded above by $(M^{k+1} - M)/(N[M - 1])$, which is vanishingly small for fixed k as M/N converges to zero. For more on this sort of justification of myopia, see Ellison (1993).

——— *Markets and Hierarchies and (Mathematical) Economic Theory* ———

her rivals will act for the rest of time (contingent on formation her rivals will receive as time passes), and then solves precisely the infinite horizon dynamic programming problem, Find a strategic response that maximizes (say) discounted expected payoffs.

Myopic decision criteria, whether extreme or an intermediate form, are one expression of bounded rationality in these models. But the main way in which bounded rationality appears is in the players' adaptive assessments. Players begin with some form of prior assessment about the actions of their rivals, and they update based on the history of their rivals' play through time. In some studies, very specific updating rules are used; e.g. players use Bayes' rule on an initially given prior assessment on their rivals' full (infinite-horizon) strategies. This includes as a special case instances where each prior is that the sequence of actions by one's rivals at each date forms an exchangeable sequence, and Bayes' rule is used to update the prior on the limiting frequencies. In others, it is assumed (only) that the updating rules satisfy certain asymptotic properties; an example is asymptotic empiricism, which is that the behavior assessed of rival Y in a given situation converges together with the empirical frequencies of the actions taken by Y in that situation, if the situation recurs infinitely often (or, in other treatments, a non-vanishing fraction of the time).

In some studies, it is assumed that the population of players is large, subject to death and replacement, and the behavior of the population has achieved a steady state, so that players are attempting to learn that steady state. (This justifies asymptotic empiricism, if the priors are sufficiently diffuse.) In others, the model is one of a small group of players interacting repeatedly, each learning and reacting to what the others do. These models involve co-learning; as players learn, they change their actions, hence each is attempting to estimate a moving target.[20]

For the most part, these models have so far been used to study the question, if players in a game are learning and acting in this fashion, will they learn to play a Nash equilibrium of the game?[21]

Inertia

Adaptive behavior would seem to be a ready source for inertia. This does not follow immediately or always; suppose for example that the players in a gen-

---

[20] For these models asymptotic empiricism is quite a leap of faith. However, one can pose statistical tests for the validity of asymptotic empiricism as a maintained hypothesis without greatly affecting the results in this literature; see Fudenberg and Kreps (1995).

[21] The literature concerns both global convergence issues—will play converge at all?, and issues connected to the nature of stable points—if play converges, will it be to a Nash equilibrium, or something stronger or weaker? For a recent survey, see Marimon (1995).

———————— *Markets and Hierarchies and (Mathematical) Economic Theory* ————————

eral repeated game have Cournotian assessments (the prediction what an opponent will do at date t is what he did at date $t - 1$). But for many models of adaptive learning, assessments of a rival's behavior at date t reflects that rival's behavior at many previous dates. In the 'extreme' case of fictitious play (or, more generally, asymptotic empiricism), assessments at date t reflect equally the rival's behavior at all previous dates. If adaptation takes this form and behavior settles into a stable state (or, as in Sonsino (1995), a stable pattern of behavior), both assessments and thus behavior will eventually be very difficult to move because of the increasingly large history that must be overcome.[22] Note the self-fulfilling feedback here: if players in the game form assessments adaptively, using data for behavior gathered over an increasing large period of time, it will take an increasingly long time to move their expectations and hence their behavior (if they are myopic or asymptotically myopic). Even a sophisticated individual (top management?) who understands the adaptive behavior of others and who optimizes accordingly will have little incentive to try to move the others from one established equilibrium to another; it will take a while to do so, which will make it unworthwhile at any reasonable discount factor.

Coordination as a game-theoretic metaphor for mutually beneficial exchange will clarify and refine these assertions. Imagine a number of individuals playing the following game.[23] At each date t, each must choose an action from some set A. The payoff to player i at date t is $v_i(\theta_t, a_i, n(a_i),)$, where θ_t is an environmental parameter (chosen by nature), a_i is the action chosen by i, and $n(a_i)$ is the number of players choosing precisely this (same) action. Imagine that v_i is strictly increasing in its third argument and that if $v_i(\theta, a, n) > v_i(\theta, a', n)$ for some n, then this inequality holds for all n. The first assumption is, essentially, that players benefit by coordinating their choices with others (and the more, the better); the second assumption is that a player's interests about where coordination takes place does not change with the level of coordination.[24]

Fix θ_t. Depending on the scale of the benefits of coordination *vis-à-vis* the 'personal preferences' of individuals (measured by the relative values of $v(\theta_t, a, 1)$ for various a), it is evident that the game at θ_t (and at date t) can have a vast number of Nash equilibria of varying efficiencies. To take a very simple example, if there are two actions a and a', even if $v_i(\theta_t, a, 1) > v_i(\theta_t, a', 1)$ for everyone, it is a Nash equilibrium for everyone to coordinate on a' if $v_i(\theta_t, a', 2) \geq v_i(\theta_t, a, 1)$. But if there are decreasing returns to scale in coordination

---

[22] This assumes convergence to strict best responses. Aficionados will recognize the problems that arise when, in the limit, more than one pure strategy is asymptotically a best response.

[23] A game of roughly this form is studied by Farrell and Shapiro (1996) on the topic of the adoption of compatible standards.

[24] This restriction is only to simplify the analysis.

——————— *Markets and Hierarchies and (Mathematical) Economic Theory* ———————

(roughly, if $v_i(\theta_p, a, n + m) - v_i(\theta_p a, n)$ is decreasing in n for fixed m), then as the total population grows, we can increasingly find equilibria for the θ_t stage game in which players coalesce into several pools; the pressures to coordinate are not sufficient so that everyone necessarily coalesces into a single lump (although a single pool almost anywhere remains a good prospect for an equilibrium).

If we look for Nash equilibria of the repeated game, inertia is not necessarily produced. Any string of single-period Nash equilibria (and more besides) give a equilibrium of the repeated game, including strings where both the actions chosen for coordination and the members of the various pools change dramatically with each date.

But, of course, such equilibria depend on players having hyper-rational expectations about the actions of their fellows. If, as seems more realistic, i's prediction about j's action choice is largely determined by how j chose in the past, then once a stable configuration is reached, it may be very hard to upset. For example, suppose that θ_t is unchanging and players begin with an equal-probability prior on how others will act and are myopic. Then $_i$ will initially choose the action $a_i{}^*$ that maximizes $v_i(a, 1)$ (where I suppress θ_t since it is momentarily constant). When these choices are noted, each player will increase the probability assessed that j will pick $a_j{}^*$. Perhaps the changed assessments will be insufficient to get anyone to abandon their personal best actions, but then after another round of seeming chaos, each will be more sure about what the others will do. At some point, someone will be moved to abandon her own personal best, to join at the best of someone else (at least, this is so if $v_i(a_i^*, 1) < v_i(a_j^*, 2)$ for some i and j. Barring a coincidental simultaneous shift, the action of coordination by these two will be self-confirming—the more often they coordinate, the more attractive coordination at this point will look to them. Then, as others become convinced that the two are coordinating there, they will be moved to join, unless they have already formed their own coordinating groups. Groups of various sizes will coalesce. There is no reason to suppose that eventually everyone will coordinate at a single action; whether a player abandons one coordinating group to join another depends on the relative sizes of the groups and the inherent attractiveness of the two actions (measured by $v_i(a, 1)$). But note that if one player drops from a coordinating group, this simultaneously makes the joined group more attractive and the group departed less.

The dynamic system depends on the precise rules for assessing what others will do, the form of myopia that is assumed, and any noise put into the system. This paper is not the place to spell out a very precise formulation and make all this specific, but five points should be clear: (i) Corresponding to the many Nash equilibria of the stage game, the dynamic

——————— *Markets and Hierarchies and (Mathematical) Economic Theory* ———————

system will have many stable configurations. Moreover, if we put some noise into the action selection process (noise pertaining, say, to how, to how one chooses among actions that are nearly equally good), the eventual limiting configuration will be random. (ii) Initial coordinating decisions will be very influential on the eventual configuration that emerges. A chance coordination at the outset by two individuals will be reinforcing and will attract others. (iii) Insofar as assessments are not much affected late in the sequence of periods by single individual actions, because there is more and more data to draw upon, once a stable configuration (a Nash equilibrium) is reached it will tend to persist. (iv) A single sophisticated individual participating in this repeated situation may find it impossible to shift the configuration. Even if she can shift it, it will take a great deal of time (spend uncoordinated with others) to do so. (v) The dynamic model has (potentially) two reinforcing sources of inertia: Stable configurations will persist, even if (say) assessments are Cournotian (the prediction of what i will do at date t is i's choice at $t - 1$. If assessments are increasingly rigid as history at a specific configuration builds up—if, say, the assessment of what i will do at date t is some sort of average of what i did at the past $\eta(t)$ dates, where $\lim_t \eta(t) = \infty$ (as in fictitious play models)—then the longer a stable configuration persists, the more persistent it becomes.

Now reintroduce variable θ_t, thinking of θ_t as a slowly evolving environmental variable. With enough variation in the θ_t, stable coalition structures may 'collapse'; player i may at some date t shift from a coalition at action a to one at a', if the ratio of $v_i(\theta_t, a', 1)/v_i(\theta_t, a, 1)$ grows sufficiently. Such a shift may occasion a cascade of further changes; when i abandons action a, everyone else who was choosing a sees less value in the choice (since $n(a)$ is reduced), and further defections may result. This effect will be stronger in small organizations (actions a with low $n(a)$) and in settings with more rapidly decreasing returns to scale in coordination, since the value of being in a larger coalition is less diluted by a single defection.[25] The picture is one of local equilibrium configurations that, once formed, persist for long periods of time, and then perhaps suddenly crumble. A configuration may be relatively efficient at date t and then become increasingly inefficient compared to other configurations that might be formed, while still staying a local equilibrium. Sophisticated individuals, getting to the process early, may strongly influence the configuration that is reached at the outset and after an unfreezing. But a single sophisticated individual may be unable to shift to a better (for her) stable configuration unless she can work directly on the assessments of

---

[25] Note in this formulation each player is concerned only with the number and not the identities of those with whom she coordinates. If player i was anxious to coordinate with a specific player j, then even if that coordination was achieved in a large cluster, it might not be any more stable in consequence.

———— Markets and Hierarchies and (Mathematical) Economic Theory ————

other individuals, and even if she can do so, it will be very expensive in time and missed coordination opportunities to do so. As a metaphor for descriptions one reads of organizational inertia, this has some appeal.

Of course, this metaphor is only a metaphor; it is far from a serious model of organizations or transactions. The coordination game with conflicting interests that has been suggested is convenient for showing how adaptive expectations can lead to inertia at any of a number of different configurations, with local adaptation but few (if any) jumps to a globally more efficient solution. But unless and until we are ready to accept coordination as an appropriate reduced form for transaction issues, it would be better to build a model of transactions that looks more like the real thing. I have not done this, so I cannot claim for certain that such a model, populated by adaptive decision-makers, will give the sort of inertial behavior the metaphor provides. But I am fairly confident it will,[26] and so the suggestion is that we ought to populate models of transactions (such as the Simon model) not with the hyperrational agents of standard game theory but with the sort of individuals who increasingly populate models of learning in (non-standard) game theory.

Some Missing Aspects of Adaptive Behavior

As we do this, we (game theorists) will need to tune up our models of adaptive behavior. There are a number of aspects of behavior that would be useful for addressing inertia (and the phenomena to be listed in Section 5) and that are currently outside of even the non-standard arsenal. There are four obvious candidates.

First, with one exception of which I am aware (Li Calzi, 1993), the models used presuppose that players are involved in repeated play of a fixed game. Inferences about what a rival will do in situation X are (usually) restricted by the past behavior of the rival in precisely that situation.[27] In real life, situations do not recur precisely as before. Instead, a situation X' may arise that seems very similar to past situations (the same rival is called upon to move, she has roughly the same options, her payoffs are roughly the same), in which case a player may use the evidence of what happened in X to assess what will happen in X'. Note my list of what makes the two situations similar—same player, roughly same options, roughly same playoffs—I have an intuition derived from experience as to what makes

---

[26] Which is to say, I think coordination with conflict will turn out to be a good metaphor for long-horizon transactions.

[27] To be clear about this, it is not typically assumed that behavior in situation X' is completely uninformative about behavior in situation X, but neither is any link presumed to hold.

———— *Markets and Hierarchies and (Mathematical) Economic Theory* ————

situations similar. More precisely, one can have many hypotheses as to what makes situations similar—call these hypotheses theories or models—which abstract from a complex real life situation a short/simple list of important attributes; and the theories are subjected through time to empirical testing, to see whether (per the data) things happen roughly the same way in similar situations. Those versed in computer science will recognize basic ideas of pattern recognition here; psychologists will recognize cognitive psychology.

Second, the literature generally assumes that players understand the underlying structure of the game that is being repeated. They know what information their rivals have, what all the options are, and so on. In real life these things are more vague, and learning models should be constructed reflecting this.

Third, players cannot be expected to learn how their rivals act in situations that recur very, very rarely (formally, a finite number of times; see Fudenberg and Levine (1993) and Fudenberg and Kreps (1994). Players, by their own actions, preclude certain observations; put the other way around, to obtain certain data, players sometimes must conduct experiments that are costly in the short-run. How is the decision made whether to experiment? The models in the literature either invoke an incredible level of sophistication (players are presumed to solve non-stationary multi-armed bandit problems precisely) or are silent on the process except to make broad-gauge assumptions such as, every action that can be taken infinitely often is taken infinitely often. Adaptive learning models in general need better models of the process of experimentation by boundedly rational decision makers, especially where the experiments take us to regions of the sort mentioned in the second point above, where the options and payoffs are *ex ante* unclear.

Finally, an important aspect of the equilibrium analysis of long-horizon relational contracts is that players reciprocate, assuming that their trading partners will reciprocate. We lack a good story on learning to reciprocate in a small numbers formulation. In the literature on small numbers interactions, most papers have very myopic decision-makers; they essentially forecast what their rivals will do in the current encounter and, at least asymptotically, choose a stage-game strategy that maximizes their stage-game expected payoff. Kalai and Lehrer (1993) give a small-numbers formulation with more far-sighted players, but their players are incredibly far-sighted and computationally sophisticated; they (each) solve a dynamic programming problem that is at least as hard as a multi-armed bandit problem with non-independent arms. Since we have stories of learning to play extensive form games (e.g. in Fudenberg and Kreps, 1994, 1995), we can imagine learning reciprocation as a general rule; Player A plays a long-

———— *Markets and Hierarchies and (Mathematical) Economic Theory* ————

horizon game against B, then another against C, then D, and so on, taking what she has learned in each interaction into the next.[28] This may be an interesting story—indeed, it makes reciprocation into something of a social phenomena rather than something internally arising between two individual players—but we would like as well a story about A and B interacting and each learning how each will reciprocate (or not) in their specific relationship.

5. Other Phenomena

Inertia is not the only phenomenon which, I believe, can be fruitfully studied with models of individual behavior that go beyond the hyper-rationality of standard economics and game theory. Among the other phenomena of interest are the following.

(1) **Consistency/comprehensibility/transparency/simplicity.** At least in the domain of employment practices, 'internal consistency' is held to be important. I am unable to give a concise definition of consistency (Potter Stewart is apposite once more); and so I resort to some examples: (i) If the organization promotes cooperation among employees in its compensation practices, it should not simultaneously base promotion on individual (relative) performance. (ii) If workers are exhorted to take risks and be forthcoming with criticisms or ideas, incentive systems should not penalize failure harshly. (iii) An organization whose compensation and promotion practices have the flavor of a competitive marketplace does better with a cafeteria-style benefits plan than with benefits configured to look like gifts.

Another form of consistency that is sometimes recommended is consistency of practices among workers otherwise undistinguished by education or other apparent demographic factors. For example, notwithstanding the obvious transaction-cost advantages, IBM found it difficult to treat differently engineers in its PC division and engineers in other parts of the firm. Firms will use artificial distinctions in some instances, such as job titles, or they will resort to things like geographic separation that prevent communication/cross-observation.

Other aspects of employment practices that are sometimes held to be efficiency-promoting are comprehensibility, transparency, and simplicity. These concepts are even harder to define than is consistency. Indeed most definitions I have formulated are internally referential. But (in the context of

---

[28] Note that this is not quite true, since Fudenberg and Kreps have a small numbers formulation. That is, to cite those papers directly, we would need A and B to play a long-horizon game, then another, and another, etc. where for some reason they are myopic between, but of course not within, each individual 'encounter'. To make up the story suggested, we would need a large numbers formulation of Fudenberg and Kreps. It does not seem difficult, but it has not (to my knowledge) been done formally.

——————— *Markets and Hierarchies and (Mathematical) Economic Theory* ———————

employment practices, at least), employers are enjoined to create HR practices that give positive answers to questions such as: do you (the employee)
understand what is expected of you?; and do you understand how your compensation and promotion prospects are determined? I hypothesize that positive answers to parallel questions for other forms of relational exchange are
associated with greater efficiency in those exchanges.

(2) **Social embeddedness.**   Employment (and other transactional) practices are embedded within the general milieu of social exchange, and the
efficiency of various practices changes with changes in the social milieu
(Grannovetter, 1985). Specifically, practices that are generally consistent
with norms for general social exchange in the society in which the transaction is embedded tend to do better than those that are at variance with those
norms. An employer with assembly plants in the USA and Thailand may
find it counterproductive to subject employees in the US plant to daily
searches by metal detectors, where such searches promote an aura of distrust
(which is then reciprocated), while such practices have lesser adverse consequences in Thailand. A handshake agreement made following joint atten-
dance at a club or at Church may take on greater sanctity than the same
agreement made in an airport hotel suite.

(3) **Gift exchange.**   Party A to a long-run transaction provides 'gifts' to
party B; extra benefits, above-market wages, free drinks during the work
day, and so on. Party B reciprocates with 'gifts' such as working extra hours
without compensation, giving consummate effort (Akerlof, 1982).

(4) **The psychology of escalating commitment and other dynamic
effects.**   Escalating commitment concerns behavior in which an individual's commitment to a goal or a relationship grows over time (as the goal is
pursued or the relationship matures), to the point where the goal/relation-
ship is pursued past the seeming point of 'economic' sense (Staw and Ross,
1986). Sunk-cost illusions are one example; firms that have invested (in a
sunk cost fashion) in a venture will continue to invest in the venture even if
it is increasingly clear that the return on continued investments is such that
the investments would not be undertaken de novo. In terms of long-horizon
contracting, party A may continue to transact with party B even if it seems a
better (more efficient) trading relation with some party C could take its
place. In a more positive aspect, parties A and B may, as their relationship
matures, become more willing to trust the other; contracts between them
may become less detailed, with greater reliance on either one-party-
determined adaptation or adaptation by unanimous consent. In terms of the

——— *Markets and Hierarchies and (Mathematical) Economic Theory* ———

repeated-game model of long-horizon contracting, it appears that the simple fact that A and B have dealt with each other over time increases the value to each of continuing to deal with each other, beyond the value that seems to arise from the economic exchanges that take place

(5) **The managerial risk of forgiveness, and high- and low-powered incentives.** As something of a special case of escalating commitment (but more besides), we have one of the reasons given by Williamson that firms cannot attain the high-powered incentives offered by markets; viz., the managerial risk of forgiveness. Markets can and do punish poor performance quite severely, and (thus) provide high-powered incentives to avoid failure. But within an organization, failure by an individual or group of individuals can be and often is forgiven, reducing the incentive to avoid failure. (I would imagine that this effect is stronger the longer the malefactor has been associated with the firm and, especially, his particular boss, assuming the relationship to date has been positive.)

(6) **Noncalculative and non-intrusive trust, and atmosphere in general.** In response to agency theory, social psychologists and sociologists often cite evidence that close monitoring of individuals and rewards based on extrinsic measures of performance may perversely (for economists, at least) increase slacking and lower effort. For the former, an individual who is closely monitored takes from the very fact the idea that he is not trusted, and thus that trust is not expected (think of common rationales for honor codes). For the latter, extrinsic reward schemes supposedly blunt the (sometimes) very powerful effect of intrinsic rewards. Moreover, the very act of calculation (of personal costs and benefits) may injure trust (Williamson, 1993b).

Each of these phenomena can be rationalized to some extent with standard-theory models. In particular, efficiency-wage theory works well with gift exchange (albeit not with the part of gift-exchange theory that stresses the symbolic importance attached to the form of the gift). But I have selected these phenomena because I believe that they will respond well to non-standard treatments of individual behavior.

First, in the real world, where no situation ever repeats precisely, predictions of how a trading partner will act will be made on the basis of similarities and 'general principles'. Moreover, *ex post* checking on adherence to an implicit contract will be made on the basis of similarly unclear criteria. A rule/principle/similarity will be more or less efficient as a basis for trade according to (i) how easily it is for the trading partners to learn, through experience or communication; (ii) how unambiguous it is to apply *ex ante* and to verify *ex post*; and (ii) how widely and efficiently it applies to contingencies that arise. Clearly these desiderata will conflict: ambiguity is likely to rise with range of applicability; letting a fixed third party arbitrate dis putes is widely applicable and relatively unambiguous (follow whatever the third party dictates), but in a world with privately held information this is likely to give less than efficient adaptation to contingencies that arise. Notwithstanding the tradeoffs that must be made, the general desirability for purposes of learnability and unambiguous applications of qualities such as simplicity, comprehensibility, and consistency seems clear. Consistency, moreover, means both internal consistency and consistency of the specific rule/principle with rules/principles found generally in society; it is easier to learn and apply a pattern of behavior that conforms with generally observed patterns of behavior than to learn and apply a pattern that mixes many gen erally observed forms, so that social embeddedness and the symbolic charac ter of actions play a role. I am uncertain how to model these aspects within (mathematical) economic models of adaptive behavior (see earlier remarks concerning similarities), but there are obvious sources to tap for insights: psychological theories of perception and cognition; sociological theories of norms; computer science theories of pattern recognition.

Second, economic models have (with rare exceptions) left untouched the notion that, putting aside expectations, one's own tastes and preferences change with experience. In particular (and particularly germane for the cur rent context), individuals internalize to greater or lesser extent the welfare of others depending on such factors as kinship, social similarity, and length of (positive or negative) interactions. Models of endogenously evolving tastes that capture these ideas ought to be very helpful refining our understanding of escalating commitment, the managerial risk of forgiveness, and the like. Models where such tastes are influenced by symbolic actions (e.g. non-calcu lative trust suggests friendship or kinship, which leads to greater internal ization of the other's welfare) may help us to understand non-calculative trust or the importance in gift exchange of the symbolic character of the gift.

6. Conclusions

Transaction-cost economics has been partially translated in the more mathe matical language of game theory over the past decade, and (I hope and believe) our understanding of the costs of transactions has been deepened, refined and extended in consequence. But the translation is incomplete. There is a lot to human behavior that standard game-theoretic models miss, and undertaking 'game theory' with more life-like models of individuals will get us much closer to phenomena that we (game theorists) currently

——— *Markets and Hierarchies and (Mathematical) Economic Theory* ———

must ignore or leave unexplained, at least insofar as we stick rigidly to the standard rules of our toolkit. Transaction-cost economics, especially the economics of relational contracts, provides an outstanding arena for these developments, because the important issues of bounded rationality and (more generally) individual behavior are central to the topic. I have suggested models that take off from recent work on adaptive co-learning as a useful starting point, but I do not mean to suggest that these models are exclusively the way to proceed: the models of reinforcement learning that have recently been studied by Erev and Roth (1995) are very attractive (and come with something of a theory of similarities); I have just argued for models with exogenously influenced and endogenously evolving levels of internalization of the welfare of others.

I can imagine responses to this thesis from economists, from social psychologists and sociologists, and from those interested primarily in the economics of transactions. Traditionalist economists will look at Section 5 especially and mark this down as an appeal to ad hockery run amok. Allowing tastes to change with, say, the social millieu, is just assuming the result. Put differently, can the program I am advocating be carried out without losing the things of value that game theory does provide, namely a strongly deductive treatment of the behavior of reasonably rational individuals? I find the position today quite similar to where game theory was in the late 1960s, just before the brilliant technical innovations of Selten (concerning the importance of dynamics in game theory) and Harsanyi (on incomplete information), which substantially increased the reach of game theory as a language for discussing and tool for analyzing economic phenomena. Those innovations, and the way they played out in economic applications, gave modelers the ability to spin a lot of 'stories'. It has been said, with substantial justice, that a lot of the armchair theorizing that went on was uninformed by facts. But deductive theory is language and not a divining rod for empirical truth. It is a high order language that allows us to check for logical consistency of our sentences and paragraphs, and it is a language that allows for fairly precise communication. But a lot of stories can be constructed in this language, only some of which will resemble real-world economic phenomena, and empirical tests are run at the level of particular (one hopes, well-constructed) paragraphs, and not at the level of the language itself. If there is a difference in the current situation, I do not see it. Of course widening what we can say will allow us to say more, and to say more garbage in consequence. But if the language is used sensibly, and the paragraphs are subjected to empirical tests (both in the field and in the lab), we ought to be better off in consequence.

Economists will also ask whether any expansion is necessary. Are not the

─────── *Markets and Hierarchies and (Mathematical) Economic Theory* ───────

tools we have already adequate? After all, each of the phenomena I have mentioned can be rationalized to some extent with standard-theory models. And per Posner (1993) and some of my high theory colleagues, I imagine that, at some level, everything having to do with bounded rationality can be reduced to a model of full rationality in a setting of incomplete information and positive costs of computation. But as a practical matter of constructing useful and illuminating models, it seems to me that those who advocate these positions bear the burden of proof; where proof is not a formal proposition to this effect, but instead a set of workable modeling techniques by which (for example) organizational theorists can come fully to grips with organizational inertia, forgiveness, etc.

Sociologists and social psychologists may wonder what is in it for them. I have written this paper as an invitation and challenge to my own (that is, to economists) and have therefore focused on what is missed in standard economic models. It ill behooves me to lecture sociologists and social psychologists on what their models miss (or, to put if more positively, what economic reasoning contributes); in any case, I have not the space left to do so. But notwithstanding comments from colleagues that I seem to be evolving into a socialist, I reaffirm my faith in models in which individuals maximize (albeit as best they can) and admit that my objective is to convert the heathens to economics by mild cooption.

And for the economics of transactions: Since most of the hard work of modeling and analyzing remains to be done, I do not have any solid returns to offer. But let me suggest a question that the models I propose may help to answer.

A central tenet of *Markets and Hierarchies* and transaction-cost economics more generally is that transactions *tend* to be arranged in a way that economizes on transaction costs or, perhaps more precisely, that maximizes the net benefits of the transaction, net of costs of the transaction. The italicized *tend* in this principle gives some scope for things like organizational inertia, it is an open question (in my mind, at least) how much scope transaction-cost economists mean to allow. Or to put it more sensibly, clearly the degree of this tendency will be influenced by environmental variables; it would be helpful to know when the economizing tendency is strong and when it is relatively weak. Based on the metaphorical model of Section 4, the strength of the tendency will be influenced by: the extent to which expectations are blindly adaptive and/or can be unfrozen by direct and explicit intervention of 'leaders'; the extent to which expectations are increasingly frozen as time passes (i.e. are expectations closer to Cournotian or closer to those suggested by fictitious play?); the extent to which participants can foresee where other stable configurations may be found.

———— *Markets and Hierarchies and (Mathematical) Economic Theory* ————

Since the model is a very bare metaphor, these are not conjectures on which I would care to stake my professional reputation. In any event, it is not at all clear (to me) how we could measure these environmental factors empirically; i.e. how we might test these conjectures. But my point for now is not that I have a good answer to the question. Instead, I assert (only) that the question is interesting, and better models of individual behavior is a good place to look for good answers.

Acknowledgements

Prepared originally for presentation at the conference celebrating the 20th anniversary of Williamson's *Markets and Hierarchies*, held in Berkeley, October 1995. My thinking on this subject has been affected by too many colleagues to list here, but I should certainly acknowledge (with gratitude) the time and effort taken by Jim Baron to educate me. The financial assistance of the National Science Foundation (Grant 92-08954) is gratefully acknowledged.

References

Aghion, P. and J. Tirole (1994), 'Formal and Real Authority in Organizations,' mimeo, IDEI and Oxford.

Akerlof, G. A. (1982), 'Labor Contracts as Partial Gift Exchange,' *Quarterly Journal of Economics*, 97, 543–569.

Amburgey, T. L., D. Kelly and W. P. Barnett (1993), 'Resetting the Clock: The Dynamics of Organizational Change and Failure,' *Administrative Science Quarterly*, 38, 51–73.

Debreu, G. (1990), 'The Mathematization of Economic Theory,' *American Economic Review*, 81, 1–7.

Ellison, G. (1993), 'A Little Rationality and Learning from Personal Experience,' mimeo, Harvard University.

Erev, I. and A. E. Roth (1995), 'On the Need for Low Rationality, Cognitive Game Theory: Reinforcement Learning in Experimental Games with Unique, Mixed Strategy Equilibria,' mimeo, University of Pittsburgh.

Farrell, J. and C. Shapiro (1993), 'The Dynamics of Bandwagons,' in J. W. Friedman (ed.), *Problems in Coordination of Economic Activity*, Kluwer: Amsterdam, 149–184.

Fudenberg, D. and D. M. Kreps (1987), 'Reputation in the Simultaneous Play of Multiple Opponents,' *Review of Economic Studies*, 54, 541–568.

Fudenberg, D. and D. M. Kreps (1994), 'Learning in Extensive-Form Games I. Self-Confirming Equilibrium,' *Games and Economic Behavior*, 8, 20–55.

Fudenberg, D. and D. M. Kreps (1995), 'Learning in Extensive-Form Games II. Experimentation and Nash Equilibrium,' mimeo, Stanford University.

Fudenberg, D. and D. Levine (1989), 'Reputation and Equilibrium Selection in Games with a Patient Player,' *Econometrica*, 57, 759–778.

Fudenberg, D. and D. Levine (1993), 'Steady State Learning and Nash Equilibrium,' *Econometrica*, 61, 523–546.

Fudenberg, D. and J. Tirole (1990), 'Moral Hazard and Renegotiation in Agency Contracts,' *Econometrica*, 58, 1279–1320.

———————— *Markets and Hierarchies and (Mathematical) Economic Theory* ————————

Grannovetter, M. (1985), 'Economic Action and Social Structure: The Problem of Embeddedness,' *American Journal of Sociology*, 91, 481–510.

Grossman, S. and O. Hart (1986), 'The Costs and Benefits of Ownership: A Theory of Vertical and Lateral Integration,' *Journal of Political Economy*, 94, 691–719.

Hannan, M. T. and J. Freeman (1977), 'The Population Ecology of Organizations,' *American Journal of Sociology*, 89, 929–964.

Hannan, M. T. and J. Freeman (1984), 'Structural Inertia and Organizational Change,' *American Sociological Review*, 49, 149–164.

Hart, O. (1990), 'Is "Bounded Rationality" and Important Element of a Theory of Institutions?' *Journal of Institutional and Theoretical Economics*, 146, 696–702.

Hart, O. (1995), *Firms, Contracts, and Financial Structure*. Clarendon Press: Oxford.

Hart, O. and M. Moore (1990), 'Property Rights and the Nature of the Firm,' *Journal of Political Economy*, 98, 1119–1158.

Kalai, E. and E. Lehrer (1993), 'Rational Learning Leads to Nash Equilibrium,' *Econometrica*, 61 1019–1045.

Kreps, D. M., R. Wilson (1982), 'Reputation and Imperfect Information,' *Journal of Economic Theory*, 27, 253–79.

Kreps, D. M. (1996), 'Economics—The Current Position,' mimeo, forthcoming in *Daedalus*.

Lazear, E. T. (1979), 'Why Is There Mandatory Retirement?' *Journal of Political Economy*, 87, 1261–1284.

Li Calzi, M. (1993), *Similarities and Learning*, PhD thesis, Stanford.

Marimon, R. (1995), 'Learning from Learning in Economics,' presentation to the Seventh World Congress of the Econometric Society, mimeo, European University Institute, Florence.

Maskin, E. and J. Tirole (1995), 'Dynamic Programming, Unforseen Contingencies, and Incomplete Contracts,' oral presentation at the Seventh World Congress of the Econometric Society, Tokyo.

Milgrom, P. N. and D. J. Roberts (1982), 'Predation, Reputation, and Entry Deterrence,' *Journal of Economic Theory*, 27, 280–312.

Posner, R. A. (1993), 'The New Institutional Economics Meets Law and Economics,' *Journal of Institutional and Theoretical Economics*, 149, 73–87.

Rubinstein, A. (1982), 'Perfect Equilibrium in a Bargaining Model,' *Econometrica*, 50, 97–109.

Schein, E. H. (1983), 'The Role of the Founder in Creating Organizational Culture,' *Organizational Dynamics*, reprinted in B. M. Staw (ed.), *Psychological Dimensions of Organizational Behavior*, 2nd edition. Prentice-Hall: Englewood Cliffs, NJ, 1995.

Simon, H. (1951), 'A Formal Model of the Employment Relationship,' *Econometrica*, 19, 293–305.

Sonsino, D. (1995), 'Learning to Learn, Pattern Recognition, and Nash Equilibrium,' Ph.D. thesis, Stanford.

Staw, B. M. and J. Ross (1986), 'Understanding Behavior in Escalation Situations,' *Science*, 246, 216–220.

Stinchcombe, A. (1965), 'Social Structure and Organizations,' in J. G. March (ed.) *Handbook of Organizations*. Rand McNally: Chicago, pp. 142–193.

Tirole, J. (1994), 'Incomplete Contracts: Where Do We Stand?,' mimeo, IDEI, Toulouse, (Walras-Bowley Lecture for 1994).

Watson, J. (1993), 'A 'Reputation' Refinement without Equilibrium,' *Econometrica*, 61, 199–206.

Williamson, O. E. (1975), *Markets and Hierarchies*. Free Press: New York.

Williamson, O. E. (1985), *The Economic Institutions of Capitalism*, Free Press: New York.

Williamson, O. E. (1993a), 'Transaction Cost Economics Meets Posnerian Law and Economics,' *Journal of Institutional and Theoretical Economics*, 149, 99–118.

Williamson, O. E. (1993b), 'Calculativeness, Trust, and Economic Organization,' *Journal of Law and Economics*, 36, 453.

[16]

International Journal of Industrial Organization 3 (1985) 365–378. North-Holland

ASSET SPECIFICITY AND ECONOMIC ORGANIZATION*

Michael H. RIORDAN

Stanford University, Stanford, CA 94305, USA

Oliver E. WILLIAMSON

Yale University, New Haven, CT 06520, USA

Final version received May 1985

This paper examines the optimization problem of firm and market organization in which both production cost and transaction cost differences are expressed as a function of asset specificity. In general, markets enjoy advantages by aggregating the demands of many buyers, thereby realizing economies of scale or scope. Such production cost savings need to be assessed in relation to the transaction cost advantages that internal organization sometimes enjoys over markets in adapting to changed circumstances. As it turns out, both production cost economies and the transaction cost differences between firm and market organization vary systematically with the characteristics of the investments. This paper employs a unified framework to assess the choice of organization form. The condition of asset specificity is featured.

1. Introduction

Transaction cost economics regards the transaction as the basic unit of analysis and holds that the organization of economic activity is largely to be understood in transaction cost economizing terms. Such economies are realized by aligning governance structures (of which firms and markets are the leading types) with the attributes of transactions in a discriminating way.

Technological features of economic organization are thus relegated to a secondary role by this approach. Given that successive stages of economic activity are technologically separable, how ought the trading interface to be organized? Vertical integration – or, in more mundane terms, the 'make-or-buy' decision – is the paradigm problem. Transaction cost economics maintains that the resolution of this issue turns on the attributes of the

*The authors are Assistant Professor of Economics, Stanford University and Gordon B. Tweedy Professor of Economics of Law and Organization. Yale University, respectively. Helpful comments from Avinash Dixit, David Sappington, Richard Schmalensee, Pablo Spiller and anonymous referees are gratefully acknowledged.

transaction, of which the condition of asset specificity is the most important.[1] A variety of related and some rather distant contractual relations turns out to be variations on this same underlying theme.[2] This is gratifying since, as Friedrich Hayek (1967, p. 50) observed, 'whenever the capacity of recognizing an abstract rule which the arrangement of these attributes follows has been acquired in one field, the same master mould will apply when the signs for those abstract attributes are evoked by altogether different elements'.

Although this transaction cost approach to contracting has been gaining wider acceptance,[3] it is not now and does not threaten to become the new orthodoxy. Even, moreover, among those who are persuaded that a transaction cost orientation is needed to get at the core issues of comparative economic organization, there is some discomfit with the apparent disjunction between neoclassical and transaction cost modes of economic analysis – where the former emphasizes production costs and views the firm as a production function, while the latter focuses on transaction costs and regards the firm as a governance structure.

Both approaches, however, maintain an economizing orientation. And plainly production and transaction costs both need to be taken into account in any effort to realize a broadly conceived economizing result. This paper is an effort to pull these two cost categories together in a common framework. It is highly preliminary, in that we (1) deal only with polar alternatives, namely neoclassical markets and hierarchical firms of very stylized kinds, (2) look at only one transaction at a time, and (3) employ a reduced form type of analysis, in that we ascribe rather than derive the basic production and governance cost competencies of firms and markets.[4]

The paper mainly confirms implications that have been advanced earlier using more heuristic arguments. In this sense, there are few surprises – though this may be a surprise to those who hold different priors. Surprises or

---

[1]The argument is advanced and assessed in the theoretical, empirical, and public policy literatures in which transaction cost economics is featured. The theory is set out in Williamson (1971, 1975, 1979, 1983, 1985), Klein et al. (1978), Masten (1982), and Alchian (1984). Corroborating evidence is developed in Stuckey (1983), Monteverde and Teece (1982), Palay (1984, 1985), Masten (1984), Walker and Weber (1984), Anderson and Schmittlein (1984), and Joskow (1985). Applications to public policy include Williamson (1976, 1982), and Joskow and Schmalensee (1983).

[2]Variations on the basic transaction cost economizing theme include applications to labor market organization, vertical restrictions of various kinds, franchising, reciprocal trading (including product exchange agreements), regulation, corporate governance, and even family organization. This last is treated by Ben-Porath (1980) and Pollak (1985). The others are discussed in Williamson (1985).

[3]Alchian, who once held otherwise, now agrees that asset specificity is the key condition on which the study of firm and market organization turns (1984, pp. 38–39). The recent treatment of vertical integration by Grossman and Hart (1984) also assumes a condition of asset specificity.

[4]It is thus akin to Masten's earlier treatment of these matters (1982). While our analysis is more expansive, his treatment and ours both employ reduced form expressions.

not, the spirit of the analysis is consonant with that of economics quite generally: use more general modes of analysis as a check on the limitations that inform more specialized types of reasoning. This paper employs a unified framework to make a modest step in the direction of formalization. While we remain somewhat agnostic – believing, as we do, that there are both costs and benefits to formalization – it is in the spirit of Kenneth Arrow's recent remarks that new theories of economic organization take on greater 'analytic usefulness when these are founded on more directly neoclassical lines' [Arrow (1985, p. 303)].

The heuristic model and the factors responsible for cost differences among firm and market modes are sketched in section 2. The main model, in which asset specificity has only cost but no demand effects, is then set out in section 3. Demand features are the object of analysis in section 4. Concluding remarks follow.

2. The heuristic model

2.1. Asset specificity

Transaction cost economics maintains that the principal factor that is responsible for transaction cost differences among transactions is variations in asset specificity. Transactions that are supported by non-specific (redeployable) investments are ones for which neoclassical analysis is well-suited to deal. As a condition of asset specificity becomes more important, however, exchange relations take on a progressively stronger bilateral trading character. The reason is that parties to such trades have a stake in preserving the continuity of the relationship. Simultaneously, however, problems of adapting bilateral contracts to changing circumstances predictably arise. Autonomous market contracting is thus supplanted by more complex forms of governance as asset specificity deepens. New forms of dispute settlement (such as arbitration) may be created. Some transactions may be removed from the market and organized internally instead. The heuristic model gives content to this firm or market (make or buy) orientation.

2.2. Governance costs

Transaction cost economics maintains that complex, bilateral contracts are invariably incomplete. Contingencies will thus arise for which the appropriate adaptations have not been expressly agreed upon ex ante. Although it is always in the mutual interest of the parties to adapt efficiently, the disposition of the gain must be resolved. As compared with unified ownership of the two stages, autonomous ownership normally gives rise to more intensive, self-interested bargaining over the allocation of the adaptive gains.

Added contract execution costs thereby result. Autonomous ownership may therefore forego some potentially beneficial adaptations altogether. The upshot is that internal organization enjoys a progressive governance cost advantage over market organization as the condition of asset specificity deepens.

These differential costs of adaptation (expressed as a function of asset specificity) are not, however, the only transaction costs that distinguish firm and market. Also important, though less well developed, are the differential incentive and bureaucratic costs of firm and market organization. As developed elsewhere [Williamson (1985, ch. 6)], markets are extraordinary institutions for delivering high-powered incentives. Best efforts to preserve market-like incentives (e.g., transfer pricing and appropriability rules) within unified ownership notwithstanding, internal organization unavoidably experiences incentive degradation. Also, internal organization experiences a series of bureaucratic distortions (management excesses, investment renewal biases, and the like) as compared with market organization. Both of these incentive and bureaucratic effects, moreover, are relatively independent of the condition of asset specificity.

Accordingly, whereas internal organization is at a transaction cost disadvantage to the market where asset specificity is slight, this disadvantage decreases and is eventually reversed as the condition of asset specificity deepens. This is shown in fig. 1 by the curve (ΔG), which shows the transaction cost difference between firm and market organization as asset specificity increases (for a given level of output). The intercept (β_0) is positive and the curve has a negative slope throughout.

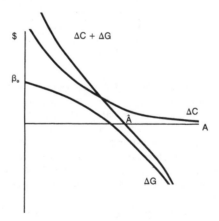

Fig. 1. Heuristic model.

2.3. Production costs

It can be and has been argued that firm and market are identical in production cost respects. To be sure, outside procurement might appear to be favored if a firm's needs for a good or service are not sufficient to support a plant of minimum efficient scale. The same would appear to be true for items that experience economies of scope. But since the firm can always realize the same scale or scope economies as an outside supplier, by selling product that exceeds its own needs on the market, the firm need not and presumably will not experience production cost diseconomies of either kind.

This argument assumes, however, that a firm can sell to others, including, often, its rivals, as effectively as can an independent supplier. It also ignores the possibility that the incentive and bureaucratic costs referred to above have cumulative features. Upon making allowance for these, the firm would appear to be at a production cost disadvantage in relation to the market.

These production cost diseconomies, however, are also a function of asset specificity. The diseconomies are arguably great where asset specificity is slight, since the outside supplier here can produce to the needs of a wide variety of buyers using the very same (large scale) production technology. As asset specificity increases, however, the outside supplier specializes his investment in relation to the buyer. This is the meaning of non-redeployability. As these assets become highly unique, moreover, the firm can essentially replicate the investments of an outside supplier without penalty. The firm and market production technology thus become indistinguishable at this stage.

Production cost differences between firm and market, whereby the firm experiences a production cost penalty when asset specificity is slight but these cost differences asymptotically approach zero as asset specificity becomes great, are shown by the curve ΔC in fig. 1. As with the ΔG curve, the ΔC curve is drawn for a fixed level of output.

2.4. Combined effects

Total cost differences of firm and market organization are given by the vertical sum, $\Delta C + \Delta G$. This curve is positive initially but has a negative slope throughout and becomes zero at $\hat{A}$. The heuristic model of firm and market organization thus supports the following general conclusions: (1) market organization is the least cost mode if the optimal value of asset specificity is small; (2) internal organization is the least cost mode if the optimal value of asset specificity is great; and (3) neither mode enjoys a significant advantage (that is, it doesn't matter much which mode is chosen) for asset specificity values in the neighborhood of $\hat{A}$.

These results are obtained, however, by assuming that both modes produce the same level of output and that the optimal level of asset specificity is the same for each. What happens when these simplifying assumptions are relaxed? More generally, what happens when the above relations of firm and market organization are digested in a maximizing framework of the more familiar neoclassical kind?

3. The main model

The cost differences discussed above are responsible for the reduced form geometry shown in fig. 1. The main model examined here is in the same spirit. The resulting models are somewhat more general, however. We examine their first-order maximizing and comparative statics properties. It will facilitate the argument to assume initially that firm and market have the identical production cost technology. This assumption will be relaxed in section 3.2. Demand features of asset specificity are reserved for section 4.

3.1. Common production technology

Revenue is given by $R = R(X)$, and production costs of market and internal procurement are assumed to be given by the relation

$$C = C(X, A; \alpha), \qquad C_X > 0, \quad C_A < 0, \quad C_{XA} < 0,$$

where the parameter α is a shift parameter, a higher value of α yielding greater cost reducing consequences to asset specificity,

$$C_{A\alpha} < 0, \qquad C_{X\alpha} < 0.$$

Asset specificity is assumed to be available at the constant per unit cost of γ. The neoclassical profit expression corresponding to this statement of revenue and production costs is given by

$$\pi^*(X, A; \alpha) = R(X) - C(X, A; \alpha) - \gamma A.$$

Governance costs are conspiciously omitted from this profit relation, there being no provision for such costs in the neoclassical statement of the problem.

We assume that this function is globally concave. At an interior maximum the decision variables X^*, A^* are determined from the zero marginal profit conditions

$$\pi_X^*(X, A; \alpha) = 0, \qquad \pi_A^*(X, A; \alpha) = 0.$$

Consider now the governance costs of internal and market organization.

Let the superscripts i denote internal and m denote market organization. Governance cost expressions congruent with the cost differences described above are given by

$$G^i = \beta + V(A), \qquad \beta > 0, \quad V_A > 0,$$

$$G^m = W(A), \qquad W_A > 0,$$

where $W_A > V_A$, evaluated at common A.

The corresponding profit expressions for internal market procurement in the face of positive governance costs are

$$\pi^i = R(X) - C(X, A; \alpha) - \gamma A - (\beta + V(A)),$$

$$\pi^m = R(X) - C(X, A; \alpha) - \gamma A' - W(A).$$

The zero marginal profit conditions for internal procurement are

$$\pi^i_X = R_X - C_X = 0, \qquad \pi^i_A = -C_A - \gamma - V_A = 0.$$

Those for market procurement are

$$\pi^m_X = R_X - C_X = 0, \qquad \pi^m_A = -C_A - \gamma - W_A = 0.$$

In each instance, therefore, optimal output, given asset specificity, is obtained by setting marginal revenue equal to the marginal costs of production, while optimal asset specificity, given output, is chosen to minimize the sum of production and governance costs.

Given that $\pi^*_{XA} = -C_{XA} > 0$, the neoclassical locus of optimal output given asset specificity and the corresponding locus of optimal asset specificity given output will bear the relations shown by $\pi^*_X = 0$ and $\pi^*_A = 0$ in fig. 2. The corresponding loci for internal and market organization are also shown. Inasmuch as the zero marginal profit expressions for output for all three statements of the maximand are identical, the loci $\pi^i_X = 0$ and $\pi^m_X = 0$ track $\pi^* = 0$ exactly. The zero marginal profit expressions for asset specificity, however, differ. Given that $W_A > V_A > 0$, the locus $\pi^m_A = 0$ is everywhere below $\pi^i_A = 0$, which in turn is below $\pi^*_A = 0$. Accordingly, we observe that profit maximizing values of X and A for these three statements of the optimization problem bear the following relation to each other: $X^* > X^i > X^m$ and $A^* > A^i > A^m$. The output effects are indirect or induced effects, attributable to shifts in the zero marginal profit asset specificity loci.

Of course, the X^* and A^* choices are purely hypothetical since, in reality, a zero transaction cost condition is not a member of the feasible set. The

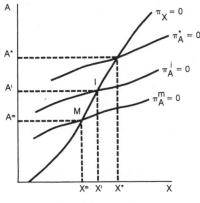

Fig. 2. For $\pi_{XA} > 0$.

relevant choices thus reduce to using input combinations *I* under internal procurement or *M* under market procurement. An immediate implication is that if the firm were operating in two identical markets and was constrained to buy in one and to make in the other, it would sell more goods of a more distinctive kind in the region where it produced to its own needs.

Ordinarily, however, the firm will not be so constrained but will choose to make or buy according to which mode offers the greatest profit in each region. Fig. 3 shows profit as a function of asset specificity, the choice of output assumed to be optimal for each value of *A*. Whereas there is a family of π^i curves, one for each value of the bureaucratic cost parameter β, there is

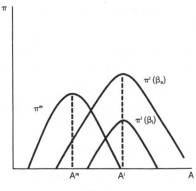

Fig. 3

only a single π^m curve. Which mode is favored depends on which has the highest peak. This is the internal mode for $\beta = \beta_0$ but the market mode for $\beta = \beta_1$, where $\beta_1 > \beta_0$. The optimal value of A and X depends only on the mode selected and not on β, however, since β does not influence the marginal conditions.

The comparative statics ramifications of the production cost parameter α are more central to our interests. Applications of the envelope theorem reveal that

$$\pi_\alpha^m = -C_\alpha(X^m, A^m; \alpha), \qquad \pi_\alpha^i = -C_\alpha(X^i, A^i; \alpha).$$

Inasmuch as $X^i > X^m$ and $A^i > A^m$, it follows from our earlier production cost assumptions that $\pi_\alpha^i > \pi_\alpha^m$. In other words, as asset specificity has greater cost reducing impact, internal organization is progressively favored.

3.2. Production cost differences

Consider now the case, to which we referred earlier and is arguably the more realistic, where the firm is unable to aggregate demands and sell product that exceeds its own demands without penalty. Let $H(X, A)$ denote the production cost disadvantage per unit of output associated with internal organization. The production costs of the two modes then are

$$C^m = C(X, A; \alpha), \qquad C^i = C(X, A; \alpha) + H(X, A)X.$$

Assume that $H_X < 0$ and $H_A < 0$ but that $H(X, A)X$ is positive and asymptotically approaches zero as X and A approach infinity. Denote the marginal production cost disadvantage by $M(X, A) = H_X(X, A)X + H(X, A)$.

The analysis depends on the way in which the total production cost disadvantage experienced by internal organization changes for outputs within the relevant range. At low levels of output, decreasing unit cost disadvantages will normally be attended by an increasing total cost, whence $M(X, A) > 0$. Beyond some threshold level of output, however, the total production cost disadvantage of internal organization will begin to decline. Indeed, as the firm progressively increases in relation to the size of the market, the production cost disadvantage presumably approaches zero – since firm and market have access to identical economies of scale as a monopoly condition evolves. Accordingly, $M(X, A) < 0$ once this threshold is crossed.

Our main results are strengthened within the (large output) range where $M(X, A) < 0$: $X^m < X^i$; $A^m < A^i$; and $\pi_\alpha^i > \pi_\alpha^m$. Within the (small output) range, however, where $M_X > 0$, the marginal production cost disadvantage of internal organization and the marginal governance cost disadvantage of market procurement operate in opposite directions. An unambiguous ordering of optimal output and asset specificity is not possible in terms of the above-described qualitative features of the problem in this instance. An anomaly thus arises that was not evident in the heuristic presentation in section 2.

4. Demand effects

Another possibility is that asset specificity yields design benefits but has no direct effect on production costs. Thus suppose that a die can be shaped to produce a very special effect (a tailfin on an automobile), a semi-special effect (in that the die can be redeployed, albeit at reduced value), or a standard product. Production cost differences may be (and will be assumed to be) insubstantial. The main effects take the form of demand shifts and governance cost changes.

The three profit expressions corresponding to this statement of the problem are

$$\pi^* = R(X, A; \delta) - C(X) - \gamma A,$$

$$\pi^m = R(X, A; \delta) - C(X) - \gamma A - W(A),$$

$$\pi^i = R(X, A; \delta) - C(X) - \gamma A - (\beta + V(A)),$$

where $R_A > 0$, $R_{XA} > 0$, $R_{A\delta} > 0$, $R_{X\delta} > 0$ and δ is a demand shift parameter.

Again, the locus of optimal X given A will be identical for each of these profit expressions, while the locus of optimal A given X will move progressively down from neoclassical to internal to market in that order. The output and asset specificity relations reported under the main model are thus preserved. Increases in the demand enhancement parameter δ, moreover, have the expected effect: internal organization is relatively favored over market organization as the demand enhancement effects of added specificity increase. The differential advantage of internal organization is explained by the respective marginal governance cost penalties that accrue to asset specificity under firm and market modes.

5. Conclusions

The foregoing demonstrates that conventional demand and production cost analysis can be augmented to include governance cost features. The comparative institutional ramifications of the two can then be explored. The apparent gap between the orthodox theory of the firm and the transaction cost economics approach to the study of firm and market structures is thus narrowed as a consequence.

Extensions to this approach are, moreover, possible. A progressive operationalization of the economics of transaction costs will thereby result. A high priority for further research should be an assessment of comparative transaction costs within more specific models of organizational choice.

With reference to consumer welfare, the main implication of the argument is this: firms that decide for profitability reasons to integrate (produce to their own needs) will produce more and realize lower costs than if they were constrained by public policy to procure from the market. Note in this connection that we treat all costs – production and governance, market and internal – as social costs. Market governance costs do not therefore reflect rents but rather are added costs due to maladaption [being off the 'shifting contract curve', in the language of Masahiko Aoki (1984)] and haggling costs. These are real costs for which full social cost valuation is warranted.

The models and the above welfare argument make *no provision*, however, *for strategic behavior*. Strategic incentives to integrate intrude where integration by a firm that is large in relation to the market, and for which integration promises little in the way of cost savings, nevertheless disadvantage actual and potential rivals – because the remaining market is too small to support competitive supply and rivals experience cost penalties should they produce to their own needs [Williamson (1974)]. In circumstances, therefore, where the preconditions for strategic behavior are satisfied – namely, in dominant firms or highly concentrated industries where the condition of entry is difficult – decisions to integrate cannot be accepted with equanimity but need also to be assessed with reference to their strategic consequences. The difficult cases, of course, are those where vertical integration economies and entry impediments are both non-trivial. Integration, however, that gives rise to negligible economies (maybe even, in consideration of the adverse incentive and bureaucratic cost consequences of internal organization, diseconomies) and is responsible for severe entry impediments is plainly problematic if not outright antisocial.

Note that we treat asset specificity as being all of a kind. In fact, asset specificity takes at least four different forms: site, physical, human, and dedicated assets [Williamson (1983)]. These different forms of asset specificity, moreover, have somewhat different ramifications for the economics of organization. The empirical tests discussed below do not make these distinctions and thus can be further refined.

The crude argument is instructive nevertheless. It predicts that vertical integration will be more common where (1) cost savings that accrue to asset specificity are great, (2) design features deter asset redeployment to alternative uses, (3a) economies of scale are small or, (3b) as among firms of different sizes, that larger firms will be more integrated than smaller, and (4) bureaucratic cost consequences of internal organization are less severe. These are all plausible propositions and appear to be consonant with the data –

although these matters have only recently come under review and the data need much more systematic development. We nevertheless submit that corroborative support for each of the propositions can be found – and in some cases is bountiful. The following are illustrative:

(1)   Forward integration out of manufacturing into distribution is much more common for durable products that require idiosyncratic knowledge of product attributes, in order effectively to sell and service an item, than it is for products which lack these features. Human asset specificity in sales and service thus favors forward integration out of manufacturing into distribution. American experience at the turn of the century appears to correspond with this prediction [Porter and Livesay (1971), Chandler (1977), Williamson (1985, ch. 5)].

(2)   Rolling stock that is easily redeployable among shippers is owned by carriers while that which is specialized to shipper needs and cannot be redeployed except at great sacrifice is owned by shippers [Palay (1984)]. This is also consonant with the hypothesis.

(3)   Casual observation suggests, though the data, to our knowledge, are not very well developed in this respect, that larger firms are more integrated than smaller rivals. [See Monteverde and Teece (1982) for support in the automobile industry.]

(4)   Social scientists have not given a great deal of attention to bureaucratic costs. Comparative assessments are especially few, which is especially regrettable.[5] Alfred Chandler has nevertheless interpreted the shift from the functional (or U-form) to the multidivisional (or M-form) organization as being driven in part by the bureaucratic distortions in the former that are alleviated by the latter. This is responsible for the M-form hypothesis: *'the organization and operation of the large enterprise along the lines of the M-form favors goal pursuit and least-cost behavior more nearly associated with the neoclassical profit maximization hypothesis than does the U-form organizational alternative'* [Williamson (1970, p. 134)]. Although the evidence is not extensive, it appears again to be broadly corroborative [Armour and Teece (1978), Steer and Cable (1978)].

We conclude with a caveat: the argument throughout has emphasized polar firm and market choices. This facilitates the analysis, but it ignores an important class of hybrid modes of organization – of which joint ventures, franchising, and a variety of complex forms of 'relational contracting' are examples. Recent studies of economic organization disclose that these hybrid modes are much more important than had hitherto been realized [MacNeil

---

[5]The sociology literature often documents managerial discretion, but rarely in a comparative institutional way. [An example is Dalton (1959).] Thus if all forms of organization are subject to identical distortions in relation to a hypothetical ideal, then none afford relief. Distortions that are irremediable lack comparative institutional significance.

(1974), Goldberg (1976), Klein (1980), Joskow (1985), Williamson (1985)]. Future descriptive, theoretical, and empirical studies of economic organization will presumably make more adequate provision for these hybrid modes.

References

Alchian, Armen, 1984, Specificity, specialization, and coalitions, Journal of Institutional and Theoretical Economics 140, 34–49.

Anderson, Erin and David Schmittlein, 1984, Integration of the sales force: An empirical examination, The Rand Journal of Economics 15, 385–395.

Aoki, Masahiko, 1984, The cooperative game theory of the firm (Oxford University Press, London).

Arrow, Kenneth, 1985, Informational structure of the firm, American Economic Review 75, 303–307.

Ben-Porath, Yoram, 1980, The F-connection: Families, friends, and firms and the organization of exchange, Population and Development Review 6, 1–30.

Chandler, Alfred, 1966, Strategy and structure (Doubleday, New York).

Chandler, Alfred, 1977, The visible hand (Belknap Press, Cambridge).

Dalton, Melville, 1959, Men who manage (Wiley, New York).

Goldberg, Victor, 1976, Toward an expanded economic theory of contract, Journal of Economic Issues 10, 45–61.

Grossman, Sanford and Oliver Hart, 1984, The costs and benefits of ownership: A theory of vertical integration, Unpublished manuscript (University of Chicago, Chicago, IL).

Hayek, Friedrich, 1967, Studies in philosophy, politics, and economics (Routledge and Kegan Paul, London).

Joskow, Paul, 1985, Vertical integration and long term contracts: The case of coal burning electric generating plants, Journal of Law, Economics, and Organization 1, 25–64.

Joskow, Paul and Richard Schmalensee, 1983, Markets for power (MIT Press, Cambridge, MA).

Klein, Benjamin, 1980, Transaction cost determinants for 'unfair' contractual arrangements, American Economic Review 70, 356–362.

Klein, Benjamin, Robert Crawford and Armen Alchian, 1978, Vertical integration, appropriable rents, and the competitive contracting process, Journal of Law and Economics 21, 297–326.

MacNeil, Ian, 1974, The many futures of contracts, Southern California Law Review 47, 691–816.

Masten, Scott, 1982, Transaction costs, institutional choice, and the theory of the firm, Unpublished Ph.D. dissertation (University of Pennsylvania, Philadelphia, PA).

Masten, Scott, 1984, The organization of production: Evidence from the aerospace industry, Journal of Law and Economics 27, 403–418.

Monteverde, Kirk and David Teece, 1982, Supplier switching costs and vertical integration in the automobile industry, Bell Journal of Economics 12, 206–213.

Palay, Thomas, 1984, Comparative institutional economics: The governance of rail freight contracting, Journal of Legal Studies 13, 265–288.

Palay, Thomas, 1985, The avoidance of regulatory constraints: The use of informal contracts, Journal of Law, Economics, and Organization 1, 140–162.

Pollak, Robert, 1985, A transaction cost approach to households, Journal of Economic Literature 23, 581–608.

Porter, Glenn and Harold Livesay, 1971, Merchants and manufacturers (Johns Hopkins University Press, Baltimore, MD).

Stuckey, John, 1983, Vertical integration and joint ventures in the international aluminum industry (Harvard University Press, Cambridge, MA).

Walker, Gordon and David Weber, 1984, Transaction cost approach to component make or buy decisions, Administrative Science Quarterly 29, 373–391.

Williamson, Oliver, 1970, Corporate control and business behavior (Prentice-Hall, Englewood Cliffs, NJ).

Williamson, Oliver, 1971, The vertical integration of production: Market failure considerations, American Economic Review 61, 112–123.

Williamson, Oliver, 1975, Markets and hierarchies: Analysis and antitrust implications (Free Press, New York).

Williamson, Oliver, 1976, Franchise bidding for natural monopolies – in general and with respect to CATV, Bell Journal of Economics 7, 73–104.

Williamson, Oliver, 1979, Transaction-cost economics: The governance of contractual relations, Journal of Law and Economics 22, 233–261.

Williamson, Oliver, 1983, Credible commitments: Using hostages to support exchange, American Economic Review 73, 519–540.

Williamson, Oliver, 1985, The economic institutions of capitalism (Free Press, New York).

[17]

RAND Journal of Economics
Vol. 32, No. 3, Autumn 2001
pp. 387–407

Incentives versus transaction costs: a theory of procurement contracts

Patrick Bajari*

and

Steven Tadelis*

Inspired by facts from the private-sector construction industry, we develop a model that explains many stylized facts of procurement contracts. The buyer in our model incurs a cost of providing a comprehensive design and is faced with a tradeoff between providing incentives and reducing ex post transaction costs due to costly renegotiation. We show that cost-plus contracts are preferred to fixed-price contracts when a project is more complex. We briefly discuss how fixed-price or cost-plus contracts might be preferred to other incentive contracts. Finally, our model provides some microfoundations for ideas from Transaction Cost Economics.

1. Introduction

■ The procurement problem has attracted much attention in the economics literature. The main focus of this literature has been on procurement by the public sector, in part because of its sheer importance to the economy: procurement by federal, state, and local government accounts for at least 10% of gross domestic product in the United States. (Recent books are Laffont and Tirole (1993) and McAfee and McMillan (1987), which include references to many other studies of government procurement.) Many private-sector transactions are also governed by procurement contracts. Prominent examples include electronics components, custom software, automobile production, and building construction.

Modern economic theories of procurement use mechanism design to model the procurement problem as one of *ex ante* asymmetric information coupled with moral hazard. (See Laffont and Tirole (1993) for a summary of this literature.) Namely, the seller has information about production costs that the buyer does not have. The buyer *screens* the seller by offering a *menu of contracts* from which the seller selects a particular contract, thus revealing his private information.

---
* Stanford University; bajari@stanford.edu, stadelis@stanford.edu.

We thank Tim Bresnahan, Avner Greif, Oliver Hart, John Kennan, Eric Maskin, Antonio Rangel, Ilya Segal, Curtis Taylor, Mike Whinston, and especially Paul Milgrom for insightful discussions. We have also benefited from comment; by Igal Hendel, Chad Jones, Jon Levin, Scott Masten, Preston McAfee, John McMillan, Eric Rasmusen, Michael Riordan, Eric Van den Steen, Oliver Williamson, Jeff Zwiebel, and many seminar participants. We are grateful to Ed Schlee for detecting an error in a previous version of the article. Comments by Editor Joseph Harrington and two referees were very helpful. Financial support from the Stanford Institute for Economic Policy Research and from the NSF (grant nos. SES-0112106, SES-0122747, and SES-0079876) is gratefully acknowledged. This article stemmed from a previous working paper titled "Procurement Contracts: Fixed Price vs. Cost Plus."

This literature is normative and attempts to prescribe how the procurement problem *should* be addressed under the assumption that *ex ante* asymmetric information is the main concern.

By contrast, the descriptive engineering and construction management literature (summarized in Section 2) suggests that menus of contracts are not used. Instead, the vast majority of contracts are variants of simple fixed-price (FP) and cost-plus (C+) contracts. (In fixed-price contracts, the buyer offers the seller a prespecified price for completing the project. A cost-plus contract does not specify a price, but rather reimburses the contractor for costs plus a stipulated fee.) While carefully examining the literature and speaking with industry participants, we have found little evidence that either the contractor or the buyer has private information at the onset of a procurement project. They both, however, share uncertainty about many important design changes that occur *after* the contract is signed and production begins, such as design failures, unanticipated site and environmental conditions, and changes in regulatory requirements.

An illustrative example of the significance of *ex post* adaptation is the building of the Getty Center Art Museum in Los Angeles, which is a 24-acre, $1 billion facility that took over 8 years to construct. (See *Engineering News-Record*, 1994 and 1997.) The project design had to be changed due to site conditions that were hard to anticipate. The geology of the project included canyons, slide planes, and earthquake fault lines, which posed numerous challenges for the team of architects and contractors. For instance, contractors "hit a slide" and unexpectedly moved 75,000 cubic yards of earth. More severely, in 1994 an earthquake struck. Cracks in the steel welds of the building's frame caused the contractors to reassess the adequacy of the seismic design standards that were used. The project design also had to be altered due to the regulatory environment—107 items had to be added to the building's conditional use permit. These problems were very hard to predict, both for the buyer and the contractor. However, it seems reasonable that once problems arose, the contractor had superior information about the costs and methods to implement changes.

These observations suggest that the procurement problem is primarily one of *ex post adaptations* rather than *ex ante screening*. While it is probably true that there is some asymmetric information about costs before the contract is signed, the choice of contract may not be the mechanism that deals with such asymmetries. Other mechanisms seem to be important in solving the adverse-selection problem. These include competitive bidding, reputation, and bonding companies that insure the buyer against default by the contractor. Accordingly, this article tries to shed light on the economic forces that determine the choice of procurement contracts, and it is motivated by two specific questions. First, if one restricts attention to FP and C+ contracts, when should each type of contract be used? Second, what can explain the widespread use of these two simple contracts?

To answer these questions we develop a simple model (Section 3) that formalizes the procurement problem and is helpful for organizing thoughts. We ignore *ex ante* hidden information and concentrate on problems of adaptation when the initial design is *endogenously incomplete*. Our buyer wishes to procure a product from a seller, where the latter can exert cost-reducing effort that is not contractible. The buyer provides the seller with an *ex ante* design of the product. The more complete the design, the lower the likelihood that both parties will need to renegotiate changes *ex post*. A more complete *ex ante* design, however, imposes higher *ex ante* costs on the buyer. When renegotiation occurs, the seller has private information about the costs of changes to the original design.

Our central analysis in Section 4 compares FP with C+ contracts. We show that simple projects (which are cheap to design) will be procured using FP contracts and will be accompanied by high levels of design completeness (that is, a low probability that adaptations are needed). More complex projects will be procured using C+ contracts and will be accompanied by low levels of design completeness (that is, a high probability that adaptations are needed). This is consistent with the stylized facts that we have found in the construction industry and with facts from other industries as well. We then offer some insight as to why FP and C+ contracts are so prevalent. We point at possible discontinuities (or nonconvexities) in procurement that are plausible explanations for the prevalence of extreme and simple compensation schemes.

The intuition for our central result stems from a tension between providing *ex ante* incentives and avoiding *ex post* transaction costs due to costly renegotiation. Clearly, high incentives (FP) reduce costs, but we show that these same incentives dissipate *ex post* surplus due to renegotiation under asymmetric information. Low incentives (C+), however, do not erode *ex post* surplus but obviously discourage cost-saving efforts. Thus, our model demonstrates a link between *ex ante* incentives and *ex post* renegotiation costs. This is consistent with the documented facts that demonstrate a significant difference in disputes under these two contracts.

Our model is novel in that it treats the choice both of incentives and of design (contractual) incompleteness as *endogenous* variables in the procurement problem. Our analysis demonstrates how the empirical regularities in which these contracting components seem to move together are consistent with the complexity of the project being procured. In Section 5 we discuss how our analysis may shed light on another procurement problem, the celebrated "make-or-buy" decision. Our insights resonate with themes that are central to Transaction Cost Economics (TCE), pioneered by Williamson (1975, 1985). In fact, Williamson expresses the idea that low incentives are good to accommodate *ex post* adaptations and writes (1985, p. 140) that "low powered incentives have well-known adaptability advantages. That, after all, is what commends cost-plus contracting. But, such advantages are not had without cost—which explains why cost-plus contracting is embraced reluctantly." We contribute to the TCE literature by providing a microfoundation for the different transaction/governance costs associated with weak incentives (internal production) and those with strong incentives (market procurement). By focusing on the effect of design-intensive attributes of the product (complexity), our model implies testable predictions that are consistent with several empirical investigations that evaluate TCE.

All proofs are in Appendix A.

2. The building construction industry

■ **Overview.** In 1992, there were 2 million establishments in the U.S. construction industry that completed $528 billion of work. These firms directly employed 4.7 million workers and had a payroll of $118 billion (U.S. Department of Commerce, 1992a, 1992b, 1992c). In 1997, the construction industry comprised 8% of U.S. GDP, and worldwide the construction industry was a $3.2 trillion market (*Engineering News-Record*, 1998).

In general contracting, there is a division of labor between creating the technical specifications, drawings, and designs for the project and the actual construction. The buyer typically first hires an architectural firm to design the project, and the architect often helps the buyer to monitor the contractor's performance while the project is being completed.[1]

Since every construction project is unique, the coordination and management of change are important aspects of successful project management. For example, coordinating construction work at the Getty Center was an extremely complex task. There were over 240 subcontractors and between 900 and 1,200 workers at any given time performing approximately $100 million per year of construction. The general contractor created a special division of 75 managers and supervisors to oversee construction. The general contractor was brought into the contract four years before construction even began, to help in project planning. Access to the project site posed a major and costly coordination problem. Since there was only one road to the site, a traffic coordinator scheduled access. Traffic was described as a "logistical nightmare." Long backlogs of ready-mix trucks were not uncommon since, in addition to deliveries to specialty contractors, 260,000 cubic yards of concrete were poured. (See *Engineering News-Record*, 1994, 1997.)

An important cost of change is the disruption of the schedule between the general contractor, subcontractors, and suppliers. The general contractor must carefully coordinate the work of many

---

[1] Other possible organizational forms include design-and-build contracts, force accounting, and construction management, among others. For general descriptions of the building industry, contracting practices and project management, see Bartholomew (1998), Clough and Sears (1994), Finkel (1997), Hinze (1993), and U.S. Department of Commerce (1992a, 1992b, and 1992c).

subcontractors and the deliveries of material suppliers. Schedules are highly interrelated because building construction needs to proceed sequentially—a delay on the part of one subcontractor or supplier can have a domino effect throughout the project. It is our understanding that the costs of coordination are better known to the contractor, which motivates our modelling approach of the renegotiation stage (Section 3).

□   **Construction contracts.** There is a surprising amount of standardization in the contracts used in building construction. The American Institute of Architects (AIA) and the Associated General Contractors (AGC) provide standard forms of contract that are used by many buyers as general conditions for private-sector building. These documents have the advantage that the central clauses are well understood in the industry, and there exists a significant body of case law on the interpretation of the contract conditions. While there are many forms of alternative contractual arrangements used in the industry, cost-plus and fixed-price contracting appear to be the most commonly used.[2] Fixed-price contracts in the private sector tend to be awarded through competitive bidding, while cost-plus contracts are frequently negotiated between a buyer and contractor. Occasionally there are cost incentives in cost-plus contracts that reward (or penalize) contractors for having actual costs below (or above) a cost target that is set at the start of the contract. Cost-incentive contracts are not the industry standard because of difficulties with implementing incentives in the face of changes. A leading problem is the difficulty in establishing fair and equitable cost targets. Any changes due to design failure, buyer priorities, goals, or other factors beyond the contractor's control will require a renegotiation of incentive provisions and cost targets. As a consequence, the working relationship between the buyer and contractor can be spoiled. Ashley and Workman (1986) claim that at a minimum, project engineering must be 40–60% complete to establish reasonable cost and schedule targets. In a survey of contractors and buyers, Ashley and Workman report that only 12% of the respondents use contracts with cost incentives. They also report that incentives on time-to-completion, commonly referred to as liquidated damages, appear to be more commonly used than incentives on costs. A typical set of documents in the contract includes, but is not limited to, bidding documents, general conditions of the contract, specifications, drawings, and reports of investigations of physical site conditions. The general conditions define the roles of the buyer, architect, and engineer, describe the warranty, provide provisions for dispute resolution, outline procedures for adjusting the design and how the payment will be changed, among other provisions. The drawings are also considered a part of the contract documents. The drawings should be sufficiently clear and accurate so that if the contractor conforms to them, a well-constructed product will arise.

□   **Change orders.** The courts have recognized that contractors are entitled to fair compensation for changes to the plans and specifications in a fixed-price contract. For example, Sweet (1994) discusses the case of *Watson Lumber Company* v. *Guennewig* argued in the Appellate Court of Illinois. Watson Lumber Company, a building contractor, was awarded compensation for extras in a building contract for William and Mary Guennewig. In its decision the court stated:

In a building and construction situation, both the owner and the contractor have interests that must be kept in mind and protected. The contractor should not be required to furnish items that were clearly beyond and outside of what the parties originally agreed that he would furnish. The owner has a right to full and good faith performance of the contractor's promise, but has no right to expand the nature and extent of the contractor's obligation. On the other hand, the owner has a right to know the nature and extent of his promise, and a right to know the extent of his liabilities before they are incurred.

Therefore, in a fixed-price contract, the general contractor will not be willing to perform duties beyond those to which he is contractually bound without additional compensation. Two contractual procedures used to adjust compensation in fixed-price contracts are called *change orders* and *change directives*.

---

[2] A commonly used fixed-price contract is AIA Document A101, and a commonly used cost-plus contract is AIA Document A111. Variants of fixed-price contracts occasionally used are unit-price contracts, a series of fixed-price contracts and fixed-price with escalation. (See Business Roundtable (1987), Bartholomew (1998), Clough and Sears (1994), Hinze (1993), and Sweet (1994) for an overview).

A change order is a written amendment to the contract that describes additional work the contractor must undertake and the compensation he will receive. AIA document A201 defines a change order as a

written instrument prepared by the Architect and signed by the Owner, Contractor and Architect, stating their agreement upon all of the following: (1) a change in the work; (2) the amount of the adjustment in the Contract sum, if any; and (3) the extent of the adjustment in the contract time, if any.

The work and the conditions in a change order are generally determined by bargaining between the buyer, contractor, and architect.

If the parties are unable to reach an agreement, in many contracts the architect has the power to issue a change directive. A change directive is described as

a written order prepared by the Architect and signed by the Owner and Architect, directing a change in the Work and Stating a proposed basis for adjustment... A construction Change Directive shall be used in the absence of total agreement on the terms of a Change order.

If the contract amount cannot be agreed to by bargaining between the parties, the contractor may be paid by what is called *force accounting*, which is described as follows:

If the contractor does not respond promptly or disagrees with the method for adjustment in the Contract sum, the method and the adjustment shall be determined by the Architect on the basis of reasonable expenditures and savings of those performing the Work attributable to the change, including, in the case of an increase in the Contract Sum, a reasonable allowance for overhead and profit.

(For more details on change orders, directives, and force accounting, see AIA document A201.)

Change directives give the buyer significant bargaining power in the case of a dispute, and they may be viewed as the threat point in the bargaining process over compensation for changes. This clause gives the buyer the right to reimburse the contractor at cost for all change orders (although in many cases, allowances for profit and overhead are included). In practice, however, the buyer may not choose to do this because of the costs involved. First, writing construction change directives is time consuming and requires considerable administrative effort. Second, excessive changes may lead to indirect costs, such as scheduling problems between the general contractor and subcontractors. Such time delays may be a source of liability for the buyer. Last, a buyer may acquire a reputation for being difficult to work with, causing higher construction costs for future projects. All this implies that under fixed-price contracting, performing changes is accompanied by frictions between the contractor and the buyer, which is a central motivation for our model of renegotiation.

□   **Empirical evidences on contractual arrangements.** There is ample evidence that *ex post* changes are the rule rather than the exception. Hester, Kuprenas, and Chang (1991) study change orders and other forms of disputes in construction projects and document the value of changes as a percentage of the total contract price, as well as the sources of change across several studies of fixed-price contracting. Defective plans and specifications, changes in scope, and unpredictable site conditions account for many of the necessary changes to the original design. In many cases these changes have significant effects on the total costs of the project.

Ibbs et al. (1986) quantify the impact of 96 different contractual clauses on project performance in building construction. The study consisted of a survey of buyers and contractors for 36 building construction projects. The study claimed to verify the conventional wisdoms about cost-plus and fixed-price contracting that are summarized in Table 1.[3]

The first two facts should be no surprise to economists: the allocation of risk is trivial, and a simple multitask model can explain how cost-reducing incentives adversely affect quality (see Holmström and Milgrom, 1991). The other points, however, have not, to the best of our knowledge, been analyzed in the economics literature. Namely, changes are more easily agreed upon under

---

[3] The dataset collected by the researchers was quite unique, but the usefulness of the analysis is limited by two major factors. First, the hypothesis testing used by these researchers does not explicitly account for the fact that the choice of contractual form is endogenous. Second, in collecting the data, the researchers signed confidentiality arrangements with the firms. These arrangements prohibit us from viewing the survey responses tabulated by survey respondents.

TABLE 1	Comparing FP with C+ Contracts in Construction	
	Fixed Price	Cost Plus
Risk allocation mainly on	Contractor	Buyer
Incentives for quality	Less	More
Buyer administration	Less	More
Good to minimize	Costs	Schedule
Documentation efforts	More	Less
Flexibility for change	Less	More
Adversarial relationship	More	Less

C+ contracting, while FP contracts require the buyer to invest more in design and specification. This leads to an advantage of C+ contracting in that the design of the project and the construction of the project can take place simultaneously. This generally reduces total time to project completion but requires more administrative costs. (This is sometimes referred to as "fast-tracking" of the project.)

3. The model

■ **Project design.** Consider a buyer who wishes to procure an exogenously given project for her use, such as a production plant. This requires her to hire a contractor (or seller) who will perform the work according to the buyer's specifications. The buyer's value of the project is $v > 0$ (which is common knowledge) if the project is completed, and zero if not. The time horizon consists of three stages: In the first stage there is uncertainty about how to build the project given realizations that occur during construction. The buyer must supply the seller with a design, which is a specification of instructions that inform and guide the seller on how to proceed with production under different scenarios. Examples of contingencies in design can be (1) what type of foundations are needed given the type of soil, (2) what to do if the prices of alternative building materials change, (3) what air-conditioning system should be installed in case the current choice is discontinued, and (4) how to change plans in case a regulator passes restrictions such as "historic sites" or height limits. In the second stage a contractor is hired and construction begins. In the third stage the actual needs of the buyer are revealed, and the contractor proceeds with construction. In the event that the plans do not account for the realized needs, the parties can renegotiate from the specified status quo. This renegotiation process is modelled in a subsection below.

We proceed by developing a simple model of project complexity and design uncertainty that will motivate an operational reduced form. Let T be the number of states of nature that can occur *ex post*, and let $\pi_t > 0$ be the probability that state $t \in \{1, \ldots, T\}$ occurs (states that occur with zero probability are ignored). For example, a state of nature would include the type of foundation needed given the actual soil type, or the specifications of the air-conditioning system given the type of machinery that will be used in the completed building.

Each state must be *ex ante* specified to completely design the project, and we assume that the cost of specifying a state of nature is $k > 0$ regardless of the state of nature. We also assume that $\pi_t > \pi_{t+1}$ for all $t \in \{1, \ldots, T - 1\}$. These two assumptions imply that from a cost-benefit analysis it is better to first specify a design for state 1, then for 2, and so on. Keeping v fixed, a project is characterized by the pair $\langle T, \{\pi_t\}_{t=1}^{T} \rangle$.

Definition. Project $\langle T, \{\pi_t\}_{t=1}^{T} \rangle$ is *more complex* than project $\langle T', \{\pi_t'\}_{t=1}^{T} \rangle$ if

    (i) $T > T'$,

(ii) $\sum_{t=1}^{S} \pi_t < \sum_{t=1}^{S} \pi_t'$ for all $1 \leq S \leq T'$, and

(iii) $\forall S' < T', \exists S < T$ such that $\sum_{t=1}^{S'} \pi_t' = \sum_{t=1}^{S} \pi_t$.

Parts (i) and (ii) imply first-order stochastic dominance. Part (iii) captures the idea that a more complex project is a finer partition of the probabilities over states. This definition is a simple operational way of ordering projects along some scale of complexity, but it provides only a partial ordering over the possible space of projects. We restrict attention to a subset of this space for which condition (i) in the definition above implies conditions (ii) and (iii) and vice versa. This restriction implies that a project can be characterized only by the number of states, so that project T is more complex than project T' if and only if $T > T'$. Alternatively, if the project space is not restricted, our comparative statics will be defined over the relevant subset of ordered projects.

Consider a buyer who wishes to provide a design for project T to guarantee that the project is well specified with probability at least $\tau \in [0, 1]$. The cost of design can be written as the following value:

$$d(\tau, T) = \min_{S \in \{1, \dots, T\}} Sk \qquad \text{subject to } \sum_{t=1}^{S} \pi_t \geq \tau.$$

Lemma 1. $d(\tau, T)$ is nondecreasing in τ and T and exhibits increasing differences in (τ, T).

Proof. All proofs are found in the Appendix.

The economic implications are straightforward: First, for a given level of complexity, design costs are increasing in the probability that the project is well specified *ex post*. Second, the cost of guaranteeing a fixed probability of *ex post* specification is increasing in complexity. Finally, the more complex a project, the higher the marginal cost of increasing the probability of specification.

Using Lemma 1, we continue our analysis with a reduced-form model of project design as follows. Given the project complexity $T > 0$, the buyer chooses a design that is well specified with probability $\tau \in [0, 1]$. The cost of design is given by the function $d(\tau, T)$ that is increasing in T and τ and supermodular in T and τ. Thus, we hereafter treat T as a primitive exogenous parameter, τ as an endogenous choice variable, and $d(\tau, T)$ as the (derived) cost of design.

With probability τ the original design accurately describes the project, and if followed, it gives the buyer a value of v. With probability $1 - \tau$, however, the design fails and modifications are needed to obtain the full value of v. We make the extreme assumption that if the original design fails, and no design changes are made, then the buyer's valuation of the product built *per original design* is zero. This assumption simplifies the analysis and sets simple threat points for the renegotiation stage that follows.

Remark 1. This setup is easily generalized to projects that are given as distributions over a countable number of states, or a continuum. For a continuum, let $G_A(\cdot)$ and $G_B(\cdot)$ be two such distributions for projects A and B respectively. We say that project A is more complex than project B if and only if $G_A(\cdot)$ first-order stochastically dominates $G_B(\cdot)$, and the density is everywhere lower over the support where *both densities are positive*. Indeed, this will mean that $G_A(\cdot)$ has a "fatter" upper tail, and that more states need to be specified in order to achieve the same level of completeness.

Remark 2. Notice that due to our assumption that $\pi_t > \pi_{t+1}$, the increments in design costs are increasing in τ, which seems sensible from an engineering perspective. This is not convexity, since our derived $d(\tau, T)$ is a step function of τ. We will, however, treat this function as continuous in (τ, T) and convex in τ. Convexity is not needed for our comparative statics results, for which only increasing differences are required. Without convexity in τ we will have corner ("bang-bang") solutions, but the qualitative comparative statics will still hold.

Remark 3. A more realistic model of complexity and design uncertainty would account for realizations for which the original design is "close" to the actual needs. For example, without changes the original design will result in a payoff of $\gamma(\tau, T) \cdot v$, where $\gamma(\tau, T) < 1$ reflects the loss from not implementing changes. The gross benefit from renegotiation will then be $[1 - \gamma(\tau, T)]v$, which can easily be incorporated into the analysis. The shape of $\gamma(\tau, T)$ will have bearing on the meaning of complexity, which itself would have to be revisited to ensure a condition of increasing differences for $d(\tau, T)$. It is extremely interesting to fully characterize a general and more realistic model of project complexity and design uncertainty, but this is beyond the scope of the current article and is left for future research.

☐   **Construction and change orders.** Following design, a contractor is hired to build the project. We assume that the contractor engages in cost-reducing effort denoted by $e \geq 0$ that is not contractible. The technology is given by the product's cost function $c(e) \geq 0$, which is assumed to be decreasing and strictly convex in e (i.e., $c'(e) < 0$, $c''(e) > 0$). Given effort e, the cost of production *per original design* is perfectly known, but design changes will add noise, as described below. Effort imposes a private cost on the contractor denoted by $g(e) \geq 0$, which is assumed to be increasing and convex (i.e., $g'(e) > 0$, $g''(e) \geq 0$), and we assume that $g(0) = 0$. This specification leads to a standard moral hazard problem.

Design changes are implemented during construction if both parties agree to depart from the original design during renegotiation. (The renegotiation game is fully specified in a subsection below.) Recall that a change is needed if the initial design was inadequate, i.e., the realized state of nature was not specified in the design, which occurs with probability $1 - \tau$. In this case, "filling in" the design should be equivalent to specifying what to do for this particular state, at a cost of k. Aside from the cost of completing the design, the change itself entails production costs. We assume that the cost of change is *ex post* private information for the contractor and is equal to some value $m \in [0, v - k]$ that is distributed according to the cumulative distribution function $F(\cdot)$ (with density $f(\cdot) > 0$), which is common knowledge. Together with the assumption that the whole value v is lost unless renegotiation occurs, $m \leq v - k$ implies that it is always first-best optimal to describe and implement the change.

☐   **Contracting.** Following the discussion in Section 2, a contract includes two elements. The first is the *specifications, drawings, and reports*, which are summarized by τ. The second is a *compensation scheme*, $p(c)$, which defines a transfer from the buyer to the seller upon completion of the project. Since costs are verifiable in our model, we allow the compensation scheme to depend on c.

Note that if changes are not required, then contracting on costs c is equivalent to contracting on effort e, since there is a one-to-one correspondence between $c(e)$ and e. The problem is not trivial, however, since the possibility of design changes provides noise and generates tradeoffs. This requires the following assumption about cost-based compensation:

Assumption 1. The product's total costs are verifiable, but the costs of modifications cannot be independently measured.

This assumption implies that when modifications are needed, the original costs $c(e)$ and the added costs m cannot be disentangled. For example, in the middle of construction the buyer might ask to raise the height of the first floor. This would entail additional labor and material that is used *in parallel* to the original plan's specifications, and it would be impossible to accurately measure the incremental costs associated with the modification. Another way to view this is that the costs of counterfactuals (the abandoned original design) cannot be measured, so incremental costs due to changes in the original design likewise cannot be measured. Clearly, monitoring technologies that would undermine this assumption would cause different optimal contracts to arise, as discussed below. In summary, Assumption 1 rules out compensation schemes that are based on the costs of modification, which is important in our analysis and is discussed further at the end of this section.

We assume that there is a competitive market of potential sellers, so that *ex ante* the buyer can offer a contract that guarantees the seller zero expected profits. This zero-profit condition will be useful for our analysis, but allowing the seller to capture some positive *ex ante* surplus will not alter our qualitative results.

Finally, we will restrict attention to linear contracts of the form $P(c) = \alpha + \beta c$, where $\beta \in \{0, 1\}$ can take on only two extreme values. Notice that $\beta = 0$ is a fixed-price contract with a price of α, whereas $\beta = 1$ is a cost-plus contract that reimburses the contractor for costs and gives him an additional compensation of α. In our framework the restriction to linear contracts is without loss, as shown in Appendix B. The restriction to the two extreme values is arbitrary, but in Section 4 we shall offer some plausible explanations for the prevalence of these extreme contracts.

□ **Renegotiation.** With probability $1 - \tau > 0$ the parties will have to renegotiate the contract for the buyer to receive the value v. From the setup above, the disagreement payoffs are well defined. Regardless of the realized state of nature, the contractor can complete the project per original design and receive his payment of $\alpha + \beta c$, paid for by the buyer. The buyer's benefit, however, does depend on the state of nature; she receives the benefit v when the design covers the particular state, while she receives zero otherwise, unless the parties agree to modify the design.

We model the renegotiation stage as a reduced-form game: with probability $\lambda > 0$ the buyer makes the seller a take-it-or-leave-it (TIOLI) offer, and with probability $1 - \lambda > 0$ the seller makes the buyer a TIOLI offer. Clearly, the party making the offer will capture all the surplus from renegotiation. However, given that the seller has private information, there is scope for *ex post* inefficiencies, as will indeed be demonstrated shortly.[4] For analytical convenience both parties are assumed to be risk neutral.

Renegotiating fixed-price contracts. If a FP contract is chosen, then when the buyer makes a TIOLI offer she chooses a payment w to maximize her expected *ex post* payoff given by

$$F(w) \cdot (v - w) - k,$$

which yields the first-order condition with respect to w, $f(w) \cdot (v - w) - F(w) = 0$, or

$$w^* = v - \frac{F(w^*)}{f(w^*)} < v. \tag{1}$$

Thus, we get the standard distortion of a monopoly facing a downward-sloping demand curve, where this demand curve is generated from the private information of the seller. If $F(w)/f(w)$ is increasing in w (satisfied by any log-concave distribution of m, such as uniform), then there is a unique solution to (1), and $w^* < v$ implies that there is a positive probability that renegotiation breaks down.

If the seller is making the TIOLI offer he will clearly ask for v, since this is what the buyer has to gain, and this leaves the buyer with the sunk cost of additional design k and the seller with the *ex post* profits $v - m$. Therefore, if the status quo contract is a FP contract, then we can summarize the expected utility of the buyer and the expected profits of the seller from renegotiation as

$$Eu_{RNG}^{FP} = \lambda F(w^*)(v - w^*) - k,$$

$$E\pi_{RNG}^{FP} = \lambda \left(F(w^*)w^* - \int_0^{w^*} m \, dF(m) \right) + (1 - \lambda) \left(v - \int_0^{v-k} m \, dF(m) \right).$$

Renegotiating cost-plus contracts. Now imagine that the relationship is governed by a C+ contract. When the buyer makes a TIOLI offer, she can do no better than to offer the contractor to do the change *without amending* the C+ contract. The added costs due to the change, m, are less or equal to the benefit $v - k$, and thus following the original C+ contract gives the buyer all the surplus. When the seller makes the TIOLI offer he can extract no more than the buyer's expected benefit, which is $v - E[m]$ (where E is the expectations operator). Therefore, when the status quo contract

---

[4] We thus assume full commitment for the party making the offer, so that rejection causes loss of all surplus. This is a simplifying assumption. The conclusion that incomplete information causes bargaining inefficiencies is consistent with a wide class of bargaining models.

is a C+ contract, we can summarize the expected utility of the buyer and the expected profits of the seller from renegotiation as

$$Eu_{RNG}^{C+} = \lambda \left(v - \int_0^{v-k} m \, dF(m) \right) - k,$$

$$E\pi_{RNG}^{C+} = (1-\lambda) \left(v - \int_0^{v-k} m \, dF(m) \right).$$

Notice that the right to *demand* changes is *not* part of the C+ contract. Instead, the complete flexibility is achieved by the fact that a C+ contract is a well-defined compensation scheme that guarantees the seller his outside option of zero. When the seller makes a TIOLI offer in our model, he extracts the buyer's surplus and α increases as a result (*ex ante* individual rationality). When the buyer makes the TIOLI offer, the seller is set to his outside option, which is zero, and the C+ contract does not change. It is interesting to note that in our model, the seller is offered an initial compensation that does not cover his expected costs. This follows from the fact that the seller expects to get positive expected *ex post* surplus when changes are required. This is a rather realistic aspect of the model. (In reality, bigger changes include both more costs and more time to implement them. If the contractor's outside opportunity is not zero, as reality suggests, then bigger changes would require more compensation. Choosing $\beta > 1$, which is common but cost inefficient (it gives incentives to increase costs), may be a response to reduce haggling over the contractor's willingness to continue under C+ contracts.)

Several points are warranted given the stark and crude structure of our renegotiation game. First, if the seller had all the bargaining power, then no inefficiency would arise at the renegotiation stage. In fact, if the parties can commit in the *ex ante* contract that the seller has all the bargaining power in case of design failure, then they can circumvent this inefficiency. This scheme, however, would undermine our reduced-form bargaining game. Thus, it is implicitly assumed by our reduced-form game that design failure is not verifiable. With nonverifiable design failures the seller would hold up the buyer's design investment and always claim that failure occurred. Indeed, nonverifiability of design failure and the potential for seller holdup would be a good reason to grant the buyer the bargaining power. This is consistent with the practice of change directives as described in Section 2.

Second, after renegotiation the parties continue with the same type of contract they began with, either FP or C+. This implicitly assumes that the parties can't measure total cost after renegotiation accurately unless they chose a C+ contract *ex ante*. If we allow for such shifts at the renegotiation stage from a FP to a C+ contract, then the optimal contract is to start with FP and renegotiate to C+, which reduces incentives (through the seller's correct foresight of renegotiation) but eliminates renegotiation costs. To restore *ex ante* selection of C+ contracts, we would need to add noise to the construction costs $c(e)$, as is standard in moral hazard models. This would restore the bargaining inefficiencies because inefficiencies arise either from unknown postbargaining payoffs (our case in FP) or from unknown disagreement points (the result of a random $c(e)$).

Third, in reality one would expect that the buyer too has some private information at the renegotiation stage with respect to her value from the change. It is easy to extend the model in this way so that when the seller makes his TIOLI offer then an inefficiency will arise for both types of contract, while the buyer's TIOLI offer still has no inefficiencies when a C+ contract is in place. (For example, if the value from the change is $v \in [\underline{v}, \overline{v}]$ and $m \in [0, \underline{v} - k]$.) This would cause more bargaining inefficiencies under FP contracts, which would preserve the nature of our analysis.

In summary, there is a fundamental difference between having a FP or C+ contract governing the relationship. A C+ contract is a *well-defined compensation scheme* for both the initial design and any modifications that are requested, as long as compensation is based on total costs. If a FP contract was initially chosen, then the compensation scheme is a *specific performance*

FIGURE 1
SEQUENCE OF EVENTS

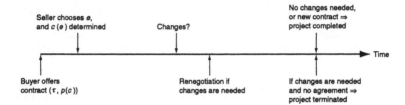

compensation scheme and cannot account for modifications, resulting in *ex post* inefficient bargaining. The time line in Figure 1 is provided to clarify the sequence of events.

Remark. Asymmetric information at the renegotiation stage implies that a menu of contracts should be offered by the uninformed principal. This is indeed the case with FP contracts: the TIOLI offer explicitly states two continuations, perform or quit. With C+ a menu would not improve utilities. This all follows from our all-or-nothing assumption on the buyer's value. If there are several potential changes with different costs and benefits, more elaborate menus should be used, but our qualitative results on selective friction would not change. It would be reasonable to argue that the role of negotiations is to nail down the choice from such a menu.

4. Fixed price or cost plus?

■   We turn to our first question: If the buyer was restricted to choose between a FP and a C+ contract, when should each be chosen? We begin by examining the *ex ante* expected payoffs under the two extreme contractual arrangements we consider here.

☐   ***Exante* payoffs: FP.** A FP contract has $\alpha > 0$ and $\beta = 0$, so that the seller's *ex ante* expected profit is

$$E\pi^{FP} = \alpha - c(e) - g(e) + (1 - \tau)E\pi^{FP}_{RNG}$$
$$= \alpha - c(e) - g(e)$$
$$+ (1 - \tau)\left[\lambda\left(F(w^*)w^* - \int_0^{w^*} m\,dF(m)\right) + (1 - \lambda)\left(v - \int_0^{v-k} m\,dF(m)\right)\right].$$
(2)

The seller maximizes (2) to obtain his optimal effort choice under a fixed-price contract, e^{FP}. Notice that the seller bears all the construction costs, $c(e)$, and the private costs of effort, $g(e)$, implying that his choice of effort will be first-best optimal. The buyer's expected utility is given by

$$Eu^{FP} = \tau v - \alpha - d(\tau, T) + (1 - \tau)Eu^{FP}_{RNG}$$
$$= \tau v - \alpha - d(\tau, T) + (1 - \tau)\left[\lambda F(w^*)(v - w^*) - k\right],$$

which she maximizes taking the seller's effort e^{FP} as given. Recall that by assumption the seller earns zero expected profits, so we can substitute α from equating (2) above with zero, and simple algebra yields the following representation for the buyer's utility:

$$Eu^{FP} = v - c(e^{FP}) - g(e^{FP}) - d(\tau, T)$$
$$- (1 - \tau)\lambda(1 - F(w^*))v$$

$$- (1 - \tau) \left[\int_0^{v-k} md\, F(m) - \lambda \int_{w^*}^{v-k} md\, F(m) + k \right]. \tag{3}$$

The first line captures the value from having the project completed, less the costs of construction, effort, and design. The second line represents the loss of efficiency due to bargaining under asymmetric information: with probability $(1 - \tau)\lambda(1 - F(w^*))$ the buyer will make a TIOLI offer that is rejected, and lose the gross value v. The third line represents the expected cost of modifications.

In other words, the buyer gets the benefits v, bears all the costs of construction, effort, and design, and finally will bear a *friction* in case the design fails due to inefficient *ex post* bargaining under asymmetric information. This friction is the loss of gains from renegotiation, which is equal to

$$(1 - \tau)\lambda(1 - F(w^*))v - (1 - \tau)\lambda \int_{w^*}^{v-k} md\, F(m). \tag{4}$$

Notice also that w^* is not a function of τ, so the gross loss (the first part of (4)) can be rewritten as $(1 - \tau)\sigma v$, where $\sigma \equiv \lambda(1 - F(w^*))$ is the *endogenous friction* arising from inefficient *ex post* bargaining. We can now rewrite (3) as

$$Eu^{FP} = v - c(e^{FP}) - g(e^{FP}) - d(\tau, T) - (1 - \tau)\sigma v - (1 - \tau)K_1, \tag{5}$$

where $K_1 \equiv \int_0^{v-k} md\, F(m) - \lambda \int_{w^*}^{v-k} md\, F(m) + k$ is the expected costs of modifications following renegotiation. Thus, (5) represents a reduced form for the derived expected utility of the buyer from a FP contract.

□ *Exante* **payoffs: C+.** A C+ contract has $\beta = 1$, and α derived to guarantee the seller expected zero profits *ex ante*. The seller's *ex ante* expected profit is

$$E\pi^{C+} = \alpha - c(0)g(e) + (1 - \tau)E\pi_{RNG}^{C+}$$

$$= \alpha - c(0)g(e) + (1 - \tau)(1 - \lambda)\left(v - \int_0^{v-k} md\, F(m) \right). \tag{6}$$

This problem clearly implies that the seller will choose no effort, $e^{C+} = 0$, which is suboptimal. As before, this is not affected by the buyer's choice of design, τ.

Turning to the buyer, her expected utility is given by

$$Eu^{C+} = \tau v - \alpha - d(\tau, T) + (1 - \tau)Eu_{RNG}^{C+}$$

$$= \tau v - \alpha - d(\tau, T) + (1 - \tau)\left[\lambda(v - \int_0^{v-k} md\, F(m)) - k \right],$$

which she maximizes over τ taking the seller's effort $e = 0$ as given. As before, substitute α from equating (6) above with zero, and simple algebra yields the following representation for the buyer's utility:

$$Eu^{C+} = v - c(0) - g(0) - d(\tau, T) - (1 - \tau)K_2, \tag{7}$$

where $K_2 \equiv \int_0^{v-k} md\, F(m) + k$. That is, the buyer gets the benefits, v, and bears all the costs of construction, effort, design, and the expected cost of modifications. Notice that with C+ contracts the value of design is not reducing friction, just reducing the expected costs from modifications.

□ **Comparative analysis.** Notice the differences between the C+ problem, (7), and the FP problem, (5). C+ contracting has no friction, since the inefficiencies due to asymmetric information do not arise, even though there is still asymmetric information. Thus, our model demonstrates that the efficiency of *ex post* renegotiation is affected by the *ex ante* contract that the parties sign, which implies that renegotiation costs, or transaction costs, are endogenous. This plays a key role in the costs and benefits of the two contracting arrangements.

Benchmark: exogenous design. We describe two benchmark cases to illustrate the simple economic forces that describe the tradeoff between FP and C+ contracts in the model. First, consider the extreme case in which the buyer is given a product that comes with a complete specification and requires no initial resources for design. That is, $\tau = 1$ is given exogenously, and the cost of design, $d(\cdot)$, is zero. Following the analysis described in Section 4, if a FP contract is chosen, then the contractor will choose effort e^{FP}, and from (5), the buyer's expected utility from a FP contract is given by

$$Eu^{FP} = v - c(e^{FP}) - g(e^{FP}),$$

since there will be no renegotiation given the complete design ($\tau = 1$). If, however, a C+ contract is chosen, then $e^{C+} = 0$ and the buyer's expected utility is given by

$$Eu^{C+} = v - c(0).$$

In this benchmark case, we obtain the following result:

Lemma 2. If $\tau = 1$ is exogenously given, then FP contracts dominate C+ contracts.

The intuition for this result is quite straightforward. If there is no cost to complete the design, then FP contracting gives the contractor an incentive to invest optimally in cost reduction, and *ex ante* competition transfers these cost savings directly to the buyer. Since no costly renegotiation occurs, a FP contract induces (first-best) cost reduction without introducing renegotiation costs.

Now consider the opposite extreme case, in which the buyer has a project T, but $\tau = 0$ is exogenously set. In this case the buyer's expected utility from a FP contract is given by

$$Eu^{FP} = -c(e^{FP}) - g(e^{FP}) + (1 - \sigma)v - K_1, \tag{8}$$

since renegotiation will occur with probability one when no *ex ante* design is provided. If a C+ contract is chosen, then $e = 0$, and the buyer's expected utility is

$$Eu^{C+} = v - c(0) - K_2. \tag{9}$$

In this benchmark case of $\tau = 0$, comparing (8) with (9) shows that a C+ contract dominates a FP contract if and only if

$$\sigma v + g(e^{FP}) \geq c(0) - c(e^{FP}) + K_2 - K_1.$$

The intuition is again straightforward. If $\tau = 0$ is exogenously set, then the gains from choosing a C+ contract over a FP contract are the incentives for cost-reducing effort, $c(0) - c(e^{FP})$, and saving modification costs when renegotiation breaks down, $K_2 - K_1$. The costs of a FP contract are that first, the contractor needs to be compensated for his effort by the amount $g(e^{FP})$, and second, a proportion σ of the remaining surplus will be dissipated through inefficient renegotiation. When the costs outweigh the benefits, then choosing a C+ contract is optimal.

This subsection demonstrated that FP contracts create strong cost-reducing incentives, which benefit the buyer through the *ex ante* competition between potential contractors. But if the design fails, then some surplus will be eroded by the frictions of *ex post* renegotiation The next subsection completes the analysis by endogenizing the choice of design completeness and then demonstrating the comparative analysis between the two contractual arrangements.

Endogenous design. To proceed, let $x \in \{0, 1\}$ denote the contractual compensation choice of the buyer, where $x = 1$ is a FP contract and $x = 0$ is a C+ contract. The buyer then maximizes

$$\max_{\substack{x \in \{0,1\} \\ \tau \in [0,1]}} x \left[v - c(e^{FP}) - g(e^{FP}) - (1 - \tau)(\sigma v + K_1) \right]$$
$$+ (1 - x)[v - c(0) - (1 - \tau)K_2] - d(\tau, T).$$

Proposition 1. The buyer's optimal choices $x(T)$ and $\tau(T)$ are monotone nonincreasing in T.

To put the proposition in words, more complex products have a less complete design and are more likely to be procured using C+ contracts. The intuition is almost identical to that described in the previous subsection, in which the design was considered exogenous. The effect of complexity on endogenous design is linked to the choice of the compensation scheme by the complementarity characteristics of the derived function $d(\tau, T)$. When a C+ contract is chosen, then savings on design costs (lower τ) are warranted because renegotiation friction is eliminated. When a FP contract is chosen, then to reduce inefficient *ex post* renegotiation there is a need to have a more complete design (higher τ). As described earlier, when design is fairly complete the gains from cost incentives outweigh the losses from inefficient renegotiation. When the design is fairly incomplete the losses from inefficient renegotiation outweigh the benefits from cost incentives. Notice that $\tau(T)$ nonincreasing does not mean that as complexity increases then the buyer specifies fewer states if, for example, the contractual choice does not change from FP to C+. What this means is that even if more states are specified, the design is (weakly) less complete and τ is (weakly) smaller.

This conclusion is consistent with the stylized facts described in Table 1. Our result explains why more design documentation is linked to the choice of FP contracts, and it can shed light on the tradeoff between cost reduction and time to completion. Namely, if one considers T to be a combined measure of complexity per unit of time invested in design, then saving time is equivalent to less design in our model. Thus, a buyer who wishes to engage in "fast tracking" is indeed better off choosing a C+ contract as observed in the stylized facts (Section 2).

Remark. Notice that Assumption 1 (total costs are measurable but modification costs are not) prevents the buyer from writing an initial FP contract and later requesting changes using a C+ contract. If such a contract is feasible, it clearly is optimal: it provides efficient incentives and has no *ex post* inefficient bargaining. Though the intuition of the tradeoff between incentives and bargaining costs is rather straightforward, without this assumption the tradeoff would not be generated by our model. In a sense, this observation is due to the model, and discussions with practitioners verify the validity of this assumption.

☐ **The comparative statics of friction.** In the reduced-form representation of the buyer's maximization problem, the friction is characterized by $\sigma > 0$. It is interesting to ask the following question: If renegotiation friction increases due to more severe asymmetric information (or other sources of friction), what will the effects on the contractual arrangement be? The following result answers this question.

Proposition 2. The buyer's optimal choice $x(\sigma)$ is monotone nonincreasing in σ, and her optimal choice $\tau(\sigma)$ is nonmonotonic in σ.

The intuition is simple. As friction increases, the loss from inefficient renegotiation of a FP contract increases, making it less desirable. As for the completeness of design, this depends on the choice of the compensation scheme. If parameters are such that a FP contract is chosen ($x = 1$), and friction increases without changing the optimal choice of x, then it will be beneficial to provide more design to mitigate the loss from renegotiation of a FP contract. If the optimal regime is a C+ contract, and friction increases, then the optimal contract will still remain a C+ contract, and design completeness will be unchanged. The difficulty arises when an increase in friction causes the regime to change from FP to C+. In this case there will be a discontinuous reduction in τ because of the shift to frictionless renegotiation due to the C+ contract.

This suggests that reducing friction is beneficial for three reasons. First, it trivially reduces the *ex post* inefficiencies from costly renegotiation. Second, it may allow the buyer to save on design costs and face a higher probability of renegotiation. Finally, it increases the use of FP contracts, which generate cost incentives and lower construction costs. The interesting question is how buyers and sellers can cause frictions to be lower. One answer may be by using third parties as arbitrators, which seems to be a common practice in the construction industry. Clearly, this finding begs for more careful analysis of how costly renegotiation can be reduced in different procurement settings.

☐ **Optimality of extreme contracts.** Consider the more general problem in which all linear contracts $\beta \in [0, 1]$ are considered. Under the continuity conditions we have assumed, the objective function over the domain $\beta \in (0, 1)$ is continuous in β. Thus, we can find functional forms and parameter values to support any $\beta \in (0, 1)$ as a solution, and in this more general problem the analogy to Proposition 1 is that $\beta(T)$ and $\tau(T)$ are monotone nonincreasing in T. Why then are most observed contracts either FP or C+? Two simple observations seem to make the procurement problem "nonconvex" at these extreme contracts, and this subsection will outline two simple ways to modify our model and address these issues. We refrain from performing the actual analysis, since it seems quite predictable, and further algebra would add very little.

First, we argue that there is a fundamental difference between a FP contract ($\beta = 0$) and any other cost-sharing contract with $\beta \in (0, 1]$. This follows because a FP contract *does not require the measurement of construction costs*, whereas any cost-sharing contract requires such measurement. This obvious fact, which is documented in the engineering-management literature, leads to a clear nonconvexity in the cost of measuring and monitoring product costs. An immediate implication of introducing measurement costs is that FP contracts will dominate contracts that are "close" to FP, and as it becomes costlier to measure costs, FP contracts will dominate a larger set of incentive contracts.

Second, we argue that there may be a fundamental difference between a C+ contract with $\beta = 1$ and other incentive contracts with $\beta < 1$. Consider a richer model in which the seller engages in two tasks, as introduced by Holmström and Milgrom (1991). For example, the seller can exert effort in cost reduction, e_c, and effort in quality enhancement, e_q. Holmström and Milgrom impose two extreme assumptions: (1) the tasks are perfect substitutes in the seller's private cost function, $g(e_c + e_q)$, and (2) costs are verifiable but quality is not. With these extreme assumptions Holmström and Milgrom show that giving the seller incentives to reduce costs will cause him to ignore quality considerations completely and engage only in cost reductions.[5] Thus, in our simple model that ignores quality considerations, there exist solutions β close to 1 (close to C+) that are no longer optimal once quality concerns are introduced.

McAfee and McMillan (1986) analyze a model in which risk-averse agents (contractors) bid and the buyer is faced with both adverse selection and moral hazard. In their model the tradeoff between risk sharing, incentives, and information revelation cause incentive contracts that lie between FP and C+ to be generally desirable. In fact, C+ contracts are never optimal in their model because they give the contractor no incentive to bid aggressively. McAfee and McMillan acknowledge that most government contracts are FP, and some are C+, and they use their results to encourage more use of incentive contracts. Our arguments shift the focus of attention and try to rationalize the use of these extreme contracts.

It is hard to assess the magnitude of such nonconvexities, though their existence is suggested by the stylized facts. Furthermore, our stylized model cannot address the relative performance of these extreme contracts compared to intermediate ones, since it is hard to imagine that these nonconvexities are so extreme as to eliminate all intermediate contracts. Clearly, other sources of monitoring costs would affect the choice of contracts, such as the ability to monitor quality and performance *ex post*. Trying to understand the prevalence of these extreme contracts is very much still an open question, and we can only offer limited insights at this stage. Note that these nonconvexities, together with the need for design specification, are related to the problem of measurement introduced by Barzel (1982).

5. Discussion

■ **Relation to the literature.** We depart from many of the central themes illustrated by the standard theoretical literature on procurement contracting. First, we depart from the mechanism-design approach of Laffont and Tirole (1993) by assuming no *ex ante* hidden information. While

---

[5] In a different context, Manelli and Vincent (1995) show that if the buyer cares a lot about quality, using an auction mechanism (which is associated with a fixed price) is not efficient.

it is probably true that there is some asymmetric information about costs before the contract is signed, the optimal choice of contract may not be the mechanism that deals with such asymmetries. Other mechanisms, like competitive bidding, reputation, and third-party bonding companies, seem to be important in solving the adverse-selection problem.

As for its positive implications, the mechanism-design methodology predicts that (i) screening of sellers should occur via menus of contracts; (ii) we should see various strengths of incentives, not primarily FP or C+; (iii) the likelihood of renegotiation is not related to types of contract;[6] (iv) the distribution of "types" should affect incentives, rents, and compensation; and (v) project complexity/design are ignored and thus not related to the choice of contract. As we describe in Section 2, the facts do not seem to support predictions (i), (ii), and (iii), and the mechanism-design approach cannot account for the strong empirical regularities that (iv) ignores. The comparative statics of (iv) on the distributions of types are not very useful, since it is possible to rationalize any choice of contracts with the right asymmetry of information. Finally, the mechanism-design approach assumes that sellers do not compete for projects, which is instrumental in deriving the results of that literature. This assumption seems to be inadequate for many industries.

Second, we depart from the standard contracting literature by making the product design and specification endogenous.[7] At one extreme, the mechanism-design literature assumes that writing contracts is costless, while at the other extreme, the incomplete-contracts literature pioneered by Grossman and Hart (1986) assumes that writing contracts is prohibitively expensive. In our model, both the form of compensation and the completeness of design are endogenous choice variables and are related in a systematic way: FP contracts feature high levels of design, strong incentives, and significant friction when changes are required. C+ contracts feature low levels of design, weak incentives, and small amounts of friction. Another contrast to the incomplete-contracts literature is that we do not assume efficient *ex post* renegotiation. We endogenously derive a relationship between *ex ante* incentives and *ex post* renegotiation that results in selective friction. The selective friction we derive seems consistent with the stylized facts on the intensity of contract disputes.

□ **Evidence from other industries.** It is evident that *ex post* adaptation is important in other industries and procurement settings. For example, change orders are common in defense procurement, as Rogerson (1994, p. 67) notes: "Significant unanticipated changes almost always occur, which leads to renegotiation where there is an inevitable tendency to ascribe all cost overruns to the changes." Our analysis suggests that if the likelihood of changes to a design is large, then the buyer should choose weak incentives, whereas strong incentives should govern purchases that are less likely to involve changes. Crocker and Reynolds (1993) find that Air Force engine procurement contracts are based more on cost reimbursements and adjustments at initial production stages. These initial stages are those where changes are expected (initial batches of production). Later production stages involve fixed-price contracts. These later stages are performed after initial production problems were resolved by change orders. This is consistent with our predictions.

A recent study by Banerjee and Duflo (2000) examines the choice of contracts in the Indian customized software industry. They construct and analyze a dataset of 236 contracts, which are either FP or C+ (time and material) contracts. Their main empirical finding is that older firms (sellers) are more likely to be engaged in cost-plus contracts compared to young firms. They interpret age as a measure of reputation and conclude that a seller's reputation affects his contract. They also show that older firms, and firms that are ISO-certified, do on average larger and more

---

[6] More precisely, in a dynamic mechanism-design model, contracts will be renegotiated to change the incentive structure after the buyer learns information about the seller. In reality, renegotiation seldom changes the overall compensation scheme but rather changes the product specification in return for added compensation. In C+ contracts the added compensation is well specified *ex ante*.

[7] Endogenous incomplete contracts arise in the analysis of Dye (1985), who developed a model with costly specification of contingent actions in a competitive equilibrium framework. Battigalli and Maggi (2000) offer a different, but related, approach to modelling contractual incompleteness. These articles do not link *ex post* renegotiation to the incentives of the *ex ante* contract.

complex products than younger or non-ISO-certified firms. These results are not inconsistent with our model. A software project that is simple, or small, will be easy to design, which in turn calls for a FP contract. It is reasonable to argue that in the software industry, young (small) firms will generally bid lower and more aggressively to establish themselves as capable, or because larger and more established firms have higher overhead and greater profit margins. If, however, the project is complex or large, then design is more costly, resulting in less complete design and a C+ contract. In the latter case, since competitive bidding is not an option, then the buyer needs to select a firm using other criteria. If there are concerns about a software firm's ability to carry out a complex project (ignored in our model), then we would expect the buyer to care about reputation, which indeed may be evaluated by age or, more likely, by certification. Thus, a similar correlation identified would be interpreted by a different causality: the type of product determines the contract, and the latter determines the type of firm selected.

☐   **The make-or-buy decision.** Our framework may shed some light on the celebrated "make-or-buy" question that lies at the heart of what determines a firm's boundaries: which activities should be performed inside the firm, and which should be procured across the market?[8] To apply our insights to this question, consider a buyer (firm) who faces the decision of whether an input component will be produced inside the firm (make) or purchased on the market (buy). A "make" decision has the buyer bear all the costs of producing the component, and the relationship between the buyer and the "unit" that produces the good is like a C+ contract. Similarly, a "buy" decision has the seller (a different firm) bear all the cost of producing the component.

Our analysis then suggests that the complexity of the component determines the buyer's choice. Namely, a simple component that is easy to define will be bought, while a complex component will be procured internally. These insights resonate with Williamson (1975, 1985), who addressed the tradeoff between incentives and governance costs and noted that "internal organization often has attractive properties in that it permits the parties to deal with uncertainty/complexity in an adaptive, sequential fashion..." (1975, p. 25) and that "a high degree of bilateral dependency exists in those circumstances and high powered incentives impair the ease with which adaptive, sequential adjustments to disturbances are accomplished" (1985, p. 91). However, Williamson did not spell out *why* it is that *ex post* adaptation is easier in the firm compared to the market.

Riordan and Williamson (1985) extend Williamson's arguments to include neoclassical choices such as scope and scale, and their analysis of binary institutional choice is similar to our reduced-form structure. However, Riordan and Williamson "employ a reduced-form type of analysis, in that we ascribe rather than derive the basic production and governance cost competencies of firms and markets" (p. 366). Given that their reduced form is tailored to the vertical-integration decision, and the ascribed governance costs are not derived from a structural model, it is difficult to adapt their analysis to the choice of procurement contracts or to understand what might drive such results. In contrast, our model derives, rather than ascribes, the costs and benefits of different contractual forms based on specific tradeoffs between incentive provision and renegotiation costs.

Our approach contributes to the TCE literature in two ways. First, we formalize how the product's complexity affects the choice of incentives, and we highlight the endogenous transaction costs that arise from *ex post* bargaining. This, together with our agency approach, erects a comprehensive bridge between the less formal TCE literature and the more formal models of modern agency theory. Second, by focusing on product complexity as the determinant of the make-or-buy decision, our approach has clear empirical predictions. Indeed, several well-known empirical studies provide evidence that supports this conclusion. For the aerospace industry, Masten (1984) shows that both a higher degree of specialization (specificity) and a higher level of complexity will increase the probability of internal procurement. For the automobile industry,

---

[8] This agenda was pioneered by Coase (1937) and developed further by Williamson (1975, 1985), Klein, Crawford, and Alchian (1978), Grossman and Hart (1986), Hart and Moore (1990), and others. (See Holmström and Roberts (1998) for an excellent summary.)

Monteverde and Teece (1982) show that more complexity, identified by more engineering investment, will increase the likelihood of internal procurement. More recent work has further supported these empirical regularities. (See, for example, Novak and Eppinger (2001) and Knez and Simester (forthcoming).)

☐ **Concluding remarks.** We develop a model that illustrates what we believe to be a fundamental problem of procurement contracting. An important aspect of contractual arrangements is their ability to accommodate adaptation, thus creating a tradeoff between transaction costs that are due to changes and incentives to reduce costs. On one hand, FP contracts provide the strongest incentives for cost reduction. On the other hand, if the design is left incomplete, then the cost of renegotiating FP contracts is high. When C+ contracts are used the cost-reducing incentives disappear, but the process of adaptation is far smoother because the reimbursement process is simple, well defined, and leaves little room for haggling. Evidence from procurement contracts in private construction, defense, and software acquisition are consistent with the results of our model.

The implications of our analysis are relevant to both the private and public sector as to how procurement should be conducted. As the Federal Acquisition Rules (FARs) prescribe, government procurement is guided almost solely by fixed-price contracts. A common justification is that competitive bidding reduces the risk of ad hoc selection and corruption. But for complex systems, particularly in defense and aerospace, this approach may have high costs. Following the unsuccessful mission of NASA's Mars Polar Lander at the end of 1999, in an interview on PBS,[9] Liam P. Sarsfield, a senior policy analyst with the Science and Technology Policy Institute at RAND, wondered how "NASA [can] ask the contractor community—it's done this many times—to build some of these very exotic spacecraft—cutting-edge spacecraft—on really fixed-price budgets... the private sector that builds these spacecraft is being asked really to develop a spacecraft the way you and I would buy a car. And there is so much that is unknown up front." In response to this concern, Lori Garver, NASA's associate administrator for policy and plans, suggested that "NASA has been on the cutting edge of trying to get fixed-based cost contracting, and we may need to look at other incentives to provide commercial companies who work with NASA the ability to have more flexibility." This anecdote highlights the central theme of our article, and we believe that our analysis provides some guidance as to when relaxing stringent fixed-price rules is warranted.

Appendix A

■ Proofs of Lemmas 1–2 and Propositions 1–2 follow.

Proof of Lemma 1. The fact that $d(\tau, T)$ is increasing in τ and T follows immediately from the definition of $d(\tau, T)$. To see that $d(\tau, T)$ exhibits increasing differences, consider two projects $T > T'$, and fix some $\tau < 1$. Since project T is more complex than T', then by definition $\pi_t < \pi'_t$ for all t, and there exist integers S and S', $S \geq S'$, such that

$$\sum_{t=1}^{S-1} \pi_t < \tau \leq \sum_{t=1}^{S} \pi_t \quad \text{and} \quad \sum_{t=1}^{S'-1} \pi'_t < \tau \leq \sum_{t=1}^{S'} \pi'_t,$$

and $d(\tau, T') = S'k \leq Sk = d(\tau, T)$. Now consider an increase from τ to $\tau + \varepsilon$. Since project T is more complex than T', then there exist integers $K \geq K'$ such that

$$\sum_{t=1}^{S+K-1} \pi_t < \tau + \varepsilon \leq \sum_{t=1}^{S+K} \pi_t \quad \text{and} \quad \sum_{t=1}^{S'+K'-1} \pi'_t < \tau + \varepsilon \leq \sum_{t=1}^{S'+K'} \pi'_t,$$

and $d(\tau + \varepsilon, T') = (S' + K')k \leq (S + K)k = d(\tau + \varepsilon, T)$. It then follows that

---

[9] *The Newshour with Jim Lehrer*, December 7, 1999. Transcript available at http://www.pbs.org/newshour/bb/science/july-dec99/mars_12-7.html.

$$d(\tau + \varepsilon, T) - d(\tau, T) \geq d(\tau + \varepsilon, T') - d(\tau, T'),$$

which proves the result.   *Q.E.D.*

Proof of Lemma 2. The optimal FP contract for the exogenous design case $\tau = 1$ ($\alpha = c(e^{FP}) + g(e^{FP})$ and $\beta = 0$) dominates the optimal C+ contract for this case ($\alpha = 0$ and $\beta = 1$) if and only if $Eu^{FP} \geq Eu^{C+}$, which reduces to

$$c(0) \geq c(e^{FP}) + g(e^{FP}). \tag{A1}$$

Now consider the contractor's problem with a FP contract. By revealed preference, he prefers choosing e^{FP} over $e = 0$, which implies that

$$\max_{e} E\pi^{FP} = \alpha - c(e^{FP}) - g(e^{FP}) \geq \alpha - c(0),$$

which is equivalent to (A1) above.   *Q.E.D.*

Proof of Proposition 1. From well-known results in monotone comparative statics (see Vives (1999), and also Milgrom and Shannon (1994) and Topkis (1998)), if the buyer's objective function has increasing differences in $(x, \tau, -T)$, then the optimal response functions $x(T)$ and $\tau(T)$ are monotone decreasing. Define the buyer's objective function as $f(x, \tau, -T, \sigma)$. To show that the buyer's objective function exhibits increasing differences in $(x, \tau, -T,)$, it suffices to show that the cross partials of $f(\cdot, \cdot, \cdot, \cdot)$ with respect to these three variables are nonnegative. We first compute two of the partial derivatives:

$$\frac{\partial f}{\partial \tau} = x(\sigma v + K_1 - K_2) - \frac{\partial d(\tau, T)}{\partial \tau} \tag{A2}$$

$$\frac{\partial f}{\partial (-T)} = \frac{\partial d(\tau, T)}{\partial T}. \tag{A3}$$

Differentiating (A3) with respect to x and τ respectively gives

$$\frac{\partial^2 f}{\partial x \partial(-T)} = 0, \quad \text{and} \quad \frac{\partial^2 f}{\partial \tau \partial(-T)} = \frac{\partial^2 d(\tau, T)}{\partial \tau \partial T} > 0,$$

where the inequality follows from the supermodularity of the derived function $d(\tau, T)$. Differentiating (A2) with respect to x gives

$$\frac{\partial^2 f}{\partial x \partial \tau} = \sigma v + K_1 - K_2$$

$$= \lambda(1 - F(w^*))v + \int_0^{v-k} m\, dF(m) - \lambda \int_{w^*}^{v-k} m\, dF(m) + k - \int_0^{v-k} m\, dF(m) - k$$

$$= \lambda \left[(1 - F(w^*))v - \int_{w^*}^{v-k} m\, dF(m) \right] > 0,$$

where the last inequality follows from the fact that the losses from renegotiation are positive, and this is indeed (4) from the analysis in Section 4 above. This shows that $f(\cdot, \cdot, \cdot, \cdot)$ has increasing differences in $(x, \tau, -T)$, completing our proof. *Q.E.D.*

Proof of Proposition 2. From (A2) we obtain $\partial^2 f/\partial x \partial(-\sigma) = (1 - \tau)v > 0$, while $\partial^2 f/\partial \tau \partial(-\sigma) = -xv \leq 0$. *Q.E.D.*

Appendix B: Optimality of linear contracts

■   This Appendix shows that the restriction to linear contracts is without loss of generality due to the risk neutrality of the parties. Consider general contracts of the form $p(c)$. The seller's *ex ante* expected profits are given by

$$E\pi = p(c) - c(e) - g(e) + (1 - \tau)E\pi_{RNG}.$$

Notice that the expected renegotiation payoffs of the seller do not depend on his choice of effort. This follows because the continuation gains from trade are not a function of the initial compensation scheme, or of the choice of effort. The following compensation scheme will trivially implement effort level e^*:

406 / THE RAND JOURNAL OF ECONOMICS

$$p(c) = \begin{cases} c(e^*) + g(e^*) - (1-\tau)E\pi_{RNG} & \text{if } c = c(e^*) \text{ or if the parties renegotiate} \\ -\varepsilon & \text{otherwise.} \end{cases}$$

This works as follows: if the design is complete, and there is no renegotiation, then by choosing e^* the seller guarantees zero profit, while other levels of effort cause a loss. In the event that the parties renegotiate, the seller would maximize his expected profits by choosing the first-best effort level, which may be different from e^*. But by choosing ε large enough, this discontinuous scheme will implement e^*, thus giving the seller an expected profit of zero.

Now we show that the same effort e^* can be implemented with a linear contract, and the expected payoffs are the same as from the discontinuous contract above. With a linear contract the seller's expected utility is given by

$$E\pi = \alpha + \beta c(e) - c(e) - g(e) + (1-\tau)E\pi_{RNG},$$

and the seller's necessary and sufficient first-order condition is

$$\beta c'(e) - c'(e) - g'(e) = 0.$$

Now let

$$\beta^* = 1 + \frac{g'(e^*)}{c'(e^*)} \le 1,$$
$$\alpha^* = c(e^*) + g(e^*) - \beta^* c(e) - (1-\tau)E\pi_{RNG}.$$

It is easy to see that (α^*, β^*) implement effort level e^* and give the seller zero expected profits by construction. This exercise works because the seller and buyer are assumed to be risk neutral.

References

ASHLEY, D. AND WORKMAN A. "Incentives in Construction Contracts." Document SD-8, Austin, Tex.: The Construction Industry Institute, 1986.
BANERJEE, A.V. AND DUFLO, E. "Reputation Effects and the Limits of Contracting: A Study of the Indian Software Industry." *Quarterly Journal of Economics*, Vol. 115 (2000), pp. 989–1018.
BARTHOLOMEW, S.H. *Construction Contracting: Business and Legal Principles.* Upper Saddle River, N.J.: Prentice-Hall, Inc., 1998.
BARZEL, Y. "Measurement Cost and the Organization of Markets." *Journal of Law and Economics*, Vol. 25 (1982), pp. 27–48.
BATTIGALLI, P. AND MAGGI, G. "Imperfect Contracting." Working Paper in Economic Theory no. 00S12, Department of Economics, Princeton University, 2000.
BUSINESS ROUNDTABLE. *Contractual Arrangements.* Report A-7. New York: Business Roundtable, 1987.
CLOUGH, R.H. AND SEARS, G.A., EDS. *Construction Contracting,* 6th ed. New York: Wiley, 1994.
COASE, R. "The Nature of the Firm." *Economica,* Vol. 4 (1937), pp. 386–405.
CROCKER, K.J. AND REYNOLDS, K.J. "The Efficiency of Incomplete Contracts: An Empirical Analysis of Air Force Engine Procurement." *RAND Journal of Economics,* Vol. 24 (1993), pp. 126–146.
DYE, R.R. "Costly Contract Contingencies." *International Economic Review,* Vol. 26 (1985), pp. 233–250.
ENGINEERING NEWS-RECORD. "Getting to the Top: Getty Center Builders Say Elevating Art in L.A. Is No Small Task." December 12, 1994, p. 30.
———. "Getty Center Wraps Up Work Eight Years and $1 Billion Later." October 15, 1997, p. 19.
———. "The World Is a $3.2 Trillion Construction Market." November 30, 1998, p. 36.
FINKEL, G. *The Economics of the Construction Industry.* New York: Sharpe, 1997.
GROSSMAN, S.J. AND HART, O.D. "The Costs and Benefits of Ownership: A Theory of Vertical and Lateral Integration." *Journal of Political Economy,* Vol. 94 (1986), pp. 691–719.
HART, O. AND MOORE, J. "Property Rights and the Nature of the Firms." *Journal of Political Economy,* Vol. 98 (1990), pp. 1119–1158.
HESTER, W., KUPRENAS, J., AND CHANG, T. *Construction Changes and Change Orders: Their Magnitude and Impact.* Document SD-66, Austin, Tex.: The Construction Industry Institute, 1991.
HINZE, J. *Construction Contracts.* Boston: Irwin McGraw-Hill, 1993.
HOLMSTRÖM, B. AND MILGROM, P. "Multitask Principal-Agent Analyses: Incentive Contracts, Asset Ownership, and Job Design." *Journal of Law, Economics and Organization,* Vol. 7 (1991), pp. 24–51.
——— AND ROBERTS, J. "The Boundaries of the Firm Revisited." *Journal of Economic Perspectives,* Vol. 12 (1998), pp. 73–94.

IBBS, C.W., WALL, D.E., HASSANEIN, M.A., BACK, W.E., DEL LA GARZA, J.M., TWARDOCK, R.K., KIM, J.J., AND SCHRAN, S.M. "Determining the Impact of Various Construction Contract Types and Clauses on Project Performance: Volumes I and II." Documents SD-10 and SD-11, Austin, Tex.: The Construction Industry Institute, 1986.

KLEIN, B., CRAWFORD, R.E., AND ALCHIAN, A.A. "Vertical Integration, Appropriable Rents, and the Competitive Contracting Process." *Journal of Law and Economics*, Vol. 21 (1978), pp. 297–326.

KNEZ, M. AND SIMESTER, D. "Direct and Indirect Bargaining Costs and the Scope of the Firm." *Journal of Business*, forthcoming.

LAFFONT, J.-J. AND TIROLE, J. *A Theory of Incentives in Procurement and Regulation.* Cambridge, Mass.: MIT Press, 1993.

MANELLI, A.M. AND VINCENT, D.R. "Optimal Procurement Mechanisms." *Econometrica*, Vol. 63 (1995), pp. 591–620.

MASTEN, S.E. "The Organization of Production: Evidence from the Aerospace Industry." *Journal of Law and Economics*, Vol. 27 (1984), pp. 403–417.

MCAFEE, R.P. AND MCMILLAN, J. "Bidding for Contracts: A Principal-Agent Analysis." *RAND Journal of Economics*, Vol. 17 (1986), pp. 326–338.

——— AND ———. *Incentives in Government Contracting.* Toronto: University of Toronto Press, 1988.

MILGROM, P. AND SHANNON, C. "Monotone Comparative Statics." *Econometrica*, Vol. 62 (1994), pp. 157–180.

MONTEVERDE, K. AND TEECE, D.J. "Supplier Switching Costs and Vertical Integration in the Automobile Industry." *Bell Journal of Economics*, Vol. 13 (1982), pp. 206–213.

NOVAK, S. AND EPPINGER, S. "Sourcing by Design: Product Architecture and the Supply Chain." *Management Science*, Vol. 47 (2001), pp. 189–204.

RIORDAN, M.H. AND WILLIAMSON, O.E. "Asset Specificity and Economic Organization." *International Journal of Industrial Organization*, Vol. 3 (1985), pp. 365–378.

ROGERSON, W.P. "Economic Incentives and the Defense Procurement Process." *Journal of Economic Perspectives*, Vol. 8 (1994), pp. 65–90.

SWEET, J. *Legal Aspects of Architecture, Engineering and the Construction Process*, 5th ed. Minneapolis/St. Paul, Minn.: West Publishing Company, 1994.

TOPKIS, D.M. *Supermodularity and Complementarity.* Princeton, N.J.: Princeton University Press, 1998.

U.S. DEPARTMENT OF COMMERCE, BUREAU OF THE CENSUS. "1992 Census of Construction Industries. United States Summary, Establishments With and Without Payroll." Washington, D.C.: U.S. GPO, 1992a.

———. "1992 Census of Construction Industries. General Contractors–Residential Buildings, Other Than Single-Family Houses, Industry 1542." Washington, D.C.: U.S. GPO, 1992b.

———. "1992 Census of Construction Industries. General Contractors–Nonresidential Buildings, Other Than Industrial Buildings and Warehouses, Industry 1542" Washington, D.C.: U.S. GPO, 1992c.

VIVES, X. *Oligopoly Pricing: Old Ideas and New Tools.* Cambridge, Mass.: MIT Press, 1999.

WILLIAMSON, O.E. *Markets and Hierarchies, Analysis and Antitrust Implications.* New York: Free Press, 1975.

———. *The Economic Institutions of Capitalism.* New York: Free Press, 1985.

[18]

Structure-induced equilibrium and legislative choice

KENNETH A. SHEPSLE   and   BARRY R. WEINGAST

Washington University

In the area of legislative choice, social choice theorists have focused on the equilibrium properties of pure majority rule (PMR), operating according to the implicit belief that whatever is true about the PMR mechanism also applies to institutions based upon it. This view has encouraged the study of what seemed to be the general case, thereby avoiding the narrower study of special cases such as those that might be observed in prominent real-world legislatures, e.g., the U.S. Congress. Over the past decade, the literature has marched toward increasingly general results about the nearly complete instability of PMR; a very detailed review of these developments is found in Schofield (1980). These results in the context of the operating belief noted above seem to imply that the stability of legislative outcomes is tenuous at best.

In this paper, we develop an alternative view of institutions based upon majority rule and show that PMR is a special subset of this category, if not an extreme special case. By focusing upon the manner in which institutions transform PMR into a different legislative game (such as one with a committee system), we can show the properties of legislative institutions necessary for the existence of equilibrium.

The paper proceeds as follows. In Section I, we briefly review the recent literature on voting that focuses on the instability of majority rule. In Section II, we demonstrate how stability may be induced in appropriate institutional circumstances and illustrate these circumstances with several examples. In Section III, we develop the theory behind these examples, showing the general

Mr. Shepsle is Professor of Political Science and Research Associate at the Center for the Study of American Business, Washington University. Mr. Weingast is Assistant Professor of Economics and Research Associate at the Center for the Study of American Business, Washington University. This paper was stimulated by Tullock's paper, 'Why so much stability?' We would like to thank author Tullock for sending us the early versions of this paper, and editor Tullock for encouraging us to write up our own comments and thoughts. An earlier version was presented at the Annual Meeting of the Public Choice Society, New Orleans, 1981, where it benefitted from wide-ranging discussion. We also greatly benefitted from several conversations with John Ferejohn.

Public Choice 37: 503-519 (1981) 0048-5829/81/0373-0503 $02.55.
© 1981 Martinus Nijhoff Publishers, The Hague. Printed in the Netherlands.

504

principle upon which stability is based. Finally, the concluding section draws some general implications and points to what remain, in our opinion, the important categories of unsettled questions.

We have been impelled to write up these ideas by the provocative question raised by Professor Tullock in a recent essay of the same title, *viz.* 'Why so much stability?' There he confronts the impossibility/instability theorems of PMR with the apparent fact that real-world legislatures exhibit a good deal of stability. Absent from these real institutions are the manifestations of instability and disequilibrium – constantly shifting majorities, endless cycling, policy reversals – that one would expect of a PMR system. He resolves this apparent contradiction, and in turn answers the question he posed. In his view, logrolling and vote-trading (hereafter called 'legislative exchange') reverse the otherwise bleak hopes for PMR implied by a decade's worth of social choice theory. We propose an alternative resolution of this anomaly. In our view, real-world legislative practices constrain the instability of PMR by *restricting* the domain and the content of legislative exchange. The latter, in our view, is part of the problem (though by no means the only part) with PMR, not part of the solution. Throughout, then, we hope to convey what we believe is a compelling case for answering Tullock's question, 'Why so much stability?' with 'Institutional arrangements do it!' It is the transformation[1] of PMR into a more complex institutional arrangement, not logrolling and other forms of exchange, that produces 'so much' stability.

Section I: Instability of pure majority rule

Starting with Plott (1967), students of majority rule have focused on the extreme and special nature of the conditions necessary for the existence of equilibrium; generally no such equilibrium exists. This literature has matured over the past decade and includes the work, among others, of Kadane (1972), Sloss (1973), Kramer (1973), McKelvey (1976, 1979), McKelvey and Wendell (1976), Slutsky (1977), Cohen (1979), Schofield (1978), and Cohen and Matthews (1980). These results are by now quite familiar to readers of this journal and may be summarized as follows. Assume an m-dimensional policy space, X, of feasible outcomes, and consider choice over X by an n-person legislature. The legislature operates under a system of pure majority rule (PMR) in which any legislator (or group of legislators) may make proposals to alter the status quo, x^0. Any proposal that commands a majority against x^0 beats it. In this setting, a *majority rule equilibrium* (MRE) is an element of the feasible set that is unbeaten by any other element of X in paired comparison. The results cited above show that under all but extreme circumstances – specifically, smooth and convex preferences distributed in a precisely symmetrical fashion (see Plott, 1967; McKelvey and Wendell, 1976) – no MRE exists. Rather, for any point, $x \in X$, there is a non-empty set of points, $W(x)$, called the *majority-rule win set at* x, each element of which commands the support of a majority against x. The lack of equilibrium implies that for all $x \in X$, $W(x) \neq \emptyset$. As a consequence, majority rule cycles exist, cycles which can be shown to extend over the entire policy space (McKelvey, 1976, 1979; Cohen, 1978; Schofield, 1978, 1980).

It may be noted, moreover, that no form of legislative exchange can obviate these results *as long as the pure majority rule structure is maintained*. That is, no form of logrolling, whether implicit or explicit, coalition formation, or individual bargaining, can eliminate the inherent instability that follows from the non-existence of an MRE. No matter what form of exchange is postulated, any point is dominated by some other proposed point that benefits a decisive coalition. For example, suppose some policy x is arrived at through logrolling or coalition formation. Then, because $W(x)$ is non-empty at x, the losers, in combination with some of the winners at x, may propose some $y \in W(x)$ that makes this new majority better off at y than at x. And nothing in the rules of the PMR game prohibits the new majority from forming and displacing its predecessor. This is the very essence of the nonexistence of equilibrium.[2]

The principal features of PMR, and the inefficaciousness of vote-trading in the resolution of disequilibrium, are illustrated in Figure 1. Here we consider the case of a five-person legislature using PMR. Each legislator has strictly quasi-convex preferences (in fact, so-called Type I preferences) and ideal point labeled $\bar{x}^i$. For an arbitrary point $x^0 \in X$, the five petal-shaped shaded regions displayed in the figure constitute the set of points that three or more legislators

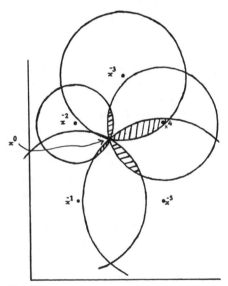

Figure 1.

506

prefer to x^0; that is, their union is $W(x^0)$. The thrust of Plott's theorem is that $W(x) \neq \emptyset$ for all $x \in X$ except possibly for those points (if any) satisfying Plott's extreme symmetry condition. Thus, no point is an equilibrium; the core of the PMR game is empty; and these results remain in force for any legislature of cardinality $n \geq 3$ and any issue characterization of dimensionality $m \geq 2$.

To make our point most forcefully, let us briefly consider the quintessential logrolling circumstance – the pork barrel. For simplicity we develop a highly symmetric example, though the force of our argument is not compromised by further complexities. Let each legislator in an n-person legislature represent a geographical constituency which seeks a pork-barrel project. A project is parametrized by a scalar – x_j for the jth district – measuring project size. Thus, an outcome in this context is an n-dimensional vector, $(x_1, \ldots, x_n)$, describing the various scales at which projects in each of the n districts are to be built. Associated with each project are benefits concentrated exclusively in the district in which the project is sited – $b_i(x_j) = 0$ if $i \neq j$ – and costs distributed across all districts according to a fixed tax-sharing rule, $t_i c(x_j)$ being district i's tax burden for district j's project. The maximand for the jth legislator, assuming here that it is based exclusively on the net benefits secured by his district, is

$$N_j(x_1, \ldots, x_n) = b_j(x_j) - t_j \sum_{i=1}^{n} c(x_i).$$

If project benefits are increasing at a marginally diminishing rate in project scale ($b' > 0, b'' < 0$) and costs are increasing at a marginally increasing rate ($c' > 0, c'' > 0$), then the level sets of the $N_j(x)$ functions are smooth and quasi-convex. The ideal point of the jth legislator is given by the vector x^j in which the ith component is zero for $i \neq j$ and the jth component is the value for which $b_j'(x_j) = t_j c'(x_j)$.

That is, the pork-barrel PMR game is the n-dimensional version of Figure 1 with each legislator bliss point located along its own dimension so as to satisfy the above first-order condition. Consequently, the generic instability associated with that earlier example applies here as well. The no-project vector, $(0, \ldots, 0)$, is defeated by a coalition D consisting of the collection of $d = \frac{n+1}{2}$ (n odd) projects, each set at the scale x_j^* for which $b_j(x_j^*) > t_j \sum_{i \in D} c_i(x_i^*)$. This vector of projects, in turn, is defeated by the bribe coalition (Fiorina, 1980) consisting of the $n - d$ losers agreeing to build only one of the d previous projects, thereby bribing its legislator into their coalition. In this case, all members of the new winning coalition have diminished their respective tax burdens by this move. Finally, coming full circle, the no-project vector defeats the bribe vector by a vote of $n - 1: 1$.

The point here is that there is no natural stopping point for this choice institution so long as losers are not denied access to the agenda. And it does not matter that, as Tullock points out, the efficient policy that builds all projects at their most efficient scale, x^e, yields legislators highest *ex ante* payoffs.[3] Since at any proposal the majority win set is non-empty, it is always in the interests of those who prefer elements of this set to the original point to propose them. And, since nothing in the rules prevents them from doing so, they will. All we wish to note at this point is that x^e, like any other point under PMR, has a non-empty win set: $W(x^e) \neq \emptyset$. It is therefore vulnerable and holds no privileged theoretical status under PMR. We would, however, distinguish this argument from another entirely different argument, namely that x^e might comprise the basis of an *ex ante* agreement among legislators to *alter institutional rules* in order to guarantee x^e as the outcome. This latter argument, which may well be what Tullock has in mind, involves *transforming* PMR into a different legislative game, namely one constrained by prior agreements on rules (see note 1).

This transformation differs from logrolling and other forms of legislative exchange within PMR. Consequently, we must further emphasize in this context, since Tullock makes so much of it in his paper, *that logrolling accomplishes nothing*. If projects are voted on one at a time, in non-cooperative fashion, then any such project will lose $n - 1: 1$ and the outcome is the zero vector, x^0. Logrolling, either of the explicit form in which an omnibus of projects is voted on or of the implicit form in which, through vote-trading agreements, individual projects are approved, provides no new opportunities for equilibrium. As Kadane (1972) demonstrated, either the zero vector is an equilibrium or none is; and, since $W(x^0) \neq \emptyset$, the latter is true. Indeed, what this suggests is that logrolling and other forms of legislative exchange *destroy*, not enhance, the possibility of equilibrium. We conclude, consequently, that the promising direction of research involves an examination of transformations of the PMR game, transformations that *constrain* the prospects of logrolling, not enhance it. To this endeavor we now turn.

Section II: Inducing stability

The multidimensional formulation above, as well as its specialization to the pork barrel, covers a multitude of sins associated with PMR. We have suggested above, moreover, that legislative exchange cannot rescue PMR from disequilibrium and may, in fact, exacerbate the instability. In this section, we show that institutional modifications of PMR may induce stability. Specifically, we show that *institutional restrictions on the domain of exchange* induce stability, not legislative exchange per se. To see how this works, note that though at all points $W(x)$ is non-empty, if at some point y, the rules of the game prohibit proposals in $W(y)$ from being placed on the agenda, or at least prohibit the would-be gainers from making these proposals, then y may remain invulnerable or stable. This is not because there do not exist points that beat y but rather because those favoring these points cannot place them on the agenda for consideration.

Example 1: In this first example, we illustrate our point through a set of stringent restrictions on the proposal mechanism; other examples allow for more realistic sets of restrictions. Consider the following modifications to the PMR pork-barrel choice institution in a five-person legislature. Suppose that the decision to build projects is made by majority rule vote between the status quo vector, $x^0 = (0, 0, 0, 0, 0)$, and an omnibus proposal that is put together in the following manner. Any legislator that wishes his project built may simply elect to add it to the omnibus without prior approval of other legislators, providing it is proposed at the efficient scale, x_i^e (see note 3). In this case, the agenda facing the legislature is fixed and the amendments extremely pro-scribed, allowing only a *majority rule comparison* between the vector x^e and the status quo. All legislators are better off under the omnibus than under the status quo (assuming an even distribution of tax burdens, since $b_i > c_i$ at x_i^e); therefore this beats the status quo. Moreover, since no amendments are allowed, this point remains invulnerable. Even though there exists a large collection of policies that command the support of a majority against this point, they cannot arise for a vote and therefore cannot replace the entire package. Put differently, because the ability of a subset of individuals to logroll is *attenuated*, they cannot upset this equilibrium as under PMR. As a result of the institutional structure circumscribing individual proposal power, stability is induced.

Example 2: Consider another modification of the pork-barrel example sug-gested by Fiorina (1980). Given an initial proposed vector of projects, amend-ments to this proposal may only be of the following form:

(1) strike a project;
(2) add a project;
(3) substitute one project for another.

Under these amendment control rules, it can be shown that a stable policy choice exists, namely x^c – the vector of d cheapest projects (where d is the size of a simple majority). Indeed, Fiorina derives the following proposition:

> *Proposition:* Under the specified rules, the omnibus representing x^c is stable:
> (1) All expansion amendments fail, 1: $n - 1$;
> (2) All deletion amendments fail,[4] $n - d$: d;
> (3) All substitution amendments fail, 1: $n - 1$.

Stability results here as a consequence of the restrictions on proposal power. At the equilibrium, x^c, there exists many packages of projects that command a majority against this one. However, because amendments are limited to changing one element of the package at a time, none of these may arise for comparison. Consequently, stability is induced.

In this example the amendment rule permitting changes restricted to a single project does not prohibit exchanges across several moves; it just makes it difficult. While vote trading is not precluded, the functional equivalent of contracts may be costly to formulate and costly to enforce. If, for example, the secret ballot is in use, enforcement may be prohibitive. Collaboration, more importantly, if it manages to develop across projects despite high costs, *destabilizes* the situation; it renders x^c vulnerable, while producing some different outcome which, itself, is vulnerable. Put more constructively, institutional arrangements that attach costs to exchange may induce stability that would otherwise not be forthcoming under PMR.

Example 3 (Tullock, 1967): Here we begin with the general multidimensional case, but add the following modifications to the PMR institution. For any point x, no point within a certain distance, d, may be placed on the agenda. That is, all points within the ball $D(x)$ of radius d around x are not feasible; a presiding officer may rule any such motion dilatory and, therefore, out of order. This requirement may be thought of as a rule that prohibits what Tullock refers to as 'small changes.' We can show that this limitation on the

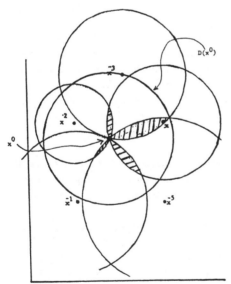

Figure 2.

510

ability of members to propose changes may induce stability under certain circumstances. Suppose that d is fixed, and hence for any policy, x, we specify the set of *infeasible proposals* as $D(x)$. If, at some point, x^0, the majority rule win set, $W(x^0)$, is wholly contained within $D(x^0)$, then x^0 is invulnerable in the sense that none of the points that command a majority against x^0 may arise for a vote. Because of this added institutional detail proscribing 'small changes,' x^0 remains a stable choice. This is illustrated in Figure 2. Figure 2 is identical to Figure 1 with the heavily outlined circle $D(x^0)$ superimposed. It is quite transparent that x^0 is stable (though the radius of $D(x^0)$ in this particular example may not satisfy some as proscribing 'small' changes inasmuch as it contains nearly the entire Pareto set). It should also be apparent that, for any fixed radius d, the existence of equilibrium points depends on the configuration of preferences. If the ideal points of legislators 4 and 5, for example, were placed at somewhat more southeastern locations in Figure 2, x^0 would no longer be invulnerable, even though 'small changes' were proscribed. More generally, for any given d there appear to be no obvious conditions that guarantee $W(x) \subseteq D(x)$ for some x.[5]

Example 4 (McKelvey, 1979): Social choice theorists have long noted the potential of an 'agenda setter' or convenor for manipulating the final outcome. Several scholars study examples of this type (Plott and Levine, 1978; Issac and Plott, 1979; McKelvey, 1979; Miller, 1979; Romer and Rosenthal, 1979; and Weingast, 1981). It is now well known that under unlimited agenda control by one individual (or set of perfectly conspiring individuals) an agenda may be devised the final outcome of which is his ideal point. In Figure 1, for example, where individual 1 has complete agenda power and no other individual may make proposals, there are no restrictions on individual 1's ability to achieve any desired point. There exists a particular sequence of motions, commencing with x^0 and ending with $\bar{x}^1$, with the property that each motion defeats its predecessor by a majority. Here again, even though the majority win set is non-empty (i.e., $W(\bar{x}^1) \neq \emptyset$), none of the legislators preferring elements of this set may propose them. The only one with the power to do so, legislator 1, has no incentive to do so.

Example 5 (Shepsle, 1979): In our final example, we again modify the five-person legislature of Figure 1. Suppose, instead of the unlimited proposal power of each individual, that legislators were restricted to proposing alternatives that change only one dimension of the status quo at a time. No restrictions are placed on the number of amendments nor on which individuals may propose alternatives. Under these circumstances, it can be proved that the vector of medians is an equilibrium. Here again, even though there remain many policies that beat this point, these may not be achieved because of the nature of the restrictions on changes in policy. This is illustrated in

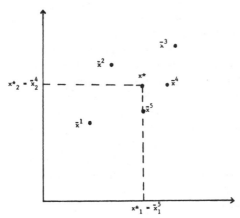

Figure 3.

Figure 3. Here, all proposals that change only one component of x^* $= (x_1^*, x_2^*)$, where x_i^* is the median position along dimension i, are dominated by x^*. As we noted at the end of Example 2, vote-trading agreements across dimensions may allow sophisticated players to subvert x^* in favor of some other y. It, in turn, is vulnerable to still other points. Hence, this form of logrolling is destabilizing and surely cannot constitute an answer to Tullock's question, 'Why so much stability?'

Section III: Equilibrium in a class of legislative institutions

The examples of the previous two sections may be summarized as follows. The results by McKelvey et al. show that for any PMR institution, $W(x)$ is non-empty for all x. As a consequence, all policies are vulnerable and hence unstable under PMR. The lack of restrictions on the ability of the losers at x to place alternatives before the legislature account for this inherent instability. However, the five examples of the previous section show that restrictions on the ability of individuals or groups to make proposals is one fundamental way in which *institutions may induce stability*. This is not because the results of McKelvey et al. are irrelevant, but because of the way in which restrictions on proposals neutralize the destabilizing effect of non-empty $W(x)$ sets. In order to understand this kind of stability, therefore, we must look at those features which systematically transform PMR into an institution with appropriate restrictions on the proposal power of individuals. *In this sense, the instability of majority rule hinges upon the unrestricted richness of coalition and logrolling possibilities under PMR. Institutions different from PMR may exhibit stability*

512

precisely because they restrict logrolling behavior and therefore the potential for legislative exchange to upset an equilibrium.

Consider a legislature with n members. Let $C(x, y)$ be the majority rule choice function, i.e., $x = C(x, y)$ iff the number of legislators preferring x to y exceeds the number preferring y to x. As before, the majority rule win set at any point x is $W(x) = \{y | y = C(x, y)\}$. In a PMR institution, there are no restrictions on proposal or agenda power. The search for equilibrium in past research consequently focused upon $W(x)$. Little explicit attention needed to be given to the set of feasible proposals since this set always comprised the entire space. However, a wide class of institutions based upon majority rule, including the examples offered in Section II, may be described in terms of restrictions on proposal sets available to individuals (or particular sets of individuals). Indeed, we formalize this by defining the family of majority rule legislative institutions.

For any coalition, s, composed of one or more members, let $g_s(x)$ be the set of feasible points open to s to propose at a given point x. These sets capture the idea that some institutions single out different roles for institutional actors, and that the behavioral discretion of these roles may be dependent upon the prevailing state, x. For example, in the extreme case of some individual, i, with complete agenda power, then $g_i(x) = X \,\forall\, x$ and $g_j(x) = \emptyset \,\forall j \neq i$ and $\forall x$. In a similar manner, we may define an institution that delegates agenda power to a specific subset or committee. Other examples include restrictions on amendment possibilities, such as a germaneness rule, or on the structure of the order of vote, such as a rule requiring that the status quo be voted upon last.

In addition to knowing the opportunities available to s at any point x, it is convenient to know whether s has an incentive to make proposals at this point, that is, whether the members of s prefer some element in $g_s(x)$ to x. Let these points be $P_s(x)$, where $P_s(x) = \{y \in g_s(x) | y$ preferred to $x \,\forall\, i \in s\}$. In the case where s consists of a single legislator i, then $P_i(x) = \{y \in g_i(x) | U^i(y) > U^i(x)\}$.

Definition: A point x is *vulnerable* iff $\exists y$ such that
(i) $y \in P_s(x)$ for some s, and
(ii) $y \in W(x)$.

Otherwise, a point is said to be invulnerable.

We are now in a position to define our notion of equilibrium.

Definition: A point x^* is a *structure induced equilibrium* (SIE) iff it is invulnerable (Shepsle, 1979a, 1979b).

Thus, x^* is a SIE iff $W(x^*) \cap P_s(x^*) = \emptyset \,\forall\, s$. This says that a point x^* is an SIE if and only if those points which defeat x^* either can be proposed only by those who do not prefer to do so, or cannot be proposed at all. Conversely, if this intersection were non-empty, then x^* could not be an equilibrium since there remain points which some s is empowered and disposed to propose and which, in turn, are capable of defeating x^*. Since s could do better in this case, x^* cannot be an equilibrium.

The concepts of vulnerability and structure-induced equilibrium define in a precise manner the notion of stability exhibited in the examples in Section II. Within this framework, we may easily see why there are no structure-induced equilibria for PMR. Since the proposal set of all legislators is the entire set at any status quo, there are no restrictions on the ability of individuals who prefer elements of $W(x)$ from proposing them. That is, at any x, $g_i(x) = X$ for all i. Moreover, at any x, there exists an i such that for some $y \in W(x)$, $U^i(y) > U^i(x)$ so that $W(x) \cap P_i(x) \neq \emptyset$. Since this intersection property holds at all x, we have shown that no SIE exists for PMR.

However, we may demonstrate, through a series of examples, the usefulness of this approach for studying legislative voting institutions other than PMR. These contrast with the so-called Chaos Theorem of McKelvey et al., inasmuch as the rules limit the set of feasible alternatives to which the status quo is vulnerable.

In our first example, we show the implications of a *convenor* with exclusive power over the agenda; that is, the only feasible replacements for the status quo are those proposed by him. The situation can be seen in Figure 1 for the status quo, x^0, with Mr. 2 assumed to be the convenor. $W(x^0)$, representing all the points that command a majority against x^0, is given by the shaded petals. Yet, only those proposed by the convenor may arise for a vote. The convenor will structure a sequence of votes that leads to his ideal point, $\bar{x}^2$. The nonemptiness of $W(x^0)$ guarantees this possibility.[6] The convenor's ideal point, $\bar{x}^2$, is a structure-induced equilibrium, even though $W(\bar{x}^2)$ is non-empty. This is because the set of points preferred to $\bar{x}^2$ by the *convenor* is empty – $P_2(\bar{x}^2) \cap W(\bar{x}^2) = \emptyset$, so that even though there exist points that beat $\bar{x}^2$, these will never arise for a vote.

We next study several rules employed in the U.S. Congress to illustrate restrictions on legislative choice:

(a) *The status quo voted on last:* This rule means that no matter where votes on alternatives prior to the last one move through the space (by McKelvey, this process can lead anywhere), the last vote is against the prevailing social state, x^0. Hence, the only outcomes of this process are x^0 or some point in $W(x^0)$. It will be the latter if the penultimate survivor in the process is in $W(x^0)$; otherwise, it will be the former. Referring back to Figure 1, PMR as amended by the rule of voting the status quo last is a restricted and well-behaved decision process, in which the final result is contained in the shaded area $W(x^0)$. In contrast, the results on PMR by McKelvey imply that the final outcome could lie in any region of the space.

514

(b) *Committee proposal power:* In the House of Representatives, committees (with minor exceptions) initiate the proposal process within their respective areas of policy jurisdiction. The rules of the House require that in addition to voting the status quo last, a committee proposal, B, is voted on second to last. This implies that any successful amendment, A, to B must satisfy two conditions: (i) $A \in W(B)$; and (ii) $A \in W(x^0)$. The first is necessary if A is to defeat B in the penultimate vote. The second is necessary if A, having defeated B, is to prevail against x^0. We have previously seen that voting the status quo last restricts outcomes dramatically. We now learn that granting a committee the power to propose the penultimate alternative further constrains the process; the set of final outcomes now consists of $W(x^0) \cap W(B)$.

(c) *Rules Committee:* In the House of Representatives, each bill must go to the Rules Committee after being passed by its committee but before it reaches the House floor. The purpose is to grant the bill a 'rule' governing debate and the amendment process. If a rule is not granted, the bill is effectively killed since it may not be forwarded to the full House for a vote. In the days of Judge Smith, autocratic chairman of the House Rules Committee, this veto power was exercised with some frequency. It is clear that this institutional feature further restricts the outcomes of an institutionalized majority rule system. Specifically, to avoid a Rules Committee veto, a committee bill must be contained in the Rules Committee 'preferred to' set, i.e., $B \in P_R(x^0)$.

Like institutional practices (a), (b), and (c) above, other features in current use in the legislative process are amenable to similar analyses, including: conference committee agreements, the executive veto, germaneness rules, rules of recognition, and so on. The point of these examples discussed above is to show that the rules employed by legislatures significantly restrict the potential outcomes of the legislative process. Our model provides a technology for studying these effects. The somewhat startling conclusion, in contrast to the McKelvey results that anything may happen, is that the number of potential replacements for a given status quo may be restricted. The reason is simple. Even though the majority rule win-sets are everywhere non-empty, the rules of the legislature may prohibit elements of this set from arising for comparison, thus leaving other points invulnerable.

Section IV: Conclusion

Professor Tullock has raised a central question in the confrontation between abstract models of PMR and majority rule as practiced in real institutions. We believe the decision making stability of real-world legislatures lies in the way these legislatures institutionalize majority rule. Logrolling, vote trading, coalition formation, and bargaining are red herrings in this argument. Rather, it is the restrictions on such legislative exchange that promote structure-induced equilibrium. Put differently, institutional arrangements place constraints on the completeness of the majority rule relation by restricting social comparisons.

The framework developed here shows that an assumption implicit in the discussions of many majority rule theorists fails to hold. In part, the implicit rationale for focusing upon PMR was that results proved for this rule were presumed to hold for *any* institution based on PMR. In one sense this remains true, namely, that the majority rule win sets, $W(x)$, are everywhere non-empty. In another sense, however, it is not true that all properties of institutions based upon majority rule are inherited from PMR. The theory outlined above shows that stability may not be as elusive as theorists of PMR have concluded.

The concept of equilibrium developed in the last section incorporates the major features of prominent choice institutions as well as capturing the special cases in the literature cited in Section II. We now turn to a brief discussion of future work. We address the question that remains, in our opinion, the salient one in the study of institutions and their effect on policy choice, namely, understanding the factors governing the choice of one institutional arrangement over another.

Throughout this paper, we have distinguished agreements that transform the rules from agreements (or vote-trades) that take place within a given set of rules. In principle, anything attainable under the former could also be attained under the latter if there were some form of mechanism to enforce vote-trades as contracts. Under such a rubric, complex legislative agreements in the form of contingent contracts achieve the desired result without resorting to the institutionalization of a rule. In practice, however, there are several problems with vote-trading agreements as contracts. First, the cost of writing these contracts is often quite high due to the number of potential contingencies for which provision must be made. Second, and more important, PMR lacks an enforcement mechanism. Individual parties to contracts in market settings have recourse to the courts. This provides protection beyond the assurance of good faith and brand names. No comparable institution exists within the legislature to supplement the natural though imperfect brand name phenomenon (i.e., that of 'keeping one's word' to preserve and enhance credibility for future trades).

While the legislature could create a court or committee to monitor contracts and enforce agreements, alternatively, it could simply impose a rule binding upon everyone which insured the outcome sought. Of the two alternative institutions, the latter probably economizes on transaction costs, particularly for those situations that recur with some frequency. With a rule, a new contract need not be negotiated each time between new sets of players. Moreover, a contingency clause might easily be appended to a rule to cover cases where there is widespread agreement that it is inappropriate. For

516

example, in the Congress a special majority may vote to suspend the rules (note that if only a simple majority were required, then this would be no different from PMR).[7] In sum, logrolling solutions to the problem of forging agreements are unworkable because they lack enforcement mechanisms. Logrolling, then, cannot constitute an answer to the question, 'Why so much stability?'[8]

If institutional rules are to constitute an answer to Tullock's stability question, then we must confront the manner in which those rules are chosen. There are very few theories about the choice of rules – exceptions include Buchanan and Tullock (1962), Buchanan (1975, 1979), and contributions in the property rights literature. Even in the absence of a theory, we may still worry that constitutional choice processes (the choice of rules) are vulnerable to the same instabilities found in PMR. We term this the 'Riker Objection' since this issue was recently posed by Riker (1980). If institutional constraints create equilibrium – that is, if transformations of a PMR institution into a non-PMR institution create a situation of equilibrium from one without an equilibrium – then preferences over outcomes lead naturally to an *induced* set of preferences over institutional arrangements. In this sense, an individual prefers one institution over another if he prefers the equilibrium policy state of one over the equilibrium (or unpredictability) of the other. In the case of multiple equilibria, an individual prefers the institution that yields the highest expected utility given a probability distribution over equilibrium states (Plott, 1972).

As long as preferences for policy states differ, then preferences over institutions with differing equilibrium states (distribution of equilibria) should also differ. The Riker Objection suggests that a simple extension of McKelvey's Chaos Theorem predicts endless cycles here so long as PMR governs the choice over institutions. In this sense, the existence of institutions and their stability must remain, like policy choices under PMR, tenuous – what Riker calls 'unstable constants.' Nevertheless, empirically we observe institutions persisting for long periods; in light of the Riker Objection, Tullock's question applies at this level as well.

We may make several observations that imply an attenuation of endless cycling at the institutional-choice level. First, typically, non-PMR rules govern the choice of new rules. Second, it is risky to attempt to change the status quo contrary to the interests of those currently in control. Since failure may lead to the imposition of sanctions, expected gains must be weighed against the certainty of these sanctions. While this does not rule out changes, it will reduce the number of attempts. This is surely the conclusion to be drawn from a reading of the history of the U.S. Congress. The comparison between choice in this setting and the McKelvey world, then, is not parallel since proposals are costless to make in the latter but not in the former. Finally, there often exists a well-defined status quo alternative. In the case of the social

517

contract, the status quo is the Hobbesian state of nature. For the case of the U.S. Constitutional Convention, it was the Articles of Confederation (Riker, 1979). In these and similar settings, even though there may be no formal rule that the status quo must literally be voted last, this restriction nevertheless may hold de facto. Consequently, the constitutional outcome is either the status quo ante or an alteration that cannot be vetoed, i.e., an element in the 'win set' of the status quo. With these qualifications in mind, the effect of the Riker Objection is mitigated. Even at the constitutional level, then, restrictions on the ability of individuals to make proposals may induce equilibrium.

NOTES

1. We wish to distinguish legislative exchange as it occurs in a particular institutional context – for example, vote-trading and logrolling in support of a specific bill – from that which occurs in the process that transforms one institutional arrangement into another. As we shall demonstrate, legislative exchange in these two contexts have different effects. We defer until the final section a discussion of legislative exchange in the process transforming PMR into a more complex institutional arrangement.
2. There are illustrations in the literature, e.g., Vickrey's 'self-policing property,' of circumstances in which players entertain rational expectations about continued play. Various conceptions of sophisticated behavior contain this idea as well. With this idea, it is possible to construct contingencies in which the expectation of adverse consequences if the game is permitted to continue induces an aversion to change (continued cycling) by a decisive set of players. It is doubtful, however, whether Tullock's condition of 'so much' stability can be accounted for in this fashion.
3. The efficient vector is $x^e = (x^e_1, \ldots, x^e_e)$, where x^e_j satisfies the first-order condition $b'_j(x^e_j) = c'(x^e_j)$. For details, see Weingast (1979) and Shepsle and Weingast (1981). In these papers, as well as in Tullock (1981), it is shown that the certainty of x^e is preferred by all legislators to the expected value of net benefits on the assumption that some minimal winning coalition will ultimately form, each equally likely.
4. Fiorina's proposition is not quite right in this particular instance inasmuch as it is not at all clear why $d - 1$ of the members of the winning coalition oppose striking the project of the remaining coalition member. With one fewer project, their tax burdens all would be reduced. Fiorina notes, however, that he has some form of sophisticated behavior in mind (see note 2 above) according to which members of the winning coalition rationally expect (fear) the strategy of 'striking a project' to be a ploy to destroy the winning coalition; they therefore oppose it.
5. Schofield (1978) gives some analytical precision to a related problem – namely a demonstration of instability in the context in which *only* small departures from an existing state (incrementalism) are permitted.
6. McKelvey (1977) actually has designed an algorithm by which to accomplish this result.
7. This is the same rationale that underpins the Uniform Commercial Code and other areas of the law of contracts. To cover situations that occur quite regularly, certain standard procedures are written into the law and are automatically a part of any agreement or exchange. This significantly lowers transaction costs (contracts need not be negotiated *sui generis*), and in those circumstances where the standard is inappropriate, the parties may simply contract around it. Similar results occur in most areas of the common law. For further discussion, see Posner (1976).
8. This reasoning justifies our separation throughout the text of choices within a given institution

518

and choices among institutions. This distinction is a natural one, dating back to Buchanan and Tullock's *The Calculus of Consent*. There they analyze separately the constitutional calculus of choice over voting rules and the behavior under a specific voting rule.

REFERENCES

Buchanan, J. M. (1975). *The limits of liberty*. Chicago: University of Chicago Press.
Buchanan, J. M. (1979). *What should economists do?* Indianapolis: Liberty Press.
Buchanan, J. M., and Tullock, G. (1962). *The calculus of consent*. Ann Arbor: University of Michigan Press.
Cohen, L. (1979). Cyclic sets in multidimensional voting models. *Journal of Economic Theory* 20: 1-12.
Cohen, L., and Matthews, S. (1980). Constrained Plott equilibria, directional equilibria, and global cycling sets. *Review of Economic Studies* 47: 975-986.
Fiorina, M. P. (1980). Legislative facilitation of government growth: Universalism and reciprocity practices in majority rule institutions. *Research in Public Policy Analysis and Management* 1: forthcoming.
Isaac, R. M., and Plott, C. R. (1978). Cooperative game models of the influence of the closed rule in three person majority rule committees: Theory and experiments. In P. C. Ordeshook (Ed.), *Game theory and political science*. New York: New York University Press. 283-322.
Kadane, J. B. (1972). On division of the question. *Public Choice* 13: 47-55.
Kramer, G. H. (1973). On a class of equilibrium conditions for majority rule. *Econometrica* 41: 285-297.
McKelvey, R. D. (1976). Intransitivities in multidimensional voting models and some implications for agenda control. *Journal of Economic Theory* 12: 472-482.
McKelvey, R. D. (1977). Constructing majority paths between arbitrary points. Paper delivered at American Economic Association Meetings. New York.
McKelvey, R. D. (1979). General conditions for global intransitivities in formal voting models. *Econometrica* 47: 1085-1111.
McKelvey, R. D., and Wendell, R. E. (1976). Voting equilibria in multidimensional choice spaces. *Mathematics of Operations Research* 1: 144-158.
Miller, G. J. (1979). Experimental results in two-party agenda setting: What's it worth to be a party? Working paper. Michigan State University.
Plott, C. R. (1967). A notion of equilibrium and its possibility under majority rule. *American Economic Review* 57: 787-806.
Plott, C. R. (1972). Individual choice of a political-economic process. In R. G. Niemi and H. F. Weisberg (Eds.), *Probability models of collective decision making*. Columbus: Charles E. Merrill Publishing Co. 83-101.
Plott, C. R., and Levine, M. E. (1978). A model of agenda influence on committee decisions. *American Economic Review* 68: 146-160.
Posner, R. A. (1977). *Economic analysis of law*. 2nd Edition. Boston: Little-Brown.
Riker, W. H. (1979). The verification of scientific generalizations by historical case studies: The genesis of the American Constitution. Presented at Meeting of Social Science History Association. Cambridge, Mass.
Riker, W. H. (1980). Implications from the disequilibrium of majority rule for the study of institutions. *American Political Science Review* 74: 432-447.
Romer, T., and Rosenthal, H. (1978). Political resource allocation, controlled agendas, and the status quo. *Public Choice* 33: 27-45.
Schofield, N. (1978). Instability of simple dynamic games. *Review of Economic Studies* 45: 575-594.
Schofield, N. (1980). Formal political theory. *Quality and Quantity* 14: 249-275.

519

Shepsle, K. A. (1979a). Institutional arrangements and equilibrium in multidimensional voting models. *American Journal of Political Science* 23: 27-59.

Shepsle, K. A. (1979b). The role of institutional structure in the creation of policy equilibrium. In D. W. Rae and T. J. Eismeier (Eds.), *Public choice and public policy*. Beverly Hills: Sage. 249-283.

Shepsle, K. A., and Weingast, B. R. (1980). Political solutions to market problems: The political incidence of economic benefits and costs. Delivered at Meetings of Public Choice Society. San Francisco.

Shepsle, K. A., and Weingast, B. R. (1981). Political preferences for the pork barrel: A generalization. *American Journal of Political Science* 25: 96-112.

Sloss, J. (1973). Stable outcomes in majority rule voting games. *Public Choice* 15: 19-48.

Slutsky, S. M. (1977). A voting model for the allocation of public goods: Existence of an equilibrium. *Journal of Economic Theory* 14: 299-325.

Tullock, G. (1967). The general irrelevance of the general impossibility theorem. *Quarterly Journal of Economics*, May 1967, p. 256. Reprinted in *Towards a mathematics of politics*, 1967, University of Michigan Press, Ann Arbor, Michigan, p. 37.

Tullock, G. (1981). Why so much stability? *Public Choice* 37: 189-202.

Weingast, B. R. (1979). A rational choice perspective on Congressional norms. *American Journal of Political Science* 24: 245-263.

Weingast, B. R. (1981). Regulation, reregulation, and deregulation: The political foundations of agency-clientele relationships. *Law and Contemporary Problems* 44: 147-177.

Part IV
Some Major Issues

[19]

Introductory Observations

If the project of turning economics into a hard science could succeed, it would be worth doing. . . . There are, however, some reasons for pessimism about the project. (Solow 1985, 331)

The central message of the New Institutional Economics is that institutions matter for economic performance. This is, of course, an old and inherently plausible intellectual position. Even writers in the strict neoclassical tradition such as Marshall (1920, 200) have recognized that institutional structure exerts an important influence on behavior. In more recent times, however, as the technical development of neoclassical theory has progressed and economic models have become increasingly abstract, institutional phenomena have received less and less attention. Thus, in what may be regarded as mainstream theory through the 1980s (exemplified by welfare economics and the general equilibrium models of Arrow-Debreu), institutions play virtually no role at all. Emphasis is on allocative efficiency, and different institutional arrangements are seen merely as "alternative means" for meeting the conditions required for Pareto optimality.

> The optimality conditions, being simply technical requirements, contain no ideological implications. They apply equally to capitalism, socialism, or any other "ism." Whatever the political ideology of a country, it could make all of its citizens better off by ensuring that production and allocation satisfied the optimality conditions. (Lancaster 1969, 276)

On this accounting, microeconomics is, in effect, institutionally neutral, a circumstance that represents both a strength and a weakness of neoclassical economics. The orthodox approach is useful because it permits the theorist to show the basics of economic efficiency under ideal-typical conditions of perfect information and foresight. Moreover, the role of relative prices in economic decision making can be made clear despite the absence of any institutional analysis. Contemporary theory, however, does have sharp limitations. Its weakness resides precisely in its institutional neutrality or its predisposition to

2   Institutions and Economic Theory

neglect serious consideration of institutional constraints and transaction costs. Neoclassical economic theory, therefore, can only be applied in a highly abstract sense to questions of resource allocation.

The deficiencies of neoclassical theory were, of course, not unknown to earlier generations of economists. Indeed, dissenters to the classical and neoclassical theoretical line have always existed in the profession, and, at times, these critics have had substantial influence. Representatives of the German historical school such as Roscher, Hildebrand, and later Schmoller reacted strongly against English classical economics, as did American institutionalists such as Commons. But these writers were basically hostile to abstract theoretical work in the sense of marginalism, utility or profit maximization, and the weighing of alternatives.[1] By contrast, the exponents of modern institutional economics apply the analytical apparatus of neoclassical theory (and newer techniques) to explain the workings and evolution of institutional arrangements and thus to expand the scope and predictive power of microeconomics.

1.1. Some Basic Assumptions and Terms

The body of thought that is now known as the New Institutional Economics began simply as an attempt to extend the range of applicability of neoclassical theory. During the postwar period, there was increasing dissatisfaction with, and criticism of, the traditional models of production and exchange. Nevertheless, neoinstitutionalism did not come into being as a result of any planned or coordinated effort to develop a new doctrine. In particular, marginalism was not rejected. What was desired primarily was change in certain key assumptions. Thus, modern institutionalism, while similar in many respects to standard neoclassical analysis, is distinct and is characterized by a significantly different perspective on microeconomic phenomena.

The following concepts and hypotheses are particularly relevant in modern institutional economics.

1. *Methodological individualism:* An entirely new interpretation is given to the role of individual decision makers. Methodological individualism emphasizes that people are different and have different and varied tastes, goals, purposes, and ideas. Hence, the implication is that "society," "the state," "the firm," "political parties," and so on are *not* to be understood as collective entities that behave as though they were individual agents. The organization or collectivity per se is no longer the main focus. Rather, it is thought that a theory of social phenomena must start with and base its explanations on the views and

---

1. On the German Younger Historical School, of which Schmoller was the leading figure, see for example, the critical remarks by Wagner (1907, 15): "political economy dissolves into a descriptive economic and cultural history."

behaviors of the individual members whose actions give rise to the phenomena being studied.

2. *The maximand:* Individuals are assumed to seek their own interests as they perceive them and to maximize utility subject to the constraints established by the existing institutional structure. Contrary to conventional practice in neoclassical theory, the dichotomy between the theory of consumer choice and the theory of the firm is ended by extending the utility maximization hypothesis to *all* individual choices. It follows, therefore, that a decision maker, whether he be the manager of a capitalist firm, a state bureaucrat, a politician, or whatever, is presumed to make his own choices and pursue his own goals within the limits allowed by the organizational structure in which he is operating.

3. *Individual rationality:* The neoinstitutionalist literature reveals that at least two distinct approaches are taken by economists in current attempts to interpret the concept of "individual rationality." The situation can be understood as follows. First, there are theorists who adhere closely to the traditional neoclassical view of *perfect individual rationality.* The assumption here is that all decision makers possess consistent and stable preferences—whether they are consumers, entrepreneurs, or bureaucrats. In other words, it is possible to conceive of an ideal case in which individuals display purposeful, rational behavior of a very high order. Thus:

> A completely rational individual has the ability to foresee everything that might happen and to evaluate and optimally choose among available courses of action, all in the blink of an eye and at no cost. (Kreps 1990b, 745)

Such complete or perfect individual rationality is assumed in the earlier work of representatives of the New Institutional Economics, and the view still dominates thinking in agency theory, the economic analysis of law, and public choice theory.

To approach the conditions of the real world more closely, contemporary writers have given increasing attention to the idea of *imperfect individual rationality.* From this perspective, the preferences of decision makers are recognized as incomplete and subject to change over time. Among the new institutional economists, this point is stressed particularly by North (1978, 972ff.).[2] What must be recognized, however, is that once positive transaction costs are

---

2. "The study of tastes—or writ large, ideology—can certainly be ignored by economists in dealing with many economic issues; it cannot be ignored by economists exploring the political and judicial process and certainly cannot be ignored by economic historians studying the changing constraints of an economic system over time" (North 1978, 973).

4   Institutions and Economic Theory

introduced into a microeconomic model, the universe being considered changes fundamentally, and decision makers cannot be assumed to be "completely" informed. The acquisition of unlimited knowledge simply becomes too expensive, or plainly impossible, insofar as future developments are concerned. Moreover, when transaction costs are posited, it is an easy step to the further understanding that individuals have restricted ability to handle data and formulate plans. Simon (1957) uses the term *bounded rationality* to signify the fact that decision makers are not omniscient and have real difficulties in processing information. Thus, while people can be seen as intendedly rational, they are not "hyperrational."

The assumption of imperfect individual rationality is dominant in transaction-cost analysis, in the more recent work on property rights, and in the new institutional approach to economic history. Williamson (1985) has consistently emphasized the importance of transaction costs in economic relations, and he has pointed out that, inter alia, limited rationality means that all economic exchange cannot be organized by market contracting. The situation under bounded rationality (and nonzero transaction costs) is such that it is impossible to deal with complex reality in all contractually relevant respects. As Kreps (1990b, 745) says:

> A boundedly rational individual attempts to maximize but finds it costly to do so and, unable to anticipate all contingencies, and aware of this inability, provides ex ante for the (almost inevitable) time ex post when an unforseen contingency will arise. Given this insight, the theory of incomplete contracts emerges as an inevitable development.

4. *Opportunistic behavior:* Qualities other than rationality per se have been attributed to decision makers. For example, Brunner and Meckling (1977, 71) describe the model of man developed in economics as the "resourceful, evaluating, maximizing man" (or REMM). This characterization implies that man is more than a brainy but heartless calculating machine. The literature also recognizes, however, that not all human qualities are attractive or praiseworthy. As Williamson has argued (1975), some individuals are likely to be dishonest in the sense that they may disguise preferences, distort data, or deliberately confuse issues. The existence of such behavior is important because, while bounded rationality prevents the writing of complete contracts, there could be general reliance on incomplete contracts if economic agents were *wholly trustworthy*. But realistically, since there is, in Williamson's phrase, "self-seeking with guile," and since it is normally very costly to distinguish opportunistic from nonopportunistic actors ex ante, comprehensive contracting must break down.

5. *Economic society:* From the most general standpoint, economic society can be said to involve individuals and a set of rules or norms that assign sanctioned property rights to each member of society. Property rights, in the economist's widest sense of the term, embrace the right to use and gain benefits from physical objects or intellectual works and the right to demand certain behavior from other individuals. The latter condition implies that contract rights exist—for example, in the requirement that the promised performance of a labor contract or loan agreement be fulfilled.[3] Society must, of course, be concerned with contract rights and the social arrangements that regulate the transfer of property rights.

Characteristically, neoclassical economics considers a special type of society in which the transfer of property rights by the use of physical force or other forms of compulsion is excluded. This convention means, inter alia, that the formation of pressure groups is ruled out. In other words, no attention is given to those coalitions whose purpose is to improve the welfare of their memberships at the expense of other individuals in the system through the use, for example, of government authority. In the neoclassical world, the only coalitions considered operate so as to produce Pareto improvements for their members by adhering to the principle of voluntary association and voluntary exchange.[4] Competition and free choice are assumed to dominate. Thus, transfer payments (including taxes) are to be understood as voluntary transfers within a cooperative coalition.

6. *Governance structure:* At any time, the property-rights configuration existing in an economy is determined and guaranteed by a governance structure[5] or order.[6] The latter can be understood as a system of rules plus the instruments that serve to enforce the rules. In general, an order may be enforced by "purely subjective" mechanisms (value-rational, religious, etc.) or by "the expectations of specific external effects" (Weber 1968, 33). Institutional economics usually deals with the second case—specifically, with a system that

---

3. Fisher (1912, 20) explains this as follows: "Lawyers distinguish between property rights and personal rights; but, to the economist, all rights are proprietary . . . logical convenience is served by adopting the broader definition of wealth, which includes human beings even when free, and by adopting also a coexistensively broad definition of property so as to include all rights known to jurisprudence. This being premised, it follows that every right is a property right. . . . Property rights, then, consist of rights to the uses or services of wealth." These are necessarily future services and they are therefore uncertain: "A strictly complete definition of property rights, therefore would read as follows: A property right is the right to the chance of obtaining some or all of the future services of one or more articles of wealth . . . Wealth and property . . . are correlative terms. Wealth is the concrete thing owned; property is the abstract right of ownership."

4. Essentially, that is the main concern of the theory of the core.

5. See Williamson (1979).

6. Weber uses the term *legitimate order* (1968, 31). Terms such as *structure, system,* and *social organization* have also been used (see Coleman 1991, 8).

6   Institutions and Economic Theory

restricts the possible behaviors of individuals through the use of sanctions. The sanctions are themselves established either by law or by custom (including the social enforcement of ethical and moral codes of conduct).

7. *Institutions:* It is tempting to try to secure some precision in formulating a definition for so basic a concept as the "institution," but, as Arrow has noted, "since research in this area is still in its early stages, undue exactness must be avoided" (1970, 224). In any event, for the purposes of this book, an institution will be defined as a set of formal and informal rules, including their enforcement arrangements (Schmoller 1900, 61). The purpose of an institution is, of course, to steer individual behavior in a particular direction. And, insofar as it is successful in realizing this objective, an institution provides structure to everyday activity and thus reduces uncertainty (North 1990, 239). In effect, institutions "define the incentive structure of societies and specifically economies" (North 1994, 4). This general conception of an institution can be elaborated, and it may be useful now to introduce Ostrom's fuller definition:

> "Institutions" can be defined as the sets of working rules that are used to determine who is eligible to make decisions in some arena, what actions are allowed or constrained, what aggregation rules will be used, what procedures must be followed, what information must or must not be provided, and what payoffs will be assigned to individuals dependent on their actions. . . . All rules contain prescriptions that forbid, permit, or require some action or outcome. Working rules are those actually used, monitored, and enforced when individuals make choices about the actions they will take . . . (1990, 51)

Schmoller (1900, 61) understands an institution to be

> a partial order for community life which serves specific purposes and which has the capacity to undergo further evolution independently. It offers a firm basis for shaping social actions over long periods of time; as for example property, slavery, serfhood, marriage, guardianship, market system, coinage system, freedom of trade.

How institutions come to be established is another question of interest, and the literature suggests at least two basic explanations. At one extreme, institutions are said to arise "spontaneously" (as a spontaneous order) on the basis of the self-interest of individuals. In such cases, they may organize themselves "without any agreement, without any legislative compulsion, even without any consideration of public interest" (Menger [1883] 1963, 154). Hayek (1973, 5) uses the term *evolutionary rationalism* to describe the situation. It is also recognized, however, that at the other extreme institutions may be the product of deliberate design. Some authority (parliament, a dictator, an entrepreneur, a team, etc.), acting with complete rationality, may be able to introduce a particular institutional structure that it deems appropriate. In the words of Hayek (1973), this is the case of a "made order" as opposed to a "spontaneous" or "grown order." Williamson (1991, 3) speaks of the respective situations as "intentional" and "spontaneous" governance. Coleman (1991, 8) uses the terms *constructed* and *spontaneous* social organization.

Institutions so defined are, so to speak, the grin without the cat, the rules of the game without the players. The functioning of an institution, though, depends in part on the individuals who use it. Thus, it follows that: "You cannot construct foolproof institutions" (Popper 1957, 66). Indeed, as Popper further notes: "Institutions are like fortresses. They must be well designed *and* properly manned" (66).

From the standpoint of institutional economics, there is interest not only in studying the characteristics of institutions but in making them integral elements of a general economic model. The endogenization of institutions is, therefore, crucial to the ongoing program of the New Institutional Economics.

8. *Organizations:* Institutions together with the people taking advantage of them are called organizations (North 1990) or in Schmoller's (1900, 61) terms "the personal side of the institution." Relative to the two explanations of institutional evolution mentioned above, the following associations hold. We speak, in the constructivist case, of formal organizations (a firm, a city council, etc.) and, in the spontaneous case, of informal organizations (such as a market community). De facto, there are neither pure formal nor pure informal organizations[7] to be found in the real world. Modern institutional economics deals with both institutions and organizations—that is, with institutions sine and cum people. Therefore, the New Institutional Economics includes, as a special case, the so-called new economics of organization (Moe 1984; Williamson 1991). A formal organization is defined by Arrow (1970, 224) as "a group of individuals seeking to achieve some common goals, or, in different language, to maximize an objective function." The problem of organizational control is, according to Arrow (225), answered by what we have termed an order.[8] Ideally, the order is constructed in such a way as to precisely maximize the organization's objective function. If this interpretation is accepted, it would seem that the economic theory of formal organizations (i.e., those that are deliberately "made") has some elements in common with neoclassical theory but still fits into the general body of institutional economics.

---

7. This terminology follows Weber (1968, 40, 48).

8. In the words of Arrow (1970, 225), this consists of a set of operating rules "instructing the members of the organization how to act" and a corresponding set of enforcement rules "to persuade or compel them to act in accordance with the operating rules."

8   Institutions and Economic Theory

It is apparent that real resources are required in order to create and operate any institution (or organization) and guarantee obedience to its rules. In other words, costs are involved, and these costs are referred to, broadly, as *transaction costs*. Once the assumption of a "frictionless" economic system is abandoned, analysis must change radically. Given frictions, property or contractual rights cannot be defined, monitored, and enforced instantly and without the use of resources. Rather, all of these essential activities imply transaction-cost outlays. Similarly, if property rights or contractual rights are to be transferred, transaction costs are inevitable. Specifically, there are costs attached to using the market (e.g., search and bargaining costs), and there are the costs of administrative coordination within a hierarchical organization (Chandler 1977, 490), including the setup costs of hierarchies. In short, transaction costs are both ubiquitous and significant in a modern economic system.

1.2. The Strange World of Costless Transactions

Although the fact has not always been recognized explicitly, the neoclassical model is based squarely on the assumption that transaction costs are zero. At first glance, such a simplification may appear to be both innocuous and highly useful to analysis. This assessment, however, is dubious. The concept of costless transactions has very far reaching consequences for microeconomic theory and leads to a model of the economic universe that is difficult to interpret consistently. In the rarefied world of zero transaction costs, decision makers can, supposedly, acquire and process any information they wish instantly and costlessly. They possess perfect foresight and, hence, are able to write complete contracts—contracts that can be monitored and enforced with absolute precision.[9] Force, in all its forms, is perfectly monopolized by the state. Consequently, there can exist no strikes, no boycotts, no sit-ins, no need for political correctness or other forms of social pressure. The power of coercion is exclusively in the hands of the state. Quite simply, then, it seems that, under neoclassical thinking, the setting in which economic activity is assumed to take place is remarkably specialized and remote from reality. While abstraction can be useful, there is good reason to believe that the neoclassical approach is overly abstract and incapable of dealing adequately with many current problems of interest to theorists and policymakers.

It is important to note that the assumption of costless transactions has great significance for the way institutions are viewed by neoclassical theory. The general impression conveyed is that institutional arrangements play an inconsequential role in the economic process. There is recognition that politi-

---

9. Note that "perfect foresight" does not necessarily imply that a decision maker knows precisely what the future will bring. Normally, the term is used to mean that the decision maker is aware of all future contingencies and knows the probabilities attaching to these contingencies.

cal, legal, monetary, and other institutions exist, but they are regarded as *neutral* in their effect on economic outcomes and largely ignored. In other words, institutions are taken as "allocationally neutral" in the sense that it does not matter, for example:

1. whether goods and services are exchanged by the use of money or otherwise (Samuelson 1968)
2. how production is organized—by the price mechanism across markets or within a hierarchically organized firm (Coase 1937)
3. whether the factors of production are owned or rented by their users (see Samuelson 1957, 894: "Remember that in a perfectly competitive market it really doesn't matter who hires whom: so have labor hire 'capital,' . . .").
4. who holds property rights in the productive factors, individuals or society (see, e.g., the arguments in favor of market socialism by Lange [1938] or of the labor-managed economy by Vanek [1970])
5. whether or not the ownership and control of a firm are separated (the market value rule is imposed by the forces of the market for corporate control, e.g., through the threat of hostile takeovers [Manne 1965])
6. whether the factors of production employed by a firm are financed by money loans or shares ("the market value of any firm is independent of its capital structure and is given by capitalizing its expected return at the rate . . . appropriate to its risk class" [Modigliani and Miller 1958, 268])
7. whether transactions are undertaken singly as transactions between "faceless strangers" or are repeated frequently between the same parties (Macneil 1974)
8. whether a good is supplied by a monopolist or by a large number of independent firms (in either case, unrestricted bargaining is said to lead to a Pareto-efficient equilibrium (Buchanan and Tullock 1962, 88; Demsetz 1968b, 61)[10]
9. whether legal rights are assigned to the party generating an externality or the party harmed by the externality (whatever the law, the allocation of resources will be identical [Coase 1960] because "people can always negotiate without cost to acquire, subdivide, and combine rights whenever this would increase the value of production" [Coase 1988b, 14])
10. whether an economy is based on the operations of decentralized individuals who rely on price signals and require no extensive infor-

---

10. From a game-theoretical viewpoint, this implies that every individual knows every other individual's payoff (utility, profit, or whatever function of the strategies played [Arrow 1979, 24]).

10   Institutions and Economic Theory

mation on the system's data or by a command structure based on a
central agent who possesses complete knowledge of individual preferences, technological alternatives, resources, and so on.

Given the diversity and importance of the cases just summarized, it is
clear that the idea of neutral institutions is strongly entrenched in neoclassical
theory. It may be true that, in some instances, the downplaying of institutional
arrangements does not seem to make much difference to the conclusions that
can be reached by economic analysis. What has to be remembered, however, is
that all of the explanations in points 1 through 10 are tied to the assumption of
costless transactions, and this assumption implies that decision makers operate
with perfect information and perfect foresight. But the presumption that hyper-
rational individuals exist necessarily affects outcomes. The precise and unambiguous solutions that can be reached in a frictionless world are simply not
possible in the real world. As Stigler has said: "The world of zero transaction
costs turns out to be as strange as the physical world would be without friction"
(1972, 12). The central inference to be drawn is that, because of its treatment of
institutions, neoclassical theory will not be able to discriminate between certain economic situations that are, in fact, quite different. For example, if the
conventional neoclassical position is taken, a money-using economy cannot be
distinguished from a barter economy or a private-ownership economy from a
socialist economy. Yet we know that, in these cases, systems having the same
initial data will show quite different results.

It should also be noted at this point that, in neoclassical theory, the price
system is the *only* (explicitly modeled) device that is identified as a means for
coordinating different activities. Administrative coordination is disregarded
because it is generally not thought to be necessary in a market-driven system.
Thus, coordination within institutions such as firms is viewed as taking place in
a "black box." That is, whatever is presumed to happen beyond straightforward
market transactions is not modeled.[11]

In general, the representatives of the NIE have not been content to merely
criticize orthodox neoclassical theory. Rather, they have attempted to produce
new theoretical constructs capable of explaining areas of economic life that
have previously been ignored and of showing why certain neoclassical theorems cannot be validated in real life. A first step was to consider why the
existence of positive transaction costs makes it necessary to view institutions
as endogenous variables in the economic model. The answer, of course, is that
in the real world institutional structure affects both transaction costs and individual incentives and hence economic behavior. Once this set of relations is

---

11. Arrow (1970, 232) says: "Some intra-organizational transactions will have the same
economic content as price-mediated transactions . . . [but] there are limits to its application."

acknowledged, it follows that new, more refined economic models must appear. In the chapters that follow, this book will attempt to describe some of these innovations.

1.3. The Ideal Type of the Classical Liberal State

General equilibrium theory can be understood as an approach that tries to establish the main features of the ideal type of liberal capitalist state in terms of a system of simultaneous equations. The state or society envisioned here is supposed to

> abstain from all attention to the personal wealth of its citizens and to go not a step further than necessary to secure its citizens against themselves and foreign enemies; for no other final purpose the State should restrict their freedom. (Humboldt [1792] 1967, 52)

Consequently, the elementary *constitutional rules* are based on the principle of the inviolability of individual property rights. This demands an elementary legal order, plus its enforcement mechanism, regulating: (1) the *property rights* of individuals according to the general principles of private property, (2) the *transfer* of these rights by consent according to the principle of freedom of contract,[12] and (3) individual *liability* for contractual obligations or in case of tortious acts.

Unfortunately, freedom of contract does not necessarily guarantee "voluntary exchange." To secure the latter, at least in general equilibrium theory, the principle of freedom of contract has to be *limited*. Individuals must not be permitted to contract in order to form coalitions whose purpose is predatory. That is, any coalition that is organized so as to improve the lot of its members at the expense of individuals outside the coalition must be ruled out. This restriction means, technically speaking, that there will be no resource allocations outside the core.[13] As a practical matter, there can be no pressure groups, no cartels, or, indeed, any coalition possessed of monopoly power. As noted, force is monopolized by the state, but the state's power of coercion is strictly limited by law—that is, by the state's constitution. Nevertheless, even if the state's powers are perfectly controlled, there remains the problem of the formation of pressure groups and the control of private coercive power.

The principle of freedom of contract can destroy itself through the evolution (via contract) of pressure groups, monopolies, and so on—Eucken (1952,

---

12. The individual has the right to regulate his contractual relations with a freely chosen partner in a mutually binding agreement.

13. Zero transaction costs do not imply the nonexistence of pressure groups. Actually, because of zero monitoring and enforcement costs, pressure groups are quite imaginable. See Furubotn (1991).

12   Institutions and Economic Theory

48), therefore, rightly demands that the constitutional state must protect its citizens not only from the coercive power of government but also from arbitrary acts by other citizens.[14] It follows that the formation of the institutional framework of the economy should not be left to itself.[15] Finally, the observance of this elementary legal order for the liberal state can be perfect provided that all activities can be monitored and proper behavior enforced at *zero cost.*

The basic legal structure implicit in the neoclassical model leaves room for the creation of "law" (*Recht*) by *private individuals,* and it is assumed that individuals take advantage of this opportunity. Given the existence of zero transaction costs (and the consequent full information status of decision makers), any private contracts made will be complete in the sense that they account for all contingencies. As a result of the private activity, the honeycomb of the legal order provided by the state is filled out by a network of complete (classical) contracts between individuals. Collectively, these contracts constitute a "voluntary legal order" built up spontaneously from below by utility-maximizing individuals (Hippel 1963, 27). In effect, freedom of contract is the institutional counterpart of the principle of economic decentralization—which is presupposed by competitive market models.[16]

According to the logic of the decentralized capitalist model, individual "atoms" negotiate with each other until they reach a state of the economy in which no one can improve his position without hurting someone else—that is, until Pareto efficiency is achieved. Since pressure groups are excluded by assumption and the number of bargaining parties is very large, the principle of free contracting described in this section is also the optimal means of achieving fair conciliation of interests. In other words, the presumption is that private contracting will be undertaken in such a way that the content of contracts will not be dictated by the more powerful agents in society.

1.4. The Ideal Type of Market Socialism

From a technical standpoint, general equilibrium models are institutionally neutral, but, in much of the literature, such models are discussed against the background of a competitive capitalist system. Consequently, the first-best configuration of the economy, which is supposed to be attained when all of the

---

14. "If the constitutional State (Rechtsstaat) was able to protect its citizens from arbitrary acts of the State itself, it was unable to save them from the arbitrary acts by other citizens" (Eucken 1952, 52). Eucken warns that the constitutional state is only able to succeed completely if together with its public legal order an "adequate" economic order is realized (52).

15. Eucken has noted that: "The realization of the laissez-faire principle causes the tendency for its abolition" (1952, 55).

16. German legal literature speaks in this context of *Privatautonomie,* the principle that each individual is free to regulate the circumstances of his life himself.

Pareto conditions are met, is associated with idealized capitalism. This association, however, is not necessary or inevitable. As some socialist writers have attempted to show, the same general equilibrium model may also be used to characterize the role of prices (or shadow prices) in the democratic socialist state (whose operation mimics that of a laissez faire system). In the socialist case, of course, the elementary legal framework has to be changed accordingly. Perhaps the best-known model of the socialist market economy is the one Lange (1938) proposed in seeking to answer Mises's assertion that a socialist economy could not provide for consistent and efficient factor allocation. Under socialism, the material means of production belong to "society" or the state— which may be regarded as a coalition of all individuals who are members of the economic system under consideration. Unfortunately, this arrangement leads to the loss of normal (capitalistic) markets for production goods, natural resources, and so on, but, as Lange argues, artificial markets can be created. That is, the state planning authorities, with the aid of so-called industry managers, can set arbitrary prices and then, through a trial-and-error process, range in on meaningful scarcity prices.

Since the liberal socialist blueprint normally provides for free markets for consumer goods and labor, only certain sectors of the system require the use of the trial-and-error approach. In any event, if all activities go forward as Lange suggests, the economy will achieve a first-best equilibrium solution and show allocative efficiency equal to that promised in an ideal capitalist state. Moreover, certain added advantages are said to hold for socialism. Pressure groups such as unions do not exist and are not necessary. Since all enterprise profits revert to the state, the socialist economy is able to pay "social dividends" to the public at large and bring about a more egalitarian (and supposedly more "fair") distribution of income than that found in capitalist societies. Ownership and control of capital are perfectly separated in the socialist case. This separation, however, poses no problem in a zero-transaction-cost world. Of course, "ownership" under socialism has limited meaning; ownership rights are severely attenuated, and no private individual possesses either permanent or transferable rights in collective assets. Finally, what must be emphasized here is that the assumption of costless transactions is crucial to the results Lange and other theorists obtain. Given an environment in which perfect monitoring and enforcement are possible, even an authoritarian socialist state can be made to seem appealing.

The literature indicates that it is possible to construct other elementary legal orders and secure variant types of economic systems. Thus, for example, the institutional framework of socialist labor management has been studied, by Vanek (1970) among others. The system envisioned relies heavily on the existence of competition and is similar to capitalism in that profit maximization by firms is encouraged. Workers are accorded certain control rights in the firm

14   Institutions and Economic Theory

and are expected to make key decisions for the firm.[17] Reward is based on the success of the firm's operations but is limited to usus fructus. In all cases, the productive capital required is leased to the labor-managed firms at a centrally or democratically determined leasing rate (Vanek 1990, 191), which, in the end, will become equal to the long-run equilibrium rate.

It is interesting to note that, in the zero-transaction-cost world of neo-classical economics, the two economic systems that have been viewed as the arch rivals of this century, capitalism and socialism, can be modeled by general equilibrium systems. Granted, the analysis of the respective cases proceeds only with regard to the role of the price system as a device meant to coordinate activities. No real attention is paid to the significance of changes in ownership (or property rights) for economic behavior. And this is true despite the fact that ownership, in another sense, constitutes a central issue for socialism. Indeed, the complete disregard of the economic role of ownership is astounding. To "prove" the workability of a socialist market economy by means of an institutionally neutral model (e.g., the Walrasian system) is as meaningless as if we were to use this model to "prove" that a barter economy is in reality as efficient as a monetary economy.

The essential point to be noted is this. In attempting to answer the question of whether a competitive market economy with or without private ownership rights in firms is the more efficient social arrangement, one needs a model in which property-rights structure plays a central role. Institutionally neutral general equilibrium theory is simply not appropriate for the purpose of comparing different institutional arrangements (Richter 1992a). In general, the concept of economic efficiency needs rethinking when something other than the frictionless neoclassical world is considered. And the problems of efficiency definition are compounded when the issue is one of proper institutional choice (Furubotn and Richter 1991, 11ff.).

1.5. Constructed or Spontaneous Orders?

Earlier discussion indicated that there exist, in principle, two types of (formal) institutions—one created and protected "from above" by the central agent of an organization, the other created "from below" by independent individuals but also protected "from above." In the case of the classical liberal state, the two types of formal institutions are: (1) institutions in the sense of *law* (e.g., the German constitution or the German Civil Code), and (2) institutions in the sense of *rights* (e.g., concrete claims arising out of a voluntarily agreed upon labor contract).

---

17. The principle of freedom of contract excludes labor contracts for productive purposes and trade in land and capital goods.

In the neoclassical world of costless transactions and perfect foresight, such institutions, (constitutions, laws, individual contracts, and so on) are complete and perfect. Their provisions, which are perfectly enforceable by law, will be observed with absolute precision. Courts work without cost in resources and time. Moreover, in this special environment, it is known in advance how courts will decide in the event of litigation. Lawsuits could be carried out by computers because of perfect information and perfect laws and contracts. Strictly speaking, there will be no need for lawsuits because decision makers understand the conditions of the system and act with perfect rationality. This, then, is the neoclassical vision. It is the ideal world of the public administrator who dreams of perfect social engineering.

In real life, of course, neither the formal rules of society nor individual contracts are perfect, and individuals do not behave with complete rationality. Characteristically, the gaps in the formal constraints are covered, to some degree, by informal rules. The latter, however, cannot be fully enforced by law. From a historical standpoint, we know that informal conventions existed before the formal, legally enforceable rules came into being. In tribal societies, "a dense social network leads to the development of informal structures with substantial stability" (North 1990, 38). These arrangements make exchange possible, though only on a limited scale.[18] Since people have limited capacities to acquire and process information, uncertainty and asymmetric information must exist, and these conditions represent unavoidable obstacles to "perfect" institutional design.

As a result of the imperfections found in the real world, formal institutional arrangements such as constitutions, laws, contracts, and charters are inevitably *incomplete*. This inherent limitation should be recognized and dealt with as far as possible. Important instruments of the type noted should be written in such a way as to leave room for their rapid adaption to unforseen circumstances through the spontaneous development of informal rules. Following this flexible approach, the difficulties caused by uncertainty and asymmetric information can be reduced. Thus, during the last ten to fifteen years, the New Institutional Economics has placed increasing emphasis on the need to view institutional design from the perspective of unavoidable incompleteness.

1.6. The Work of the Invisible Hand Can Be Accelerated

The invisible hand, if unaided by supporting institutions, tends to work slowly and at high cost. For example, we know that in primitive societies the absence of effective government contributes to limited exchange in property (Posner

---

18. For a good description, see Collson (1974).

16   Institutions and Economic Theory

1980). Fortunately, however, the work of the invisible hand can be accelerated substantially, and transaction costs lowered remarkably, by planned collective action undertaken through either public or private auspices. The "construction" of institutions is feasible because certain factors that are important to the successful fashioning of institutional arrangements are relatively well known to the public and largely independent of future events.

In the first place, a community normally has knowledge of the elementary "objects" in the system that require regulation or control through the functioning of institutional rules. Characteristic regulatory objects would include property, money, marriage, and contracts. Elementary property laws or rules, for example, have to regulate the use of an asset (usus), the appropriation of the returns from an asset (usus fructus), and the change of its form, substance, and location (abusus). The last element implies that the owner has the freedom to transfer some or all of his property rights in an asset to another individual at a mutually agreed upon price (as in selling or renting a house).

When money is introduced into a barter economy or when a new monetary system is created (such as the planned European Monetary Union), rules are again necessary. An elementary monetary order has to regulate four basic issues: the unit of account, its real anchor (i.e., the standard of coinage or the price target of monetary policy), the means of payment, and the organization of the money supply.[19]

Second, in addition to general knowledge of the regulatory objects of any particular institutional arrangement, society can have a rather clear understanding of how, on the average, individuals behave under certain circumstances. That is why comedies or tragedies can be written so convincingly that, sometimes at least, people in the audience laugh or cry at the right moment. That is also the reason why economics, as a science, is feasible at all. In trying to forecast tomorrow's interest rate, or the levels that will be reached by the prices of shares, economists have no great advantage over others. But economists can predict with some confidence what is likely to happen to a piece of property, say a forest, that operates as a common property resource. And economists know that the fate of the forest would be quite different if it were privately owned and subject to sale by its owner to any qualified purchaser. Similarly, reasonable predictions can be made of the circumstances under which a vendor will, on the average, adhere to his promises (or at least avoid gross infringements of the rules of good faith and fair dealing) and when not. Further, relative to the use of money, we can imagine quite well how, in general, the individual money user will protect his financial assets in the case of serious inflation. We can also tell broadly what kind of problems will arise if a manager does not own the business he runs.

---

19. See Richter (1989a, chap. 4).

In all of these illustrative cases, it is necessary to consider "human nature as we know it" (Knight 1922, 270) to make good forecasts. In particular, we have to identify "moral hazard" as an endemic condition with which economic organization must contend. The ideal of the perfectly honest, or perfectly controllable, homo oeconomicus of neoclassical theory cannot be sustained. This conclusion is basic to the approach taken by modern institutional economics.[20]

1.7. Rational Incompleteness

Several thousand years of human history have made it clear that a lawmaker, however dedicated and ambitious, must accept incompleteness in any fabricated order. All of the contingencies of real life cannot be anticipated ex ante. Thus, a rational lawmaker does not try to regulate everything to the last detail. Rather, he recognizes the wisdom of leaving reasonable gaps in his design. The gaps in question can be closed over time, as circumstances dictate, by for example, "jurisprudence and legal practice."[21]

As noted, the fundamental problem in this area arises because of our relative ignorance. If everything were known in advance, "something could be done and specified in advance by rule. This would be a world fit for 'mechanical jurisprudence'" (Hart 1961, 125). But, as we know: "Plainly this is not our world; human legislators can have no such knowledge . . ." (125). One technique to deal legally with the difficulties created by "gaps" is to apply certain accepted principles—for example, the common judgment of what is "reasonable." Hart says: "The most famous example of this technique in Anglo-American law is the use of the standard of due care in cases of negligence" (129).

For obvious reasons, a judge is not free to decide cases according to his whims. He has to apply some principle[22] that, ideally, is understandable,

---

20. Although institutional economics is still in the process of development, economists are able to make predictions about how particular institutional arrangements affect behavior and economic outcomes. Indeed, in some areas, as in state ownership of the means of production, we know with considerable precision what the consequences of given institutional frameworks are likely to be.

21. A typical example of this general approach is found in German civil law. In Article 929 of the German Civil Code, which is concerned with the transfer of physical objects, the phrase "agreement and delivery" is used. Whether "agreement" in this context is to be understood only in the sense of "contract" (i.e., contractual transfer of ownership) or has a broader meaning is left to the dictates of "Wissenschaft und Praxis" (Motive 1888, 332).

22. Legal principles, not rules, are cited by courts as justification for adopting and applying a new rule. On the role of principles in reaching particular decisions of law, see, for example, Dwarkin (1977, 28ff). He discusses the positivists' tenet "that the law of a community is distinguished from other social standards by some test in the form of a master rule" (44). North

18   Institutions and Economic Theory

reconstructible, and predictable. Unavoidably, bargaining is pervasive. And this process seems to obey some implicitly or explicitly agreed upon principles. In any case, the rational lawmaker knows that additional rules will evolve over time. Changes will come about partly by the extension of judge-made law, or through the writing of individual contracts, and partly through the generation of informal rules. This informal area is the sphere in which the invisible hand still works, slowly but powerfully. Such action may help to stabilize a necessarily incomplete formal institutional structure (as in the development of property laws in the West), or it may destabilize a system (as in the property regulations in the East under socialism). In either case, the inevitable residual activity of the invisible hand, via the continuous bargaining between private or public agents, is an important source of institutional change.

Not only constitutions and formal bodies of law but also private contracts are necessarily incomplete. Indeed:

> The parties [to a contract] will quite rationally leave out many contingencies, taking the point of view that it is better to 'wait and see what happens' than to try to cover a large number of individually unlikely eventualities. Less rationally, the parties will leave out other contingencies that they simply do not anticipate. Instead of writing very long-term contracts the parties will write limited-term contracts, with the intention of renegotiating these when they come to an end. (Hart 1987, 753)

It is true, of course, that in considering contracting activities decision makers are forced to take due account of transaction costs.

The parties to a contract must agree, either explicitly or tacitly, "about the procedure [the 'constitution'] that will be employed to deal with problems that may arise in the future" (Macneil 1974, 753). Moreover, it is accepted that negotiations on matters of concern will be carried on more or less continuously. Many of the different types of contracts found in the business world have emerged on the basis of this set of procedures. In the academic literature, Williamson (1985) especially has stressed the ongoing nature of contractual relations and has criticized models that assume all contractual problems are solved, once and for all, during the initial period.

Room for the development of informal rules in a formal organization is generally of vital importance. Barnard (1938, 120) has argued that "formal organizations are vitalized and conditioned by informal organizations. . . .

(1978, 976) suggests that it is useful to analyze "legal principles" from the standpoint of "ideology." See section 1.10.

[T]here cannot be one without the other."[23] All this has obvious significance for the New Institutional Economics. The evolution of informal rules is seen, once again, as the force that in the end may lead to institutional change. Informal rules, as expressed by certain empirical uniformities, are called "custom" (*Sitte*) if the practice is based upon long-standing behavior (cf. Weber 1968, 29). Important for the viability of a custom is what Schlicht (1997) calls the "clarity of its informal rules."

Any custom refers to regularities that must be perceived, learned, memorized, and passed on. Unclear and complicated rules cannot be handled in this way and cannot, therefore, be coded by custom. This constrains possible customary patterns. Clarity eases encoding, while unclarity smothers it (Schlicht 1997).[24]

1.8. Enforcement

Bounded rationality makes institutional incompleteness inevitable, and the existence of incompleteness causes problems not only for the design of an institution's behavioral rules but also for its enforcement rules. The basic difficulty is that, in the case of an incomplete institution, legal enforcement is of limited use. The perfect constitutional state (*der "perfekte Rechtsstaat"*) simply does not exist in practice. Thus, legal enforcement rules must be supplemented by extralegal guarantee instruments such as hostages, collateral, tit-for-tat strategies, reputation, and so on. In other words, various "private" guarantees against "bad" behavior by an institution's members are needed during their unavoidably ongoing relationship. The rational designer of an incomplete institution has to take into account a priori the human tendency toward opportunistic behavior—that is, the predisposition toward self-seeking with guile (Williamson 1985, 47).

It is true, of course, that conflicts may also arise because of honest disagreement among parties (Alchian and Woodward 1988, 66). In general, then, the rational designer of an incomplete institution must plan for strategic or "noncooperative" behavior on the part of the participants during their ongo-

---

23. One of the indispensable functions of informal organizations operating within a formal organization is communication. "Another function is that of maintenance of cohesiveness in formal organizations through regulating the willingness to serve and the stability of objective authority. A third function is the maintenance of the feeling of personal integrity, of self-respect, of independent choice" (Barnard [1938] 1962, 122). Barnard also stresses the importance of personal knowledge on the part of management. The "clarity view" of custom is elaborated by Schlicht (1997). The clarity view stresses the motivational aspect of custom as well as its unifying force.

24. *Bargaining,* understood in the widest sense of the word, includes as a limiting case the possibility of delegating all decision making to one party, an "authority."

20   Institutions and Economic Theory

ing bargaining process.[25] The designer has to make sure that the members or parties of an institution agree ex ante to guarantees against ex-post opportunism (noncooperative behavior). As might be expected, transaction costs play an important role in this context. Because they require resources, activities undertaken to enforce an institution's operating rules should be treated as a standard economic problem (Wiggins 1991). And this cost issue looms large in comparative institutional analysis. Differences in institutional design may be attributed in large degree to the need to overcome enforcement problems. Full understanding of institutions must, in fact, rest on a more complete understanding of the enforcement process (Wiggins 1991, 33).

In a general sense, the enforcement problem turns on the matter of how to make incomplete agreements "binding" and thus credible. The credibility problem was "discovered," as an important issue, by economic theorists pursuing different specialties. For example, monetary economists were concerned with credibility in their analysis of monetary policy formation (Persson and Tabellini 1990). Similarly, industrial organization economists focused on this issue in their research on the purchase of experience goods (Klein and Leffler 1981).[26]

Characteristically, the establishment and enforcement of institutional norms requires some kind of *collective* action, private or public. This is precisely what the New Institutional Economics analyses, and it is this recognition of the need for collective action that sets the NIE apart from orthodox neoclassical theory. The latter accepts the metaphor of the invisible hand and supposes harmony of individual actions because enforcement is seen as automatic in a zero-transaction-cost world. Once frictions are posited, however, the operation of the invisible hand cannot be accepted without qualification. In what follows, then, economic behavior will be assumed to include the development of enforcement rules and the necessary collective action to support the rules.

Arrow mentions the role of ethical and moral codes in connection with the enforcement problem. "It is useful for individuals to have some trust in each other's word. In the absence of trust, it would become very costly to arrange for alternative sanctions and guarantees, and many opportunities deriving from mutually beneficial cooperation would have to be foregone. Banfield (1958) has argued that lack of trust is indeed one of the causes of economic underdevelopment" (Arrow 1969, 62).

The observations made by Arrow represent a recognition of the instru-

---

25. Commitment problems play a central role in shaping the structure of firms, contracts, and most long-term relationships (see Wiggins 1991).

26. See also Dewatripont (1986) on the problem of "renegotiation proofness" in the context of labor markets.

mental role of morality, the overlap of economics and practical ethics.[27] Social morality (or trust) cannot simply be bought. Within limits, it can be produced through "education"—a collective undertaking that requires a considerable amount of real resources and time to become effective. Such education may be costly, but it is crucially important for keeping society together.

1.9. The Political Process

The political process is intimately involved in bringing about institutional change, but many economists, at least in this century, have tended to abstract from political phenomena in conducting their analyses. Realistically, though, political and economic processes cannot be separated.

People are not merely consumers and producers; they are also citizens in a variety of polities that not only regulate markets but can expropriate directly the resources markets allocate. Correspondingly, it is impossible to predict market outcomes without also predicting the political response that alternative outcomes engender (Ordeshook 1990, 9). That is the hard lesson for people who favor free markets. The hard lesson for socialists is that "whatever institutional structure the state takes, the laws governing market forces cannot be abrogated—the forces of supply and demand operate regardless of culture, ethnic identity, socialization patterns, ideology, and political system" (9). It is therefore apparent that the NIE is related to the New Political Economy in the sense of Black 1958, Downs 1957, Buchanan and Tullock 1962, Olson 1965, and so on. But, strangely, these authors have not shown much interest in utilizing the methods of the NIE for analysis. On the other hand, among the representatives of the NIE, North (1990) probably comes closest to dealing with the subject matter of Public Choice Theory with his observations on what he calls the "institutional environment." Some political scientists, too, such as Keohane, Shepsle, Weingast, and Levi, have concerns with institutional questions and have produced works that show affinity with the neoinstitutionalist approach.

Political and economic decisions are necessarily interconnected in the real world where positive transaction costs exist and no party has a complete monopoly on violence. Decisions are constrained by formal economic and political rules. Both have to be consistent, and both are necessarily incomplete. That is, informal rules develop in both fields through the functioning of the "invisible hand." The problem with state and governmental activity is that "formal political rules, like formal economic rules, are designed to facilitate

---

27. For example, Adam Smith [1776] 1976) has spoken of the great importance of rules of conduct: "Those general rules of conduct, when they have been fixed in our mind by habitual reflection, are of great use in correcting misrepresentation of self-love concerning what is fit and proper to be done in our particular situation" (quoted in Sen 1990, 87).

22   Institutions and Economic Theory

exchange but democracy in the polity is not to be equated with competitive markets in the economy" (North 1990, 51). Dealings in the arena of "power" are, apparently, much more difficult to explain by means of the workings of some sort of invisible hand than are market phenomena in the case of economic exchange. Nevertheless, even in the political sphere, decentralization, and thus competition, is possible, too. As a political counterpart to the market economy, one may consider a federalist state such as Switzerland. Federalism may enhance political competition (Weingast 1995) and thus help to check the power of the state as the owner of some kind of "monopoly of violence." However, the transaction costs associated with political markets are high, and for this reason institutional inefficiency tends to persist (North 1990, 52).

Another important point to consider is that the coercive power of the state can be used to economize on transaction costs (Arrow 1969, 60). And, as Arrow points out: "Political policy is not made by voters. . . . It is in fact made by representatives in one form or another. Political representation is an outstanding example of the principle-agent relation" (61).

Disregard of the interrelationship between economic development and political processes by Western academic advisers is responsible for the malaise of development economics and the slow and hesitant economic transformation of postcommunist countries. As Riker and Weimer (1995, 85) point out, Western advisers have not been as alert to the political side of political economy as they have been to the economic. Consequently, they "initially proposed reforms for a well-operating market for free trade. But when these reforms were undertaken, without solicitation of popular political support for the new economic system, the voters often became hostile to the reforms, which seemed to offer immediate suffering for only the prospect of future benefits." The authors continue: "Only in the Czech Republic . . . did the government undertake economic reform balanced with a search for political support" (85).

1.10. Agency

The legal construct of agency plays a prominent role as an analytical concept in modern institutional economics. The basic idea conveyed is simple. The agent acts on behalf of the principal, but the principal faces difficulties in trying to monitor the actions of his agent. What the principal sees, essentially, are results. For example, if the principal is the owner of a firm and the agent serves as the firm's manager, the results are the profits at the end of the year. Provided there were no exogenous disturbances (e.g., variations in the weather), the principal could assess the firm's results and draw conclusions about the behavior (e.g., the effort level) of his agent. However, if outside disturbances that could influence results did occur, the agent may have valid excuses for bad results, and the principal cannot determine definitively what the reason is for the results observed.

In theory, a situation can be envisioned in which the principal is "blind" as a direct monitor of his agent but otherwise has full knowledge of his agent's personality (the agent's preference function) as well as precise knowledge of the distribution function of the external shocks (disturbances). Under these special circumstances, the principal can design a remuneration plan for the agent that could induce or "bribe" the agent to act advantageously for the principal. This is, broadly speaking, what the economic principal-agent theory is about.

Of course, informational difficulties (i.e., transaction costs) are ubiquitous in real life and not confined to one or a few activities. Indeed, once we reject the notion of the omniscient decision maker who is "completely rational" (Kreps 1990b, 745), the existence of positive transaction costs everywhere in the system is assured. The implication is that complete agency contracts (in the sense of the preceding paragraph) will be impossible. Incomplete contracts must rule in practice. Thus, one of the central interests of the New Institutional Economics is the search for optimal incomplete agency contracts.

The field of application of the principal-agent model is very wide. What can be included, besides the familiar problem of separation of ownership from control in the firm, is, for example, the issue of rules versus discretion in economic policy making. A basic point is this: insofar as positive transaction costs and incomplete foresight exist, it is not feasible to write a complete set of rules that monetary or fiscal policymakers must observe. Discretionary powers for agents are, within limits, unavoidable. The problem, then, is how principals in the form of money users or taxpayers can protect themselves against opportunistic behavior on the part of their agents (the policy authorities).

1.11. Institutional Stability

The problem of institutional stability becomes evident once consideration is given to the possibility that institutions may evolve and show changes in their structures over time. Change (or distortion) can come to any type of institution (constitution, contract, etc.) and, in each case, it is important to understand the causes and consequences of change. For formal institutions (so-called made orders) key questions are: what set of informal rules will grow into the gaps in the formal institutional framework and how long will the spontaneous growth process continue? Is it likely that some stable endpoint will be reached that represents a *complete* institutional arrangement? And, if such an endpoint does appear, can it be viewed as a true institutional equilibrium position?

Presumably, an institutional equilibrium would mean that an original set of formal rules remains in active use despite the fact that a supplementary set of

24   Institutions and Economic Theory

informal rules and enforcement characteristics has grown up to complete the total structure. Then, an institutional equilibrium may be said to be essentially stable: (1) if it is achieved "automatically" in the sense that the informal rules reach some stable endpoint of the new (complete) institutional arrangement without destroying the original formal framework, or (2) if, after a disturbance of an initial institutional equilibrium, a new institutional equilibrium (not necessarily the original) will be reached. The central concern expressed here is with the adaptive capabilities of institutions such as markets (Hayek 1945) or hierarchies (Barnard 1938).[28]

It should be noted that a theory of institutions may not lead to the conclusion that unique institutional equilibria will always emerge (Schotter 1981, 12). Note further that political and economic processes cannot be separated in this context. The New Institutional Economics is therefore closely related to the new political economics (public choice and constitutional economics) and political science proper.

Even a tentative understanding of the nature of institutional stability permits us to recognize that it is impossible to impose any ad libitum constructed institutional framework on people and expect that it will function normally. In general, we know that institutional change can be the result of institutional instability in the sense of "bad design." Change may, however, come about as a consequence of economic growth or decline or because of technical, intellectual, or cultural shifts. History suggests that there is no easy way to forestall institutional instability; certainly, attempts to simply arrest change through the use of force have proved ineffective.[29]

An example of institutional instability drawn from experience can be instructive. Thus, consider the European Monetary System (EMS) of 1979. It

---

28. Barnard was particularly interested in the adaptability of internal organizations. He writes that "the survival of an organization depends upon the maintenance of an equilibrium of complex character. . . . [This] calls for readjustment of processes internal to the organization. . . . [Hence] the *center of our interest* is the processes by which [adaptation] is accomplished" ([1938] 1962, 6). Williamson asks in this connection: "If, however, the 'marvel of the market' [Hayek] is matched by the 'marvel of internal organization' [Barnard], then wherein does one outperform the other?" (1991, 163)

29. In considering the Platonic State, Popper makes the comment:

Arresting political change is not the remedy, it cannot bring happiness. We can never return to the alleged innocence and beauty of the closed society. Our dream of heaven cannot be realized on earth. Once we begin to rely on our reason, and to use our powers of criticism, once we feel the call of personal responsibilities, and with it, the responsibility of helping to advance knowledge, we cannot return to a state of implicit submission to tribal magic. For those who have eaten of the tree of knowledge, paradise is lost. The more we try to return to the heroic age of tribalism, the more surely we arrive at the Inquisition, at the Secret Police, and at a romanticized gangsterism. Beginning with the suppression of reason and truth, we must end with the most brutal and violent destruction of all that is human. (1945, 1:200)

formally was organized in such a way that no "key currency" existed. The system, however, developed so that the D-mark "automatically" assumed the role of a key currency and the Bundesbank the role of a "stability leader" for the system. The general result was that the formal part of the European Monetary System was not stable in the sense described. The informal rules that grew into the formal institutional framework led to an institutional disequilibrium manifested by the desire of some members of the EMS to create the European Monetary Union (EMU). The motivation for this suggested change in structure was presumably the wish on the part of some member states to avoid German monetary hegemony. This, of course, represented a political rather than an economic reason. What can be expected now is that the formal institutional framework of the European Monetary Union will, again, be necessarily incomplete. The question that arises, then, is what kind of informal institutional extension will grow into the new formal hull of the EMU. Will the EMU, given the present individual interests of Europeans and in light of their individual endowments, organization, and technical knowledge, move to a stable endpoint, to an institutional equilibrium? To answer this question, both political and economic forces have to be taken into account. There are, however, good reasons to expect that the EMU will not be a stable system—provided it will in fact be realized.

1.12. Once More with Feeling

In the discussion so far, it has been argued that the working of the "invisible hand" can be accelerated by the introduction of a set of rationally designed formal institutions into a system. It is true, however, that even the best attempts at such construction cannot be expected to yield perfect or "complete" institutions. Rationally designed formal institutions have to leave room for the development of informal arrangements. Moreover, if the so-called made institutional framework is to be *stable,* the structure must be established so as to take account of "human nature as we know it" and must, of course, remain open for the inevitable growth of informal process and enforcement rules.

Affectual social relationships "determined by the actor's specific affects and feeling states" have a role to play in shaping the general environment in which economic activity takes place, as do the traditional social relationships that are determined by "ingrained habituation" (Weber 1968, 25). Feelings or traditions cannot be created ad hoc by rational acts, and time often is involved. To illustrate this point, it will be useful to consider the phenomenon of trust among people. Without a large measure of general trust, "society itself would disintegrate" (Simmel 1978, 178). Obviously, trust cannot be created instantaneously—for example, by the use of force or money. Trust is the product of an evolutionary process that takes time. Among other things, it requires the

26   Institutions and Economic Theory

development of common values (social consensus) and the adaptation of values to new conditions. Credible commitments by the agents of society are also crucial in this connection. We know that, to a great extent, the past rules the present, that history matters.

Take the institution of money; without trust, money transactions would collapse. Simmel argues that it is important to think of trust not only in the sense of, for example, confidence in next year's harvest, but also as

> a further element of social-psychological quasi-religious faith. The feeling of personal security that the possession of money gives is perhaps the most concentrated and pointed form and manifestation of confidence in the sociopolitical organization and order. (Simmel 1978, 179)

Dasgupta (1988, 51) speaks of "trust" as involving correct expectations about the *actions* of other people who influence one's own choice of action when that action must be chosen before it is possible to *monitor* the actions of these others. He emphasizes that the inability to monitor others' actions in his definition of trust is crucial. Logically, this is "trust" viewed in terms of the "moral hazard" version of the principal-agent problem previously described.

From the standpoint of motivation, it can be argued that feelings and emotions are the proximate causes of most behavior (Frank 1990). The psychological reward mechanism that guides individual choices can and does compete with feelings that spring from rational calculations about material payoffs. Frank's thesis is that understanding of this interaction has direct relevance for the commitment problem that underlies the matter of trust.

Commitment problems in close personal relationships are better solved by moral sentiments than by awkward formal contracts. The best insurance against a change in future material incentives is a strong bond of love. If ten years from now one partner falls victim to a lasting illness, the other's material incentive will be to find a new partner. But a deep bond of affection will render this change in incentive irrelevant, which opens the door for current investments in the relationship that might otherwise be too risky (Frank 1990, 76).

Presumably, the ideal outcome just described can be realized only if feelings are equally strong on both sides. There are, of course, clues to behavioral predispositions, but it is also true that emotional attitudes can be falsified and misleading signals given. In any event, Frank finds it useful to distinguish between the *commitment model* and the *self-interest* model. As suggested, the former relates to situations in which seemingly irrational behavior may be explained by emotional predispositions that help solve commitment problems, while the latter concerns situations in which people always act "efficiently" in the pursuit of narrow self-interest.

Feelings are important not only in the context of private relationships but also in the public domain. Thus, the connection between feelings and ideologies must be considered. Ideologies, or comprehensive systems of cognitive and moral beliefs, figure prominently in social life and require study (North 1978, 972ff.).[30]

Ideologies are shared frameworks of mental models possessed by groups of individuals that provide both an interpretation of the environment and a prescription as to how that environment should be ordered (North 1994, 363, n.6).[31]

They may be understood as implicit agreements about informal rules for social action that help to reduce uncertainty. They may or may not become social norms or "ethical systems." Whatever the outcome here, the quality of trust an individual has in the word of others is correlated with the quality of the system of informal rules established in society in the large or in the small. The formation of implicit agreements (social relationships) leads to a structure that has some persistence over time. These agreements need not only be seen as components of social structure but as resources for individuals. Indeed, the term *social capital* has been used to describe these resources (see, e.g., Schlicht 1984; and Coleman 1990, 300).[32]

Of course, change in ideology, or implicit agreements, can take place over time and a hysteresis effect may be observed. As Arrow has pointed out:

> [Social] agreements are typically harder to change than individual decisions. When you have committed not only yourself but many others to an enterprise, the difficulty of changing becomes considerable . . . (1974, 128)

---

30. North argues that: "The study of ideology has been bedeviled by its origins in the writings of Marx . . . and Mannheim . . . on the relativity of knowledge to one's social position. . . . But ideology can be studied as a positive science, and empirically testable propositions can be derived as Robert Merton (1949) pointed out . . . in examining the literature on the sociology of knowledge" (1978, 975). North goes on to suggest two propositions about ideology that bear exploration by economic historians. These are: (1) all societies invest substantial resources to convince their constituents that the existing system is legitimate, and (2) the political and judicial structure results in legislators and judges making many decisions about property rights (and therefore resource allocation) based on their set of moral and ethical views about the "public good." It follows, from the latter point especially, that: "Any study of the independent judiciary must make ideology central to analysis" (976).

31. Schmoller (1900, 70), like North, argues that: "The nature of Weltanschauung, the moral system, is to give a holistic view of the world. Such a system therefore always contains some hypothesis and belief . . ."

32. Other such terms are *moral capital* (Schlicht 1984) and *organizational capital* (Weizsäcker 1971).

28   Institutions and Economic Theory

He goes on to say that what may be hardest of all to change are unconscious agreements, agreements whose very purpose is lost to mind.

> A commitment to war or revolution or to religion is typically one that is very hard to reverse, even if conditions have changed from the time when the thing started. Even if experience has shown the unexpectedly undesirable consequences of a commitment, the past may continue to rule the present. (128)

Examples are provided by contemporary developments in Eastern Europe. For the reasons indicated, then, rational institutional change cannot help but be path dependent. The working of the invisible hand can be accelerated only within limits by "piecemeal social engineering," as Popper (1957, 64) calls it.[33]

Popper's arguments in favor of policies that seek only modest change in social arrangements seems to speak against a restructuring of the Eastern European economy by means of shock therapy. There is little doubt that attempts at swift and radical change pose dangers, and this fact must be kept in mind even though it seems essential to repair the consequences of misleading socialist ideology and to reestablish modern market economies in Eastern Europe. Some grounds for optimism may exist because these troubled societies had functioning market systems fifty to eighty years ago, and reversion to a historically known position is not quite the same thing as moving into a completely new and untried institutional framework. Nevertheless, a new social consensus, a consensus ideology, has to be developed, and a new system of informal rules has to grow into the gaps of the formal market framework, if a successful economic reconstruction of Eastern Europe is to be achieved. At best, this transformation will take time and resources and is, politically, a tricky exercise. Reconstruction requires, besides patience and sufficient popular confidence in the new policy, substantial specific investments in the political, educational, intellectual, and other sectors of these societies.

To summarize the main themes of this general line of discussion, we can say the following. The rules and enforcement characteristics of specific institutions involve elements that can, for the most part, be "rationally expected" by lawmakers, contracting parties, organizers, and so on. The basic objects of regulation are known in advance. Moreover, as for the rules to be applied for these objects, we know pretty well from experience and introspection how individuals behave on the average under certain circumstances. Inferring from this, we are able to formulate general principles according to which the rules

---

33. This is understood to be distinct from what he calls "holistic" or "utopian" engineering. "It aims at remodeling the 'whole of society' in accordance with a definite plan" (Popper 1957, 67).

and enforcement characteristics of a particular institution are to be written. Differently expressed, the presumption is that society is able to use incentive and disincentive effects rationally in setting up the basic structure of an institution. It is also understood that complete or perfect rationality is impossible in social planning because of transaction costs and an unavoidable lack of knowledge of what the future will bring. Institutional arrangements will, of necessity, be incomplete, and therefore they should be planned from the outset, as incomplete. That is, institutional arrangements should be sufficiently flexible and open ended so that they will be able to adapt swiftly and at low cost to new circumstances. Enforcement through credible commitments plays a vital role in this connection. Costs also have to be considered because considerable amounts of real resources are needed to establish, operate, and adapt institutions.

Brief mention can be made of other factors that affect institutional development. Agency relationships influence social processes and raise special problems because of informational asymmetries. Inevitably, there are important interconnections between economic and political activities. And, finally, we know that history matters for the success or failure of institutional change and that there are limits to institutional engineering. The path dependency of institutional change and the ideological and emotional predispositions of the public always have to be taken into account.

1.13.   The New Institutional Economics and Modern Institutionalism

The various issues described in the preceding sections illustrate the types of problems addressed by modern institutional economists. Such writers, however, do not all follow the same analytic approach. Rather, they deal with problems selectively and often use quite different methods. Thus, it is important to emphasize that, in the present book, we shall concentrate attention on one particular mode of analysis—the New Institutional Economics. This line of investigation, also called the New Theory of Organization, is associated with the work of Armen Alchian, Ronald Coase, Douglass North, Oliver Williamson, and others.[34] Analysis here is based on the elementary insight that the creation of institutions and organizations, and their day-to-day use, requires the input of real resources. In short, the existence of transaction costs is recognized. And nonzero transaction costs mean, in turn, that resources have significance at several levels. Resources serve as transaction inputs in production and distribution activities and as necessary factors in maintaining the framework within which all economic operations take place. It follows, of course, that the

---

34. The term *New Institutional Economics* was coined by Williamson (1975, 1).

30   Institutions and Economic Theory

assignment and formation of individual property rights in resources have direct influence on the economic results achieved by a society.

Transaction costs, property rights, and contractual relations constitute basic elements in the literature of the New Institutional Economics. All these concepts have far-reaching consequences that require exploration. For example, it is possible to argue that, because of transaction costs, the neoclassical assumption of perfect rationality has to be abandoned and replaced by some notion of "bounded rationality." Thus, consistent with these understandings, the following chapters are organized around the three themes just noted. We begin with a chapter each on transaction costs and property rights and continue with two chapters on contract rights. The first of the contract chapters covers writings cast largely in literary terms, while the second takes up contributions made in the mathematical style by information or contract theorists such as Stiglitz and Holmstrom. Uniformity of approach does not obtain in these fields, and, indeed, disagreement exists about how the research should be pursued. On the new institutionalist side, there is skepticism concerning the usefulness of the formal approach. This is so primarily because formal contract theory stays relatively close to neoclassical preconceptions and assumes, inter alia, that decision makers possess a capacity for highly rational behavior. It is this rationality assumption that neoinstitutionalists see as unacceptable because it is inconsistent with their belief that transaction costs and bounded rationality make anything like mathematically precise economic calculation impossible for individuals.[35] Nevertheless, in order to present a full survey of the divergent methods applied in the New Institutional Economics and its immediate neighborhood, an investigation of formal contract models is unavoidable. (This presentation will be undertaken in simplified form so that readers possessing basic knowledge of standard microeconomic theory will be able to follow it readily.)

As planned, the first part of the book is devoted to a description and explanation of the analytical tools of the New Institutional Economics. In the second part, the objective is to illustrate the application of the new research style to certain significant problems. Specifically, understanding of three fundamental types of institutions will be sought—namely, the market, the firm, and the state. It is hoped that the examples provided here are sufficiently diverse to give the reader an idea of the flexibility of the new institutionalist research procedures and to show how they can be applied to a variety of real world problems. Given this background, the power of the NIE approach to yield valuable insights into economic phenomena should become evident.

---

35. Indeed, some leading figures in the new institutionalist group, such as Frey and Williamson, argue that formalization may actually be counterproductive and impede further advances in the understanding of basic institutional questions.

The analytical methods based on the fundamental building blocks of the New Institutional Economics were, of course, not developed at one stroke in the systematic manner outlined in this book. The new approach, which is still in the process of refinement, came about as the result of groundbreaking studies in various subfields of what is now known as modern institutional economics. These subfields included the following.

1. *Transaction-cost economics:* Transaction costs arise in connection with the exchange process, and their magnitude affects the ways in which economic activity is organized and carried out. Included within the general category of transaction costs are search and information costs, bargaining and decision costs, and policing and enforcement costs. Transaction-cost economics is concerned particularly with the effect such costs have on the formation of contracts. Contributors in this area include Coase, Williamson, Alchian, Klein, Demsetz, and Barzel.

2. *Property-rights analysis:* The system of property rights in an economic system defines the positions of individuals with respect to the utilization of scarce resources. Since the allocation of property rights influences incentives and human behavior in ways that are generally predictable, a basis exists for studying the impact of property-rights arrangements on economic outcomes. Contributors in this area include Coase, Alchian, Demsetz, DeAlessi, Furubotn, and Pejovich.

3. *Economic theory of contracts:* As a "relative" of both transaction-cost economics and property-rights analysis, contract theory deals with incentive and asymmetric information problems. The latter fall into two distinct categories. There can be asymmetric information between the parties to a contract and asymmetric information between the contractual parties on one side and a third party (e.g., the court) on the other. Accordingly, we may distinguish between two variant types of contract theories.

a. *Agency theory* deals with problems of asymmetric information between contractual parties. The asymmetric information in question can exist either before or after a transaction has taken place. The theoretical approach adopted in these cases may rely largely on verbal analysis or on the use of formal models. Contributors to verbal ("positive") agency theory include Jensen, Meckling, Fama, Alchian, and Demsetz. Contributors to the mathematical ("normative") agency literature include Stiglitz, Holmstrom, Spence, and Shavell.

b. *Relational and incomplete contract theory* focuses on informational asymmetries that can arise between the parties to a (usually longer-term) contract on one side and a third party on the other. An important objective of such contracts is to overcome the postcontractual opportunism that may result from the difficulties courts or other third parties face in verifying the execution of contractual obligations. Credible commitments and self-enforcing commitments are important topics in this field. Contributors to relational contract theory include Macauly, Macneil, Goldberg, Williamson, and Alchian. Writers such as Grossman and Hart have contributed to the literature of formal incomplete contract theory, while Telser, Klein, Leffler, and Kreps have produced less formal models of self-enforcing contracts.

4. *The new institutional approach to economic history:* The work of economic historians following this methodological line is concerned with the application and extension of concepts such as transaction costs, property rights, and contractual relationships to historical experience. One important objective is to establish a theory of the institutional structure of society as a whole. As would be expected, writers in this field are especially concerned with making institutions endogenous variables within a general economic model. Contributors in this area include North, Thomas, Wallis, Weingast, Hoffman, Eggertsson, Libecap, and Greif.

5. *The new institutional approach to political economics:* In recent years, the New Institutional Economics movement has given impetus to the development of the so-called New Economics of Organization (NEO). This approach, pioneered by Williamson and drawing on ideas developed independently by North, has been applied in various fields of political science. The areas affected include the theory of the state (Levi 1988), government organization (Shepsle and Weingast 1987), public administration (Weingast 1984; Moe 1990), international organization (Keohane 1984), and the emergence and change of (political) institutional arrangements (Knight and Sened 1995), among others. In general, it can be said that the close relationship between the political and economic sides of social systems, which has been the basic object of study for political economy, is now viewed from the perspective of transaction costs and their effects on property rights and contractual arrangements. These observations provide a link to constitutional economics.

6. *Constitutional economics:* Buchanan (1987, 585) describes this field as one that attempts "to explain the working properties of alternative sets of legal-institutional-constitutional rules that constrain the choices in activities of political and economic agents." Moreover, since these "rules" can be interpreted as formal or informal social devices that constrain behavior, procedures for making selections among alternative constraints must be examined along with the constraints themselves. In particular, interest attached to the study of how society chooses the rules for making the rules under which the system operates ("public choice"). This focus on institutional choice suggests that some of the recent work on constitutional economics may be regarded as an American version of German Ordnungspolitik. American representatives include Buchanan, Wagner, and Tollison. German representatives include Eucken, Böhm, Miksch, and Watrin. Significantly, the new view of pressure groups initiated by Olson (1965) has developed into an important topic of its own.

It is also interesting to observe that in recent years there has been an increased willingness among sociologists to apply rational-action-based theory to social problems. This movement has stimulated the development of areas of mutual interest among economists, including representatives of the NIE and sociologists. According to Swedberg (1990), economists with sociological interests include such scholars as Becker, Akerlof, and Williamson. On the other side, Coleman, White, Granovetter, Lindenberg, and Opp can be mentioned as sociologists with economic interests.

These various subfields, which underlie our presentation of the New Institutional Economics, overlap to greater and lesser degrees. Collectively, they comprise a considerable part of modern institutional economics. Nevertheless, subsequent discussions in this book will give only limited attention to some of these specialties. Complete coverage is not feasible (and is hardly desirable) in a book of limited size. Further, certain important subareas of institutionalist scholarship, such as the economic analysis of the law and the field of public choice, will not be covered at all. We believe that these areas of concern are somewhat remote from our central interest in the methodology and application of transaction-cost/property-rights analysis. It is also true, of course, that in both of the fields just mentioned there already exist good systematic surveys and introductory books. On the economic analysis of law, there are volumes by Posner (1972b) and Cooter and Ulen (1988); on public choice, a number of works are available.

Finally, we must point out that two other interesting areas of study, ones that lie close to modern institutional economics, have been largely disregarded in the present book. These fields are neo-Austrian economics (e.g., Kirzner 1973) and the evolutionary approach to economics (e.g., Nelson and Winter 1982). Although the writings in these areas project lines of thought that complement the research program of the New Institutional Economics, the two fields are sufficiently distinct in their essential content to warrant separate treatment. Langlois (1986) provides a useful introduction to some of the parallelism here.

1.14. Some Notes on the History of the Old Institutional Economics

An excellent review of this area has been provided by Hutchison (1984). The old institutionalists, he writes, "were a rather loose and mixed group of economists, and institutionalism, as a brand, or type of economics, is a rather fuzzy, opaque term" (20). It is true, of course, that institutions or organizations were never totally excluded from consideration by economists; institutions played a role in the work of "orthodox" theorists such as Adam Smith, J. S. Mill, and Alfred Marshall, though not a central one. The adjective *institutional* was

34   Institutions and Economic Theory

applied, expressis verbis, to the American economists Veblen, Commons, and Mitchell. Of these three, John R. Commons was the most important from the standpoint of the NIE. This is so because his work, due to its direction, had particular significance for the development of modern institutionalism. He advanced the proposition that the *transaction* (the transfer of ownership) should be regarded as the ultimate unit of economic investigation. This view contrasts with classical economic theory, Commons (1934, 57) argues, whose units were "commodities and individuals with ownership omitted." To Commons, the "collective control of individual transactions" represented the basic conceptual contribution of institutional economics to political economy (6). Commons argued that classical and neoclassical doctrine was misleading because it failed to recognize that it is not harmony but "conflict of interests" among individuals that is predominant in transactions. Unlike Marx, however, he did not believe that conflict of interests represented the only relevant principle. Also important are mutual dependence of people and maintenance of order by collective action. Indeed, Commons defines an institution as "collective action in control of individual action" (69).[36]

According to Commons's analysis, cooperation emerges, in the end, not as a result of any presupposed harmony of interests, as in classical or neoclassical economics, but as a consequence of deliberate action designed to bring about a new harmony of interests among the hoped-for cooperators (1934, 6). A major objective of Commons was "to give to collective action, in all its varieties, its place throughout economic theory" (5).

Also helpful to the development of modern institutional economics was the work of Knight (1922). He acknowledged the importance of studying "human nature as we know it" (1922, 270) and identified "moral hazard as an endemic condition with which economic organization must contend" (quoted in Williamson 1985, 3).

The German Historical School might be classified as still another branch of "institutional" economics. Gustav Schmoller, the leader of the so-called Younger German Historical School, assumed the most prominent role in this intellectual movement. Significantly, Schumpeter (1926, 355) described him as the "father" of American institutionalism. Schmoller's critique of classical economics is strikingly similar to that made more recently by Ronald Coase— the "father" of the New Institutional Economics. Selected quotations from the writings of these two influential economists illustrate the parallelism in their thinking. Thus:

---

36. Collective action ranges all the way from unorganized custom to many organized going concerns such as the family, the corporation, the holding company, the trade association, the trade union, the federal reserve system, the "group of affiliated interests," and the "State" (Commons 1934, 69).

The old [classical] economics, submerged in the analysis of prices and the phenomena of circulation, represents the attempt to provide an economic physiology of the juices of the social body without anatomy. (Schmoller 1900, 64)

The objection [to what most economists have been doing] essentially is that the theory floats in the air. It is as if one studied the circulation of the blood without having a body. Firms have no substance. Markets exist without laws. . . . (Coase 1984, 230)[37]

Consistent with this thinking, Schmoller (1900, 64) insisted on the importance of comparative institutional analysis—something the exponents of the NIE insist on today. He also considered such topics as evolution, feelings, and norms, as some modern institutional economists do. Yet Schmoller's model of man is more that of homo sociologicus, whose behavior is driven by passions (26–41) and controlled by norms (41–59), than of homo oeconomicus, the self-seeking, purposive, rational individual of classical and neoclassical theory. Indeed, Schmoller abhored the latter theories (92). In general, then, Schmoller's *Grundriss* (1900) offers a sociological analysis of institutions (linked to strong ethical goals) not an economic one.[38] Max Weber (1968), a representative of the "Younger" Historical School (Schumpeter 1955, 816), developed an institutional theory similar in spirit and scope to that developed recently by North (1990). Hamilton and Feenstra (1995, 59) point out that:

Weber assumed that participants in the market economies reach decisions based on rational means-end calculations of interests. These calculations occur in institutionalized contexts, where only a range of specific options and an array of specific economic organizations are present. In such contexts, economic calculations are conditioned by the fact that economic actions are "carried" by an existing set of "economic orgnizations" (i.e., corporations, cartels and business groups) and are channeled by an existing set of "economically regulative organizations," a category including everything from "medieval village assocations" to "the modern state."

What may be interpreted as a mixture of English classical economics and the teachings of the German Historical School forms the intellectual base for

---

37. See Richter 1996a for similar parallels between the writings of Douglas North, and Schmoller.

38. "The natural forces of the economy, as far as they concern human action, go back not only to natural feelings but to feelings transformed through spiritual and moral evolution to ethicized instincts, to an ordered combination of natural and higher feelings, that is, essentially moral feelings, to virtues and habits (which are due to the ethical community life)" (Schmoller 1900, 60). For further details, see Richter 1996a.

36   Institutions and Economic Theory

the Freiburg School. The leading economist of the Freiburg group was Walter Eucken (1952), about whom Lutz remarks that his "academic training followed, in the first instance, the lines of the Historical School. What was best in the Historical School he absorbed as part of his intellectual make-up: that is, the urgent concern with the real world" (quoted in Hutchison 1984, 22). It should be said, however, that in general Eucken was strongly opposed to Schmoller's research methods (Eucken 1940).

As is well known, Eucken was one of the originators of German "Ordnungspolitik." The fundamental idea behind this theoretical approach is to create and maintain an institutional framework that guarantees the proper functioning of a free market economy. As guidelines to this end, Eucken developed a set of principles to be observed by lawmakers and public administrators. These principles include the three classical concepts of private ownership, freedom of contract, and acceptance of obligation (Hume [1739–40] 1969, 542). In addition, stress is placed on the need for open markets, the stability of economic policy, and the primacy of monetary policy. It can be observed that, in general, the teachings of German Ordnungspolitik (cf. Schmidtchen 1984) are quite similar to those of American constitutional economics as represented in more recent years by Buchanan (1987).

Ordnungspolitik, rather than Keynesian macropolicy, was applied at the time of the West German currency reform of June 1948 and achieved great success. Similarly, it proved valuable during the following years of the Wirtschaftswunder (Richter 1979). Nevertheless, Ordnungspolitik is open to criticism because it tended to disregard the costs of establishing and running institutions—as did American institutionalism and the German Historical School. The failure to account adequately for costs is no small matter. The German public (and a large part of the economics profession) learned this through experience after German reunification! If there were any doubts previously, it is now abundantly clear that the reorganization of an institutional framework, the creation of viable markets, is an extremely costly and time-consuming affair.

On the classical or neoclassical side of old institutional economics, we have to mention the evolutionary approach in the tradition of the Austrian School: Carl Menger ([1883] 1963) and later Mises and Hayek. This approach involves the application of the concept of convention (a regularity in behavior) between rational individuals to explain the spontaneous evolution of such institutions as language, law, and money.

The idea can also be found in David Hume's ([1739–40] 1969) explanation of the origin of "justice and property." Hume writes that it is human conventions without promise that gradually establish institutions like the three just mentioned plus those of property rights and obligation. Famous became his example of two men pulling the oars of a boat in rhythm by convention, "though they have never given promises to each other" (542). In technical terms, we have here cooperation without ex ante binding promises. This is a rather special case that assumes a harmony of interests. In the more general case, cooperation between individuals may not be possible without ex ante binding agreements, that is, without enforcement characteristics. To consider this became a major issue of the New Institutional Economics.

1.15. Suggested Readings for Chapter 1

Chapter 1 deals with general issues, and the readings should be correspondingly general. We suggest the following.

One may begin with some introductory readings on formal organizations. An excellent beginning is provided by Arrow's presidential address delivered to the international meeting of the Institute of Management Science, Tokyo, in 1963 (Arrow 1970) in combination with his booklet on *The Limits of Organization* (1974). Somewhat special but also very readable is Arrow's statement prepared for the Joint Economic Committee of the Ninety-first Congress, first session, on "The Organization of Economic Activity" (Arrow 1969), which is one of the first contributions in which transaction costs and general equilibrium theory are confronted. With regard to institutions, in the sense of institutional frameworks (rules of the game), North (1990) provides a fine introduction to the problems involved. Also stimulating is the presidential address to the Royal Economic Society by R. C. O. Matthews (1986) on "The Economics of Institutions and the Source of Growth." A short introduction to the early history of the New Institutional Economics is provided by Williamson (1985, 1–14; 1996, 3–20).

As for the history of thought of the old institutional economics, we would suggest, as a first step, to read David Hume, *A Treatise of Human Nature,* part 2, section 2, of *The Origin of Justice and Property.* Hume explains justice and property as the result of human convention. One could continue with Carl Menger ([1883] 1963), who argues along the same lines and attacks the German Historical School. Schmoller's (1883) unfavorable review of this book and Menger's (1884) bitter reply began the original Methodenstreit. The differences in methods stemmed from fundamental differences in worldviews, with the individualist outlook of Menger standing in sharp contrast to the more collectivist outlook of the German Historical School. For readers who know German, it would be interesting to read Schmoller's exposition on custom, law, and morality and on the relationship between economic and ethical life in his *Grundriß der Allgemeinen Volkswirtschaftslehre* (1900, 48–72). A more balanced view of the two positions is given by Commons (1934), whose introductory chapter 1 is a suggested reading.

38   Institutions and Economic Theory

Institutional economics helps to improve understanding of economic history, and therefore plays an increasing role in modern economic history, as illustrated by North (1990). Still, the warning by Popper in his book *The Poverty of Historicism* (1957) should not be forgotten. No scientific theory of historical development can serve as a basis for historical prediction (which Popper calls historicism). Of particular interest here is the section on "Piecemeal versus Utopian Engineering" (64–70) together with the rest of the chapter.

References

Alchian, A. A., and S. Woodward. 1988. "The Firm is Dead; Long Live the Firm: A Review of Oliver E. Williamson's *The Economic Institutions of Capitalism.*" *Journal of Economic Literature* 26:65–79.

Arrow, K. J. 1969. "The Organization of Economic Activity: Issues Pertinent to the Choice of Market versus Non-Market Allocation." In *The Analysis and Evaluation of Public Expenditures: The PBB-System*, Joint Economic Committee, 91st Cong., 1st sess., vol. 1. Washington, D.C.: Government Printing Office.

Arrow, K. J. 1970. *Essays in the Theory of Risk-Bearing*. Amsterdam: North-Holland.

Arrow, K. J. 1974. *The Limits of Organization*. New York: W. W. Norton.

Arrow, K. J. 1979. "The Property Rights Doctrine and Demand Revelation under Incomplete Information." In M. J. Boskin, ed., *Economics and Human Welfare: Essays in Honor of Tibor Scitovsky*, 23–39. New York: Academic Press.

Banfield, E. C. 1958. *The Moral Basis of a Backward Society*. New York: Free Press.

Barnard, C. [1938] 1962. *The Functions of the Executive*. 15th ed. Cambridge: Harvard University Press.

Black, D. 1958. *The Theory of Committees and Elections*. Cambridge: Cambridge University Press.

Brunner, K., and W. H. Meckling. 1977. "The Perception of Man and the Conception of Government." *Journal of Money, Credit, and Banking* 3:70–85.

Buchanan, J. M. 1987. "Constitutional Economics." In J. Eatwell, M. Milgate, and P. Newman, eds., *The New Palgrave: A Dictionary of Economics*, 1:585–88. London et al.: Macmillan.

Buchanan, J. M., and Tullok, G. 1962. *The Calculus of Consent*. Ann Arbor: University of Michigan Press.

Chandler, A. D., Jr. 1977. *The Visible Hand: The Managerial Revolution in American Business*. Cambridge: Harvard University Press.

Coase, R. H. 1937. "The Nature of the Firm." *Economica* 4:386–405.

Coase, R. H. 1960. "The Problem of Social Cost." *Journal of Law and Economics* 3:1–44.

Coase, R. H. 1984. "The New Institutional Economics." *Journal of Institutional and Theoretical Economics* 140:229–31.

Coase, R. H. 1988b. *The Firm, the Market, and the Law*. Chicago and London: University of Chicago Press.

Coleman, J. S. 1990. *Foundations of Social Theory*. Cambridge: Belknap Press of Harvard University Press.

Coleman, J. S. 1991. "Constructed Organization, First Principles." *Journal of Law, Economics, and Organization* 7:7–23.

Colson, E. 1974. *Tradition and Contract: The Problem of Order*. Chicago: Aldine.

Commons, J. R. 1934. *Institutional Economics*. Madison: University of Wisconsin Press.

Cooter, R., and T. Ulen. 1988. *Law and Economics*. Glenview, Ill.: Scott, Foresman.

Dasgupta, P. 1988. "Trust as a Commodity." In D. Gambetta, ed., *Trust: Making and Breaking Cooperative Relations*, 49–72. Oxford: Basil Blackwell.

Demsetz, H. 1968b. "Why Regulate Utilities?" *Journal of Law and Economics* 11:55–66.

Dewatripont, M. F. 1986. "On the Theory of Commitment with Applications to the Labor Market." Ph.D. diss. Harvard University, Department of Economics.

Downs, A. 1957. *An Economic Theory of Democracy*. New York: Harper and Row.

Dwarkin, R. 1977. *Taking Rights Seriously*. London: Duckworth.

Eucken, W. 1940. "Wissenschaft im Stile Schmollers." *Weltwirtschaftliches Archiv* 52:468–506.

Eucken, W. 1952. *Grundsätze der Wirtschaftspolitik*. Edited by E . Eucken and K. P. Hensel. Tübingen: J. C. B. Mohr (Paul Siebeck).

Fisher, I. 1912. *The Nature of Capital and Income*. New York and London: Macmillan.

Frank, R. H. 1990. "A Theory of Moral Sentiments." In J. J. Mansbridge, ed., *Beyond Self-Interest*, 71–96. Chicago and London: University of Chicago Press.

Furubotn, E. G. 1991. "General Equilibrium Models, Transaction Costs, and the Concept of Efficient Allocation in a Capitalist Economy." *Journal of Institutional and Theoretical Economics* 147:662–86.

Furubotn, E. G., and R. Richter. 1991. "The New Institutional Economics: An Assessment." In E. G. Furubotn and R. Richter, eds., *The New Institutional Economics*, 1–32. Tübingen: J. C. B. Mohr (Paul Siebeck).

Hamilton, G. G., and R. C. Feenstra. 1995. "Varieties of Hierarchies and Markets: An Introduction." *Industrial and Corporate Change* 4:51–92.

Hart, H. L. A. 1961. *The Concept of Law*. Oxford: Clarendon.

Hart, O. D. 1987. "Incomplete Contracts." In J. Eatwell, M. Milgate, and P. Newman, eds., *The New Palgrave: A Dictionary of Economics*, 2:752–59. London: Macmillan.

Hayek, F. A. 1945. "The Use of Knowledge in Society." *American Economic Review* 35:519–30.

Hayek, F. A. 1973. *Law, Legislation, and Liberty*. Vol. 1. Chicago: University of Chicago Press.

Hippel, E. von. 1963. *Die Kontrolle der Vertragsfreiheit nach anglo-amerikanischem Recht*. Frankfurt: Klostermann.

Humboldt, W. Von. [1792] 1967. *Ideen zu einem Versuch, die Grenzen der Wirksamkeit des Staates zu bestimmen*. Stuttgart: Philipp Reclam, Jr.

Hume, D. [1739–40] 1969. *A Treatise of Human Nature*. Edited by E. C. Mossner. London: Penguin.

Hutchison, T. W. 1984. "Institutionalist Old and New." *Journal of Institutional and Theoretical Economics* 140:20–29.

Keohane, R. O. 1984. *After Hegemony: Cooperation and Discord in the World Political Economy*. Princeton: Princeton University Press.

Kirzner, I. M. 1973. *Competition and Entrepreneurship*. Chicago: University of Chicago Press.

Klein, B., and K. B. Leffler. 1981. "The Role of Market Forces in Assuring Contractual Performance." *Journal of Political Economy* 89:615–41.

Knight, F. 1922. *Risk, Uncertainty, and Profit*. New York: Harper and Row.

Knight, J., and I. Sened, eds. 1995. *Explaining Social Institutions*. Ann Arbor: University of Michigan Press.

Kreps, D. M. 1990b. *A Course in Microeconomic Theory*. New York: Harvester.

Lancaster, K. 1969. *Introduction to Modern Microeconomics*. Chicago: Rand McNally.

Lange, O. 1938. "On the Economic Theory of Socialism." In O. Lange, F. M. Taylor, and B. E. Lippincott, eds., *On the Economic Theory of Socialism*, 57–143. Minneapolis: University of Minnesota Press.

Levi, M. 1988. *Of Rule and Revenue*. Berkeley: University of California Press.

Macneil, I. R. 1974. "The Many Futures of Contracts." *Southern California Law Review* 47:691–816.

Manne, H. G. 1965. "Mergers and the Market for Corporate Control." *Journal of Political Economy* 73:110–20.

Marshall, A. 1920. *Principles of Economics*. 8th ed. London: Macmillan.

Menger, C. [1883] 1963. *Problems of Economics and Sociology*. Translated by F. J. Nock from the German edition of 1883. Edited by L. Schneider. Urbana: University of Illinois Press.

Merton, R. 1949. *Social Theory and Social Structure*. New York: Free Press.

Modigliani, F., and M. Miller. 1958. "The Cost of Capital, Corporation Finance, and the Theory of Investment." *American Economic Review* 48:261–97.

Moe, T. M. 1984. "The New Economics of Organization." *American Journal of Political Science* 28:739–77.

Moe, T. M. 1990. "Political Institutions: The Neglected Side of the Story." *Journal of Law, Economics, and Organization, Special Issue* 6:213–53.

Motive 1888. *Motive zu dem Entwurfe eines Bürgerlichen Gesetzbuches für das Deutsche Reich*. Band III, *Sachenrecht*. Berlin and Leipzig: J. Guttentag.

Nelson, R., and S. G. Winter. 1982. *An Evolutionary Theory of Economic Change*. Cambridge: Belknap Press of Harvard University Press.

North, D. C. 1978. "Structure and Performance: The Task of Economic History." *Journal of Economic Literature* 16:963–78.

North, D. C. 1990. *Institutions, Institutional Change, and Economic Performance*. Cambridge: Cambridge University Press.

North, D. C. 1994. "Economic Performance through Time." *American Economic Review* 84:359–68. Alfred Nobel Memorial Prize Lecture in Economic Science.

Olson, M. 1965. *The Logic of Collective Action: Public Goods and the Theory of Groups*. Cambridge: Harvard University Press.

Ordeshook, P. C. 1990. "The Emerging Discipline of Political Economy." In J. E. Alt and S. Shepsle, eds., *Perspectives on Positive Political Economy*, 9–30. Cambridge: Cambridge University Press.

Persson, T., and G. Tabellini. 1990. *Macroeconomic Policy, Credibility, and Politics.* Chur: Harwood Academic.

Popper, K. R. 1945. *The Open Society and Its Enemies.* Vol. 1: *The Spell of Plato.* London: Routledge and Kegan Paul.

Popper, K. R. 1957. *The Poverty of Historicism.* 2d ed. London: Routledge and Kegan Paul.

Posner, R. A. 1972b. *The Economic Analysis of Law.* Boston and Toronto: Little, Brown.

Posner, R. A. 1980. "A Theory of Primitive Society with Special Reference to Primitive Law." *Journal of Law and Economics* 23:1–53.

Richter, R. 1979. "Currency and Economic Reform: West Germany after World War II, a Symposium, Editorial Preface." *Zeitschrift für die gesamte Staatswissenschaft/ Journal of Institutional and Theoretical Economics* 135:297–300.

Richter, R. 1989a. *Money: Lectures on the Basis of General Equilibrium Theory and the Economics of Institutions.* Heidelberg: Springer.

Richter, R. 1992a. "A Socialist Market Economy: Can It Work?" *Kyklos* 45:185–207.

Richter, R. 1996a. "Bridging Old and New Institutional Economics: Gustav Schmoller, the Leader of the Younger German Historical School, Seen with Neoinstitutionalists' Eyes." *Journal of Institutional and Theoretical Economics* 152:568–92.

Riker, W. H., and D. L. Weimer. 1995. "The Political Economy of Transformation: Liberalization and Property Rights." In J. S. Banks and E. A. Hanushek, eds., *Modern Political Economy: Old Topics, New Directions,* 80–107. Cambridge: Cambridge University Press.

Samuelson, P. A. 1957. "Wage and Interest: A Modern Dissection of Marxian Economic Models." *American Economic Review* 47:884–912.

Samuelson, P. A. 1968. "What Classical and Neoclassical Monetary Theory Really Was." *Canadian Journal of Economics* 1:1–15.

Schlicht, E. 1984. "Cognitive Dissonance in Economics." In H. Todt, ed., *Normengeleitetes Verhalten in den Sozialwissenschaften,* 61–82. Berlin: Duncker und Humblot.

Schlicht, E. 1997. *On Custom in the Economy.* Oxford: Clarendon Press.

Schmidtchen, D. 1984. "German 'Ordnungspolitik' as Institutional Choice." *Zeitschrift für die gesamte Staatswissenschaft/Journal of Institutional and Theoretical Economics* 140:54–70.

Schmoller, G. von. 1900. *Grundriss der Allgemeinen Volkswirtschaftslehre.* Munich and Leipzig: Duncker and Humblot.

Schotter, A. 1981. *The Economic Theory of Social Institutions.* Cambridge: Cambridge University Press.

Schumpeter, J. A. 1926. "Gustav Schmoller und die Probleme von heute." *Schmollers Jahrbuch für Gesetzgebung und Verwaltung* 50:337–88.

Schumpeter, J. A. 1955. *History of Economic Analysis.* New York: Oxford University Press.

Sen, A. 1990. *On Ethics and Economics.* Oxford: Basic Blackwell.

Shepsle, K. A., and B. R. Weingast. 1987. "The Institutional Foundations of Committee Power." *American Political Science Review* 81:85–104.

Simmel, G. 1978. *The Philosophy of Money.* Translated by T. Bottomore and D. Frisby. London: Routledge and Kegan Paul.

Simon, H. A. 1957. *Models of Man.* New York: Wiley.

Smith, A. [1776] 1976. *An Inquiry into the Nature and Causes of the Wealth of Nations.* General editors R. H. Campbell and A. S. Skinner, Textual editor W. B. Todd. Oxford: Clarendon Press.

Solow, R. M. 1985. "Economic History and Economics." *American Economic Review, Papers and Proceedings* 75:328–31.

Stigler, G. J. 1972. "The Law and Economics of Public Policy: A Plea to Scholars." *Journal of Legal Studies* 1:1–12.

Swedberg, R. 1990. *Economics and Sociology, Redefining Their Boundaries: Conversations with Economists and Sociologists.* Princeton: Princeton University Press.

Vanek, J. 1970. *The General Theory of Labor-Managed Market Economics.* Ithaca, N.Y.: Cornell University Press.

Vanek, J. 1990. "On the Transition from Centrally Planned to Democratic Socialist Economies." *Economic and Industrial Democracy* 11:179–203.

Wagner, A. 1907. *Theoretische Sozialökonomik oder Allgemeine und Theoretische Volkswirtschaftslehre: Grundriss tunlichst in prinzipieller Behandlungsweise.* Erste Abteilung. Leipzig: C. F. Winter'sche.

Weber, M. 1968. *Economy and Society: An Outline of Interpretative Sociology.* Edited by G. Roth and C. Wittich. Berkeley: University of California Press.

Weingast, B. R. 1984. "Congressional-Bureaucratic System: A Principal Agent Perspective (with Applications to SEC)." *Public Choice* 44:147–91.

Weingast, B. R. 1995. "The Economic Role of Political Institutions: Market Preserving Federalism and Economic Development." *Journal of Law, Economics, and Organization* 11:1–31.

Weizsäcker, C. C. 1971. "Die zeitliche Struktur des Produktionsprozesses und das Problem der Einkommensverteilung zwischen Kapital und Arbeit." *Weltwirtschaftliches Archiv* 106:1–33.

Wiggins, S. N. 1991. "The Economics of the Firm and Contracts: A Selective Survey." *Journal of Institutional and Theoretical Economics* 147:603–61.

Williamson, O. E. 1975. *Markets and Hierarchies: Analysis and Antritrust Implications.* New York: Free Press.

Williamson, O. E. 1979. "Transaction-Cost Economics: The Governance of Contractual Relations." *Journal of Law and Economics* 22:233–61.

Williamson, O. E. 1985. *The Economic Institutions of Capitalism.* New York: Free Press.

Williamson, O. E. 1991. "Economic Institutions: Spontaneous and Intentional Governance." *Journal of Law, Economics, and Organization* 7:159–87.

[20]

A Contractarian Paradigm for Applying Economic Theory

By JAMES M. BUCHANAN*

The object for economists' research is "the economy," which is, by definition, a *social organization*, an interaction among separate choosing entities. I return deliberately to this element in our primer, because I think that it has been too often overlooked. By direct implication, the ultimate object of our study is not itself a choosing, maximizing entity. "The economy" does not maximize, and we may substitute "the polity" here without change in my emphasis. No one could quarrel with these simplistic statements. The inference must be, however, that there exists no one person, no single chooser, who maximizes *for* the economy, *for* the polity. To impose a maximizing construction on the models that are designed to be helpful in policy is to insure sterility in results.

Where did economics, as a discipline, take the wrong turn? My own suggestion is that Lionel Robbins marks a turning point. His book defined "the economic problem" as the location of maxima and minima. Almost simultaneously with this, the Edward H. Chamberlin and Joan Robinson books marked a turning inward, so to speak, a shift toward the maximizing problem of a specific decision-making

* University Professor and General Director, Center for Study of Public Choice, Virginia Polytechnic Institute and State University. The author is indebted to Amoz Kats and Gordon Tullock for helpful comments.

entity. The economics of the firm was born, to be followed by the Hicksian elaboration of the economics of consumer choice. Paul Samuelson put this all together in his *Foundations of Economic Analysis*. Importantly, he extended the maximizing construction to welfare economics, extolling the virtues of A. Bergson's social welfare function as the tool through which such extension was made possible. For a quarter of a century, we have witnessed many variations on this theme, with economists hither and yon maximizing objective functions subject to specific constraints.

I should not imply that the maximizing models have held monolithic dominance. The institutional economists, and their successors, have continued their sometimes inarticulate critique of economic theory. Frank Knight, and some of his students, continued to lay stress on the social-organization aspects of the discipline. Game theory, in its solution rather than its strategy search, offered partial redirection of emphasis. More importantly for my purposes, public choice theory emerged as the positive theory of politics, a theory that necessarily treats individual decision takers as participants in a complex interaction that generates political outcomes.

But let me return to mainstream efforts of economists in the years since World

War II. I have no quarrel with the elaborations and refinements of the maximizing models for individual and firm behavior, although I have argued that many of these contributions belong, appropriately, to home economics or to business administration rather than to political economy. My strictures are directed exclusively at the extension of this basic maximizing paradigm to social organization where it does not belong. This is the bridge which economists should never have crossed, and which has created major intellectual confusion. "That which emerges" from the trading or exchange process, conceived in its narrowest or its broadest terms, is not the solution to a maximizing problem, despite the presence of scarce resources and the conflict among ends. "That which emerges" is "that which emerges" and that is that.

Return to game theory for analogy. The solution to a game with defined rules is not a maximum, and an external observer of the game would not attempt to seek improvements by operating directly on solutions. He would, instead, look at the prospects for changing the rules, and observed solutions would be information inputs in his evaluation of the game. Solutions are not directly "chosen" by a welfare function that embodies the preferences of the players, and solutions are not themselves ordered in terms of such a function. In game theory, the attempt to force such a construction would appear (and be) absurd. Yet this seems to me to be precisely what economists try to do within their analogous domain. Game theorists would indeed be surprised if someone should find that solutions could, in fact, be ordered in any manner that was consistent with the values of individual players. And they would not be profoundly shocked, to say the least, if someone should prove that such an ordering could not be made. Yet is this not what

most economists experienced when Kenneth Arrow published his famous impossibility theorem in 1951?

My own initial reaction to Arrow's work was, and remains, one of nonsurprise (see Buchanan 1954). Who would have expected any social process to yield a consistent ordering of results? Only economists who had made the critical methodological error of crossing the bridge from individual to social maximization without having recognized what they were doing would have experienced intellectual-ideological disappointment.

There is no need to limit discussion to Arrow's theorem, although I shall return to this. Economists crossed the bridge from individual to social maximization because they wanted to be able to say something about policy alternatives. They desperately needed some instrument which would allow them to play the social engineer even if they eschewed the explicit intrusion of their own values in the process.[1] With the social welfare function construction, they could then talk as if their policy statements were operationally meaningful, and this ability provided them with a certain inner satisfaction. They have remained unwilling to utilize the Pareto criterion as a mere classification scheme, which Ragnar Frisch had advised them to do, and they have not followed my own suggestion (1962) about shifting the application of the criterion back to the level of institutional choice, where prospects for mutuality of agreement are enhanced.

How would the abandonment of the social maximization paradigm have changed the research thrust of economic theory, especially its potential relevance for social policy? The Pareto criterion

---

[1] I am indebted to Charles Plott for suggesting this explanation of the Bergson-Samuelson approach, which is a more sympathetic explanation than the one which I have elsewhere suggested.

VOL. 65 NO. 2   MICROECONOMIC THEORY   227

classifies all positions into two mutually exclusive sets. Once an initial position is explicitly identified to be "nonoptimal" or "inefficient," we know that there exists at least one means of moving from this position to a position that falls within the optimal or efficient set. The initial position must be dominated, for all persons, by at least one position in the efficient set.

There is no issue here, but what should be the role for the economist who has completed these first steps in applying his expertise? He should neither revert to nihilism nor seek the escapism of social welfare functions. His productivity lies in his ability to search out and to invent social rearrangements which will embody Pareto-superior moves.[2] If an observed position is inefficient, there must be ways of securing agreement on change, agreement which signals mutuality of expected benefits. In the limiting case, compensation schemes can be worked out which will achieve Wicksellian unanimity. Yet how many economists do we observe working out such schemes? How many economists bother with proposed compensations (which must, of course, include structural-institutional rearrangements) to those who will be overtly harmed by the effects of a public or governmental policy shift?[3] Instead of this potentially constructive effort, we find our colleagues continuing to express opposition to tariffs, quotas, minimum wages, price controls, depletion allowances, monopolies, tax loopholes, etc., whether these be existing or proposed. And they continue to stand surprised when the political process, as it operates, pays little or no heed to their advice. As Knut Wicksell noted eighty years ago,

[2] This is essentially the suggestion that I made in my paper in 1959.

[3] An exception is W. H. Hutt. In a much neglected small book published in 1943, he proposed that the postwar British economy be swept clear of all market restrictions through the device of compensating all persons and groups who would lose by the change.

economists act as if they are advising a benevolent despot, in which case their post-Robbins, post-Bergson stance would, of course, be entirely fitting.

There is a place for efficiency in my suggested scheme of things. In this sense, there is little wrong with economic theory per se. Efficiency, as an attribute, is necessarily present when there is a demonstrated absence of possible agreed-on changes. The trading process, broadly conceived, is the means through which the "potentially realizable surplus" is exploited. But there is no uniquely determinate outcome of the trading process, since exchanges must be made and contracts enforced at preequilibrium and, hence, disequilibrium prices. Under the standard assumptions, simple exchange insures that an efficient or optimal position is attained, but this is only one from among a set containing a subinfinity of possible positions. Economists should be satisfied with this result. Within theory itself, search for uniqueness seems to be misguided effort. When the standard assumptions are not descriptive, the simple exchange process will not generate efficient results, and more complex arrangements may be called for. But these arrangements may still be examined in a contractual framework. The specification of these complex contractual arrangements may challenge the skill of the practicing political economist. In facilitating these complex exchanges, which may require the inclusive membership of the whole group, collective-governmental institutions may be necessary. And even though unanimous agreement for change may be conceptually possible, the costs of reaching agreement may be acknowledged to be prohibitively high. This suggests, in turn, that rules or institutions for reaching collective or group decisions may be preselected at some constitutional stage of "trade." It becomes possible in this way to apply the basic contractarian paradigm to the discussion of possible agreement on rules, even if it is anticipated that conflict will emerge at some final stage of application.

Whether the contractarian paradigm is applied at the level of simple exchange, within the constraints of well-defined rules, or at the most basic constitutional level where institutions themselves are the objects upon which agreement must be reached, or at any intermediate level, the emergent results of the trading process are properly summarized as a set of optimal positions, each one of which represents a possible outcome, and no one of which dominates any other in the set. This statement is enough to suggest my prejudices toward game-theoretic explorations into mathematics as opposed to the intricacies of complex maximization. The continuing search for solution concepts— the J. von Neumann-O. Morgenstern solution set of imputations, the several cores along with other more sophisticated concepts—seems to me to reflect and in turn to foster an attitude in the theorist that is consistent with, and contributory to, the contractarian approach that I am here suggesting.

The modern efforts to prove that competitive equilibrium exists and lies in the core of an economy are within my own limits for methodological legitimacy. The complementary emphasis here should be placed on the multiplicity of possible equilibria, on the absence of uniqueness. The devices of the Walrasian auctioneer or Edgeworthian perfect recontracting have been required for the proofs here, but I urge those skilled in this particular mathematics to search for theorems that require less stringent assumptions, that incorporate trading at disequilibrium prices.

Now let me return, as promised, to the Arrow impossibility theorem. In his Nobel Prize lecture, Arrow (1974) offers a lucid summary of modern economic theory, and he concludes with a discussion of his impossibility theorem. Unfortunately, Arrow does not seem to have gone beyond his initial failure to appreciate the inconsistency between his norms for a social welfare function, or choosing process, and the precepts for a society of free men. In his lecture, Arrow makes it clear that the Bergsonian requirement of "collective rationality" is prior to the set of reasonable conditions that he lays down for his social ordering. Having long ago proved that these conditions cannot be met, Arrow continues to hold that "the philosophical and distributive implications of the paradox of social choice are still not clear." This statement is both surprising and personally disappointing, since it indicates that Arrow has paid no heed to the arguments which I have made, along with many others, against the whole notion of collective rationality.

The so-called paradox may be used as a single and simple illustration of the profound difference between the maximization paradigm and the contractarian one. There are three voters, A, B, and C, and three alternatives, 1, 2, and 3. The collective choice rule is simple majority voting. Through a series of pairwise comparisons, individual preference orderings may be such that 1 is majority-preferred to 2, and 2 is majority-preferred to 3, while 3 is majority-preferred to 1. This cyclical result is disturbing only to those who seek uniqueness in outcome, who seek to impose the maximization paradigm on a social interaction process where it does not belong. By contrast, to those who accept the contractarian paradigm, who seek only to explain and to understand the behavior of persons who interact, one with another, there is nothing at all disturbing in the paradox. On the assumptions that all side payments have been made, or that institutional constraints are invariant, the tools of economics enable us to classify all three positions, 1, 2, and 3, as falling within the Pareto optimal or efficient set, and no one of these positions dominates the other. If individual preferences produce this set of results, we should be content with this and forego the essentially misleading searches for "philosophical implications" which simply are not there.

In this paper I have restated a position that I have presented in bits and pieces over almost two decades. Knight's favorite quotation from Herbert Spencer says that, "only by varied reiteration can alien conceptions be forced on reluctant minds." I hope that I have at least varied the reiteration sufficiently to avoid boredom. I would not presume to think that my own views on methodology would convince more than a minority of my professional colleagues, and I am under no illusions as to the continued dominance of the maximization paradigm in modern economics. Nonetheless, I think that progress has been made during the last twenty years. Game theory, after a series of disappointing attempts to work out optimal strategies for players, has shifted toward a more comprehensive, and more appropriate, consideration of solution concepts. Public choice has emerged as a subdiscipline in its own right, and one that is currently thriving, both within economics and in political science. But intellectual developments have perhaps been overshadowed in effect by the march of events. As persons, both from the streets and the ivory towers, observe modern governmental failures, they can scarcely fail to be turned off by those constructions which require beneficent wisdom on the part of political man. And they can hardly place much credence in the economist consultant whose policy guidelines apply only within institutions that embody such wisdom. Something is amiss, and economists are necessarily being forced to take stock of the social productivity of their efforts. When, as, and if they do so, they will, I think, come increasingly to share what I have called the contractarian paradigm.

As I have argued elsewhere (1964, 1969), economics comes closer to being a "science of contract" than a "science of choice." And with this, the "scientist," as political economist, must assume a different role. The maximizer must be replaced by the arbitrator, the outsider who tries to work out compromises among conflicting claims. The Edgeworth-Bowley box becomes the first diagram in our elementary textbooks; the indifference curve-budget line construction is relegated to subsidiary treatment. Eugen v. Böhm-Bawerk's horse traders are the basic examples, not the housewife who shops for groceries in the supermarket. Game theory, in its most comprehensive sense, becomes the basic mathematics for the professional, and solutions to n-person games replace the nth order conditions for maxima and minima. The unifying principle becomes *gains-from-trade*, not maximization. These principles merge, of course, at the level of the individual chooser's calculus, but they become quite distinct when attention shifts to the social interaction that we call "the economy."

REFERENCES

K. Arrow, *Social Choice and Individual Values*, New York 1951.

———, "General Economic Equilibrium: Purpose, Analytic Techniques, Collective Choice," *Amer. Econ. Rev.*, June 1974, *64*, 253–72.

A. Bergson, "A Reformulation of Certain Aspects of Welfare Economics," *Quart. J. of Econ.*, 1938, *52*, 310–34.

J. M. Buchanan, "Social Choice, Democracy, and Free Markets," *J. of Pol. Econ.*, 1954, *62*, 114–23.

———, "Positive Economics, Welfare Economics, and Political Economy," *J. of Law and Econ.*, 1959, *2*, 124–38.

——, "The Relevance of Pareto Optimality," *J. of Conflict Resolution*, 1962, *6*, 341–54.

——, "What Should Economists Do?," *Southern Econ. J.*, Jan. 1964, *30*, 213–22.

——, "Is Economics the Science of Choice?," in E. Streissler, ed., *Roads to Freedom: Essays in Honor of F. A. Hayek*, London 1964, 47–64.

E. H. Chamberlin, *The Theory of Monopolistic Competition*, Cambridge, Mass. 1932.

R. Frisch, "On Welfare Theory and Pareto Regions," *Int. Econ. Papers*, 1959, *9*, 39–92.

J. R. Hicks, *Value and Capital*, London 1939.

W. H. Hutt, *A Plan for Reconstruction*, London 1943.

L. Robbins, *An Essay on the Nature and Significance of Economic Science*, London 1932.

J. Robinson, *Economics of Imperfect Competition*, London 1933.

P. A. Samuelson, *Foundations of Economic Analysis*, Cambridge, Mass. 1947.

J. von Neumann and O. Morgenstern, *Theory of Games and Economic Behavior*, Princeton 1944.

K. Wicksell, *Finanztheoretische Untersuchungen*, Jena 1896.

[21]

Public Choice 48: 3-25 (1986).
© *1986 Martinus Nijhoff Publishers, Dordrecht. Printed in the Netherlands.*

An agenda for the study of institutions*

ELINOR OSTROM
Department of Political Science, Indiana University, 513 North Park, Bloomington,
IN 47405, and
Workshop in Political Theory & Policy Analysis, Indiana University, Bloomington,
Indiana

1. The multiple meanings of institutions

Recently, public choice theorists have evidenced considerable interest in the study of institutions. William Riker (1982: 20) recently observed, for example, that 'we cannot study simply tastes and values, but must study institutions as well.' Little agreement exists, however, on what the term 'institution' means, whether the study of institutions is an appropriate endeavor, and how to undertake a cumulative study of institutions.

Riker defines institutions as 'rules about behavior, especially about making decisions' (1982: 4). Charles Plott also defines institutions to mean 'the rules for individual expression, information transmittal, and social choice ...' (1979: 156). Plott uses the term 'institutions' in his effort to state the fundamental equation of public choice theory. Using ⊕ as an unspecified abstract operator, Plott's fundamental equation is:

$$\text{preferences} \oplus \text{institutions} \oplus \text{physical possibilities} = \text{outcomes} \quad (1)$$

Plott himself points out, however, that the term institution refers to different concepts. He ponders:

> Could it be, for example, that preferences and opportunities *alone* determine the structure of institutions (including the constitution)? These questions might be addressed without changing 'the fundamental equation' but before that can be done, *a lot of work must be done on determining exactly what goes under the title of an 'institution.'* Are customs and ethics to be regarded as institutions? What about organizations such as coalitions? These are embarassing questions which suggest the 'fundamental equation' is perhaps not as fundamental as we would like (Plott, 1979: 160; my emphasis).

* This paper was delivered as the Presidential address at the Public Choice Society meetings, Hilton Hotel, Phoenix, Arizona, March 30, 1984. I appreciate the support of the National Science Foundation in the form of Grant Number SES 83–09829 and of William Erickson-Blomquist, Roy Gardner, Judith Gillespie, Gerd-Michael Hellstern, Roberta Herzberg, Larry Kiser, Vincent Ostrom, Roger Parks, Paul Sabatier, Reinhard Selten, Kenneth Shepsle, and York Willbern who commented on earlier drafts.

4

Plott's questions are indeed embarassing. No scientific field can advance far if the participants do not share a common understanding of key terms in their field. In a recent volume entitled *The Economic Theory of Social Institutions*, Andrew Schotter specifically views social institutions as standards of behavior rather than the rules of the game. What Schotter calls 'social institutions':

> are not rules of the game but rather the alternative equilibrium standards of behavior or conventions of behavior that evolve from a given game described by its rules. In other words, for us, institutions are properties of the equilibrium of games and not properties of the game's description. We care about what the agents do with the rules of the game, not what the rules are (Schotter, 1981: 155).

Schotter sees his enterprise as a positive analysis of the regularities in *behavior* that will emerge from a set of rules and contrasts this with a normative approach that attempts to examine which rules lead to which types of behavioral regularities. Schotter draws on a rich intellectual tradition that stresses the evolution of learned strategies among individuals who interact with one another repeatedly over a long period of time (Menger, 1963; Hayek, 1976; 1978; see also, Ullman-Margalit, 1978; Taylor, 1976; Nozick, 1975). Rawls characterizes this view of how individuals come to follow similar strategies over time as 'the summary view of rules' (Rawls, 1968: 321).

Still another way or viewing 'institutions' is equivalent to the term 'political structure.' This view differs from that of Schotter in that it does not equate institutions with behavioral regularities. It differs from that of Riker and Plott in that it does not focus on underlying rules. Institutions, defined as political structure, refer to attributes of the current system such as size (Dahl and Tufte, 1973), degree of competition (Dye, 1966; Dawson and Robinson; 1963), extent of overlap (ACIR, 1974), and other attributes of a current system.

The multiplicity of uses for a key term like 'institution' signals a problem in the general conception held by scholars of how preferences, rules, individual strategies, customs and norms, and the current structural aspects of ongoing political systems are related to one another. Over time we have reached general agreement about how we will use such key theoretical terms as 'preferences,' 'actions,' 'outcomes,' 'coalitions,' and 'games.' Further, we have a general agreement about how these concepts are used in our theories to generate predicted outcomes.

The multiple referents for the term 'institutions' indicates that multiple concepts need to be separately identified and treated as separate terms. We cannot communicate effectively if signs used by one scholar in a field have different referents than the same sign used by another scholar in the same field. As scholars, we are in our own game situation - a language generating game. The 'solution' is the result of our choice of strategies about the use of a set of terms to refer to the objects and relations of interest in our field.

5

No one can legislate a language for a scientific community. Scholars begin to use a language consistently when terms are carefully defined in a manner perceived by other scholars as useful in helping to explain important phenomena. In this presentation, I do not try to resolve the debate over *which* of the definitions of institution is the 'right definition.' Instead, one concept - that of rules - is used as a referent for the term 'institution,' and defined. I distinguish rules from physical or behavioral laws and discuss the prescriptive nature of rules. Then I show how theorists use rules in public choice analysis. Two methodological issues are raised. One relates to the configurational character of rules. A second relates to the multiple levels of analysis needed for the systematic study of rules. In the last section, I propose an alternative strategy that takes into account the configurational character of rules and the need for a self-conscious study of multiple levels of analysis.

2. What is meant by rules

Focusing specifically on the term 'rule' does not immediately help us. Even this narrower term is used variously. Shimanoff (1980: 57) identified over 100 synonyms for the term 'rule' (see also Ganz, 1971). Even among political economists the term is used to both refer to personal routines or strategies (e.g., Heiner, 1983) as well as to a set of rules used by more than one person to order decision making in interdependent situations. In game theory, 'the rules of the game include not only the move and information structure and the physical consequences of all decisions, but also the preference systems of all the players' (Shubik, 1982: 8).

Rules, as I wish to use the term, are potentially linguistic entities (Ganz, 1971; V. Ostrom, 1980; Commons, 1957) that refer to prescriptions commonly known and used by a set of participants to order repetitive, interdependent relationships. Prescriptions refer to which actions (or states of the world) are *required, prohibited*, or *permitted*. Rules are the result of implicit or explicit efforts by a set of individuals to achieve order and predictability within defined situations by: (1) creating positions (e.g., member, convener, agent, etc.); (2) stating how participants enter or leave positions; (3) stating which actions participants in these positions are required, permitted, or forbidden to take; and (4) stating which outcome participants are required, permitted, or forbidden to affect.

Rules are thus artifacts that are subject to human intervention and change (V. Ostrom, 1980)). Rules, as I wish to use the term, are distinct from physical and behavioral laws. I use the term differently than a game theorist who considers linguistic prescriptions as well as physical and behavioral laws to be 'the rules of the game.' If a theorist wants only to analyze a given game or situation, no advantage is gained by distinguishing between rules,

6

on the one hand, and physical or behavioral laws, on the other hand. To change the outcomes of a situation, however, it is essential to distinguish rules from behavioral or physical laws. Rules are the means by which we intervene to change the structure of incentives in situations. It is, of course, frequently difficult in practice to change the rules participants use to order their relationships. Theoretically, rules can be changed while physical and behavioral laws cannot. Rules are interesting variables precisely because they are potentially subject to change. That rules can be changed by humans is one of their key characteristics.

That rules have prescriptive force is another characteristic. Prescriptive force means that knowledge and acceptance of a rule leads individuals to recognize that, if they break the rule, other individuals may hold them accountable (see Harré, 1974). One may be held accountable directly by fellow participants, who call rule infraction to one's attention, or by specialists - referees or public officials - who monitor performance. The term 'rules' should *not* be equated with formal laws. Formal laws may become rules when participants understand a law, at least tacitly, and are held accountable for breaking a law. Enforcement is necessary for a law to become a rule. Participants may design or evolve their own rules or follow rules designed by others.

An unstated assumption of almost all formal models is that individuals are, in general, rule followers. Even when theorists like Becker (1976) have overtly modeled illegal behavior, some probability is presumed to exist that illegal actions will be observed, and if observed by an enforcer, that penalties will be extracted. Most public choice analysis is of the rules in use - or working rules as John R. Commons (1957) called them. Many interesting questions need exploration concerning the origin of rules, the relationship of formal laws to rules, and processes for changing rules. But, these topics cannot be addressed here.

Considerable dispute exists over the prescriptive force of 'permission.' Ganz (1971) and Shimanoff (1980) argue that prescriptive force is restricted to 'obligation' and 'prohibition' and does not include 'permission,' while Commons (1957), von Wright (1968), V. Ostrom (1980), and Toulmin (1974) all overtly include 'permission' in their conception of rules. Part of this difficulty stems from efforts to predict behavior directly from specifying rules rather than viewing rules as a set of variables defining a structured situation. In this rule-structured situation, individuals select actions from a *set of allowable actions* in light of the full set of incentives existing in the situation.

Instead of viewing rules as directly affecting behavior, I view rules as directly affecting the structure of a situation in which actions are selected. Rules rarely prescribe one and only one action or outcome. Rules specify sets of actions or sets of outcomes in three ways:

7

(1) A rule states that some particular actions or outcomes are forbidden. The remaining physically possible or attainable actions and outcomes are then permitted. The rule states what is forbidden. A residual class of actions or outcomes is permitted. (Most traffic laws regarding speed are of this type. The upper and lower bounds of the permitted speed are delimited by forbidding transit above and below specific speeds.)
(2) A rule enumerates specific actions or outcomes or states the upper and lower bound of permitted actions or outcomes and forbids those that are not specifically included. (Most public agencies are authorized to engage in only those activities specifically enumerated in the organic or special legislation that establishes them.)
(3) A rule requires a particular action or outcome. (Recent efforts to constrain judical discretion are rules of this type. A judge must impose a particular sentence if a jury concludes that a defendant is guilty of a particular crime.)

Only the third type of rule requires that an individual take one and only one action rather than choose from a set of actions. The third type of rule is used much less frequently to structure situations than the first two.

In the everyday world, rules are stated in words and must be understood (at least implicitly) for participants to use them in complex chains of actions. For analysis, however, rules can be viewed as relations operating on the structure of a situation. Rules can be formally represented as relations, whose domain are the set of physically possible variables and their values, and whose range are the values of the variables, in the situation under analysis. (See below for further elaboration.) Viewing rules as directly affecting the structure of a situation, rather than as directly producing behavior, is a subtle but extremely important distinction.

3. How rules are used in public choice theory

Most public choice theorists 'know' that multiple levels of analysis are involved in understanding how rules affect behavior. But this tacit knowledge of the multiple levels of analysis and how they intertwine is not self-consciously built into the way we pursue our work. Plott, for example, has been engaged in a sophisticated research program related to the theoretical and experimental study of rules. Yet, as discussed above, he poses the central question of our discipline as a *single* equation, rather than as a set of equations. We have not yet developed a self-conscious awareness of the methodological consequences of the multiple levels of analysis needed to study the effects of rules on behavior and outcomes.

Most public choice theorists also 'know' that *configurations* of rules,

8

rather than single rules, jointly affect the structure of the situations we analyze. Again, this tacit knowledge is not reflected in the way we proceed. Most of our theoretical work has proved theorems about the expected results of the use of one rule in isolation of other rules as if rules operated separably rather than configurationally.

To illustrate the multiple levels of analysis and the configurational character of rules, I will use several examples from public choice literature. The first example combines the work of several scholars who have studied how citizen's preferences for public goods are translated through two arenas - an electoral arena and a bargaining arena - into an agreement that a bureau will produce a particular quantity of goods for a particular budget. The second example is from an experimental study of Grether, Isaac, and Plott (1979) of the combination of default condition rules used in conjunction with aggregation rules. The third example is from McKelvey and Ordeshook (1983) who conducted an experimental study of the conjunction of three rules.

3.1 *Rules as they affect outcomes in electoral and bargaining arenas*

In a classic model of the election arena, Anthony Downs (1957) concludes that electoral procedures based on plurality vote will constrain a governing party to select (and therefore produce) the output-cost combination most preferred by a median voter within a community. The Downsian model predicts an optimal equilibrium in terms of allocative efficiency. Downs's prediction of optimal performance results from his analysis of the behavior of elected officials under the threat of being voted out of office by a competing party. It is the presence of a competitor ready to snatch any advantage that pushes the government party toward constant attention to what citizens prefer.

When William Niskanen (1971) examines how bureaucracy affects the linkage between citizen preferences and government performance, he focuses on the process of bargaining between the team of elected officials (called the *sponsor* by Niskanen) and *bureau chiefs* assigned the responsibility to direct agencies producing the desired goods and services. Niskanen assumes that a bureau chief attempts to obtain as large a budget as possible in order to secure the most private gain and to produce the most goods and services for a community. Niskanen's elected officials, like Downs's, know the preferences of the citizens that elect them. So do the bureau chiefs. However, elected officials do not know the production costs of the bureau. The equilibrium predicted by Niskanen is not responsive to citizen preferences since more than optimal levels of output are produced. The predicted result is technically efficient, but unresponsive to the preferences of those served.

Niskanen's model is based on an assumption that bureau chiefs could threaten elected officials with *no* output if the officials did not agree to the initial demand. Romer and Rosenthal (1978) argue that a more realistic assumption would be that the budget reverts to the status quo budget (the one used for the previous year) if the officials (or, the general public in a referendum) did not agree to the initial budgetary request. Changing this assumption in the model, Romer and Rosenthal continue to predict that the equilibrium budget-output combination represents a nonoptimal, over-supply. Their predicted outcome is, however, less than that predicted by Niskanen.

A dramatic change in assumptions is made by McGuire, Coiner, and Spancake (1979) who introduce a second bureau to compete with the monopoly bureau chief in the bargaining arena.[1] Whatever offer is made by one bureau can then be challenged by the second bureau. Over time the offers will approach the same optimal level as predicted by Downs. If one bureau proposes too high a budget, the other will be motivated to make a counteroffer of a more optimal budget-output combination. As the number of bureaus increases beyond two, the pressure on all bureaus to offer an optimal budget-output combination also increases.

The above models focus primarily on the structure of an operational situation and only indirectly on the rules yielding that structure. Without *explicit* analysis of the rules and other factors affecting the structure of a situation - such as the attributes of goods and the community - *implicit* assumptions underlying the overt analysis may be the most important assumptions generating predicted results.[2] In the analysis of electoral and bargaining arenas, all theorists used similar assumptions about the nature of goods and community norms. Goods are modeled as divisible in production and subject to a known technology. In regard to norms, all presume a high level of cutthroat competition is acceptable. These assumptions are not responsible for the differences among predicted outcomes.

The models have, however, different implicit or explicit assumptions about some of the rules affecting the situation. The models developed by Niskanen and by Romer and Rosenthal both give the bureau chief the capacity to make a 'take it or leave it' offer. Both of these models assume an authority rule giving the bureau chief full control over the agenda. Both models also assume that the aggregation rule between the bureau chief and the sponsors is unanimity. The models differ, however, in regard to the default specified in the aggregation rule. Niskanen presumed this rule would allow the budget to revert to zero. No agreement - no funds! An aggregation rule with such a default condition can be formally stated as:

$$B_{t+1} = \{ B_{bc} \text{ iff } B_{bc} = B_s; 0 \text{ otherwise} \}, \text{ where} \qquad (2)$$
$$B_{t+1} = \text{the budget-output combination for the next period,}$$

10

B_{bc} = the budget-output proposal of the bureau chief,
B_s = the budget-output proposal accepted by the sponsor.

In other words, the aggregation rule affecting the structure of this situaction requires unanimity among the participants and sets the budget for the next time period to zero if such agreement is not reached. The first part of this rule states the outcome when there is unanimous agreement. The second part of this rule states the outcome when there is no agreement, or the default condition.

Romer and Rosenthal presumed the rule would be to continue the budget in effect for the previous year. No agreement - continuance of the status quo! Their rule can be formally stated as:

$$B_{t+1} = \{ B_{bc} \text{ iff } B_{bc} = B_s; B_t \text{ otherwise} \}, \tag{3}$$
where B_t is the level of the current budget-output combination.

Niskanen and McGuire, Coiner, and Spancake agree on unanimity and the default condition of the aggregation rule, but differ on the boundary rules allowing entry of potential producers into the bargaining arena. Once a position rule has defined a position, S_i, such as a bureau chief, a formal boundary rule consistent with the Niskanen model could be stated as:

$$\text{Let } S_i = \{1\} \tag{4}$$

A boundary rule consistent with the McGuire, Coiner, and Spancake model would be the following:

$$\text{Let } S_i = \{1, \ldots, n\} \tag{5}$$

Assuming that the other rules are similar, we can array the configuration of rules that differ in the various analyses as shown in Figure 1. The Downsian model is placed in the upper left cell since he made a similar assumption about the default condition of the aggregation rule as Romer and Rosenthal (see Downs, 1957: 69), but had to assume implicitly that elected officials controlled the agenda in their bargaining relationships with bureau chiefs (see Mackay and Weaver, 1978). Consequently, the difference in the results predicted by Downs, by Niskanen, and by Romer and Rosenthal can be related to changes in authority rules and aggregation rules holding other rules constant.

McGuire, Coiner, and Spancake accepted the Niskanen presumption of a zero reversion level while changing the boundary rules allowing producers to enter the bargaining process. This change in boundary rules generates a different situation leading to a prediction of relatively optimal performance

11

Figure 1. Predicted equilibrium budget/output combinations under different rule configurations

Authority rules	Boundary rules	
Aggregation rules	Entry to bargaining process restricted to one bureau	Allow multiple bureaus to enter bargaining process
Open agenda Reversion level is status quo	Downs (1957) Equilibrium is the most preferred budget/output combination of the median voter. Thus, preferences of median voter dominate decision.	Parks and E. Ostrom (1981) Even if no direct competition between two producers serving same jurisdiction, presence of comparison agencies in same urban area will reduce costs of monitoring and increase pressure toward an equilibrium producing the highest net value for the community.
Reversion level is zero budget	No model yet developed for this combination of rules.	No model yet developed for this combination of rules.
Restricted agenda controlled by bureau chief Reversion level is status quo	Romer and Rosenthal (1978) Equilibrium is the highest budget/output combination that provides the median voter with at least as much value as the status quo	No model developed for this combination of rules, but given McGuire, Coiner, and Spancake (1979) status quo reversion level can only enhance tendency of equilibrium to move toward highest net value for the community.
Reversion level is zero budget	Niskanen (1971; 1975) Equilibrium is the largest budget/output combination capable of winning majority approval in an all-or-nothing vote. Preference of median voter is only a constraint.	McGuire, Coiner, and Spancake (197) Equilibrium tends over time toward budget/output combination producing the highest net value for the community.

as contrasted to Niskanen's prediction of nonoptimality. The change in boundary rules opens up a new column of potential operational situations under varying conditions of authority and aggregation rules. An effort that Parks and Ostrom (1981) made to examine the effect of multiple producers in metropolitan areas upon the efficiency of public agencies is closely related to the rule conditions specified in the upper right-hand cell. The implica-

12

tions of the situations created by the other combinations of rules
represented in the second column have not yet been explored.

In this discussion I wanted to illustrate what I meant by a 'rule configuration'. Figure 1 presents a visual display of the configuration of rules that
are consistent with the models of Downs, Niskanen, Romer and Rosenthal,
and McGuire, Coiner, and Spancake. The results predicted in a situation,
using one rule, are dependent upon the other rules simultaneously in force.
Both Niskanen, and Romer and Rosenthal assume that only one bureau can
be present in the bargaining. The boundary rule is the same. Their different
results stem from the variation in the default condition of the aggregation
rule. Both Niskanen and McGuire, Coiner, and Spancake agree on the
default condition, but differ in regard to the boundary rule. Different
results are predicted dependent on the configuration of rules, rather than
any single rule, underlying the operational situation.

Second, I wanted to illustrate the multiple levels of analysis involved. The
overt models presented by these theorists are all at one level. By examining
the rules affecting the structure of these models, I have focused on a second
level of analysis.

3.2 *Committee decisions under unanimity and varying default conditions*

A second example of the study of rules by public choice theorists is a recent
set of experiments conducted by Grether, Isaac, and Plott (1979) who examine the effect of various rules for assigning airport slots. Under one experimental condition, the Grether, Isaac, and Plott situation involves a
committee of 9 or 14 individuals that had to divide a discrete set of objects
('cards' or 'flags') using a unanimity rule. Three default conditions are used
if unanimity is not reached:

> (a) If the committee defaulted, each committee member received his/her 'initial alloca-
> tion' of slots that was unambiguously specified and known before the meeting began.
> (b) If the committee defaulted, slots were allocated randomly.
> (c) If the committee defaulted, slots were taken at random only from those with large in-
> itial allocations and given to those with small or no initial allocation (Grether, Isaac,
> and Plott, 1979: V-2).

All three of these rules can be stated in a form similar to that of equations
(2) and (3) above.

While Romer and Rosenthal make a theoretical argument that the particular default condition used as part of an unanimity rule affects the
predicted outcomes, Grether, Isaac, and Plott provide evidence that default
conditions markedly affect behavior. The decisions about slot allocations
reached by committees tended to shift directly to the value specified in each
of the default conditions.

In summary, the committee decisions are substantially influenced if not completely determined by the consequences of default. Under the grandfather arrangement, 'hardnosed' committee members will simply default rather than take less than the default value. Social pressures do exist for those with 'large' initial endowments to give to those with 'small' endowments, but even if there is no default because of concessions to social pressure the final outcome is not 'far' from the 'grandfather'alternative. On the other hand, when the consequence of default is an equal chance lottery, the slots will be divided equally, independent of the initial allocation .... Default values literally determine the outcomes in processes such as these (Grether, Isaac, and Plott, 1979: V-7).

It has frequently been presumed that aggregation rules varied unidimensionally across one continuum from an 'any one' rule to a unanimity rule (Buchanan and Tullock, 1962). What should now be recognized is that most prior analysis of aggregation rules has implicitly or explicitly assumed only one of the possible default conditions that work in combination with the voting rule to yield incentives in the operational situation. There is nothing inherently conservative about a unanimity rule unless the default condition is the status quo.

Cumulative knowledge from the analysis of these diverse situations requires that we understand that Romer and Rosenthal and Grether, Isaac, and Plott are examining the effect of variations of the same rule given the preferences of participants. If some participants strongly prefer other outcomes to that stated in a default rule, a strong bargainer can threaten them with the default unless the final outcome is moved closer to his own preferred outcome. But when some participants prefer the outcome stated in the default rule, they can afford to block any proposals that do not approach this condition (see Wilson and Herzberg, 1984).

To enhance cumulation, we need to develop formal representations for rules themselves as well as for the action situations on which rules operate. Most formal analyses loosely state the rules affecting the structure of the action situation: (1) in the written paragraphs leading up to the formal representation of the situation, (2) in footnotes justifying why the presentation of the situation is modeled in a particular manner, or (3) even worse, leave them unstated, as implicit assumptions underlying the formal analysis of the situation itself.[3]

3.3 *PMR, germaneness, and open versus closed information rules*

An experiment conducted by McKelvey and Ordeshook strongly demonstrates the configurational relationships when pure majority rule (PMR) is combined with one 'germaneness' rule and two information rules. PMR and a loose operationalization of a germaneness rule – a change in outcome can be made in only one dimension on any one move – is used throughout the experiment.[4] McKelvey and Ordeshook use a closed or an

14

open information rule. Under their 'closed' rule, members of a five-person committee can speak only if recognized by the chair, can address only the chair, and can make comments solely related to the particular motion immediately being considered. Under their 'open' rule, participants can speak without being recognized, can talk to anyone, and can discuss future as well as present motions.

McKelvey and Ordeshook find that the distribution of outcomes reached under the closed information rule, when used in combination with PMR and their germaneness rule, to be significantly different than the distributions of outcomes reached under the open information rule. The experiment is a good example of how rules operate configurationally.

Rules affecting communication flow and content affect the type of outcomes that will be produced from PMR combined with a particular germaneness rule. McKelvey and Ordeshook, however, interpret their own results rather strangely. Their overt hypothesis is 'that the ability to communicate facilitates circumventing formal procedural rules' (p. 8). A close examination of their series of experiments finds no evidence of participants breaking the rules laid down by the experimenters. What they *do* test is whether *a rule giving capabilities or assigning limitations on communication patterns* changes the way in which PMR and their germaneness rule operate. They test the configurational operation of rule systems. And, they find that the operation of one rule depends upon the operation of other rules in a rule configuration.

4. Consequences of the configurational character of rules on the appropriate strategies of inquiry

These three examples provide strong evidence for the configurational or, nonseparable, attribute of rules. This leads me to argue against an implicitly held belief of some scholars that what we learn about the operation of one rule in 'isolation' from other rules will hold across all situations in which that rule is used. I will characterize this view as a belief in the separable character of rules. I presume that rules combine in a configurational or interactive manner. If rules combine configurationally rather than separably, this dramatically affects the scientific strategy we should take in the study of rules and their effects.

A key example of the problems resulting from the view of the separable character of rules is the way theorists have approached the study of PMR as an aggregation rule. Many scholars, who have studied PMR, have self-consciously formulated their models in as general a manner as possible. By proving a theorem in a general case, it is presumed that the theorem will hold in all specific cases that contain PMR.

The penchant for generality has been interpreted to mean a formulation devoid of the specification of any rule, other than PMR. A set of N individuals somehow forms a committee or legislature. Position rules are rarely mentioned. The implicit assumption of most of these models is one and only one position exists - that of member. No information is presented concerning boundary rules. We do not know how the participants were selected, how they will be retained, whether they can leave, and how they are replaced. The participants compare points in n-dimensional space against one point in the same space called the status quo. We have no idea how that policy space came into being and what limits there may be on the policies that could be adopted. (One might presume from the way such general models are formulated that no constitutional rules protect against the taking of property without due process or prohibiting infringements on freedom of speech.) Authority rules are left unstated. We must guess at what actions individual participants are authorized to take. From the way that the models are decribed, it appears that any participant can make any proposal concerning movement to any place in policy space. We do not know anything about the information rules. Everyone appears to be able to talk to everyone and provides information about their preferences to everyone. PMR is the only rule specified.

In this general case, in which only a single rule is formulated, theorists typically make specific assumptions about preference orderings. This suggests that the concepts of 'generality' and 'specificity' are used arbitrarily. Specific assumptions about preference orderings are accepted as appropriate in general models, while efforts to increase the specificity of the rules in these same models are criticized because they are too specific.

The search for equilibria has occurred predominantly within the context of such 'general' models. And, in such 'general' models, equilibria are virtually nonexistent and are fragile to slight movements of preferences or the willingness of participants to dissemble (Riker, 1981). McKelvey and Ordeshook (1983: 1) are willing to state that 'the principal lesson of social choice theory is that preference configurations which yield majority undominated outcomes are rare and almost always are fragile and thus are unlikely to be found in reality.'

If rules combine in a configurational manner, however, theorems proved about a 'zero' institutional arrangement will not necessarily be true when other rules are fully specified. Shepsle and his colleagues at Washington University have repeatedly shown that when several other rules are overtly combined with PMR, equilibria outcomes are more likely. Shepsle and Weingast (1981) have summarized the effects of:

> (1) Scope rules that operate to limit the set of outcomes that can be affected at a node in a process, e.g., amendment control rules (Shepsle, 1979a; 1979b), 'small change' rules (Tullock, 1981), rules requiring the status quo outcome to be considered at the last

16

decision node, and rules requiring a committee proposal to be considered at the penultimate decision node.

(2) Authority rules that operate to create and/or limit the action sets available to participants in positions, e.g., rules that assign a convener special powers to order the agenda (McKelvey, 1979; Plott and Levine, 1978; Isaac and Plott, 1978), rules that assign a full committee, such as the Rules Committee in the House of Representatives, authority to set the procedures for debate and even to exclude a bill from consideration, and rules that constrain the action sets of members in regard to striking part of a motion, adding a part of a motion, and/or substituting a part of a motion (Fiorina, 1980).

Structure-induced equilibria are present in many situations where scope rules, that limit the outcomes that can be reached, or authority rules, that constrain the actions of the participants in particular positions, are combined with PMR. This leads to an optimistic conclusion that equilibria are more likely, than previously argued, in committees and assemblies using majority rule to aggregate individual votes. This substantive optimism is tempered somewhat when one recognizes the methodological consequences of rejecting the belief that rules can be studied as separable phenomena.

The methodological problem rests in the logic of combinatorics. If we were fortunate enough to be studying separable phenomena, then we could simply proceed to study individual rules out of context as we have done with PMR. We could then proceed to study other rules, out of context, and derive separable conclusions for each type of rule. Eventually, we could add our results together to build more complex models. This is an appropriate scientific method for the study of separable phenomena.

However, if the way one rule operates is affected by other rules, then we cannot continue to study each rule in isolation from others. A simple, scientific program is more difficult to envision once the configurational nature of rules is accepted. A configurational approach affects the way we do comparative statics. Instead of studying the effect of change of one rule on outcomes, regardless of the other rules in effect, we need to carefully state which other rules are in effect which condition the relationships produced by a change in any particular rule. We cannot just assume that other variables are controlled and unchanging. We need to know the value of the other variables affecting the relationship examined in a comparative statics framework.

Thus, we have much to do! It is more comforting to think about proving theorems about the effects of using one particular rule out of context of the other rules simultaneously in effect. If, however, combinations of rules work differently than isolated rules, we had better recognize the type of phenomena with which we are working and re-adjust our scientific agenda. We do, however, need a coherent strategy for analyzing and testing the effects of combinations of rules. How can we isolate a key set of generally formulated rules that provide the core of the rules to be studied? How can we build on the results of previous analytical work in our field?

5. Multiple levels of analysis and alternate strategy of inquiry

I have no final answers to these questions, but I do have an initial stategy to propose. This strategy relates to my earlier stress on the multiple levels of analysis involved in the study of rules. We have a relatively well developed body of theory related to the study of situations such as markets, committees, elections, and games in general. Thus, we already know what variables we must identify to represent one level of analysis. We can build on this knowledge as we develop the second level of analysis.

5.1 *The structure of an action situation*

The particular form of representation differs for neoclassical market theory, committee structures, and games in extensive form. However, in order to analyze any of these situations, an analyst specifies and relates together seven variables that form the structure of a situation.

(1) The set of positions to be held by participants.
(2) The set of participants (including a random actor where relevant) in each position.
(3) The set of actions that participants in positions can take at different nodes in a decision tree.
(4) The set of outcomes that participants jointly affect through their actions.
(5) A set of functions that map participant and random actions at decision nodes into intermediate or final outcomes.
(6) The amount of information available at a decision node.
(7) The benefits and costs to be assigned to actions and outcomes.

These seven variables plus a model of the decision maker must be explicitly stated (or are implicitly assumed) in order to construct any formal model of an interdependent situation. We can consider these seven to be a universal set of necessary variables for the construction of formal decision models where outcomes are dependent on the acts of more than a single individual. This is a minimal set in that it is not possible to generate a prediction about behavior in an interdependent situation without having explicitly or implicitly specified something about each of these seven variables and related them together into a coherent structure. I call the analytical entity created when a theorist specifies these seven variables an action situation.

The most complete and general mathematical structure for representing

18

an action situation is a game in extensive form (Selten, 1975; Shubik, 1982). The set of instructions given to participants in a well constructed laboratory experiment is also a means of representing an action situation. Using these variables, the simplest possible working model of any particular type of situation whether a committee, a market, or a hierarchy can be constructed.[5] A change in any of these variables produces a different action situation and may lead to very different outcomes. More complex models of committees, markets, or other interdependent situations are constructed by adding to the complexity of the variables used to construct the simplest possible situations.[6]

5.2 *An action arena: Models of the situation and the individual*

In addition to the seven universal variables of an action situation, an analyst must also utilize a model of the individual, which specifies how individuals process information, how they assign values to actions and outcomes, how they select an action, and what resources they have available. The model of the individual is the animating force that allows the analyst to generate predictions about likely outcomes given the structure of the situation (Popper, 1967). When a specific model of the individual is added to the action situation, I call the resulting analytical entity an 'action arena.' An action arena thus consists of a model of the situation and a model of the individual in the situation (see E. Ostrom, 1985).

When a theorist analyzes an action arena, the model of the situation and the model of the individual are assumed as givens. At this level of analysis, the task of the analyst is viewed as one of predicting the type of behavior and results, given this structure. Questions concerning the presence or absence of retentive, attractive, and/or stable equilibria and evaluations of the efficiency and equity of these results are pursued at this level. The key question at this level is: Given the analytical structure assumed, how does this situation work to produce outcomes?

5.3 *Rules as relations*

Let me return now to the point I made above that all rules can be represented as relations. I can now be more specific. From sets of physically possible actions, outcomes, decision functions, information, positions, payoffs, and participants, rules select the feasible sets of the values of these variables. The action situation is the intersection of these feasible sets. In regard to driving a car for example, it is physically possible for a 13 year old to drive a car at 120 miles per hour on a freeway. If one were to model the action situation of a freeway in a state with well enforced traffic laws, one would posit the position of licensed drivers traveling an average of 60 to 65 miles per hour

19

(depending on the enforcement patterns of the state). The values of the variables in the action situation are constrained by physical and behavior laws, and then, further contained by the rules in use. Most of formal analyses, to date, are of action situations; this is the surface structure that our representations model. The rules are part of the underlying structure that shapes the representations we use.

But, how do we overtly examine this part of the underlying structure? What rules should be examined when we conduct analysis at a deeper level? The approach I recommend is that we focus on those rules that can directly affect the structure of an action situation. This strategy helps us identify seven broad types of rules that operate configurationally to affect the structure of an action situation. These rules include:

(1) *Position rules* that specify a set of positions and how many participants hold each position.

(2) *Boundary rules* that specify how participants are chosen to hold these positions and how participants leave these positions.

(3) *Scope rules* that specify the set of outcomes that may be affected and the external inducements and/or costs assigned to each of these outcomes.

(4) *Authority rules* that specify the set of actions assigned to a position at a particular node.

(5) *Aggregation rules* that specify the decision function to be used at a particular node to map actions into intermediate or final outcomes.

(6) *Information rules* that authorize channels of communication among participants in positions and specify the language and form in which communication will take place.

(7) *Payoff rules* prescribe how benefits and costs are to be distributed to participants in positions.

Given the wide diversity of rules that are found in everyday life, social rules could be classified in many ways. The method I am recommending has several advantages. First, rules are tied directly to the variables of an analytical entity familiar to all public choice theorists, economists, and game theorists. From this comes a strategy, or a heuristic, for identifying the rules affecting the structure of that situation. For each variable identified in the action situation, the theorist interested in rules needs to ask what rules produced the variable as specified in the situation. For example, in regard to the number of participants, the rule analyst would be led to ask: Why are there N participants? How did they enter? Under what conditions can they leave? Are there costs, incentives, or penalties associated with entering or exiting? Are some participants forced into entry because of their residence or occupation?

In regard to the actions that can be taken, the rule analyst would ask: Why these actions rather than others? Are all participants in positions assigned

20

the same action set? Or, is some convener, or other position, assigned an action set containing options not available to the remaining participants? Are sets of actions time or path dependent?

In regard to the outcomes that can be affected, the rule analyst would ask: Why these outcomes rather than others? Are the participants all principals who can affect any state variable they are defined to own? Or, are the participants fiduciaries who are authorized to affect particular state variables within specified ranges but not beyond? Similar questions can be asked about each variable overtly placed in a model of an action situation.

Answers to these sets of questions can then be formalized as a set of relations that, combined with physical and behavioral laws, produce the particular values of the variables of the situation. I am not arguing that there is a unique set of relations that produce any particular model of a situation. Given the pervasiveness of situations with the structure of a Prisoners' Dilemma, one can expect that multiple sets of rules may produce action situations with the same structure. This is not problematic when one focuses exclusively on predicting behavior within the situation. It poses a serious problem when the question of how to change that structure. To change a situation, one must know which set of rules produce the situation.

Other factors also affect this structure. We know, for example, that rules which generate a competitive market produce relatively optimal equilibria when used to allocate homogeneous, divisible goods from which potential consumers can be excluded. The same rules generate less optimal situations when goods are jointly consumed and it is difficult to exclude consumers. But the theorist interested in how changes in rules affects behavior within situations must hold other factors constant while an analysis is conducted of changes in the rules.

Besides providing a general heuristic for identifying the relevant rules that affect the structure of a situation, a second advantage of this approach is that it leads to a relatively natural classification system for sets of rules. Classifying rules by what they affect enables us to identify sets of rules that all directly affect the same working part of the situation. This should enhance our capabilities for developing a formal language for representing rules themselves. Specific rules used in everyday life are named in a non-theoretical manner - frequently referring to the number of the rule in some written rule book or piece of legislation. Theorists studying rules tend to name the rule they are examining for some feature related to the particular type of situation in which the rule occurs.

For systematic cumulation to occur, we need to identify when rules, called by different names, are really the same rule. It is important that scholars understand, for example, that Romer and Rosenthal and Grether, Isaac, and Plott all examined consequences of default conditions of aggregation rules. Proceeding to formalize the rules used by Grether, Isaac, and Plott

21

in their series of experiments would help other scholars identify which rules, called by other everyday terms, are similar to the 'grandfather' default condition, to the random default condition, or to 'taking from the large and giving to the small' default condition.

By paying as much care to the formalization of the rules affecting an action situation as we do to formalizing the action situation itself, we will eventually establish rigorous theoretical propositions concerning the completeness and consistency of rules themselves. From Romer and Rosenthal and from Grether, Isaac, and Plott, we now know that any specification of a unanimity rule without an explicit default condition is incomplete. I am willing to speculate that any aggregation rule without a default condition is incomplete.

6. Some concluding thoughts

Given the multiple referents for the term 'institutions,' our first need is for a consistent language if public choice scholars are going to return to a major study of institutions. To begin this task, I have focused on one term - that of rules - used by some theorists as a referent for the term institutions. My effort is intended to clarify what we mean by rules, how rules differ from physical or behavioral laws, how we can classify rules in a theoretically interesting manner, and how we can begin to formalize rule configurations. I have not answered the question, 'What are institutions?' This involves an argument over which referent is 'the' right or preferred referent. Rather, I try to clarify one referent and leave the clarification of other referents to other scholars.

Secondly, I provided several examples of how public choice analysts have studied rules. These examples illustrate two points. First, rules operate configurationally rather than separably. Second, the study of rules involves multiple levels of analysis rather than a single level of analysis. The configurational character of rules significantly affects the strategies we use to analyze rules. One approach has been to posit a single rule and examine the type of equilibria, or absence of equilibria, likely to result from the operation of this single rule. Scholars have concluded that stable equilibria do not exist in situations in which individuals use majority rule aggregation procedures. This is not consistent with empirical observation. Further, when scholars introduce rules constraining actions and outcomes into majority rule models, it is then possible to predict stable equilibria. The methodological consequence of the configurational character of rules is that theorists need to specify a set of rules, rather than a single rule, when attempting to ask what consequences are produced by changes in a particular rule.

22

Once this conclusion is accepted, a method to identify sets of rules is essential if we hope to develop any cumulative knowledge about the effects of rules. If more than one rule need be specified, the key question is how many different rules must be specified to know that we have identified a rule configuration. My preliminary answer is that we need to identify seven types of rules that directly affect the seven types of variables we use to construct most of the action situations we analyze. When we analyze changes in one of these rules, we should identify the specific setting of the other variables that condition how the changes in the first rule affects outcomes.

The analysis of rules needs at least two levels. We can represent these levels by reformulating Plott's fundamental equation into two equations:

$$\text{Structure of an Action Situation} \oplus \text{Model of a Decision Maker} = \text{Outcomes} \tag{6}$$

$$\text{Rules} \oplus \text{Physical Laws} \oplus \text{Behavioral Laws} = \text{Structure of an Action Situation} \tag{7}$$

Equation (6) is the one most public choice theorists use in their work. As we delve somewhat deeper into the analysis of rules themselves, previous work that has focused on action situations themselves can be integrated into a broader framework. Equation (7) involves the specification of the rules, as well as the physical and behavioral laws, that affect the values of the variables in an action situation. The seventh equation is the one we must use when we want to analyze how rules change the structure of a situation leading, in turn, to a change in outcomes (see V. Ostrom, 1982; 1984). The seventh equation makes apparent the need to study the effects of rules where physical and behavioral laws are invariant.

In light of these characteristics, much future work needs to be done. We need a formal language for the representation of rules as functions affecting the variables in an action situation. We also need to address questions concerning the origin and change of rule configurations in use. How do individuals evolve a particular rule configuration? What factors affect the likelihood of their following a set of rules? What affects the enforcement of rules? How is the level of enforcement related to rule conformance? What factors affect the reproducibility and reliability of a rule system? When is it possible to develop new rules through self-conscious choice? And, when are new rules bound to fail?

NOTES

1. Niskanen had himself suggested that an important structural change that could be made to improve bureau performance was to increase the competition between bureaus.

23

2. See Kiser and E. Ostrom (1982) for a discussion of how rules, goods, and attributes of a community all contribute to the structure of a situation.

3. It is surprising how often one reads in a public choice article that prior models had implicit assumptions that drove the analysis. A recent example is in Mackay and Weaver (1978: 143) where they argue that:

> Standard demand side models of the collective choice process, in which fiscal outcomes are considered representative of broad-based citizen demands, implicitly assume not only that a 'democratic' voting rule is employed to aggregate citizen-voters' demands but also that the agenda formation process is characterized by both free access and unrestricted scope.

4. They do not specifically mention that they intend to operationalize the concept of germaneness, but it would appear from the 'dicta' that they think they have done so. However, as Shepsle (1979a; 1979b) conceptualized this rule, decisions about one dimension of a policy space would be made sequentially. Once a decision about a particular dimension had been reached, no further action on that dimension would be possible. Allowing members to zig-zag all over the policy space, one dimension at a time, is hardly a reasonable operationalization of the germaneness rule as specified by Shepsle.

5. The simplest possible representation of a committee, for example, can be constructed using the following assumptions:

(1) One position exists; that of member.

(2) Three participants are members.

(3) The set of outcomes that can be affected by the member contains two elements, one of which is designated as the status quo.

(4) A member is assigned an action set containing two elements: (a) vote for the states quo and (b) vote for the alternative outcome.

(5) If two members vote for the alternative outcome, it is obtained; otherwise, the status quo outcome is obtained:

(6) Payoffs are assigned to each participant depending on individual actions and joint outcomes.

(7) Complete information is available about elements (1) through (6).

For this simplest possible representation of a committee, and using a well-defined model of the rational actor, we know that an equilibrium outcome exists. Unless two of the members prefer the alternative outcome to the status quo and both vote, the status quo is the equilibrium outcome. If two members do prefer and vote for the alternative outcome, it is the equilibrium outcome. The prediction of outcoms is more problematic as soon as a third outcome is added. Only when the valuation patterns of participants meet restricted conditions can an equilibrium outcome be predicted for such a simple committee situation with three members and three potential outcomes using majority rule (Arrow, 1966; Plott, 1967).

6. A more complex committee situation is created, for example, if a second position, that of a convener, is added to the situation, and the action set of the convener includes actions not available to the other members (e.g., Isaac and Plott, 1978; Eavey and Miller, 1982). See also Gardner (1983) for an analysis of purges of recruitment to committees. Gardner's approach is very similar to the general strategy I am recommending.

REFERENCES

Advisory Commission on Intergovernmental Relations (1974). *Governmental functions and processes: Local and areawide. Volume IV of substate regionalism and the federal system.* Washington, D.C.: U.S. Government Printing Office.

Arrow, K. (1966). *Social choice and individual values*, 2nd edition. New York: Wiley.

24

Becker, G.S. (1976). *The economic approach to human behavior.* Chicago: The University of Chicago Press.

Buchanan, J.M., and Tullock, G. (1962). *The calculus of consent.* Ann Arbor: University of Michigan Press.

Commons, J.R. (1957). *Legal foundations of capitalism.* Madison: University of Wisconsin Press.

Dahl, R.A., and Tufte, E.R. (1973). *Size and democracy.* Stanford, Calif.: Stanford University Press.

Dawson, R.E., and Robinson, J.A. (1963). Interparty competition, economic variables and welfare policies in the american states. *Journal of Politics* 25: 265–289.

Downs, A. (1957). *An economic theory of democracy.* New York: Harper and Row.

Dye, T.R. (1966). *Politics, economics, and the public.* Chicago: Rand McNally.

Eavey, C.L., and Miller, G.J. (1982). Committee leadership and the chairman's power. Paper delivered at the Annual Meetings of the American Political Science Association, Denver, Colo., September 2–5.

Fiorina, M.P. (1980)). Legislative facilitation of government growth: Universalism and reciprocity practices in majority rule institutions. *Research in Public Policy Analysis and Management* 1: 197–221.

Ganz, J.S. (1971). *Rules: A systematic study.* The Hague: Mouton.

Gardner, R. (1983). Variation of the electorate: Veto and purge. *Public Choice* 40(3): 237–247.

Grether, D.M., Isaac, R.M., and Plott, C.R. (1979). Alternative methods of allocating airport slots: Performance and evaluation. A report prepared for the Civil Aeronautics Board.

Harré, R. (1974). Some remarks on 'rule' as a scientific concept. In T. Mischel (Ed.), *Understanding other persons,* 143–183. Oxford, England: Basil-Blackwell.

Hayek, F.A. (1976). *The mirage of social justice.* Chicago: University of Chicago Press.

Hayek, F.A. (1978). *New studies in philosophy, politics, economics, and the history of ideas.* Chicago: University of Chicago Press.

Heiner, R.A. (1983). The origin of predictable behavior. *American Economic Review* 83(4): 560–597.

Isaac, R.M., and Plott, C.R. (1978). Comparative game models of the influence of the closed rule in three person, majority rule committees: Theory and experiment. In P.C. Ordeshook (Ed.), *Game theory and political science,* 283–322. New York: New York University Press.

Kiser, L., and Ostrom, E. (1982). The three worlds of action: A meta-theoretical synthesis of institutional approaches. In E. Ostrom (Ed.), *Strategies of political inquiry,* 179–222. Beverly Hills: Sage Publications.

Mackay, R.J., and Weaver, C. (1979). Monopoly bureaus and fiscal outcomes: Deductive models and implications for reform. In G. Tullock and R.E. Wagner (Eds.), *Policy analysis and deductive reasoning,* 141–165. Lexington, Mass.: Lexington Books.

McGuire, T., Coiner, M., and Spancake, L. (1979). Budget maximizing agencies and efficiency in government. *Public Choice* 34(3/4): 333–359.

McKelvey, R.D. (1979). General conditions for global intransitivities. *Econometrica* 47: 1,085–1,111.

McKelvey, R.D., and Ordeshook, P.C. (1984). An experimental study of the effects of procedural rules on committee behavior. *Journal of Politics* 46(1) 185–205.

Menger, K. (1963). *Problems in economics and sociology.* (Originally published in 1883 and translated by Francis J. Nock.) Urbana: University of Illinois Press.

Niskanen, W.A. (1971). *Bureaucracy and representative government.* Chicago: Aldine-Atherton.

Nozick, R. (1975). *Anarchy, state, and utopia.* New York: Basic Books.

Ostrom, E. (1985). A method of institutional analysis. In F.X. Kaufmann, G. Majone and V. Ostrom (Eds.), *Guidance, control, and performance evaluation in the public sector.* Berlin, New York: de Gruyter, forthcoming.

Ostrom, V. (1980). Artisanship and artifact. *Public Administration Review* 40(4): 309–317.

Ostrom, V. (1982). A forgotten tradition: The constitutional level of analysis. In J.A. Gillespie and D.A. Zinnes (Eds.), *Missing elements in political inquiry: Logic and levels of analysis*, 237–252. Beverly Hills: Sage Publications.

Ostrom, V. (1985). Constitutional considerations with particular reference to federal systems. In F.X. Kaufmann, G. Majone and V. Ostrom (Eds.), *Guidance, control, and performance evaluation in the public sector.* Berlin, New York: de Gruyter, forthcoming.

Parks, R.B., and Ostrom, E. (1981). Complex models of urban service systems. In T.N. Clark (Ed.), *Urban policy analysis: Directions for future research.* Urban Affaire Annual Reviews 21: 171–199. Beverly Hills: Sage Publications.

Plott, C.R. (1967). A notion of equilibrium and its possibility under majority rule. *American Economic Review* 57(4): 787–807.

Plott, C.R. (1979). The application of laboratory experimental methods to public choice. In C.S. Russell (Ed.), *Collective decision making: Applications from public choice theory*, 137–160. Baltimore, Md.: Johns Hopkins University Press.

Plott, C.R., and Levine, M.E. (1978). A model for agenda influence on committee decisions. *American Economic Review* 68: 146–160.

Popper, K.R. (1967). La rationalité et le statut du principle de rationalité. In E. M. Classen (Ed.), *Les foundements philosophiques des systemes economiques: Textes de Jacques Rueff et essais redigés en son honneur 23 acut 1966*, 145–50. Paris, France: Payot.

Rawls, J. (1968). Two concepts of rules. In N.S. Care and C. Landesman (Eds.), *Readings in the theory of action*, 306–340. Bloomington, Ind.: Indiana University Press. Originally printed in the *Philosophical Review* 4(1955).

Riker, W.H. (1982). Implications from the disequilibrium of majority rule for the study of institutions. In P.C. Ordeshook and K.A. Shepsle (Eds.), *Political equilibrium*, 3–24. Boston: Kluwer-Nijhoff. Originally published in the *American Political Science Review* 74(June 1980): 432–447.

Romer, T., and Rosenthal, H. (1978). Political resource allocation, controlled agendas, and the status quo. *Public Choice* 33(4): 27–43.

Schotter, A. (1981). *The economic theory of social institutions.* Cambridge, England: Cambridge University Press.

Selten, R. (1975). Reexamination of the perfectness concept for equilibrium points in extensive games. *International Journal of Game Theory* 4: 25–55.

Shepsle, K.A. (1979a). Institutional arrangements and equilibrium in multidimensional voting models. *American Journal of Political Science*, 23(1): 27–59.

Shepsle, K.A. (1979b). The role of institutional structure in the creation of policy equilibrium. In D.W. Rae and T.J. Eismeier (Eds.), *Public policy and public choice*, 249–283. Sage Yearbooks in Politics and Public Policy 6. Beverly Hills: Sage Publications.

Shepsle, K.A., and Weingast, B.R. (1981). Structure-induced equilibrium and legislative choice. *Public Choice* 37(3): 503–520.

Shimanoff, S.B. (1980). *Communication rules: Theory and research.* Beverly Hills: Sage Publications.

Shubik, M. (1982). *Game theory in the social sciences: Concepts and solutions.* Cambridge, Mass.: The MIT Press.

Taylor, M. (1976). *Anarchy and cooperation.* New York: Wiley.

Toulmin, S. (197). Rules and their relevance for understanding human behavior. In T. Mischel (Ed.), *Understanding other persons* 185–215. Oxford, England: Basil-Blackwell.

Tullock, G. (1981). Why so much stability? *Public Choice* 37(2): 189–205.

Ullman-Margalit, E. (1978). *The emergence of norms.* New York: Oxford University Press.

von Wright, G.H. (1968). The logic of practical discourse. In Raymond Klibansky (Ed.), *Contemporary philosophy*, 141–167. Italy: La Nuava Italia Editrice.

Wilson, R., and Herzberg, R. (1984). Voting is only a block away: Theory and experiments on blocking coalitions. Paper presented at the Public Choice Society meetings, Phoenix, Ariz., March 29–31.

[22]

Acta Sociologica (1992) 35:3–11

Economic Institutions as Social Constructions: A Framework for Analysis

Mark Granovetter
Department of Sociology, State University of New York at Stony Brook

Institutional economics has moved from a position, earlier in the twentieth century, of drawing eclectically on several other disciplines, to a stance of building its arguments almost entirely out of neoclassical materials. This paper argues that such a stance cannot provide a persuasive account of economic institutions, and suggests a broader foundation based on classical sociological arguments about the embeddedness of economic goals and activities in socially oriented goals and structures. Emphasis is placed on how economic activity comes to be coordinated by groups of people rather than carried out by isolated individuals. Firms in developing countries, business groups, and the origins of the electrical utility industry in the United States are posed as cases of the 'social construction of economic institutions'. It is argued that, although proper analysis of such cases involves a high level of contingency, these contingencies can be taken into account in a systematic theoretical argument, and that historicist pitfalls can be avoided. Such an argument is posed as the distinctive agenda for a new economic sociology.

Mark Granovetter, Department of Sociology, State University of New York at Stony Brook, Stony Brook, NY 11794-4356, USA.

1. Introduction: the new economic sociology

The discipline of economics has seen two strong and, at first glance, mutually inconsistent trends over the past twenty years: a return to dominance by the pure neoclassical tradition, after a period of contention with competing paradigms, and an attempt by economists to greatly broaden their subject matter. This odd, simultaneous narrowing and broadening of perspective has resulted from the virtual demise of institutional economics in its midcentury form.

Earlier contention had resulted from the inability of the neoclassical synthesis to explain the broad institutional framework within which economic transactions take place. The resulting theoretical vacuum was filled by 'institutionalist' economics, whose explanations drew on historical, political,

sociological and legal factors, with minimal use of formal economic reasoning. Such widely followed American figures as Thorstein Veblen, John Commons, Wesley Clair Mitchell and John Dunlop often seemed as closely allied to other disciplines as to economics.

A broad counterattack began in the 1960s, spearheaded by Gary Becker, later joined by many of the best and brightest mathematical economists. They inventively applied rigorous neoclassical arguments to problems previously abandoned to the institutionalists. The expansion of educational institutions, long considered a cultural phenomenon, was declared the outcome of rational individuals investing in their own capacities (Becker (1964), followed by a vast outpouring of literature on 'human capital'. See the critical review in Blaug (1976)). Rigid wages and long tenures in internal labor markets were attributed not to social pressures or a 'new industrial feudalism' (a metaphor common in 1950s labor economics), but to 'implicit contracts' optimally structured by rational employers and employees faced with otherwise difficult problems of shirking and bad faith. (See the extended discussion in Granovetter (1988)). Huge wage discrepancies between categories of workers resulted not from restrictions on entry based on differences in group power, but from optimal arrangements for distributing talent in society (e.g. Rosen 1982). Vertical integration occurred not because of the suppliers' 'conspiracy against the public' denounced by Adam Smith, but as an arrangement to reduce transaction costs in markets where business had become too complex to conduct between independent units (see especially Williamson (1975, 1985)).

This 'New Institutional Economics' – distinguished from the old by its reliance on arguments for the economic efficiency of observed institutions – was closely allied to the 'New Economic History', which made similar claims for historical settings. Property rights, enclosures, and all manner of political and legal institutions came to be interpreted as the efficient outcome of rational individuals pursuing their self-interest (e.g. North & Thomas 1973; Ransom & Sutch 1982). And these new interpretations were applied even to spheres far from economists' traditional domain, such as the family, crime, altruism and animal behavior (e.g. Becker 1976, 1981). Representative of the claims of this optimistic new school is Jack Hirshleifer's comment, in a 1985 article entitled 'The Expanding Domain of Economics', that 'economics really does constitute the universal grammar of social science' (p. 53).

One unifying theme of my current work is that the new economic imperialism attempts to erect an enormous superstructure on a narrow and fragile base. A more solid foundation can be constructed on the basis of three classic sociological assumptions: (1) the pursuit of economic goals is normally accompanied by that of such non-economic ones as sociability, approval, status and power; (2) economic action (like all action) is socially situated, and cannot be explained by individual motives alone; it is embedded in ongoing networks of personal relations rather than

carried out by atomized actors (for an earlier programmatic statement see Granovetter (1985)); (3) economic institutions (like all institutions) do not arise automatically in some form made inevitable by external circumstances, but are 'socially constructed' (Berger & Luckmann 1966).

The extreme version of methodological individualism that dominates much of modern economics makes it difficult to recognize how economic action is constrained and shaped by the structures of social relations in which all real economic actors are embedded. Economists who want to reform the discipline typically attack its psychology – proposing a more realistic model of decision-making (see, e.g., Leibenstein 1976). While the psychology in neoclassical models may well be naive, I claim that the main difficulty lies elsewhere: in the neglect of social structure. Psychological revisionism has a following in part because it does not require economists to give up the assumption of atomized actors making decisions in isolation from broader social influences.

Mid-century economic sociology operated at the fringes of economic activity, ceding the central topics of production, distribution and consumption to economists. The more recent generation of economic sociologists, who constitute what I call the 'New Economic Sociology', have looked much more at core economic institutions, and are closer to such intellectual forebears as Emile Durkheim and Max Weber – who regarded economic action as a subordinate and special case of social action – than to the accommodationist stance of mid-century sociologists.[1]

An important part of this focus is a sociological theory of the construction of economic institutions. Such a theory must make dynamics central, in contrast to most neoclassical economic work on institutions which (like many branches of economics) emphasizes the comparative statics of equilibrium states. Without explicit dynamic argument, we have the irony that economics, despite its devotion to methodological individualism, finds itself with no ready way to explain institutions as the outgrowth of individual action, and so falls back to accounts based on gross features of the environment. There are two such main accounts: culturalism and functionalism.

Culturalist accounts explain economic institutions as arising from cultural beliefs that predispose a group to the observed behavior, as in the claim that the stress in Japanese culture on 'organic' unity and hierarchical loyalty produces trouble-free industrial organization. Functionalist accounts argue backwards from the characteristics of institutions to the reason why they must be present. Andrew Schotter, in his *Economic Theory of Social Institutions* (1981) states this principle in unusually candid (and a sociologist might add, pre-Mertonian) form – that to understand any social institution requires us to 'infer the evolutionary problem that must have existed for the institution as we see it to have developed. Every evolutionary economic problem requires a social institution to solve it' (p. 2). This implicitly assumes a system in equilibrium, since a still-evolving institution might not reveal by inspection what problem it had evolved to solve. These highly elliptical and often tautological culturalist and functionalist accounts become superfluous once the social construction of institutions is properly understood.

But it is not enough merely to chip away at the insufficiencies of neoclassical economics. A theoretically persuasive economic sociology must also provide an attractive alternative that improves upon the explanatory power and predictive ability of existing accounts. Though I argue repeatedly against the reductionist methodological individualism of modern economics, I have no taste for the historicist views of some of its other opponents, who suppose that every case is unique and anything can happen. I stress the contingencies associated with historical background, social structure and collective action, and the constraints imposed by already existing institutions; but my aim is still that of finding general principles, correct for all times and places. This requires that the contingencies themselves be systematically explored and incorporated into the theoretical structure. It also requires us to understand under what circumstances economic institutions are malleable by the forces of social structure and collective action, or 'locked in' in such a

way that these forces are mainly irrelevant. Finally, and closely related to this last issue, a sophisticated economic sociology will neither throw the valuable corpus of economic reasoning out the window, nor be so seduced by it as to produce a 'rational choice' argument that loses touch with the classic sociological tradition; rather, it will seek to understand how modern economics can be integrated with a social constructionist account of economic institutions, and what the division of labor must therefore be between sociology and economics.

2. Over- and undersocialized conceptions of human action

Before discussing institutions as such, I want to make some general comments on conceptions of human action. I begin by referring to Dennis Wrong's (1961) article 'The Oversocialized Conception of Man in Modern Sociology'. Wrong complained that sociologists saw people as *so* sensitive to the opinions of others that they automatically obeyed commonly held norms for behavior. This 'oversocialized' view resulted from an attempt to compensate for the *neglect* of social effects in (what Talcott Parsons (1937) called) the utilitarian tradition, whose view of economic action I would call 'undersocialized'. (For a fuller account of this distinction, see Granovetter (1985)). As Albert Hirschman (1982) has pointed out, in classical and neoclassical economics, traders in competitive markets are price-takers and thus interchangeable. The details of their social relations are irrelevant.

The classical economists thus treated these relations only as a drag on perfect competition. In a famous line from The Wealth of Nations, Adam Smith denounced the use of social occasions by traders to fix prices. Implicitly he recognized that his image of competitive markets was inconsistent with a world where economic actors knew one another personally well enough to collude. In recent years, a different tendency has emerged in economists' treatment of social influences: that is to take them

5

seriously but in terms close to Dennis Wrong's 'overocialized' conception: e.g. James Duesenberry's (1960) quip that 'economics is all about how people make choices; sociology is all about how they don't have any choices to make', or E. H. Phelps-Brown's description of the 'sociologists' approach to pay determination' as assuming that people act in 'certain ways because to do so is customary, or an obligation, or the "natural thing to do", or right and proper, or just and fair' (1977).

This conception of 'social influences' is oversocialized because it assumes that people follow customs, habits or norms automatically and unconditionally; nearly all economists' treatment of 'norms' has this flavor, and discussions of 'conventions' also run the risk of sliding into an oversocialized treatment. But this points to an irony of great theoretical importance: the oversocialized approach has in common with the undersocialized a conception of action uninfluenced by peoples' existing social relations.

In the undersocialized account this atomization results from the narrow pursuit of self-interest; in the oversocialized one – which originated as a corrective to the undersocialized one – atomization results nevertheless because behavioral patterns are treated as having been internalized and thus unaffected by ongoing social relations.

This surprising convergence of under and over-socialized views helps explain why economists who try to incorporate social influences on economic action fall so easily into oversocialized arguments. Thus it is common to attribute distinctive styles of decision-making to members of different social classes, as the result either of class cultures or of each class's distinctive experience in the eductional system (cf. Piore 1975; Bowles & Gintis 1982). But this conception of how society influences individual economic action is too mechanical: once we know someone's social class, everything else in his behavior is automatic, since he is so well socialized – I would say 'oversocialized'. Thus, I attempt in my work to thread my way between under and over-socialized views, by analyzing how behavior is embedded in concrete, ongoing systems of social relations.

3. The social construction of economic institutions

I now proceed to discuss the impact of this 'embeddedness' on the social construction of economic institutions by focusing on a problem traditionally given little attention in economic theory: how and why economic activities are carried out not by isolated individuals, but by groups that entrepreneurs get to cooperate in such larger entities as firms, industries and inter-industry groups. In other words, I recast the problem of economic institutions as one involving the mobilization of resources for collective action, which opens it up to a whole stream of thought in sociology and political science previously considered irrelevant.

Following Schumpeter (1926), one may call those who coordinate the economic activity of otherwise separate individuals, 'entrepreneurs'. But the neoclassical theory of the firm ignores the entrepreneur because, as William Baumol points out, its model 'is essentially an instrument of optimality analysis of well-defined problems, and it is precisely such . . . problems which need no entrepreneur for their solution' (1968:67). This comment suggests that the emphasis in economic theory on the comparative analysis of equilibrium states discourages attention to entrepreneurship, which can best be thought of as involving situations where markets are out of equilibrium.[2] Related to the failure to provide dynamics is the tendency to abstract away from institutions on the grounds that opportunities for profit will automatically be taken; if there are institutional or other barriers to the taking of such profit, these will be breached, and since one can count on this taking place, the actual process by which it occurs is not of much theoretical interest. Correspondingly, institutions that encourage or discourage entrepreneurship are neglected since it is assumed that it will emerge if there are profits to be made.[3]

This helps explain the remarkable fact that in the recently burgeoning economic literature on *why* firms exist, exemplified by Oliver Williamson's work on 'transaction cost economics' (1975, 1985), entrepreneurs still make no appearance and *how* firms come to exist receives no attention. Instead, it is assumed that firms emerge when needed to reduce transaction costs. In the functionalist style of the New Institutional Economics, this emergence is taken to be automatic.

But economic institutions do not emerge automatically in response to economic needs. Rather, they are constructed by individuals whose action is both facilitated and constrained by the structure and resources available in social networks in which they are embedded. We can see this in many accounts from developing countries where firms would greatly reduce transactions costs but cannot be constructed. What are the difficulties?

Traditional development theory took a dim view of social structures where economic activity was embedded in non-economic obligations, supposing that this would prevent efficient operations. But where this embedding is in fact absent, and many individuals appear to be rational profit maximizers – approximating the 'undersocialized' model of human action I have described above – economic activity is often stymied by lack of the interpersonal *trust* required to delegate authority or resources to others (see, e.g., Dewey 1962; Geertz 1963; Davis 1973; D. Szanton 1971). But if such problems of trust are overcome, the problem forecast by traditional theories does indeed come to pass: the fledgling firm is often swamped by the claims of friends and relatives for favors and support. As one abdicated king in Bali told anthropologist Clifford Geertz, firms 'turn into relief organizations rather than businesses' (1963:123). That is, the welfare of the local community is put ahead of that of the business as such.

Certain groups, however, such as the overseas Chinese in Southeast Asia, consistently overcome both problems. Trust is available because the community is so close-knit that malfeasance is not only difficult to conceal or execute, but often even hard to imagine. Many accounts thus indicate that Chinese businesses extend credit, pool capital and delegate authority without fear of default or deceit. How, then, do the businesses avoid the second problem, that

of excessive claims based on non-economic ties?

Part of the answer is that overseas Chinese are typically a small minority, and there are simply not *enough* of them for such claims to cause trouble. But the organization of social networks also limits claims, because people belong to non-overlapping groups. Kinship is so clearcut that the number of relatives with credible claims on a business is small and well-defined. People also divide into groups based on recency of immigration and on home area in China. Particular businesses are organized along such kinship and organizational lines, and it is thus sharply defined which individuals can make claims. By contrast, most non-Chinese Southeast Asian kinship patterns are more diffuse, so it is hard to limit the number of relatives with legitimate claims; and people typically belong to many overlapping interest groups, so that if one is the core of a business, its members may still be subject to claims from fellow members of others (Geertz 1963; Dewey 1962; Davis 1973; Lim & Gosling 1983).

Briefly put, overseas Chinese social structure has a pattern of coupling and decoupling that produces highly cohesive groups that are sharply delimited from one another; thus trust is available but non-economic claims are illegitimate beyond these group boundaries. These mechanisms of coupling and decoupling, that define the boundaries of trust and social affiliation, must become central matters for a theory of economic institutions. It would be a fair generalization to say that across such boundaries, economic actors may appear to act as if following the undersocialized model of action, and within them, as if oversocialized – following the dictates of the group. But this way of viewing the matter shows that the fundamental issue is not to get the right model of individual action, but rather to understand properly how variations in social structure create behavior that appears to follow one model or the other. The locus of explanation moves away from the isolated individual to a larger and more social frame of reference.

Following out this logic, note that the argument about Chinese firms implies that under some conditions, it is possible to use connections of family and friendship to develop efficient firms. But one may suspect that the consequent overwhelming importance of trust in such firms drastically limits expansion even when it would be economically rewarding. How can such a limitation be overcome? In many countries this occurs as the result of alliances of families into 'business groups'. This widespread phenomenon goes under many names: the old zaibatsu and their modern successors in Japan; the chaebol in Korea, the grupos economicos in Latin America, the 'twenty-two families' of Pakistan, and on and on.

Though there are analyses of such groups in particular countries and regions, we have so far no sustained analysis of the phenomenon as a whole, and little realization that this is a central aspect of modern capitalism. The groups vary in size, structure and legal organization, and have originated in a number of different ways. One dimension of variation, for example, is the extent to which these groups originated in a single family group which then extended its domain through acquisition or alliance, as in Japan and Korea, or in the coalescence of a number of strong family or other groups that began independently and later joined, as is more the case in Latin America. But whatever the origin and structure, it is common for them to span a number of firms and industries, and to coordinate their investment and production decisions, often through a bank that is formed through and closely identified with the group. Such groups have a strong and sometimes dominating role in the economies and polities of their countries.

And despite the variations in history and structure, it is typical for such groups to be composed of participants who are, to quote one economist who has studied them, 'linked by relations of interpersonal trust, on the basis of a similar personal, ethnic or communal background' (Leff 1979:663). In some cases, tne network of personal relations that initially builds the group becomes formalized into institutional patterns such as holding companies as in Nicaragua (Strachan 1979) or patterns of mutual stockholding as in Japan (Gerlach 1991). And then the shape of these institutions results more from the original structure of

personal relations than from the exigencies of the market – they are, in effect, congealed social networks.

Economists studying these groups in developing countries, interpret them as responses to market imperfections, arguing that they will vanish as more 'sophisticated' markets appear (e.g. Leff 1979). But when economists come upon them in advanced economies, as in Japan, Korea, France, West Germany and others, they either argue that they are vestigial and will fade – as used to be argued for Japan, though this is now increasingly implausible – or that they arise in just those economic circumstances that make them efficient. The arguments for developing and developed economies alike are functionalist tautologies that avoid the central tasks of understanding *how* such alliances can be constructed and *why* capitalist economies, despite their great differences, rarely consist of single, unrelated firms.

Just as for firms and business groups, I argue that whether and how an industry is organized is a social construction. I use the case of the electrical utility industry in the United States from 1880 to 1930.[4] We want to explain why certain plausible alternatives to the private investor owned utilities now dominant in the United States did not occur: e.g. public ownership, or private generation of electric power by each home and large industrial company, which would have consigned utilities to a minor role.

We find a series of stages where the personal networks of a few individuals were crucial. From 1880 to 1892, Thomas Edison mobilized his considerable personal following, including substantial capital from the German Empire, in a bitter struggle to defeat banker J. P. Morgan's vision of an industry providing not electricity but generators to homes and businesses to produce their own electricity on site – the kind of system that, in the United States, became conventional for home heating.

Edison had always preferred central stations and though he was finally ousted from General Electric and the electricity industry by J. P. Morgan in 1892, the dominance of central stations was by then too entrenched for even Morgan to reverse. Note that Edison won this battle not because his solution was the technologically correct one, but rather because he was able to construct winning coalitions of key actors.

One of Edison's main assistants in this battle was his personal secretary, the Englishman Samuel Insull. In 1892, Insull moved to Chicago to take over a small, new company, Chicago Edison, and brought with him a unique set of personal ties: to financiers in Chicago, New York and London, to local political leaders, and to inventors in both the United States and Britain. Many of these had been forged as the result of his long association with Edison. His combination of financial and technical expertise and political connections allowed him to assemble capital, political favors and ways of operating that other utility companies had found impossible to implement, even though some were well aware of their potential. That is, his achievements were due to his political and entrepreneurial skills rather than to technological or organizational innovations.

A close study of the way Insull organized Chicago Edison, with the help of his extensive connections and technical skills, shows that the structure of the entire industry derived from the initial organizational decisions in what would become the largest and most successful firm. Insull also shaped the industry by encouraging regulation by states (rather than by the federal or local governments) and by developing the holding company form, that stabilized relations with local industry and with regulators. Soon, this network of firms, holding companies and regulators congealed. Personal networks still mattered, but only those of people central in the holding companies. By the 1920s, the institutional forms were in place, and the outcome that we now see in the industry was already visible.

4. Discussion

In the case of the evolution of an industry, as for the development of firms and business groups, stable economic institutions begin as accretions of activity patterns around personal networks. Their structure reflects that of the networks, and even when those are no longer in place, the institutions take on a life of their own that limits the forms

future ones can take; they become 'locked in'.[5] Thus, economic problems and technology do not call forth organizational outcomes in some automatic and unconditional way. Instead, these economic conditions restrict what the possibilities are. Then, individual and collective action, channeled through existing personal networks, determine which possibility actually occurs. So even in identical economic and technical conditions, outcomes may differ dramatically if social structures are different. Where firms are, in some sense, 'called for' by market conditions, they still may not arise if no group's social structure can sustain them; inter-industry 'groups' may or may not arise in favorable economic conditions, depending on the structure of connections among important families; and industries may be configured in quite different ways, depending on the shapes of the interpersonal networks of leading actors.

There is thus, in this argument, a high level of contingency in the outcomes. This resembles situations in economic dynamics that are characterized by multiple stable equilibrium points. Indeed, I believe that a social constructionist account can help make such dynamic economic models of institutions more sophisticated. These models are frustrating because there is little substantive way to resolve their underdetermination. As in physical cases with multiple equilibria, you can understand which state the system has reached only by looking at its history. But the contingencies involved in this history are typically outside the economic framework, and thus seem ad hoc and unsatisfying to economists; within a sociological framework, however, they can be given systematic treatment.

Notice that such multiple equilibrium models, even if underdetermined, are far from the historicist argument that every case is unique and anything is possible. In all my cases there are only a few major possibilities. In the case of electric utilities, for example, we see, in effect, three possible system equilibria – public ownership, private decentralized generation of power, or privately held utilities. What we argue is even given the constraints of the particular political, technical and economic parameters in place in late 19th century

9

America, other outcomes were unlikely, but any of these three might have occurred. Individual and collective action, channeled through existing networks of personal and political relations, determined which possibility actually did occur.

An important part of general arguments about such matters would be to characterize those circumstances under which there indeed are multiple equilibria, and networks of collective action may determine outcomes; part of my argument about the utilities was that later on, once the industry form was locked in, the other possibilities were foreclosed, and in those periods, less contingent theoretical accounts might have sufficed.

Also central to the project is to formulate some theoretical principles concerning social structure that will cut across all the cases and offer some explanatory power. One such general principle is that the level of network fragmentation and cohesion, or coupling and decoupling, is a major determinant of outcomes. That was central in the discussion of malfeasance, in the argument about the overseas Chinese and in the discussion of business groups.

Such an argument bears also on the case of electric utilities. If Samuel Insull, for example, had been socially located in a tightly-knit network of close associates, he might well have found it impossible to construct the outcomes he did. Instead, he had relatively weaker ties into several institutional spheres – financial, political and technical – that were decoupled from one another, and this was the reason for his success. The general principle may be that the actor whose network reaches into the largest number of relevant institutional realms will have an enormous advantage. This may be a case of what I have called the 'strength of weak ties' (1973). It relates also to the work of Norwegian anthropologist Fredric Barth, who considers the ability to breach traditionally closed spheres of exchange as the essence of entrepreneurship (Barth 1966).

The ultimate aim, then, is to produce a theoretical argument with a high level of contingency that nevertheless meets scientific standards of generality, and does not fall prey to ever-present temptations of his-toricism. Such an agenda, I argue, is central to the vitality of the new economic sociology.

Acknowledgements

This paper was presented at a conference sponsored by the Centre de Recherche en Epistmologie Appliqué of the Ecole Polytechnique, on 'The Economics of Conventions', Paris, 27–28 March 1991. It draws on my book-in-progress, *Society and Economy: The Social Construction of Economic Institutions*, to be published by Harvard University Press.

Received September 1991
Final version accepted December 1991

Notes

[1] For a more detailed historical account of the economic arguments of Durkheim & Weber, and of the interactions between economists and sociologists over the course of the twentieth century, see Granovetter (1990).

[2] For elaborations on this theme, see Blaug (1986) and Kirzner (1973).

[3] For a more detailed account of the ups and downs in the treatment of entrepreneurship by economists, see Granovetter (1991:Ch. 4).

[4] This section reports on collaborative work originated by Patrick McGuire and joined later by me and Michael Schwartz.

[5] The idea that institutions may become 'locked in' despite the possible greater efficiency of other conceivable forms is a generalization of the argument for lock-in of inefficient technologies by Paul David (1986) and Brian Arthur (1989). Their line of argument parallels that in industrial organization on 'first-mover' advantage.

References

Arthur, W. B. 1989. Competing Technologies and Lock-In by Historical Events. *Economic Journal* 99, No. 394 (March), 116–131.

Barth, F. 1966. Models of Social Organization. Royal Anthropological Institute Occasional Paper No. 23. London: Royal Anthropological Institute of Great Britain and Ireland.

Baumol, W. 1968. Entrepreneurship in Economic Theory. *American Economic Review (Papers and Proceedings of the 80th Annual Meeting*, 58 (May), 64–71.

Becker, G. 1964. *Human Capital: A Theoretical and Empirical Analysis*. New York: Columbia University Press.

10

Becker, G. 1976. *The Economic Approach to Human Behavior*. Chicago: University of Chicago Press.

Becker, G. 1981. *Treatise on the Family*. Cambridge MA: Harvard University Press.

Berger, P. & Luckmann, T. 1966. *The Social Construction of Reality*. New York: Doubleday.

Blaug, M. 1976. The Empirical Status of Human Capital Theory: A Slightly Jaundiced Survey. *Journal of Economic Literature* 14 (December).

Blaug, M. 1986. *Economic History and the History of Economics*. New York: New York University Press.

Bowles, S. & Gintis, H. 1976. *Schooling in Capitalist America*. New York: Basic.

David, P. 1986. Understanding the Necessity of QWERTY: the Necessity of History. *Economic History and the Modern Economist. In* W. N. Parker (ed.), London: Blackwell.

Davis, W. G. 1973. *Social Relations in a Philippine Market: Self-Interest and Subjectivity*. Berkeley, CA: University of California Press.

Dewey, A. 1962. *Peasant Marketing in Java*. Glencoe, IL: Free Press.

Duesenberry, J. 1960. Comment on 'An Economic Analysis of Fertility'. *In* National Bureau Committee for Economic Research (ed.), *Demographic and Economic Change in Developed Countries*, Princeton: Princeton University Press.

Geertz, C. 1963. *Peddlers and Princes*. Chicago: Univesity of Chicago Press.

Gerlach, M. 1991. *Alliance Capitalism: The Social Organization of Japanese Business*. Berkeley: University of California Press.

Granovetter, M. 1973. The Strength of Weak Ties. *American Journal of Sociology* 78, 1360–1380.

Granovetter, M. 1985. Economic Action and Social Structure: The Problem of Embeddedness. *American Journal of Sociology* 91, 481–510.

Granovetter, M. 1988. The Sociological and Economic Approach to Labor Markets: A Social Structural View. *In* G. Farkas & P. England (eds.), *Industries, Firms and Job: Sociological and Economic Approaches*. New York: Plenum Press.

Granovetter, M. 1990. The Old and the New Economic Sociology: A History and an Agenda. *In* R. Friedland & A. F. Robertson (eds.), *Beyond the Marketplace: Rethinking Economy and Society*. New York: Aldine.

Hirshleifer, J. 1985. The Expanding Domain of Economics. *American Economic Review* 85, 53–68.

Hirschman, A. 1982. Rival Interpretations of Market Society: Civilizing, Destructive or Fee-

ble? *Journal of Economic Literature* 20, 1463–1484.

Kirzner, I. 1973. *Competition and Entrepreneurship*. Chicago: University of Chicago Press.

Leff, N. 1979. Entrepreneurship and Economic Development: The Problem Revisited. *Journal of Economic Literature* 17 (March), 46–64.

Leibenstein, H. 1976. *Beyond Economic Man*. Cambridge, MA: Harvard University Press.

Lim, Y. C. & Gosling, L. A. P. (eds.), 1983. *The Chinese in Southeast Asia, Volume I: Ethnicity and Economic Activity*. Singapore: Maruzen Asia.

McGuire, P. 1986. The Control of Power: The Political Economy of Electric Utility Development in the United States, 1870–1930. PhD Dissertation, Department of Sociology, State University of New York at Stony Brook.

North, D. & Thomas, R. 1973. *The Rise of the Western World: A New Economic History*. New York: Cambridge University Press.

Parsons, T. 1937. *The Structure of Social Action*. New York: McGraw Hill.

Phelps, B. & Henry, E. 1977. *The Inequality of Pay*. Berkeley: University of California Press.

Piore, M. 1975. Notes for a Theory of Labor Market Stratification. *In* R. Edwards, M. Reich & D. Gordon (eds.), *Labor Market Segmentation*. Lexington, MA: D. C. Heath.

Ransom, R. Sutch, R. & Walton, G. 1982. *Explorations in the New Economic History: Essays in Honor of Douglass C. North*. New York: Academic Press.

Rosen, S. 1982. Authority, Control and the Distribution of Earnings. *Bell Journal of Economics* 13, 311–323.

Schotter, A. 1981. *The Economic Theory of Social Institutions*. New York: Cambridge University Press.

Schumpeter, J. 1979 [1926]. *The Theory of Economic Development*. Second Edition. New Brunswick, NJ: Transaction Press.

Smith, A. 1776 (1976). *The Wealth of Nations*. Chicago: University of Chicago Press.

Strachan, H. 1979. Nicaragua's Grupos Economicos: Scope and Operations. *In* S. Greenfield, A. Strickon & R. Aubey (eds.), *Entrepreneurs in Cultural Context*. Albuquerque, NM: University of New Mexico Press.

Weber, M. 1921 (1968). *Economy and Society*. Edited and translated by Guenther Roth and Claus Wittich. New York: Bedminster Press.

Williamson, O. 1975. *Markets and Hierarchies*. New York: Free Press.

Williamson, O. 1985. *The Economic Institutions of Capitalism*. New York: Free Press.

Wrong, D. 1961. The Oversocialized Conception of Man in Modern Sociology. *American Sociological Review* 26, 183–196.

[23]

THE ECONOMIC JOURNAL

DECEMBER 1986

The Economic Journal, **96** (*December* 1986), 903–918
Printed in Great Britain

THE ECONOMICS OF INSTITUTIONS
AND THE SOURCES OF GROWTH*

R. C. O. Matthews

I

'The chief fault in English economists at the beginning of the [nineteenth] century was...that they did not see how liable to change are the habits and institutions of industry.' Thus Marshall in his inaugural lecture as Professor of Political Economy in Cambridge, referring to Ricardo (Marshall 1885, p. 155). In the circumstances of that occasion, the remark may have been intended in some part as an olive branch, because the only other serious contender for the Chair had been the High Tory economic historian William Cunningham, Archdeacon of Ely, famous as an anti-theoretical institutionalist and famous also as a polemicist – he was the clergyman who once told his congregation that for him the bliss of Heaven would be incomplete if it lacked the pleasures of controversy. (Perhaps *he* should be regarded as the spiritual father of the Cambridge school.) Be that as it may, nothing much came for a long time of the research programme implicitly proposed by Marshall. Instead, the economic theorists of the first half of the twentieth century concerned themselves more with the part of the subject that Marshall (no doubt wrongly) regarded as relatively well established – the theory of the interaction of unchanging utility-maximising individuals in a *given* institutional structure. Some opposing voice came from the so-called institutionalist school in America, including Veblen, but they had little impact, largely because their doctrines were too ill-defined: rather like 'structuralists' in our own times, they agreed that there was something seriously wrong with neoclassical economics, but that was about the only clear message.

In the last few decades, of course, things have greatly changed. The economics of institutions has become one of the liveliest areas in our discipline. It has, moreover, brought us more closely in touch with a number of other disciplines within the social sciences. A body of thinking has evolved based on two propositions: (i) institutions do matter, (ii) the determinants of institutions are susceptible to analysis by the tools of economic theory. I propose in this address first to say what seem to me to be the central concepts in this body of thinking and then to consider its application to one particular topic.

* Presidential Address to the Royal Economic Society, given in Cambridge on 9 April 1986 at the Royal Economic Society/Association of University Teachers of Economics Conference.

Thinking has come from a number of different angles. Generally speaking, the approaches converge, but the emphasis has been rather different, and there have been differences too in the underlying definitions of an institution. Let me enumerate.

The first identifies alternative economic institutions with alternative systems of *property rights* laid down by the law. Coase (1960) argued that any system of property rights is capable of leading to Pareto-efficiency provided it is a complete system, a complete system meaning one where all rights to all the benefits from all scarce resources are imputed to someone and are tradeable; but that a complete system is never possible, because of transaction costs; and that some incomplete systems, i.e. some institutions, are more conducive to Pareto-efficiency than others. This property-rights line of approach is connected with the now enormous literature on law and economics.

The second approach is about institutions in the sense of *conventions* or norms of economic behaviour, regarded as a supplement to law and in some circumstances one that is more effective than law because less subject to transaction costs. Some people use the word institution in this sense exclusively. This approach has affinities with moral philosophy.

The third approach concerns institutions in the sense of *types of contract* in use: whether insurance is available for a given class of risk, whether labour is employed on a lifetime basis or by the hour, whether companies are liable to take-over bids, and such like.

The fourth and last heading is really a subhead of the previous one, but with great ramifications of its own. It is about institutions in the sense of what kind of contracts are in use about *authority*, about who decides what. This line also owed its present-day origin to Coase, in his 1937 article about the influence of transaction costs on the relative domains of the market and of the command system that exists within the firm. In a broader sense it can be taken to include more complex and qualified grants of authority than 'command' would suggest; for example, it embraces cartels and coalitions, since they too involve some surrender of the authority of the individual economic agent. Furthermore the question of authority arises to some extent in all contracts except the very simplest, because it is usually impossible to provide in advance for every contingency that may arise during the period of a contract, so an element of discretion must remain and the question is how large it should be and who should exercise it. A further word may be said about this. Treating authority in a private-enterprise system as a matter of contract has sometimes been objected to as giving too much emphasis to the voluntary element and not enough to disparities in power. Disparities of power may undoubtedly exist. A contract may matter more to one of the parties than to the other, and this may affect the terms of the bargain struck. But that is true of any contract, whether it involves the grant of authority or not. Disparities of power can also arise *ex post*, once the contract has been made, in so far as there are differences between the parties in the extent to which the assets they own are specific to their dealings with each other (a major topic in the literature). Various means are available *ex ante*, in the formulation of the contract, to protect yourself from being exploited *ex post* on account of your asset-specificity: the study of these is part of the study of institutions. One way is to incorporate as much detail as possible in the contract, narrowing down the range of discretion, probably at some cost in efficiency. Another is the 'hostage' system (Williamson, 1985), under which one party reserves for itself discretion in an area which it has no particular desire to control as such but which offers countervailing power against the danger of objectionable use of discretion by the other. An example is provided by the insistence of the teachers in their recent dispute that certain duties should be classed as voluntary.

The word 'institution' is sometimes used in a quite different sense to mean an organisation (ICI, Cambridge University). I shall not be using it in that sense, though a case can be made for regarding an organisation as consisting of a *set* of institutions in the sense I *am* using.

The common feature of the four approaches I have enumerated – property rights, conventions, types of contract, and authority – is the concept of institutions as sets of rights and obligations affecting people in their economic lives. Some of these rights and obligations are unconditional and do not depend on any contract (other than the fictitious 'social contract'); these may or may not be inalienable. Others are acquired voluntarily, by entering into contracts. Some contracts are explicit, others are implicit in conventions recognised by both parties. Contracts may relate to the exchange of goods or services or money or authority in varying proportions. A system of institutions can thus be described more or less equivalently in the legal kind of parlance I have been using, as the set of rights and obligations in force; or in the parlance of sociology and social anthropology, as a role-system or status-system; or in the parlance of economics, as defining:

(i) what markets exist, taking market in the broadest sense, to include all voluntary exchanges, and
(ii) how economic relations are regulated in areas where markets do not exist.

The emphasis on markets in this economic definition is appropriate for an economy where a substantial part of economic transactions are voluntary. In an economy ruled mainly by governmental controls or by inherited customs, unconditional rights and obligations may dominate, so that attention has to be focused mainly on (ii). The scope for economic reasoning of the conventional kind in that case is likely to be reduced and the scope for political science enlarged, but economic reasoning may still be relevant to the study of the origins and consequences of the command structure or the inherited customs as the case may be.

The foregoing economic definition requires supplementation in a couple of respects. First, it is sensible to have regard not only to the existence of markets but also to the extent of their use: a country with 90 % owner-occupation of dwellings and 10 % tenancy can reasonably be described as institutionally different from a country where the proportions are the other way round, even though both arrangements *exist* in both countries. Secondly, the enforcement of contracts is not at all a matter that can be taken for granted, so different

27-2

mechanisms for enforcing a given type of contract can be taken to mark a difference in institutions.

The relation of institutions and institutional change to *transaction costs* has likewise been seen in rather different ways by different authors, but without major conceptual disagreement. The fundamental idea of transaction costs is that they consist of the costs of arranging a contract *ex ante* and monitoring and enforcing it *ex post*, as opposed to production costs, which are the costs of executing the contract. To a large extent transaction costs are costs of relations between people and people, and production costs are costs of relations between people and things, but that is a consequence of their nature rather than a definition (it would not do as a definition – for example, the cost of personal services are production costs, but they do not necessarily involve things). Naturally, there are grey areas. Some writers treat as transaction costs only costs dependent on the existence of *opportunism* (defined by Williamson as self-interest-seeking with guile). That seems to me too narrow: there are purely cognitive costs of organising and monitoring transactions, for example in calculating the bill or monitoring the other party's competence, even if his honesty is not in doubt. In one respect transaction cost is rather an unfortunate term, because it conveys the suggestion of a cost specifically tied to one individual transaction. That is true of some, such as the traditional jobber's turn; but others, such as the cost of drawing up a company's articles of asso-ciation, are overheads of conducting a set of transactions (making for a difference between marginal and average transaction costs); and yet others are overheads of maintaining the system of property rights generally, such as the costs of security.

Institutions have a static aspect and a dynamic aspect. In considering eco-nomic *change*, the relation between change in transaction costs and change in institutions is similar to the relation between change in production costs and change in product or process. Just as a change in production costs which is exogenous to an industry may or may not make it worth while to alter its products or processes, so an exogenous change in transaction costs may or may not make it worth while to change institutions. Likewise, just as a new product or process may emerge either because of a new idea – an innovation in the narrow sense – or because changes in costs have made an existing idea worth adopting for the first time, so also institutional changes may come about either because of new ideas or because of externally originating changes in costs.

The objective of the economic agent is not to minimise transaction costs as such, but to minimise the sum of transaction costs and production costs. There may be tradeoffs between the two. Choice of technique or choices of institution may affect both, in opposite directions. That can be illustrated by what is perhaps the most important of all long-run institutional changes that have occurred in advanced economies, namely decline in the importance of the family as a productive unit. Family production tends to make for high production costs because it restricts exploitation of scale economies and may create mis-matches between talents and occupation. On the other hand it tends to reduce transaction costs, because if instead you have a lot of dealing with strangers

you have to devote more resources to checking up on their personal characteristics and safeguarding yourself against opportunism. In that example a given
change – greater division of labour – inherently both calls for higher transaction
costs and permits lower production costs. However, interaction may also occur
by substitution as a result of innovations that in themselves affect only one class
of costs. For example, suppose that there is a reduction in telecommunication
costs, which reduces transaction costs. This could be enjoyed simply as a cost
reduction, without any other change, but it might also permit finer division of
labour, thereby saving production costs but possibly leading to an actual
increase in the total spent on transaction costs. Douglass North (1984) has
argued that progressive increase in the division of labour has produced an
enormous increase in transaction costs, both by itself and because it has
increased alienation and hence opportunism. He suggests that the increase has
been of such an extent that transaction costs in advanced economies today
account for about half of GDP; he interprets the rise in white-collar jobs in this
way. The natural interpretation of North's contention is that innovation has
been biased (in the Hicksian sense) in the direction of being production-cost-
saving: our skills in dealings with things have improved more than our skills in
dealing with other people. That interpretation implies a less than unit elasticity
of substitution between transaction inputs and production inputs. But at least
in principle the interpretation could be the other way round: it could be that
innovation has been *transaction*-cost-saving but that the elasticity of substitution
has been greater than one. That probably is not the most plausible interpretation in that particular instance, at least not for the economy as a whole over
the long period, but it serves to show that the bias of cost-saving cannot
necessarily be inferred from trends in the ratio of total expenditures on production costs and on transaction costs.

The economics of institutions and the economics of transaction costs (I shall
from now on be taking them as representing a single approach) have been
applied to many areas: industrial organisation and corporate governance;
labour economics; public choice; development; and economic history. Intel-
lectually it has points of contact not only with law, moral philosophy, sociology,
and social anthropology, which I have already mentioned, but also with
information theory, organisation theory, and, particularly, with game theory.
Politically it is neutral: it has been invoked in support of both market pessimism
and market optimism. On the left-wing, anti-market, side, it has been argued
that textbook theoretical vindications of the hidden hand depend on institutional assumptions that are invalid, like Walrasian *tâtonnement*, or else presuppose institutions that exist only in certain types of country – an argument
often used by left-wing development economists. On the other side, it can be
argued, and has been argued, that study of institutions opens up a whole new
domain where the dexterity of the hidden hand is revealed: not only does the
market achieve the best results within any given institutional framework, but
it does better, it selects the institutional framework that is most Pareto-efficient.
The institutional approach can also be used by people who are optimists but
not market optimists, that is to say people who believe that the most efficient

institutions do evolve but who do not hold that those institutions necessarily consist of a universal system of competitive markets with individual property rights. That sort of view has been taken by some schools of social anthropologists, and it could also be taken to be implied by the title that A. D. Chandler gave to his famous book on the American corporation, *The Visible Hand*.

II

I propose to devote most of the rest of this address to a particular area of application of the economics of institutions, namely the contribution of institutional change to economic growth. I shall identify economic growth with income per head and I shall assume, for the sake of simplicity, that a Pareto-improvement conduces to economic growth so defined.

The analogy between institutional innovations and technical innovations creates a presumption, no more, that institutional change has made a positive contribution to economic growth. The presumption is that in the course of time people have discovered and adopted institutional arrangements that enabled them to co-operate with one another more efficiently than they did before. Whether this has in fact happened, and if so how important it has been as a contributory factor in economic growth, are ultimately empirical questions. In this address I shall not be offering empirical material, except occasionally by way of illustration only. But some of the deductive considerations suggested by the economics of institutions may be helpful in organising one's thoughts.

The idea of institutional change as a source of economic growth has taken two distinctly different forms.

The first recognises that institutions need continual adaptation in face of a changing environment of technology and tastes, but holds that this adaptation occurs very quickly, if not instantaneously (at least in the absence of malign government interference). On this reckoning, institutional change is a necessary part of economic growth but not an independent source of it – rather in the same way as capital accumulation is a necessary part of steady state growth in a Solow-type growth model but is not ultimately the source of growth. At any given time institutions are about as efficient as they can be, so the efficiency of institutions is not a point of difference between periods. That view naturally limits the amount of interest that attaches to institutions as a source of economic growth. Not many people have put it forward in quite the bald form just stated, but it is quite often implied by Panglossian remarks made in other contexts. In its extreme form it would be rather difficult to defend, if only because institutions are quite obviously subject to serious inertia, for reasons I shall be considering presently. However, the importance of adaptation, probably *not* instantaneous, of institutions to changes arising from other sources is common ground.

The alternative view sees the movement towards Pareto-superior institutions not as something that is achieved almost at once but as a very long run, possibly permanent, process. This process can come about by the continual emergence and diffusion of institutional innovations, comparable to technological innovations. Alternatively, it can come about in the manner of a repeated game, in which people gradually learn or are selected against if they do not. Either way, institutional change is seen as possibly intertwined with technical change, but without either of them being regularly the senior partner. The long-run trend can be viewed as something that was observed to happen in a particular phase of history – the way Hicks viewed the emergence of the market in his *Theory of Economic History*. Or larger claims may be made about the existence of an inherent trend in that direction, on the ground that people can be expected to find ways of progressively reducing transaction costs for much the same reasons as they find ways of progressively reducing production costs – recognising, of course, that there may sometimes be periods of institutional retrogression, just as there are periods of technical retrogression.

The concept of an institutional innovation is most plainly exemplified by innovations that are consciously introduced by individual economic agents. They may consist of changes in the internal organisation of firms, like the introduction of the M-form – the multi-divisional corporation with divisional autonomy – whose origins in du Pont and General Motors were traced in Chandler's earlier book (1962). This can be compared to a process innovation. Or they may consist of a new kind of contract offered to customers, like, say, the new kind of financial service pioneered by the Halifax Building Society in the inter-war period, comparable to a product innovation. The idea of deliberate institutional innovations was interestingly developed in the 1950s and 1960s by Frederick Barth, who introduced the so-called transactional approach into social anthropology (apparently without being aware of the similar movement in economics). Barth (1966) saw the entrepreneur as someone who initiates transactions between values that were previously incommensurable, in other words someone who creates a new market. The deliberate introduction of new types of organisation or contract is the plainest example of institutional inno-vations, but similar consequences can follow from institutional changes that evolve much more gradually, involve many people, possibly owe their origin to chance and depend for their diffusion on competitive selection rather than conscious optimisation.

Given that institutional innovations do take place, in principle one could seek to do a Denison. One could try to establish what proportion of economic growth between two dates was due to institutional change, as opposed to technological change, capital accumulation, and the other standard sources of growth. I call attention here, in parenthesis, to the strikingly different treatments of institutional factors customarily given (not by Denison himself) to the two types of Denisonian question that exist: namely, the sources of differences in income per head (i) between different dates in a given country and (ii) between different countries at a given date. Some sources, like capital per head, are usually regarded as contributing in much the same way to both kinds of difference. But whereas people often say that inter-country differences, say between the United States and the United Kingdom, reflect institutional causes to an important extent, it is not so usual to postulate progressive insti-tutional improvement as a source of growth over time.

In practice a Denisonian kind of calculation would obviously run into severe difficulties because of the interactions between institutional and non-institutional factors. To take an example from the time of the Industrial Revolution: the factory system, which was set up originally, some historians say, for the institutional purpose of preventing embezzlement of materials by outworkers, made possible technical advance represented by the use of water-power and later of steam-power. How is the contribution of the institutional component to be separated out? This is exactly the same as the problem of identifying the contribution of a single technical advance (railways) when it had linkages with other *technical* advances.

So we can scarcely look forward to a time when it will have been established, say, that institutional progress in the United Kingdom has accounted for 27 % of the growth of income per head. However, the qualitative question about its importance remains a reasonable one to ask, because qualitatively different answers can be put forward without any of them being necessarily absurd. For example, it might be held that institutional change has on balance made a *negative* contribution to growth, at least in some periods, leaving correspondingly more to be explained by other sources. A member of the Mont Pelerin Society might take such a view of the first three-quarters of the twentieth century, because of the all-pervasive increase in the economic activities of the state. Or it might be held, along the lines already mentioned, that institutional change is entirely responsive to technical change and provides no independent motive power. Marxian historical materialism could be applied to yield that conclusion; at a quite different level of aggregation so can the work of organisation theorists, like Joan Woodward (1965), who trace different methods of factory organisation entirely to the underlying technology.

In addressing the qualitative question, it is helpful to review the kind of forces that influence economic change. This is the area where the new institutional economics purports to be able to do better than the old.

One can reasonably start with some sort of very general presumption that the pursuit of self-interest tends to promote the evolution of efficient institutions. However, that presumption is subject to some serious qualifications and complications.

First of all, the role of the state cannot be disregarded, even at a first approximation. The state's involvement with institutions is inherent, in a way that it is not with technology. This is because the state is the ultimate guarantor of property rights. It has to decide what kinds of rights and obligations it is prepared to recognise and enforce. The range of its involvement is indicated by the titles on the standard shelf of legal textbooks; tort, bills of exchange, landlord and tenant, bankruptcy, company law, and so on. This responsibility remains even if the state tries to be a non-interventionist as possible. Moreover – a separate point, also important – the state is likely to find it easier to alter institutions than private parties do: one of the main obstacles to privately initiated institutional changes is the need to secure the consent of other affected parties (a matter I shall revert to presently), whereas the use of compulsion is the speciality of the state, indeed its *raison d'être*.

The involvement of the state clouds any presumption there might be about the evolution of institutions being wholly shaped by the pursuit of the individual self-interest of the parties involved, and all that might follow from that. It was in this connection that Richard Posner (1977) made his ingenious attempt to extend the doctrine of the hidden hand to the evolution of the law itself, in so far as it consists of the Common Law, very sharply distinguished here from Statute Law. His contention was that judges, for various reasons that I have not time to discuss today, lean towards rulings that move the law in a Pareto-improving direction and also that even if they did not, and their rulings were made at random, non-Pareto-efficient rulings would have a more than average chance of being appealed against and hence of being overturned. Several of Posner's assumptions are very special, particularly his assumptions about the motivations of judges. While I suppose that *other things equal* Pareto-efficient rulings may commend themselves to judges, any stronger conclusion can hardly be at all general. More interesting, because less *a priori*, is a particular application that has been made of Posner's idea. It has been held that, specifically in the United States, judicial rulings made a contribution to economic growth because American judges significantly altered the English Common Law tradition by giving more weight to the effects of their rulings on economic progress and less weight to considerations of equity, particularly in the period between the War of Independence and the Civil War (Hughes, 1983, pp. 135–50).

The role of the state more generally, as opposed to the role of judge-made law alone, brings in all the issues that arise in the theory of public choice. Public choice is concerned not only with Pareto-efficiency or economic growth (not only with economics, for that matter). Its economic concerns include also the distribution of income. It would be naïve to suppose that as a matter of history this has necessarily meant redistribution of income in favour of the poor. It has tended to mean particular concern for the interests of people with the most political influence, who may or may not have been the poor or people like the median voter. It is easy to point to instances where, as a result of concern about distribution of income, the effect of institutional changes promoted by the state has not at all been to shape institutions so as to accommodate more efficiently changes signalled by non-institutional forces but on the contrary has served to frustrate those forces. An interesting historical example was provided by Domar (1970) in his hypothesis about the origins of Russian serfdom. According to this story, the territorial expansion of the Muscovite state in the sixteenth century increased the supply of land relative to labour and led to the emigration of peasants from the central areas of the state, to the disadvantage of the landowners there. The state had a military interest in the well-being of the landowners and therefore the landowners were able to procure the introduction of the institution of serfdom to prevent the peasants from moving. In that instance the parties under threat from market forces were able to transfer their case to another court where their voices carried more weight. The change that was brought about in property rights served to frustrate the achievement of Pareto-efficiency through market forces, not to facilitate it. Less exotic examples readily come to mind from more recent times: the introduction of protectionist measures against cheap new sources of supply; the formalisation through job protection legislation of the concept of property in jobs and of the distinction between the rights of the employed and the unemployed at just the moment in the 1970s when jobs were becoming scarcer. It would be interesting to speculate on what proportion of state-promoted changes in institutions have belonged to this class. I do not mean to imply that all measures of that sort were necessarily undesirable, only that they did the opposite of promoting economic growth.

So the involvement of the state does have some distinctive consequences, to put it no more strongly.

However, important as the state is, it is not all-important. Changes in the internal organisation of firms, like the transition to the multi-divisional corporate form, have not been due to the state in any direct way. Nor have the innumerable changes that go on at the most micro level in the governance of individual organisations and the way they do their business. Several of the most important long-run institutional changes that have occurred were not traceable to government, or at least not to the conscious purposes of government. One I have already mentioned – the decline in the family as a productive unit, accompanied by the decline in family and personal connections more generally in the conduct of business. Another is the emergence of the joint-stock company as the dominant form of business organisation. That did require legislation on limited liability and the emergence of a body of company law, but the spread of the company form followed only very gradually after the legislation that made it possible, and there is no reason to suppose that it was any part of the intention of legislators that the ultimate transformation should go as far as it did. Another major trend, associated with those two, has been the enormous and progressive increase in the average size of the concern in which people are typically employed. That increase was partly due to the increase in the importance in the government itself as an employer, granted, but it was also largely due to the increase in the size of private sector units, a trend which governments have sometimes encouraged but sometimes discouraged. I call your attention in passing to the partially opposing effects of those grand trends on the extent of the domain of the market: the decline in the importance of the family has tended to enlarge the domain of impersonal market forces, while the increase in the size of the business unit has diminished their domain by substituting intra-organisational 'command'.

So despite what I said a moment ago it *is* worth while to think about the forces that make for institutional change independently of government and consider their significance for economic growth. Let me now go on to that.

The element of truth in the optimistic hypothesis is obvious. There is no call to underestimate it. People surely will have *some* tendency to seek out and find institutional arrangements that are mutually advantageous and to adjust old ones in the light of changing circumstances. And surely there will be *some* tendency for inefficient institutions to be selected against evolutionarily. But the process of change is subject to complicating features. These open up possibilities of there being differences between countries and sectors and periods in the effects of institutional change, including retrogression sometimes. Let me refer to three features prominent in recent literature.

The first is that the mutual impingement of economic agents is not exclusively through agreed contracts. In many circumstances where people's actions affect one another, transaction costs prevent contracts, even though in principle it might be mutually advantageous to regulate the effects by contract, with side-payments if necessary. In some circumstances transaction costs may be so obviously prohibitive that the possibility of regulating things by contract will not seriously enter anyone's mind. Certain kinds of congestion situations are a case in point. Schelling (1978) has dealt with a fascinating range of examples. Even when a contract does exist, the transaction costs of enforcing it at all rigorously may be prohibitive. The situation then assumes a game-theoretic character, with certainly no presumption of Pareto-efficiency and with some possibility of a slide into gravely pathological situations of the Prisoners' Dilemma kind. Hence a possible reason why on occasion the trend over time may actually be for the worse. The theory of repeated games has shown the possibility of a more cheerful outcome, even with a Prisoners' Dilemma game: the game may end with a more or less co-operative outcome if it is played often enough (Axelrod, 1984). This has been an important theoretical development. But no one claims that the co-operative outcome is inevitable. Incidentally it is not very clear in the literature what sort of period in calendar time (as opposed to number of 'moves') is supposed to elapse before the co-operative outcome is arrived at – is it months or is it decades? If a fairly short period is being envisaged, as I think it usually is, we are talking about a process that may help to explain observed co-operative situations rather than a process that contributes to continuous economic growth.

The second complicating feature is inertia. Inertia is inherent in a large proportion of institutions by their nature. Of the four types of institution I mentioned at the beginning, the one least subject to inertia is type of contractual arrangement, and sometimes fairly rapid changes of that sort do occur, especially in cases where the contract is capable of exact definition, as in the financial field. But even that kind of institution has to persist for long enough for the contract to be brought to a conclusion, which may be quite a long time, for example with an explicit or implicit contract for lifetime employment with periodical promotion; also time may be needed for the use of a new kind of contract to attain the minimum critical mass to establish a market, reduce transaction costs enough to permit general adoption, and permit future plans to be made in the confidence that the market will continue to exist. Inertia *is* inherent in the other three categories of institution: property rights, conventions, and the granting of authority. None of these would serve much purpose if they were continually changing. Institutional arrangements are about interpersonal relations and, as Arrow (1974) pointed out, there are inherent reasons why it should be more difficult to make changes where other people's consent is needed than where they can be made by individual *fiat*. Previous arrangements have to be undone, possibly arrangements that were arrived at after long bargaining with many people. Trust has to be recreated. New codes have to be established and new methods of monitoring devised and made credible. Some people are always likely to lose from an institutional change and these vested interests are continuously being recreated as long as the institution remains in force. One can explain in this way the persistence of some institutional pathologies that do not belong obviously to the Prisoners' Dilemma class. Excessive reliance on overtime working in British industry may be one example. Others are familiar to us in universities, and no doubt they have parallels in most other large organisations.

Institutional inertia is not *necessarily* to be regarded as a pathology. Institutions provide the framework for economic life. A completely flexible framework is a contradiction in terms. It is a matter for study what determines the strength of the inertia and how it varies in different contexts. Casual observation suggests that it is relatively weak in financial institutions and particularly strong in the institutions of land-tenure. It is also a matter for study in what circumstances institutional inertia hinders economic growth and in what circumstances it contributes to it. The hypothesis of Mancur Olson (1982) comes to mind in this connection that war, particularly defeat in war, promotes economic growth by overcoming the inertia of growth-retarding institutions in the form of cartels and restrictive practices. War sweeps away the barnacles that have accumulated in long periods of social stability. Granted for the sake of argument that war or defeat does overcome institutional inertia, a lot must depend on whether, after the cataclysm, circumstances do or do not foster the emergence of an appropriate new set of institutional arrangements. Very different economic paths were followed by Japan after World War II and by the American South after the Civil War, although General MacArthur and General Sherman both did a thorough job in the barnacle department.

The other feature of institutions that complicates their evolution is their own complexity. This refers both to the institutional arrangements themselves and to the purposes they serve. If interpersonal economic relations were not inherently complex, a large proportion of existing institutions would be redundant. We could have a simple system of property rights and universal auction markets, as the textbooks suppose. One of the most important contributions of the new institutional economics has been to show that the purposes served by a given institution may be much more complicated than appears on the surface. Consequently it may be quite difficult to see why an institution has arisen and what purposes it currently serves.

As an example, let me take a familiar institution which I have already mentioned in passing: promotion in hierarchical organisations. This is so familiar that it is easy to overlook just how complicated it is. Typically it has all the following features. There is a system of ranks; responsibilities go with rank; so does pay and usually pension, so that rank maximisation becomes the proxy for income maximisation; promotion takes place only by one step at a time; there is property in rank, in the sense that demotion occurs seldom or never, poor performance being penalised instead by lack of further promotion or in extreme cases by dismissal; there is a retirement age, after which responsibilities fall at a stroke from a lifetime high to zero. One consequence of the system is that most top positions are held by men in their fifties, in contrast to the much more gerontocratic outcome of purely hereditary, wealth-based, systems of governance (non-human capital having no retiring age), in contrast also to the much lower average age of maximum performance and responsibility in new entrepreneurial firms, to say nothing of non-economic areas of endeavour. What forces have caused the promotion system to spread from its presumably military origins and develop the way it has? A number of quite different possibilities suggest themselves. The rationale of the system could lie in the learning process; in screening; it could be a system of deferred pay, serving to discourage mobility and enable employers to recoup training costs; the one-step-at-a-time feature could be the combined result of incomplete information on the part of the bosses, who are not well informed about the people more than one or two steps below them on the ladder, and opportunism on the part of the people in the middle, who cannot be expected to recommend their subordinates for promotion over their own heads; the non-demotion could be a restrictive agreement; or the dominant factor in the whole thing could be inertia, created by the need to safeguard the expectations of the people currently on the ladder. It is extremely difficult to say which of these elements, or others, has been dominant historically, and it is also extremely difficult to say whether the system is Pareto-efficient or not in the contexts where it is used.

The significance of complexity in the context of economic change is that complexity and inertia reinforce each other. Complex arrangements are difficult to alter radically, so they foster inertia. Inertia makes it easier to respond to changing circumstances and incorporate new institutional ideas by patching up existing institutions and so making them more complicated still rather than by starting again from scratch.

As a result, each new step in the process of institutional change is determined by its starting point and itself in turn contributes to shaping later developments. History matters. Since the choice at each step is also likely to be affected more or less strongly by stochastic elements, the process assumes some of the character of a random walk. Institutional change acquires a life of its own.

Recapitulating, then, I have suggested a number of reasons why institutional change is not likely to be *merely* a matter of Pareto-improving innovations and adaptations: the involvement of the state, non-voluntary interactions (externalities), and inertia and complexity, with their tendency to produce a random walk. Since the parallel with technical change has been underlying much of this address, it is appropriate now to ask to what extent the two types of change differ in these and related respects.

There are important respects in which technical change *is* affected by considerations of the same sort. The direction of technical advance is conditioned by its starting point and affects what follows. Technical change may be affected by linkages and require a minimum critical mass to get established. It may depend on the consent of affected parties.

At the same time there are significant respects in which technical change is subject to fewer potential obstacles and distortions than institutional change:

(i) although it *may* depend on other people's consent, the dependence is not so inherent as it is with institutional change;

(ii) institutional change is in its nature more complicated, hence more difficult, than technical change, because people are more complicated than things – this is much the same as the reason why the social sciences have more difficulty in making progress than the natural sciences and

(iii) that is a point of importance in its own right too, because in modern times the advance of pure science has provided a more solid base for technical change than anything social scientists have been able to offer to practical institution makers;

(iv) complexity arises not only because of the complexity of man but because of the scope for strategic plays. When man invented the wheel, Nature did not answer back. There is not the same danger of being caught up in a Prisoners' Dilemma.

Another point that may also be relevant concerns international competition. Institutions are liable to be less industry-specific than technology. That clearly applies to legally laid down property rights, perhaps also to conventions. In so far as it applies generally, institutions may not have much effect on a country's *comparative* advantage. Hence efficient or inefficient institutions may be less prone than efficient or inefficient technologies are to be rewarded or punished by competitive selection through international competition. There are grounds on which this could be debated and I put it forward tentatively.

However, there are also certain forces tending to make technological change *more* difficult than institutional change. For example, technological change may need to be embodied in expensive capital equipment. The effect of the role of the state on this issue is ambivalent. Its compulsory powers do not extend to the laws of nature, so there is every reason to suppose that the state's involvement serves to speed up and facilitate institutional *change* relative to technical change. Sometimes this may be synonymous with facilitating the emergence of institutions that conduce to economic growth; but sometimes it may be the reverse.

These considerations are extremely general and non-quantitative, but the balance of them does perhaps give some warrant to the belief that in most circumstances technical progress is easier to achieve than advances in institutional efficiency. Hence it creates some presumption that production costs should have a stronger downward trend than transaction costs. But the considerations do not all pull the same way. Moreover no presumption is created by these considerations about the relative importance of institutional and technical change in bringing about *differences* in growth rates between countries and periods.

III

It is conventional on an occasion like this for a speaker to say that his chosen theme is tremendously important. I am not so bold as to say whether or not the institutional contribution to economic growth has been tremendously important, either as a source of growth generally or as an explanation of differences in growth performance between countries or periods. I think we do not know. But I do think it is an important question to address.

This leads me on to two general remarks I should like to make by way of conclusion. The first is about policy and advice on policy. Politicians of all parties are great believers in institutional change as a source of economic improvement – not surprisingly, because that is the sort of change they are well placed to bring about. Economists give them advice to this end, often with no less enthusiasm. Yet among the main features of institutional change are its complexity and the unforeseeable nature of its consequences, setting us off on random walks to goodness knows what destination. Institutional experiment by a single firm is fine, because it does not much matter for the economy as a whole if it does not work. Institutional experimentation at the level of the whole economy gives one more pause. Reflection along these lines can easily lead to timid conservatism. The decisions do have to be made (sometimes). But if we are to abide by scholarly standards, we have to recognise candidly that institutional changes can easily lead in the long run to results that are quite different from intended – rather in the same way as wars have been found to do.

My other concluding point is about the direction of research. Theory has made an indispensable contribution in recent times to advances of understanding in this area. But it seems to me that in the economics of institutions theory is now outstripping empirical research to an excessive extent. No doubt the same could be said about other fields in economics, but there is a particular point about this one. Theoretical modelling may or may not be more difficult in this field than in others, but empirical work in it is confronted by a special difficulty. Because economic institutions are complex, they do not lend themselves easily to quantitative measurement. Even in the respects in which they do, the data very often are not routinely collected by national statistical offices. As a result, the statistical approach which has become the bread and butter of applied economics is not straightforwardly applicable. Examples of it do exist, the literature on the economics of slavery being perhaps the most fully developed – not surprisingly, because slavery is an institution that is sharply defined. But to a large extent the empirical literature has consisted of case-studies which are interesting but not necessarily representative, together with a certain amount on legal court cases, which are almost certainly *not* representative. Is this the best we can do? There is a challenge here on the empirical side to economists to see what is the best way forward.

Clare College, Cambridge

REFERENCES

Arrow, K. J. (1974). *The Limits of Organization*. New York: Norton.
Axelrod, R. (1984). *The Evolution of Cooperation*. New York: Basic Books.
Barth, F. (1966). *Models of Social Organization*. London: Royal Anthropological Institute of Great Britain and Ireland.
Chandler, A. D., Jr. (1962). *Strategy and Structure: Chapters in the History of the American Industrial Enterprise*. MIT Press.
—— (1977). *The Visible Hand: The Managerial Revolution in American Business*. Harvard: University Press.
Coase, R. H. (1937). 'The nature of the firm.' *Economica*, vol. 16 (N.S.), pp. 386–405.
—— (1960). 'The problem of social cost.' *Journal of Law and Economics*, vol. 3, pp. 1–44.

Domar, E. D. (1970). 'The causes of slavery or serfdom: a hypothesis.' *Journal of Economic History*, vol. 30, pp. 18–32.

Hicks, J. R. (1969). *A Theory of Economic History*. Oxford: Oxford University Press.

Hughes, J. R. T. (1983). *American Economic History*. Glenview, Illinois: Scott Foresman.

Marshall, A. (1885). 'The present position of economics.' In *Memorials of Alfred Marshall* (ed. A. C. Pigou), pp. 152–74. Macmillan, 1926.

North, D. C. (1984). 'Transaction costs, institutions, and economic history.' In Symposium on The New Institutional Economics. *Zeitschrift für die gesamte Staatswissenschaft*, no. 140, pp. 7–17.

Olson, M. (1982). *The Rise and Decline of Nations*. Yale University Press.

Posner, R. A. (1977). *Economic Analysis of Law*, 2nd ed. Boston: Little, Brown.

Schelling, T. C. (1978). *Micromotives and Macrobehaviour*. New York: Norton.

Williamson, O. E. (1985). *The Economic Institutions of Capitalism*. New York: The Free Press.

Woodward, J. (1965). *Industrial Organization: Behaviour and Control*. Oxford: Oxford University Press.

[24]

The Japanese Economic Review
Vol. 47, No. 1, March 1996

TOWARDS A COMPARATIVE INSTITUTIONAL ANALYSIS: MOTIVATIONS AND SOME TENTATIVE THEORIZING*

By MASAHIKO AOKI

Stanford University

1. Introduction

It is only in the past decade or so that a variety of critical comparative institutional issues have risen in international and national policy arenas and that economists have started looking earnestly into those issues by broadening the theoretical perspective of economics. This may indicate that the emergence of a new field, *Comparative Institutional Analysis* (CIA), is brewing. As I will discuss below, the CIA field is co-evolving with Historical Institutional Analysis (HIA) and Transition Economics. All these fields recognize that "institutions matter", and share methodological and analytical orientations and interests in many important ways. In the first half of this paper, I hope to motivate the study of CIA and, in the second half, I present some tentative, general insights, that are suggested by the CIA approach.[1]

Major comparative institutional issues which have recently attracted the keen interest of economists include the following:

(1) It has been increasingly recognized that within developed market systems there is a variety of institutional arrangements and that the differences between these may be important in determining national or regional advantage and disadvantage in industrial productivity and international competitiveness. Trade imbalances between nations have often escalated disputes over institutional differences between trading partners. Do, should, or could institutional arrangements become convergent across economies? Or, is there any gain from diversity? If so, what is the best way of exploiting it?

(2) In Eastern Europe the state apparatus of centrally planned economies suddenly collapsed. In spite of initial euphoria, however, the transition to market economies has turned out neither to be trivial, nor automatic through privatization. On the other hand, in China and Vietnam, where the transition has been gradual and the role of the state has been pivotal in designing new market-oriented institutional arrangements, economic performances seem to have excelled those of Eastern European counterparts

---

* This paper is a revised version of the Presidential Address delivered at the Annual Meeting of the Japan Association of Economics and Econometrics held at Gakushuin University in Tokyo on 23–24 September 1995. In preparing this paper, I owe much to discussions and dialogues with Serdar Dinc, Avner Greif, Kiminori Matsuyama, Paul Milgrom, Kevin Murdock, Tetsuji Okazaki, Masahiro Okuno-Fujiwara and Ying-yi Qian over the last few years. I have also benefited from reading Greif's unpublished manuscript (1995). Bo Li provided helpful research assistance and comments on the manuscript. Of course, I am responsible for views expressed in this paper.

1) For HIA and Transitional Economics, there are excellent surveys addressed by Avner Greif, John McMillan and Mathias Dewatripont and Gerald Roland at the 7th World Congress of the Econometric Society.

The Japanese Economic Review

so far. Can the transition be free from the historical constraint of communist legacies? Have China and Vietnam performed better in terms of economic growth simply because of their relatively lagged developmental stage? Should the transition be made in the Big-Bang manner or by the gradualist approach? In what sequence? If there is a variety of institutional arrangements in market economies, at what model should transitional economies aim as a terminal state?

(3) The publication of *The East Asian Miracle: Economic Growth and Public Policy* by the World Bank signalled a new stage of debate on the role of state in particular, and that of institutions in general, in the development process. The report documented various features of institutional arrangements allegedly common to East Asian economies and discussed their possible contributions to the high economic performance of that region relative to other developing regions. Does the East Asian state function as a response to pervasive market failures or rather as a complement to the enhancement of private order institutions which stimulates individual incentives? Is an observable difference in total factor productivity between Japan and other East Asian economies attributable to a difference in institutional infra-structure? Is it true that East Asian bureaucracies are less susceptible to unproductive rent-seeking behaviour? If so, why? Are East Asian institutional arrangements only effective at the developmental stage and should they be eventually replaced by a more advanced, universalistic model of Western type?[2]

Although I have quoted above partial, representative institutional issues drawn from advanced market economies, transitional economies, and developing economies respectively, it is immediately clear that they are partially overlapped and should not be analysed in complete independence from each other. I also argue below that they cannot be satisfactorily dealt with by the deductive approach of neoclassical economics and that they call for a new, interactive CIA approach which combines comparative information across various economies with context-specific micro modelling based on recently developed game theory, contract theory and information economics.

2. Institutions and their interdependencies

On several occasions above, I have referred to "institutional arrangements" in the economy. What are institutions? How are they arranged and inter-related? According to North (1990), "institutions are the rules of the game in a society or, more formally, are the humanly devised constraints that shape human interaction" (p. 3). He argues that such constraints evolve as an outcome of the (political) interplay of self-interest seeking groups. Greif (1994) sees that North's two alternative definitions—rules and constraints—are not quite the same, as the latter is inclusive of the former. He submits that "[g]iven the technologically determined rules of the game, institutions—the non-technological constraints on human interactions—are composed of two interrelated elements: cultural beliefs (how individuals expect others to act in various contingencies) and organizations (the endogenous human constructs that alter the rules of the game and that, whenever applicable, have to be in equilibrium." (p. 943) Hurwicz (1993)

---

2) For a summary of current issues see Aoki, Murdock and Okuno-Fujiwara (1995).

gives a functional definition of institution: The role of institution is "restricting the type of mechanisms that is admissible. It is a rule about rules. This means specifying which type of choice domain or of outcome function is admissible ... However, not all restrictions are candidates for institutions." (p. 59–60) He argues that restrictions need to be self-enforcing (and discusses a conceptual difficulty associated with this aspect of restriction, to which I shall return later).

There are subtle differences in emphasis and possible analytical implications in the above definitions. However, consensus seems to view institutions as humanly devised constraints on economic interactions or mechanisms which are in some type of equilibrium. Let us accept such conceptualization at this moment without much ado. I will present a more formal, game theoretic conceptualization of institutions in the second half of the paper.

As humanly devised constraints on economic interactions, we may think of the following devices:

—markets and money
—legal and political rulings by the state
—contracts and (private order) organizations
—cultural beliefs and social norms

The markets allows the voluntary exchange of goods (with the intermediary of money) among economic players. For this institution to evolve and function, property rights to economic assets need to be clearly defined and enforced. In many cases they are defined by legal rules. In some situations, however, *de facto* property rights may be created without the intervention of the state. For example, rights to a job may be created by the custom of a workshop (organizational form), but even such *de facto* right may be reinforced by legal ruling to support the custom *ex post*.

Contracts may be enforced by the state, if their contents are simple and their defaults are easily verifiable as in the case of the transfer of property rights to physical goods. However, in many instances, the fulfilment of agreements may not be verifiable by a third party (the court) and needs to be self-enforceable. The Folk Theorem suggests that, if defection can trigger a mechanism of inflicting sanctions on the defector in the future, far-sighted agents may refrain from defecting out of concern not to lose their reputations. Reputational mechanisms in the situation where agents change their partners over time are considered as constituting the basis for social norms. It is often interpreted that the long hand of the future is sufficient for the contract (cooperation) to be self-enforceable. However, this may be misleading. As the social network expands, it may become more efficient to create a formal organization to collect, keep, and make available information about deviant behaviours of agents (Milgrom, North and Weingast 1990) or up-to-date labelling of each individual based on such information (membership, licence, credit card—Kandori 1992). Also, outside options which will be available to possible defectors may be defined by a fabric of outside institutional arrangements. They may include coordinated expectations on the consequences of deviant behaviour (cultural beliefs—Greif (1994)), which may reflect past organizational forms. Alternatively, but not unrelatedly, they may be defined by available alternative contracting (e.g., alternative employment contracts) so that there may be strong complementarity among various contracts.

Also, contracts may not be able to specify all possible contingencies relevant to

– 3 –

The Japanese Economic Review

their implementation and they may only specify general rules to be followed. For example, Grossman and Hart (1986) argued that, if that is the case, it is generally the most efficient to ascribe rights to decide on the use of assets in unspecified contingencies (residual rights of control) to the owner of assets. But, if assets in cooperation are diverse and their ownerships are diffusive (as in the case of involving job rights), such a principle cannot specify the organizational mode uniquely. More elaborate, explicit organizational rules may become necessary. Recent experiences in transitional economies (e.g., Poland and China) show that a huge improvement in the performance of un-privatized firms has been brought about without a change in property rights, but by the delegation of authority (McMillan, 1995). The organizational design (the delegation of authority) and the property rights allocation cannot be identified, yet there may be some type of correlation between them (Aghion and Tirole, 1994).

The brief comments above are intended only to indicate that there may be interdependencies among various institutions: property rights, legal rulings, markets, organizations, contracts, cultural beliefs and social norms. *What is the nature of these interdependencies?* It is by a difference in perception and analysis in this regard that the emergent CIA is differentiated from the neoclassical approach and partially from New Institutional Economics as well. What has given rise to the CIA is not merely to recognize that "institutions matter".

3. The market centricism of neoclassical economics

The focus of neoclassical economics is on the market institution. Simply put, other institutions (e.g., cultural factors) are exogenous to the economic system, or they (e.g., the state and organizations) are "substitutes" for the markets when the latter are incomplete or when it is costly to find efficient prices.

Neoclassical economics adopts a deductive approach starting from the presumption of an idealized, generic situation in which property rights for all primary resources and goods are exogenously defined. Technological possibilities for transforming primary resources to final goods are exogenously given by engineering data. Cultural factors may be implicit in the preference (pay-off) function of individual agent. But, the preference is also regarded as data. From such suppositions, the well-known Fundamental Welfare Theorem is derived: if competitive markets are created for all goods and primary resources through which property rights to their uses can be voluntarily exchanged, Pareto efficient outcome will result. This state of Walrasian equilibrium forms the universalistic norm of resource allocation.

If the creation of markets for certain goods is impossible or too costly for technical reasons, alternative institutions will emerge as a substitute. For some, the failure of complete markets to emerge justifies state activism. The state intervention through taxes and subsidies is interpreted as analogous to the creation of quasi-markets which simulate, together with existing markets, the function of a complete set of Walrasian markets.[3]

---

3) It is interesting to note that there is no disagreement between the neoclassical economists and their major opponents in the debate on the role of government in the East Asian economy, the developmental state theorists (e.g., Wade), in that the state is viewed as a substitute for markets when the latter fail.

M. Aoki: Towards a Comparative Institutional Analysis: Motivations and Some Tentative Theorizing

It was the insight of Coase to regard the emergence of another type of non-market institution, organizations, as contractual arrangements aimed at maximizing efficiency in response to the market's absence or imperfection rather than engineering data. This insight eventually led to the paradigmatic development of contract theory in the last two decades. As discussed below, the theoretical achievements of the principal-agent theory provide CIA with important analytical tools. However, I would also like to note the possible pitfalls of becoming complacent with the present state of principal-agent theory as "the theory of institution".

4. Principal-agent theory

Principal-agent theory aims at understanding institutions as contractual arrangements between the principal and the agent(s) under the condition of asymmetric information. In designing contracts, the principal is constrained by the agents' incentive compatibility condition and participation constraint. The Revelation Principle à la Myerson allows the designer of a contract, without loss of generality, to limit attention to contracts that make it optimal for the agent to be truthful (thus the imposition of the incentive-compatibility condition). The Principle seems innocuous if one examines its formal logic. However, its implicit assumption is that there are no communication costs other than agents' incentives not to disclose private information unless there is the provision of information rents. There is no other barrier to the transmission of information. Its institutional implication is that any non-cooperative equilibrium outcome of an arbitrary organization can be replicated by a centralized two-tier structure where agents communicate their entire private information to the principal in exchange for information rents and there is no interaction among agents (Melumad, Mookherjee and Reichelstein, 1991).

But it is an obvious fact of reality that most organizations are characterized by multi-layered hierarchies in which real authorities are delegated to agents. Also, agents are engaged in vertical and horizontal side trades of various kinds among themselves (pecuniary and nonpecuniary, implicit and explicit) that are not directly controlled by the principal. In fact, there can be many barriers to communications which are not exclusively attributable to incentives. Private information of agents may take the form of expert knowledge which cannot be fully understood by others lacking the expertise. Some information may not be easily codifiable and cannot be communicated without noise, the reduction of information values, time delay, etc. Bounded rationality of the principal may find it impossible to communicate directly with all agents in the organization without causing excessive information costs. The efficiency of lateral interactions within the framework of principal-agent theory has been investigated by assuming that there is private information among agents which cannot be communicated to the principal (Varian (1990), Holmstrom and Milgrom (1990), Itoh (1992)). Under such a situation, allowing side-contracting among agents may become optimal for the principal.

This development of principal-agent theory suggests that optimal organizational

---

The major difference seems to be only that the latter views market failure at the developmental stage as pervasive, while the former views it as limited to a certain restricted sphere. See Aoki, Murdock and Okuno-Fujiwara (1995).

– 5 –

The Japanese Economic Review

design from the viewpoint of incentives may depend on the information structure of the organization (how information is distributed within agents, how efficiently information can be communicated). However, once the bounded rationality of agents is admitted, the information structure of the organization itself may not be technological data. As agents may be limited in their capacity and scope of processing information, organizational design may entail the design of the information structure (what information to be processed by whom and how much—Aoki (1995b)) as well as incentive design. The integration of these two aspects of organization is still at an extremely primitive stage of development in economics.

Another apparently innocuous element of principal-agent theory is the participation constraint. However, the outside options of agents may not be completely determined by the market institution alone. In his pathbreaking historical institutional analysis of agency-contracting among Maghribi traders with that of Genoese traders in late medieval overseas trade, Avner Greif (1994) showed how a difference in cultural beliefs conditioned optimal contracting as well as subsequent institutional develop-ments in response to market expansion. He identified cultural beliefs with expectations with respect to the fate of agents who cheated, or more formally, expectations with respect to off-the-path-of-play that constrain on-the-path-of-play behaviour. He distinguished between Maghribis collective value and Genoese individualistic value. In the former the trader expected that the cheater would not be employed by other traders, while in the latter the opposite is the case. The Genoese trade organizations eventually came to dominate, but Greif pointed out that it was not clear that it was because their contracting was more efficient. Contracting based on individualistic value was more adept, however, at responding to expanding markets and generating institutional innovations (e.g., permanent family company).

In the spirit of Holmstrom (1982), Aoki (1994) showed that the moral hazard in teams (organizations) may be controllable by the introduction of a third party who is committed to a menu of interventions—liquidation, rescue, surplus extraction, non-intervention—contingent on observable outcome jointly determined by team efforts and stochastic events. Such third-party intervention becomes more effective in controlling moral hazard in teams, the lower the outside option value for team members is in the event of liquidation. An implication of this is that it is complementary to the third-party monitoring scheme that organizations are mutually formed as teams and the workers are not mobile across different teams without losing their potential value. Further, incentives for the third party to commit itself to the contingent action menu need to be provided. It should properly be engaged in applying sanctions when necessary, while it should not abuse its right to punish.

An example of the theoretical construct of the third-party-monitoring scheme is main banks in Japan. It has been suggested that an implicit contract arrangement among main banks to mutually delegate monitoring responsibilities, together with a regulatory framework to assure rents to main banks for the fulfilment of their responsibility, may provide an institutional framework for the main banks neither to be too soft nor too hard in monitoring (Aoki and Patrick, 1994).

This and previous examples suggest that the effectiveness of contracts and organizations is supported by a fabric of institutions which define outside options for organizational participants and constrain individual and organizational behaviour. The organizational (contractual) environment may consist not only of markets, but also other parallel or super-imposed organizations, as well as cultural beliefs. A corollary of this observation is that at present it is desirable to accumulate context-specific models for a deeper understanding of the function of institutions. Specifically, it seems necessary to make the assumptions on information constraints of organizations and outside participation constraints more explicit, based on comparative information. The present state of contract theory is far from generating a general theory of institutions, even if such a thing may potentially exist. By accumulating context-specific models and testing their predictions in the light of comparative evidence, we may gradually advance in understanding the nature of the inter-relatedness of various institutions, and thus that of economic systems in general.

5. Failure of neoclassical deductive approach

Recently a serious public-policy failure of the deductive approach of neoclassical economics became evident in the area of transition economics. When the communist political regimes in Eastern European economies collapsed in the early 1990s, the high hope was that their economies would be able to convert to market economies à la Walrasian by quickly privatizing property rights in productive assets. It was expected that if the state-owned enterprises were privatized, then a market for shares in the privatized corporation would quickly emerge as an effective monitoring mechanism for its management. However, as soon as the initial euphoria over the sudden demise of authoritarian regimes subdued, it turned out that the transition to market economies was not so trivial a matter.

The transition involves three facets: the initial condition or the legacy of communist regime, the terminal target—what type of market system should be targeted, and the process for moving from the former to the latter, e.g., sequencing, speed of transition, etc. The neoclassical advocates perceived the Walrasian norm as the target and insisted that the best route for achieving this was to escape from the initial condition as soon as possible by the Big Bang approach.

However, the political reality of the communist legacy seemed to have made such an approach untenable. Toward the dusk of the communist regime, the central planner had already yielded much of the authority for economic management to the director of the state owned enterprise. The workers had acquired vested interests in their enterprise in terms of job security and other economic and social benefits including housing, pensions, health and child care, holidays and recreational facilities, kiosks, etc. Privatization of the state-owned enterprise was not possible without making political compromises with these insider vested interests, unless there were a powerful privatization agency as in former East Germany. Fearful of the possibility that the property rights to the privatizing enterprise would be captured by the ex-planning bureaucrats, reformist privatization agencies were also ready to make such compromise (Boycko et al, 1993). The result was the emergence of "insider control" of privatized enterprise: the directors of the former state-owned enterprises gained the majority rights in privatized corporations, in collusion with middle managers and workers (Aoki and Kim, 1995). They became virtually free from capital market control except for possible bankruptcy. Even this possibility is mitigated by continued state subsidy disguised as credits.

The Chinese authority which has observed the development of insider control in

The Japanese Economic Review

Eastern Europe is proceeding more cautiously in the transition to a market economy. Instead of aiming at developing securities markets as a means of controlling enterprises, it consciously tries to nurture the development of a commercial banking system by reforming state-owned ex-specialized banks and allowing the gradual entry of new banks. On the other hand, it has been proposed to decentralize the asset management of state-owned enterprises to decentralized state-asset controlling agencies (including enterprises, the ministerial level holding companies and the provincial level holding companies), depending on the size of enterprise (Chinese Government—World Bank Conference, 1995: particularly the paper by Q. Jian). These approaches are intended to depart gradually from the initial constraint of state-controlled economy and grope to the market economy, but the final target is not yet clearly envisioned even by reforming administrators.[4]

The Chinese approach may be criticized as *ad hoc*, slow, ambiguous, etc. However, her economic performance in terms of economic growth per capita compares favourably with that of her Eastern European counterparts. In contrast to the radical, deductive approach in Eastern Europe which was doomed to fail by its inconsistency with the historical constraints of the transition, however, the gradual, inductive approach of China may allow for evolutionary selection among various experiments, e.g., joint ventures with foreign companies, township and village enterprises, partial spinning-off or gradual privatization of subsidiaries by the state-owned enterprises, which are coexistent with initial constraints. We do not know yet whether or not they will succeed in the transition. However, their experimental approach and its relative success may be sufficient to cast a doubt on the universal validity of the neoclassical deductive approach toward policy making.

6. New institutional economics

If, as neoclassical economics presupposes, institutions other than markets emerge only as substitutes for efficiency-maximizing markets, every economy would tend to converge to an ideal Walrasian type as a result of competitive selection. However, as I noted at the beginning of this paper, there are many examples indicating that this is not likely to be the case. Why do different institutional arrangements emerge in each economy? Why do inefficient institutions remain? These questions have been earnestly pursued by New Institutional Economics (NIE) under the intellectual leadership of D. North.

In contrast to the neoclassical economics which views non-market institutions, such as the state and organizations, as substitutes for markets, NIE considers that the state may play a complementary role in enhancing market institutions or may prevent their development because of its own interests. As trade opportunities expand, technologies develop and populations grow, gains from exchange may be better exploited by complementary changes in laws and regulations defining and enforcing property rights. Property rights may be defined and redefined through the interplay of the state, its bureaucracy and various organizations, i.e., through "political markets". The existing allocation of property rights defines transaction costs, and thus players' incentives to

---

4) Deng Xiao-ping described the process as "crossing the river by exploring stones" (mozhe shitou guo he).

exchange, acquire knowledge and innovate, and ultimately promote institutional changes. Institutional changes, the essence of which is changes in property-right definition and allocations, can be brought about endogenously through the equilibriating process in political markets. However, an economy may be also locked into an inefficient institutional arrangement due to sunk cost in existing institutions and network externalities among institutions. Also the same factors can explain distinct historical trajectories of institutional development and economic growth for different economies.

I consider that NIE has made a major contribution in bringing issues of institutions to the forefront of economics, especially in clarifying the path-dependent nature of institutional development, interdependencies (complementarity) of various institutions, the nature of political structure as providing foundations for market institutions (rather than the substitute for the latter), etc. However, I should like to register a tentative reservation as regards its view that institutional arrangements are basically politically determined. This view seems to be related to North's distinction between institutions and organizations. According to North, "[a] crucial distinction ... is made between institutions and organizations ... Conceptually, what must be clearly differentiated are the rules from the players. The purpose of the rules is to define the game as played. But the objective of the team within the set of rules is to win the game—by a combination of skills, strategy, and coordination; by fair means and sometimes by foul means. Modelling the strategies and the skills of the team as it develops is a separate process from modelling the creation, evolution, consequences of the rules." (1990, pp. 4–5)

I will argue later that organization forms may also emerge as a human device restricting and enforcing individual player's admissible strategy domains, i.e., as an institution. However, once organizational forms evolve as such, organizations may become a part of the set of players in the game actually played in the economy. Thus, the dual aspects of organizations as institutions and players are conceptually reconcilable (I formalize this later). However, my reservation is more substantial. I submit that there are cases when the spontaneous evolution of a private order organizational form is an important driving force of institutional change, triggering complementary changes in the nature of other institutional arrangements. A notable comparative study by Saxenian (1994) on why Silicon Valley is flourishing today after the severe downturn of the early 1980s while Route 128 continues to decline may be read from this perspective. I present my case in relation to a current debate on the nature of contemporary Japanese institutional arrangements. The case may appear idiosyncratic. However, the CIA is aiming at accumulating comparative information before presenting a sweeping general theorizing which fits only a subset of economic systems. As such, my argument may be also interpreted as a rebuttal of the neoclassical paradigm with the Walrasian equilibrium state as the universalistic norm.

7. Are Japanese institutional arrangements an aberration from the neoclassical norm?

The impact of state intervention in Japan during the war time (1939–45) on subsequent institutional evolution are now well documented by economic historians (Nakamura,

– 9 –

ⓒ Japan Association of Economics and Econometrics 1996.

The Japanese Economic Review

Hara, Teranishi, and Okazaki among others). An emergent consensus view in the Japanese public forum seems to be that institutions which prevailed during the post-war high growth period and are still prevailing had their origins in war (Okazaki and Okuno-Fujiwara, 1994; Noguchi, 1995).[5] However, it seems to me that the controversy still remains regarding the nature of subsequent institutional development and its implications for present public policy debate. Is it, as Noguchi (1995) seems to argue, that the prevailing institutional arrangement is just the artifice of the wartime regime (what he calls the "1940s regime") and should be regarded as an aberration from the laissez-faire regime (the neoclassical norm)?

One may consider à la North that a series of state actions, such as replacing stockholders' rights in the corporation with bureaucratic intervention in corporate governance, the introduction of the designated banking system and the organization of industrial control associations as planning intermediaries, was aimed at reducing transaction costs for the bureaucracy to implement war-economy planning. Such measures were initially in serious conflict with the property rights of large capitalists and their managers. Their introduction was made possible only by the extraordinary political power of the military and associated bureaucrats at that time. However, as Okazaki (1987) convincingly argued, the objective of the military-bureaucracy alliance to reduce the transaction costs of war-economy planning did not materialize, not simply because of the destruction of productive assets and the critical shortage of resources but largely because of the overriding costs of sacrificing price incentives for managers. Then, why is it that an institutional arrangement created for the purpose of centralized control seems to have survived up to the present time? Is it simply because bureaucrats have compromised with the private incentives of managers? This is a puzzle to which those who subscribe to the theory of the 1940s regime must find an answer.

My own hypothetical argument may be summarized as follows: in parallel with and subsequent to the centralization efforts by the state bureaucracy, there was spontaneous evolution in private work organizations and the institutional arrangements introduced by the wartime government were transformed in their function to the one which fits this private sector evolution after the war (I elaborate this theme in a recent article (1995c)).

Although it is becoming increasingly popular to regard that the behaviour of Japanese firms in the 1920s in markets for products, labour, and capital as conforming to the neoclassical norm, I suspect that their internal organizations at that time were still far from conventionalized. Many firms retained classical authoritarian hierarchies in which the boss ordered and the workers obeyed. Some government-run model factories, as in steel and shipbuilding, recruited German engineers to train the workers, but their engineering approach was often at odds with the indigenous craft-oriented approach of the workers to learning. Some paternalistic capitalist firms were tolerant of less authoritarian industrial relationships, allowing more team-oriented work organization. In the sense that diverse work organizations coexisted and no convention

---

5) I also argued (1988, pp. 184–6) that some aspects of post-war Japanese "arbitrative" management originated in the pre-war and wartime periods. But, my argument placed more emphasis on the evolutionary nature of institutional changes rather than state actions, the point which I would like to amplify below.

had evolved, the situation was "far from equilibrium". The contemporaneous situation in the U.S. was similar, except that scientific management based on formal job classification schemes was being widely experimented with on a wider scale in advanced industries such as public utilities and financing.

It was during the war that the tendency toward an organizational convention began to occur in both economies, but on different trajectories. In Japan the labour administration perceived that authoritarian hierarchies were not conducive to productive efficiency under the extreme labour shortage that made the threat of discharge an ineffective discipline. In order to enhance workers' morale at strategically important plants the government sponsored the Industrial Patriotic Society movement. The movement was responsible for reducing status differentials between the boss and the subordinates, the white-collar workers and the blue-collar workers, while placing severe peer pressure on the workers to maximise effort. Because of the shortage of materials and tools, emergencies on the shop floor had to be met by the collective improvisation of the workers. In this way, the evolution of a collective approach to work organization was triggered.

It was with the same objective of increasing war production that the U.S. labour administration sponsored the spread of the scientific labour management movement and the job classification scheme in manufacturing industries during the war (Baron et al, 1986). Thus, from positions far removed from equilibria, the bifurcation of organizational convention began to emerge: the collective scheme in Japan and the specialization scheme in the U.S. As I analysed elsewhere (Aoki, 1995b), the managements of each economy mutually learned from the accomplishment of the other at various phases of post-war development when they perceived critical productivity disadvantage *vis-à-vis* the other. They also refined the respective schemes by organizational and engineering innovations as well as by relying on improved information processing capacity of the workers. However, the bifurcate trajectories seem to have retained distinctive characteristics.

It is my contention that the institutional arrangements initially introduced by the wartime Japanese government became viable in the post-war period by finding fits, after their democratic transformation, with the evolutionary trajectory of private work organizations. The removal of shareholders' control made it possible for the workers to gain shares in property rights in their firms in terms of job security, accumulation of retirement benefits, opportunities to advance to managerial positions. Their position in the firm as stakeholders provides incentives to invest in team-oriented skills. The potential moral hazard of "insider control" is effectively checked by the prospect of bank intervention contingent on the bad performance of teams (Aoki, 1994). The industrial association puts peer discipline on member firms not to recruit workers from employees of other member firms, which enhanced the effectiveness of the threat of bank discipline on badly-performing firms by reducing outside option values for the workers. On the other hand, the industrial association acted as an intermediary to protect property rights of the stakeholders of member firms *vis-à-vis* outsiders and feed their interests into the bureaucratic process of industrial policy-making and budget allocations.

The differences between my view and the emergent theory of the "1940s" regime are as follows. The latter claims that prevailing institutional arrangements were created by the state as substitutes for markets and are an aberration from the neoclassical norm previously existing. An obvious public policy implication of this view is to

- 11 -

The Japanese Economic Review

revert to the neoclassical market-supremacy norm. In contrast, I submit that team-oriented work organization began to emerge at the same time as the sweeping institutional changes were introduced by the government in the sphere of finance, corporate governance and industrial associations. The last of these were initially intended as substitutes for markets, but that aim failed. The reason that they have outlived the wartime economy was that they gradually evolved as complementary institution arrangements for subsequent private organizational innovations on the trajectory initially laid out during the war. Although the fit was not an intended one, the government-induced institutions and private order organizational forms together came to form a coherent system, exhibiting competitive advantage in certain industries. Because of its coherence, however, the system is difficult to change in a piecemeal way, even if it seems to start losing consistency with emerging configuration of technological and market parameters. On the other hand, adaptive institutional change will be likely to come only on its own evolutionary path rather than a jump towards the neoclassical norm.

8. State of play

Let me summarize the points made so far. By inductive reasoning, I submitted a critique on both the neoclassical approach which views non-market institutions as substitute for markets as well as on NIE which attaches the secondary importance to private-order institutions such as organization forms. An implied proposition is that various institutions such as property rights and markets, contracts and organizations, cultural norms and beliefs, are interdependent, mutually substitutes or complementary, shaping or shaped. They, as a whole, form a coherent system of self-enforceable constraints on economic behaviour as far as exogenous technological parameters remain within certain admissible ranges.

Once a coherent set of institutional arrangements is regarded as a system, its diversity is easily recognizable. CIA is an emergent field which tries to understand why there is a *variety of institutional arrangements across economies and what are the public policy implications of the diversity*. Is the diversity only a transitory departure from the uniformity? Is it brought about merely by the inefficient deterrence of competitive selection process by elements of monopoly, state coercive power, "irrational" cultural factors, etc? Or, alternatively, is it understood as representing some kind of multiple equilibria? If so, how is a distinct equilibrium selected in each economy? Should institutional arrangements be made uniform to benefit from competition on a level playing field? Or can there by any potential gains from the diversity?

Obviously these questions cannot be answered overnight. They can be tackled only by gradually accumulating rich comparative information and submitting it for analysis. In order to avoid the pitfall of the deductive approach leading to a premature general theorizing about institutions, CIA adopts an interactive approach combining comparative information and "context specific micro modelling" using game theory, information economics, and contract theory. The assumptions of models should be based on comparative and historical information, and their predictions should be confronted with comparative and historical evidences.

9. Differences between CIA and the neoclassical approach

CIA is an infant field and it can hardly be said to signal the emergence of a new paradigm. However, to highlight its possible differences from the market-centric neoclassical approach I venture to list a few tentative general insights which have been generated or suggested by the interactive CIA approach and submit them for possible refutation.

9.1 Institutions as equilibria

The fundamental nature of institutions is systemic and sustainable constraints on types of admissible strategic choices of players (including human deviced organizations) approximate to equilibrium strategies of a game played in the economy. Institutions may serve to reduce costs of information, implementation, and enforcement, as well as costs of disequilibrium imposed by mutants. Since they approximate to equilibrium strategies, the institutional arrangements of an economic system are self-enforceable.

Games are defined by a set of players and rules specifying for each player a strategy set and a pay-off function defined on the product of strategy sets of all the players. Let us call a game with the following property an original game: players are composed only of individual persons, and strategy sets and pay-off functions are inclusive of all technologically feasible possibilities. The original game may yet be devoid of social structuring. A structure to the original game is provided by restricting the types of admissible strategy domain for each player (for the moment let us suppose that restrictions are exogenous). Such constraints may be self-enforceable among the original players, if they share cultural beliefs, social norms. Or, constraints must be enforced by "the third party" (e.g., the court), or by the creation of an "organization" which can alter the technologically-determined pay-off functions for the original players (e.g., the state, financial institutions, labour unions, etc.). In the latter case the original game is modified to one (derivative game) defined by an augmented set of players composed of individual persons and organizations, endogenously determined rules on strategy domain and pay-off function for each players (Hurwicz, 1993). In either case, the restriction on the original game can become self-enforceable and thus viable only when equilibrium strategies of underlying games, original or derivative, fall within the restriction.[6] When they do, we may call the restrictions *institutions*.

The next question is whether equilibrium is unique relative to exogenous technological parameters. If so, institutions can be interpreted as endogenously determined by exogenous parameters alone and we can have a closed game theory of institutions. However, the next proposition asserts that is not likely to be the case.

---

6) This notion of self-enforceability of institutions distinguishes our approach from Schotter's. According to him, "A social institution is a regularity in social behavior that is agreed to by all members of society, specifies behavior in recurrent situations, and is either self-policed or policed by some external authority." (1981) He identifies a social institution with the von Neumann-Morgenstern concept of a solution in a cooperative game. Therefore the existence of external enforcer is exogenous and the problem of what mechanism makes the enforcer's commitment credible is left unexplained. Further, as Hurwicz argues, the cooperative game solution is a set of outcomes determined partly by the rule of the game (partly by technology) and not the rule itself.

The Japanese Economic Review

9.2 Multiplicity of equilibria

Even for the same exogenous parameters, equilibrium of games is likely to be multiple. Thus a diversity of institutional arrangements is possible.

In the Darwinian learning model of choice of skill type by Aoki (1993, 1995a) and that of coordination game by Matsui and Okuno-Fujiwara (1994), multiple equilibria arise because of strategic complementarity in random matching games played by bounded-rational players. Different equilibria may be supported by different organizational forms (conventions) or cultural norms respectively. In the repeated-game model of financial contracting by Dinc (1995), the sustainability of both relational banking and arm's length banking arises for a certain range of parameter values because of strategic complementarity between entrepreneurs and investors. In Greif (1994), collective cultural belief and individualistic cultural belief, as expectations with respect to off-the-path-of-play that constrained on-the-path-of-play behaviour, are both sustainable and support the two distinct contracting arrangements between traders and their overseas agents in the context of medieval trade.

In the randomized Darwinian dynamic models of Kandori, Mailath and Rob (1993) and Young (1994), continual mutations occurring at the individual level with a very small probability will assure the long-run stochastic convergence of repeated coordination games to risk-dominant equilibrium. However, in large-scale social games, mutations may be controlled by institutionalizing (locally stable) equilibrium strategies as endogenous rules of games (or rules in "stronger sense" than an established pattern of behaviour (Sugden, 1989)). Thus, a diversity of economic institutions may not disappear.

9.3 Equilibrium selection, institutional complementarity and institutional path dependence

We need some exogenous factor other than technological parameters to explain the selection of an equilibrium. The economic system as a cluster of institutions may be difficult to change in a piecemeal fashion because of complementarity existing among element institutions. Also an institution may become sustainable because of sunk costs, even if initial factors allowing for its emergence subsequently disappear.

I indicated that the usual technological parameters alone cannot endogenously determine the selection of institutional arrangements. An additional structuring factor is necessary (Field, 1981).[7] In the model of Darwinian dynamics by Aoki (1993, 1995a) involving imperfect expectational coordination among entrepreneurs, the dynamic adjustment path bifurcates à la Krugman-Matsuyama at "far from

---

7) Incidentally, Field (1981) criticized the game-theoretic equilibrium characteristization of institutions by saying that it is only a variant of neoclassical theory of institutions which in vain tries to explain the selection of institutions by exogenous technological parameters alone. However, as noted already, equilibria may be multiple due to bounded rationality (evolutionary games), differences in expectation with respect to off the path-of-play contingencies (Greif), increasing returns, strategic complementarity, etc. Further, those equilibria may not be Pareto-rankable as we will see presently. Thus, the game theory of institutions cannot be identified with the neoclassical theory of institutions which views existing institutions as efficient response to exogenous parameters. This distinction is clearly made by Nelson (1995). However, as a traditional evolutionary theorist he recorded "uneasiness" with the game theoretic equilibrium concept of institutions (p. 81).

M. Aoki: Towards a Comparative Institutional Analysis: Motivations and Some Tentative Theorizing

equilibria". At far from equilibria, the dynamic path may go either to a Pareto superior equilibrium or a Pareto inferior equilibrium. There is nothing in the model which can explain path selection except for "pure accident". It is because of this uncertainty that the deductive neoclassical approach cannot provide a complete theory of institutions and we must consider how they start to evolve. In that sense, CIA and HIA (Historical Institutional Analysis) are complementary.

Once an equilibrium is selected and has become institutionalized, it is difficult for the economy to jump to another equilibrium. Playing equilibrium strategies are made implicit or explicit rules of games. Information channels to sustain the equilibrium strategies are sunk as organizational capital (David, 1992). When institutional arrangements reflect equilibrium strategies which are mutually complementary, element institutions also become mutually complementary. I term such phenomena *institutional complementarity*.

Aoki (1994) analysed complementarity existing in the Japanese system between employment contracting and financial contracting. The former is characterized by its implicit long-term employment, while the latter involves the contingent governance structure in which corporate control automatically shifts between the insiders and the main bank contingent on the financial state of the corporation. Even if the long-term employment contract is not efficient for certain technological parameters, contracts of another type may not be viable unless a complementary financial contract also co-evolves.

Dinc (1995) showed in the model referred to above that the possibility of relational banking contracts emerging over arm's length banking contracts becomes greater if the amount of bond market financing is repressed, say by regulation. However, once relational banks are established, at least some of them will survive even if the bond markets are deregulated afterwards or the economy is integrated with competitive foreign bond markets. The reason is that reputational costs are already sunk by the relational banks while the sunk costs deter a new entry to relational banking.

Freeman (1995) argued that the welfare state in Nordic economies is a tightly-knit system composed of complementary institutional elements, such as high income tax regimes and comprehensive state-run welfare programmes, supportive government regulations of markets, and social partner centralized bargaining agreements. Using an analogy from Kauffman's model of rugged fitness landscapes (the so-called NK model), he suggests that under the condition of strong complementarity it is difficult to improve matters by making a single change or local adaptation, but "long jumps are more important in achieving good outcomes" (p. 20).

It is true that it is not easy to change a coherent system locally. However, it is not yet settled whether "long jumps" are necessary all at once, or whether they can be induced by a strategic move, which may be local, but will trigger chain reactions in other spheres by the very reason of dynamic complementarity. The intensive debate in transitional economics over the similar issue of Big-Bang approach vs. gradualism is neatly surveyed by Dewatripont and Roland (1995).

9.4 Non-optimality of institutional arrangements

Since exogenous parameters do not uniquely determine the selection of equilibrium (thus institutional arrangement), there is no guarantee that institutional arrangements

The Japanese Economic Review

are efficient or converge to an efficient one. The relative efficiency of various institutions depends on the value of exogenous parameters.

In Aoki (1993, 1995a), two distinct organizational forms can emerge in different economies as a result of the strategic choice of agents over types of skill to be invested in. If the majority of agents are committed to investing in skills useful in the specific context of an organization, the type of organization that relies on collective efforts of the workers may become more viable. But the workers make such a commitment only if the organizational type has become conventionalized in the economy. On the other hand, if the workers have invested in specialized functional skills, the type of reorganization that relies on the functional division of tasks may become more viable. But the workers will invest in that way only if this organizational type has become conventionalized. Within organizations, information tends to be assimilated in the former type and differentiated in the latter type. The relative efficiency of the two organizational types depends on technological parameters of industry, such as complementarity and stochastic correlation among tasks within the organization, and neither of them has absolute advantage (Aoki, 1995b).

More generally, the relative economic success of (particular sectors in) particular economies at a particular point of time may be generated not by the intrinsic superiority of their institutional arrangements but by the extent to which their path-dependent institutional arrangements are efficient for a particular configuration of exogenous factors at that particular time. For example, the productivity gain of the Japanese automobile firms in the 1980s did not imply the superiority of the Japanese system as a whole, while the innovative edge of American information technology in the 1990s does not necessarily imply the inherent superiority of the American system in all other respects (e.g., the poor provision of safety nets for the disadvantaged).

9.5 Gains from cross-economy institutional diversity

Since a universalistic institutional arrangement (e.g., neoclassical complete markets) which is optimal for any configuration of exogenous parameters is not viable, there are synchronic and diachronic gains from a diversity of institutional arrangements.

Again, according to Aoki (1993, 1995a), the relative efficiency of two organizational forms, assimilated and differentiated information structure, implies that organizational conventions may become a source of comparative advantage to nations (Krugman and Obstfeld 1994) or regions (Saxenian 1994). However, when an organizational innovation which has absolute advantage in some industry occurs in a small economy, the gains from trade may exclusively accrue to that economy as quasi-rents. When two economies of relatively equal size internalizing different conventions engage in trade, both of them may benefit from diversity by mutually specializing in advantageous industries. The gains are not complete (except for accidental configuration of exogenous parameters) in comparison with the case where the optimal organizational diversity can be internalized in each economy. However, it is not easy to see how a diversity of organizational conventions can be internalized in one economy as each convention may have to be supported by a matrix of complementary institutions (such as labour markets, financial systems, regulations, etc.).

As noted above, the shift from one equilibrium to another is not easy, but the cost of transition measured in terms of the necessary minimum size of mutants to upset the old equilibrium will be reduced if the productivity gap between the two equilibria can be enlarged. This suggests that the perception of a large productivity gap with a relatively more advanced foreign convention or innovations may trigger a successful organizational change based on emulation. In reality, however, experiments based on emulation and learning are likely to lead to the modification of the old convention rather than a complete transition to the new convention.

On the organizational dynamic paths of the US and Japan in the last fifty years, external shock-induced organizational evolutions are evident (Aoki, 1995b). Japan's perception of lagged productivity gap in the 1950s and learning of American scientific management method eventually ignited a collective, path dependent organizational innovation of quality and inventory control. The resulting increased productivity of the Japanese assembly industry provided a reciprocal shock to American industry in the late 1970s and 1980s. American's own conceptualization of Japanese organizational innovation as the "lean production method", combined with its own technological innovation in communications and information technology, led to the rise of new network-based coordination beyond the legal boundaries of corporations, providing a new competitive edge in high technology industry. In turn, Japan seems to be perceiving the widening productivity gap as an alarming demonstration of the urgency of overhauling the prevailing institutional arrangement. Whatever the outcome of evolving experiments may be, its nature may be predicted as path-dependent, however.

9.6 Linkage of different games

When the system moves from an equilibrium of a (derivative) game to another equilibrium (of a possibly different derivative game), expectations crystallized as a part of equilibrium strategies in the former may provide a focal point for the selection of new equilibrium or the initial condition in a dynamic adjustment process through which a new equilibrium is reached (Greif, 1995).

Institutional changes, i.e., changes from one (derivative) game to another have not yet been analysed in game theory, but this proposition is intuitive and supported by some of Greif's own historical analysis. Although it is not explicitly game theoretic, Qian and Xu (1993) analyses how differences in coordination mode between planning regimes in the USSR and China may affect the speed, effectiveness, mode of transition to a market economy. In the USSR, planning was coordinated through centralized ministerial hierarchies organized on a functional (industrial) basis, whereas in China coordination tended to be decentralized on a geographical basis in a locally integrated manner. Regional decentralization in Communist China was deliberately pursued as Mao's strategy to thwart possible disaster that might be inflicted by external attack. This Communist legacy seems to make the gradualist transition in China viable as well as to foster the development of a more decentralized market economy.

10. Conclusion

In this paper, the neoclassical deductive approach to institutions has been challenged. It has been suggested that, in order to understand the nature and public policy implications of diverse institutional arrangements across economies, it is desirable to

The Japanese Economic Review

adopt the comparative, interactive approach by which comparative information is accumulated, context specific models are constructed and analysed, and their predictions are confronted with comparative evidence.

Some recent work on these lines has been overviewed. One of the insights gained from these works is that the relationship between markets and other institutions, including legal rulings, contracts and organizations, cultural beliefs and norms, is not necessarily that of simple substitute, but may be understood as reflecting equilibrium strategies in underlying economic games. For a given configuration of parameter values, there may well be multiple equilibria, leading to a diversity of institutional arrangements across economies. Distinct institutional arrangements have evolved because of the path-dependent nature of equilibrium selection, and they may not necessarily be Pareto-rankable. It was suggested that there may be gains from a diversity of institutional arrangements. However, these insights are as yet only tentative.

The CIA approach needs to be developed much further before it can provide a sensible guide for a number of important public policy issues. I hope that this paper will stimulate the interests of economists of the younger generation in this infant, yet promising, new field.

Final version accepted October 23, 1995.

REFERENCES

Aghion, P. and J. Tirole (1994) "Formal and Real Authorities in Organizations," mimeo., IDEI, Toulouse.
Aoki, M. (1988) *Information, Incentives and Bargaining in the Japanese Economy*, Cambridge: Cambridge University Press.
—— (1993) "Organizational Conventions and the Gains from Diversity: an Evolutionary Game Approach," mimeo., Stanford University.
—— (1994) "The Contingent Governance of Teams: Analysis of Institutional Complementarity," *International Economic Review*, Vol. 35, pp. 657–676.
—— (1995a) *Keizai Sisutemu no Shinka to Tagensei* (An Evolving Diversity of Economic System), Tokyo: Toyo-Keizai Shinposha.
—— (1995b) "An Evolving Diversity of Organizational Mode and its Implications for Transitional Economies," to appear in *The Journal of the Japanese and International Economies*.
—— (1995c). "Unintended Fit," mimeo., Stanford University.
—— and H. Kim (eds.) (1995) *Corporate Governance in Transition Economy: Insider Control and the Role of the Banks*, Washington: World Bank.
—— K. Murdock and M. Okuno-Fujiwara (1995) "Beyond the East Asian Miracle: Introducing the Market-enhancing View," Introductory chapter to M. Aoki, H-K. Kim and M. Okuno-Fujiwara, eds., *The Role of Government in East Asian Economic Development: Comparative Institutional Analysis*, World Bank, forthcoming.
—— and H. Patrick (eds.) (1994) *The Japanese Main Bank System: its Relevance for Developing and Transforming Economies*, Oxford: Oxford University Press.
Baron, J. N., F. R. Dobbin and P. Devereaux (1986) "War and Peace: The Evolution of Modern Personnel Administration in U.S. Industry," *American Journal of Sociology*, Vol. 9, pp. 350–383.
Boycko, M., A. Shleifer and R. W. Vishny (1993) "Privatizing Russia," *Brookings Paper on Economic Activity*, Vol. 2, pp. 139–192.
Chinese Government and the World Bank (1995) *Beijing Conference on Enterprise Reform*, Beijing.
Coase, R. (1938) "The Nature of the Firm," *Economica*, Vol. 4 (NS), pp. 386–405.
David, P. (1992) "Why are Institutions the 'Carriers of History'?," SITE working paper, Stanford University.
Dewatripont, M. and G. Roland (1995) "Transition as a Large Scale System Change," presented at a symposia on economic history in the Econometric Society, Seventh World Congress, Tokyo.
Dinc, S. (1995) "Integration of Financial Systems and Institutional Path Dependence," mimeo., Stanford University.

– 18 –

M. Aoki: Towards a Comparative Institutional Analysis: Motivations and Some Tentative Theorizing

Field, A. (1981) "The Problem with Neoclassical Institutional Economics: A Critique with Special Reference to the North-Thomas Model of Pre-1500 Europe," *Explorations in Economic History*, Vol. 18, pp. 174–198.

Freeman, R. (1995) "The Welfare State as a System," *American Economic Review*, Vol. 85, pp. 16–21.

Greif, A. (1994) "Cultural Beliefs and the Organization of Society: A Historical and Theoretical Reflection on Collectivist and Individualist Societies," *Journal of Political Economy*, Vol. 102, pp. 912–950.

—— (1995) "Micro Theory and the Study of Economic Institutions through Economic History: Reflections on Recent Development," presented at a symposia on economic history in the Econometric Society, Seventh World Congress, Tokyo.

Grossman, S. and O. Hart (1986) "The Costs and Benefits of Ownership: A Theory of Vertical and Lateral Integration," *Journal of Political Economy*, Vol. 94, pp. 691–719.

Holmstrom, B. (1992) "Moral Hazard in Teams," *Bell Journal of Economics*, Vol. 13, pp. 324–340.

—— and P. Milgrom (1990) "Regulating Trade Among Agents," *Journal of Institutional and Theoretical Economics*, Vol. 146, pp. 324–340.

Hurwicz, L. (1993) "Toward a Framework for Analysing Institutions and Institutional Change," in S. Bowles, H. Gintis and B. Gustafsson, eds., *Markets and Democracy*, Cambridge: Cambridge University Press, pp. 51–67.

Itoh, H. (1992) "Cooperation in Hierarchical Organizations: An Incentive Perspective," *Journal of Law, Economics and Organization*, Vol. 8, pp. 321–345.

Jian, Q. (1995) "Some Thoughts on Reforming the Management System of State-owned Assets," mimeo., Beijing.

Kandori, M. (1992) "Social Norms and Community Enforcement," *Review of Economic Studies*, Vol. 59, pp. 63–80.

—— G. Mailath and R. Rob (1993) "Learning, Mutation, and Long Run Equilibria in Games," *Econometrica*, Vol. 61, pp. 29–56.

Krugman, P. and Obstfeld (1994) *International Economics: Theory and Policy*, third edition, New York: Harper Collins College Publisher.

McMillan, J. (1995) "Markets in Transition," presented at a symposia on transition in the Econometric Society, Seventh World Congress, Tokyo.

Matsui, A. and M. Okuno-Fujiwara (1994) "Evolution and Interaction of Cultures," mimeo., Universities of Pennsylvania and Tokyo.

Melumad, N., D. Mookherjee and S. Reichelstein (1991) "Hierarchical Decentralization of Incentive Contracts," mimeo, Stanford University.

Milgrom, P., D. North and B. Weingast (1990) "The Role of Institutions in the Revival of Trade: The Law Merchant, Private Judges, and the Champagne Fairs," *Economics and Politics*, Vol. 2, pp. 1–23.

Myerson, R. (1979) "Incentive Compatibility and the Bargaining Problem," *Econometrica*, Vol. 47, pp. 61–74.

Nelson, R. (1995) "Recent Evolutionary Theorizing about Economic Change," *Journal of Economic Literature*, Vol. 33, pp. 48–90.

Noguchi, Y. (1995) *1940 nen Taisei* (1940s Regime), Tokyo: Toyo Keizai Shinpo-sha.

North, D. (1990) *Institutions: Institutional Change and Economic Performance*, Cambridge: Cambridge University Press.

Okazaki, T. (1987) "Senji Keikau Keizai to Kakaku Tosei (Wartime Planning Economy and Price Control)," *Kindai Nihon Kenkyu*, Vol. 9, pp. 175–198.

—— and M. Okuno-Fujiwara (1994) *Gendai Nihon Keizai Sisutemu no Genryu* (The Origin of the Contemporary Japanese Economic System), Tokyo: Toyo Keizai Shinpo-sha.

Qian, Y. and C. Xu (1993) "Why China's Economic Reforms Differ: The N-Form Hierarchy and Entry/Expansion of the Non-State Sector," *Journal of Economic Transition*, Vol. 1, pp. 135–170.

Saxenian, S. (1994) *Regional Advantage*, Cambridge, Mass.: Harvard University Press.

Schotter, A. (1981) *The Economic Theory of Social Institutions*, Cambridge: Cambridge University Press.

Sugden, R. (1989) "Spontaneous Order," *Journal of Economic Perspectives*, Vol. 3, pp. 85–97.

Varian, H. (1990) "Monitoring Agents with other Agents," *Journal of Institutional and Theoretical Economics*, Vol. 146, pp. 153–174.

Wade, R. (1990) *Governing the Market: Economic Theory and the Role of the Government in East Asian Industrialization*, Princeton: Princeton University Press.

Young, H. P. (1994) "The Evolution of Conventions," *Econometrica*, Vol. 61, pp. 85–97.

[25]

ELSEVIER

Journal of Economic Behavior and Organization
Vol. 28 (1995) 161–182

JOURNAL OF
Economic Behavior
& Organization

Markets as institutions versus organizations as markets?
Disentangling some fundamental concepts

Claude Ménard *

Université de Paris I-Panthéon-Sorbonne, 90 rue de Tolbiac, 75634 Paris Cedex 13, France

Received 20 April 1993; revised 7 November 1994

Abstract

This paper argues that ambiguities in concepts as important as "institutions", "markets", and "organizations", undermine progress of research programs intending to take these components seriously into account. After a short review of some current confusions (section I) section II discusses recent literature to arrive at definitions that encapsulate fundamental characteristics into "pure categories". In section III, exceptions and qualifications are introduced so as to operationalize the concepts: in the "real" world (i) organizations and markets are embedded in an institutional framework, and (ii) they overlap, giving birth to "hybrid forms". However, the conclusion contends that it is essential to maintain distinct concepts in order to understand these complex arrangements.

JEL classification: A1; D2; L

Keywords: Institutions; Markets; Organizations; Hybrid forms

1. Introduction

Major developments have occurred in economics, over the last two decades, that have significantly increased our understanding of the nature of institutions and of the roles of organizations and markets in a competitive economy. Transaction

---

* Fax: 331-53790270

SSDI 0167-2681(95)00030-5

162   C. Ménard / J. of Economic Behavior & Org. 28 (1995) 161–182

costs economics made some of the most significant contributions to these developments. But these constructs are also a focal point of attention in property rights analysis, and, to a lesser degree, in game theory and in the literature on incomplete contracts. Indeed, we now frequently come across statements about the emergence of a "New Institutional Economics" [1].

As often happens with new ideas, there is also a great deal of conceptual confusion. Variations in the meanings of the terms are not purely formal; they frequently reflect diverging analyses [2]. This can be illustrated by the ambiguities involved in the concept of *organization*. It is often used as identical to that of the firm (Williamson (1975); Milgrom and Roberts (1991)). But several authors emphasize the structural similarities with other forms, such as non-profit businesses and public agencies (Fama and Jensen (1983a); Fama and Jensen (1983b); Simon (1991)), and therefore they expect the theory to be valid for all of these forms-as it is assumed to be in the tradition of "Organization Theory". On the other hand, many contemporary economists have emphasized that an organization is an *institution* (Williamson (1985), Chap. 1) or an institutional arrangement (Davis and North (1971); Jensen and Meckling (1976); and, relatedly, Coase (1991)). Others have adopted a different view and, underlining the contractual nature of organizations, and especially of firms, have defined them as merely a variant of market activities (Alchian and Demsetz (1972)). At the extreme end of this spectrum, Fama (1980) suggested that organizations should be considered as purely "legal entities", as "fictions" as far as economics is concerned, while Cheung (1983) suggested considering forms of contractualization, not organizations, as the appropriate object of analysis. Conversely, some economists conceptualize markets as specific organizational forms (Arrow (1974)), or as "one large organization" (Arrow (1964); Hurwicz (1987)), while others consider markets as institutions (Hodgson (1988)), or as a specific "institutional arrangement", a variety of "governance structure" (Williamson (1991b)).

This review may overstate the prevailing confusion. But I contend that these ambiguities in key terminology undermine our capacity to embed more firmly the new institutional economics in modern economic analysis. They reduce the credibility of that research program among fellow economists, particularly those committed to formal economics, and they preclude the integration of these concepts into an analytical framework. In the tradition of Russell and Whitehead (1910); see also Jensen (1983)), I would argue that we must clarify the basic concepts in order to identify the appropriate questions to be raised and the data to be collected.

---

[1] This is explicitly claimed by Williamson (1985). Eggertsson (1990) suggested a distinction between "Neoinstitutional Economics", understood as an extension of the rational-choice model to the study of institutions, and "New Institutional Economics" which, as in Williamson, would reject some elements of the hard core of neoclassical economics.

[2] See, for example, the vigorous discussion of transaction cost economics in Demsetz (1988).

C. Ménard / J. of Economic Behavior & Org. 28 (1995) 161–182   163

The purpose of this paper is to contribute to this clarification. I intend to do so in the continuation of the tri-dimensional program suggested by Coase's title, *The Firm, the Market, and the Law* (Coase (1988a)). The characterizations I will suggest can also be understood as an extension of Davis and North's (Davis and North (1971)) fruitful distinction between "institutional environment" and "institutional arrangements" [3]. In section II, I examine and discuss some fundamental characteristics of "institutions", "markets", and "organizations", to arrive at definitions that encapsulate these characteristics into *"pure categories"*. Section III introduces exceptions and qualifications, in order to demonstrate more clearly (i) how actual organizations and markets are embedded in an "institutional environment" and (ii) how they overlap, giving birth to "hybrid forms" that are crucial to the understanding of market economies. But I challenge the view that we are confronted with a pure *continuum* of forms.

My main argument is twofold. *First*, I develop the idea that institutions, markets, and organizations operate at different levels, with institutions being an overarching class that subsumes both organizations and markets. *Second*, I maintain that, while markets and organizations do overlap, they each also have unique features of their own.

2. Exploring the basic concepts

Economists have long concentrated almost exclusively on the analysis of purely competitive market structures, in which agents are individuals, or, within institutional frameworks that are exogenously determined and very weakly specified, nevertheless behave as individuals. The Arrow–Debreu model can be considered as the intellectual achievement of this approach, focusing on the price system. Demsetz (1988) argued that this model, which fails to address either the organization of firms or the legal institutions involved in a competitive market place, could best be explained in terms of its intellectual origins: the eighteenth-century debate between mercantilists and free traders was about the proper scope of government in economic affairs, not about competition per se, nor about the nature and properties of organizations involved in competition.

It is more and more recognized, though, that this model falls short of characterizing market economies in which the price system operates with costs, and necessitates specific institutions, and in which firms are more than purely rhetorical devices. Current debates on the requisite conditions for a transition from command economy to market economy illustrate the importance of these extra-market aspects (Day (1993); Joskow (1994)).

---

[3] I see this last concept as very close to that of "governance structures" developed by Williamson. Maki et al. (1993) suggested similarities between the distinction made by Davis and North (1971), and the one made by Lachman between "internal" and "external" institutions.

164 C. Ménard / J. of Economic Behavior & Org. 28 (1995) 161–182

In order to disentangle the dimensions involved, this section discusses some recent contributions, not as a survey, but to demonstrate major differences between an institutional framework and the pure "governance structures" operating within this framework. Going to a courtroom to have a contract enforced is intuitively different than going to meet a boss to negotiate a wage increase, or than visiting several salesrooms to buy a car. While all of these activities involve contracts, the nature of the relationship between the agents involved is very different in each situation. But what exactly are these differences?

2.1. A structuring "environment": institutions

Institutions operate at a higher level of generalization than do markets and organizations: they delineate the rules of the game within which such "governance structures" actually operate. As an illustration, the legal system, which most economists would agree on calling an institution, is a framework that defines the social acceptability of possible actions, e.g. the ways in which property rights can be implemented and enforced. The institution of the law largely contributes to socially embed markets and organizations (Granovetter (1985); North (1981)). In order to explore further some fundamental characteristics of this embedding, let us start with three examples deliberately chosen from very different approaches. These examples are from formal models, rather than from historical analyses such as those developed by North, because I want to emphasize the analytical content of the concept of institution that I will propose hereafter.

The *first* example specify more precisely the idea that institutions define *an abstract set of-rules*. Stiglitz (1974) and Hurwicz (1987) suggested the importance of underlying institutional rules in their discussions of the following simple relationship governing the distribution of rewards. Let r be a reward to agents involved in the production of a specific output, q the income generated by these agents or a subset of these agents, and a and b two parameters defined respectively on $[0,1]$ and on $\mathbb{R}$. We can then write a familiar expression of the type:

$$r = aq + b \qquad (1)$$

Traditionally, price theory focuses all of the attention on the relationships between r and q, and considers a and b as exogenously determined. But what if we shift our attention to the properties of the parameters? If a and b are not known a priori, the two-dimensional parameter space (a,b) then defines the class of a priori admissible institutional patterns for the distribution of rewards. If a is strictly positive and b is zero, the equation describes a pure sharecropping system. If a is zero and b strictly positive, the equation describes a wage earner system. If b is negative, the worker pays a fixed fee for the use of resources. We could continue to explore possible institutional environments by varying a and b. Hence, this simple model can describe specific forms, in a limited number if

C. Ménard / J. of Economic Behavior & Org. 28 (1995) 161–182   165

empirical constraints are taken into consideration, with well-defined rules of distribution of rewards. More generally, such models point out the importance of the underlying institutional framework, and the possibility of *identifying* abstract sets of rules. However, these models fail to account for the *emergence* of these rules, nor do they describe either the mechanisms that constrain agents to accept these rules, or the implementation and enforcement of those mechanisms.

My *second* example is chosen to show how other models deal with aspects of these difficulties by linking institutions to a "common knowledge" shared by rational agents, so that the implementation of rules depends on individual behavior. The illustration comes from a game theoretic approach, which is not surprising, considering the renewed interest in that field as a way of understanding institutions [4]. It is so because the rigorous definition of a "game form" involves specifying "strategies" (i.e., the actions available to the agents) and determining a priori the "outcome functions" (i.e., what the consequences of these actions will be), and because such a definition also requires understanding how these actions can be coordinated. In an often quoted page (Schotter, 1981, chap. 1, p. 11), referring explicitly to Lewis (1969), suggested the following definition of an institution:

"A regularity R in the behavior of the members of a population P when they are agents in a recurrent situation K is an *institution* if and only if it is true and is common knowledge in R that (1) everyone conforms to R; (2) everyone expects everyone else to conform to R; and (3) either everyone prefers to conform to R on the conditions that the others do so, if K is a coordination problem, in which case uniform conformity to R is a coordination equilibrium; or (4) if anyone ever deviates from R it is known that some or all of the others will also deviate and the payoffs associated with the recurrent play of K using these deviating strategies are worse for all agents than the payoff associated with R".

The crucial point of comparison with the previous example, is that the set of possible rules is restricted to "regularities" based on "common knowledge" acquired by the agents who behave *rationally*: they conform to these regularities because they can calculate the advantages of doing so. Therefore, institutions are conceptualized as *patterns of behavior* implemented through repeated actions of agents as they deal with recurrent problems. Emphasis is shifted from rules to regularity of behavior (Maki et al. (1993), p. 13). Institutions are non-cooperative Nash equilibria, with characteristics ultimately determined by individuals acting selfishly (Aumann (1985); Sugden, this issue). There are several difficulties involved, though. First, regularities develop through repeated actions which are necessary for "common knowledge" to emerge: the extension of such repetitiveness is not well specified, while the calculative resources of agents must be very large (outcome functions are well-defined). Second, it is implicitly assumed that

---

[4] See in this special issue, papers by Goyal and Janssen, and Sugden.

such "institutions" are totally self-enforcing, as it appears with conditions (3) and (4) (we have either "uniform conformity" or "it is known" by agents that deviating strategies are worse for all agents) [5]. Third, in order for such coordination to be efficient, agents must have access to very dense information. But we know, thanks to new institutional economics, that this can be extremely costly, and that institutions are often developed to reduce such costs.

This informational requirement is precisely at the center of my *third* example. In order to better understand how an "institution" can coordinate, Hurwicz (1987) suggested a much more restrictive definition than Schotter's (Schotter (1981)). In his model, an institution is conceptualized as the *information mechanism* that coordinates the actions of different agents. "Regularities", as defined above, would be structured by a *pre-assigned set of social outcomes*. If I represents the institution, then it can be defined by the following pair:

$$I = (M; O(m)) \tag{2}$$

where M is the space of all messages that any agent can send to the "coordinating device", and $O(\cdot)$ represents the outcome function,

$$O: M^n \rightarrow a \in A$$

so that O is mapping each n-upple m, $m = (m_1, m_2, \ldots, m_n)$, into an a, with A the set of all possible actions. Such an "institutional mechanism", understood as the *pairing of messages and outcomes*, defines a game form. In Lewis's perspective, the acceptance of the institution depended on the nature and commonality of "common knowledge"; for Hurwicz, acceptability depends both on the quality of the system of signals and on the efficiency of the transmission mechanism. Hurwicz himself acknowledged that this model falls short of a complete definition of an institution. He emphasized that a more comprehensive view would have to specify: (1) the prior human actions on which the mechanism is based (the "emergence" of the institution [6]); (2) an enforcement process (which could be interpreted as an augmented game: but this raises the problem of infinite regression); and (3) the universality constraint (the rules must apply over an extended period of time to all persons and situations qualifying in a given category). The basic question remains: how does such an institution induce agents to behave in particular (and pre-determined) ways to signals they receive?

Notwithstanding the differences, these three examples have in common certain characteristics that can help to define a more comprehensive concept of institution. First, institutions are viewed as specific forms which are stable over long periods of time and which operate as constraints on agents. On the other hand, these

---

[5] For a related critique, see Langlois and Csontos (1993) and Maki et al. (1993).

[6] Some game theoreticians are quite skeptical about the ability of Game Theory to explain the emergence of rules (see, for example, Kreps (1991)). Recent models in "evolutionary" game theory intend to go farther on that problem of the emergence of rules (see Sugden, this issue).

C. Ménard / J. of Economic Behavior & Org. 28 (1995) 161–182   167

models tend to ignore that every institution has a historical dimension that describes the specific conditions of its emergence. Knowledge of an institution's history is essential for an understanding of the very nature of its operations: institutions regulating financial markets in the US have a historical background which shapes the differences of their forms as compared to those in Germany or Japan. Second, Institutions transcend individuals and organizations such as firms. They involve the implementation of an *abstract* set of rules which are *impersonal*, in that they must apply to all members of specified categories and preclude individual choices [7], and *non-arbitrary*, in that they are perceived to be the same for all members of a certain category. These rules are encapsulated in specific mechanisms, be they tradition, custom, or laws (Weber (1947)). Think about the fiscal system, which divides citizens into subsets, and taxes them accordingly. Third, Institutions are normative in that they intend to establish distinctions between what is acceptable and what will be considered as illegitimate: they define behavioral norms that delineate the "limited set of alternatives available at any moment in a society" (North (1986)). That is, the norms delimit the domain of choices available to agents, or define what they can and cannot do. Hence, most institutional models describe individuals as acting according to norms, not in relation to choices. Ideally, these norms would be internalized, implementing patterns of behavior that are experienced by agents as "proper, legitimate, or expected modes of action. (Parsons (1940), p. 190)" [8] . Most of the time, however, these norms require specific mechanisms of implementation and enforcement. To illustrate, property rights define norms to be respected in the transfer of goods and services, while laws are designed to implement these norms and the court system to enforce them.

To summarize these characteristics in order to facilitate comparison with the concepts of markets and organizations, I suggest this definition: *An* institution *is manifested in a long-standing historically determined set of stable, abstract and impersonal rules, crystallized in traditions, customs, or laws, so as to implement and enforce patterns of behavior governing the relationships between separate social constituencies* [9].

It is within this limited set of alternatives that specific "governance structures" such as markets and organizations occur.

2.2. A specific institutional arrangement: markets

Institutions are of major interest to the economist because they delineate the conditions under which goods and services are produced and exchanged. In Davis

---

[7] This idea could be related to Hayek's view of institutions as spontaneous and self organizing entities. Differently, see also Williamson (1991a).

[8] Relatedly, Maki et al. (1993) emphasizes the ability of institutions to generate "reciprocal beliefs and expectations" among agents.

[9] For related definitions see Parsons (1940) and North (1986).

and North's terms, they provide the *environment* in which specific arrangements can be defined. The best known such arrangement, or "governance structure", is the market.

Now it is paradoxical how variously and vaguely defined the concept of market is [10]. It has long been approximated as the abstract *space of exchange* in which frequent intercourse among buyers and sellers determines prices [11]. Differently, Jevons identified markets as extensive "business relations" which generate a "community of knowledge", namely the ratio of exchange [12]. The predominant view of this shared knowledge is that it is produced by the famous but mysterious Invisible Hand (Smith (1776); Hahn (1984)).

The most widely accepted modern representation of this Smithian view, and probably the most precise definition of markets available so far, is the Arrow–Debreu model of general equilibrium [13]. Under the now well-known assumptions about: (a) commodities, assumed to be measurable; (b) consumers, assumed to be able to order every pair of consumption plans within a consumption set, so that the ordering is complete, transitive, and continuous; (c) firms, "owned" by a subset of consumers and assumed to be technologically able to produce a specific plan within a production set supposed to be convex; and (d) several other specific assumptions [14], *equilibrium* is defined as a price vector P^*, technically the dual of the commodity vector, so that:

$$P^* y_j^* \geq P^* y_j \; y_j \in Y_j \text{ for all } j;$$ (3)

$$P^* x^i \leq \sum_j d_{ij} P^* y_j^* + P^* w^i \text{ for all } i;$$ (4)

$$\sum_i x^i = \sum_i w^i + \sum_j y_j$$ (5)

with y_j a production vector of firm j within the production set Y, x^i a consumption vector of consumer i within the consumption set X, d_{ij} a share of firm j "owned" by consumer i, and w^i the initial endowment of consumer i.

---

[10] See Vroey (1990a); DeVille (1990) and Hodgson (1988).

[11] "It is well known that by *market*, economists mean, not a certain place where purchases and sales are carried on, but the entire territory of which the parts are so united by the relations of unrestricted commerce that prices there take the same level throughout, with ease and rapidity" (Cournot (1838), chap. 4, par. 23).

[12] "By a market, I shall mean two or more persons dealing in two or more commodities, whose stocks of those commodities and intentions of exchanging are known to all. It is also essential that the ratio of exchange between any two persons should be known to all others. It is only so far as this *community of knowledge* extends that the market extends" (Jevons (1970), chap. 4; emphasis is mine, C.M.).

[13] For an elegant mathematical presentation, see Balasko (1988).

[14] Such as non satiability and the capacity of any agent to survive (so that trading will occur only if mutually beneficial).

C. Ménard / J. of Economic Behavior & Org. 28 (1995) 161–182   169

Such an equilibrium, if it exists, characterizes the concept of a *perfect market*, understood as a situation in which autonomous agents will be induced to make *mutually compatible plans*. In the perfectly decentralized economy described by this model, which Demsetz (1988) described as "an extreme *decentralization* model of resource allocation", the price system thus represents Adam Smith's Invisible Hand, and it is the backbone of Jevons' "community of knowledge" among traders.

But this representation also means that the price mechanism *is* the market, i.e., the fundamental and exclusive "institutional arrangement" for coordinating economic activities. What, precisely, is this mechanism, and what are its prerequisites? That the answer to these questions is not at all obvious has been made clear through the past thirty years of exploration of the properties that might explain how such an equilibrium can be reached and maintained [15]. The severe restrictions imposed by the assumptions of the "pure" Arrow–Debreu model are now well-known [16]. In the perspective of this paper, which is to emphasize similarities and differences between institutional prerequisites, e.g. the auctioneer in the Walrasian model, and specific institutional arrangements, such as markets and hierarchies (Williamson (1975)), the most significant restrictions are that firms do not exist [17], except as "legal fictions" (Famo, 1980), and that institutions necessary for a price system to exist and to perform efficiently, as required by the theory, are left totally unspecified. In this representation of markets, the rationality of agents has no internal limits that could explain either the incentive to cooperate or the necessity of some authority, as within firms. The property rights are left unspecified, transactions are considered to be costless and to need no enforcement. There is no regulatory power [18], and no political process is involved in decision-making. In the words of Demsetz (1988) "⟨⟨Firm⟩⟩ in the theory of price is simply a rhetorical device adopted to facilitate discussion of the price system".

Hence the question, always a source of heated debate: Can this model be an adequate "base camp" (Vroey (1990b)) for analyzing a market economy in which there are institutions and firms? Whatever the answer to this question is or will be,

---

[15] Critical surveys of problems involved can be found in Fisher (1983) and Hahn (1984). Let it be remembered that, so far, there is no satisfying solution to the "stability" problem. All tentative solutions, though, do involve institutional specification.

[16] In relation to this paper, the most significant ones are: (1) the absence of bankruptcy, since all agents must meet their budget constraint (hence, firms must have an infinite horizon of life); (2) the absence of money and of institutions to enforce its use (see Garretsen and van Es, this issue); (3) the necessity for all trades to be done at the beginning of time, since there is no reopening of markets at later dates; (4) the absence of significant asymmetry of information (otherwise there would be inefficiencies); and (5) the inexistence of increasing returns to scale (otherwise some traders could have some "market power").

[17] What exist are technological units of production.

[18] But it can be argued that the Walrasian auctioneer is the most centralized regulatory power, since no exchange can be proceeded before he determines P^*.

170   *C. Ménard / J. of Economic Behavior & Org. 28 (1995) 161–182*

both the achievements and the shortcomings of the Arrow–Debreu model can help us to specify what we are looking for in a more appropriate definition of a market.

First, we need a much more explicit description of the prerequisite institutional environment, one that specifies the conditions (laws, governmental apparatus, regulation) necessary for structuring and enforcing the transfer of property rights. Second, we need a much more extensive analysis of the specific mechanism of control that constrains traders' choices, namely *competition*, which operates through prices [19]. Third, we have learned, and this is a major contribution of general equilibrium models, that transactions must be *repeated among varying agents*, in order to create both regularities and interchangeability, at least in the sense that there *are always possible substitutes* for any trader. Last, and this is fundamentally different from what we will develop to characterize organizations, there is a *reversibility* of positions among traders that does not exist within an authority structure: in markets, a buyer can always become a seller.

These characteristics can be summarized into the following synthetic definition: *a market is a specific institutional arrangement consisting of rules and conventions that make possible a large number of voluntary transfers of property rights on a regular basis, these reversible transfers being implemented and enforced through a specific mechanism of regulation, the competitive price system* [20].

Recent approaches to the theory of the firm make it clear that this definition does not entirely cover either transaction activities or the allocation of resources. Therefore, we must now turn our attention to another institutional arrangement, the organization.

2.3. Organizations as an alternative arrangement

Many decisions to create or allocate resources are made by organizations or, at least, within organizations. For most theorists of organizations, since Barnard (1938) and Simon (1947), firms and, more generally, organizations, have structural properties that strongly influence how agents behave and what types of decisions they make. As emphasized by March and Olsen (1984), organizations act *coherently* and are *autonomous*, so that they are not conceptually reducible to conglomerations of their individual members. One can also view Williamson's pioneering book, in which he contrasts "markets" with "hierarchies", as a particularly significant step toward the inclusion of the firm within the scope of economic analysis.

However, many economists have asserted that firms are not an appropriate object of analysis. In their widely quoted paper, Alchian and Demsetz (1972)

---

[19] But we must be aware that: (1) competition should not be reduced to "pure and perfect competition"; and (2) the efficiency of the price system may also involve specific qualities of traders, as when reputation plays an important role.

[20] Partially related views can be found in Polanyi (1944); Davis and North (1971); Hess (1983); and Hodgson (1988).

questioned the idea that the concept of "authority" should be used to identify the coordinating device typical of firms. They denied that the complex contractual relationships within firms are in any sense different from market relationships: they described employees and their employer as being in positions analogous to those of shoppers and their local grocer. Similarly, Cheung (1983) posited a continuum of arrangements, from markets to firms, with the process of transactions rather than "discrete forms" (such as firms) as the proper "unit" of analysis. Fama (1980) drew the same conclusion, though from a different point of view, in stating that firms are nothing but "a legal fiction", or a "nexus of contracts."

Using the word "fiction" suggests that the legal framework of a firm is not fundamentally relevant to an understanding of its economic functions. Whether the specificities of this institutional arrangement matter or not may be a major point of divergence among economists. Transaction costs economists consider that the nature of the arrangement does matter: the characteristics of the "institutional structure of production" (Coase (1991)) are highly relevant to an understanding of how an organization works. It is the specificity of that structure that Chester Barnard already wanted to emphasize when he described organizations in terms of their capacity to create "a field of gravity" among their members, so that "energies" from participating agents "become organization forces only when certain conditions obtain within the field, and are evidenced only by certain phenomena such as words and other actions, or are inferred by concrete results imputed to such action. But neither the persons nor the objective results are themselves the organization" (Barnard (1938), chap. 6, footnote 7). While this description of organizations is virtually taken for granted among organization theorists, it is still heatedly debated among economists, as noted above.

There are, however, significant signs of an evolution in the direction of more universal recognition of organizations as entities in themselves. "Revisiting" the theory of the firm, Demsetz (1988) expressed regret that "the study of the price system, characterized as it is by Marshall's representative firm and Walras' auctioneer, undermines serious consideration of the firm as a problem solving institution". He went even further in describing how "the real tasks of management", such as discovering markets, products, and techniques, and orienting the actions of employees, are, at worst, ignored, or, at best, are mentioned only rhetorically by mainstream economists. Charging that the role of "giving *directions*" (his emphasis) is crucial to the understanding of what firms are, he laid the groundwork for a revision in status of the role of authority in organizations, toward a position of central importance [21]. In the same special issue of the *Journal of Law, Economics, and Organization*, Sidney Winter went even further, in his assertion that "large corporations are, as *organizations* (his emphasis),

---

[21] Such a conception is explicitly developed by Radner (1992) and Menard (1994a).

172   *C. Ménard / J. of Economic Behavior & Org. 28 (1995) 161–182*

among society's most significant repositories of the productive knowledge that they exercise, and not merely an economic contrivance of the individuals currently associated with them'' [22].

These reformulations call on us, as economists, to take into account the impact of the structural properties of organizations on the nature of their productive activities and on the characteristics of the transactions they make. Organizations, and especially firms, are specific institutional arrangements, different from those of markets, in that they exist to coordinate specific assets through *discretionary rules* (Williamson (1991a); Williamson (1991b)). There are important implications of this characterization, in relation to how we defined institutions and markets. First, organizations are based on formal agreements, where *voluntarity* is crucial: hierarchy can constrain individual choices within organizations, such as when a new job is assigned, but one can always quit. *Second*, organizations differ from institutions in being "a system of consciously coordinated personal activities or forces" (Barnard (1938)), chap. 6), with this *conscious coordination* defining the "governance structure" of this specific arrangement. *Third*, organizations cannot operate exclusively through command: they require also *cooperation* from their members, which involves their commitment to specific goals, their willingness to endorse or transform existing routines, and their responsiveness to incentives *deliberately designed* to maintain or improve their participation.

Formally, an organization must therefore be characterized by: (1) the presence of a set of members M, $m = 1, 2, \ldots, n$, with $n \in N$, with specific conditions that can qualify an individual as a "member"; (2) a set of possible actions A, $A = \{a_1, a_2, \ldots, a_k\}$ where $a_1, a_2, \ldots, a_k$ are subsets, with A defining the scope of the organization; (3) an internal rule s, determining the relationship among members, based on *"fiat"* (s is usually referred to as a *supervisory relation*, with s irreflexive, asymmetric, and acyclic); and (4) an external law t, let us call it a "treaty" (of which contracts are a subset), which describes the arrangement within which specific actions or subsets of actions are performed [23].

These characteristics can be summarized as follow: *an* organization *is an institutional arrangement designed to make possible the conscious and deliberate coordination of activities within identifiable boundaries, in which members associate on a regular basis through a set of implicit and explicit agreements, commit themselves to collective actions for the purpose of creating and allocating resources and capabilities by a combination of command and cooperation.*

This definition leaves unresolved the problem of identifying the factors that distinguish an organization from the sum of its individual members [24]. Two

---

[22] He then added, quoting a previous paper of his: "...it is the firms, not the people who work for the firms, that know how to make gasoline, automobiles, and computers".

[23] For a similar view, see Beckmann (1988), chap. 1 and 2.

[24] Barnard (1938) already examined this problem, and looked for a solution in the concept of *"zone of acceptance"*. For more recent approaches, see Winter (1988) and Menard (1994b).

C. Ménard / J. of Economic Behavior & Org. 28 (1995) 161–182   173

complementary approaches may be particularly helpful toward that end: (a) the idea that an organization is a structured combination of specific assets; and (b) the idea that this combination transforms organizations into significant producers and repositories of productive knowledge.

3. Toward a continuum?

I will now compare the three concepts defined above, so as to elucidate the major differences among institutions (or "institutional environment"), on one hand, and the two specific "governance structures", markets and organizations, on the other hand. I will show too that there are areas of overlap between organizations and markets, which can be described as "hybrid forms" (Williamson (1985)). The existence of hybrid forms raises the fundamental question: Do institutional arrangements comprise _a continuum_ of combinations of elements? If so, are our conceptually pure categories invalid? I will argue that this is not the case, and that the existence of deviations from the pure concepts does not undermine the importance of the differences I have already delineated.

3.1. Comparative characteristics

In order to facilitate comparisons, I will tabulate the properties already identified, under three headings: (i) Foundations, i.e., the principles of consistency at work within each structure; (ii) Modes of Coordination, i.e., the specific devices by which each structure implements its activities; and (iii) "Raisons d'Etre", i.e., the specific functions of these devices, either explicit or implicit.

	FOUNDATIONS	MODES OF COORDINATION	RAISON D'ETRE
INSTITUTIONS	Stable, Universal, and impersonal set of rules	Traditions, Customs, And Laws	Implementation and enforcement of the « rules of the game »
MARKETS	Noncooperative arrangements (substitutability, repetivity, and reversibility)	Monetary Prices (Competition)	Transfer of Property Rights and open access to substitutes
ORGANIZATIONS	Formal and voluntary agreements to coordinate	Conscious governance through Fiat	Combination of specific assets into collective action

174   C. Ménard / J. of Economic Behavior & Org. 28 (1995) 161–182

While necessarily oversimplified, this table makes it easier to underline some basic differences among the three concepts under examination. It makes it clear that institutions operate as an overarching class, of which markets and organizations are members. Moreover, a closer examination reveals significant areas of overlap between these two pure "governance structures". Hence, the necessity to qualify our "polar cases" and to bring into the picture these shadowy areas.

3.2. Delineating some fundamental ambiguities

It should be clear from the preceding definitions, as well as from my numerous references to North and to Williamson, that I see both markets and organizations as firmly *embedded* in institutions, but also as *discrete* structures. However, it is essential to clarify these qualifications because there still remains disagreement about this among economists, including among "new institutionalists".

First, let us consider the embeddedness problem, i.e, how the two polar "governance structures" defined above are viewed in relation to the institutional environment.

Markets and *institutions* are often defined in ways that make it difficult to differentiate between the concepts. Long ago, Commons (1934) advocated that markets should be understood as institutions, a point recently repeated by Hodgson (1988, chap. 8). Similarly, Okun (1981) underlined the importance of what he suggested calling "custom markets". As noted by Granovetter (1985), the tendency to identify markets by the institutional environment within which they necessarily operate may reflect a trend toward "oversocializing" their characteristics. This is particularly so when markets are closely regulated or when they are about activities defined by "natural monopolies" and subject to strong political control. Conversely, others have argued that several non-economic institutions do operate as markets. Becker (1981) viewed the institution of the family in this way. More recently, Weingast and Marshall (1988) interpreted the relationships among politicians, and those between politicians and their constituencies, as typical of transaction arrangements, which implies that the polity can be understood as a form of market (North (1990) shares some aspects of this view).

There are also ambiguities about the relationship between the concepts of *organizations* and *institutions*. These confusions may go back to Marshall (1920), who explicitly characterized the institutions of a market economy as organizations, while identifying firms etc... as "business organizations". More recently, Oliver E. Williamson published in close juxtaposition two books, whose contents cover much the same territory. One is characterized as about "institutions" (Williamson (1985)), the other as about "organizations" (Williamson (1986)). And Moe (1991), who was strongly influenced by the literature on transaction costs, went further in asserting that institutions *are* organizations. Conversely, there are firms that have operated over long periods of time, that have developed some characteristics similar to those of institutions as I define them above. A key to the

C. Ménard / J. of Economic Behavior & Org. 28 (1995) 161–182   175

interpretation of these difficulties may be provided by North. In a recent paper (1990), he suggested that the blurring of the distinction occurs because there is "*a symbiotic relationship between institutions and the consequent organization*" (my emphasis, C.M.). As I see it, North's most important word here is *consequent*: it underlines both the importance of distinguishing between institutions and organizations, and the fact that very often an organization is the way to implement and operationalize the "rules of the game" as they are defined by the institutional environment. To illustrate, one can think of Central Banks: they are embedded in those institutions necessary to define the legal tender of money; but they operate as organizations. Therefore, one source of confusion is that institutions are made operational through "secular arms", i.e., organizations whose role is to monitor, enforce and manage the set of rules these institutions have defined.

Second, there are important areas of *overlap* between these two "*governance structures*", markets and organizations.

A major contribution of the recent literature on transactions is the demonstration of the fundamental importance of "hybrid forms", between the polar cases of markets and hierarchies (see particularly Cheung (1983); and Williamson (1990), Williamson (1991b)). Hybrid forms are characterized by specific combinations of markets incentives and modalities of coordination involving some forms of hierarchical relationship. They develop essentially when transactions involve assets that are specific, but not specific enough to justify integration, and/or when the frequency of transactions is rather low and involves developing personal relationships among traders. Hence, many market transactions are strongly coordinated by mechanisms well beyond the price adjustments involved in competition. An illustration is provided by very long term contracts, in which short term fluctuations in prices that are at the very core of market adjustments, have minor impact on the terms of contracts and on the coordination process. Crucial clauses are left incomplete, and certain major decisions, even including adjustments in prices, are made over the course of time by agreements of a more or less informal nature, in which the personal relationships between decision-makers of the interacting firms can play an important role, as it has been documented in the railroad industry (Palay (1984)) and in the coal-electricity complex (Joskow (1985)).

More formalized "relational contracting" (Hodgson (1988)) can also be so strong that transactions are made almost "as if" within a single organization. Illustrations can be found in the New York market for diamonds (Ben-Porath (1980)) and in labor relations in the British docks (Edwards (1990)). In these cases, markets are coordinated through strongly codified relationships, often embedded in cultural values shared by traders, so that we have a mix of "governance structures" filled with characteristics of the institutional environment. Ouchi (1979) suggested that we identify such situations as being of a "clannish" nature, distinct from markets or "bureaucracies" (i.e., what most economists would call "hierarchies" or "organizations"). As an example, he quoted Light (1972), who described revolving-credit societies that perform the functions of investment banks, but with participation strictly limited by birthright, and with crucial variables such as the rate of interest to be paid by borrowers, left unspecified. In all of these situations, the market activities are significantly permeated with organizational factors, while simultaneously embedded in institutions.

Conversely, *organizations can be internally structured as quasi-markets*. In their now classical study, Doeringer and Piore (1971) analyzed large firms in terms of internal labor markets. More radically, for reasons mentioned earlier, Alchian and Demsetz (1972), and then Jensen and Meckling (1976), argued that organizations could be reduced to a nexus of "contracts". If this were so, and if contracts characterized hybrid forms as well, then there would be a *continuum* between markets and hierarchies. This is the challenging view developed by Cheung (1983), based on a study of different forms of agreements at work in Hong Kong, ranging from contracts among independent workers, through networks established by a middleman, to the contractual arrangement typical of a "classical" firm. Differently, Williamson increasingly acknowledged the importance of forms in which organizational governance combines with market relations. Franchising, when very strict standards are imposed on independent participants, is a case in point (see Williamson, 1985, chap. 13). Classification becomes particularly difficult when firms are interconnected by a dense web of transactions, with strong commitments to each other and complementarities of their assets, but without formal agreements and, moreover, with property rights on these firms clearly maintained as distinct. This has been shown for large Japanese corporations in relation to their suppliers (Aoki (1984); Aoki et al. (1990)), as well as for American auto manufacturers (Bensaou and Venkatraman (1992)). Thorelli (1986) has examined such networks, based on long term relationships that are very stable, although only weakly contractualized, where linkages are rooted in technological complementarities, organizational synergies or, simply, by personal familiarity among traders (see also Macaulay (1963); Ben-Porath (1980)). But, in Williamson's view, and this is crucial to my previous analysis, these "hybrid forms" do not invalidate the existence of discrete structures: characteristics of the polar cases, in terms of incentives at work, of property rights involved, and of the absence or presence of "fiat" as a mode of coordination, are maintained.

3.3. Where are we left?

All the above examples show the large variety of forms involved in economic activities, and the multiplicity of linkages that are neither pure "markets", nor pure "hierarchies", and that emerge partially in response to institutional constraints (but also to technological factors, for sure).

Does this variety mean that *"pure categories"* or *"pure concepts"* should be abandoned and that we should rather concentrate on the *continuum of agreements* between these forms? Should we treat organizations and institutions as pure

C. Ménard / J. of Economic Behavior & Org. 28 (1995) 161–182   177

derivatives from the market forms, as suggested by Alchian and Demsetz (1972) for the former, and by Weingast and Marshall (1988) for the later? Should we go even further and, in conformity with Cheung's proposal (Cheung (1983)), should we drop these forms from our research agenda and focus our attention exclusively on what would be the (universal) underneath contractual arrangements?

It is my contention that this would be erroneous, because the abandonment of "discrete analysis" would remove from economic analysis such fundamental problems as organizational (non-monetary) incentives, transactions without transfer of property rights, and the role of *command*. That there is an *institutional structure of production* does not mean that an understanding of the organization of a productive activity can be reduced to the identification of the institutional framework necessary for such an organization to exist. Let me suggest an analogy from the field of biology. Abandoning the distinction between markets and hierarchies would be like arguing that there are no significant differences between mammals and fishes, since they are all vertebrates (or, even more radically, that animals and plants are the same because they are all made from cells). I submit that the deep significance of the New Institutional Economics is to have delineated fundamental differences among the complex components of a market economy, and to have initiated studies leading to a subtle articulation of these dimensions.

I would like to go a little further and suggest that there are two complementary reasons that can explain the tendency, among so many economists, to deny the importance of considering "discrete structures".

First, the prevailing methodology focuses on *individual choices* to explain all economic structures. If collective actions are reducible to individual choices, if there are no structural characteristics of entities such as firms, then one cannot see why organizations should be analyzed per se: their properties would be identical to those of mutual agreements among individuals. Moreover, this is true for markets and for institutions as well: hence, the emergence of institutions should be interpreted as a process of convergence of individual choices [25], and markets should be analyzed by examining those exchanges in which individuals freely decide to trade because of their mutual interest (so that the perfectly decentralized model developed by Arrow and Debreu would be the most adequate to interpret all of these specific "forms").

Second, the *contractual approach* conjugated itself to that methodology, suggesting that organizations would be but a "nexus of contracts" (understood as a set of agreements among individuals), and institutions would arise out of repeated games among non-cooperating players. It should be noted that, in the process, the very concept of contract has been expanded up to the point that it has almost been dissolved: once considered as a formal agreement (Macaulay (1963)), it was then

---

[25] A view partially supporting some analysis of this special issue: see Sugden, and Orlean.

used to describe ''implicit contracts'', and is now often used almost synonymously with transactions. But contracts, as central as they are, do not fully explain the structuring of economic activity. Studies on innovations, be they technological or organizational, strongly support this view. Inventions, to become economic innovations, i.e., processes or products that are brought to the marketplace on a regular basis, require a complex of factors that far exceeds contractual capabilities of agents. They are depending on the institutional environment (laws regulating patents, rules constraining experimentation); and they are embedded in constituencies (research laboratories, firms, banks, government agencies) that must cooperate or be commanded. They also have to be implemented through markets, both to attract the necessary financial resources and to satisfy an already existing demand or to develop a new one (Orsenigo (1989); Green (1991)). Similarly, the development of the M-Form as an innovative organizational structure, was not the outcome of contracts, but the result of changes in strategies within some major organizations, in market conditions (new demands, new technological possibilities as with transportations), and in the institutional environment (Williamson (1975), chap. 8; Lazonick (1993)).

It is more and more recognized that we need these concepts, and the related structural properties, for the understanding of how market economies work. To illustrate, let me mention three on-going research programs. In a special issue, now a book (Williamson and Winter (1991)), celebrating the publication of Coase's paper on ''The Nature of the Firm'' (Coase (1988b)), Williamson defined a three-stage research program, of which the first stage is ''comparative contractual analysis''; the second, an examination of ''alternative forms of governance-market, hybrid, and hierarchy''; and the third, an extension to intertemporal process. Revisiting the theory of the firm, Demsetz adopted a different view, but similarly emphasized the importance of considering the role of ''substantive managed coordination'' based on authority and command. Some pages later, Sidney Winter characterized the contribution of evolutionary theory in its emphasis on firms as ''repositories of knowledge'', strongly denying that this can be reduced to the contributions of individuals composing a firm.

4. Conclusion

In this paper, I have delineated as precisely as possible the three concepts of institutions, markets and organizations. I used as a starting point Davis and North's very fruitful distinction (Davis and North (1971)) between *''institutional environment''* and *''institutional arrangements''*. This paper can be seen as a reinterpretation of recent literature guided by that distinction, and an extension of the distinction in order to better identify and characterize the two major categories of institutional arrangements, organizations and markets. Elucidating these ''pure concepts'' also helps to explain the status of hybrid forms, and, more generally,

C. Ménard / J. of Economic Behavior & Org. 28 (1995) 161–182   179

how these concepts interact in the interpretation of economic phenomena in the "real" world.

The guideline of this conceptual exploration is: while the concepts do intersect, they nevertheless remain distinct. I emphasized several possible confusions in this paper, in order to show that much more than semantics is involved. On one hand, the many ambiguities are a positive signal, because they arise out of proliferating research over the last twenty years, in directions and on topics previously ignored or considered as marginal by almost all economists. On the other hand, well-defined concepts are essential to the implementation of a progressive research program in New Institutional Economics, and to its diffusion throughout modern economic theory.

Total priority has long been given to the study of a purely decentralized market structure, operating solely through prices. I contend in this paper that the vigorously renewed interest in institutions and governance structures defines a new research program that is transforming our understanding of how market economies function, and even of what "markets" are. To develop this program, we must better understand how the rules governing institutional arrangements such as markets and organizations are created and changed, i.e., how *institutions emerge and are stabilized.*

Acknowledgements

Previous versions of this paper were presented and discussed at the Universities of Louvain-La-Neuve, Berkeley, Concordia, and Paris (Pantheon-Sorbonne). I am indebted to all participants, but I owe a more specific debt to Marina Bianchi, Harry Garretsen, Maarten Janssen, Neil de Marchi, Pablo Spiller, Michel de Vroey, and Oliver E. Williamson. Two anonymous referees made extensive comments and suggestions. Linda Davenport significantly improved the style of the paper, and, therefore, its content. The usual disclaimer obviously applies.

References

Alchian, Armen and Harold Demsetz, 1972, Production, information costs and economic organizations, American Economic Review, 62 (5), 777–795.

Aoki, Masahiko (ed.), 1984, The economic analysis of the Japanese firm, North Holland, Amsterdam.

Aoki et al. (eds.), 1990, The firm as a nexus of treaties, Sage Publications, London.

Arrow, Kenneth J., 1964, Control in large organizations, Management Science, 10 (3), 397–408.

Arrow, Kenneth J., 1974, The limits of organization, Norton and Co., New York.

Aumann, Robert J., 1985, Repeated games, In: Georges Feiwel (ed.) Issues in contemporary micro-economics and welfare, MacMillan, London, 209–243.

Balasko, Yves, 1988, Foundations of the theory of general equilibrium, Academic Press, London.

Barnard, Chester I., 1938, The functions of the executive, Harvard University Press, Cambridge.

Becker, Gary, 1981, A treatise on the family, Harvard University Press, Cambridge.

Beckmann, Martin, 1988, Tinbergen lectures on organizational theory, Springer Verlag, New York.

Ben-Porath, Yoram, 1980, The f-connection: families, friends, and firms and the organization of exchange, Population and Development Review, 6 (March), 1–30.

Bensaou, Ben and N. Venkatraman, 1992, Configurations of inter-organizational relationships, IN-SEAD and MIT, Working Paper.

Cheung, Steven, 1983, The contractual nature of the firm, Journal of Law and Economics, 26 (1), 1–22.

Coase, Ronald, 1988a, The firm, the market, and the law, University of Chicago Press, Chicago.

Coase, Ronald, 1988b, The nature of the firm: origin, meaning, and influence, Journal of Law, Economics, and Organization, 4 (1), 3–59.

Coase, Ronald, 1991, The institutional structure of production, Stockholm, Nobel Foundation.

Commons, John, 1934, Institutional economics. Its place in political economy, MacMillan, New York.

Cournot, Antoine A., 1838, Researches into the mathematical principles of the theory of wealth, Macmillan, New York; English translation, N. Bacon, 1897.

Davis, Lance E. and Douglass C. North, 1971, Institutional change and American economic growth, Cambridge University Press, Cambridge, UK.

Day, Richard H., 1993, Bounded rationality and the coevolution of market and state, In, R.H. Day, G. Eliasson and C. Wihlborg (eds) The markets for innovation, ownership and control, Forthcoming.

DeVille, Philippe, 1990, Comportements concurrentiels et equilibre general, de la necessite des institutions, Economie Appliquee, 43 (3), 9–34.

Doeringer, P. and Michael Piore, 1971, Internal labor markets and manpower analysis, D.C. Heath, Lexington, MA.

Edwards, P.K., 1990, The politics of conflict and consent, how the labor contract really works, Journal of Economic Behavior and Organization, 13 (1), 41–61.

Fama, Eugene, 1980, Agency theory and the theory of the firm, Journal of Political Economy, 88 (1), 288–307.

Fama, Eugene and Michael Jensen, 1983a, Separation of ownership and control, Journal of Law and Economics, 26 (2), 301–325.

Fama, Eugene and Michael Jensen, 1983b, Agency problems and residual claims, Journal of Law and Economics, 26 (2), 327–349.

Fisher, Franklin, 1983, Disequilibrium. Foundations of equilibrium economics, Cambridge University Press, Cambridge, UK.

Granovetter, Mark, 1985, Economic action and social structure, the problem of embeddedness, American Journal of Sociology, 91 (3), 481–510.

Green, Kenneth A., 1991, Shaping technologies and shaping markets, creating demand for biotechnology, Technological Assessment and Strategic Management, 3 (1), 57–76.

Hahn, Frank, 1984, Macroeconomics and money, Basic Blackwell, London.

Hess, James, 1983, The economics of organization, North Holland, Amsterdam.

Hodgson, Geoffrey, 1988, Economics and institutions, a manifesto for a modern institutional economics, University of Philadelphia Press, Philadelphia.

Hurwicz, Leonid, 1987, Inventing new institutions, the design perspective, American Journal of Agricultural Economics, 69 (2), 395–402.

Jensen, Michael and W.H. Meckling, 1976, Theory of the firm, managerial behavior, agency cost, and ownership structure, Journal of Financial Economics, (3), 304–360.

Jensen, Michael, 1983, Organization theory and methodology, The Accounting Review, 58 (2), 319–339.

Jevons, William S., 1871, The theory of political economy, Penguin, Harmondsworth (UK), 1970.

Joskow, Paul L., 1985, Vertical integration and long term contracts, the case of coal-burning electric generating plants, Journal of Law, Economics, and Organization, 1 (1), 33–80.

Joskow, Paul L., 1994, Privatization in Russia, what should be a firm?, Working Paper, In Transaction Costs Economics, Recent Developments, Sorbonne

C. Ménard / J. of Economic Behavior & Org. 28 (1995) 161–182   181

Kreps, David, 1991, Game theory and economic modeling, Oxford University Press, Oxford.

Langlois, Richard N. and Laszlo Csontos, 1993, Optimization, rule-following, and the methodology of situational analysis, In Maki et al., 1993.

Macaulay, Stewart, 1963, Non contractual relations in business, a preliminary study, American Sociological Review, 28 (1), 55–67.

Maki, Uskali, Bo Gustafsson and Christian Knudsen, 1993, Rationality, institutions, and economic methodology, Routledge, London.

March, James G. and Johan P. Olsen, 1984, The new institutionalism, organizational factors in political life, American Political Science Review, 78 (3), 734–749.

Marshall, Alfred, 1920, Principles of economics, Macmillan, London, 8th ed.

Menard, Claude, 1994a, Organizations as coordinating devices, Metroeconomica 45 (3), 224–247.

Menard, Claude, 1994b, Comportement rationnel et cooperation, le dilemme organisationnel, Cahiers d'economie politique, 24–25, pp. 163–186.

Milgrom, Paul and John Roberts, 1991, Economics of organization and management, Prentice-Hall, New York.

Moe, Terry M., 1991, Politics and the theory of organization, Journal of Law, Economics, and Organization, 7 (Sp), 106–129.

North, Douglass C., 1981, Structure and change in economic history, Norton and Co, New York.

North, Douglass C., 1986, The new institutional economics, Journal of Institutional and Theoretical Economics, 142 (1), 230–237.

North, Douglass C., 1990b, A Transaction cost theory of politics, Political Economy Working Paper, nr. 144., St Louis, Washington University.

Orsenigo, Luigi, 1989, The emergence of biotechnology, institutions and markets in industrial organization, Pinter, London.

Ouchi, William G., 1979, A conceptual framework for the design of organizational control mechanisms, Management Science, 25 (9), 833–848.

Palay, Thomas M., 1984, Comparative institutional economics, the governance of the rail freight contract, Journal of Legal Studies, 13 (June), 265–288.

Parsons, Talcott, 1940, The motivation of economic activities, Canadian Journal of Economics and Political Sciences, 6, 187–203.

Polanyi, Karl, 1944, The great transformation, The Free Press, New York.

Radner, Roy, 1992, Hierarchy, the economics of managing, Journal of Economic Literature, 30 (3), 1382–1415

Russell, Bertrand and Alfred N. Whitehead, 1910, Principia mathematica, Cambridge University Press, Cambridge, UK.

Schotter, Andrew, 1981, The economic theory of social institutions, Cambridge University Press, Cambridge, UK.

Simon, Herbert A., 1947, Administrative behavior.

Simon, Herbert A., 1991, Organizations and markets, Journal of Economic Perspective, 5 (2), 25–44.

Smith, Adam, 1776, An inquiring into the nature and causes of the wealth of nations, (reed E. Cannan, University of Chicago Press/Chicago, 1976.

Stiglitz, Joseph, 1974, Incentives and risk sharing in sharecropping, Review of Economic Studies, 41 (June), 219–256.

Thorelli, Hans B., 1986, Networks, between markets and hierarchies, Strategic Management Journal, 7 (1), 37–51.

Vroey, Michel de, 1990a, S'il te plait, dessine-moi un marche, Economie Appliquee, 43 (3), 67–87.

Vroey, Michel de, 1990b, The base camp paradox, Economics and Philosophy, 6, 235–253.

Weber, Max, 1947, The theory of social and economic organization, Trans. Talcott Parsons, Free Press, Glencoe, IL.

Weingast, Barry R. and Marshall, William, 1988, The industrial organization of congress, Journal of Political Economy, 96 (Feb.), 135–163.

Williamson, Oliver E., 1975, Markets and hierarchies, Free Press, New York.

Williamson, Oliver E., 1985, The economic institutions of capitalism, Free Press-MacMillan, New York.

Williamson, Oliver E., 1986, Economic organization, firms, markets, and policy control, New York University Press, New York.

Williamson, Olviver E., 1990, A comparison of alternative approaches to economic organization, Journal of Institutional and Theoretical Economics, 146 (1), 61–71.

Williamson, Oliver E., 1991a, Economic institutions, spontaneous and intentional governance, Journal of law, Economics, and Organization, 7 (Sp), 159–187.

Williamson, Oliver E., 1991b, Comparative economic organization, the analysis of discrete structural analysis, Administrative Science Quarterly, 36 (2), 269–296.

Williamson, Oliver E. and Sidney G. Winter (eds), 1991, The nature of the firm, Oxford University Press, Oxford.

Winter, Sidney G., 1988, On Coase, competence, and the corporation, In: Oliver E. Williamson and Sidney G. Winter (eds), 1991, pp. 179–195.

[26]

THE NEW INSTITUTIONAL ECONOMICS†

The New Institutional Economics

By Ronald Coase*

It is commonly said, and it may be true, that the new institutional economics started with my article, "The Nature of the Firm" (1937) with its explicit introduction of transaction costs into economic analysis. But it needs to be remembered that the source of a mighty river is a puny little stream and that it derives its strength from the tributaries that contribute to its bulk. So it is in this case. I am not thinking only of the contributions of other economists such as Oliver Williamson, Harold Demsetz, and Steven Cheung, important though they have been, but also of the work of our colleagues in law, anthropology, sociology, political science, sociobiology, and other disciplines.

The phrase, "the new institutional economics," was coined by Oliver Williamson. It was intended to differentiate the subject from the "old institutional economics." John R. Commons, Wesley Mitchell, and those associated with them were men of great intellectual stature, but they were anti-theoretical, and without a theory to bind together their collection of facts, they had very little that they were able to pass on. Certain it is that mainstream economics proceeded on its way without any significant change. And it continues to do so. I should explain that, when I speak of mainstream economics, I am referring to microeconomics. Whether my strictures apply also to macroeconomics I leave to others.

Mainstream economics, as one sees it in the journals and the textbooks and in the courses taught in economics departments has become more and more abstract over time, and although it purports otherwise, it is in fact little

† Roundtable discussion.

* University of Chicago Law School, 1111 East 60th Street, Chicago, IL 60637-2786.

concerned with what happens in the real world. Demsetz has given an explanation of why this has happened: economists since Adam Smith have devoted themselves to formalizing his doctrine of the invisible hand, the coordination of the economic system by the pricing system. It has been an impressive achievement. But, as Demsetz has explained, it is the analysis of a system of extreme decentralization. However, it has other flaws. Adam Smith also pointed out that we should be concerned with the flow of real goods and services over time—and with what determines their variety and magnitude. As it is, economists study how supply and demand determine prices but not with the factors that determine what goods and services are traded on markets and therefore are priced. It is a view disdainful of what happens in the real world, but it is one to which economists have become accustomed, and they live in their world without discomfort. The success of mainstream economics in spite of its defects is a tribute to the staying power of a theoretical underpinning, since mainstream economics is certainly strong on theory if weak on facts. Thus, for example, in the *Handbook of Industrial Organization*, Bengt Holmstrom and Jean Tirole (1989 p. 126), writing on "The Theory of the Firm," remark that "the evidence/theory ratio ... is currently very low in this field."

This disregard for what happens concretely in the real world is strengthened by the way economists think of their subject. In my youth, a very popular definition of economics was that provided by Lionel Robbins (1935 p. 15) in his book *An Essay on the Nature and Significance of Economic Science*: "Economics is the science which studies human behaviour as a relationship between ends and scarce means that have alternative uses." It is the study of human behavior as a relationship. These days economists are more likely to refer to their subject as "the science of human choice" or they talk about "an economic approach." This is not a recent development. John Maynard Keynes said that the "Theory of Economics ... is a method rather than a doctrine, an apparatus of the mind, a technique of thinking, which helps the possessor to draw correct conclusions" (introduction in H. D. Henderson, 1922 p. v). Joan Robinson (1933 p. 1) says in the introduction to her book *The Economics of Imperfect Competition* that it "is presented to the analytical economist as a box of tools." What this comes down to is that economists think of themselves as having a box of tools but no subject matter. It reminds me of two lines from a modern poet (I forget the poem and the poet but the lines are indeed memorable):

I see the bridle and the bit all right
But where's the bloody horse?

I have expressed the same thought by saying that we study the circulation of the blood without a body.

In saying this I should not be thought to imply that these analytical tools are not extremely valuable. I am delighted when our colleagues in law use them to study the working of the legal system or when those in political science use them to study the working of the political system. My point is different. I think we should use these analytical tools to study the economic system. I think economists do have a subject matter: the study of the working of the economic system, a system in which we earn and spend our incomes. The welfare of a human society depends on the flow of goods and services, and this in turn depends on the productivity of the economic system. Adam Smith explained that the productivity of the economic system depends on specialization (he says the division of labor), but specialization is only possible if there is exchange—and the lower the costs of exchange (transaction costs if you will), the more specialization there will be and the greater the productivity of the system. But the costs of exchange depend on the institutions of a country: its legal system, its political system, its social system, its educational system, its culture, and so on. In effect it is the institutions that govern the performance of an econ-

omy, and it is this that gives the "new institutional economics" its importance for economists.

That such work is needed is made clear by another feature of economics. Apart from the formalization of the theory, the way we look at the working of the economic system has been extraordinarily static over the years. Economists often take pride in the fact that Charles Darwin came to his theory of evolution as a result of reading Thomas Malthus and Adam Smith. But contrast the developments in biology since Darwin with what has happened in economics since Adam Smith. Biology has been transformed. Biologists now have a detailed understanding of the complicated structures that govern the functioning of living organisms. I believe that one day we will have similar triumphs in economics. But it will not be easy. Even if we start with the relatively simple analysis of "The Nature of the Firm," discovering the factors that determine the relative costs of coordination by management within the firm or by transactions on the market is no simple task. However, this is not by any means the whole story. We cannot confine our analysis to what happens within a single firm. This is what I said in a lecture published in *Lives of the Laureates* (Coase, 1995 p. 245): "The costs of coordination within a firm and the level of transaction costs that it faces are affected by its ability to purchase inputs from other firms, and their ability to supply these inputs depends in part on their costs of coordination and the level of transaction costs that they face which are similarly affected by what these are in still other firms. What we are dealing with is a complex interrelated structure." Add to this the influence of the laws, of the social system, and of the culture, as well as the effects of technological changes such as the digital revolution with its dramatic fall in information costs (a major component of transaction costs), and you have a complicated set of interrelationships the nature of which will take much dedicated work over a long period to discover. But when this is done, all of economics will have become what we now call "the new institutional economics."

This change will not come about, in my view, as a result of a frontal assault on mainstream economics. It will come as a result of economists in branches or subsections of economics adopting a different approach, as indeed is already happening. When the majority of economists have changed, mainstream economists will acknowledge the importance of examining the economic system in this way and will claim that they knew it all along.

REFERENCES

Coase, Ronald H. ''The Nature of the Firm.'' *Economica*, November 1937, *4*, pp. 386–405.

_____. ''My Evolution as an Economist,'' in William Breit and Roger W. Spencer, eds., *Lives of the laureates*. Cambridge, MA: MIT Press, 1995, pp. 227–49.

Henderson, H. D. *Supply and demand*. London: Nisbet, 1922.

Holmstrom, Bengt and Tirole, Jean. ''The Theory of the Firm,'' in Richard Schmalensee and Robert D. Willig, eds., *Handbook of industrial organization*. Amsterdam: North-Holland, 1989, pp. 61–128.

Robbins, Lionel. *An essay on the nature and significance of economic science*. London: Macmillan, 1935.

Robinson, Joan. *The economics of imperfect competition*. London: Macmillan, 1933.

Name Index

Von Wright, G.H. 432

Wade, R. 480
Wagner, A. 382, 412
Walker, G. 327
Wallis, J.J. 412
Walras, V. 73, 506
Watrin 412
Watson, J. 301
Weaver, C. 436, 449
Weaver, W. 95
Weber, D. 327
Weber, M. 385, 387, 399, 405, 415, 453, 459, 502
Weber, R.J. 223
Weimer, D.L. 402
Weingast, B. 269, 368, 375, 401–2, 412, 441, 479, 509, 512
Weitzman, M.L. 220, 223
Weizsäcker, C.C. 407
Wendell, R.E. 362
Whinston, A. 175

Whinston, G. 196
White, H.J. 67
White, L. 413
Whitehead, A.N. 497
Wicksell, K. 425
Wiggins, S.N. 400
Williamson, O.E. 223–4, 248, 291–2, 320, 324, 327, 329, 336–8, 342, 356, 384, 387, 398–9, 404, 409–14, 453, 455, 463–4, 497, 504–5, 507–8, 510–11, 513, 518
Wilson, R. 310
Wilson, R. 439
Winter, S.G. 413, 506, 513
Woodward, J. 468
Woodward, S. 399
Workman, A. 343
Wrong, D. 454–5

Young, A.A. 115
Young, H.P. 269, 288, 490

Zu, C. 492